CONTENTS

Geographers' A-Z Map Company Ltd.
Fairfield Road, Borough Green, Sevenoaks, Kent TN15 8PP
Telephone : 01732 781000 (Enquiries & Trade Sales)
01732 783422 (Retail Sales)

Edition 19 2011   Copyright © Geographers' A-Z Map Company Ltd.
No reproduction by any method whatsoever of any part of this publication is
permitted without the prior consent of the copyright owners.
An AtoZ publication

REFERENCE | Légende | Zeichenerklärung

English	Français	Deutsch
MOTORWAY	Autoroute	Autobahn
MOTORWAY UNDER CONSTRUCTION	Autoroute en construction	Autobahn im Bau
MOTORWAY PROPOSED	Autoroute prévue	Geplante Autobahn
MOTORWAY JUNCTIONS WITH NUMBERS — Unlimited interchange / Limited interchange	Echangeur numéroté — Echangeur non limité / Echangeur limité	Autobahnanschlußstelle mit Nummer — Unbeschränkter Fahrtrichtungswechsel / Beschränkter Fahrtrichtungswechsel
MOTORWAY SERVICE AREA — with access from one carriageway only	Aire de services d'autoroute — à sens unique	Rastplatz oder Raststätte — Einbahn
MAJOR ROAD SERVICE AREAS with 24 hour Facilities — Primary Route / Class A Road	Aire de services de route prioriataire Ouverte 24h sur 24 — Route à grande circulation / Route de type A	Raststätte Durchgehend geöffnet — Hauptverkehrsstraße / A-Straße
TRUCKSTOP (Selected)	Choix d'aire pour poids lourds	Auswahl von Fernfahrerrastplatz
PRIMARY ROUTE	Route à grande circulation	Hauptverkehrsstraße
PRIMARY ROUTE JUNCTION WITH NUMBER	Echangeur numéroté	Hauptverkehrsstraßenkreuzung mit Nummer
PRIMARY ROUTE DESTINATION **DOVER**	Route prioritaire, direction **DOVER**	Hauptverkehrsstraße Richtung **DOVER**
DUAL CARRIAGEWAYS (A & B Roads)	Route à deux chaussées séparées (route A & B)	Zweispurige Schnellstraße (A- und B-Straßen)
CLASS A ROAD A129	Route de type A A129	A-Straße A129
CLASS B ROAD B177	Route de type B B177	B-Straße B177
NARROW MAJOR ROAD (Passing Places)	Route prioritaire étroite (possibilité de dépassement)	Schmale Hauptverkehrsstraße (mit Überholmöglichkeit)
MAJOR ROADS UNDER CONSTRUCTION	Route prioritaire en construction	Hauptverkehrsstaße im Bau
MAJOR ROADS PROPOSED	Route prioritaire prévue	Geplante Hauptverkehrsstraße
GRADIENT 1:5(20%) & STEEPER (Ascent in direction of arrow)	Pente égale ou supérieure à 20% (dans le sens de la montée)	20% Steigung und steiler (in Pfeilrichtung)
TOLL	Péage	Gebührenpflichtig
MILEAGE BETWEEN MARKERS 8	Distance en milles entre les flèches 8	Strecke zwischen Markierungen in Meilen 8
RAILWAY AND STATION	Voie ferrée et gare	Eisenbahnlinie und Bahnhof
LEVEL CROSSING AND TUNNEL	Passage à niveau et tunnel	Bahnübergang und Tunnel
RIVER OR CANAL	Rivière ou canal	Fluß oder Kanal
COUNTY OR UNITARY AUTHORITY BOUNDARY	Limite des comté ou de division administrative	Grafschafts- oder Verwaltungsbezirksgrenze
NATIONAL BOUNDARY	Frontière nationale	Landesgrenze
BUILT-UP AREA	Agglomération	Geschlossene Ortschaft
VILLAGE OR HAMLET	Village ou hameau	Dorf oder Weiler
WOODED AREA	Zone boisée	Waldgebiet
SPOT HEIGHT IN FEET · 813	Altitude (en pieds) · 813	Höhe in Fuß · 813
HEIGHT ABOVE SEA LEVEL 400'-1,000' 122m-305m; 1,000'-1,400' 305m-427m; 1,400'-2,000' 427m-610m; 2,000'+ 610m+	Altitude par rapport au niveau de la mer 400'-1,000' 122m-305m; 1,000'-1,400' 305m-427m; 1,400'-2,000' 427m-610m; 2,000'+ 610m+	Höhe über Meeresspiegel 400'-1,000' 122m-305m; 1,000'-1,400' 305m-427m; 1,400'-2,000' 427m-610m; 2,000'+ 610m+
NATIONAL GRID REFERENCE (Kilometres) ¹00	Coordonnées géographiques nationales (Kilometres) ¹00	Nationale geographische Koordinaten (Kilometer) ¹00
PAGE CONTINUATION 48	Suite à la page indiquée 48	Seitenfortsetzung 48

Tourist Information		Information		Touristeninformationen	
AIRPORT	⊕	Aéroport	⊕	Flughafen	⊕
AIRFIELD	✛	Terrain d' aviation	✛	Flugplatz	✛
HELIPORT	🚁	Héliport	🚁	Hubschrauberlandeplatz	🚁
BATTLE SITE AND DATE	⚔ *1066*	Champ de bataille et date	⚔ *1066*	Schlachtfeld und Datum	⚔ *1066*
CASTLE (Open to Public)	⛫	Château (ouvert au public)	⛫	Schloss / Burg (für die Öffentlichkeit zugänglich)	⛫
CASTLE WITH GARDEN (Open to Public)	⛫	Château avec parc (ouvert au public)	⛫	Schloß mit Garten (für die Öffentlichkeit zugänglich)	⛫
CATHEDRAL, ABBEY, CHURCH, FRIARY, PRIORY	✝	Cathédrale, abbaye, église, monastère, prieuré	✝	Kathedrale, Abtei, Kirche, Mönchskloster, Kloster	✝
COUNTRY PARK	⛺	Parc régional	⛺	Landschaftspark	⛺
FERRY (Vehicular, sea)	⛴	Bac (véhicules, mer)	⛴	Fähre (Autos, meer)	⛴
(Vehicular, river)	⛴	(véhicules, rivière)	⛴	(Autos, fluß)	⛴
(Foot only)	👥	(Piétons)	👥	(nur für Personen)	👥
GARDEN (Open to Public)	✿	Jardin (ouvert au public)	✿	Garten (für die Öffentlichkeit zugänglich)	✿
GOLF COURSE (9 Hole)	⛳	Terrain de golf (9 trous)	⛳	Golfplatz (9 Löcher)	⛳
(18 Hole)	⛳	(18 trous)	⛳	(18 Löcher)	⛳
HISTORIC BUILDING (Open to Public)	🏛	Monument historique (ouvert au public)	🏛	Historisches Gebäude (für die Öffentlichkeit zugänglich)	🏛
HISTORIC BUILDING WITH GARDEN (Open to Public)	🏛	Monument historique avec jardin (ouvert au public)	🏛	Historisches Gebäude mit Garten (für die Öffentlichkeit zugänglich)	🏛
HORSE RACECOURSE	🐎	Hippodrome	🐎	Pferderennbahn	🐎
LIGHTHOUSE	🗼	Phare	🗼	Leuchtturm	🗼
MOTOR RACING CIRCUIT	🏁	Circuit automobile	🏁	Automobilrennbahn	🏁
MUSEUM, ART GALLERY	🖼	Musée	🖼	Museum, Galerie	🖼
NATIONAL PARK	——	Parc national	——	Nationalpark	——
NATIONAL TRUST PROPERTY (Open)	*NT*	National Trust Property (ouvert)	*NT*	National Trust-Eigentum (geöffnet)	*NT*
(Restricted Opening)	*NT*	(heures d'ouverture)	*NT*	(beschränkte Öffnungszeit)	*NT*
(National Trust for Scotland)	*NTS NTS*	(National Trust for Scotland)	*NTS NTS*	(National Trust for Scotland)	*NTS NTS*
NATURE RESERVE OR BIRD SANCTUARY	🦃	Réserve naturelle botanique ou ornithologique	🦃	Natur- oder Vogelschutzgebiet	🦃
NATURE TRAIL OR FOREST WALK	🍂	Chemin forestier, piste verte	🍂	Naturpfad oder Waldweg	🍂
PLACE OF INTEREST	*Monument* •	Site, curiosité	*Monument* •	Sehenswürdigkeit	*Monument* •
PICNIC SITE	⛱	Lieu pour pique-nique	⛱	Picknickplatz	⛱
RAILWAY, STEAM OR NARROW GAUGE	🚂	Chemin de fer, à vapeur ou à voie étroite	🚂	Eisenbahn, Dampf- oder Schmalspurbahn	🚂
THEME PARK	🎡	Centre de loisir	🎡	Vergnügungspark	🎡
TOURIST INFORMATION CENTRE	ℹ	Syndicat d'initiative	ℹ	Information	ℹ
VIEWPOINT (360 degrees)	☀	Vue panoramique (360 degrés)	☀	Aussichtspunkt (360 Grade)	☀
(180 degrees)	☀	(180 degrés)	☀	(180 Grade)	☀
VISITOR INFORMATION CENTRE	ℹ	Centre d'information touristique	ℹ	Besucherzentrum	ℹ
WILDLIFE PARK	⚘	Réserve de faune	⚘	Wildpark	⚘
WINDMILL	⚙	Moulin à vent	⚙	Windmühle	⚙
ZOO OR SAFARI PARK	🐘	Parc ou réserve zoologique	🐘	Zoo oder Safari-Park	🐘

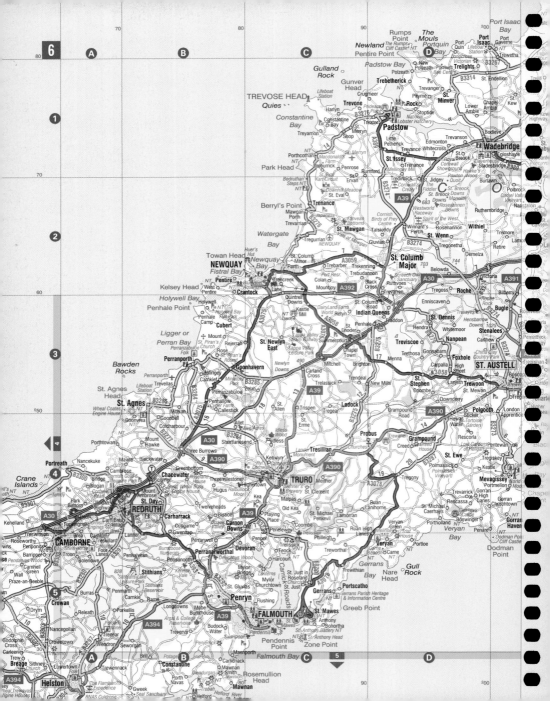

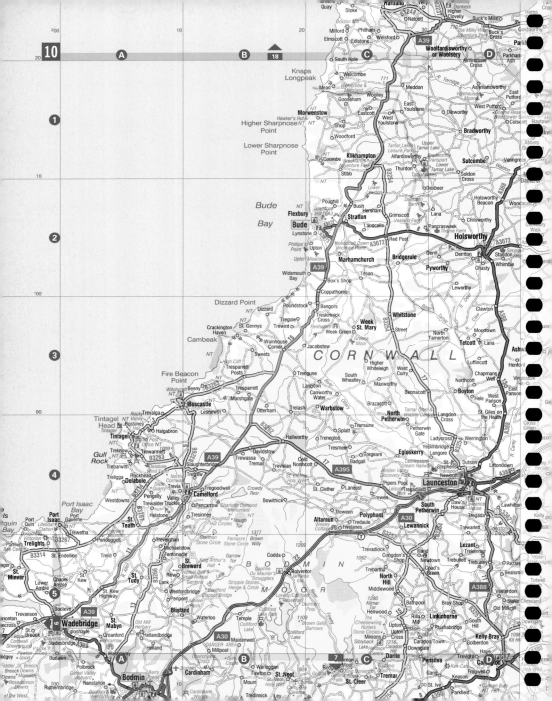

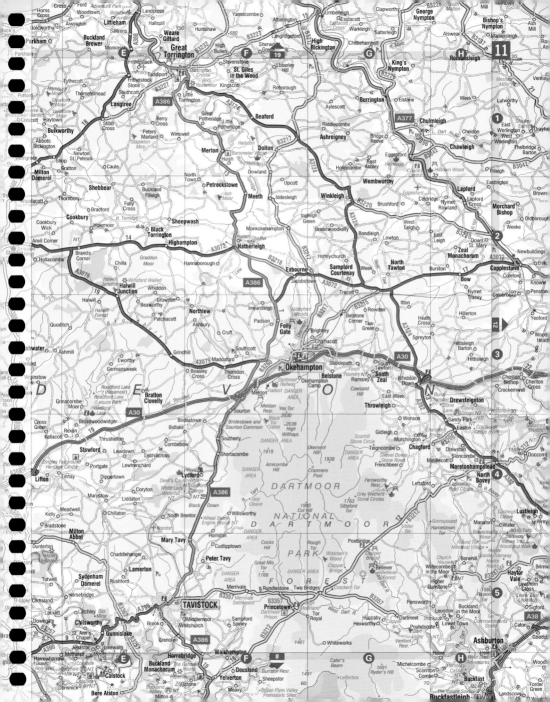

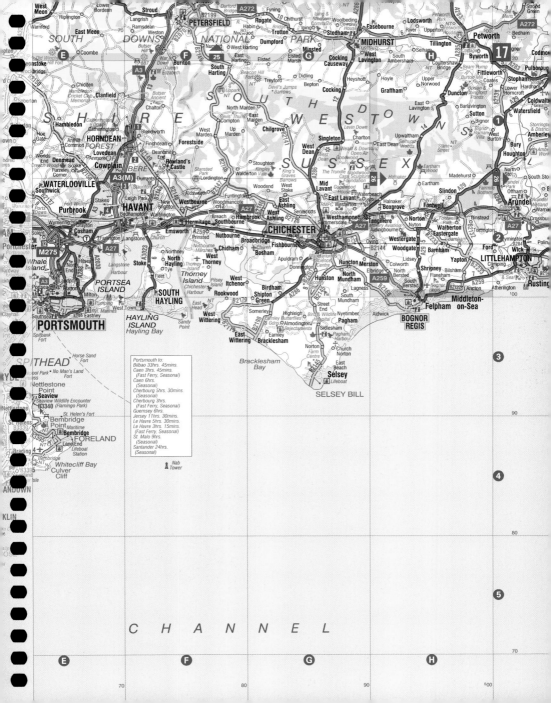

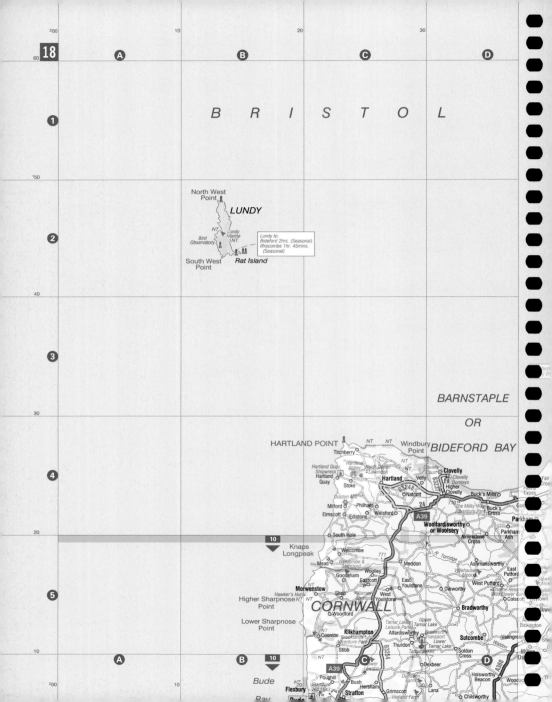

B R I S T O L

North West
Point
LUNDY

Bird
Observatory

NT

Lundy
Marine
NT

NT

South West
Point

Rat Island

Lundy to:
Bideford 2hrs. (Seasonal)
Ilfracombe 1hr. 45mins.
(Seasonal)

BARNSTAPLE

OR

HARTLAND POINT

NT

NT

Windbury
Point

BIDEFORD BAY

Titchberry

NT

Hartland Quay
Shipwreck
Hartland
Quay

Docton Mill

Milford

Hartland
Abbey

Beach Damsel
+ Lawondsd

Clovelly
Court

Clovelly

Clovelly
Donkeys

Higher
Clovelly

Velly

Hartland

B3248

B3237

Buck's Mills

Fair
Cross

Hone
Cross

Stoke

Philham

Elmscott

Edistone

Welsford

South Hole

Welcombe

Natcott

The Milky Way
Adventure Park

24

A39

Buck's
Cross

Woolfardisworthy
or Woolsery

Parkham

Parkham
Ash

Gold

Parkha

Arminstone
Cross

Ashmansworthy

Knaps
Longpeak

Mead

Welcombe &
Marsland

771'

R. Torridge

Woolsery Transport

Meddon

Woolley

Gooseham

Eastcott

East
Yuolstone

Dinworthy

East
Putford

West Putford

Colscot

CORNWALL

Morwenstow

Hawker's Hut
NT

Higher Sharpnose
Point

Shop

Lower Sharpnose
Point

Woodford

Stanbury
Springs

West
Yuolstone

Bradworthy

Sutcombe

Vealingem

Bickington

St

kw

Kilkhampton

Coombe

Tamar Lakes
Leisure Park

Brocksworthy
Adventure Park

Thurdon

Stibb

Upper
Tamar Lake

Woolsery
Transport
Lower
Tamar Lake

Alfardisworthy

B3254

Tamar Lake

Soldon
Cross

Veangreen

Mi

Da

NT

A39

Lower
Leworthy

C

Poughill

Bush

Hersham

Oxbexber

Dizzard
Farm

Holsworthy
Beacon

A388

Woolac

Stibb

Bude

Flexbury

Stratton

Stamford
Hill 643 ft

NT
20

Bude

Grimscott

Lana

Vealand Farm

Chilsworthy

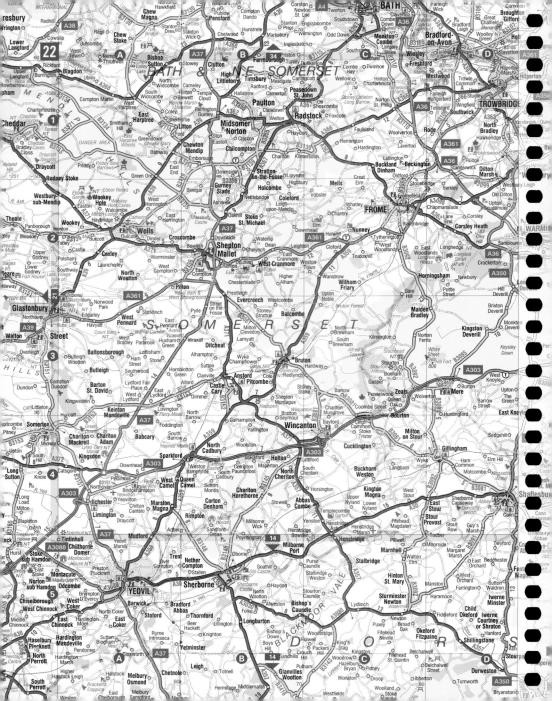

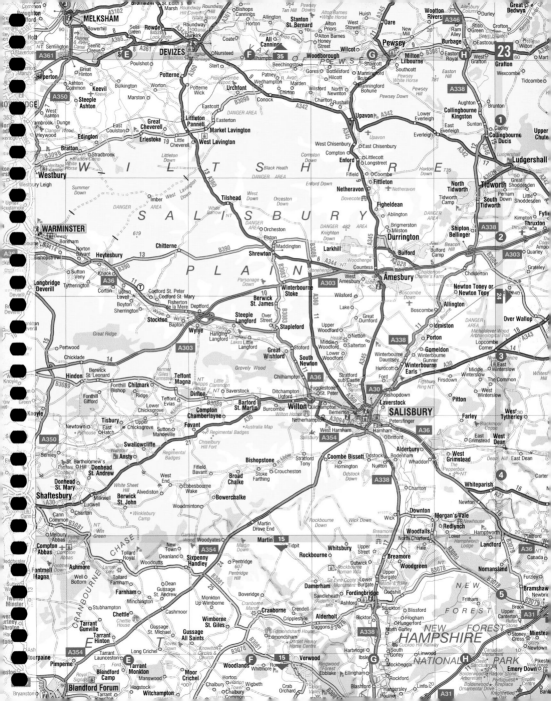

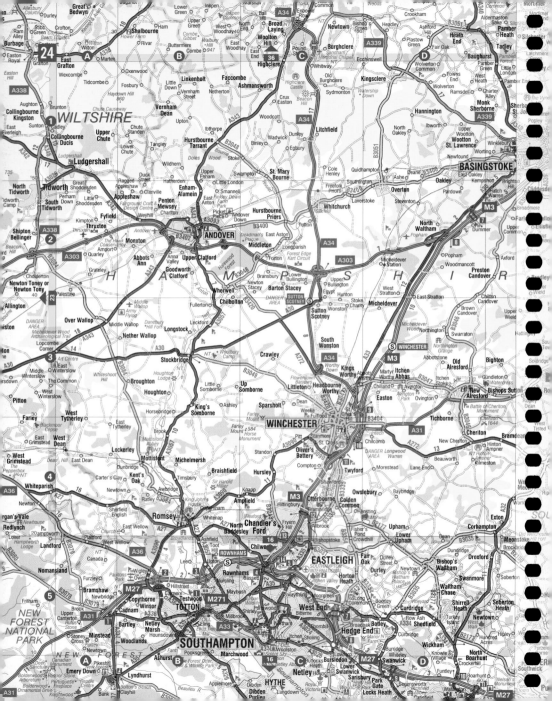

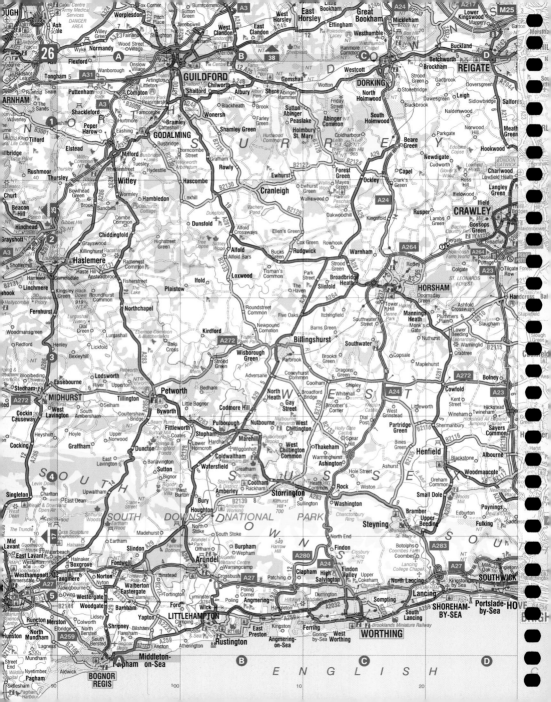

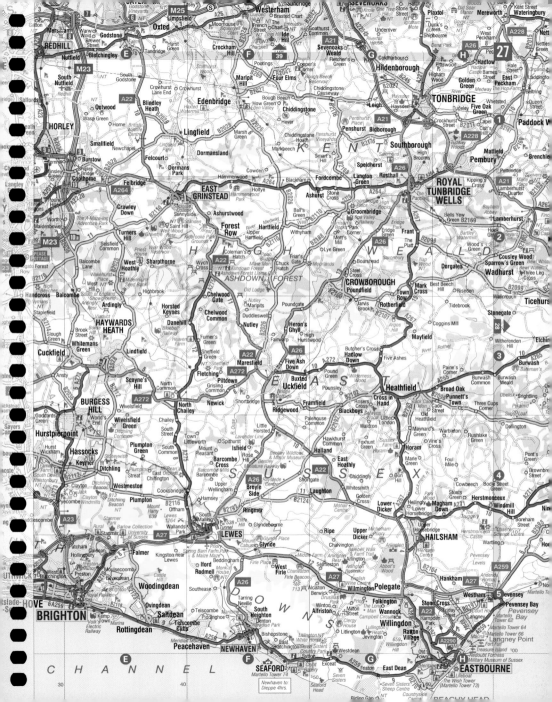

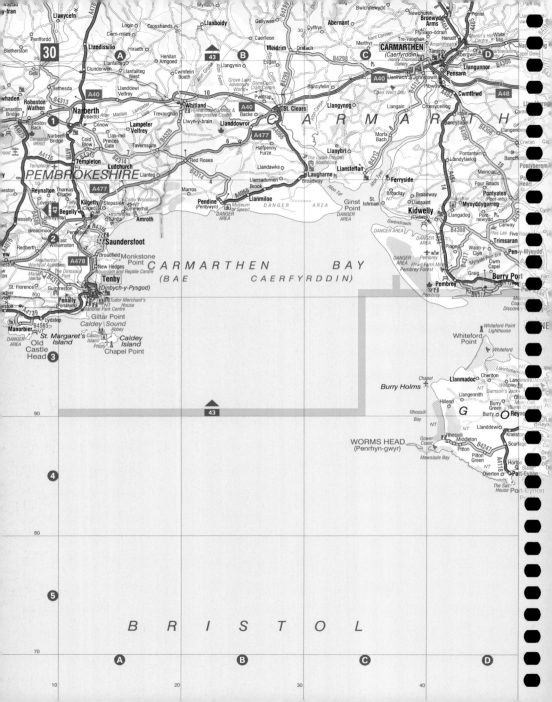

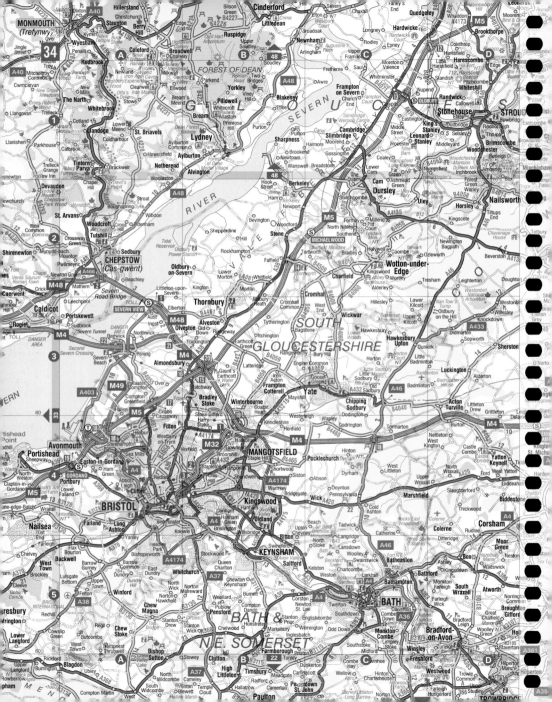

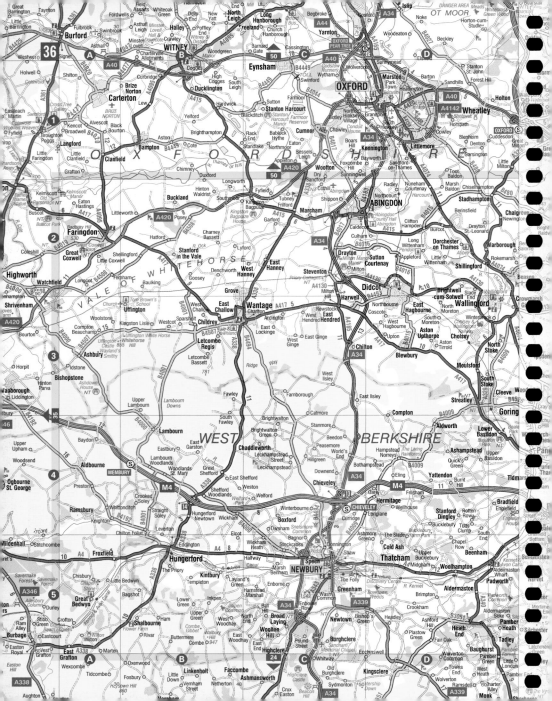

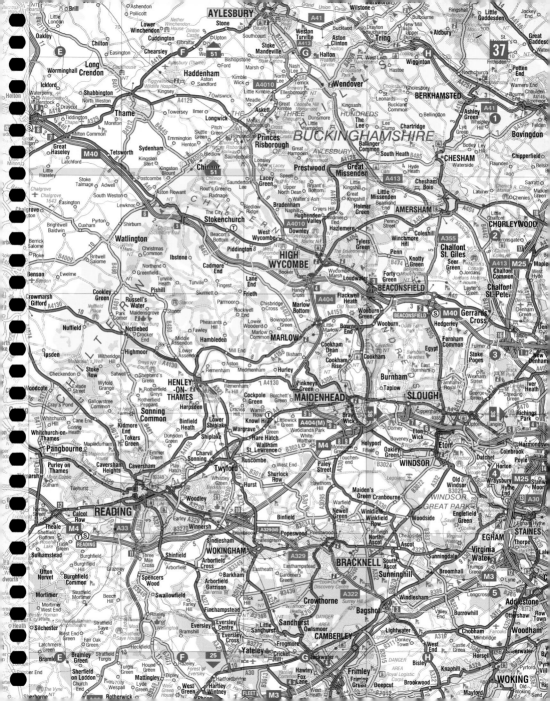

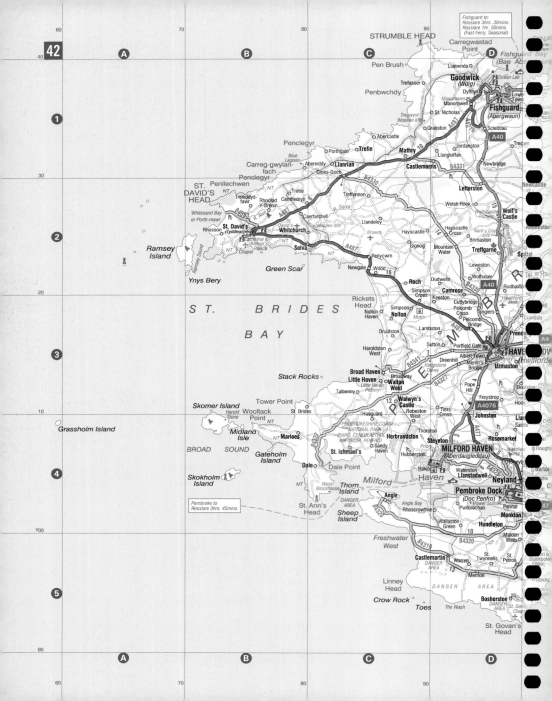

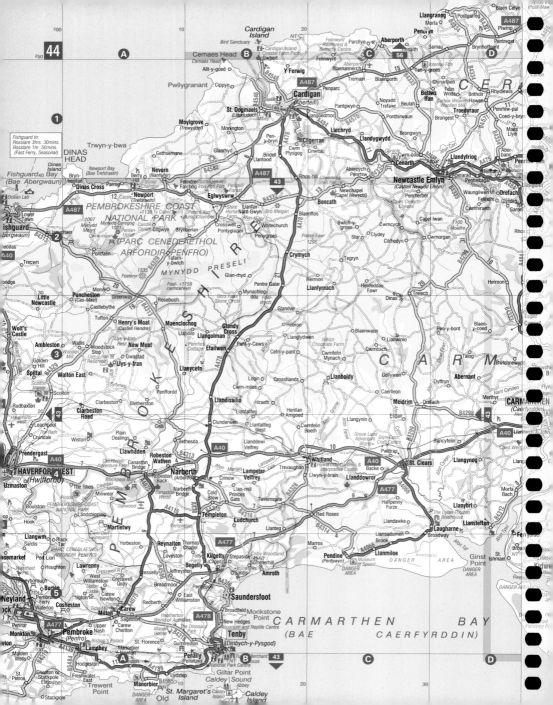

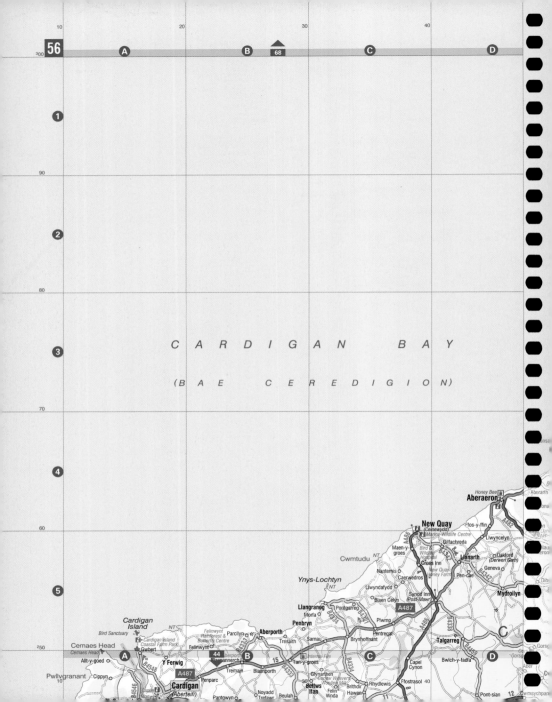

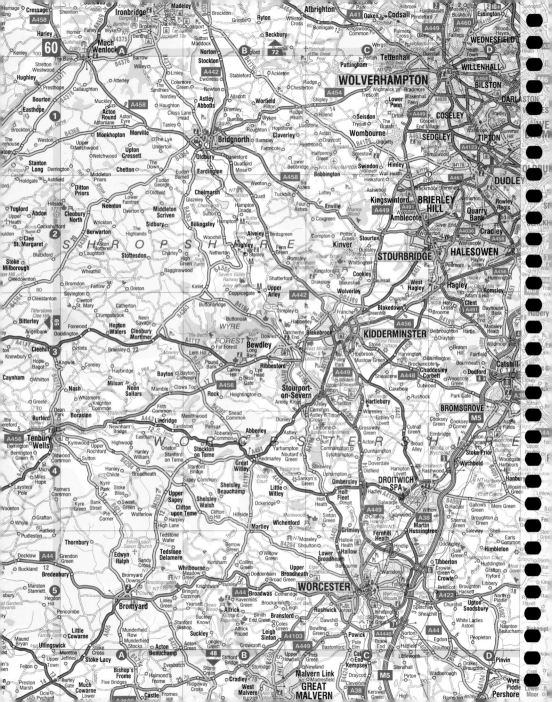

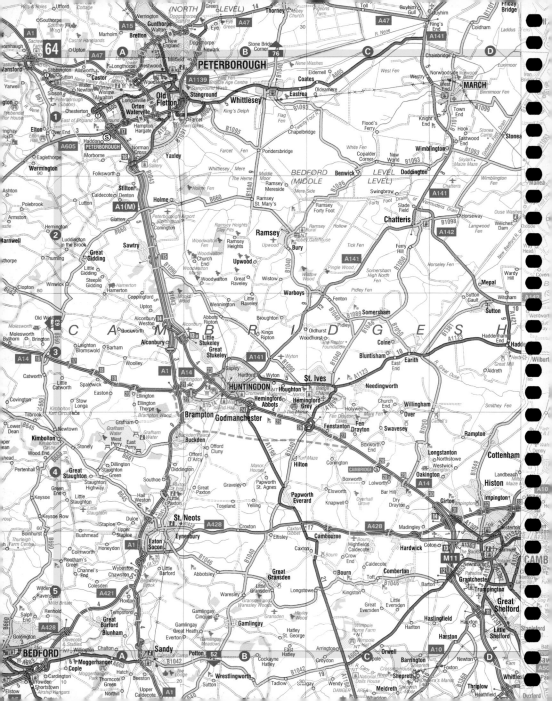

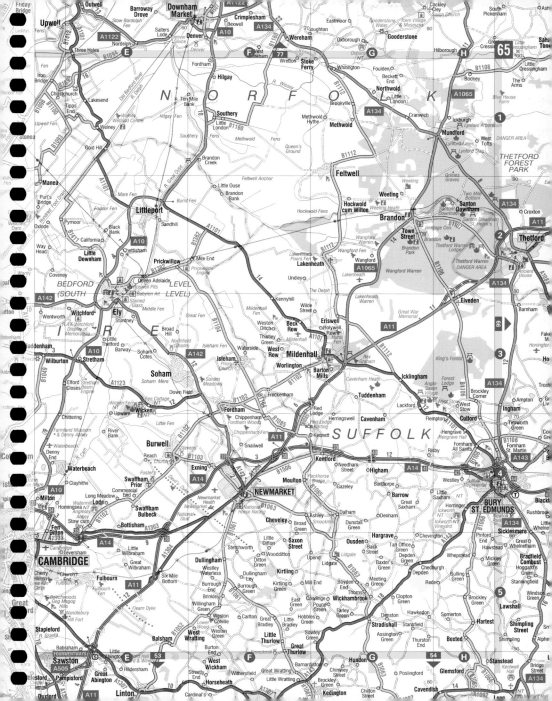

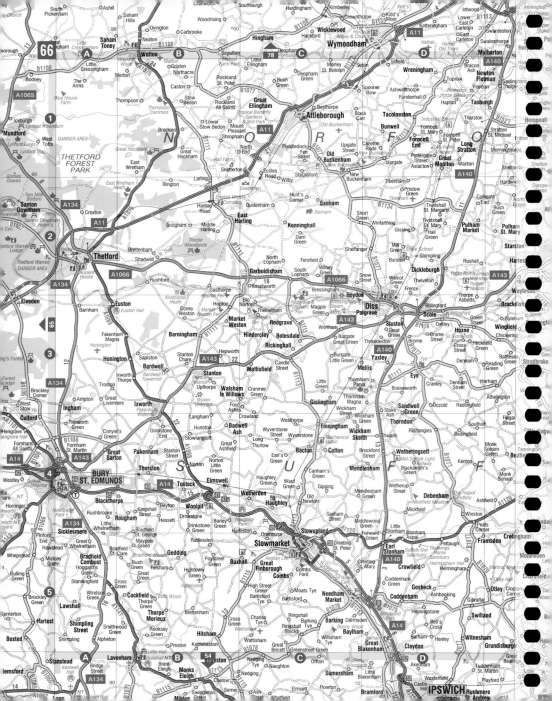

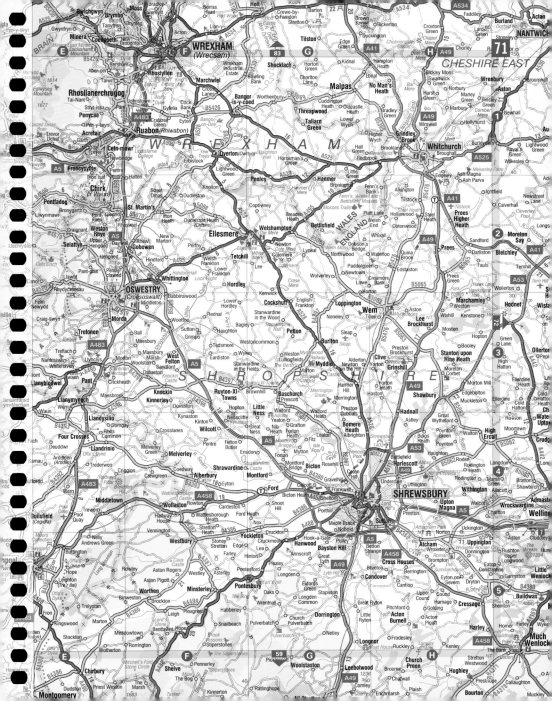

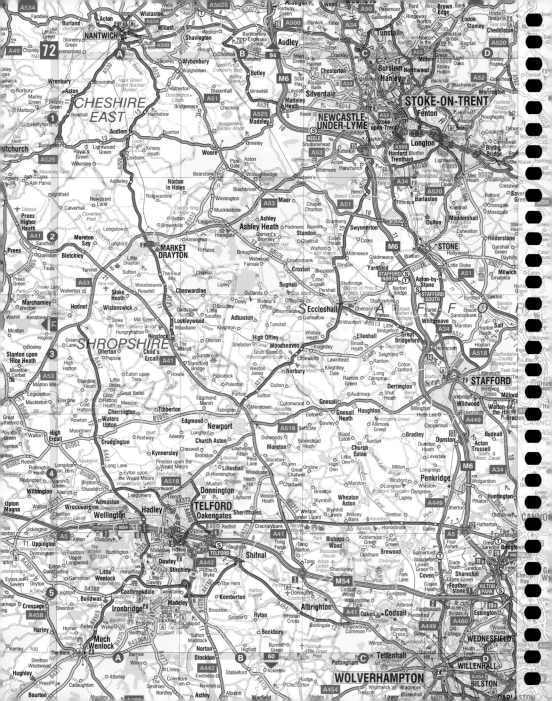

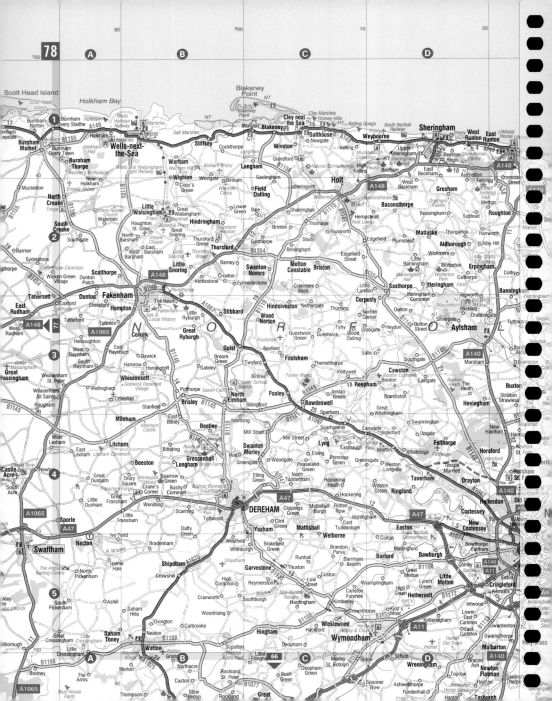

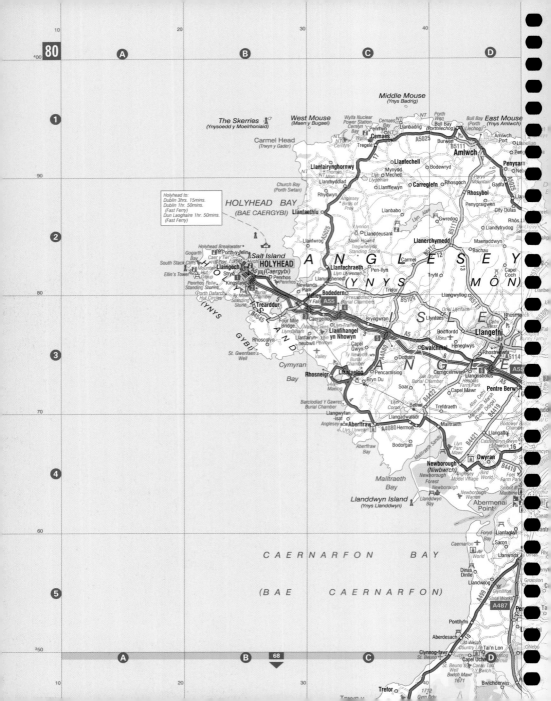

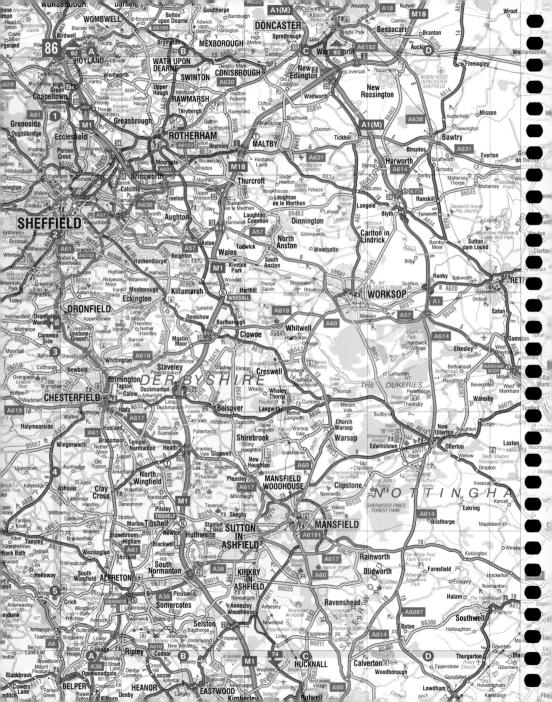

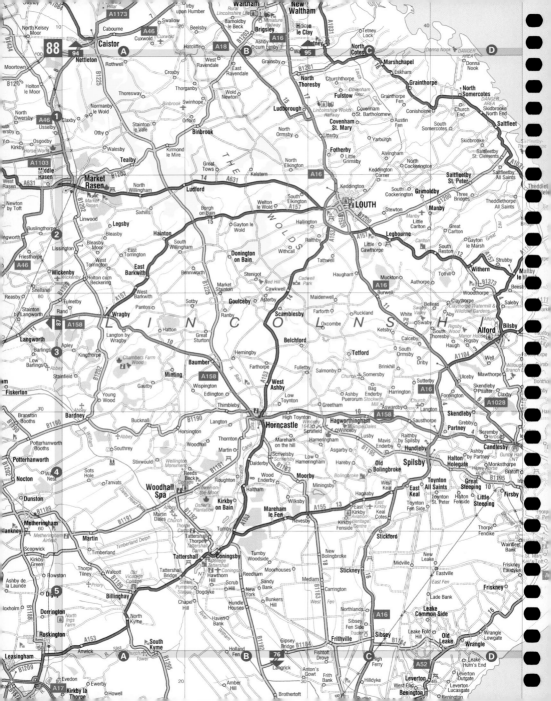

E   F   G   H

50   60   70   80   400

1

N O R T H

S E A

90

2

80

Saltfleetby-
Theddlethorpe
Dunes

Theddlethorpe
St. Helen

Seal
Sanctuary

Meers
Bridge

Mablethorpe

Ye Olde
Curiosity

Trusthorpe

Thorpe

Sutton on Sea

Maltby
le Marsh

Sandilands

Hannah

Markby

Thurlby

Huttoft

Anderby
Creek

Farlesthorpe

Anderby

Drainage

Cumberworth

Mumby

Authorpe
Row

3

70

Helsey

Borthorpe

Chapel
St. Leonards

Willoughby

Hogsthorpe

Sloothby

Slackholme
End

Hardy's
Animal
Farm

Hasthorpe

Addlethorpe

Ingoldmells

Welton
Marsh

Ingoldmells
Point

Orby

Orby
Marsh

Skegness
Ingoldmells
Water
Leisure Park

Butlin's
Resort

Winthorpe

Seathorne

4

Burgh
le Marsh

Church
Farm

Natureland
Seal Sanctuary

60

SKEGNESS

Model Village

Thorpe
St. Peter

Croft

Seacroft

Croft Marsh

Gibraltar Point

Bateman's
Brewery

Magdalen

Wainfleet
All Saints

Wainfleet
St. Mary

Gibraltar

Key's Toft

A52

DANGER AREA

5

350

Deeps

Boston

E   F   77   G   H

50   60   70   80

Scolt Head
Island

Scolt Head
Island NT

Scolt Head
Island

Brancaster Bay

Holkham Bay

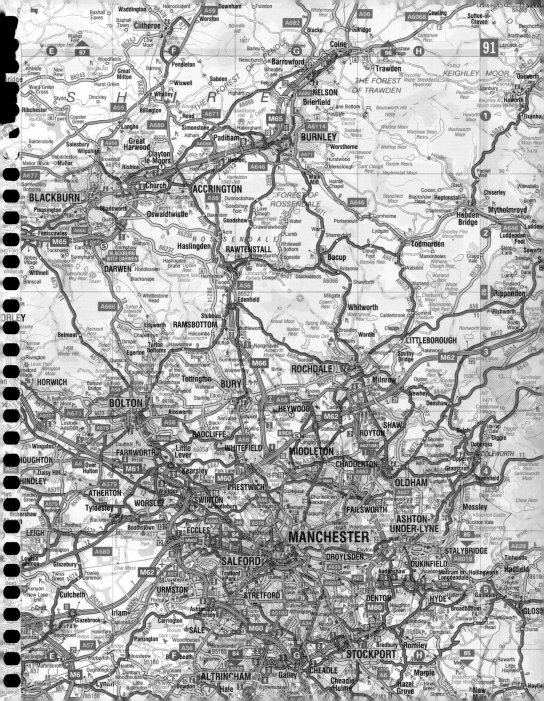

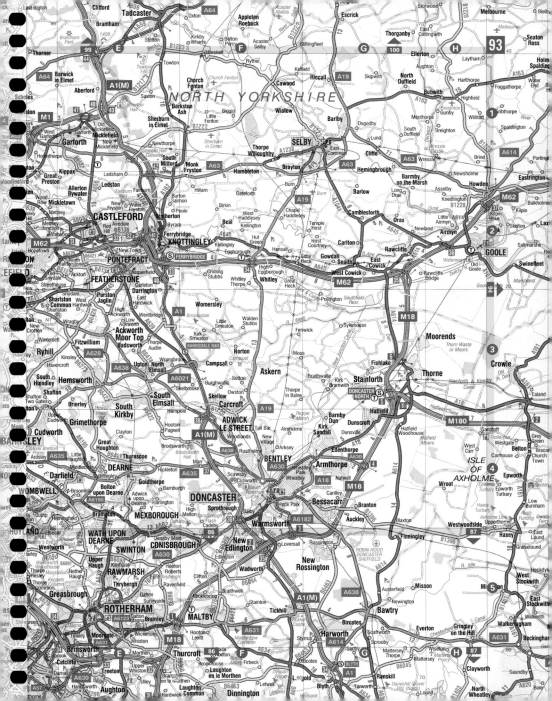

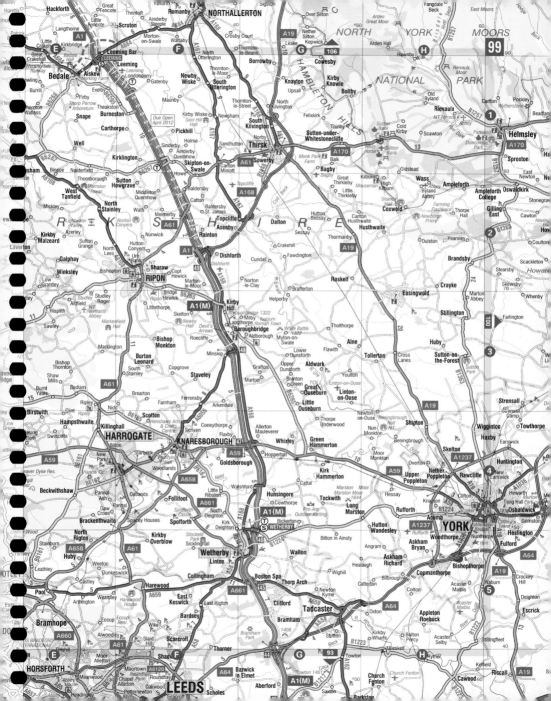

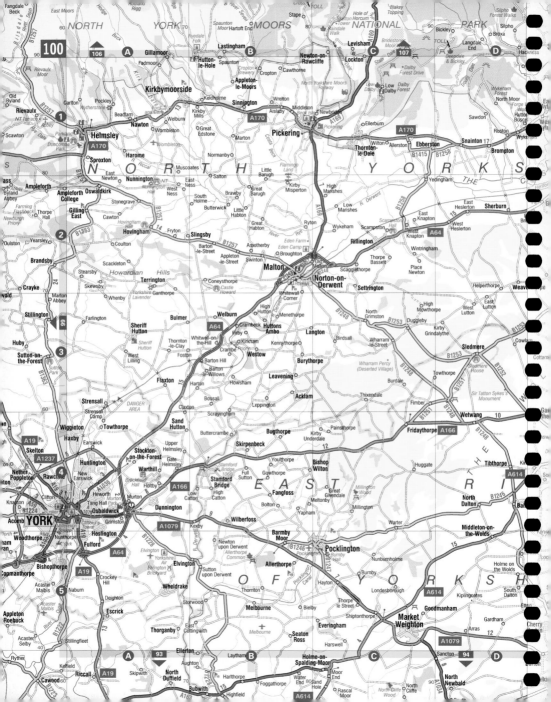

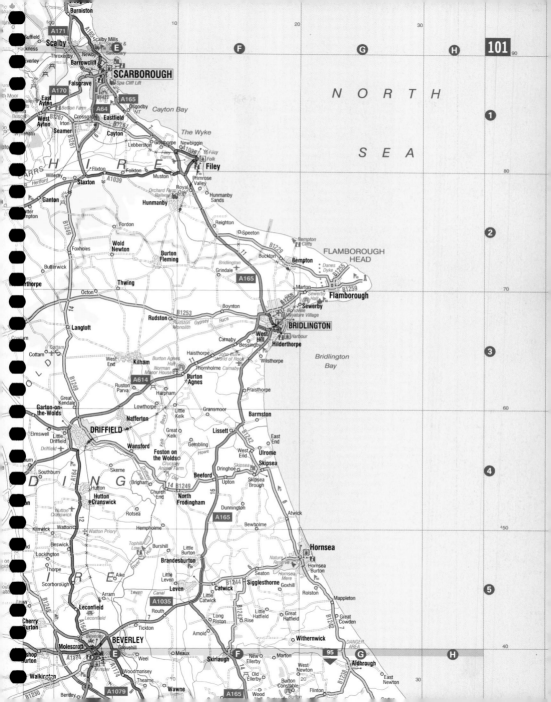

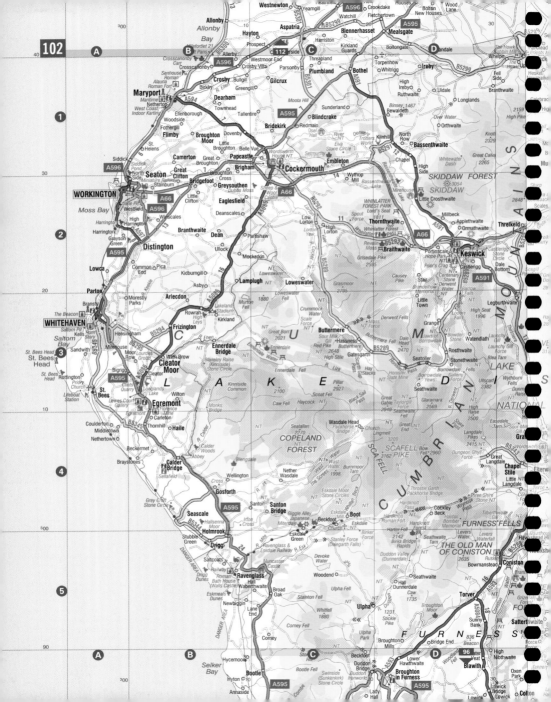

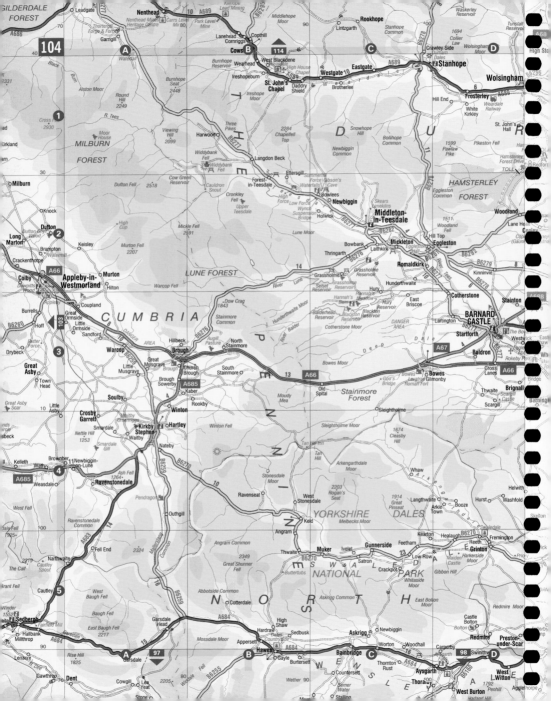

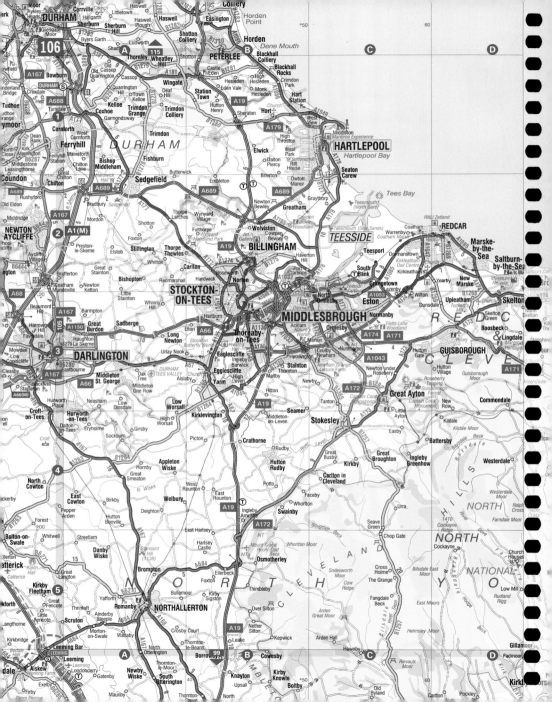

POINT OF AYRE

Rue Point
The Ayres
NT
Manx
The Ayres

Cranstal

Cronk y
Bing
The
Lhen
Dhowin
Bride

Jurby
East
Andreas
Shellag Point

Jurby
West
Crosses

Jurby Head
B3
Regaby

Ballasalla
Sandygate
Close
Sartfield
St.
Judes
Ramsey
Bay

The
Cronk
Civil War
Fort
Dhoor
Ramsey

Orrisdale
Ballaugh
Sulby
Churchtown
Lhergy
Frissel
Port e Vullen

Orrisdale Head
Ravensdale
Glen
Auldyn
Maughold
Head

Bishopscourt
Glen
Gate
Lewaigue
Maughold
Crosses

Kirk Michael
Glen
Dhoo
1854
North Barrule
Ballajora
Port Mooar

Ballaleigh
Corrany
Cornaa
Manx
Electric
Railway

Ballacarnane Beg
Glen
Mooar
Slieau Dhoo
SNAEFELL
Glen
Mona
Port Cornaa

Gob y Deigan
Barregarrow
1601
Clagh Ouyr
Dhoon
NT Manx
Dhoon Glen

Knocksharry
Cronk-y-Voddy
Sulby
Resr.
Mountain
Railway
Bulgham Bay

St. Patrick's Isle
Lambfell
Moar
1599
Colden
Injebreck
Resr.
Great Laxey
Mine Wheel
Old
Laxey
Laxey Head

Peel
Ballagyr
Glen Helen
Ballaugh
Laxey

Contrary Head
Ballig
Greeba
Castle
Ballaheannagh
Old
Laxey
Ballacannell

Patrick
Glen
Maye
St. John's
1570
Baldwin
Laxey Bay

ISLE OF MAN
Crosby
Glen
Vine
Hillberry
Baldrine
Clay Head

Dalby Point
Lower
Foxdale
Strang
Onchan
Port Groudle
Groudle Glen
Railway

Dalby
Foxdale
Fairy
Union Mills
Willaston
Onchan Head

Niarbyl Bay
Dalby
Moorland
1586
Hill
South
Fort Barule
Garth
Spring
Valley
DOUGLAS

Stroin Vuigh
Close
Clark
St.
Mark
Braaid
Cooil
Kewaigue
Douglas Bay

Fleshwick
Bay
Ballamodha
Newtown
Quine's
Hill
Horses
Home
Douglas Head

Lingague
Ronague
Grenaby
Port
Soderick
Little Ness

Bradda Head
Bradda
Surby
Colby
Ballabeg
Kentraa
Santon Head

Port Erin
Port
St. Mary
Ballasalla

The Howe
Four
Roads
Castletown
ISLE OF MAN

Chambered Cairn
The Sound
Kitterland
Cregneash
Derby
Fort
St. Michael's Island
Derbyhaven

NT Manx
Calf of Man
National
Folk
NT Manx
Scarlett
Nautical
Old House
of Keys

SPANISH HEAD
Dreswick
Point

Calf of Man

PAGE NOT CONTINUED

Douglas to:
Belfast 2hrs. 45mins.
(Fast Ferry, Seasonal)
Birkenhead 4hrs. 15mins.
(Seasonal)
Heysham 3hrs. 30mins.
Dublin 2hrs. 45mins.
(Fast Ferry, Seasonal)
Liverpool 2hrs. 30mins.
(Fast Ferry, Seasonal)

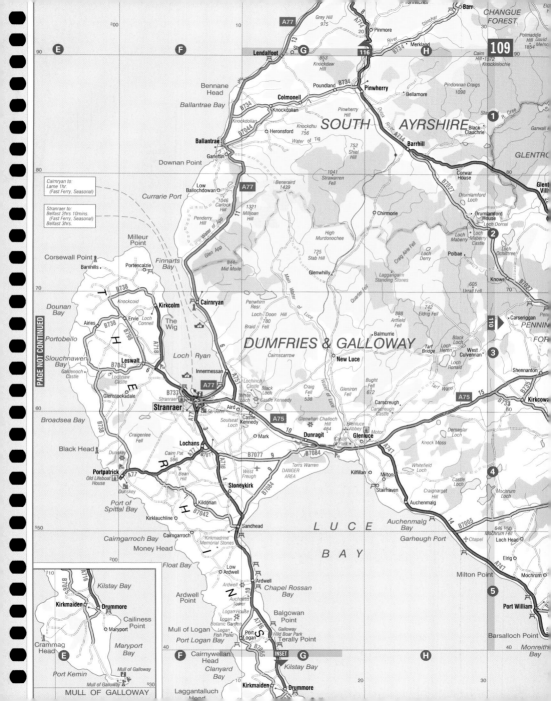

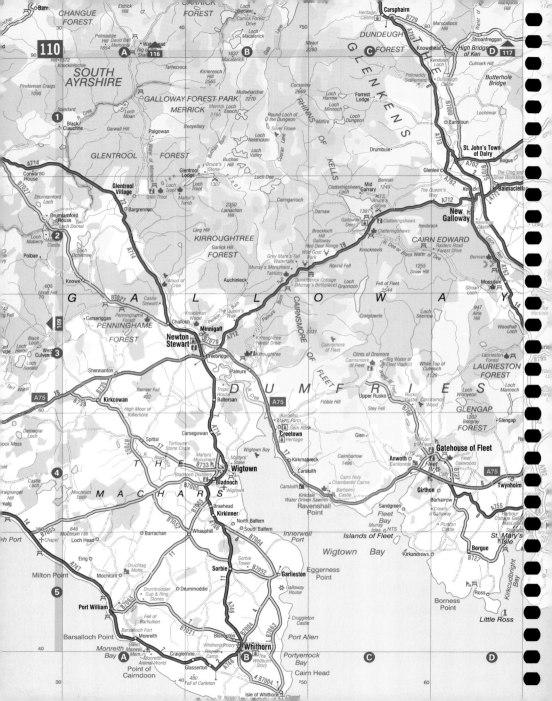

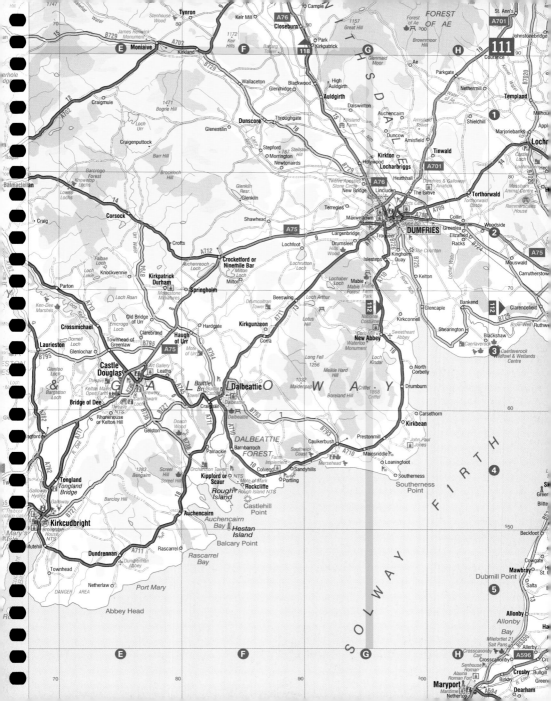

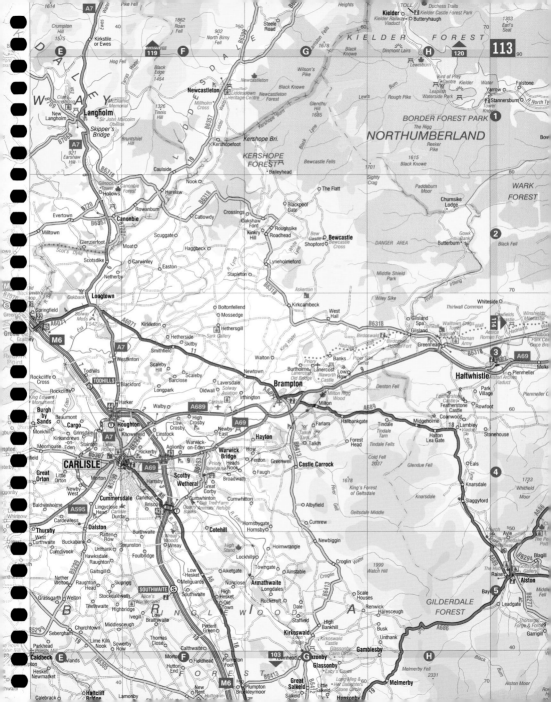

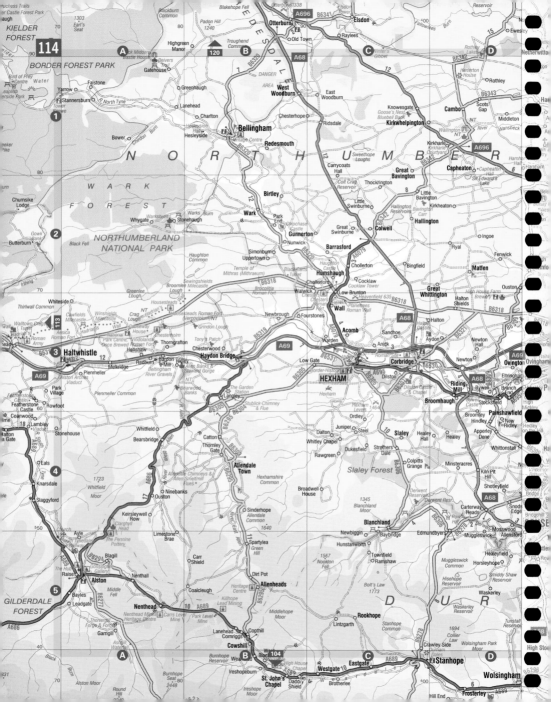

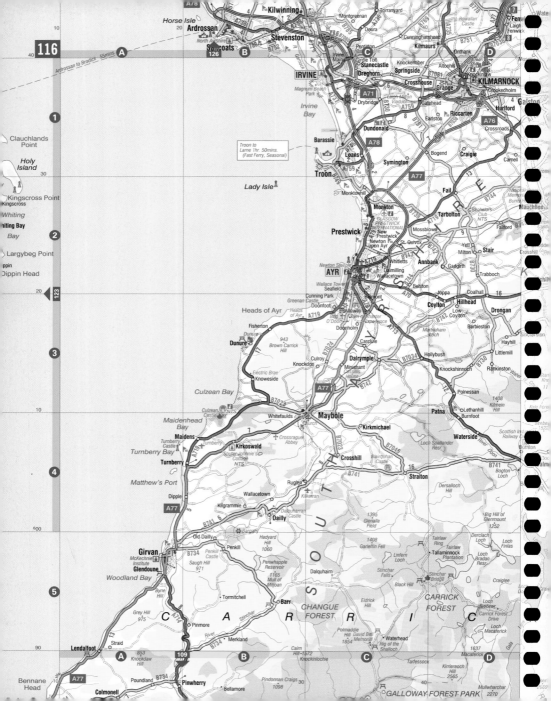

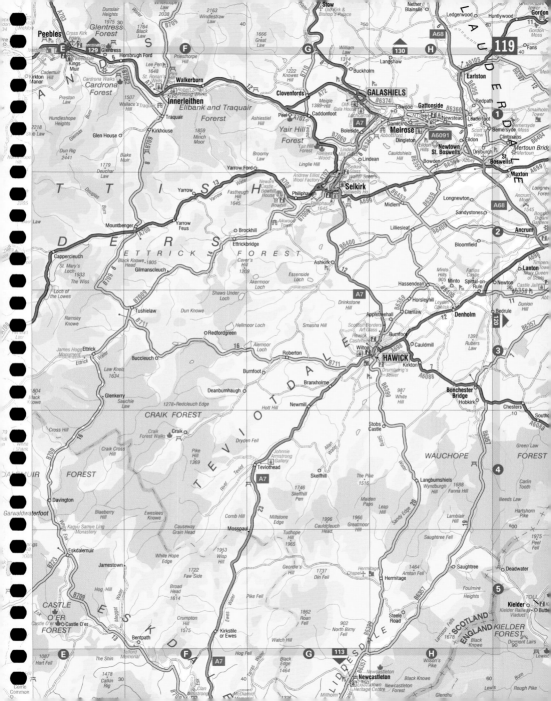

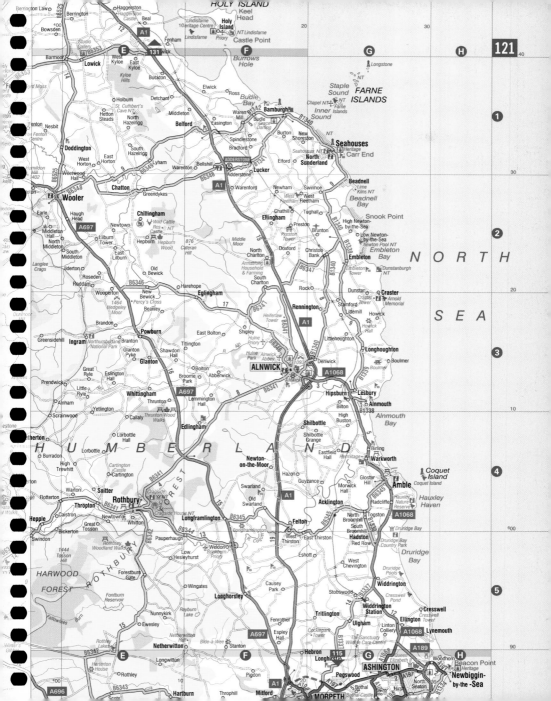

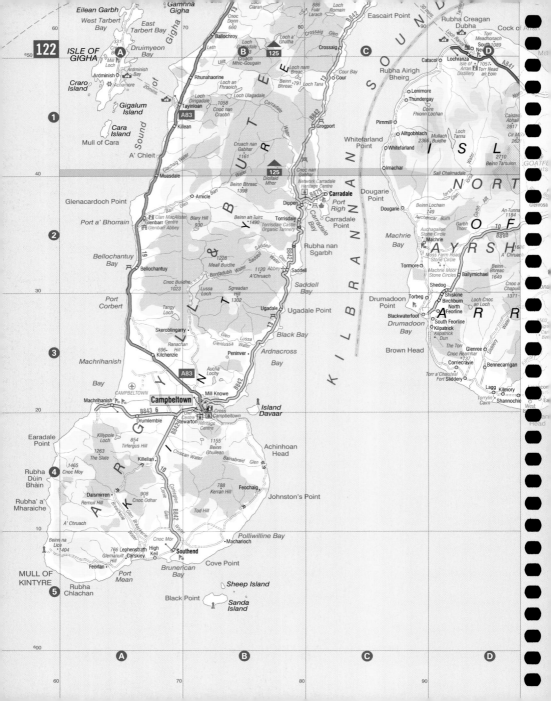

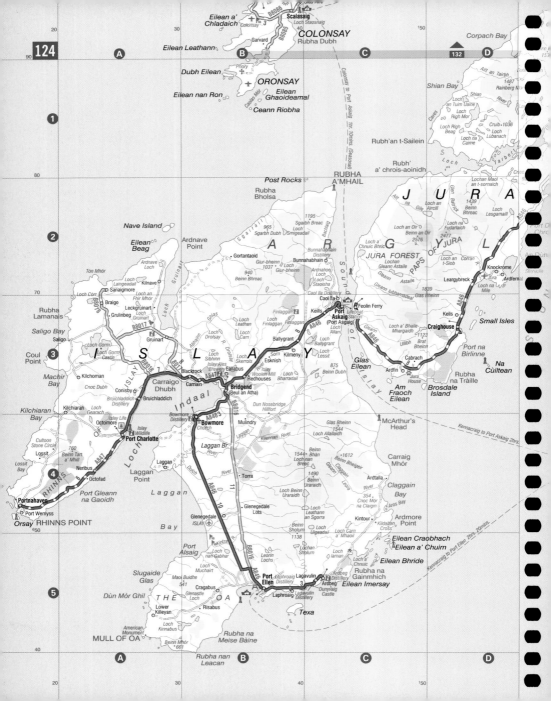

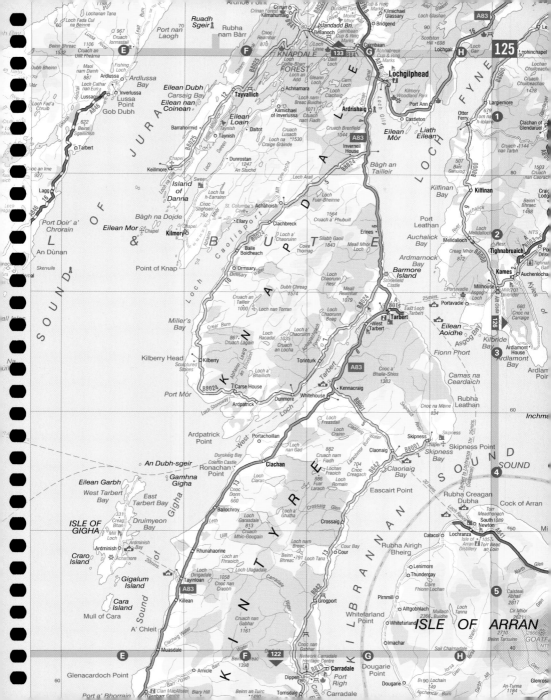

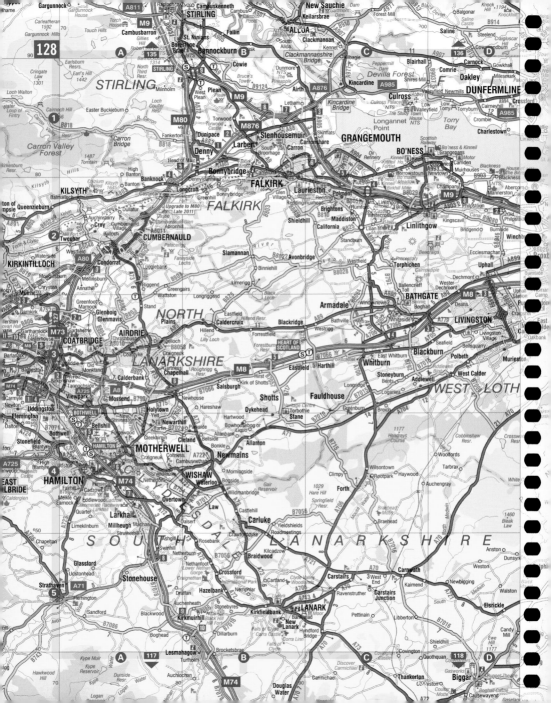

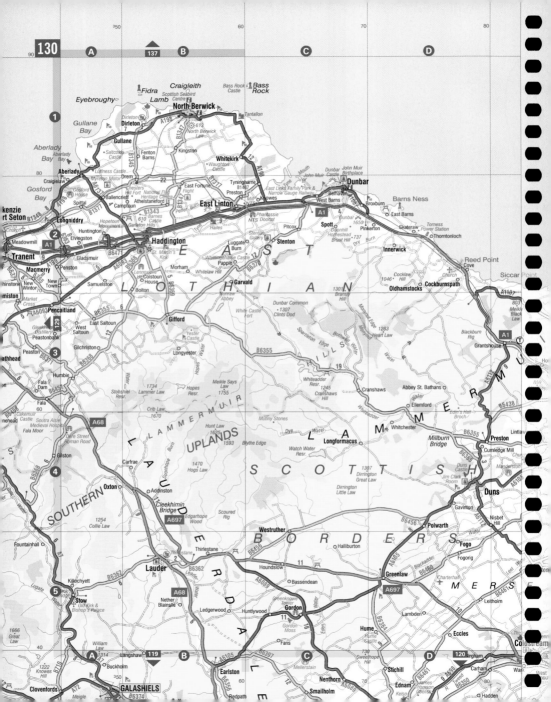

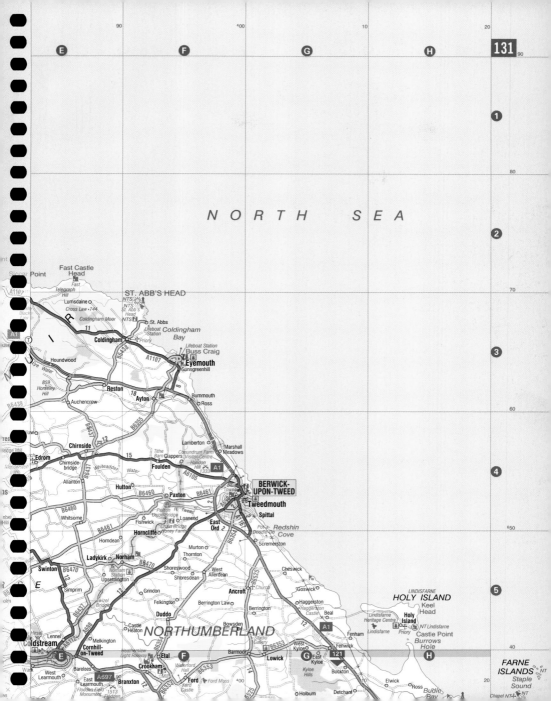

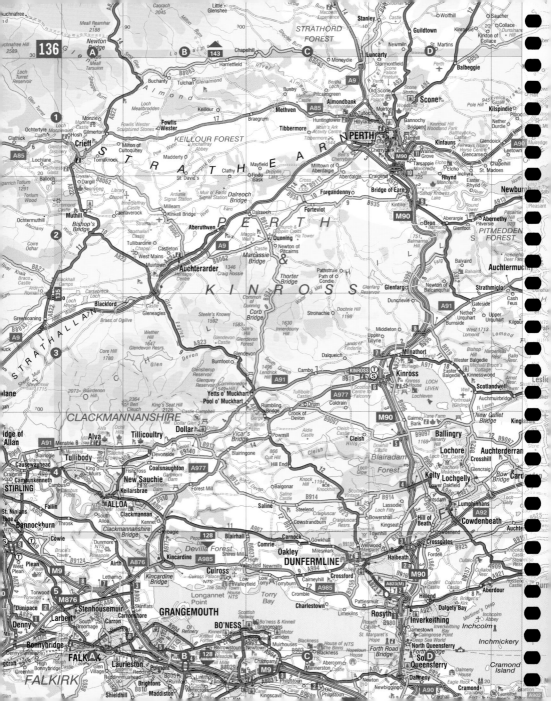

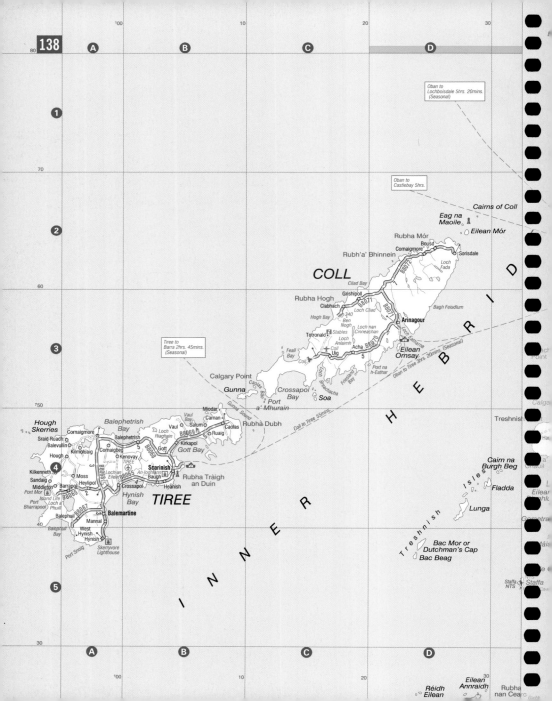

80

A   B   C   D

1

70

Oban to
Lochboisdale 5hrs. 20mins.
(Seasonal)

2

Oban to
Castlebay 5hrs.

Cairns of Coll

Eag na
Maoile

Eilean Mór

Rubha Mór

Bousd

60

Rubh' a' Bhinnein

Cornaigmore

Sorisdale

COLL

Loch
Fada

B8072

Cliad Bay

Grishipoll

H   E   B   R   I   D

Rubha Hogh

Loch Clad

Bagh Feisdlum

Clabhach

B8071

3

Hogh Bay

340
Ben
Nogh

Stables

Arinagour

B8071

Tiree to
Barra 2hrs. 45mins.
(Seasonal)

Totronald

Loch
Anlaimh

Loch nan
Cinneachan

Acha

Eilean
Ornsay

Feall
Bay

Coll

Uig

Coll

5

Port na
h-Eathar

Loch Airneanan

B8070

Point

Calgary Point

Crossapol
Bay

Loch Breachacha

Friesland Bay

Oban to Tiree 3hrs. 20mins. (Seasonal)

Calga

Gunna

Soa

Coll to Tiree 55mins.

Port
a' Mhurain

Caolas Bàn

Gunna Sound

Treshnish

Hou

Hough
Skerries

Balephetrish
Bay

Miodar

Vaul
Bay

Carnan

Rubhà Dubh

Chaoll

Cairn na
Burgh Beg

Sraid Ruadh

Cornaigmore

Balephetrish

Vaul

Salum

Caolas

B8069

Ruaig

Loch
Riaghain

Gott

Kirkapol

Eilean

Fladda

Balevullin

Kilmoluaig

Cornaigbeg

Kenovay

TIREE

Gott Bay

Lunga

Gometra

Hough

B8068

An-Iochdan

Scarinish

4

Kilkenneth

Moss

Loch an
Eilein

Baugh

Rubha Tràigh
an Duin

Treshnish   Isles

Nàis

Sandaig

Heylipol

Crossapol

Heanish

Middleton

Barrapol

Island Life

2

Port Mor

Loch a'
Phuill

Hynish Bay

TIREE

Bac Mor or
Dutchman's Cap

Port
Bharrapol

B8067

Balephuil

Balemartine

Bac Beag

Mannal

Balephuil
Bay

40

West
Hynish

Hynish

Port Snoig

Skerryvore
Lighthouse

Staffa
NTS

Staffa

5

30

A   B   C   D

I   N   N   E   R

100

10

20

30

Réidh
Eilean

Eilean
Annraidh

Rubha
nan Cear

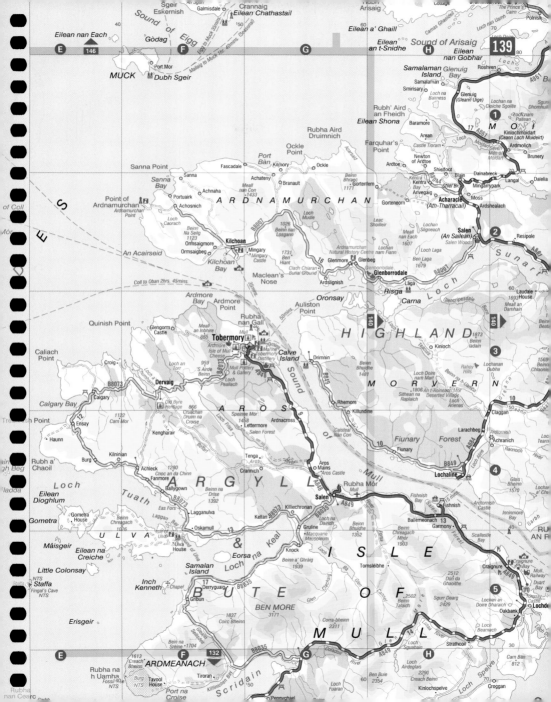

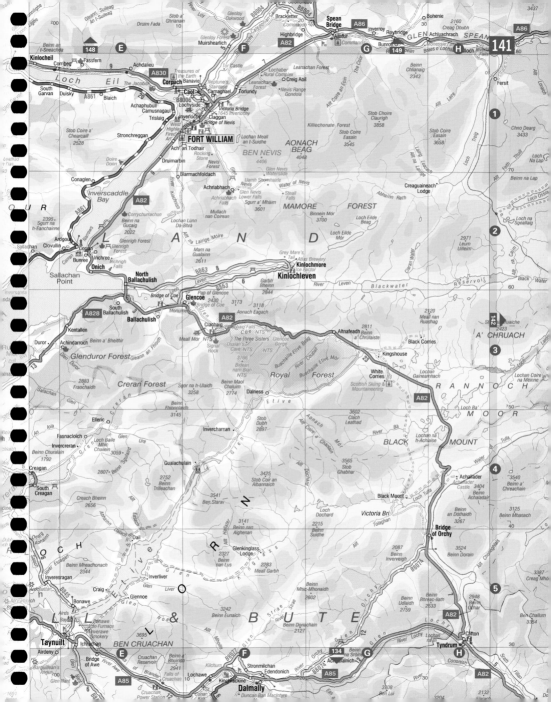

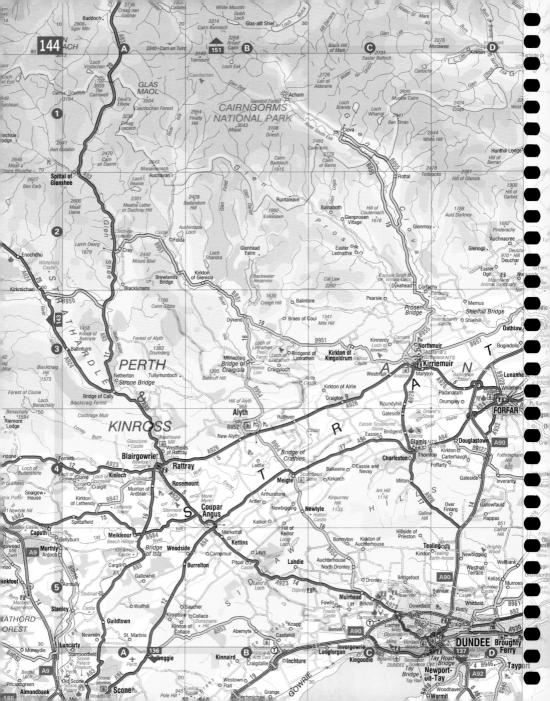

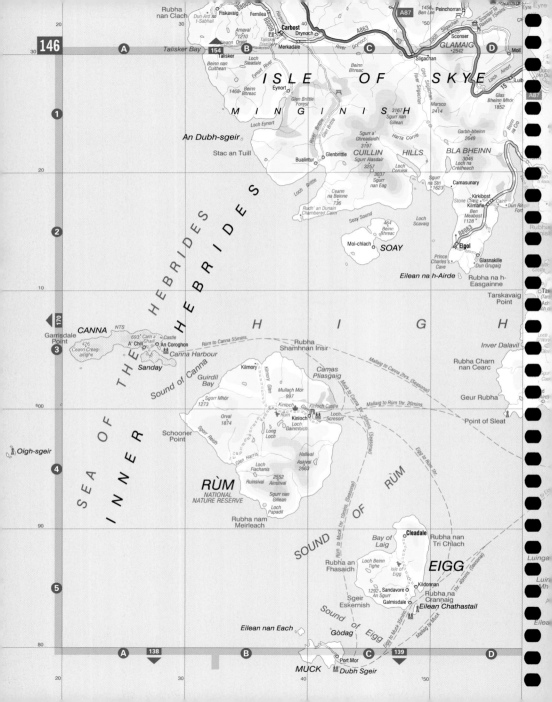

ISLE OF SKYE

MINGINISH

CUILLIN HILLS

BLA BHEINN

SOAY

THE HEBRIDES

THE HEBRIDES

SEA OF THE INNER HEBRIDES

H I G H

CANNA

Canna Harbour
Sanday

RÙM
NATIONAL
NATURE RESERVE

SOUND OF RÙM

SOUND OF EIGG

EIGG

MUCK

Oigh-sgeir

Rubha
nan Clach

Fiskavaig
Fernilea
Arnaval
1210
Talisker
Distillery
Carbost
Drynoch
Merkadale
River Drynoch
A863
Sligachan
GLAMAIG
•2542
Sconser
Moll

Talisker Bay
Talisker
Loch
Sleadale
Eynort River
Beinn nan
Cuithean
Beinn
Bhreac
Glen
Drynoch
Peinchorran
Ben Lee
1456·
Sconser to
Raasay 15mins
Suisnish
Eyre

A87

Eynort
Glen Brittle
Forest
Beinn
Bhreac
Marsco
2414
Glas
Bheinn Mhòr
1852

An Dubh-sgeir
Stac an Tuill

Loch Eynort

Loch
Brittle
Sgurr a'
Ghreadaidh
3197
Sgurr Alasdair
3257
3037
Sgurr
nan Eag
3167
Sgurr nan
Gillean
Harta Corrie
Garbh-bheinn
2649

Bualintur
Glenbrittle

Ceann
na Beinne
736
Ruadh' an Dunain
Chambered Cairn

Loch
Coruisk
3046
Loch na
Crèitheach

Sgùrr
na Strì
1623·
Camasunary

Kirkibost
Kilmarie
Ben
Meabost
1128·
Dùn Ringill
Fort

Soay Sound
464
Beinn
Bhreac

Loch
Scavaig

Stone Circle
Cairn

Moi-chlach

Prince
Charles's
Cave

Elgol

Glasnakille
Dùn Grugaig

Eilean na h-Airde

Rubha na h-
Easgainne

Tarskavaig
Point

Garrisdale
Point

NTS
693· Carn a'
Ghaill
·426
Ceann Creag-
airighe
A' Chill
Castle
Coroghon

Rùm to Canna 55mins
Rubha
Shamhnan Insir

Inver Dalavil

Rubha Charn
nan Cearc

Sound of Canna

Kilmory
Kilmory
Glen
Camas
Pliasgaig

Mallaig to Canna 2hrs (Seasonal)

Geur Rubha

Guirdil
Bay
Sgorr Mhòr
1273
Mullach Mòr
997

Mallaig to Rùm 1hr. 20mins.
Mallaig to Canna 1hr

Point of Sleat

Schooner
Point
Orval
1874

Kinloch
Glen Kinloch Castle
Kinloch
Loch
Scresort
Loch.
Gainmhich

Long
Loch

Egg to Rùm 1hr.

Rùm to Muck 10mins. (Seasonal)

Mallaig to Rùm 1hr. (Seasonal)

Glen Harris.
Loch
Fiachanis
2552
Ainshval
Hallival
Askival
2663
Ruinsival
Sgurr nan
Gillean

Rubha nam
Meirleach
Loch
Papadil

SOUND OF RÙM

Eigg to Rùm 1hr.

Cleadale
Rubha nan
Trì Chlach

Luinga

Luira
Mh

Bay of
Laig
Rubha an
Fhasaidh
Loch Beinn
Tighe
Isle of
Eigg

Rùm to Muck 10mins. (Seasonal)

Sgeir
Eskernish
1292
An Sgurr
Sandavore
Galmisdale
Kildonnan
Rubha na
Crannaig
Eilean Chathastail

Eilean

Eilean nan Each

Gòdag

Port Mor
MUCK
Dubh Sgeir

Eigg to Muck 30mins.
Mallaig to Muck

154
170
138
139

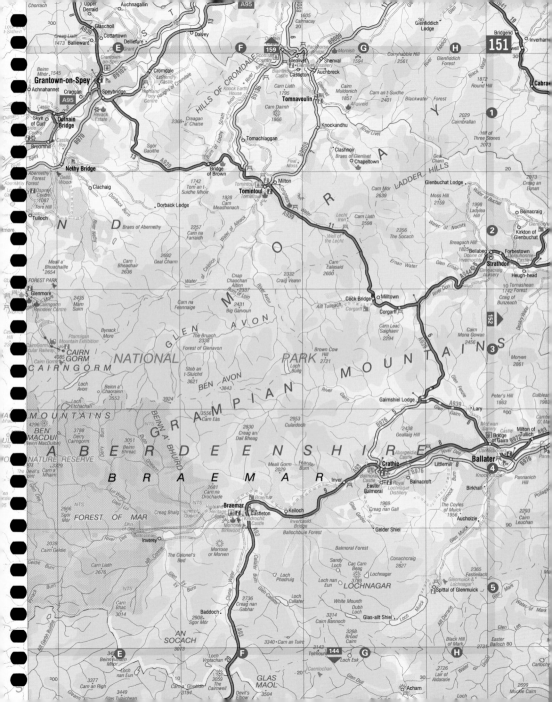

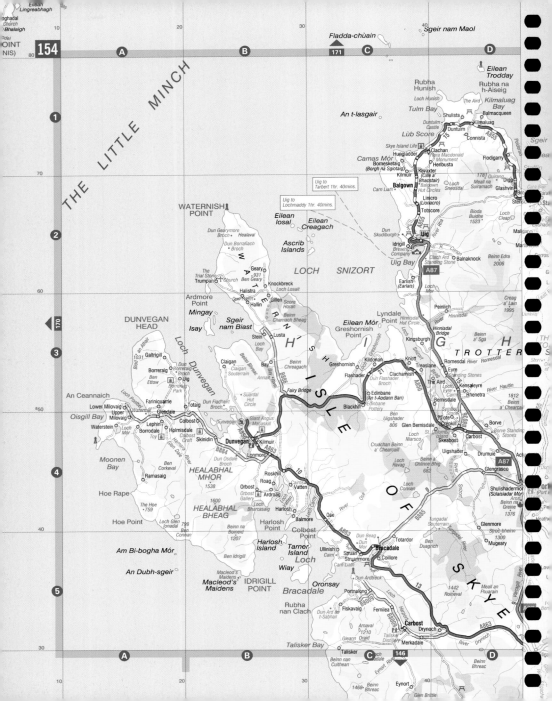

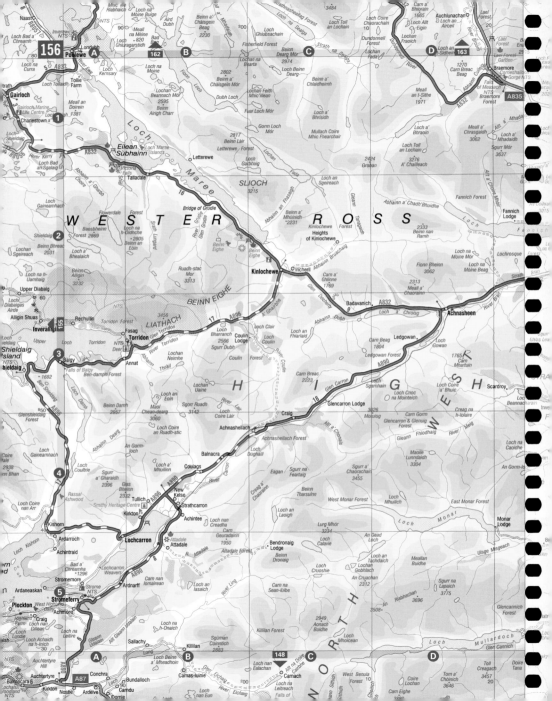

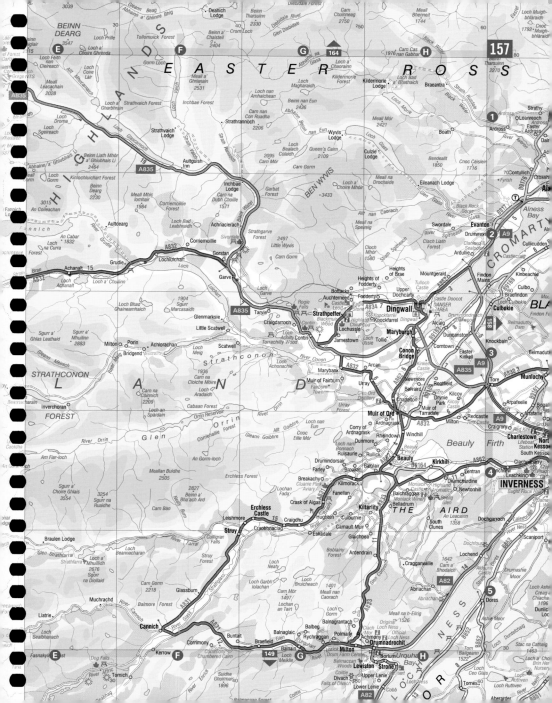

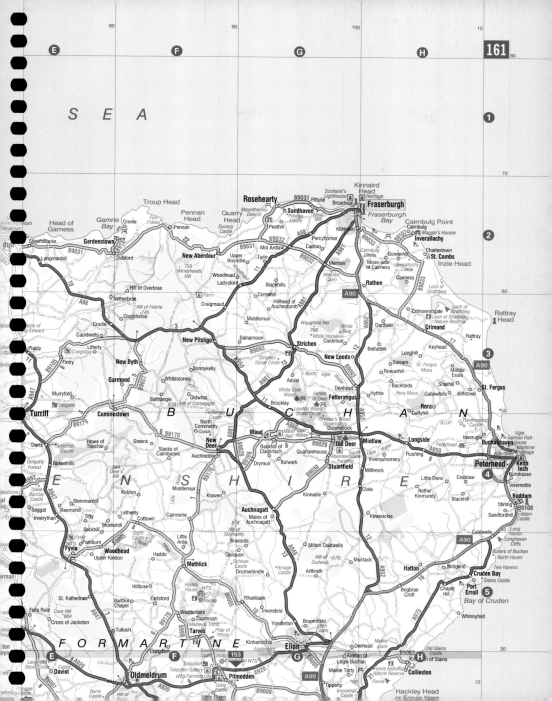

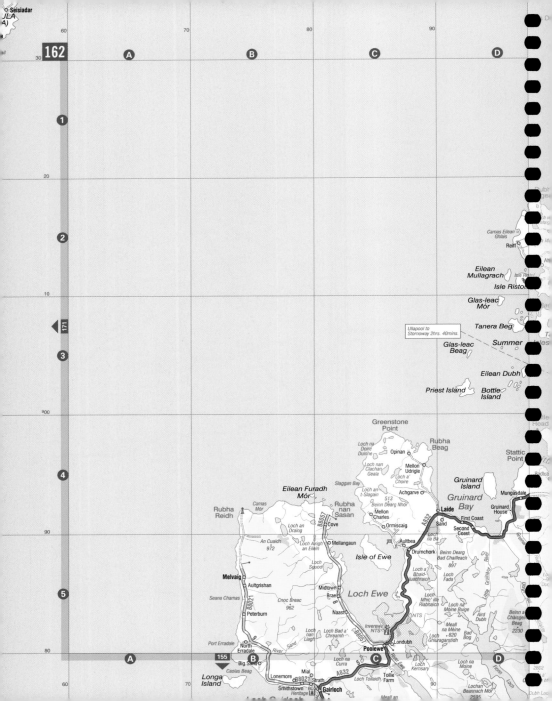

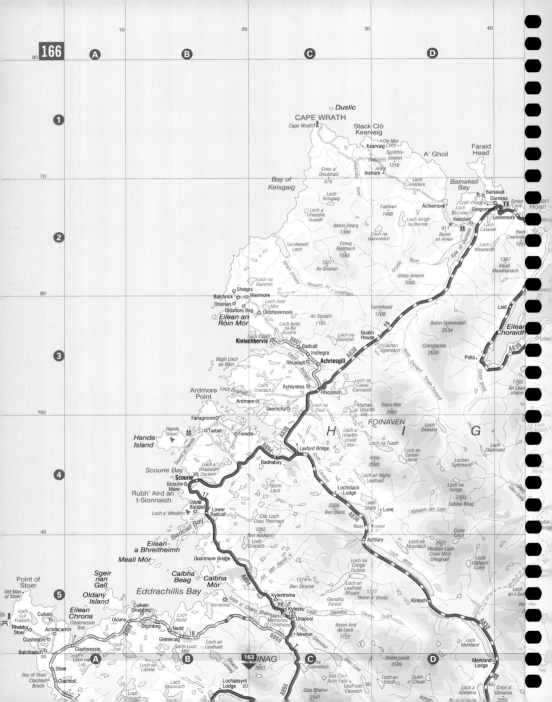

PENTLAND FIRTH

Burwick
B9041 Chambered Cairn
Brough Tomb of the Eagles
Liddle

Island of Stroma
Nethertown
Uppertown

Pentland Skerries

DUNNET HEAD
Dunnet Head 374
Burifa Hill
Long Loch
Dunnet Hill 398
Loch of Bushta
Mary-Ann's Cottage
Hunspow
West Dunnet
St. John's Loch
Corsback
Brough
Ham
Rattar
Castle of Mey
Loch of Mey
Mey
Scarfskerry
Tang Head
East Mey
Gills
Gills Bay
Kirkstyle
Warse
Seater
Huna
John o' Groats
Last Ho.
Duncansby Stacks

St. John's Point
Boars of Duncansby
DUNCANSBY HEAD
Stacks of Duncansby

A836
Barrock
Inkstack
Upper Gills
Canisbay
Brabster
Warth Hill 406

Dunnet
Dunnet Bay
Castletown
Olrig
Greenland
Greenland Mains
Lochend
Slickly
Freswick
Tofts
Freswick Bay
Skirza
Skirza Head
Ness Head

Murkle
Murkle
Tain
Reaster
Alterwall
Kirk Burn
Gill Burn
A99

Hillclay
Durran
Bowermadden
Lyth
Sortat
Howe
Mireland
Keiss
Keiss Castle
Tang Head
Arts Centre
Northlands Viking Centre
Auckengill
Nybster
Brough Head

Stemster
Corsback
B874
Bowertower
Halcro
North Watten
Kirk
B870
Myrelandhorn
Loch of Wester
Westerloch
Sinclair's Bay

Clayock
Loch Scarmclate
Gillock
Loch of Lyth
Knapperfield
Killimster
Reiss
Sinclair Girnigoe
Noss Head

Larel
A882
Oldhall
Loch Watten
B874
Winless
Bilster
Sibster
Ackergill
Ackergillshore
Sealky Head

Watten
N
D
Strath
Wick River
Haster
Milton
Janetstown
Staxigoe
Papigoe
Broadhaven
WICK Heritage Centre
Staxigoe

Archie Sinclair Fossil Centre
Loch of Toftingall
B870
Acharole
Burn of Acharole
A882
Wick
Wick Bay

Badlipster
Tannach
Loch Hempriggs
Newton
Whiterow
Old Wick
Gote o' Tram
Helman Head
Pulteney Distillery
A99
South Head

Hill of Olickett 462
Gansclet
Thrumster
Raggra
Borrowston
Sarclet
Sarclet Head

Hill of Rangag •623
Achavanich
Loch Stemster Standing Stones •815 Stemster Hill
Camster
Grey Cairns of Camster
Cnoc an Earranaiche 692
Loch of Yarrows
'South Yarrows Cairns'
Cairn o' Get

Sheppardstown
Roster
East Clyth
Uibster
A99

Crofts of Benachielt
Rumster Forest
Osclay
Bruan
Hill o' Many Stanes
Upper Lybster
Mid Clyth
Halberry Head

A9
Achow
Swiney
Clyth
Overton
Upper Latheron
A99
Lybster
Waterlines
Burrigill
Forse
Forse Castle
Clan Gunn Heritage Centre
Inveshore
Standing Stones

Landhallow
Latheron
Latheronwheel
Knockinnon
Laidhay Croft
Dormin Centre

BUTT OF LEWIS
(RUBHA ROBHANAIS)

NA H-EILEANAN AN IAR
(WESTERN ISLES)

O U T E R   H E B R I D E S

I S L E   O F   L E W I S   (E I L E A N   L E O D H A I S)

STORNOWAY
(STEORNABHAGH)

T H E   M I N C H

Cellar Head

Tolsta Head
(Ceann Tholastaidh)

Broad Bay

EYE PENINSULA
(AN RUBHA)

SOUND OF SHIANT
(CAOLAS NAN EILEAN)

Shiant Islands
(Na H-Eileanan Mora)

PARK
(PAIRC)

NORTH HARRIS
(CEANNA TUTATH
NA HEARADH)

SOUTH HARRIS
(CEANNA DEAS
(NA HEARADH))

Leverburgh
(An t-Ob)

Rennish Point
(Rubha Reinis)

Toe Head
(Gob an Tobha)

Taransay
(Tarasaigh)

Great Bernera
(Bearnaraigh)

Scarp

Rubha na h-Aiseig

ISLE OF SKYE

Uig

Waternish Point

L I T T L E   M I N C H

Scale: 9.72 miles to 1 inch   1:615,730

| 0 5 10 15 Miles |
| 0 5 10 15 20 Kilometres |

Stornoway to
Ullapool 2hrs. 40mins.

Tarbert to
Uig 1hr. 40mins.

Lochmaddy to:
Uig 1hr. 40mins.

Uig to:
Lochmaddy 1hr. 40mins.
Tarbert 1hr. 40mins.

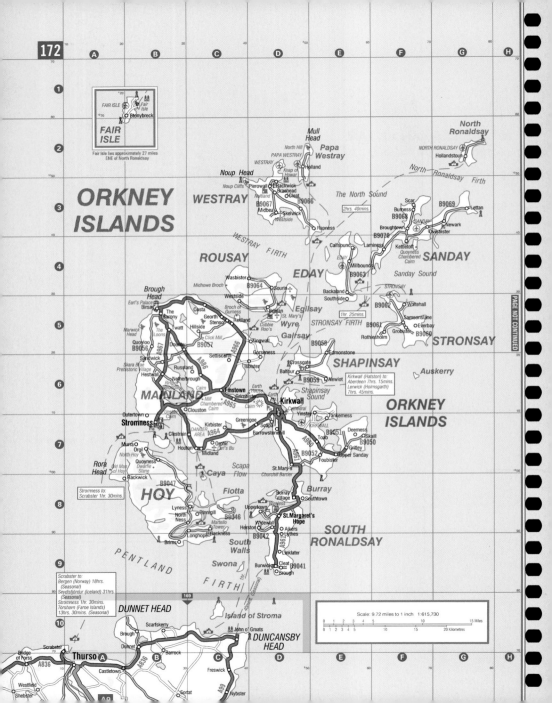

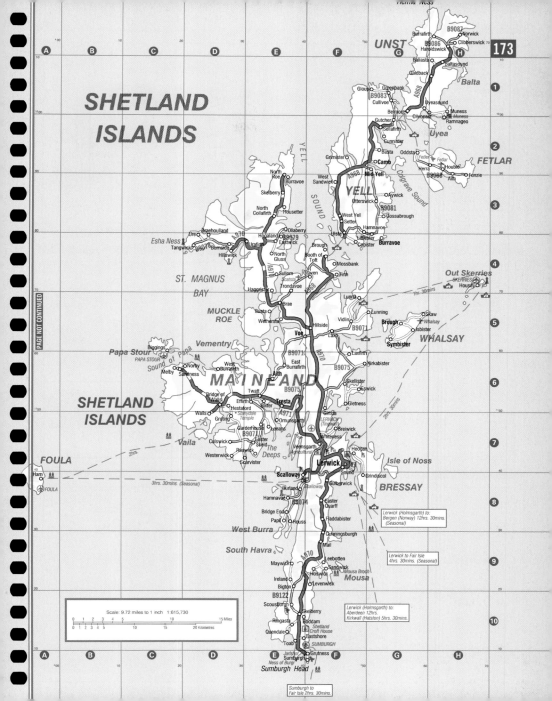

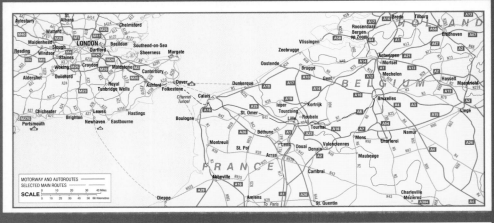

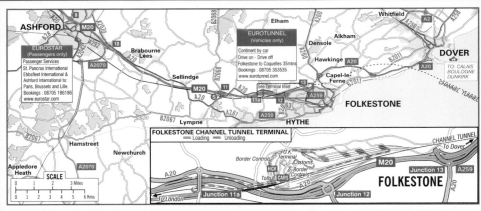

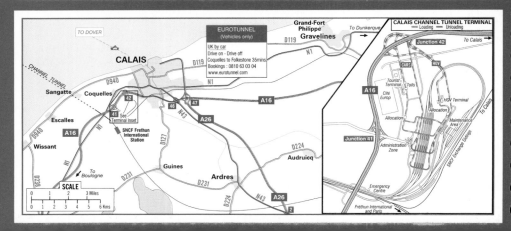

Mileage Chart

The distances for the mileage chart have been compiled by using a combination of Primary Routes and Motorways between any two towns shown.

To find the distance between any two towns shown, follow the horizontal line of one town and the vertical line of the other; at the intersection read off the mileage.

ie : Horizontal - LONDON

Vertical - LIVERPOOL

Intersection 216 miles

178 **179** **176** **177**

Key to Route Planning Map Pages

PRIMARY ROUTES, shown in green throughout this Atlas, are a national network of recommended through routes which complement the motorway system. Selected places of major traffic importance are known as Primary Route Destinations and, on road signs, have a green background.

```
ABERDEEN
449 ABERYSTWYTH
181 324 AYR
400 114 272 BIRMINGHAM
330 159 196 124 BRADFORD
562 258 441 169 263 BRIGHTON
503 122 375 88 215 129 BRISTOL
447 198 366 102 156 117 167 CAMBRIDGE
505 106 377 106 233 168 42 201 CARDIFF
217 232 89 183 107 345 286 256 288 CARLISLE
437 134 297 18 124 157 102 84 129 200 COVENTRY
397 137 269 41 88 188 134 99 159 180 43 DERBY
340 192 239 95 40 232 184 117 210 150 94 57 DONCASTER
558 315 477 195 284 81 194 118 233 393 180 208 244 DOVER
125 340 75 284 198 466 377 326 379 91 303 266 212 444 EDINBURGH
553 199 425 161 282 170 75 232 107 336 166 213 257 244 439 EXETER
148 430 136 391 305 568 478 456 486 198 415 387 345 591 131 549 FORT WILLIAM
148 322 36 291 203 468 378 355 384 96 313 282 245 491 46 449 100 GLASGOW
445 109 317 53 171 152 35 132 53 228 59 93 149 189 331 107 435 324 GLOUCESTER
520 258 411 170 224 130 203 64 234 323 152 167 185 129 397 262 524 419 171 HARWICH
443 96 315 151 158 330 204 252 209 226 167 156 169 358 316 279 423 323 189 331 HOLYHEAD
107 492 198 449 353 620 536 490 558 260 458 421 369 601 157 607 63 162 496 554 481 INVERNESS
505 268 420 156 210 125 206 54 240 311 138 155 171 127 381 264 510 409 177 21 307 538 IPSWICH
269 182 139 151 62 324 235 215 232 50 170 136 99 344 141 307 248 146 200 279 180 310 268 KENDAL
357 235 255 139 68 243 228 134 239 165 123 94 37 254 230 290 367 255 195 204 218 387 189 127 KINGSTON UPON HULL
316 171 198 119 9 256 209 144 226 111 117 74 32 275 190 279 309 208 167 217 162 345 197 72 60 LEEDS
407 155 294 43 99 163 118 70 140 214 24 30 73 183 282 189 412 312 83 146 182 431 125 166 98 97 LEICESTER
376 208 249 87 80 207 170 88 192 178 76 53 41 206 247 241 376 274 135 152 204 402 124 140 46 72 52 LINCOLN
327 120 199 99 67 267 180 179 169 110 113 90 89 294 201 240 308 213 142 265 95 370 236 75 126 73 110 118 LIVERPOOL
321 128 204 87 37 252 167 159 188 117 99 58 51 273 208 239 315 215 132 230 120 363 211 72 96 42 95 87 34 MANCHESTER
273 233 181 174 69 316 265 196 287 92 175 130 84 316 147 337 279 192 230 266 226 306 253 77 88 64 154 127 134 106 MIDDLESBROUGH
230 266 146 209 98 345 300 232 312 58 209 165 115 350 104 369 237 153 260 302 262 269 289 207 113 168 197 264 295 152 129 25 264 287 88 130 96 188 153 167 136 40 NEWCASTLE UPON TYNE
476 270 348 163 185 174 234 62 256 280 142 146 142 169 351 284 478 378 193 72 289 505 44 249 145 178 112 103 222 177 221 252 NORWICH
381 155 267 54 78 191 140 84 165 188 52 15 48 210 256 218 386 286 108 165 177 410 140 141 92 72 27 37 107 68 128 159 118 NOTTINGHAM
485 151 335 68 167 106 73 92 106 267 57 101 138 142 358 151 465 365 47 104 208 515 128 253 175 166 98 97 LEICESTER
680 301 552 269 394 279 184 343 218 463 278 316 369 355 551 109 663 561 217 374 388 715 375 419 412 391 310 359 353 344 449 481 393 323 261 PENZANCE
87 366 85 336 245 509 412 370 422 134 346 309 254 485 43 487 103 59 362 439 360 113 424 184 273 233 326 290 244 254 191 148 394 299 404 598 PERTH
589 232 461 203 325 206 111 274 159 372 209 254 300 286 485 43 592 490 150 305 322 648 305 348 326 323 231 284 299 281 379 412 327 255 193 75 529 PLYMOUTH
575 231 440 147 274 50 95 132 138 357 132 184 231 137 448 127 555 455 114 161 303 603 158 308 268 245 166 209 254 237 315 360 200 191 83 235 486 170 PORTSMOUTH
526 180 399 103 213 79 77 92 110 312 90 138 184 115 402 141 506 406 75 129 349 569 109 260 207 213 136 167 212 196 288 321 227 159 98 145 456 170 31 READING
529 178 383 121 245 82 53 140 101 312 113 159 207 158 400 91 510 408 73 177 262 569 177 265 251 230 132 187 213 208 287 318 200 162 65 201 443 132 43 57 SALISBURY
355 173 235 79 42 245 163 121 193 154 75 35 21 268 230 245 352 252 133 185 164 387 176 102 66 33 68 46 74 40 102 133 147 36 142 173 171 55 118 311 287 241 201 147 168 50 35 183 199 SHEFFIELD
388 73 260 47 100 216 116 140 107 171 64 67 114 249 262 175 369 267 77 215 104 424 195 125 163 102 79 123 59 67 166 203 196 86 105 286 309 218 195 147 150 85 SHREWSBURY
547 213 401 128 235 64 75 129 122 330 114 167 201 150 433 106 528 426 98 157 287 590 162 276 249 230 136 189 235 215 288 320 190 162 66 217 476 149 20 47 23 206 175 SOUTHAMPTON
520 258 431 152 220 85 177 64 211 342 129 168 185 89 395 226 548 438 152 57 303 569 57 283 200 213 139 156 255 225 262 299 99 160 105 337 439 269 117 98 132 197 173 126 SOUTHEND-ON-SEA
374 108 243 47 75 217 127 137 140 150 64 36 74 236 241 202 348 248 95 201 122 410 179 121 117 78 55 87 56 36 142 173 171 55 118 311 267 241 201 147 168 50 35 183 199 STOKE-ON-TRENT
496 76 368 124 220 209 80 222 116 150 184 244 263 57 293 76 177 469 267 249 262 229 174 226 168 187 293 323 286 178 144 266 446 196 175 147 136 202 124 159 245 159 SWANSEA
213 584 304 557 461 728 644 589 640 352 552 529 475 706 262 715 169 293 604 657 589 108 654 402 492 453 544 510 463 471 410 367 613 519 621 823 220 758 709 662 664 506 523 682 659 502 631 THURSO
437 96 309 29 135 162 62 119 73 220 46 68 124 197 306 136 418 311 28 168 151 480 174 169 166 146 72 118 108 101 203 229 180 85 72 244 350 177 146 91 105 103 49 124 150 65 97 572 WORCESTER
312 193 201 129 34 269 227 151 237 116 129 84 33 269 187 289 314 214 181 232 185 344 200 81 38 24 108 76 96 65 48 83 176 84 174 400 230 331 257 217 244 54 132 244 214 114 268 450 164 YORK
501 206 390 118 203 53 118 58 150 305 97 128 165 76 373 171 503 403 101 79 264 527 76 264 188 196 102 143 216 200 246 278 114 130 55 282 416 214 74 39 84 161 160 78 43 160 187 636 110 203 LONDON
```

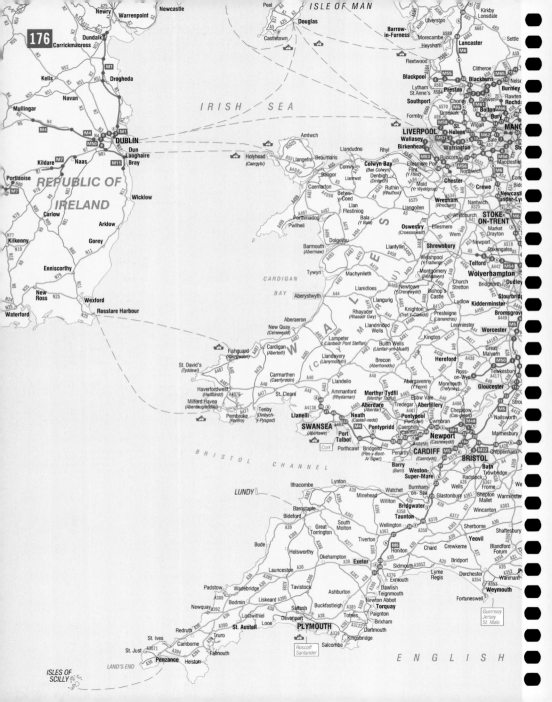

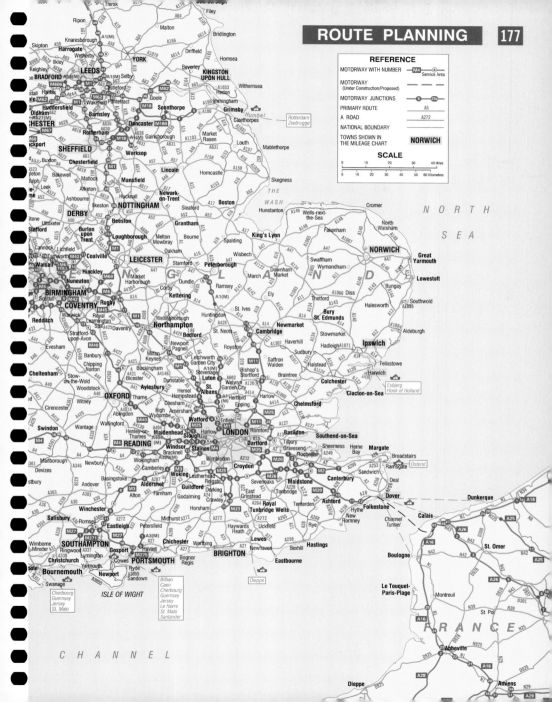

REFERENCE

MOTORWAY WITH NUMBER	M4 Service Area
MOTORWAY (Under Construction/Proposed)	- - -
MOTORWAY JUNCTIONS	
PRIMARY ROUTE	A5
A ROAD	A272
NATIONAL BOUNDARY	
TOWNS SHOWN IN THE MILEAGE CHART	**NORWICH**

SCALE

0   10   20   30   40 Miles
0   10   20   30   40   50   60 Kilometres

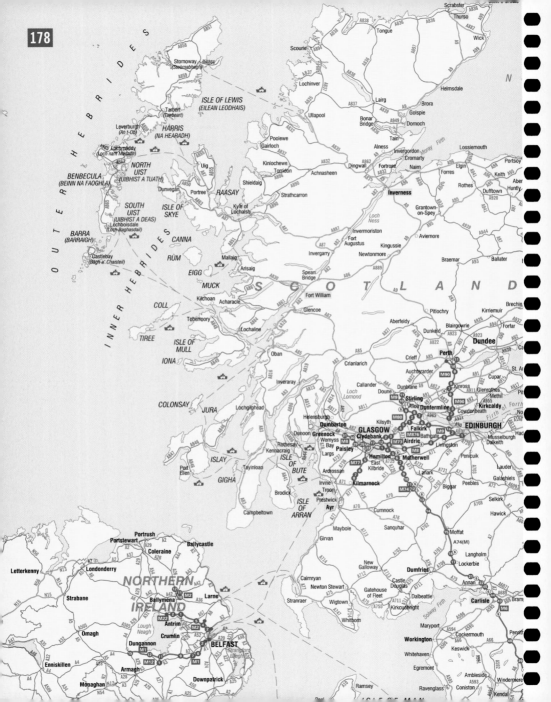

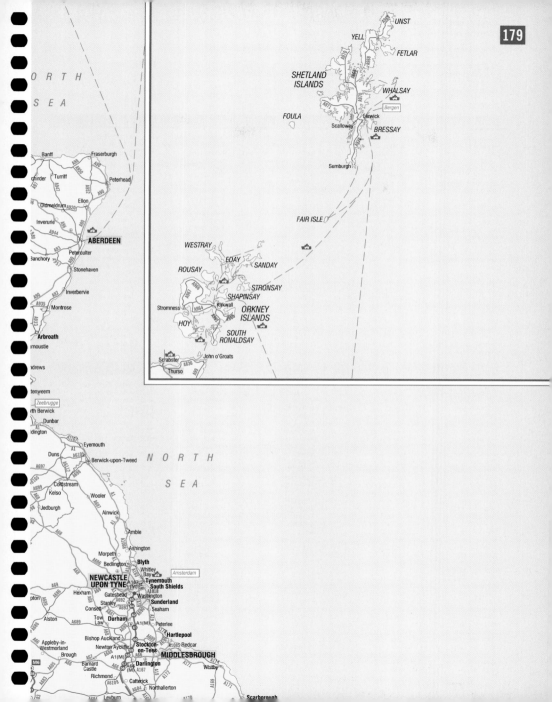

INDEX TO CITIES, TOWNS, VILLAGES, HAMLETS & LOCATIONS

(1) A strict alphabetical order is used e.g. An Dùnan follows Andreas but precedes Andwell.

(2) The map reference given refers to the actual map square in which the town spot or built-up area is located and not to the place name.

(3) Where two or more places of the same name occur in the same County or Unitary Authority, the nearest large town is also given; e.g. Achiemore. *High* . . . .2D **166** (nr. Durness) indicates that Achiemore is located in square 2D on page **166** and is situated near Durness in the Unitary Authority of Highland.

(4) Only one reference is given although due to page overlaps the place may appear on more than one page.

(5) Major towns are shown in bold, i.e. **Abercynon**. *Rhon* 2D **32**

COUNTIES and UNITARY AUTHORITIES with the abbreviations used in this index

Aberdeen : *Aber*
Aberdeenshire : *Abers*
Angus : *Ang*
Argyll & Bute : *Arg*
Bath & N E Somerset : *Bath*
Bedford : *Bed*
Blackburn with Darwen : *Bkbn*
Blackpool : *Bkpl*
Blaenau Gwent : *Blae*
Bournemouth : *Bour*
Bracknell Forest : *Brac*
Bridgend : *B'end*
Brighton & Hove : *Brig*
Bristol : *Bris*
Buckinghamshire : *Buck*
Caerphilly : *Cphy*
Cambridgeshire : *Cambs*
Cardiff : *Card*
Carmarthenshire : *Carm*
Central Bedfordshire : *C Beds*
Ceredigion : *Cdgn*
Cheshire East : *Ches E*
Cheshire West & Chester : *Ches W*
Clackmannanshire : *Clac*
Conwy : *Cnwy*
Cornwall : *Corn*
Cumbria : *Cumb*
Darlington : *Darl*
Denbighshire : *Den*

Derby : *Derb*
Derbyshire : *Derbs*
Devon : *Devn*
Dorset : *Dors*
Dumfries & Galloway : *Dum*
Dundee : *D'dee*
Durham : *Dur*
East Ayrshire : *E Ayr*
East Dunbartonshire : *E Dun*
East Lothian : *E Lot*
East Renfrewshire : *E Ren*
East Riding of Yorkshire : *E Yor*
East Sussex : *E Sus*
Edinburgh : *Edin*
Essex : *Essx*
Falkirk : *Falk*
Fife : *Fife*
Flintshire : *Flin*
Glasgow : *Glas*
Gloucestershire : *Glos*
Greater London : *G Lon*
Greater Manchester : *G Man*
Gwynedd : *Gwyn*
Halton : *Hal*
Hampshire : *Hants*
Hartlepool : *Hart*
Herefordshire : *Here*
Hertfordshire : *Herts*
Highland : *High*

Inverclyde : *Inv*
Isle of Anglesey : *IOA*
Isle of Man : *IOM*
Isle of Wight : *IOW*
Isles of Scilly : *IOS*
Kent : *Kent*
Kingston upon Hull : *Hull*
Lancashire : *Lanc*
Leicester : *Leic*
Leicestershire : *Leics*
Lincolnshire : *Linc*
Luton : *Lutn*
Medway : *Medw*
Merseyside : *Mers*
Merthyr Tydfil : *Mer T*
Middlesbrough : *Midd*
Midlothian : *Midl*
Milton Keynes : *Mil*
Monmouthshire : *Mon*
Moray : *Mor*
Neath Port Talbot : *Neat*
Newport : *Newp*
Norfolk : *Norf*
Northamptonshire : *Nptn*
North Ayrshire : *N Ayr*
North East Lincolnshire : *NE Lin*
North Lanarkshire : *N Lan*
North Lincolnshire : *N Lin*
North Somerset : *N Som*

Northumberland : *Nmbd*
North Yorkshire : *N Yor*
Nottingham : *Nott*
Nottinghamshire : *Notts*
Orkney : *Orkn*
Oxfordshire : *Oxon*
Pembrokeshire : *Pemb*
Perth & Kinross : *Per*
Peterborough : *Pet*
Plymouth : *Plym*
Poole : *Pool*
Portsmouth : *Port*
Powys : *Powy*
Reading : *Read*
Redcar & Cleveland : *Red C*
Renfrewshire : *Ren*
Rhondda Cynon Taff : *Rhon*
Rutland : *Rut*
Scottish Borders : *Bord*
Shetland : *Shet*
Shropshire : *Shrp*
Slough : *Slo*
Somerset : *Som*
Southampton : *Sotn*
South Ayrshire : *S Ayr*
Southend-on-Sea : *S'end*
South Gloucestershire : *S Glo*
South Lanarkshire : *S Lan*
South Yorkshire : *S Yor*

Staffordshire : *Staf*
Stirling : *Stir*
Stockton-on-Tees : *Stoc T*
Stoke-on-Trent : *Stoke*
Suffolk : *Suff*
Surrey : *Surr*
Swansea : *Swan*
Swindon : *Swin*
Telford & Wrekin : *Telf*
Thurrock : *Thur*
Torbay : *Torb*
Torfaen : *Torf*
Tyne & Wear : *Tyne*
Vale of Glamorgan, The : *V Glam*
Warrington : *Warr*
Warwickshire : *Warw*
West Berkshire : *W Ber*
West Dunbartonshire : *W Dun*
Western Isles : *W Isl*
West Lothian : *W Lot*
West Midlands : *W Mid*
West Sussex : *W Sus*
West Yorkshire : *W Yor*
Wiltshire : *Wilts*
Windsor & Maidenhead : *Wind*
Wokingham : *Wok*
Worcestershire : *Worc*
Wrexham : *Wrex*
York : *York*

INDEX

Altrua—Ashford

Altrua. *High* 4E **149**
Alva. *Clac* 4A **136**
Alvanley. *Ches W* 3G **83**
Alvaston. *Derb* 2A **74**
Alvechurch. *Worc* 3E **61**
Alvecote. *Warw* 5G **73**
Alvediston. *Wilts* 4E **23**
Alveley. *Shrp* 2B **60**
Alverdiscott. *Devn* 4F **19**
Alverstoke. *Hants* 3D **16**
Alverstone. *IOW* 4D **16**
Alverthorpe. *W Yor* 2D **92**
Alverton. *Notts* 1E **75**
Alves. *Mor* 2F **159**
Alvescot. *Oxon* 5A **50**
Alveston. *S Glo* 3B **34**
Alveston. *Warw* 5G **61**
Alvie. *High* 3C **150**
Alvingham. *Linc* 1C **88**
Alvington. *Glos* 5B **48**
Alwalton. *Cambs* 1A **64**
Alweston. *Dors* 1B **14**
Alwington. *Devn* 4E **19**
Alwinton. *Nmbd* 4D **120**
Alwoodley. *W Yor* 5E **99**
Alyth. *Per* 4B **144**
Amatnatua. *High* 4B **164**
Am Baile. *W Isl* 7C **170**
Ambaston. *Derbs* 2B **74**
Ambergate. *Derbs* 5H **85**
Amber Hill. *Linc* 1B **76**
Amberley. *Glos* 5D **48**
Amberley. *W Sus* 4B **26**
Amble. *Nmbd* 4G **121**
Amblecote. *W Mid* 2C **60**
Ambler Thorn. *W Yor* 2A **92**
Ambleside. *Cumb* 4E **103**
Ambleston. *Pemb* 2E **43**
Ambrosden. *Oxon* 4E **50**
Amcotts. *N Lin* 3B **94**
Amersham. *Buck* 1A **38**
Amerton. *Staf* 3D **73**
Amesbury. *Wilts* 2G **23**
Amisfield. *Dum* 1B **112**
Amlwch. *IOA* 1D **80**
Amlwch Port. *IOA* 1D **80**
Ammanford. *Carm* 4G **45**
Amotherby. *N Yor* 2B **100**
Ampfield. *Hants* 4B **24**
Ampleforth. *N Yor* 2H **99**
Ampleforth College. *N Yor* 2H **99**
Ampney Crucis. *Glos* 5F **49**
Ampney St Mary. *Glos* 5F **49**
Ampney St Peter. *Glos* 5F **49**
Amport. *Hants* 2A **24**
Ampthill. *C Beds* 2A **52**
Ampton. *Suff* 3A **66**
Amroth. *Pemb* 4F **43**
Amulree. *Per* 5G **143**
Amwell. *Herts* 4B **52**
Anaheilt. *High* 2C **140**
An Àird. *High* 3D **147**
An Camus Darach. *High* 4E **147**
Ancaster. *Linc* 1G **75**
Anchor. *Shrp* 2D **58**
Anchorsholme. *Bkpl* 5C **96**
Anchor Street. *Norf* 3F **79**
An Cnoc. *W Isl* 4G **171**
An Coroghon. *High* 3A **146**
Ancroft. *Nmbd* 5G **131**
Ancrum. *Bord* 2A **120**
Ancton. *W Sus* 5A **26**
Anderby. *Linc* 3E **89**
Anderby Creek. *Linc* 3E **89**
Anderson. *Dors* 3D **15**
Anderton. *Ches W* 3A **84**
Andertons Mill. *Lanc* 3D **90**
Andover. *Hants* 2B **24**
Andover Down. *Hants* 2B **24**
Andoversford. *Glos* 4F **49**
Andreas. *IOM* 2D **108**
An Dùnan. *High* 1D **147**
Andwell. *Hants* 1E **25**
Anelog. *Gwyn* 3A **68**
Anfield. *Mers* 1F **83**
Angarrack. *Corn* 3C **4**
Angelbank. *Shrp* 3H **59**
Angersleigh. *Som* 1F **13**
Angerton. *Cumb* 4D **112**
Angle. *Pemb* 4C **42**
Angmering. *W Sus* 5B **26**
Angmering-on-Sea. *W Sus* 5B **26**
Angram. *N Yor* 5B **104** (nr. Keld)
Angram. *N Yor* 5H **99** (nr. York)
Anick. *Nmbd* 3C **114**
Ankerbold. *Derbs* 4A **86**
Ankerville. *High* 1C **158**
Anlaby. *E Yor* 2D **94**
Anlaby Park. *Hull* 2D **94**
An Leth Meadhanach. *W Isl* 7C **170**
Anmer. *Norf* 3G **77**
Anmore. *Hants* 1E **17**
Annan. *Dum* 3D **112**
Annaside. *Cumb* 1A **96**
Annat. *Arg* 1H **133**
Annat. *High* 3A **156**
Annathill. *N Lan* 2A **128**
Anna Valley. *Hants* 2B **24**
Annbank. *S Ayr* 2D **116**
Annesley. *Notts* 5C **86**
Annesley Woodhouse. *Notts* 5C **86**
Annfield Plain. *Dur* 4E **115**
Annscroft. *Shrp* 5G **71**
An Sailean. *High* 2A **140**
Ansdell. *Lanc* 2B **90**
Ansford. *Som* 3B **22**
Ansley. *Warw* 1G **61**
Anslow. *Staf* 3G **73**
Anslow Gate. *Staf* 3F **73**
Ansteadbrook. *Surr* 2A **26**
Anstey. *Herts* 2E **53**
Anstey. *Leics* 5C **74**
Anston. *S Lan* 5D **128**
Anstruther Easter. *Fife* 3H **137**
Anstruther Wester. *Fife* 3H **137**
Ansty. *Warw* 2A **62**
Ansty. *W Sus* 3D **27**
Ansty. *Wilts* 4E **23**
An t-Aodann Ban. *High* 3C **154**
An t Ath Leathann. *High* 1E **147**
An Teanga. *High* 3E **147**
Anthill Common. *Hants* 1E **17**
Anthorn. *Cumb* 4C **112**
Antingham. *Norf* 2E **79**
An t-Ob. *W Isl* 9C **171**
Anton's Gowt. *Linc* 1B **76**
Antony. *Corn* 3A **8**
An t-Òrd. *High* 2E **147**
Antrobus. *Ches W* 3A **84**
Anvil Corner. *Devn* 2D **10**
Anwick. *Linc* 5A **88**
Anwoth. *Dum* 4C **110**
Apethorpe. *Nptn* 1H **63**
Apeton. *Staf* 4C **72**
Apley. *Linc* 3A **88**
Apperknowle. *Derbs* 3A **86**
Apperley. *Glos* 3D **48**
Apperley Dene. *Nmbd* 4D **114**
Appersett. *N Yor* 5B **104**
Appin. *Arg* 4D **140**
Appleby. *N Lin* 3C **94**
Appleby-in-Westmorland. *Cumb* 2H **103**
Appleby Magna. *Leics* 5H **73**
Appleby Parva. *Leics* 5H **73**
Applecross. *High* 4G **155**
Appledore. *Devn* 3E **19** (nr. Bideford)
Appledore. *Devn* 1D **12** (nr. Tiverton)
Appledore. *Kent* 3D **28**
Appledore Heath. *Kent* 2D **28**
Appleford. *Oxon* 2D **36**
Applegarthtown. *Dum* 1C **112**
Applemore. *Hants* 2B **16**
Appleshaw. *Hants* 2B **24**
Applethwaite. *Cumb* 2D **102**
Appleton. *Hal* 2H **83**
Appleton. *Oxon* 5C **50**
Appleton-le-Moors. *N Yor* 1B **100**
Appleton-le-Street. *N Yor* 2B **100**
Appleton Roebuck. *N Yor* 5H **99**
Appleton Thorn. *Warr* 2A **84**
Appleton Wiske. *N Yor* 4A **106**
Appletree. *Nptn* 1C **50**
Appletreehall. *Bord* 3H **119**
Appletreewick. *N Yor* 3C **98**
Appley. *Som* 4D **20**
Appley Bridge. *Lanc* 4D **90**
Apse Heath. *IOW* 4D **16**
Apsley End. *C Beds* 2B **52**
Apuldram. *W Sus* 2G **17**
Arabella. *High* 1C **158**
Arasaig. *High* 5E **147**
Arbeadie. *Abers* 4D **152**
Arberth. *Pemb* 3F **43**
Arbirlot. *Ang* 4F **145**
Arborfield. *Wok* 5F **37**
Arborfield Cross. *Wok* 5F **37**
Arborfield Garrison. *Wok* 5F **37**
Arbourthorne. *S Yor* 2A **86**
Arbroath. *Ang* 4F **145**
Arbuthnott. *Abers* 1H **145**
Arcan. *High* 3H **157**
Archargary. *High* 3H **167**
Archdeacon Newton. *Darl* 3F **105**
Archiestown. *Mor* 4G **159**
Arclid. *Ches E* 4B **84**
Arclid Green. *Ches E* 4B **84**
Ardachu. *High* 3D **164**
Ardalanish. *Arg* 2A **132**
Ardaneaskan. *High* 5H **155**
Ardarroch. *High* 5H **155**
Ardbeg. *Arg* 1C **126** (nr. Dunoon)
Ardbeg. *Arg* 5C **124** (on Islay)
Ardbeg. *Arg* 3B **126** (on Isle of Bute)
Ardcharnich. *High* 5F **163**
Ardchiavaig. *Arg* 2A **132**
Ardchonnell. *Arg* 2G **133**
Ardchrishnish. *Arg* 1B **132**
Ardchronie. *High* 5D **164**
Ardchullarie. *Stir* 2E **135**
Ardchyle. *Stir* 1E **135**
Ard-dhubh. *High* 4G **155**
Arddleen. *Powy* 4E **71**
Arddlîn. *Powy* 4E **71**
Ardechive. *High* 4D **148**
Ardeley. *Herts* 3D **52**
Ardelve. *High* 1A **148**
Arden. *Arg* 1E **127**
Ardendrain. *High* 5H **157**
Arden Hall. *N Yor* 5C **106**
Ardens Grafton. *Warw* 5F **61**
Ardentinny. *Arg* 1C **126**
Ardeonaig. *Stir* 5D **142**
Ardersier. *High* 3B **158**
Ardery. *High* 2B **140**
Ardessie. *High* 5E **163**
Ardfern. *Arg* 3F **133**
Ardfernal. *Arg* 2D **124**
Ardfin. *Arg* 3C **124**
Ardgartan. *Arg* 3B **134**
Ardgay. *High* 4C **164**
Ardgour. *High* 2E **141**
Ardheslaig. *High* 3G **155**
Ardindrean. *High* 5F **163**
Ardingly. *W Sus* 3E **27**
Ardington. *Oxon* 3C **36**
Ardlamont House. *Arg* 3A **126**
Ardleigh. *Essx* 3D **54**
Ardler. *Per* 4B **144**
Ardley. *Oxon* 3D **50**
Ardlui. *Arg* 2C **134**
Ardlussa. *Arg* 1E **125**
Ardmair. *High* 4F **163**
Ardmay. *Arg* 3B **134**
Ardminish. *Arg* 5E **125**
Ardmolich. *High* 1B **140**
Ardmore. *High* 3C **166** (nr. Kinlochbervie)
Ardmore. *High* 5E **164** (nr. Tain)
Ardnacross. *Arg* 4G **139**
Ardnadam. *Arg* 1C **126**
Ardnagrask. *High* 4H **157**
Ardnamurach. *High* 4G **147**
Ardnarff. *High* 5A **156**
Ardnastang. *High* 2C **140**
Ardoch. *Per* 5H **143**
Ardochy House. *High* 3E **148**
Ardpatrick. *Arg* 3F **125**
Ardrishaig. *Arg* 1G **125**
Ardroag. *High* 4B **154**
Ardross. *High* 1A **158**
Ardrossan. *N Ayr* 5D **126**
Ardshealach. *High* 2A **140**
Ardsley. *S Yor* 4D **93**
Ardslignish. *High* 2G **139**
Ardtalla. *Arg* 4C **124**
Ardtalnaig. *Per* 5E **142**
Ardtoe. *High* 1A **140**
Arduaine. *Arg* 2E **133**
Ardullie. *High* 2H **157**
Ardvasar. *High* 3E **147**
Ardvorlich. *Per* 1F **135**
Ardwell. *Dum* 5G **109**
Ardwell. *Mor* 5A **160**
Arean. *High* 1A **140**
Areley Common. *Worc* 3C **60**
Areley Kings. *Worc* 3B **60**
Arford. *Hants* 3G **25**
Argoed. *Cphy* 2E **33**
Argoed Mill. *Powy* 4B **58**
Aridhglas. *Arg* 2B **132**
Arinacrinachd. *High* 3G **155**
Arinagour. *Arg* 3D **138**
Arisaig. *High* 5E **147**
Ariundle. *High* 2C **140**
Arivegaig. *High* 2A **140**
Arkendale. *N Yor* 3F **99**
Arkesden. *Essx* 2E **53**
Arkholme. *Lanc* 2E **97**
Arkle Town. *N Yor* 4D **104**
Arkley. *G Lon* 1D **38**
Arksey. *S Yor* 4F **93**
Arkwright Town. *Derbs* 3B **86**
Arlecdon. *Cumb* 3B **102**
Arlescote. *Warw* 1B **50**
Arlesey. *C Beds* 2B **52**
Arleston. *Telf* 4A **72**
Arley. *Ches E* 2A **84**
Arlingham. *Glos* 4C **48**
Arlington. *Devn* 2G **19**
Arlington. *E Sus* 5G **27**
Arlington. *Glos* 5G **49**
Arlington Beccott. *Devn* 2G **19**
Armadail. *High* 3E **147**
Armadale. *High* 3E **147** (nr. Isleornsay)
Armadale. *High* 2H **167** (nr. Strathy)
Armadale. *W Lot* 3C **128**
Armathwaite. *Cumb* 5G **113**
Arminghall. *Norf* 5E **79**
Armitage. *Staf* 4E **73**
Armitage Bridge. *W Yor* 3B **92**
Armley. *W Yor* 1C **92**
Armscote. *Warw* 1H **49**
Arms, The. *Norf* 1A **66**
Armston. *Nptn* 2H **63**
Armthorpe. *S Yor* 4G **93**
Arncliffe. *N Yor* 2B **98**
Arncliffe Cote. *N Yor* 2B **98**
Arncroach. *Fife* 3H **137**
Arne. *Dors* 4E **15**
Arnesby. *Leics* 1D **62**
Arnicle. *Arg* 2B **122**
Arnisdale. *High* 2G **147**
Arnish. *High* 4E **155**
Arniston. *Midl* 3G **129**
Arnol. *W Isl* 3F **171**
Arnold. *E Yor* 5F **101**
Arnold. *Notts* 1C **74**
Arnprior. *Stir* 4F **135**
Arnside. *Cumb* 2D **96**
Aros Mains. *Arg* 4G **139**
Arpafeelie. *High* 3A **158**
Arrad Foot. *Cumb* 1C **96**
Arram. *E Yor* 5E **101**
Arras. *E Yor* 5D **100**
Arrathorne. *N Yor* 5E **105**
Arreton. *IOW* 4D **16**
Arrington. *Cambs* 5C **64**
Arrochar. *Arg* 3B **134**
Arrow. *Warw* 5E **61**
Arscaig. *High* 2C **164**
Artafallie. *High* 4A **158**
Arthington. *W Yor* 5E **99**
Arthingworth. *Nptn* 2E **63**
Arthog. *Gwyn* 4F **69**
Arthrath. *Abers* 5G **161**
Arthurstone. *Per* 4B **144**
Artington. *Surr* 1A **26**
Arundel. *W Sus* 5B **26**
Asby. *Cumb* 2B **102**
Ascog. *Arg* 3C **126**
Ascot. *Wind* 4A **38**
Ascott-under-Wychwood. *Oxon* 4B **50**
Asenby. *N Yor* 2F **99**
Asfordby. *Leics* 4E **74**
Asfordby Hill. *Leics* 4E **74**
Asgarby. *Linc* 4C **88** (nr. Horncastle)
Asgarby. *Linc* 1A **76** (nr. Sleaford)
Ash. *Devn* 4E **9**
Ash. *Dors* 1D **14**
Ash. *Kent* 5G **41** (nr. Sandwich)
Ash. *Kent* 4H **39** (nr. Swanley)
Ash. *Som* 4H **21**
Ash. *Surr* 1G **25**
Ashampstead. *W Ber* 4D **36**
Ashbocking. *Suff* 5D **66**
Ashbourne. *Derbs* 1F **73**
Ashbrittle. *Som* 4D **20**
Ashbrook. *Shrp* 1G **59**
Ashburton. *Devn* 2D **8**
Ashbury. *Devn* 3F **11**
Ashbury. *Oxon* 3A **36**
Ashby. *N Lin* 4B **94**
Ashby by Partney. *Linc* 4D **88**
Ashby cum Fenby. *NE Lin* 4F **95**
Ashby de la Launde. *Linc* 5H **87**
Ashby-de-la-Zouch. *Leics* 4A **74**
Ashby Folville. *Leics* 4E **74**
Ashby Magna. *Leics* 1C **62**
Ashby Parva. *Leics* 2C **62**
Ashby Puerorum. *Linc* 3C **88**
Ashby St Ledgars. *Nptn* 4C **62**
Ashby St Mary. *Norf* 5F **79**
Ashchurch. *Glos* 2E **49**
Ashcombe. *Devn* 5C **12**
Ashcott. *Som* 3H **21**
Ashdon. *Essx* 1F **53**
Ashe. *Hants* 1D **24**
Asheldham. *Essx* 5C **54**
Ashen. *Essx* 1H **53**
Ashendon. *Buck* 4F **51**
Ashey. *IOW* 4D **16**
Ashfield. *Hants* 1B **16**
Ashfield. *Here* 3A **48**
Ashfield. *Shrp* 2H **59**
Ashfield. *Stir* 3G **135**
Ashfield. *Suff* 4E **66**
Ashfield Green. *Suff* 3E **67**
Ashfold Crossways. *W Sus* 3D **26**
Ashford. *Devn* 3F **19** (nr. Barnstaple)
Ashford. *Devn* 4C **8** (nr. Kingsbridge)
Ashford. *Hants* 1G **15**
Ashford. *Kent* 1E **28**

Bagby—Barrow

Bagby. *N Yor* 1G 99
Bag Enderby. *Linc* 3C 88
Bagendon. *Glos* 5F 49
Bagginswood. *Shrp* 2A 60
Baggrave. *Leics* 5D 74
Bàgh a Chàise. *W Isl* 1E 170
Bàgh a' Chaisteil. *W Isl* 9B 170
Bagham. *Kent* 5E 41
Baghasdal. *W Isl* 7C 170
Bagh Mor. *W Isl* 3D 170
Bagh Shiarabhagh. *W Isl* 8C 170
Bagillt. *Flin* 3E 83
Baginton. *Warw* 3H 61
Baglan. *Neat* 2A 32
Bagley. *Shrp* 3G 71
Bagley. *Som* 2H 21
Bagnall. *Staf* 5D 84
Bagnor. *W Ber* 5C 36
Bagshot. *Surr* 4A 38
Bagshot. *Wilts* 5B 36
Bagstone. *S Glo* 3B 34
Bagthorpe. *Norf* 2G 77
Bagthorpe. *Notts* 5B 86
Bagworth. *Leics* 5B 74
Bagwy Llydiart. *Here* 3H 47
Baildon. *W Yor* 1B 92
Baildon Green. *W Yor* 1B 92
Baile Ailein. *W Isl* 5E 171
Baile an Truiseil. *W Isl* 2F 171
Baile Boidheach. *Arg* 2F 125
Baile Glas. *W Isl* 3D 170
Bailemeonach. *Arg* 4A 140
Baile Mhanaich. *W Isl* 3C 170
Baile Mhartainn. *W Isl* 1C 170
Baile Mor. *Arg* 2A 132
Baile Mor. *W Isl* 2C 170
Baile nan Cailleach. *W Isl* 3C 170
Baile Raghaill. *W Isl* 2C 170
Bailey Green. *Hants* 4E 25
Baileyhead. *Cumb* 1G 113
Bailiesward. *Abers* 5B 160
Bail' Iochdrach. *W Isl* 3D 170
Baillieston. *Glas* 3H 127
Bailrigg. *Lanc* 4D 97
Bail' Uachdraich. *W Isl* 2D 170
Bail Ur Tholastaidh. *W Isl* 3H 171
Bainbridge. *N Yor* 5C 104
Bainsford. *Falk* 1B 128
Bainshole. *Abers* 5D 160
Bainton. *E Yor* 4D 100
Bainton. *Oxon* 3D 50
Bainton. *Pet* 5H 75
Baintown. *Fife* 3F 137
Baker Street. *Thur* 2H 39
Bakewell. *Derbs* 4G 85
Bala. *Gwyn* 2B 70
Balachuirn. *High* 4E 155
Balbeg. *High* 5G 157
(nr. Cannich)
Balbeg. *High* 1G 149
(nr. Loch Ness)
Balbeggie. *Per* 1D 136
Balblair. *High* 4C 164
(nr. Bonar Bridge)
Balblair. *High* 2B 158
(nr. Invergordon)
Balblair. *High* 4H 157
(nr. Inverness)
Balby. *S Yor* 4F 93
Balcathie. *Ang* 5F 145
Balchladich. *High* 1E 163
Balchraggan. *High* 4H 157
Balchrick. *High* 3B 166
Balcombe. *W Sus* 2E 27
Balcombe Lane. *W Sus* 2E 27
Balcurvie. *Fife* 3F 137
Baldersby. *N Yor* 2F 99
Baldersby St James. *N Yor* 2F 99
Balderstone. *Lanc* 1E 91
Balderton. *Ches W* 4F 83
Balderton. *Notts* 5F 87
Baldinnie. *Fife* 2G 137
Baldock. *Herts* 2C 52
Baldrine. *IOM* 3D 108
Baldslow. *E Sus* 4C 28
Baldwin. *IOM* 3C 108
Baldwinholme. *Cumb* 4E 113
Baldwin's Gate. *Staf* 2B 72
Bale. *Norf* 2C 78
Balearn. *Abers* 3H 161
Balemartine. *Arg* 4A 138
Balephretrish. *Arg* 4B 138
Balephuil. *Arg* 4A 138
Balerno. *Edin* 3E 129
Balevullin. *Arg* 4A 138
Balfield. *Ang* 2E 145
Balfour. *Orkn* 6D 172
Balfron. *Stir* 1G 127
Balgaveny. *Abers* 4D 160
Balgonar. *Fife* 4C 136
Balgowan. *High* 4A 150
Balgown. *High* 2C 154
Balgrochan. *E Dun* 2H 127
Balgy. *High* 3H 155
Balhalgardy. *Abers* 1E 153
Baliasta. *Shet* 1H 173
Baligill. *High* 2A 168
Balintore. *Ang* 3B 144
Balintore. *High* 1C 158
Balintraid. *High* 1B 158
Balk. *N Yor* 1G 99
Balkeerie. *Ang* 4C 144
Balkholme. *E Yor* 2A 94
Ball. *Shrp* 3F 71
Ballabeg. *IOM* 4B 108
Ballacannell. *IOM* 3D 108
Ballacarnane Beg. *IOM* 3C 108
Ballachulish. *High* 3E 141
Ballagyr. *IOM* 3B 108
Ballajora. *IOM* 2D 108
Ballaleigh. *IOM* 3C 108
Ballamodha. *IOM* 4B 108
Ballantrae. *S Ayr* 1F 109
Ballards Gore. *Essx* 1D 40
Ballasalla. *IOM* 4B 108
(nr. Castletown)
Ballasalla. *IOM* 2C 108
(nr. Kirk Michael)
Ballater. *Abers* 4A 152
Ballaugh. *IOM* 2C 108
Ballencrieff. *E Lot* 2A 130
Ballencrieff Toll. *W Lot* 2C 128
Ballentoul. *Per* 2F 143
Ball Hill. *Hants* 5C 36
Ballidon. *Derbs* 5G 85
Balliemore. *Arg* 1B 126
(nr. Dunoon)
Balliemore. *Arg* 1F 133
(nr. Oban)
Ballieward. *High* 5E 159
Ballig. *IOM* 3B 108
Ballimore. *Stir* 2E 135
Ballingdon. *Suff* 1B 54
Ballinger Common. *Buck* 5H 51
Ballingham. *Here* 2A 48
Ballingry. *Fife* 4D 136
Ballinluig. *Per* 3G 143
Ballintuim. *Per* 3A 144
Balliveolan. *Arg* 4C 140
Balloan. *High* 3C 164
Balloch. *High* 4B 158
Balloch. *N Lan* 2A 128
Balloch. *Per* 2H 135
Balloch. *W Dun* 1E 127
Ballochan. *Abers* 4C 152
Ballochgoy. *Arg* 3B 126
Ballochmyle. *E Ayr* 2E 117
Ballochroy. *Arg* 4F 125
Balls Cross. *W Sus* 3A 26
Ball's Green. *E Sus* 2F 27
Ballygown. *Arg* 4F 139
Ballygrant. *Arg* 3B 124
Ballymichael. *N Ayr* 2D 122
Balmacara. *High* 1G 147
Balmaclellan. *Dum* 2D 110
Balmacqueen. *High* 1D 154
Balmaha. *Stir* 4D 134
Balmalcolm. *Fife* 3F 137
Balmalloch. *N Lan* 2A 128
Balmeanach. *High* 5E 155
Balmedie. *Abers* 2G 153
Balmerino. *Fife* 1F 137
Balmerlawn. *Hants* 2B 16
Balmore. *E Dun* 2H 127
Balmore. *High* 4B 154
Balmuir. *Ang* 5D 144
Balmullo. *Fife* 1G 137
Balmurrie. *Dum* 3H 109
Balnaboth. *Ang* 2C 144
Balnabruaich. *High* 1B 158
Balnabruich. *High* 5D 168
Balnacoil. *High* 2F 165
Balnacra. *High* 4B 156
Balnacroft. *Abers* 4G 151
Balnageith. *Mor* 3E 159
Balnaglaic. *High* 5G 157
Balnagrantach. *High* 5G 157
Balnaguard. *Per* 3G 143
Balnahard. *Arg* 4B 132
Balnain. *High* 5G 157
Balnakeil. *High* 2D 166
Balnaknock. *High* 2D 154
Balnamoon. *Abers* 3G 161
Balnamoon. *Ang* 2E 145
Balnapaling. *High* 2B 158
Balornock. *Glas* 3H 127
Balquhidder. *Stir* 1E 135
Balsall. *W Mid* 3G 61
Balsall Common. *W Mid* 3G 61
Balscote. *Oxon* 1B 50
Balsham. *Cambs* 5E 65
Balstonia. *Thur* 2A 40
Baltasound. *Shet* 1H 173
Balterley. *Staf* 5B 84
Baltersan. *Dum* 3B 110
Balthangie. *Abers* 3F 161
Baltonsborough. *Som* 3A 22
Balvaird. *High* 3H 157
Balvaird. *Per* 2D 136
Balvenie. *Mor* 4H 159
Balvicar. *Arg* 2E 133
Balvraid. *High* 2G 147
Balvraid Lodge. *High* 5C 158
Bamber Bridge. *Lanc* 2D 90
Bamber's Green. *Essx* 3F 53
Bamburgh. *Nmbd* 1F 121
Bamford. *Derbs* 2G 85
Bamfurlong. *G Man* 4D 90
Bampton. *Cumb* 3G 103
Bampton. *Devn* 4C 20
Bampton. *Oxon* 5B 50
Bampton Grange. *Cumb* 3G 103
Banavie. *High* 1F 141
Banbury. *Oxon* 1C 50
Bancffosfelen. *Carm* 4E 45
Banchory. *Abers* 4D 152
Banchory-Devenick. *Abers* 3G 153
Bancycapel. *Carm* 4E 45
Bancyfelin. *Carm* 3H 43
Banc-y-ffordd. *Carm* 2E 45
Banff. *Abers* 2D 160
Bangor. *Gwyn* 3E 81
Bangor-is-y-coed. *Wrex* 1F 71
Bangors. *Corn* 3C 10
Bangor's Green. *Lanc* 4B 90
Banham. *Norf* 2C 66
Bank. *Hants* 2A 16
Bankend. *Dum* 3B 112
Bankfoot. *Per* 5H 143
Bankglen. *E Ayr* 3E 117
Bankhead. *Aber* 2F 153
Bankhead. *Abers* 3D 152
Bankhead. *S Lan* 5B 128
Bankland. *Som* 4G 21
Bank Newton. *N Yor* 4B 98
Banknock. *Falk* 2A 128
Banks. *Cumb* 3G 113
Banks. *Lanc* 2B 90
Bankshill. *Dum* 1C 112
Bank Street. *Worc* 4A 60
Bank, The. *Ches E* 5C 84
Bank, The. *Shrp* 1A 60
Bank Top. *Lanc* 4D 90
Banners Gate. *W Mid* 1E 61
Banningham. *Norf* 3E 78
Banniskirk. *High* 3D 168
Bannister Green. *Essx* 3G 53
Bannockburn. *Stir* 4H 135
Banstead. *Surr* 5D 38
Bantham. *Devn* 4C 8
Banton. *N Lan* 2A 128
Banwell. *N Som* 1G 21
Banyard's Green. *Suff* 3F 67
Bapchild. *Kent* 4D 40
Bapton. *Wilts* 3E 23
Barabhas. *W Isl* 3F 171
Barabhas Iarach. *W Isl* 2F 171
Baramore. *High* 1A 140
Barassie. *S Ayr* 1C 116
Baravullin. *Arg* 4D 140
Barbaraville. *High* 1B 158
Barber Booth. *Derbs* 2F 85
Barber Green. *Cumb* 1C 96
Barbhas Uarach. *W Isl* 2F 171
Barbieston. *S Ayr* 3D 116
Barbon. *Cumb* 1F 97
Barbourne. *Worc* 5C 60
Barbridge. *Ches E* 5A 84
Barbrook. *Devn* 2H 19
Barby. *Nptn* 3C 62
Barby Nortoft. *Nptn* 3C 62
Barcaldine. *Arg* 4D 140
Barcheston. *Warw* 1A 50
Barclose. *Cumb* 3F 113
Barcombe. *E Sus* 4F 27
Barcombe Cross. *E Sus* 4F 27
Barden. *N Yor* 5E 105
Barden Scale. *N Yor* 4C 98
Bardfield End Green. *Essx* 2G 53
Bardfield Saling. *Essx* 3G 53
Bardnabeinne. *High* 4E 164
Bardney. *Linc* 4A 88
Bardon. *Leics* 4B 74
Bardon Mill. *Nmbd* 3A 114
Bardowie. *E Dun* 2G 127
Bardrainney. *Inv* 2E 127
Bardsea. *Cumb* 2C 96
Bardsey. *W Yor* 5F 99
Bardsley. *G Man* 4H 91
Bardwell. *Suff* 3B 66
Bare. *Lanc* 3D 96
Barelees. *Nmbd* 1C 120
Barewood. *Here* 5F 59
Barford. *Hants* 3G 25
Barford. *Norf* 5D 78
Barford. *Warw* 4G 61
Barford St John. *Oxon* 2C 50
Barford St Martin. *Wilts* 3F 23
Barford St Michael. *Oxon* 2C 50
Barfrestone. *Kent* 5G 41
Bargeddie. *N Lan* 3A 128
Bargod. *Cphy* 2E 33
Bargoed. *Cphy* 2E 33
Bargrennan. *Dum* 2A 110
Barham. *Cambs* 3A 64
Barham. *Kent* 5G 41
Barham. *Suff* 5D 66
Barharrow. *Dum* 4D 110
Bar Hill. *Cambs* 4C 64
Barholm. *Linc* 4H 75
Barkby. *Leics* 4D 74
Barkestone-le-Vale. *Leics* 2E 75
Barkham. *Wok* 5F 37
Barking. *G Lon* 2F 39
Barking. *Suff* 5C 66
Barkingside. *G Lon* 2F 39
Barking Tye. *Suff* 5C 66
Barkisland. *W Yor* 3A 92
Barkston. *Linc* 1G 75
Barkston Ash. *N Yor* 1E 93
Barkway. *Herts* 2D 53
Barlanark. *Glas* 3H 127
Barlaston. *Staf* 2C 72
Barlavington. *W Sus* 4A 26
Barlborough. *Derbs* 3B 86
Barlby. *N Yor* 1G 93
Barlestone. *Leics* 5B 74
Barley. *Herts* 2D 53
Barley. *Lanc* 5H 97
Barley Mow. *Tyne* 4F 115
Barleythorpe. *Rut* 5F 75
Barling. *Essx* 2D 40
Barlings. *Linc* 3H 87
Barlow. *Derbs* 3H 85
Barlow. *N Yor* 2G 93
Barlow. *Tyne* 3E 115
Barmby Moor. *E Yor* 5B 100
Barmby on the Marsh. *E Yor* 2G 93
Barmer. *Norf* 2H 77
Barming. *Kent* 5B 40
Barming Heath. *Kent* 5B 40
Barmoor. *Nmbd* 1E 121
Barmouth. *Gwyn* 4F 69
Barmpton. *Darl* 3A 106
Barmston. *E Yor* 4F 101
Barmulloch. *Glas* 3H 127
Barnack. *Pet* 5H 75
Barnacle. *Warw* 2A 62
Barnard Castle. *Dur* 3D 104
Barnard Gate. *Oxon* 4C 50
Barnardiston. *Suff* 1H 53
Barnbarroch. *Dum* 4F 111
Barnburgh. *S Yor* 4E 93
Barnby. *Suff* 2G 67
Barnby Dun. *S Yor* 4G 93
Barnby in the Willows. *Notts* 5F 87
Barnby Moor. *Notts* 2D 86
Barnes. *G Lon* 3D 38
Barnes Street. *Kent* 1H 27
Barnet. *G Lon* 1D 38
Barnetby le Wold. *N Lin* 4D 94
Barney. *Norf* 2B 78
Barnham. *Suff* 3A 66
Barnham. *W Sus* 5A 26
Barnham Broom. *Norf* 5C 78
Barnhead. *Ang* 3F 145
Barnhill. *D'dee* 5D 145
Barnhill. *Mor* 3F 159
Barnhill. *Per* 1D 136
Barnhills. *Dum* 2E 109
Barningham. *Dur* 3D 105
Barningham. *Suff* 3B 66
Barnoldby le Beck. *NE Lin* 4F 95
Barnoldswick. *Lanc* 5A 98
Barns Green. *W Sus* 3C 26
Barnsley. *Glos* 5F 49
Barnsley. *Shrp* 1B 60
Barnsley. *S Yor* 4D 92
Barnstaple. *Devn* 3F 19
Barnston. *Essx* 4G 53
Barnston. *Mers* 2E 83
Barnstone. *Notts* 2E 75
Barnt Green. *Worc* 3E 61
Barnton. *Ches W* 3A 84
Barnwell. *Cambs* 5D 64
Barnwell. *Nptn* 2H 63
Barnwood. *Glos* 4D 48
Barons Cross. *Here* 5G 59
Barony, The. *Orkn* 5B 172
Barr. *Dum* 4G 117
Barr. *S Ayr* 5B 116
Barra Airport. *W Isl* 8C 170
Barrachan. *Dum* 5A 110
Barrahormid. *Arg* 1F 125
Barrapol. *Arg* 4A 138
Barrasford. *Nmbd* 2C 114
Barravullin. *Arg* 3F 133
Barregarrow. *IOM* 3C 108
Barrhead. *E Ren* 4G 127
Barrhill. *S Ayr* 1H 109
Barri. *V Glam* 5E 32
Barrington. *Cambs* 1D 53
Barrington. *Som* 1G 13
Barripper. *Corn* 3D 4
Barrmill. *N Ayr* 4E 127
Barrock. *High* 1E 169
Barrow. *Lanc* 1F 91
Barrow. *Rut* 4F 75
Barrow. *Shrp* 5A 72
Barrow. *Som* 3C 22

Barrow—Bennah

Barrow. Suff 4G 65
Barroway Drove. Norf 5E 77
Barrow Bridge. G Man 3E 91
Barrowburn. Nmbd 3C 120
Barrowby. Linc 2F 75
Barrowcliff. N Yor 1E 101
Barrow Common. N Som 5A 34
Barrowden. Rut 5G 75
Barrowford. Lanc 1G 91
Barrow Gurney. N Som 5A 34
Barrow Haven. N Lin 2D 94
Barrow Hill. Derbs 3B 86
Barrow-in-Furness. Cumb 3B 96
Barrow Nook. Lanc 4C 90
Barrows Green. Cumb 1E 97
Barrow's Green. Hal 2H 83
Barrow Street. Wilts 3D 22
Barrow upon Humber. N Lin 2D 94
Barrow upon Soar. Leics 4C 74
Barrow upon Trent. Derbs 3A 74
Barry. Ang 5E 145
Barry. V Glam 5E 32
Barry Island. V Glam 5E 32
Barsby. Leics 4D 74
Barsham. Suff 2F 67
Barston. W Mid 3G 61
Bartestree. Here 1A 48
Barthol Chapel. Abers 5F 161
Bartholomew Green. Essx 3H 53
Barthomley. Ches E 5B 84
Bartley. Hants 1B 16
Bartley Green. W Mid 2E 61
Bartlow. Cambs 1F 53
Barton. Cambs 5D 64
Barton. Ches W 5G 83
Barton. Cumb 2F 103
Barton. Glos 3F 49
Barton. IOW 4D 16
Barton. Lanc 4B 90
(nr. Ormskirk)
Barton. Lanc 1D 90
(nr. Preston)
Barton. N Som 1G 21
Barton. N Yor 4F 105
Barton. Oxon 5D 50
Barton. Torb 2F 9
Barton. Warw 5F 61
Barton Bendish. Norf 5G 77
Barton Gate. Staf 4F 73
Barton Green. Staf 4F 73
Barton Hartsthorn. Buck 2E 51
Barton Hill. N Yor 3B 100
Barton in Fabis. Notts 2C 74
Barton in the Beans. Leics 5A 74
Barton-le-Clay. C Beds 2A 52
Barton-le-Street. N Yor 2B 100
Barton-le-Willows. N Yor 3B 100
Barton Mills. Suff 3G 65
Barton on Sea. Hants 3H 15
Barton-on-the-Heath. Warw 2A 50
Barton St David. Som 3A 22
Barton Seagrave. Nptn 3F 63
Barton Stacey. Hants 2C 24
Barton Town. Devn 2G 19
Barton Turf. Norf 3F 79
Barton-under-Needwood. Staf 4F 73
Barton-upon-Humber. N Lin 2D 94
Barton Waterside. N Lin 2D 94
Barugh Green. S Yor 4D 92
Barway. Cambs 3E 65
Barwell. Leics 1B 62
Barwick. Herts 4D 53
Barwick. Som 1A 14
Barwick in Elmet. W Yor 1D 93
Baschurch. Shrp 3G 71
Bascote. Warw 4B 62
Basford Green. Staf 5D 85
Bashall Eaves. Lanc 5F 97
Bashall Town. Lanc 5G 97
Bashley. Hants 3H 15
Basildon. Essx 2B 40
Basingstoke. Hants 1E 25
Baslow. Derbs 3G 85
Bason Bridge. Som 2G 21
Bassaleg. Newp 3F 33
Bassendean. Bord 5C 130
Bassenthwaite. Cumb 1D 102
Bassett. Sotn 1C 16
Bassingbourn. Cambs 1D 52
Bassingfield. Notts 2D 74
Bassingham. Linc 5G 87
Bassingthorpe. Linc 3G 75
Bassus Green. Herts 3D 52
Basta. Shet 2G 173
Baston. Linc 4A 76
Bastonford. Worc 5C 60
Bastwick. Norf 4G 79
Batchley. Worc 4E 61
Batchworth. Herts 1B 38
Batcombe. Dors 2B 14
Batcombe. Som 3B 22
Bate Heath. Ches E 3A 84
Bath. Bath 5C 34
Bathampton. Bath 5C 34
Bathealton. Som 4D 20
Batheaston. Bath 5C 34
Bathford. Bath 5C 34
Bathgate. W Lot 3C 128
Bathley. Notts 5E 87
Bathpool. Corn 5C 10
Bathpool. Som 4F 21
Bathville. W Lot 3C 128
Bathway. Som 1A 22
Batley. W Yor 2C 92
Batsford. Glos 2G 49
Batson. Devn 5D 8
Battersby. N Yor 4C 106
Battersea. G Lon 3D 39
Battisborough Cross. Devn 4C 8
Battisford. Suff 5C 66
Battisford Tye. Suff 5C 66
Battle. E Sus 4B 28
Battle. Powy 2D 46
Battleborough. Som 1G 21
Battledown. Glos 3E 49
Battlefield. Shrp 4H 71
Battlesbridge. Essx 1B 40
Battlesden. C Beds 3H 51
Battlesea Green. Suff 3E 66
Battleton. Som 4C 20
Battramsley. Hants 3B 16
Batt's Corner. Surr 2G 25
Bauds of Cullen. Mor 2B 160
Baugh. Arg 4B 138
Baughton. Worc 1D 49
Baughurst. Hants 5D 36
Baulking. Oxon 2B 36
Baumber. Linc 3B 88
Baunton. Glos 5F 49
Baverstock. Wilts 3F 23
Bawburgh. Norf 5D 78
Bawdeswell. Norf 3C 78
Bawdrip. Som 3G 21
Bawdsey. Suff 1G 55
Bawdsey Manor. Suff 2G 55
Bawsey. Norf 4F 77
Bawtry. S Yor 1D 86
Baxenden. Lanc 2F 91
Baxterley. Warw 1G 61
Baxter's Green. Suff 5G 65
Baybridge. Hants 4D 24
Baybridge. Nmbd 4C 114
Baycliff. Cumb 2B 96
Baydon. Wilts 4A 36
Bayford. Herts 5D 52
Bayford. Som 4C 22
Bayles. Cumb 5A 114
Baylham. Suff 5D 66
Baynard's Green. Oxon 3D 50
Bayston Hill. Shrp 5G 71
Baythorn End. Essx 1H 53
Baythorpe. Linc 1B 76
Bayton. Worc 3A 60
Bayton Common. Worc 3B 60
Bayworth. Oxon 5D 50
Beach. S Glo 4C 34
Beachampton. Buck 2F 51
Beachamwell. Norf 5G 77
Beachley. Glos 2A 34
Beacon. Devn 2E 13
Beacon End. Essx 3C 54
Beacon Hill. Surr 3G 25
Beacon's Bottom. Buck 2F 37
Beaconsfield. Buck 1A 38
Beacontree. G Lon 2F 39
Beacrabhaicg. W Isl 8D 171
Beadlam. N Yor 1A 100
Beadnell. Nmbd 2G 121
Beaford. Devn 1F 11
Beal. Nmbd 5G 131
Beal. N Yor 2F 93
Bealsmill. Corn 5D 10
Beam Hill. Staf 3G 73
Beamhurst. Staf 2E 73
Beaminster. Dors 2H 13
Beamish. Dur 4F 115
Beamond End. Buck 1A 38
Beamsley. N Yor 4C 98
Bean. Kent 3G 39
Beanacre. Wilts 5E 35
Beanley. Nmbd 3E 121
Beanshanger. Nptn 2F 51
Beardwood. Bkbn 2E 91
Beare Green. Surr 1C 26
Bearley. Warw 4F 61
Bearpark. Dur 5F 115
Bearsbridge. Nmbd 4A 114
Bearsden. E Dun 2G 127
Bearsted. Kent 5B 40
Bearstone. Shrp 2B 72
Bearwood. Pool 3F 15
Bearwood. W Mid 2E 61
Beattock. Dum 4C 118
Beauchamp Roding. Essx 5F 53
Beauchief. S Yor 2H 85
Beaufort. Blae 4E 47
Beaulieu. Hants 2B 16
Beauly. High 4H 157
Beaumaris. IOA 3F 81
Beaumont. Cumb 4E 113
Beaumont. Essx 3E 55
Beaumont Hill. Darl 3F 105
Beaumont Leys. Leic 5C 74
Beausale. Warw 3G 61
Beauvale. Notts 1B 74
Beauworth. Hants 4D 24
Beaworthy. Devn 3E 11
Beazley End. Essx 3H 53
Bebington. Mers 2F 83
Bebside. Nmbd 1F 115
Beccles. Suff 2G 67
Becconsall. Lanc 2C 90
Beckbury. Shrp 5B 72
Beckenham. G Lon 4E 39
Beckermet. Cumb 4B 102
Beckett End. Norf 1G 65
Beckfoot. Cumb 1A 96
(nr. Broughton in Furness)
Beck Foot. Cumb 5H 103
(nr. Kendal)
Beckfoot. Cumb 4C 102
(nr. Seascale)
Beckfoot. Cumb 5B 112
(nr. Silloth)
Beckford. Worc 2E 49
Beckhampton. Wilts 5F 35
Beck Hole. N Yor 4F 107
Beckingham. Linc 5F 87
Beckingham. Notts 1E 87
Beckington. Som 1D 22
Beckley. E Sus 3C 28
Beckley. Hants 3H 15
Beckley. Oxon 4D 50
Beck Row. Suff 3F 65
Beck Side. Cumb 1C 96
(nr. Cartmel)
Beckside. Cumb 1F 97
(nr. Sedbergh)
Beck Side. Cumb 1B 96
(nr. Ulverston)
Beckton. G Lon 2F 39
Beckwithshaw. N Yor 4E 99
Becontree. G Lon 2F 39
Bedale. N Yor 1E 99
Bedburn. Dur 1E 105
Bedchester. Dors 1D 14
Beddau. Rhon 3D 32
Beddgelert. Gwyn 1E 69
Beddingham. E Sus 5F 27
Beddington. G Lon 4D 39
Bedfield. Suff 4E 66
Bedford. Bed 1A 52
Bedford. G Man 4E 91
Bedham. W Sus 3B 26
Bedhampton. Hants 2F 17
Bedingfield. Suff 4D 66
Bedingham Green. Norf 1E 67
Bedlam. N Yor 3E 99
Bedlar's Green. Essx 4F 53
Bedlington. Nmbd 1F 115
Bedlinog. Mer T 5D 46
Bedminster. Bris 4A 34
Bedmond. Herts 5A 52
Bednall. Staf 4D 72
Bedrule. Bord 3A 120
Bedstone. Shrp 3F 59
Bedwas. Cphy 3E 33
Bedwellty. Cphy 5E 47
Bedworth. Warw 2A 62
Beeby. Leics 5D 74
Beech. Hants 3E 25
Beech. Staf 2C 72
Beechcliffe. W Yor 5C 98
Beech Hill. W Ber 5E 37
Beechingstoke. Wilts 1F 23
Beedon. W Ber 4C 36
Beeford. E Yor 4F 101
Beeley. Derbs 4G 85
Beelsby. NE Lin 4F 95
Beenham. W Ber 5D 36
Beeny. Corn 3B 10
Beer. Devn 4F 13
Beer. Som 3H 21
Beercrocombe. Som 4G 21
Beer Hackett. Dors 1B 14
Beesands. Devn 4E 9
Beesby. Linc 2D 88
Beeson. Devn 4E 9
Beeston. C Beds 1B 52
Beeston. Ches W 5H 83
Beeston. Norf 4B 78
Beeston. Notts 2C 74
Beeston. W Yor 1C 92
Beeston Regis. Norf 1D 78
Beeswing. Dum 3F 111
Beetham. Cumb 2D 97
Beetham. Som 1F 13
Beetley. Norf 4B 78
Beffcote. Staf 4C 72
Began. Card 3F 33
Begbroke. Oxon 4C 50
Begdale. Cambs 5D 76
Begelly. Pemb 4F 43
Beggar Hill. Essx 5G 53
Beggar's Bush. Powy 4E 59
Beggearn Huish. Som 3D 20
Beguildy. Powy 3D 58
Beighton. Norf 5F 79
Beighton. S Yor 2B 86
Beighton Hill. Derbs 5G 85
Beith. N Ayr 4E 127
Bekesbourne. Kent 5F 41
Belaugh. Norf 4E 79
Belbroughton. Worc 3D 60
Belchalwell. Dors 2C 14
Belchalwell Street. Dors 2C 14
Belchamp Otten. Essx 1B 54
Belchamp St Paul. Essx 1A 54
Belchamp Walter. Essx 1B 54
Belchford. Linc 3B 88
Belfatton. Abers 3H 161
Belford. Nmbd 1F 121
Belgrano. Cnwy 3B 82
Belhaven. E Lot 2C 130
Belhelvie. Abers 2G 153
Belhinnie. Abers 1B 152
Bellabeg. Abers 2A 152
Belladrum. High 4H 157
Bellamore. S Ayr 1H 109
Bellanoch. Arg 4F 133
Bell Busk. N Yor 4B 98
Belleau. Linc 3D 88
Belleheiglash. Mor 5F 159
Bell End. Worc 3D 60
Bellerby. N Yor 5E 105
Bellerby Camp. N Yor 5D 105
Bellever. Devn 5G 11
Belle Vue. Cumb 1C 102
Belle Vue. Shrp 4G 71
Bellfield. S Lan 1H 117
Belliehill. Ang 2E 145
Bellingdon. Buck 5H 51
Bellingham. Nmbd 1B 114
Bellmount. Norf 3E 77
Bellochantuy. Arg 2A 122
Bellsbank. E Ayr 4D 117
Bell's Cross. Suff 5D 66
Bellshill. N Lan 4A 128
Bellshill. Nmbd 1F 121
Bellside. N Lan 4B 128
Bellspool. Bord 1D 118
Bellsquarry. W Lot 3D 128
Bells Yew Green. E Sus 2H 27
Belmaduthy. High 3A 158
Belmesthorpe. Rut 4H 75
Belmont. Bkbn 3E 91
Belmont. Shet 1G 173
Belmont. S Ayr 3C 116
Belnacraig. Abers 2A 152
Belnie. Linc 2B 76
Belowda. Corn 2D 6
Belper. Derbs 1A 74
Belper Lane End. Derbs 1H 73
Belph. Derbs 3C 86
Belsay. Nmbd 2E 115
Belsford. Devn 3D 8
Belsize. Herts 5A 52
Belstead. Suff 1E 55
Belston. S Ayr 2C 116
Belstone. Devn 3G 11
Belstone Corner. Devn 3G 11
Belthorn. Lanc 2F 91
Beltinge. Kent 4F 41
Beltoft. N Lin 4B 94
Belton. Leics 3B 74
Belton. Linc 2G 75
Belton. Norf 5G 79
Belton. N Lin 4A 94
Belton-in-Rutland. Rut 5F 75
Beltring. Kent 1A 28
Belts of Collonach. Abers 4D 152
Belvedere. G Lon 3F 39
Belvoir. Leics 2F 75
Bembridge. IOW 4E 17
Bemersyde. Bord 1H 119
Bemerton. Wilts 3G 23
Bempton. E Yor 2F 101
Benacre. Suff 2H 67
Ben Alder Lodge. High 1C 142
Ben Armine Lodge. High 2E 164
Benbuie. Dum 5G 117
Benchill. G Man 2C 84
Benderloch. Arg 5D 140
Bendish. Herts 3B 52
Bendronaig Lodge. High 5C 156
Benenden. Kent 2C 28
Benera. High 1G 147
Benfieldside. Dur 4D 115
Bengate. Norf 3F 79
Bengeworth. Worc 1F 49
Bengrove. Glos 2E 49
Benhall Green. Suff 4F 67
Benholm. Abers 2H 145
Benington. Herts 3C 52
Benington. Linc 1C 76
Benington Sea End. Linc 1D 76
Benllech. IOA 2E 81
Benmore Lodge. High 2H 163
Bennacott. Corn 3D 10
Bennah. Devn 4B 12

Bissoe—Bont-newydd

Bissoe. *Corn* 4B 6
Bisterne. *Hants* 2G 15
Bisterne Close. *Hants* 2H 15
Bitchfield. *Linc* 3G 75
Bittadon. *Devn* 2F 19
Bittaford. *Devn* 3C 8
Bittering. *Norf* 4B 78
Bitterley. *Shrp* 3H 59
Bitterne. *Sotn* 1C 16
Bitteswell. *Leics* 2C 62
Bitton. *S Glo* 5B 34
Bix. *Oxon* 3F 37
Bixter. *Shet* 6E 173
Blaby. *Leics* 1C 62
Blackawton. *Devn* 3E 9
Black Bank. *Cambs* 2E 65
Black Barn. *Linc* 3D 76
Blackborough. *Devn* 2D 12
Blackborough. *Norf* 4F 77
Blackborough End. *Norf* 4F 77
Black Bourton. *Oxon* 5A 50
Blackboys. *E Sus* 3G 27
Blackbrook. *Derbs* 1H 73
Blackbrook. *Mers* 1H 83
Blackbrook. *Staf* 2B 72
Blackbrook. *Surr* 1C 26
Blackburn. *Abers* 2F 153
Blackburn. *Bkbn* 2E 91
Blackburn. *W Lot* 3C 128
Black Callerton. *Tyne* 3E 115
Black Carr. *Norf* 1C 66
Black Clauchrie. *S Ayr* 1H 109
Black Corries. *High* 3G 141
Black Crofts. *Arg* 5D 140
Black Cross. *Corn* 2D 6
Blackden Heath. *Ches E* 3B 84
Blackditch. *Oxon* 5C 50
Blackdog. *Abers* 2G 153
Black Dog. *Devn* 2B 12
Blackdown. *Dors* 2G 13
Blackdyke. *Cumb* 4C 112
Blacker Hill. *S Yor* 4D 92
Blackfen. *G Lon* 3F 39
Blackfield. *Hants* 2C 16
Blackford. *Cumb* 3E 113
Blackford. *Per* 3A 136
Blackford. *Shrp* 2H 59
Blackford. *Som* 2H 21
(nr. Burnham-on-Sea)
Blackford. *Som* 4B 22
(nr. Wincanton)
Blackfordby. *Leics* 4H 73
Blackgang. *IOW* 5C 16
Blackhall. *Edin* 2F 129
Blackhall. *Ren* 3F 127
Blackhall Colliery. *Dur* 1B 106
Blackhall Mill. *Tyne* 4E 115
Blackhall Rocks. *Dur* 1B 106
Blackham. *E Sus* 2F 27
Blackheath. *Essx* 3D 54
Blackheath. *G Lon* 3E 39
Blackheath. *Suff* 3G 67
Blackheath. *Surr* 1B 26
Blackheath. *W Mid* 2D 61
Black Heddon. *Nmbd* 2D 115
Blackhill. *Abers* 4H 161
Blackhill. *High* 3C 154
Black Hill. *Warw* 5G 61
Blackhills. *Abers* 2G 161
Blackhills. *High* 3D 158
Blackjack. *Linc* 2B 76
Blackland. *Wilts* 5F 35
Black Lane. *G Man* 4F 91
Blackleach. *Lanc* 1C 90
Blackley. *G Man* 4G 91
Blackley. *W Yor* 3B 92
Blacklunans. *Per* 2A 144
Blackmill. *B'end* 3C 32
Blackmoor. *G Man* 4E 91
Blackmoor. *Hants* 3F 25
Blackmoor Gate. *Devn* 2G 19
Blackmore. *Essx* 5G 53
Blackmore End. *Essx* 2H 53
Blackmore End. *Herts* 4B 52
Black Mount. *Arg* 4G 141
Blackness. *Falk* 2D 128
Blacknest. *Hants* 2F 25
Blackney. *Dors* 3H 13
Blacknoll. *Dors* 4D 14
Black Notley. *Essx* 3A 54
Blacko. *Lanc* 5A 98
Black Pill. *Swan* 3F 31
Blackpool. *Bkpl* 1B 90
Blackpool. *Devn* 4E 9
Blackpool Airport. *Lanc* 1B 90
Blackpool Corner. *Devn* 3G 13
Blackpool Gate. *Cumb* 2G 113
Blackridge. *W Lot* 3C 128
Blackrock. *Arg* 3B 124
Blackrock. *Mon* 4F 47
Blackrod. *G Man* 3E 90
Blackshaw. *Dum* 3B 112
Blackshaw Head. *W Yor* 2H 91
Blacksmith's Green. *Suff* 4D 66
Blacksnape. *Bkbn* 2F 91
Blackstone. *W Sus* 4D 26
Black Street. *Suff* 2H 67
Black Tar. *Pemb* 4D 43
Blackthorn. *Oxon* 4E 50
Blackthorpe. *Suff* 4B 66
Blacktoft. *E Yor* 2B 94
Blacktop. *Aber* 3F 153
Black Torrington. *Devn* 2E 11
Blacktown. *Newp* 3F 33
Blackwall Tunnel. *G Lon* 2E 39
Blackwater. *Corn* 4B 6
Blackwater. *Hants* 1G 25
Blackwater. *IOW* 4D 16
Blackwater. *Som* 1F 13
Blackwaterfoot. *N Ayr* 3C 122
Blackwell. *Darl* 3F 105
Blackwell. *Derbs* 5B 86
(nr. Alfreton)
Blackwell. *Derbs* 3F 85
(nr. Buxton)
Blackwell. *Som* 4D 20
Blackwell. *Warw* 1H 49
Blackwell. *Worc* 3D 61
Blackwood. *Cphy* 2E 33
Blackwood. *Dum* 1G 111
Blackwood. *S Lan* 5A 128
Blackwood Hill. *Staf* 5D 84
Blacon. *Ches W* 4F 83
Bladnoch. *Dum* 4B 110
Bladon. *Oxon* 4C 50
Blaenannerch. *Cdgn* 1C 44
Blaenau Dolwyddelan. *Cnwy* 5F 81
Blaenau Ffestiniog. *Gwyn* 1G 69
Blaenavon. *Torf* 5F 47
Blaenawey. *Mon* 4F 47
Blaen Celyn. *Cdgn* 5C 56
Blaen Clydach. *Rhon* 2C 32
Blaendulais. *Neat* 5B 46
Blaenffos. *Pemb* 1F 43
Blaengarw. *B'end* 2C 32
Blaen-geuffordd. *Cdgn* 2F 57
Blaengwrach. *Neat* 5B 46
Blaengwynfi. *Neat* 2B 32
Blaenllechau. *Rhon* 2D 32
Blaenpennal. *Cdgn* 4F 57
Blaenplwyf. *Cdgn* 3E 57
Blaenporth. *Cdgn* 1C 44
Blaenrhondda. *Rhon* 2C 32
Blaenwaun. *Carm* 2G 43
Blaen-y-coed. *Carm* 2H 43
Blaenycwm. *Rhon* 2C 32
Blagdon. *N Som* 1A 22
Blagdon. *Torb* 2E 9
Blagdon Hill. *Som* 1F 13
Blagill. *Cumb* 5A 114
Blaguegate. *Lanc* 4C 90
Blaich. *High* 1E 141
Blain. *High* 2A 140
Blaina. *Blae* 5F 47
Blair Atholl. *Per* 2F 143
Blair Drummond. *Stir* 4G 135
Blairgowrie. *Per* 4A 144
Blairhall. *Fife* 1D 128
Blairingone. *Per* 4B 136
Blairlogie. *Stir* 4H 135
Blairmore. *Abers* 5B 160
Blairmore. *Arg* 1C 126
Blairmore. *High* 3B 166
Blairquhanan. *W Dun* 1F 127
Blaisdon. *Glos* 4C 48
Blakebrook. *Worc* 3C 60
Blakedown. *Worc* 3C 60
Blake End. *Essx* 3H 53
Blakemere. *Here* 1G 47
Blakeney. *Glos* 5B 48
Blakeney. *Norf* 1C 78
Blakenhall. *Ches E* 1B 72
Blakenhall. *W Mid* 1C 60
Blakeshall. *Worc* 2C 60
Blakesley. *Nptn* 5D 62
Blanchland. *Nmbd* 4C 114
Blandford Camp. *Dors* 2E 15
Blandford Forum. *Dors* 2D 15
Blandford St Mary. *Dors* 2D 15
Bland Hill. *N Yor* 4E 98
Blandy. *High* 3G 167
Blanefield. *Stir* 2G 127
Blankney. *Linc* 4H 87
Blantyre. *S Lan* 4H 127
Blarmachfoldach. *High* 2E 141
Blarnalearoch. *High* 4F 163
Blashford. *Hants* 2G 15
Blaston. *Leics* 1F 63
Blatchbridge. *Som* 2C 22
Blathaisbhal. *W Isl* 1D 170
Blatherwycke. *Nptn* 1G 63
Blawith. *Cumb* 1B 96
Blaxhall. *Suff* 5F 67
Blaxton. *S Yor* 4G 93
Blaydon. *Tyne* 3E 115
Bleadney. *Som* 2H 21
Bleadon. *N Som* 1G 21
Blean. *Kent* 4F 41
Bleasby. *Linc* 2A 88
Bleasby. *Notts* 1E 74
Bleasby Moor. *Linc* 2A 88
Blebocraigs. *Fife* 2G 137
Bleddfa. *Powy* 4E 58
Bledington. *Glos* 3H 49
Bledlow. *Buck* 5F 51
Bledlow Ridge. *Buck* 2F 37
Blencarn. *Cumb* 1H 103
Blencogo. *Cumb* 5C 112
Blendworth. *Hants* 1F 17
Blenheim. *Oxon* 5D 50
Blennerhasset. *Cumb* 5C 112
Bletchingdon. *Oxon* 4D 50
Bletchingley. *Surr* 5E 39
Bletchley. *Mil* 2G 51
Bletchley. *Shrp* 2A 72
Bletherston. *Pemb* 2E 43
Bletsoe. *Bed* 5H 63
Blewbury. *Oxon* 3D 36
Blickling. *Norf* 3D 78
Blidworth. *Notts* 5C 86
Blindburn. *Nmbd* 3C 120
Blindcrake. *Cumb* 1C 102
Blindley Heath. *Surr* 1E 27
Blindmoor. *Som* 1F 13
Blisland. *Corn* 5A 10
Blissford. *Hants* 1G 15
Bliss Gate. *Worc* 3B 60
Blists Hill. *Telf* 5A 72
Blisworth. *Nptn* 5E 63
Blithbury. *Staf* 3E 73
Blitterlees. *Cumb* 4C 112
Blockley. *Glos* 2G 49
Blofield. *Norf* 5F 79
Blofield Heath. *Norf* 4F 79
Blo' Norton. *Norf* 3C 66
Bloomfield. *Bord* 2H 119
Blore. *Staf* 1F 73
Blount's Green. *Staf* 2E 73
Bloxham. *Oxon* 2C 50
Bloxholm. *Linc* 5H 87
Bloxwich. *W Mid* 5E 73
Bloxworth. *Dors* 3D 15
Blubberhouses. *N Yor* 4D 98
Blue Anchor. *Som* 2D 20
Blue Anchor. *Swan* 3E 31
Blue Bell Hill. *Kent* 4B 40
Blue Row. *Essx* 4D 54
Bluetown. *Kent* 5D 40
Blundeston. *Suff* 1H 67
Blunham. *C Beds* 5A 64
Blunsdon St Andrew. *Swin* 3G 35
Bluntington. *Worc* 3C 60
Bluntisham. *Cambs* 3C 64
Blunts. *Corn* 2H 7
Blurton. *Stoke* 1C 72
Blyborough. *Linc* 1G 87
Blyford. *Suff* 3G 67
Blymhill. *Staf* 4C 72
Blymhill Lawns. *Staf* 4C 72
Blyth. *Nmbd* 1G 115
Blyth. *Notts* 2D 86
Blyth. *Bord* 5E 129
Blyth Bank. *Bord* 5E 129
Blyth Bridge. *Bord* 5E 129
Blythburgh. *Suff* 3G 67
Blythe Bridge. *Staf* 1D 72
Blythe Marsh. *Staf* 1D 72
Blythe, The. *Staf* 3E 73
Blyton. *Linc* 1F 87
Boarhills. *Fife* 2H 137
Boarhunt. *Hants* 2E 16
Boarshead. *E Sus* 2G 27
Boar's Head. *G Man* 4D 90
Boars Hill. *Oxon* 5C 50
Boarstall. *Buck* 4E 51
Boasley Cross. *Devn* 3F 11
Boath. *High* 1H 157
Boat of Garten. *High* 2D 150
Bobbing. *Kent* 4C 40
Bobbington. *Staf* 1C 60
Bobbingworth. *Essx* 5F 53
Bocaddon. *Corn* 3F 7
Bocking. *Essx* 3A 54
Bocking Churchstreet. *Essx* 3A 54
Boddam. *Abers* 4H 161
Boddam. *Shet* 10E 173
Boddington. *Glos* 3D 49
Bodedern. *IOA* 2C 80
Bodelwyddan. *Den* 3C 82
Bodenham. *Here* 5H 59
Bodenham. *Wilts* 4G 23
Bodewryd. *IOA* 1C 80
Bodfari. *Den* 3C 82
Bodffordd. *IOA* 3D 80
Bodham. *Norf* 1D 78
Bodiam. *E Sus* 3B 28
Bodicote. *Oxon* 2C 50
Bodieve. *Corn* 1D 6
Bodinnick. *Corn* 3F 7
Bodle Street Green. *E Sus* 4A 28
Bodmin. *Corn* 2E 7
Bodnant. *Cnwy* 3H 81
Bodney. *Norf* 1H 65
Bodorgan. *IOA* 4C 80
Bodrane. *Corn* 2G 7
Bodsham. *Kent* 1F 29
Boduan. *Gwyn* 2C 68
Bodymoor Heath. *Warw* 1F 61
Bogallan. *High* 3A 158
Bogbrae Croft. *Abers* 5H 161
Bogend. *S Ayr* 1C 116
Boghall. *Midl* 3F 129
Boghall. *W Lot* 3C 128
Boghead. *S Lan* 5A 128
Bogindollo. *Ang* 3D 144
Bogmoor. *Mor* 2A 160
Bogniebrae. *Abers* 4C 160
Bognor Regis. *W Sus* 3H 17
Bograxie. *Abers* 2E 152
Bogside. *N Lan* 4B 128
Bog, The. *Shrp* 1F 59
Bogton. *Abers* 3D 160
Bogue. *Dum* 1D 110
Bohenie. *High* 5E 149
Bohortha. *Corn* 5C 6
Bokiddick. *Corn* 2E 7
Bolam. *Dur* 2E 105
Bolam. *Nmbd* 1D 115
Bolberry. *Devn* 5C 8
Bold Heath. *Mers* 2H 83
Boldon. *Tyne* 3G 115
Boldon Colliery. *Tyne* 3G 115
Boldre. *Hants* 3B 16
Boldron. *Dur* 3D 104
Bole. *Notts* 2E 87
Bolehall. *Staf* 5G 73
Bolehill. *Derbs* 5G 85
Bolenowe. *Corn* 5A 6
Boleside. *Bord* 1G 119
Bolham. *Devn* 1C 12
Bolham Water. *Devn* 1E 13
Bolingey. *Corn* 3B 6
Bollington. *Ches E* 3D 84
Bolney. *W Sus* 3D 26
Bolnhurst. *Bed* 5H 63
Bolshan. *Ang* 3F 145
Bolsover. *Derbs* 3B 86
Bolsterstone. *S Yor* 1G 85
Bolstone. *Here* 2A 48
Boltachan. *Per* 3F 143
Boltby. *N Yor* 1G 99
Bolton. *Cumb* 2H 103
Bolton. *E Lot* 2B 130
Bolton. *E Yor* 4B 100
Bolton. *G Man* 4F 91
Bolton. *Nmbd* 3F 121
Bolton Abbey. *N Yor* 4C 98
Bolton-by-Bowland. *Lanc* 5G 97
Boltonfellend. *Cumb* 3F 113
Boltongate. *Cumb* 5D 112
Bolton Green. *Lanc* 3D 90
Bolton-le-Sands. *Lanc* 3D 97
Bolton Low Houses. *Cumb* 5D 112
Bolton New Houses. *Cumb* 5D 112
Bolton-on-Swale. *N Yor* 5F 105
Bolton Percy. *N Yor* 5H 99
Bolton Town End. *Lanc* 3D 97
Bolton upon Dearne. *S Yor* 4E 93
Bolton Wood Lane. *Cumb* 5D 112
Bolventor. *Corn* 5B 10
Bomarsund. *Nmbd* 1F 115
Bomere Heath. *Shrp* 4G 71
Bonar Bridge. *High* 4D 164
Bonawe. *Arg* 5E 141
Bonby. *N Lin* 3D 94
Boncath. *Pemb* 1G 43
Bonchester Bridge. *Bord* 3H 119
Bonchurch. *IOW* 5D 16
Bond End. *Staf* 4F 73
Bondleigh. *Devn* 2G 11
Bonds. *Lanc* 5D 97
Bonehill. *Devn* 5H 11
Bonehill. *Staf* 5F 73
Bo'ness. *Falk* 1C 128
Boney Hay. *Staf* 4E 73
Bonham. *Wilts* 3C 22
Bonhill. *W Dun* 2E 127
Boningale. *Shrp* 5C 72
Bonjedward. *Bord* 2A 120
Bonkle. *N Lan* 4B 128
Bonnington. *Ang* 5E 145
Bonnington. *Edin* 3E 129
Bonnington. *Kent* 2E 29
Bonnybank. *Fife* 3F 137
Bonnybridge. *Falk* 1B 128
Bonnykelly. *Abers* 3F 161
Bonnyrigg. *Midl* 3G 129
Bonnyton. *Ang* 5C 144
Bonnytown. *Fife* 2H 137
Bonsall. *Derbs* 5G 85
Bont. *Mon* 4G 47
Bontddu. *Gwyn* 4F 69
Bont Dolgadfan. *Powy* 5A 70
Bontgoch. *Cdgn* 2F 57
Bonthorpe. *Linc* 3D 89
Bontnewydd. *Cdgn* 4F 57
Bont-newydd. *Cnwy* 3C 82

Bontnewydd—Brampton

Bontnewydd. *Gwyn* . . . . 4D **81** (nr. Caernarfon)
Bont Newydd. *Gwyn* . . . . 1G **69** (nr. Llan Ffestiniog)
Bontuchel. *Den* 5C **82**
Bonvilston. *V Glam* 4D **32**
Bon-y-maen. *Swan* 3F **31**
Booker. *Buck* 2G **37**
Booley. *Shrp* 3H **71**
Boorley Green. *Hants* 1D **16**
Boosbeck. *Red C* 3D **106**
Boot. *Cumb* 4C **102**
Booth. *W Yor* 2A **92**
Boothby Graffoe. *Linc* 5G **87**
Boothby Pagnell. *Linc* 2G **75**
Booth Green. *Ches E* 2D **84**
Booth of Toft. *Shet* 4F **173**
Boothstown. *G Man* 4F **91**
Boothville. *Nptn* 4E **63**
Booth Wood. *W Yor* 3A **92**
Bootle. *Cumb* 1A **96**
Bootle. *Mers* 1F **83**
Booton. *Norf* 3D **78**
Booze. *N Yor* 4D **104**
Boquhan. *Stir* 1G **127**
Boraston. *Shrp* 3A **60**
Borden. *Kent* 4C **40**
Borden. *W Sus* 4G **25**
Bordlands. *Bord* 5E **129**
Bordley. *N Yor* 3B **98**
Bordon. *Hants* 3G **25**
Boreham. *Essx* 5A **54**
Boreham. *Wilts* 2D **23**
Boreham Street. *E Sus* 4A **28**
Borehamwood. *Herts* 1C **38**
Boreland. *Dum* 5D **118**
Boreston. *Devn* 3D **8**
Borestone Brae. *Stir* 4H **135**
Boreton. *Shrp* 5H **71**
Borgh. *W Isl* . . . . 8B **170** (on Barra)
Borgh. *W Isl* . . . . 3C **170** (on Benbecula)
Borgh. *W Isl* . . . . 1E **170** (on Berneray)
Borgh. *W Isl* . . . . 2G **171** (on Isle of Lewis)
Borghastan. *W Isl* 3D **171**
Borgh na Sgiotaig. *High* 1C **154**
Borgie. *High* 3G **167**
Borgue. *Dum* 5D **110**
Borgue. *High* 1H **165**
Borley. *Essx* 1B **54**
Borley Green. *Essx* 1B **54**
Borley Green. *Suff* 4B **66**
Borlum. *High* 1H **149**
Bornais. *W Isl* 6C **170**
Bornesketaig. *High* 1C **154**
Boroughbridge. *N Yor* 3F **99**
Borough Green. *Kent* 5H **39**
Borras Head. *Wrex* 5F **83**
Borreraig. *High* 3A **154**
Borrobol Lodge. *High* 1F **165**
Borrodale. *High* 4A **154**
Borrowash. *Derb* 2B **74**
Borrowby. *N Yor* . . . . 1G **99** (nr. Northallerton)
Borrowby. *N Yor* . . . . 3E **107** (nr. Whitby)
Borrowston. *High* 4F **169**
Borrowstonehill. *Orkn* 7D **172**
Borrowstoun. *Falk* 1C **128**
Borstal. *Medw* 4B **40**
Borth. *Cdgn* 2F **57**
Borthwick. *Midl* 4G **129**
Borth-y-Gest. *Gwyn* 2E **69**
Borve. *High* 4D **154**
Borwick. *Lanc* 2E **97**
Bosbury. *Here* 1B **48**
Boscastle. *Corn* 3A **10**
Boscombe. *Bour* 3G **15**
Boscombe. *Wilts* 3H **23**
Boscoppa. *Corn* 3E **7**
Bosham. *W Sus* 2G **17**
Bosherston. *Pemb* 5D **42**
Bosley. *Ches E* 4D **84**
Bossall. *N Yor* 3B **100**
Bossiney. *Corn* 4A **10**
Bossingham. *Kent* 1F **29**
Bossington. *Som* 2B **20**
Bostadh. *W Isl* 4D **171**
Bostock Green. *Ches W* 4A **84**
Boston. *Linc* 1C **76**
Boston Spa. *W Yor* 5G **99**
Boswarthen. *Corn* 3B **4**
Boswinger. *Corn* 4D **6**
Botallack. *Corn* 3A **4**
Botany Bay. *G Lon* 1D **39**
Botcheston. *Leics* 5B **74**
Botesdale. *Suff* 3C **66**
Bothal. *Nmbd* 1F **115**
Bothampstead. *W Ber* 4D **36**
Bothamsall. *Notts* 3D **86**
Bothel. *Cumb* 1C **102**
Bothenhampton. *Dors* 3H **13**
Bothwell. *S Lan* 4H **127**
Botley. *Buck* 5H **51**
Botley. *Hants* 1D **16**
Botley. *Oxon* 5C **50**
Botloe's Green. *Glos* 3C **48**
Botolph Claydon. *Buck* 3F **51**
Botolphs. *W Sus* 5C **26**
Bottacks. *High* 2G **157**
Bottesford. *Leics* 2F **75**
Bottesford. *N Lin* 4B **94**
Bottisham. *Cambs* 4E **65**
Bottlesford. *Wilts* 1G **23**
Bottomcraig. *Fife* 1F **137**
Bottom o' th' Moor. *G Man* 3E **91**
Botton. *N Yor* 4D **107**
Botton Head. *Lanc* 3F **97**
Bottreaux Mill. *Devn* 4B **20**
Botusfleming. *Corn* 2A **8**
Botwnnog. *Gwyn* 2B **68**
Bough Beech. *Kent* 1F **27**
Boughrood. *Powy* 2E **47**
Boughspring. *Glos* 2A **34**
Boughton. *Norf* 5F **77**
Boughton. *Nptn* 4E **63**
Boughton. *Notts* 4D **86**
Boughton Aluph. *Kent* 1E **29**
Boughton Green. *Kent* 5B **40**
Boughton Lees. *Kent* 1E **28**
Boughton Malherbe. *Kent* 1C **28**
Boughton Monchelsea. *Kent* 5B **40**
Boughton under Blean. *Kent* 5E **41**
Boulby. *Red C* 3E **107**
Bouldnor. *IOW* 4B **16**
Bouldon. *Shrp* 2H **59**
Boulmer. *Nmbd* 3G **121**
Boulston. *Pemb* 3D **42**
Boultham. *Linc* 4G **87**
Boulton. *Derb* 2A **74**
Boundary. *Staf* 1D **73**
Bounds. *Here* 2B **48**
Bourn. *Cambs* 5C **64**
Bournbrook. *W Mid* 2E **61**
Bourne. *Linc* 3H **75**
Bourne End. *Bed* 4H **63**
Bourne End. *Buck* 3G **37**
Bourne End. *C Beds* 1H **51**
Bourne End. *Herts* 5A **52**
Bournemouth. *Bour* 3F **15**
Bournemouth Airport. *Dors* 3G **15**
Bournes Green. *Glos* 5E **49**
Bournes Green. *S'end* 2D **40**
Bourne, The. *Surr* 2G **25**
Bournheath. *Worc* 3D **60**
Bournmoor. *Dur* 4G **115**
Bournville. *W Mid* 2E **61**
Bourton. *Dors* 3C **22**
Bourton. *N Som* 5G **33**
Bourton. *Oxon* 3H **35**
Bourton. *Shrp* 1H **59**
Bourton. *Wilts* 5F **35**
Bourton on Dunsmore. *Warw* 3B **62**
Bourton-on-the-Hill. *Glos* 2G **49**
Bourton-on-the-Water. *Glos* 3G **49**
Bousd. *Arg* 2D **138**
Boustead Hill. *Cumb* 4D **112**
Bouth. *Cumb* 1C **96**
Bouthwaite. *N Yor* 2D **98**
Boveney. *Buck* 3A **38**
Boveridge. *Dors* 1F **15**
Boverton. *V Glam* 5C **32**
Bovey Tracey. *Devn* 5B **12**
Bovingdon. *Herts* 5A **52**
Bovingdon Green. *Buck* 3G **37**
Bovinger. *Essx* 5F **53**
Bovington Camp. *Dors* 4D **14**
Bow. *Devn* 2H **11**
Bowbank. *Dur* 2C **104**
Bow Brickhill. *Mil* 2H **51**
Bowbridge. *Glos* 5D **48**
Bowburn. *Dur* 1A **106**
Bowcombe. *IOW* 4C **16**
Bowd. *Devn* 4E **12**
Bowden. *Devn* 4E **9**
Bowden. *Bord* 1H **119**
Bowden Hill. *Wilts* 5E **35**
Bowdens. *Som* 4H **21**
Bowdon. *G Man* 2B **84**
Bower. *Nmbd* 1A **114**
Bowerchalke. *Wilts* 4F **23**
Bowerhill. *Wilts* 5E **35**
Bower Hinton. *Som* 1H **13**
Bowermadden. *High* 2E **169**
Bowers. *Staf* 2C **72**
Bowers Gifford. *Essx* 2B **40**
Bowershall. *Fife* 4C **136**
Bowertower. *High* 2E **169**
Bowes. *Dur* 3C **104**
Bowgreave. *Lanc* 5D **97**
Bowhousebog. *N Lan* 4B **128**
Bowithick. *Corn* 4B **10**
Bowland Bridge. *Cumb* 1D **96**
Bowlees. *Dur* 2C **104**
Bowley. *Here* 5H **59**
Bowlhead Green. *Surr* 2A **26**
Bowling. *W Dun* 2F **127**
Bowling. *W Yor* 1B **92**
Bowling Bank. *Wrex* 1F **71**
Bowling Green. *Worc* 5C **60**
Bowlish. *Som* 2B **22**
Bowmanstead. *Cumb* 5E **102**
Bowmore. *Arg* 4B **124**
Bowness-on-Solway. *Cumb* 3D **112**
Bowness-on-Windermere. *Cumb* 5F **103**
Bow of Fife. *Fife* 2F **137**
Bowriefauld. *Ang* 4E **145**
Bowscale. *Cumb* 1E **103**
Bowsden. *Nmbd* 5F **131**
Bowside Lodge. *High* 2A **168**
Bowston. *Cumb* 5F **103**
Bow Street. *Cdgn* 2F **57**
Bowthorpe. *Norf* 5D **78**
Box. *Glos* 5D **48**
Box. *Wilts* 5D **34**
Boxbush. *Glos* 3B **48**
Box End. *Bed* 1A **52**
Boxford. *Suff* 1C **54**
Boxford. *W Ber* 4C **36**
Boxgrove. *W Sus* 5A **26**
Boxley. *Kent* 5B **40**
Boxmoor. *Herts* 5A **52**
Box's Shop. *Corn* 2C **10**
Boxted. *Essx* 2C **54**
Boxted. *Suff* 5H **65**
Boxted Cross. *Essx* 2D **54**
Boxworth. *Cambs* 4C **64**
Boxworth End. *Cambs* 4C **64**
Boyden End. *Suff* 5G **65**
Boyden Gate. *Kent* 4G **41**
Boylestone. *Derbs* 2F **73**
Boylestonfield. *Derbs* 2F **73**
Boyndlie. *Abers* 2D **160**
Boynton. *E Yor* 3F **101**
Boys Hill. *Dors* 1B **14**
Boythorpe. *Derbs* 4A **86**
Boyton. *Corn* 3D **10**
Boyton. *Suff* 1G **55**
Boyton. *Wilts* 3E **23**
Boyton Cross. *Essx* 5G **53**
Boyton End. *Essx* 2G **53**
Boyton End. *Suff* 1H **53**
Bozeat. *Nptn* 5G **63**
Braaid. *IOM* 4C **108**
Braal Castle. *High* 2D **168**
Brabling Green. *Suff* 4E **67**
Brabourne. *Kent* 1F **29**
Brabourne Lees. *Kent* 1E **29**
Brabster. *High* 2F **169**
Bracadale. *High* 5C **154**
Bracara. *High* 4F **147**
Braceborough. *Linc* 4H **75**
Bracebridge. *Linc* 4G **87**
Bracebridge Heath. *Linc* 4G **87**
Braceby. *Linc* 2H **75**
Bracewell. *Lanc* 5A **98**
Brackenfield. *Derbs* 5A **86**
Brackenlands. *Cumb* 5D **112**
Brackenthwaite. *Cumb* 5D **112**
Brackenthwaite. *N Yor* 4E **99**
Brackla. *B'end* 4C **32**
Brackla. *High* 3C **158**
Bracklesham. *W Sus* 3G **17**
Brackletter. *High* 5D **148**
Brackley. *Nptn* 2D **50**
Brackley Hatch. *Nptn* 1E **51**
Brackloch. *High* 1F **163**
Bracknell. *Brac* 5G **37**
Braco. *Per* 3H **135**
Bracobrae. *Mor* 3C **160**
Bracon. *N Lin* 4A **94**
Bracon Ash. *Norf* 1D **66**
Bradbourne. *Derbs* 5G **85**
Bradbury. *Dur* 2A **106**
Bradda. *IOM* 4A **108**
Bradden. *Nptn* 1E **51**
Bradenham. *Buck* 2G **37**
Bradenham. *Norf* 5B **78**
Bradenstoke. *Wilts* 4F **35**
Bradfield. *Essx* 2E **55**
Bradfield. *Norf* 2E **79**
Bradfield. *W Ber* 4E **36**
Bradfield Combust. *Suff* 5A **66**
Bradfield Green. *Ches E* 5A **84**
Bradfield Heath. *Essx* 3E **55**
Bradfield St Clare. *Suff* 5B **66**
Bradfield St George. *Suff* 4B **66**
Bradford. *Derbs* 4G **85**
Bradford. *Devn* 2E **11**
Bradford. *Nmbd* 1F **121**
Bradford. *W Yor* 1B **92**
Bradford Abbas. *Dors* 1A **14**
Bradford Barton. *Devn* 1B **12**
Bradford Leigh. *Wilts* 5D **34**
Bradford-on-Avon. *Wilts* 5D **34**
Bradford-on-Tone. *Som* 4E **21**
Bradford Peverell. *Dors* 3B **14**
Bradiford. *Devn* 3F **19**
Brading. *IOW* 4E **16**
Bradley. *Ches W* 3H **83**
Bradley. *Derbs* 1G **73**
Bradley. *Glos* 2C **34**
Bradley. *Hants* 2E **25**
Bradley. *NE Lin* 4F **95**
Bradley. *N Yor* 1C **98**
Bradley. *Staf* 4C **72**
Bradley. *W Mid* 1D **60**
Bradley. *W Yor* 2B **92**
Bradley. *Wrex* 5F **83**
Bradley Cross. *Som* 1H **21**
Bradley Green. *Ches W* 1H **71**
Bradley Green. *Som* 3F **21**
Bradley Green. *Warw* 5G **73**
Bradley Green. *Worc* 4D **61**
Bradley in the Moors. *Staf* 1E **73**
Bradley Mount. *Ches E* 3D **84**
Bradley Stoke. *S Glo* 3B **34**
Bradlow. *Here* 2C **48**
Bradmore. *Notts* 2C **74**
Bradmore. *W Mid* 1C **60**
Bradninch. *Devn* 2D **12**
Bradnop. *Staf* 5E **85**
Bradpole. *Dors* 3H **13**
Bradshaw. *G Man* 3F **91**
Bradstone. *Devn* 4D **11**
Bradwall Green. *Ches E* 4B **84**
Bradway. *S Yor* 2H **85**
Bradwell. *Derbs* 2F **85**
Bradwell. *Essx* 3B **54**
Bradwell. *Mil* 2G **51**
Bradwell. *Norf* 5H **79**
Bradwell-on-Sea. *Essx* 5D **54**
Bradwell Waterside. *Essx* 5C **54**
Bradworthy. *Devn* 1D **10**
Brae. *High* 5C **162**
Brae. *Shet* 5E **173**
Braeantra. *High* 1H **157**
Braefield. *High* 5G **157**
Braefindon. *High* 3A **158**
Braegrum. *Per* 1C **136**
Braehead. *Ang* 3F **145**
Braehead. *Dum* 4B **110**
Braehead. *Mor* 4G **159**
Braehead. *Orkn* 3D **172**
Braehead. *S Lan* . . . . 1H **117** (nr. Coalburn)
Braehead. *S Lan* . . . . 4C **128** (nr. Forth)
Braehoulland. *Shet* 4D **173**
Braemar. *Abers* 4F **151**
Braemore. *High* . . . . 5C **168** (nr. Dunbeath)
Braemore. *High* . . . . 1D **156** (nr. Ullapool)
Brae of Achnahaird. *High* 2E **163**
Brae Roy Lodge. *High* 4F **149**
Braeside. *Abers* 5G **161**
Braeside. *Inv* 2D **126**
Braes of Coul. *Ang* 3B **144**
Braetongue. *High* 3F **167**
Braeval. *Stir* 3E **135**
Braevallich. *Arg* 3G **133**
Brafferton. *Darl* 2F **105**
Brafferton. *N Yor* 2G **99**
Brafield-on-the-Green. *Nptn* 5F **63**
Bragar. *W Isl* 3E **171**
Bragbury End. *Herts* 3C **52**
Bragleenbeg. *Arg* 1G **133**
Braichmelyn. *Gwyn* 4F **81**
Braides. *Lanc* 4D **96**
Braidwood. *S Lan* 5B **128**
Braigo. *Arg* 3A **124**
Brailsford. *Derbs* 1G **73**
Braintree. *Essx* 3A **54**
Braiseworth. *Suff* 3D **66**
Braishfield. *Hants* 4B **24**
Braithwaite. *Cumb* 2D **102**
Braithwaite. *S Yor* 3G **93**
Braithwaite. *W Yor* 5C **98**
Braithwell. *S Yor* 1C **86**
Brakefield Green. *Norf* 5C **78**
Bramber. *W Sus* 4C **26**
Brambledown. *Kent* 3D **40**
Brambridge. *Hants* 4C **24**
Bramcote. *Notts* 2C **74**
Bramcote. *Warw* 2B **62**
Bramdean. *Hants* 4E **24**
Bramerton. *Norf* 5E **79**
Bramfield. *Herts* 4C **52**
Bramfield. *Suff* 3F **67**
Bramford. *Suff* 1E **54**
Bramhall. *G Man* 2C **84**
Bramham. *W Yor* 5G **99**
Bramhope. *W Yor* 5E **99**
Bramley. *Hants* 1E **25**
Bramley. *S Yor* 1B **86**
Bramley. *Surr* 1B **26**
Bramley. *W Yor* 1C **92**
Bramley Green. *Hants* 1E **25**
Bramley Head. *N Yor* 4D **98**
Bramley Vale. *Derbs* 4B **86**
Bramling. *Kent* 5G **41**
Brampford Speke. *Devn* 3C **12**
Brampton. *Cambs* 3B **64**

Brampton—Broadwath

Brampton. Cumb 2H 103
(nr. Appleby-in-Westmorland)
Brampton. Cumb 3G 113
(nr. Carlisle)
Brampton. Linc 3F 87
Brampton. Norf 3E 78
Brampton. S Yor 4E 93
Brampton. Suff 2G 67
Brampton Abbotts. Here 3B 48
Brampton Ash. Nptn 2E 63
Brampton Bryan. Here 3F 59
Brampton en le Morthen. S Yor 2B 86
Bramshall. Staf 2E 73
Bramshaw. Hants 1A 16
Bramshill. Hants 5F 37
Bramshott. Hants 3G 25
Branault. High 2G 139
Brancaster. Norf 1G 77
Brancaster Staithe. Norf 1G 77
Brancepeth. Dur 1F 105
Branch End. Nmbd 3D 114
Branchill. Mor 3E 159
Brand End. Linc 1C 76
Branderburgh. Mor 1G 159
Brandesburton. E Yor 5F 101
Brandeston. Suff 4E 67
Brand Green. Glos 3C 48
Brandhill. Shrp 3G 59
Brandis Corner. Devn 2E 11
Brandish Street. Som 2C 20
Brandiston. Norf 3D 78
Brandon. Dur 1F 105
Brandon. Linc 1G 75
Brandon. Nmbd 3E 121
Brandon. Suff 2G 65
Brandon. Warw 3B 62
Brandon Bank. Cambs 2F 65
Brandon Creek. Norf 1F 65
Brandon Parva. Norf 5C 78
Brandsby. N Yor 2H 99
Brandy Wharf. Linc 1H 87
Brane. Corn 4B 4
Bran End. Essx 3G 53
Branksome. Pool 3F 15
Bransbury. Hants 2C 24
Bransby. Linc 3G 87
Branscombe. Devn 4E 13
Bransford. Worc 5B 60
Bransgore. Hants 3G 15
Bransholme. Hull 1D 94
Bransley. Shrp 3A 60
Branston. Leics 3F 75
Branston. Linc 4H 87
Branston. Staf 3G 73
Branston Booths. Linc 4H 87
Branstone. IOW 4D 16
Bransty. Cumb 3A 102
Brant Broughton. Linc 5G 87
Brantham. Suff 2E 54
Branthwaite. Cumb 1D 102
(nr. Caldbeck)
Branthwaite. Cumb 2B 102
(nr. Workington)
Brantingham. E Yor 2C 94
Branton. Nmbd 3E 121
Branton. S Yor 4G 93
Branton Green. N Yor 3G 99
Branxholme. Bord 3G 119
Branxton. Nmbd 1C 120
Brassington. Derbs 5G 85
Brasted. Kent 5F 39
Brasted Chart. Kent 5F 39
Bratch, The. Staf 1C 60
Brathens. Abers 4D 152
Bratoft. Linc 4D 88
Brattleby. Linc 2G 87
Bratton. Som 2C 20
Bratton. Telf 4A 72
Bratton. Wilts 1E 23
Bratton Clovelly. Devn 3E 11
Bratton Fleming. Devn 3G 19
Bratton Seymour. Som 4B 22
Braughing. Herts 3D 53
Braulen Lodge. High 5E 157
Braunston. Nptn 4C 62
Braunstone Town. Leic 5C 74
Braunston-in-Rutland. Rut 5F 75
Braunton. Devn 3E 19
Brawby. N Yor 2B 100
Brawl. High 2A 168
Brawlbin. High 3C 168
Bray. Wind 3A 38
Braybrooke. Nptn 2E 63
Brayford. Devn 3G 19
Bray Shop. Corn 5D 10
Braystones. Cumb 4B 102
Brayton. N Yor 1G 93
Bray Wick. Wind 4G 37
Brazacott. Corn 3C 10
Brea. Corn 4A 6
Breach. W Sus 2F 17
Breachwood Green. Herts 3B 52
Breacleit. W Isl 4D 171
Breaden Heath. Shrp 2G 71
Breadsall. Derbs 1A 74
Breadstone. Glos 5C 48
Breage. Corn 4D 4
Breakachy. High 4G 157
Breakish. High 1E 147
Bream. Glos 5B 48
Breamore. Hants 1G 15
Bream's Meend. Glos 5B 48
Brean. Som 1F 21
Breanais. W Isl 5B 171
Brearton. N Yor 3F 99
Breascleit. W Isl 4E 171
Breaston. Derbs 2B 74
Brecais Àrd. High 1E 147
Brecais Iosal. High 1E 147
Brechfa. Carm 2F 45
Brechin. Ang 3F 145
Breckles. Norf 1B 66
Brecon. Powy 3D 46
Bredbury. G Man 1D 84
Brede. E Sus 4C 28
Bredenbury. Here 5A 60
Breden's Norton. Worc 2E 49
Bredfield. Suff 5E 67
Bredgar. Kent 4C 40
Bredhurst. Kent 4B 40
Bredicot. Worc 5D 60
Bredon. Worc 2E 49
Bredwardine. Here 1G 47
Breedon on the Hill. Leics 3B 74
Breibhig. W Isl 9B 170
(on Barra)
Breibhig. W Isl 4G 171
(on Isle of Lewis)
Breich. W Lot 3C 128
Breightmet. G Man 3F 91
Breighton. E Yor 1H 93
Breinton. Here 2H 47
Breinton Common. Here 2H 47
Breiwick. Shet 7F 173
Brelston Green. Here 3A 48
Bremhill. Wilts 4E 35
Brenachie. High 1B 158
Brenchley. Kent 1A 28
Brendon. Devn 2A 20
Brent Cross. G Lon 2D 38
Brent Eleigh. Suff 1C 54
Brentford. G Lon 3C 38
Brentingby. Leics 4E 75
Brent Knoll. Som 1G 21
Brent Pelham. Herts 2E 53
Brentwood. Essx 1H 39
Brenzett. Kent 3E 28
Brereton. Staf 4E 73
Brereton Cross. Staf 4E 73
Brereton Green. Ches E 4B 84
Brereton Heath. Ches E 4C 84
Bressingham. Norf 2C 66
Bretby. Derbs 3G 73
Bretford. Warw 3B 62
Bretforton. Worc 1F 49
Bretherdale Head. Cumb 4G 103
Bretherton. Lanc 2C 90
Brettenham. Norf 2B 66
Brettenham. Suff 5B 66
Bretton. Flin 4F 83
Bretton. Pet 5A 76
Brewer Street. Surr 5E 39
Brewlands Bridge. Ang 2A 144
Brewood. Staf 5C 72
Briantspuddle. Dors 3D 14
Bricket Wood. Herts 5B 52
Bricklehampton. Worc 1E 49
Bride. IOM 1D 108
Bridekirk. Cumb 1C 102
Bridell. Pemb 1B 44
Bridestowe. Devn 4F 11
Brideswell. Abers 5C 160
Bridford. Devn 4B 12
Bridfordmills. Devn 4B 12
Bridge. Corn 4A 6
Bridge. Kent 5F 41
Bridge. Som 2G 13
Bridge End. Bed 5H 63
Bridge End. Cumb 5D 102
Bridge End. Linc 2A 76
Bridge End. Shet 8E 173
Bridgefoot. Ang 5C 144
Bridgefoot. Cumb 2B 102
Bridge Green. Essx 2E 53
Bridgehampton. Som 4A 22
Bridge Hewick. N Yor 2F 99
Bridgehill. Dur 4D 115
Bridgemary. Hants 2D 16
Bridgemere. Ches E 1B 72
Bridgemont. Derbs 2E 85
Bridgend. Abers 5C 160
(nr. Huntly)
Bridgend. Abers 5H 161
(nr. Peterhead)
Bridgend. Ang 2E 145
(nr. Brechin)
Bridgend. Ang 4C 144
(nr. Kirriemuir)
Bridgend. Arg 4F 133
(nr. Lochgilphead)
Bridgend. Arg 3B 124
(on Islay)
Bridgend. B'end 3C 32
Bridgend. Cumb 3F 103
Bridgend. Devn 4B 8
Bridgend. Fife 2F 137
Bridgend. High 3F 157
Bridgend. Mor 5A 160
Bridgend. Per 1D 136
Bridgend. W Lot 2D 128
Bridgend of Lintrathen.
Ang 3B 144
Bridgeness. Falk 1D 128
Bridge of Alford. Abers 2C 152
Bridge of Allan. Stir 4G 135
Bridge of Avon. Mor 5F 159
Bridge of Awe. Arg 1H 133
Bridge of Balgie. Per 4C 142
Bridge of Brown. High 1F 151
Bridge of Cally. Per 3A 144
Bridge of Canny. Abers 4D 152
Bridge of Dee. Dum 3E 111
Bridge of Don. Aber 2G 153
Bridge of Dun. Ang 3F 145
Bridge of Dye. Abers 5D 152
Bridge of Earn. Per 2D 136
Bridge of Ericht. Per 3C 142
Bridge of Feugh. Abers 4E 152
Bridge of Forss. High 2C 168
Bridge of Gairn. Abers 4A 152
Bridge of Gaur. Per 3C 142
Bridge of Muchalls. Abers 4F 153
Bridge of Oich. High 3F 149
Bridge of Orchy. Arg 5H 141
Bridge of Walls. Shet 6D 173
Bridge of Weir. Ren 3E 127
Bridge Reeve. Devn 1G 11
Bridgerule. Devn 2C 10
Bridge Sollers. Here 1H 47
Bridge Street. Suff 1B 54
Bridgetown. Devn 2E 9
Bridgetown. Som 3C 20
Bridge Town. Warw 5G 61
Bridge Trafford. Ches W 3G 83
Bridgeyate. S Glo 4B 34
Bridgham. Norf 2B 66
Bridgnorth. Shrp 1B 60
Bridgtown. Staf 5D 73
Bridgwater. Som 3G 21
Bridlington. E Yor 3F 101
Bridport. Dors 3H 13
Bridstow. Here 3A 48
Brierfield. Lanc 1G 91
Brierley. Glos 4B 48
Brierley. Here 5G 59
Brierley. S Yor 3E 93
Brierley Hill. W Mid 2D 60
Brierton. Hart 1B 106
Briestfield. W Yor 3C 92
Brigg. N Lin 4D 94
Briggate. Norf 3F 79
Briggswath. N Yor 4F 107
Brigham. Cumb 1B 102
Brigham. E Yor 4E 101
Brighouse. W Yor 2B 92
Brighstone. IOW 4C 16
Brightgate. Derbs 5G 85
Brighthampton. Oxon 5B 50
Brightholmlee. S Yor 1G 85
Brightley. Devn 3G 11
Brightling. E Sus 3A 28
Brightlingsea. Essx 4D 54
Brighton. Brig 5E 27
Brighton. Corn 3D 6
Brighton Hill. Hants 2E 24
Brightons. Falk 2C 128
Brightwalton. W Ber 4C 36
Brightwalton Green. W Ber 4C 36
Brightwell. Suff 1F 55
Brightwell Baldwin. Oxon 2E 37
Brightwell-cum-Sotwell. Oxon 2D 36
Brigmerston. Wilts 2G 23
Brignall. Dur 3D 104
Brig o'Turk. Stir 3E 135
Brigsley. NE Lin 4F 95
Brigsteer. Cumb 1D 97
Brigstock. Nptn 2G 63
Brill. Buck 4E 51
Brill. Corn 4E 5
Brilley. Here 1F 47
Brimaston. Pemb 2D 42
Brimfield. Here 4H 59
Brimington. Derbs 3B 86
Brimley. Devn 5B 12
Brimpsfield. Glos 4E 49
Brimpton. W Ber 5D 36
Brims. Orkn 9B 172
Brimscombe. Glos 5D 48
Brimstage. Mers 2F 83
Brincliffe. S Yor 2H 85
Brind. E Yor 1H 93
Brindle. Lanc 2E 90
Brindley Ford. Stoke 5C 84
Brineton. Staf 4C 72
Bringhurst. Leics 1F 63
Brington. Cambs 3H 63
Brinian. Orkn 5D 172
Briningham. Norf 2C 78
Brinkhill. Linc 3C 88
Brinkley. Cambs 5F 65
Brinklow. Warw 3B 62
Brinkworth. Wilts 3F 35
Brinscall. Lanc 2E 91
Brinscombe. Som 1H 21
Brinsley. Notts 1B 74
Brinsty Common. Here 5A 60
Brinsworth. S Yor 2B 86
Brinton. Norf 2C 78
Brisco. Cumb 4F 113
Brisley. Norf 3B 78
Brislington. Bris 4B 34
Brissenden Green. Kent 2D 28
Bristol. Bris 4A 34
Bristol International Airport.
N Som 5A 34
Briston. Norf 2C 78
Britannia. Lanc 2G 91
Britford. Wilts 4G 23
Brithdir. Cphy 5E 47
Brithdir. Cdgn 1D 44
Brithdir. Gwyn 4G 69
Briton Ferry. Neat 3G 31
Britwell Salome. Oxon 2E 37
Brixham. Torb 3F 9
Brixton. Devn 3B 8
Brixton. G Lon 3E 39
Brixton Deverill. Wilts 3D 22
Brixworth. Nptn 3E 63
Brize Norton. Oxon 5B 50
Broad Alley. Worc 4C 60
Broad Blunsdon. Swin 2G 35
Broadbottom. G Man 1D 85
Broadbridge. W Sus 2G 17
Broadbridge Heath. W Sus 2C 26
Broad Campden. Glos 2G 49
Broad Chalke. Wilts 4F 23
Broadclyst. Devn 3C 12
Broadfield. Inv 2E 127
Broadfield. Pemb 4F 43
Broadfield. W Sus 2D 26
Broadford. High 1E 147
Broadford Bridge. W Sus 3B 26
Broad Green. Cambs 5F 65
Broad Green. C Beds 1H 51
Broad Green. Worc 3D 61
(nr. Bromsgrove)
Broad Green. Worc 5B 60
(nr. Worcester)
Broadhaven. High 3F 169
Broad Haven. Pemb 3C 42
Broadheath. G Man 2B 84
Broad Heath. Staf 3C 72
Broadheath. Worc 4A 60
Broadhembury. Devn 2E 12
Broadhempston. Devn 2E 9
Broad Hill. Cambs 3E 65
Broad Hinton. Wilts 4G 35
Broadholm. Derbs 1A 74
Broadholme. Linc 3F 87
Broadlay. Carm 5D 44
Broad Laying. Hants 5C 36
Broadley. Lanc 3G 91
Broadley. Mor 2A 160
Broadley Common. Essx 5E 53
Broad Marston. Worc 1G 49
Broadmayne. Dors 4C 14
Broadmere. Hants 2E 24
Broadmoor. Pemb 4E 43
Broad Oak. Carm 3F 45
Broad Oak. Cumb 5C 102
Broad Oak. Devn 3D 12
Broadoak. Dors 3H 13
(nr. Bridport)
Broad Oak. Dors 1C 14
(nr. Sturminster Newton)
Broad Oak. E Sus 4C 28
(nr. Hastings)
Broad Oak. E Sus 3H 27
(nr. Heathfield)
Broadoak. Glos 4B 48
Broadoak. Hants 1C 16
Broad Oak. Here 3H 47
Broad Oak. Kent 4F 41
Broadrashes. Mor 3B 160
Broadsea. Abers 2G 161
Broad's Green. Essx 4G 53
Broadshard. Som 1H 13
Broadstairs. Kent 4H 41
Broadstone. Pool 3F 15
Broadstone. Shrp 2H 59
Broad Street. E Sus 4C 28
Broad Street. Kent 1F 29
(nr. Ashford)
Broad Street. Kent 5C 40
(nr. Maidstone)
Broad Street Green. Essx 5B 54
Broad, The. Here 4G 59
Broad Town. Wilts 4F 35
Broadwas. Worc 5B 60
Broadwath. Cumb 4F 113

Broadway—Buglawton

Broadway. *Carm* 5D 45 (nr. Kidwelly)
Broadway. *Carm* 3G 43 (nr. Laugharne)
Broadway. *Pemb* 3C 42
Broadway. *Som* 1G 13
Broadway. *Suff* 3F 67
Broadway. *Worc* 2G 49
Broadwell. *Glos* 4A 48 (nr. Cinderford)
Broadwell. *Glos* 3H 49 (nr. Stow-on-the-Wold)
Broadwell. *Oxon* 5A 50
Broadwell. *Warw* 4B 62
Broadwell House. *Nmbd* 4C 114
Broadwey. *Dors* 4B 14
Broadwindsor. *Dors* 2H 13
Broadwoodkelly. *Devn* 2G 11
Broadwoodwidger. *Devn* 4E 11
Broallan. *High* 4G 157
Brobury. *Here* 1G 47
Brochel. *High* 4E 155
Brockamin. *Worc* 5B 60
Brockbridge. *Hants* 1E 16
Brockdish. *Norf* 3E 66
Brockencote. *Worc* 3C 60
Brockenhurst. *Hants* 2A 16
Brocketsbrae. *S Lan* 1H 117
Brockford Street. *Suff* 4D 66
Brockhall. *Nptn* 4D 62
Brockham. *Surr* 1C 26
Brockhampton. *Glos* 3E 49 (nr. Bishop's Cleeve)
Brockhampton. *Glos* 3F 49 (nr. Sevenhampton)
Brockhampton. *Here* 2A 48
Brockhill. *Bord* 2F 119
Brockholes. *W Yor* 3B 92
Brockhouse. *S Yor* 2C 86
Brockhurst. *Hants* 2D 16
Brocklesby. *Linc* 3E 95
Brockley. *N Som* 5H 33
Brockley Corner. *Suff* 3H 65
Brockley Green. *Suff* 1H 53 (nr. Bury St Edmunds)
Brockley Green. *Suff* 5H 65 (nr. Haverhill)
Brockleymoor. *Cumb* 1F 103
Brockmoor. *W Mid* 2C 60
Brockton. *Shrp* 2F 59 (nr. Bishop's Castle)
Brockton. *Shrp* 5B 72 (nr. Madeley)
Brockton. *Shrp* 1H 59 (nr. Much Wenlock)
Brockton. *Shrp* 5F 71 (nr. Pontesbury)
Brockton. *Staf* 2C 72
Brockton. *Telf* 4B 72
Brockweir. *Glos* 5A 48
Brockworth. *Glos* 4D 49
Brocton. *Staf* 4D 72
Brodick. *N Ayr* 2E 123
Brodie. *Mor* 3D 159
Brodiesord. *Abers* 3C 160
Brodsworth. *S Yor* 4F 93
Brogaig. *High* 2D 154
Brogborough. *C Beds* 2H 51
Brokenborough. *Wilts* 3E 35
Broken Cross. *Ches E* 3C 84
Bromborough. *Mers* 2F 83
Bromdon. *Shrp* 2A 60
Brome. *Suff* 3D 66
Brome Street. *Suff* 3D 66
Bromeswell. *Suff* 5F 67
Bromfield. *Cumb* 5C 112
Bromfield. *Shrp* 3G 59
Bromford. *W Mid* 1F 61
Bromham. *Bed* 5H 63
Bromham. *Wilts* 5E 35
Bromley. *G Lon* 4F 39
Bromley. *Herts* 3E 53
Bromley. *Shrp* 1B 60
Bromley Cross. *G Man* 3F 91
Bromley Green. *Kent* 2D 28
Bromley Wood. *Staf* 3F 73
Brompton. *Medw* 4B 40
Brompton. *N Yor* 5A 106 (nr. Northallerton)
Brompton. *N Yor* 1D 100 (nr. Scarborough)
Brompton. *Shrp* 5H 71
Brompton-on-Swale. *N Yor* 5F 105
Brompton Ralph. *Som* 3D 20
Brompton Regis. *Som* 3C 20
Bromsash. *Here* 3B 48
Bromsberrow. *Glos* 2C 48
Bromsberrow Heath. *Glos* 2C 48
Bromsgrove. *Worc* 3D 60
Bromstead Heath. *Staf* 4B 72
Bromyard. *Here* 5A 60
Bromyard Downs. *Here* 5A 60
Bronaber. *Gwyn* 2G 69
Broncroft. *Shrp* 2H 59
Brongest. *Cdgn* 1D 44
Brongwyn. *Cdgn* 1C 44
Bronington. *Wrex* 2G 71
Bronllys. *Powy* 2E 47
Bronnant. *Cdgn* 4F 57
Bronwydd Arms. *Carm* 3E 45
Bronydd. *Powy* 1F 47
Bronygarth. *Shrp* 2E 71
Brook. *Carm* 4G 43
Brook. *Devn* 5E 11
Brook. *Hants* 1A 16 (nr. Cadnam)
Brook. *Hants* 4B 24 (nr. Romsey)
Brook. *IOW* 4B 16
Brook. *Kent* 1E 29
Brook. *Surr* 1B 26 (nr. Guildford)
Brook. *Surr* 2A 26 (nr. Haslemere)
Brooke. *Norf* 1E 67
Brooke. *Rut* 5F 75
Brookend. *Glos* 5B 48
Brook End. *Worc* 1D 48
Brookfield. *Lanc* 1D 90
Brookfield. *Ren* 3F 127
Brookhouse. *Lanc* 3E 97
Brookhouse Green. *Ches E* 4C 84
Brookhouses. *Staf* 1D 73
Brookhurst. *Mers* 2F 83
Brookland. *Kent* 3D 28
Brooklands. *G Man* 1B 84
Brooklands. *Shrp* 1H 71
Brookmans Park. *Herts* 5C 52
Brooks. *Powy* 1D 58
Brooksby. *Leics* 4D 74
Brooks Green. *W Sus* 3C 26
Brook Street. *Essx* 1G 39
Brook Street. *Kent* 2D 28
Brook Street. *W Sus* 3E 27
Brookthorpe. *Glos* 4D 48
Brookville. *Norf* 1G 65
Brookwood. *Surr* 5A 38
Broom. *C Beds* 1B 52
Broom. *Fife* 3F 137
Broom. *Warw* 5E 61
Broome. *Norf* 1F 67
Broome. *Shrp* 1H 59 (nr. Cardington)
Broome. *Shrp* 2G 59 (nr. Craven Arms)
Broome. *Worc* 3D 60
Broomedge. *Warr* 2B 84
Broomend. *Abers* 2E 153
Broome Park. *Nmbd* 3F 121
Broomer's Corner. *W Sus* 3C 26
Broomfield. *Abers* 5G 161
Broomfield. *Essx* 4H 53
Broomfield. *Kent* 4F 41 (nr. Herne Bay)
Broomfield. *Kent* 5C 40 (nr. Maidstone)
Broomfield. *Som* 3F 21
Broomfleet. *E Yor* 2B 94
Broom Green. *Norf* 3B 78
Broomhall. *Ches E* 1A 72
Broomhall. *Wind* 4A 38
Broomhaugh. *Nmbd* 3D 114
Broomhill. *Bris* 4B 34
Broom Hill. *Dors* 2F 15
Broomhill. *High* 1D 151 (nr. Grantown-on-Spey)
Broomhill. *High* 1B 158 (nr. Invergordon)
Broomhill. *Norf* 5F 77
Broomhill. *S Yor* 4E 93
Broom Hill. *Worc* 3D 60
Broomhillbank. *Dum* 5D 118
Broomholm. *Norf* 2F 79
Broomlands. *Dum* 4C 118
Broomley. *Nmbd* 3D 114
Broom of Moy. *Mor* 3E 159
Broompark. *Dur* 5F 115
Broom's Green. *Glos* 2C 48
Brora. *High* 3G 165
Broseley. *Shrp* 5A 72
Brotherhouse Bar. *Linc* 4B 76
Brotheridge Green. *Worc* 1D 48
Brotherlee. *Dur* 1C 104
Brothertoft. *Linc* 1B 76
Brotherton. *N Yor* 2E 93
Brotton. *Red C* 2D 107
Broubster. *High* 2C 168
Brough. *Cumb* 3A 104
Brough. *Derbs* 2F 85
Brough. *E Yor* 2C 94
Brough. *High* 1E 169
Brough. *Notts* 5F 87
Brough. *Orkn* 9D 172
Brough. *Shet* 4F 173 (nr. Booth of Toft)
Brough. *Shet* 5G 173 (on Whalsay)
Broughall. *Shrp* 1H 71
Brougham. *Cumb* 2G 103
Brough Sowerby. *Cumb* 3A 104
Broughton. *Cambs* 3B 64
Broughton. *Flin* 4F 83
Broughton. *Hants* 3B 24
Broughton. *Lanc* 1D 90
Broughton. *Mil* 2G 51
Broughton. *Nptn* 3F 63
Broughton. *N Lin* 4C 94
Broughton. *N Yor* 2B 100 (nr. Malton)
Broughton. *N Yor* 4B 98 (nr. Skipton)
Broughton. *Oxon* 2C 50
Broughton. *Bord* 1D 118
Broughton. *Staf* 2B 72
Broughton. *V Glam* 4C 32
Broughton Astley. *Leics* 1C 62
Broughton Beck. *Cumb* 1B 96
Broughton Cross. *Cumb* 1B 102
Broughton Gifford. *Wilts* 5D 35
Broughton Green. *Worc* 4D 60
Broughton Hackett. *Worc* 5D 60
Broughton in Furness. *Cumb* 1B 96
Broughton Mills. *Cumb* 5D 102
Broughton Moor. *Cumb* 1B 102
Broughton Park. *G Man* 4G 91
Broughton Poggs. *Oxon* 5H 49
Broughtown. *Orkn* 3F 172
Broughty Ferry. *D'dee* 5D 144
Brownber. *Cumb* 4A 104
Brownbread Street. *E Sus* 4A 28
Brown Candover. *Hants* 3D 24
Brown Edge. *Lanc* 3B 90
Brown Edge. *Staf* 5D 84
Brownhill. *Bkbn* 1E 91
Brownhill. *Shrp* 3G 71
Brownhills. *Shrp* 2A 72
Brownhills. *W Mid* 5E 73
Brown Knowl. *Ches W* 5G 83
Brownlow. *Ches E* 4C 84
Brownlow Heath. *Ches E* 4C 84
Brown's Green. *W Mid* 1E 61
Brownshill. *Glos* 5D 49
Brownston. *Devn* 3C 8
Brownstone. *Devn* 2A 12
Browston Green. *Norf* 5G 79
Broxa. *N Yor* 5G 107
Broxbourne. *Herts* 5D 52
Broxburn. *E Lot* 2C 130
Broxburn. *W Lot* 2D 129
Broxholme. *Linc* 3G 87
Broxted. *Essx* 3F 53
Broxton. *Ches W* 5G 83
Broxwood. *Here* 5F 59
Broyle Side. *E Sus* 4F 27
Brù. *W Isl* 3F 171
Bruach Mairi. *W Isl* 4F 171
Bruairnis. *W Isl* 8C 170
Bruan. *High* 5F 169
Bruar Lodge. *Per* 1F 143
Brucehill. *W Dun* 2E 127
Brucklay. *Abers* 3G 161
Bruera. *Ches W* 4G 83
Bruern Abbey. *Oxon* 3A 50
Bruichladdich. *Arg* 3A 124
Bruisyard. *Suff* 4F 67
Bruisyard Street. *Suff* 4F 67
Brumby. *N Lin* 4B 94
Brund. *Staf* 4F 85
Brundall. *Norf* 5F 79
Brundish. *Norf* 1F 67
Brundish. *Suff* 4E 67
Brundish Street. *Suff* 3E 67
Brunery. *High* 1B 140
Brunswick Village. *Tyne* 2F 115
Brunthwaite. *W Yor* 5C 98
Bruntingthorpe. *Leics* 1D 62
Brunton. *Fife* 1F 137
Brunton. *Nmbd* 2G 121
Brunton. *Wilts* 1H 23
Brushford. *Devn* 2G 11
Brushford. *Som* 4C 20
Brusta. *W Isl* 1E 170
Bruton. *Som* 3B 22
Bryanston. *Dors* 2D 15
Bryant's Bottom. *Buck* 2G 37
Brydekirk. *Dum* 2C 112
Brymbo. *Cnwy* 3H 81
Brymbo. *Wrex* 5E 83
Brympton D'Evercy. *Som* 1A 14
Bryn. *Carm* 5F 45
Bryn. *G Man* 4D 90
Bryn. *Neat* 2B 32
Bryn. *Shrp* 2E 59
Brynamman. *Carm* 4H 45
Brynberian. *Pemb* 1F 43
Brynbryddan. *Neat* 2A 32
Bryncae. *Rhon* 3C 32
Bryncethin. *B'end* 3C 32
Bryncir. *Gwyn* 1D 69
Bryn-coch. *Neat* 3G 31
Bryncroes. *Gwyn* 2B 68
Bryncrug. *Gwyn* 5F 69
Bryn Du. *IOA* 3C 80
Bryn Eden. *Gwyn* 3G 69
Bryneglwys. *Den* 1D 70
Bryn Eglwys. *Gwyn* 4F 81
Brynford. *Flin* 3D 82
Bryn Gates. *G Man* 4D 90
Bryn Golau. *Rhon* 3D 32
Bryngwran. *IOA* 3C 80
Bryngwyn. *Mon* 5G 47
Bryngwyn. *Powy* 1E 47
Bryn-henllan. *Pemb* 1E 43
Brynhoffnant. *Cdgn* 5C 56
Bryn-llwyn. *Flin* 2C 82
Brynllywarch. *Powy* 2D 58
Bryn-mawr. *Blae* 4E 47
Bryn-mawr. *Gwyn* 2B 68
Brynmenyn. *B'end* 3C 32
Brynmill. *Swan* 3F 31
Brynna. *Rhon* 3C 32
Brynrefail. *Gwyn* 4E 81
Brynrefail. *IOA* 2D 81
Brynsadler. *Rhon* 3D 32
Bryn-Saith Marchog. *Den* 5C 82
Brynsiencyn. *IOA* 4D 81
Brynteg. *IOA* 2D 81
Brynteg. *Wrex* 5F 83
Brynygwenyn. *Mon* 4G 47
Bryn-y-maen. *Cnwy* 3H 81
Buaile nam Bodach. *W Isl* 8C 170
Bualintur. *High* 1C 146
Bubbenhall. *Warw* 3A 62
Bubwith. *E Yor* 1H 93
Buccleuch. *Bord* 3F 119
Buchanan Smithy. *Stir* 1F 127
Buchanhaven. *Abers* 4H 161
Buchanty. *Per* 1B 136
Buchany. *Stir* 3G 135
Buchley. *E Dun* 2G 127
Buchlyvie. *Stir* 4E 135
Buckabank. *Cumb* 5E 113
Buckden. *Cambs* 4A 64
Buckden. *N Yor* 2B 98
Buckenham. *Norf* 5F 79
Buckerell. *Devn* 2E 13
Buckfast. *Devn* 2D 8
Buckfastleigh. *Devn* 2D 8
Buckhaven. *Fife* 4F 137
Buckholm. *Bord* 1G 119
Buckholt. *Here* 4A 48
Buckhorn Weston. *Dors* 4C 22
Buckhurst Hill. *Essx* 1F 39
Buckie. *Mor* 2B 160
Buckingham. *Buck* 2E 51
Buckland. *Buck* 4G 51
Buckland. *Glos* 2F 49
Buckland. *Here* 5H 59
Buckland. *Herts* 2D 52
Buckland. *Kent* 1H 29
Buckland. *Oxon* 2B 36
Buckland. *Surr* 5D 38
Buckland Brewer. *Devn* 4E 19
Buckland Common. *Buck* 5H 51
Buckland Dinham. *Som* 1C 22
Buckland Filleigh. *Devn* 2E 11
Buckland in the Moor. *Devn* 5H 11
Buckland Monachorum. *Devn* 2A 8
Buckland Newton. *Dors* 2B 14
Buckland Ripers. *Dors* 4B 14
Buckland St Mary. *Som* 1F 13
Buckland-tout-Saints. *Devn* 4D 8
Bucklebury. *W Ber* 4D 36
Bucklegate. *Linc* 2C 76
Buckleigh. *Devn* 4E 19
Bucklers Hard. *Hants* 3C 16
Bucklesham. *Suff* 1F 55
Buckley. *Flin* 4E 83
Buckley Green. *Warw* 4F 61
Buckley Hill. *Mers* 1F 83
Bucklow Hill. *Ches E* 2B 84
Buckminster. *Leics* 3F 75
Bucknall. *Linc* 4A 88
Bucknall. *Stoke* 1D 72
Bucknell. *Oxon* 3D 50
Bucknell. *Shrp* 3F 59
Buckpool. *Mor* 2B 160
Bucksburn. *Aber* 3F 153
Buck's Cross. *Devn* 4D 18
Bucks Green. *W Sus* 2B 26
Buckshaw Village. *Lanc* 2D 90
Bucks Hill. *Herts* 5A 52
Bucks Horn Oak. *Hants* 2G 25
Buck's Mills. *Devn* 4D 18
Buckton. *E Yor* 2F 101
Buckton. *Here* 3F 59
Buckton. *Nmbd* 1E 121
Buckton Vale. *G Man* 4H 91
Buckworth. *Cambs* 3A 64
Budby. *Notts* 4D 86
Bude. *Corn* 2C 10
Budge's Shop. *Corn* 3H 7
Budlake. *Devn* 2C 12
Budle. *Nmbd* 1F 121
Budleigh Salterton. *Devn* 4D 12
Budock Water. *Corn* 5B 6
Buerton. *Ches E* 1A 72
Buffler's Holt. *Buck* 2E 51
Bugbrooke. *Nptn* 5D 62
Buglawton. *Ches E* 4C 84

C

Cadley—Carnforth

Cadley. Wilts 1H 23
(nr. Ludgershall)
Cadley. Wilts 5H 35
(nr. Marlborough)
Cadmore End. Buck 2F 37
Cadnam. Hants 1A 16
Cadney. N Lin 4D 94
Cadole. Flin 4E 82
Cadoxton-Juxta-Neath. Neat 2A 32
Cadwell. Herts 2B 52
Cadwst. Den 2C 70
Cadzow. S Lan 4A 128
Caeathro. Gwyn 4E 81
Caehopkin. Powy 4B 46
Caenby. Linc 2H 87
Caerau. B'end 2B 32
Caerau. Card 4E 33
Cae'r-bont. Powy 4B 46
Cae'r-bryn. Carm 4F 45
Caerdeon. Gwyn 4F 69
Caerdydd. Card 4E 33
Caerfarchell. Pemb 2B 42
Caerffili. Cphy 3E 33
Caerfyrddin. Carm 4E 45
Caergeiliog. IOA 3C 80
Caergwrle. Flin 5F 83
Caergybi. IOA 2B 80
Caerlaverock. Per 2A 136
Caerleon. Newp 2G 33
Caerlleon. Carm 2G 43
Caerllion. Newp 2G 33
Caernarfon. Gwyn 4D 81
Caerphilly. Cphy 3E 33
Caersws. Powy 1C 58
Caerwedros. Cdgn 5C 56
Caerwent. Mon 2H 33
Caerwys. Flin 3D 82
Caim. IOA 2F 81
Caio. Carm 2G 45
Cairinis. W Isl 2D 170
Cairisiadar. W Isl 4C 171
Cairminis. W Isl 9C 171
Cairnbaan. Arg 4F 133
Cairnbulg. Abers 2H 161
Cairncross. Ang 1D 145
Cairndow. Arg 2A 134
Cairness. Abers 2H 161
Cairneyhill. Fife 1D 128
Cairngarroch. Dum 5F 109
Cairnhill. Abers 5D 160
Cairnie. Abers 4B 160
Cairnorrie. Abers 4F 161
Cairnryan. Dum 3F 109
Caister-on-Sea. Norf 4H 79
Caistor. Linc 4E 95
Caistor St Edmund. Norf 5E 79
Caistron. Nmbd 4D 121
Cakebole. Worc 3C 60
Calais Street. Suff 1C 54
Calanais. W Isl 4E 171
Calbost. W Isl 6G 171
Calbourne. IOW 4C 16
Calceby. Linc 3C 88
Calcot. Glos 4F 49
Calcot Row. W Ber 4E 37
Calcott. Kent 4F 41
Calcott. Shrp 4G 71
Caldback. Shet 1H 173
Caldbeck. Cumb 1E 102
Caldbergh. N Yor 1C 98
Caldecote. Cambs 5C 64
(nr. Cambridge)
Caldecote. Cambs 2A 64
(nr. Peterborough)
Caldecote. Herts 2C 52
Caldecote. Warw 1A 62
Caldecott. Nptn 4G 63
Caldecott. Oxon 2C 36
Caldecott. Rut 1F 63
Calderbank. N Lan 3A 128
Calder Bridge. Cumb 4B 102
Calderbrook. G Man 3H 91
Caldercruix. N Lan 3B 128
Calder Grove. W Yor 3D 92
Calder Mains. High 3C 168
Caldermill. S Lan 5H 127
Calder Vale. Lanc 5E 97
Calderwood. S Lan 4H 127
Caldescote. Nptn 5D 62
Caldicot. Mon 3H 33
Caldwell. N Yor 3E 105
Caldy. Mers 2E 83
Calebrack. Cumb 1E 103
Caledfwlch. Carm 3G 45
Calford Green. Suff 1G 53
Calfsound. Orkn 4E 172
Calgary. Arg 3E 139
Califer. Mor 3E 159
California. Cambs 2E 65
California. Falk 2C 128
California. Norf 4H 79
California. Suff 1E 55
Calke. Derbs 3A 74
Callakille. High 3F 155
Callaly. Nmbd 4E 121
Callander. Stir 3F 135
Callaughton. Shrp 1A 60
Callendoun. Arg 1E 127
Callestick. Corn 3B 6
Calligarry. High 3E 147
Callington. Corn 2H 7
Callingwood. Staf 3F 73
Callow. Here 2H 47
Callowell. Glos 5D 48
Callow End. Worc 1D 48
Callow Hill. Wilts 3F 35
Callow Hill. Worc 3B 60
(nr. Bewdley)
Callow Hill. Worc 4E 61
(nr. Redditch)
Calmore. Hants 1B 16
Calmsden. Glos 5F 49
Calne. Wilts 4E 35
Calow. Derbs 3B 86
Calshot. Hants 2C 16
Calstock. Corn 2A 8
Calstone Wellington. Wilts 5F 35
Calthorpe. Norf 2D 78
Calthorpe Street. Norf 3G 79
Calthwaite. Cumb 5F 113
Calton. N Yor 4B 98
Calton. Staf 5F 85
Calveley. Ches E 5H 83
Calver. Derbs 3G 85
Calverhall. Shrp 2A 72
Calverleigh. Devn 1C 12
Calverley. W Yor 1C 92
Calvert. Buck 3E 51
Calverton. Mil 2F 51
Calverton. Notts 1D 74
Calvine. Per 2F 143
Calvo. Cumb 4C 112
Cam. Glos 2C 34
Camaghael. High 1F 141
Camas-luinie. High 1B 148
Camasnacroise. High 3C 140
Camastianavaig. High 5E 155
Camasunary. High 2D 146
Camault Muir. High 4H 157
Camb. Shet 2G 173
Camber. E Sus 4D 28
Camberley. Surr 5G 37
Camberwell. G Lon 3E 39
Camblesforth. N Yor 2G 93
Cambo. Nmbd 1D 114
Cambois. Nmbd 1G 115
Camborne. Corn 3D 4
Cambourne. Cambs 5C 64
Cambridge. Cambs 5D 64
Cambridge. Glos 5C 48
Cambrose. Corn 4A 6
Cambus. Clac 4A 136
Cambusbarron. Stir 4G 135
Cambuskenneth. Stir 4H 135
Cambuslang. S Lan 3H 127
Cambusnethan. N Lan 4B 128
Cambus o'May. Abers 4B 152
Camden Town. G Lon 2D 39
Cameley. Bath 1B 22
Camelford. Corn 4B 10
Camelon. Falk 1B 128
Camelsdale. Surr 2A 26
Camer's Green. Worc 2C 48
Camerton. Bath 1B 22
Camerton. Cumb 1B 102
Camerton. E Yor 2F 95
Camghouran. Per 3C 142
Cammachmore. Abers 4G 153
Cammeringham. Linc 2G 87
Camore. High 4E 165
Campbelton. N Ayr 4C 126
Campbeltown. Arg 3B 122
Campbeltown Airport.
Arg 3A 122
Cample. Dum 5B 118
Campmuir. Per 5B 144
Campsall. S Yor 3F 93
Campsea Ashe. Suff 5F 67
Camps End. Cambs 1G 53
Camp, The. Glos 5E 49
Campton. C Beds 2B 52
Camptoun. E Lot 2B 130
Camptown. Bord 3A 120
Camrose. Pemb 2D 42
Camserney. Per 4F 143
Camster. High 4E 169
Camus Croise. High 2E 147
Camuscross. High 2E 147
Camusdarach. High 4E 147
Camusnagaul. High 1E 141
(nr. Fort William)
Camusnagaul. High 5E 163
(nr. Little Loch Broom)
Camusteel. High 4G 155
Camusterrach. High 4G 155
Camusvrachan. Per 4D 142
Canada. Hants 1A 16
Canadia. E Sus 4B 28
Canaston Bridge. Pemb 3E 43
Candlesby. Linc 4D 88
Candle Street. Suff 3C 66
Candy Mill. S Lan 5D 128
Cane End. Oxon 4E 37
Canewdon. Essx 1C 40
Canford Cliffs. Pool 4F 15
Canford Heath. Pool 3F 15
Canford Magna. Pool 3F 15
Cangate. Norf 3F 79
Canham's Green. Suff 4C 66
Canholes. Derbs 3E 85
Canisbay. High 1F 169
Canley. W Mid 3H 61
Cann. Dors 4D 22
Cann Common. Dors 4D 23
Cannich. High 5F 157
Cannington. Som 3F 21
Cannock. Staf 4D 73
Cannock Wood. Staf 4E 73
Canonbie. Dum 2E 113
Canon Bridge. Here 1H 47
Canon Frome. Here 1B 48
Canon Pyon. Here 1H 47
Canons Ashby. Nptn 5C 62
Canonstown. Corn 3C 4
Canterbury. Kent 5F 41
Cantley. Norf 5F 79
Cantley. S Yor 4G 93
Cantlop. Shrp 5H 71
Canton. Card 4E 33
Cantray. High 4B 158
Cantraybruich. High 4B 158
Cantraywood. High 4B 158
Cantsdam. Fife 4D 136
Cantsfield. Lanc 2F 97
Canvey Island. Essx 2B 40
Canwick. Linc 4G 87
Canworthy Water. Corn 3C 10
Caol. High 1F 141
Caolas. W Isl 9B 170
Caolas Liubharsaigh. W Isl 4D 170
Caolas Stocinis. W Isl 8D 171
Caoles. Arg 4B 138
Caol Ila. Arg 3C 124
Caol Loch Ailse. High 1F 147
Caol Reatha. High 1F 147
Capel. Kent 1H 27
Capel. Surr 1C 26
Capel Bangor. Cdgn 2F 57
Capel Betws Lleucu.
Cdgn 5F 57
Capel Coch. IOA 2D 80
Capel Curig. Cnwy 5G 81
Capel Cynon. Cdgn 1D 45
Capel Dewi. Carm 3E 45
Capel Dewi. Cdgn 2F 57
(nr. Aberystwyth)
Capel Dewi. Cdgn 1E 45
(nr. Llandysul)
Capel Garmon. Cnwy 5H 81
Capel Green. Suff 1G 55
Capel Gwyn. IOA 3C 80
Capel Gwynfe. Carm 3H 45
Capel Hendre. Carm 4F 45
Capel Isaac. Carm 3F 45
Capel Iwan. Carm 1G 43
Capel-le-Ferne. Kent 2G 29
Capel Llanilterne. Card 4D 32
Capel Mawr. IOA 3D 80
Capel Newydd. Pemb 1G 43
Capel St Andrew. Suff 1G 55
Capel St Mary. Suff 2D 54
Capel Seion. Carm 4F 45
Capel Seion. Cdgn 3F 57
Capel Uchaf. Gwyn 1D 68
Capel-y-ffin. Powy 2F 47
Capenhurst. Ches W 3F 83
Capernwray. Lanc 2E 97
Capheaton. Nmbd 1D 114
Cappercleuch. Bord 2E 119
Capplegill. Dum 4D 118
Capton. Devn 3E 9
Capton. Som 3D 20
Caputh. Per 5H 143
Caradon Town. Corn 5C 10
Carbis Bay. Corn 3C 4
Carbost. High 5C 154
(nr. Loch Harport)
Carbost. High 4D 154
(nr. Portree)
Carbrook. S Yor 2A 86
Carbrooke. Norf 5B 78
Carburton. Notts 3D 86
Carcluie. S Ayr 3C 116
Car Colston. Notts 1E 74
Carcroft. S Yor 3F 93
Cardenden. Fife 4E 136
Cardeston. Shrp 4F 71
Cardewlees. Cumb 4E 113
Cardiff. Card 4E 33
Cardiff International Airport.
V Glam 5D 32
Cardigan. Cdgn 1B 44
Cardinal's Green. Cambs 1G 53
Cardington. Bed 1A 52
Cardington. Shrp 1H 59
Cardinham. Corn 2F 7
Cardno. Abers 2G 161
Cardow. Mor 4F 159
Cardross. Arg 2E 127
Cardurnock. Cumb 4C 112
Careby. Linc 4H 75
Careston. Ang 2E 145
Carew. Pemb 4E 43
Carew Cheriton. Pemb 4E 43
Carew Newton. Pemb 4E 43
Carey. Here 2A 48
Carfin. N Lan 4A 128
Carfrae. Bord 4B 130
Cargate Green. Norf 4F 79
Cargenbridge. Dum 2G 111
Cargill. Per 5A 144
Cargo. Cumb 4E 113
Cargreen. Corn 2A 8
Carham. Nmbd 1B 120
Carhampton. Som 2D 20
Carharrack. Corn 4B 6
Carie. Per 3D 142
(nr. Loch Rannah)
Carie. Per 5D 142
(nr. Loch Tay)
Carisbrooke. IOW 4C 16
Cark. Cumb 2C 96
Carkeel. Corn 2A 8
Carlabhagh. W Isl 3E 171
Carland Cross. Corn 3C 6
Carlbury. Darl 3F 105
Carlby. Linc 4H 75
Carlecotes. S Yor 4B 92
Carleen. Corn 4D 4
Carlesmoor. N Yor 2D 98
Carleton. Cumb 4F 113
(nr. Carlisle)
Carleton. Cumb 4B 102
(nr. Egremont)
Carleton. Cumb 2G 103
(nr. Penrith)
Carleton. Lanc 1B 90
Carleton. N Yor 5B 98
Carleton. W Yor 2E 93
Carleton Forehoe. Norf 5C 78
Carleton Rode. Norf 1D 66
Carleton St Peter. Norf 5F 79
Carlidnack. Corn 4E 5
Carlingcott. Bath 1B 22
Carlin How. Red C 3E 107
Carlisle. Cumb 4F 113
Carloonan. Arg 2H 133
Carlops. Bord 4E 129
Carlton. Bed 5G 63
Carlton. Cambs 5F 65
Carlton. Leics 5A 74
Carlton. N Yor 1A 100
(nr. Helmsley)
Carlton. N Yor 1C 98
(nr. Middleham)
Carlton. N Yor 2G 93
(nr. Selby)
Carlton. Notts 1D 74
Carlton. S Yor 3D 92
Carlton. Stoc T 2A 106
Carlton. Suff 4F 67
Carlton. W Yor 2D 92
Carlton Colville. Suff 1H 67
Carlton Curlieu. Leics 1D 62
Carlton Husthwaite. N Yor 2G 99
Carlton in Cleveland. N Yor 4C 106
Carlton in Lindrick. Notts 2C 86
Carlton-le-Moorland. Linc 5G 87
Carlton Miniott. N Yor 1F 99
Carlton-on-Trent. Notts 4F 87
Carlton Scroop. Linc 1G 75
Carluke. S Lan 4B 128
Carlyon Bay. Corn 3E 7
Carmarthen. Carm 4E 45
Carmel. Carm 4F 45
Carmel. Flin 3D 82
Carmel. Gwyn 5D 81
Carmel. IOA 2C 80
Carmichael. S Lan 1B 118
Carmunnock. Glas 4H 127
Carmyle. S Lan 3H 127
Carmyllie. Ang 4E 145
Carnaby. E Yor 3F 101
Carnach. High 1C 148
(nr. Lochcarron)
Carnach. High 4E 163
(nr. Ullapool)
Carnach. Mor 4E 159
Carnach. W Isl 8E 171
Carnachy. High 3H 167
Carnain. Arg 3B 124
Carnais. W Isl 4C 171
Carnan. Arg 4B 138
Carnbee. Fife 3H 137
Carnbo. Per 3C 136
Carn Brea Village. Corn 4A 6
Carndu. High 1A 148
Carne. Corn 5D 6
Carnell. S Ayr 1D 116
Carnforth. Lanc 2E 97

Charlesfield—Church Green

Charlesfield. *Dum* 3C **112**
Charleshill. *Surr* 2G **25**
Charleston. *Ang* 4C **144**
Charleston. *Ren* 3F **127**
Charlestown. *Aber* 3G **153**
Charlestown. *Abers* 2H **161**
Charlestown. *Corn* 3E **7**
Charlestown. *Dors* 5B **14**
Charlestown. *Fife* 1D **128**
Charlestown. *G Man* 4G **91**
Charlestown. *High* 1H **155**
(nr. Gairloch)
Charlestown. *High* 4A **158**
(nr. Inverness)
Charlestown. *W Yor* 2H **91**
Charlestown of Aberlour. *Mor* 4G **159**
Charles Tye. *Suff* 5C **66**
Charlesworth. *Derbs* 1E **85**
Charlton. *G Lon* 3F **39**
Charlton. *Hants* 2B **24**
Charlton. *Herts* 3B **52**
Charlton. *Nptn* 2D **50**
Charlton. *Nmbd* 1B **114**
Charlton. *Oxon* 3C **36**
Charlton. *Som* 1B **22**
(nr. Radstock)
Charlton. *Som* 2B **22**
(nr. Shepton Mallet)
Charlton. *Som* 4F **21**
(nr. Taunton)
Charlton. *Telf* 4H **71**
Charlton. *W Sus* 1G **17**
Charlton. *Wilts* 3E **35**
(nr. Malmesbury)
Charlton. *Wilts* 1G **23**
(nr. Pewsey)
Charlton. *Wilts* 4G **23**
(nr. Salisbury)
Charlton. *Wilts* 4E **23**
(nr. Shaftesbury)
Charlton. *Worc* 1F **49**
(nr. Evesham)
Charlton. *Worc* 3C **60**
(nr. Stourport-on-Severn)
Charlton Abbots. *Glos* 3F **49**
Charlton Adam. *Som* 4A **22**
Charlton Down. *Dors* 3B **14**
Charlton Horethorne. *Som* 4B **22**
Charlton Kings. *Glos* 3E **49**
Charlton Mackrell. *Som* 4A **22**
Charlton Marshall. *Dors* 2E **15**
Charlton Musgrove. *Som* 4C **22**
Charlton-on-Otmoor. *Oxon* 4D **50**
Charlton on the Hill. *Dors* 2D **15**
Charlwood. *Hants* 3E **25**
Charlwood. *Surr* 1D **26**
Charlynch. *Som* 3F **21**
Charminster. *Dors* 3B **14**
Charmouth. *Dors* 3G **13**
Charndon. *Buck* 3E **51**
Charney Bassett. *Oxon* 2B **36**
Charnock Green. *Lanc* 3D **90**
Charnock Richard. *Lanc* 3D **90**
Charsfield. *Suff* 5E **67**
Chart Corner. *Kent* 5B **40**
Charter Alley. *Hants* 1D **24**
Charterhouse. *Som* 1H **21**
Charterville Allotments. *Oxon* 4B **50**
Chartham. *Kent* 5F **41**
Chartham Hatch. *Kent* 5F **41**
Chartridge. *Buck* 5H **51**
Chart Sutton. *Kent* 5B **40**
Chart, The. *Kent* 5F **39**
Charvil. *Wok* 4F **37**
Charwelton. *Nptn* 5C **62**
Chase Terrace. *Staf* 5E **73**
Chasetown. *Staf* 5E **73**
Chastleton. *Oxon* 3H **49**
Chasty. *Devn* 2D **10**
Chatburn. *Lanc* 5G **97**
Chatcull. *Staf* 2B **72**
Chatham. *Medw* 4B **40**
Chatham Green. *Essx* 4H **53**
Chathill. *Nmbd* 2F **121**
Chatley. *Worc* 4C **60**
Chattenden. *Medw* 3B **40**
Chatteris. *Cambs* 2C **64**
Chattisham. *Suff* 1D **54**
Chatton. *Nmbd* 2E **121**
Chatwall. *Shrp* 1H **59**
Chaulden. *Herts* 5A **52**
Chaul End. *C Beds* 3A **52**
Chawleigh. *Devn* 1H **11**
Chawley. *Oxon* 5C **50**
Chawston. *Bed* 5A **64**
Chawton. *Hants* 3F **25**
Chaxhill. *Glos* 4C **48**
Cheadle. *G Man* 2C **84**
Cheadle. *Staf* 1E **73**
Cheadle Hulme. *G Man* 2C **84**
Cheam. *Surr* 4D **38**
Cheapside. *Wind* 4A **38**
Chearsley. *Buck* 4F **51**
Chebsey. *Staf* 3C **72**
Checkendon. *Oxon* 3E **37**
Checkley. *Ches E* 1B **72**
Checkley. *Here* 2A **48**
Checkley. *Staf* 2E **73**
Chedburgh. *Suff* 5G **65**
Cheddar. *Som* 1H **21**
Cheddington. *Buck* 4H **51**
Cheddleton. *Staf* 5D **84**
Cheddon Fitzpaine. *Som* 4F **21**
Chedglow. *Wilts* 2E **35**
Chedgrave. *Norf* 1F **67**
Chedington. *Dors* 2H **13**
Chediston. *Suff* 3F **67**
Chediston Green. *Suff* 3F **67**
Chedworth. *Glos* 4F **49**
Chedzoy. *Som* 3G **21**
Cheeseman's Green. *Kent* 2E **29**
Cheetham Hill. *G Man* 4G **91**
Cheglinch. *Devn* 2F **19**
Cheldon. *Devn* 1H **11**
Chelford. *Ches E* 3C **84**
Chellaston. *Derb* 2A **74**
Chellington. *Bed* 5G **63**
Chelmarsh. *Shrp* 2B **60**
Chelmick. *Shrp* 1G **59**
Chelmondiston. *Suff* 2F **55**
Chelmorton. *Derbs* 4F **85**
Chelmsford. *Essx* 5H **53**
Chelsea. *G Lon* 3D **39**
Chelsfield. *G Lon* 4F **39**
Chelsham. *Surr* 5E **39**
Chelston. *Som* 4E **21**
Chelsworth. *Suff* 1C **54**
Cheltenham. *Glos* 3E **49**
Chelveston. *Nptn* 4G **63**
Chelvey. *N Som* 5H **33**
Chelwood. *Bath* 5B **34**
Chelwood Common. *E Sus* 3F **27**
Chelwood Gate. *E Sus* 3F **27**
Chelworth. *Wilts* 2E **35**
Chelworth Lower Green. *Wilts* 2F **35**
Chelworth Upper Green. *Wilts* 2F **35**
Chelynch. *Som* 2B **22**
Cheney Longville. *Shrp* 2G **59**
Chenies. *Buck* 1B **38**
Chepstow. *Mon* 2A **34**
Chequerfield. *W Yor* 2E **93**
Chequers Corner. *Norf* 5D **77**
Cherhill. *Wilts* 4F **35**
Cherington. *Glos* 2E **35**
Cherington. *Warw* 2A **50**
Cheriton. *Devn* 2H **19**
Cheriton. *Hants* 4D **24**
Cheriton. *Kent* 2G **29**
Cheriton. *Pemb* 5D **43**
Cheriton. *Swan* 3D **30**
Cheriton Bishop. *Devn* 3A **12**
Cheriton Cross. *Devn* 3A **12**
Cheriton Fitzpaine. *Devn* 2B **12**
Cherrington. *Telf* 3A **72**
Cherrybank. *Per* 1D **136**
Cherry Burton. *E Yor* 5D **101**
Cherry Green. *Herts* 3D **52**
Cherry Hinton. *Cambs* 5D **65**
Cherry Willingham. *Linc* 3H **87**
Chertsey. *Surr* 4B **38**
Cheselbourne. *Dors* 3C **14**
Chesham. *Buck* 5H **51**
Chesham. *G Man* 3G **91**
Chesham Bois. *Buck* 1A **38**
Cheshunt. *Herts* 5D **52**
Cheslyn Hay. *Staf* 5D **73**
Chessetts Wood. *Warw* 3F **61**
Chessington. *G Lon* 4C **38**
Chester. *Ches W* 4G **83**
Chesterblade. *Som* 2B **22**
Chesterfield. *Derbs* 3A **86**
Chesterfield. *Staf* 5F **73**
Chesterhope. *Nmbd* 1C **114**
Chester-le-Street. *Dur* 4F **115**
Chester Moor. *Dur* 5F **115**
Chesters. *Bord* 3A **120**
Chesterton. *Cambs* 4D **64**
(nr. Cambridge)
Chesterton. *Cambs* 1A **64**
(nr. Peterborough)
Chesterton. *Glos* 5F **49**
Chesterton. *Oxon* 3D **50**
Chesterton. *Shrp* 1B **60**
Chesterton. *Staf* 1C **72**
Chesterton Green. *Warw* 5H **61**
Chesterwood. *Nmbd* 3B **114**
Chestfield. *Kent* 4F **41**
Cheston. *Devn* 3C **8**
Cheswardine. *Shrp* 2B **72**
Cheswell. *Telf* 4B **72**
Cheswick. *Nmbd* 5G **131**
Cheswick Green. *W Mid* 3F **61**
Chetnole. *Dors* 2B **14**
Chettiscombe. *Devn* 1C **12**
Chettisham. *Cambs* 2E **65**
Chettle. *Dors* 1E **15**
Chetton. *Shrp* 1A **60**
Chetwode. *Buck* 3E **51**
Chetwynd Aston. *Telf* 4B **72**
Cheveley. *Cambs* 4F **65**
Chevening. *Kent* 5F **39**
Chevington. *Suff* 5G **65**
Chevithorne. *Devn* 1C **12**
Chew Magna. *Bath* 5A **34**
Chew Moor. *G Man* 4E **91**
Chew Stoke. *Bath* 5A **34**
Chewton Keynsham. *Bath* 5B **34**
Chewton Mendip. *Som* 1A **22**
Chichacott. *Devn* 3G **11**
Chicheley. *Mil* 1H **51**
Chichester. *W Sus* 2G **17**
Chickerell. *Dors* 4B **14**
Chickering. *Suff* 3E **66**
Chicklade. *Wilts* 3E **23**
Chicksands. *C Beds* 2B **52**
Chickward. *Here* 5E **59**
Chidden. *Hants* 1E **17**
Chiddingfold. *Surr* 2A **26**
Chiddingly. *E Sus* 4G **27**
Chiddingstone. *Kent* 1F **27**
Chiddingstone Causeway. *Kent* 1G **27**
Chiddingstone Hoath. *Kent* 1F **27**
Chideock. *Dors* 3H **13**
Chidgley. *Som* 3D **20**
Chidham. *W Sus* 2F **17**
Chieveley. *W Ber* 4C **36**
Chignall St James. *Essx* 5G **53**
Chignall Smealy. *Essx* 4G **53**
Chigwell. *Essx* 1F **39**
Chigwell Row. *Essx* 1F **39**
Chilbolton. *Hants* 2B **24**
Chilcomb. *Hants* 4D **24**
Chilcombe. *Dors* 3A **14**
Chilcompton. *Som* 1B **22**
Chilcote. *Leics* 4G **73**
Childer Thornton. *Ches W* 3F **83**
Child Okeford. *Dors* 1D **14**
Childrey. *Oxon* 3B **36**
Child's Ercall. *Shrp* 3A **72**
Childswickham. *Worc* 2F **49**
Childwall. *Mers* 2G **83**
Childwick Green. *Herts* 4B **52**
Chilfrome. *Dors* 3A **14**
Chilgrove. *W Sus* 1G **17**
Chilham. *Kent* 5E **41**
Chilhampton. *Wilts* 3F **23**
Chilla. *Devn* 2E **11**
Chilland. *Hants* 3D **24**
Chillaton. *Devn* 4E **11**
Chillenden. *Kent* 5G **41**
Chillerton. *IOW* 4C **16**
Chillesford. *Suff* 5F **67**
Chillingham. *Nmbd* 2E **121**
Chillington. *Devn* 4D **9**
Chillington. *Som* 1G **13**
Chilmark. *Wilts* 3E **23**
Chilmington Green. *Kent* 1D **28**
Chilson. *Oxon* 4B **50**
Chilsworthy. *Corn* 5E **11**
Chilsworthy. *Devn* 2D **10**
Chiltern Green. *C Beds* 4B **52**
Chilthorne Domer. *Som* 1A **14**
Chilton. *Buck* 4E **51**
Chilton. *Devn* 2B **12**
Chilton. *Dur* 2F **105**
Chilton. *Oxon* 3C **36**
Chilton Candover. *Hants* 2D **24**
Chilton Cantelo. *Som* 4A **22**
Chilton Foliat. *Wilts* 4B **36**
Chilton Lane. *Dur* 1A **106**
Chilton Polden. *Som* 3G **21**
Chilton Street. *Suff* 1A **54**
Chilton Trinity. *Som* 3F **21**
Chilwell. *Notts* 2C **74**
Chilworth. *Hants* 1C **16**
Chilworth. *Surr* 1B **26**
Chimney. *Oxon* 5B **50**
Chimney Street. *Suff* 1H **53**
Chineham. *Hants* 1E **25**
Chingford. *G Lon* 1E **39**
Chinley. *Derbs* 2E **85**
Chinnor. *Oxon* 5F **51**
Chipley. *Som* 4E **20**
Chipnall. *Shrp* 2B **72**
Chippenham. *Cambs* 4F **65**
Chippenham. *Wilts* 4E **35**
Chipperfield. *Herts* 5A **52**
Chipping. *Herts* 2D **52**
Chipping. *Lanc* 5F **97**
Chipping Campden. *Glos* 2G **49**
Chipping Hill. *Essx* 4B **54**
Chipping Norton. *Oxon* 3B **50**
Chipping Ongar. *Essx* 5F **53**
Chipping Sodbury. *S Glo* 3C **34**
Chipping Warden. *Nptn* 1C **50**
Chipstable. *Som* 4D **20**
Chipstead. *Kent* 5G **39**
Chipstead. *Surr* 5D **38**
Chirbury. *Shrp* 1E **59**
Chirk. *Wrex* 2E **71**
Chirmorie. *S Ayr* 2H **109**
Chirnside. *Bord* 4E **131**
Chirnsidebridge. *Bord* 4E **131**
Chirton. *Wilts* 1F **23**
Chisbridge Cross. *Buck* 3G **37**
Chisbury. *Wilts* 5A **36**
Chiselborough. *Som* 1H **13**
Chiseldon. *Swin* 4G **35**
Chiselhampton. *Oxon* 2D **36**
Chiserley. *W Yor* 2A **92**
Chislehurst. *G Lon* 4F **39**
Chislet. *Kent* 4G **41**
Chiswell. *Dors* 5B **14**
Chiswell Green. *Herts* 5B **52**
Chiswick. *G Lon* 3D **38**
Chisworth. *Derbs* 1D **85**
Chitcombe. *E Sus* 3C **28**
Chithurst. *W Sus* 4G **25**
Chittering. *Cambs* 4D **65**
Chitterley. *Devn* 2C **12**
Chitterne. *Wilts* 2E **23**
Chittlehamholt. *Devn* 4G **19**
Chittlehampton. *Devn* 4G **19**
Chittoe. *Wilts* 5E **35**
Chivelstone. *Devn* 5D **9**
Chivenor. *Devn* 3F **19**
Chobham. *Surr* 4A **38**
Cholderton. *Wilts* 2H **23**
Cholesbury. *Buck* 5H **51**
Chollerford. *Nmbd* 2C **114**
Chollerton. *Nmbd* 2C **114**
Cholsey. *Oxon* 3D **36**
Cholstrey. *Here* 5G **59**
Chop Gate. *N Yor* 5C **106**
Choppington. *Nmbd* 1F **115**
Chopwell. *Tyne* 4E **115**
Chorley. *Ches E* 5H **83**
Chorley. *Lanc* 3D **90**
Chorley. *Shrp* 2A **60**
Chorley. *Staf* 4E **73**
Chorleywood. *Herts* 1B **38**
Chorlton. *Ches E* 5B **84**
Chorlton-cum-Hardy. *G Man* 1C **84**
Chorlton Lane. *Ches W* 1G **71**
Choulton. *Shrp* 2F **59**
Chrishall. *Essx* 2E **53**
Christchurch. *Cambs* 1D **65**
Christchurch. *Dors* 3G **15**
Christchurch. *Glos* 4A **48**
Christian Malford. *Wilts* 4E **35**
Christleton. *Ches W* 4G **83**
Christmas Common. *Oxon* 2F **37**
Christon. *N Som* 1G **21**
Christon Bank. *Nmbd* 2G **121**
Christow. *Devn* 4B **12**
Chryston. *N Lan* 2H **127**
Chuck Hatch. *E Sus* 2F **27**
Chudleigh. *Devn* 5B **12**
Chudleigh Knighton. *Devn* 5B **12**
Chulmleigh. *Devn* 1G **11**
Chunal. *Derbs* 1E **85**
Church. *Lanc* 2F **91**
Churcham. *Glos* 4C **48**
Church Aston. *Telf* 4B **72**
Church Brampton. *Nptn* 4E **62**
Church Brough. *Cumb* 3A **104**
Church Broughton. *Derbs* 2G **73**
Church Common. *Hants* 4F **25**
Church Corner. *Suff* 2G **67**
Church Crookham. *Hants* 1G **25**
Churchdown. *Glos* 4D **48**
Church Eaton. *Staf* 4C **72**
Church End. *Cambs* 5D **65**
(nr. Cambridge)
Church End. *Cambs* 2B **64**
(nr. Sawtry)
Church End. *Cambs* 3C **64**
(nr. Willingham)
Church End. *Cambs* 5C **76**
(nr. Wisbech)
Church End. *C Beds* 3H **51**
(nr. Dunstable)
Church End. *C Beds* 2B **52**
(nr. Stotfold)
Church End. *C Beds* 2H **51**
(nr. Woburn)
Church End. *E Yor* 4E **101**
Church End. *Essx* 3H **53**
(nr. Braintree)
Churchend. *Essx* 3G **53**
(nr. Great Dunmow)
Church End. *Essx* 1F **53**
(nr. Saffron Walden)
Churchend. *Essx* 1E **40**
(nr. Southend-on-Sea)
Church End. *Glos* 5C **48**
Church End. *Hants* 1E **25**
Church End. *Linc* 2B **76**
(nr. Donington)
Church End. *Linc* 1D **88**
(nr. North Somercotes)
Church End. *Norf* 4E **77**
Church End. *Warw* 1G **61**
(nr. Coleshill)
Church End. *Warw* 1G **61**
(nr. Nuneaton)
Church End. *Wilts* 4F **35**
Church Enstone. *Oxon* 3B **50**
Church Fenton. *N Yor* 1F **93**
Church Green. *Devn* 3E **13**

Clyth—Coombe

Clyth. High 5E 169
Cnip. W Isl 4C 171
Cnwcau. Pemb 1C 44
Cnwch Coch. Cdgn 3F 57
Coad's Green. Corn 5C 10
Coal Aston. Derbs 3A 86
Coalbrookdale. Telf 5A 72
Coalbrookvale. Blae 5F 47
Coalburn. S Lan 1H 117
Coalburns. Tyne 3E 115
Coalcleugh. Nmbd 5B 114
Coaley. Glos 5C 48
Coalford. Abers 4F 153
Coalhall. E Ayr 3D 116
Coalhill. Essx 1B 40
Coalpit Heath. S Glo 3B 34
Coal Pool. W Mid 5E 73
Coalport. Telf 5B 72
Coalsnaughton. Clac 4B 136
Coaltown of Balgonie. Fife 4F 137
Coaltown of Wemyss. Fife 4F 137
Coalville. Leics 4B 74
Coalway. Glos 4A 48
Coanwood. Nmbd 4H 113
Coat. Som 4H 21
Coatbridge. N Lan 3A 128
Coatdyke. N Lan 3A 128
Coate. Swin 3G 35
Coate. Wilts 5F 35
Coates. Cambs 1C 64
Coates. Glos 5E 49
Coates. Linc 2G 87
Coates. W Sus 4A 26
Coatham. Red C 2C 106
Coatham Mundeville. Darl 2F 105
Cobbaton. Devn 4G 19
Coberley. Glos 4E 49
Cobhall Common. Here 2H 47
Cobham. Kent 4A 40
Cobham. Surr 4C 38
Cobnash. Here 4G 59
Coburg. Devn 5B 12
Cockayne. N Yor 5D 106
Cockayne Hatley. C Beds 1C 52
Cock Bank. Wrex 1F 71
Cock Bridge. Abers 3G 151
Cockburnspath. Bord 2D 130
Cock Clarks. Essx 5B 54
Cockenzie and Port Seton. E Lot 2H 129
Cockerham. Lanc 4D 96
Cockermouth. Cumb 1C 102
Cockernhoe. Herts 3B 52
Cockfield. Dur 2E 105
Cockfield. Suff 5B 66
Cockfosters. G Lon 1D 39
Cock Gate. Here 4G 59
Cock Green. Essx 4G 53
Cocking. W Sus 1G 17
Cocking Causeway. W Sus 1G 17
Cockington. Torb 2F 9
Cocklake. Som 2H 21
Cocklaw. Abers 4H 161
Cocklaw. Nmbd 2C 114
Cockley Beck. Cumb 4D 102
Cockley Cley. Norf 5G 77
Cockmuir. Abers 3G 161
Cockpole Green. Wind 3G 37
Cockshutford. Shrp 2H 59
Cockshutt. Shrp 3G 71
Cockthorpe. Norf 1B 78
Cockwood. Devn 4C 12
Cockyard. Derbs 3E 85
Cockyard. Here 2H 47
Codda. Corn 5B 10
Coddenham. Suff 5D 66
Coddenham Green. Suff 5D 66
Coddington. Ches W 5G 83
Coddington. Here 1C 48
Coddington. Notts 5F 87
Codford St Mary. Wilts 3E 23
Codford St Peter. Wilts 3E 23
Codicote. Herts 4C 52
Codmore Hill. W Sus 3B 26
Codnor. Derbs 1B 74
Codrington. S Glo 4C 34
Codsall. Staf 5C 72
Codsall Wood. Staf 5C 72
Coed Duon. Cphy 2E 33
Coedely. Rhon 3D 32
Coedglasson. Powy 4C 58
Coedkernew. Newp 3F 33
Coed Morgan. Mon 4G 47
Coedpoeth. Wrex 5E 83
Coedway. Powy 4F 71
Coed-y-bryn. Cdgn 1D 44
Coed-y-paen. Mon 2G 33
Coed-yr-ynys. Powy 3E 47
Coed Ystumgwern. Gwyn 3E 69
Coelbren. Powy 4B 46
Coffinswell. Devn 2E 9
Cofton Hackett. Worc 3E 61
Cogan. V Glam 4E 33
Cogenhoe. Nptn 4F 63
Cogges. Oxon 5B 50
Coggeshall. Essx 3B 54
Coggeshall Hamlet. Essx 3B 54
Coggins Mill. E Sus 3G 27
Coignafearn Lodge. High 2A 150
Coig Peighinnean. W Isl 1H 171
Coig Peighinnean Bhuirgh. W Isl 2G 171
Coilleag. W Isl 7C 170
Coilliemore. High 1A 158
Coillore. High 5C 154
Coire an Fhuarain. W Isl 4E 171
Coity. B'end 3C 32
Cokhay Green. Derbs 3G 73
Col. W Isl 4G 171
Colaboll. High 2C 164
Colan. Corn 2C 6
Colaton Raleigh. Devn 4D 12
Colbost. High 4B 154
Colburn. N Yor 5E 105
Colby. Cumb 2H 103
Colby. IOM 4B 108
Colby. Norf 2E 78
Colchester. Essx 3D 54
Cold Ash. W Ber 5D 36
Cold Ashby. Nptn 3D 62
Cold Ashton. S Glo 4C 34
Cold Aston. Glos 4G 49
Coldbackie. High 3G 167
Cold Blow. Pemb 3F 43
Cold Brayfield. Mil 5G 63
Cold Cotes. N Yor 2G 97
Coldean. Brig 5E 27
Coldeast. Devn 5B 12
Colden. W Yor 2H 91
Colden Common. Hants 4C 24
Coldfair Green. Suff 4G 67
Coldham. Cambs 5D 76
Coldham. Staf 5C 72
Cold Hanworth. Linc 2H 87
Coldharbour. Corn 4B 6
Cold Harbour. Dors 3E 15
Coldharbour. Glos 5A 48
Coldharbour. Kent 5G 39
Coldharbour. Surr 1C 26
Cold Hatton. Telf 3A 72
Cold Hatton Heath. Telf 3A 72
Cold Hesledon. Dur 5H 115
Cold Hiendley. W Yor 3D 92
Cold Higham. Nptn 5D 62
Coldingham. Bord 3F 131
Cold Kirby. N Yor 1H 99
Coldmeece. Staf 2C 72
Cold Northcott. Corn 4C 10
Cold Norton. Essx 5B 54
Cold Overton. Leics 4F 75
Coldrain. Per 3C 136
Coldred. Kent 1G 29
Coldridge. Devn 2G 11
Cold Row. Lanc 5C 96
Coldstream. Bord 5E 131
Coldwaltham. W Sus 4B 26
Coldwell. Here 2H 47
Coldwells. Abers 5H 161
Coldwells Croft. Abers 1C 152
Cole. Som 3B 22
Colebatch. Shrp 2F 59
Colebrook. Devn 2D 12
Colebrooke. Devn 2A 12
Coleburn. Mor 3G 159
Coleby. Linc 4G 87
Coleby. N Lin 3B 94
Cole End. Warw 2G 61
Coleford. Devn 2A 12
Coleford. Glos 4A 48
Coleford. Som 2B 22
Colegate End. Norf 2D 66
Cole Green. Herts 4C 52
Cole Henley. Hants 1C 24
Colehill. Dors 2F 15
Coleman Green. Herts 4B 52
Coleman's Hatch. E Sus 2F 27
Colemere. Shrp 2G 71
Colemore. Hants 3F 25
Colemore Green. Shrp 1B 60
Coleorton. Leics 4B 74
Colerne. Wilts 4D 34
Colesbourne. Glos 4E 49
Colesden. Bed 5A 64
Coles Green. Worc 5B 60
Coleshill. Buck 1A 38
Coleshill. Oxon 2H 35
Coleshill. Warw 2G 61
Colestocks. Devn 2D 12
Colethrop. Glos 4D 48
Coley. Bath 1A 22
Colgate. W Sus 2D 26
Colinsburgh. Fife 3G 137
Colinton. Edin 3F 129
Colintraive. Arg 2B 126
Colkirk. Norf 3B 78
Collace. Per 5B 144
Collaton. Devn 5D 8
Collaton St Mary. Torb 2E 9
College of Roseisle. Mor 2F 159
Collessie. Fife 2E 137
Collier Row. G Lon 1F 39
Colliers End. Herts 3D 52
Collier Street. Kent 1B 28
Colliery Row. Tyne 5G 115
Collieston. Abers 1H 153
Collin. Dum 2B 112
Collingbourne Ducis. Wilts 1H 23
Collingbourne Kingston. Wilts 1H 23
Collingham. Notts 4F 87
Collingham. W Yor 5F 99
Collingtree. Nptn 5E 63
Collins Green. Warr 1H 83
Collins Green. Worc 5B 60
Colliston. Ang 4F 145
Colliton. Devn 2D 12
Collydean. Fife 3E 137
Collyweston. Nptn 5G 75
Colmonell. S Ayr 1G 109
Colmworth. Bed 5A 64
Colnbrook. Slo 3B 38
Colne. Cambs 3C 64
Colne. Lanc 5A 98
Colne Engaine. Essx 2B 54
Colney. Norf 5D 78
Colney Heath. Herts 5C 52
Colney Street. Herts 5B 52
Coln Rogers. Glos 5F 49
Coln St Aldwyns. Glos 5G 49
Coln St Dennis. Glos 4F 49
Colpitts Grange. Nmbd 4C 114
Colpy. Abers 5D 160
Colscott. Devn 1D 10
Colsterdale. N Yor 1D 98
Colsterworth. Linc 3G 75
Colston Bassett. Notts 2D 74
Colstoun House. E Lot 2B 130
Coltfield. Mor 2F 159
Colthouse. Cumb 5E 103
Coltishall. Norf 4E 79
Coltness. N Lan 4A 128
Colton. Cumb 1C 96
Colton. Norf 5D 78
Colton. N Yor 5H 99
Colton. Staf 3E 73
Colton. W Yor 1D 92
Colt's Hill. Kent 1H 27
Col Uarach. W Isl 4G 171
Colvend. Dum 4F 111
Colwall Green. Here 1C 48
Colwall Stone. Here 1C 48
Colwell. Nmbd 2C 114
Colwich. Staf 3E 73
Colwick. Notts 1D 74
Colwinston. V Glam 4C 32
Colworth. W Sus 5A 26
Colwyn Bay. Cnwy 3A 82
Colyford. Devn 3F 13
Colyton. Devn 3F 13
Combe. Devn 2D 8
Combe. Here 4F 59
Combe. Oxon 4C 50
Combe. W Ber 5B 36
Combe Almer. Dors 3E 15
Combebow. Devn 4E 11
Combe Common. Surr 2A 26
Combe Down. Bath 5C 34
Combe Fishacre. Devn 2E 9
Combe Florey. Som 3E 21
Combe Hay. Bath 1C 22
Combeinteignhead. Devn 5C 12
Combe Martin. Devn 2F 19
Combe Moor. Here 4F 59
Combe Raleigh. Devn 2E 13
Comberbach. Ches W 3A 84
Comberford. Staf 5F 73
Comberton. Cambs 5C 64
Comberton. Here 4G 59
Combe St Nicholas. Som 1G 13
Combpyne. Devn 3F 13
Combridge. Staf 2E 73
Combrook. Warw 5H 61
Combs. Derbs 3E 85
Combs. Suff 5C 66
Combs Ford. Suff 5C 66
Combwich. Som 2F 21
Comers. Abers 3D 152
Comhampton. Worc 4C 60
Comins Coch. Cdgn 2F 57
Comley. Shrp 1G 59
Commercial End. Cambs 4E 65
Commins. Powy 3D 70
Commins Coch. Powy 5H 69
Commondale. N Yor 3D 106
Common End. Cumb 2B 102
Common Hill. Here 2A 48
Common Moor. Corn 2G 7
Common Platt. Wilts 3G 35
Commonside. Ches W 3H 83
Common Side. Derbs 3H 85 (nr. Chesterfield)
Commonside. Derbs 1G 73 (nr. Derby)
Common, The. Wilts 3H 23 (nr. Salisbury)
Common, The. Wilts 3F 35 (nr. Swindon)
Compstall. G Man 1D 84
Compton. Devn 2E 9
Compton. Hants 4C 24
Compton. Staf 2C 60
Compton. Surr 1A 26
Compton. W Ber 3D 36
Compton. W Sus 1F 17
Compton. Wilts 1G 23
Compton Abbas. Dors 1D 14
Compton Abdale. Glos 4F 49
Compton Bassett. Wilts 4F 35
Compton Beauchamp. Oxon 3A 36
Compton Bishop. Som 1G 21
Compton Chamberlayne. Wilts 4F 23
Compton Dando. Bath 5B 34
Compton Dundon. Som 3H 21
Compton Greenfield. S Glo 3A 34
Compton Martin. Bath 1A 22
Compton Pauncefoot. Som 4B 22
Compton Valence. Dors 3A 14
Comrie. Fife 1D 128
Comrie. Per 1G 135
Conaglen. High 2E 141
Conchra. Arg 1B 126
Conchra. High 1A 148
Conder Green. Lanc 4D 96
Conderton. Worc 2E 49
Condicote. Glos 3G 49
Condorrat. N Lan 2A 128
Condover. Shrp 5G 71
Coneyhurst Common. W Sus 3C 26
Coneysthorpe. N Yor 2B 100
Coneythorpe. N Yor 4F 99
Coney Weston. Suff 3B 66
Conford. Hants 3G 25
Congdon's Shop. Corn 5C 10
Congerstone. Leics 5A 74
Congham. Norf 3G 77
Congleton. Ches E 4C 84
Congl-y-wal. Gwyn 1G 69
Congresbury. N Som 5H 33
Congreve. Staf 4D 72
Conham. S Glo 4B 34
Conicaval. Mor 3D 159
Coningsby. Linc 5B 88
Conington. Cambs 4C 64 (nr. Fenstanton)
Conington. Cambs 2A 64 (nr. Sawtry)
Conisbrough. S Yor 1C 86
Conisby. Arg 3A 124
Conisholme. Linc 1D 88
Coniston. Cumb 5E 102
Coniston. E Yor 1E 95
Coniston Cold. N Yor 4B 98
Conistone. N Yor 3B 98
Connah's Quay. Flin 4E 83
Connel. Arg 5D 140
Connel Park. E Ayr 3F 117
Connista. High 1D 154
Connor Downs. Corn 3C 4
Conock. Wilts 1F 23
Conon Bridge. High 3H 157
Cononley. N Yor 5B 98
Cononsyth. Ang 4E 145
Conordan. High 5E 155
Consall. Staf 1D 73
Consett. Dur 4E 115
Constable Burton. N Yor 5E 105
Constantine. Corn 4E 5
Constantine Bay. Corn 1C 6
Contin. High 3G 157
Contullich. High 1A 158
Conwy. Cnwy 3G 81
Conyer. Kent 4D 40
Conyer's Green. Suff 4A 66
Cooden. E Sus 5B 28
Cooil. IOM 4C 108
Cookbury. Devn 2E 11
Cookbury Wick. Devn 2D 11
Cookham. Wind 3G 37
Cookham Dean. Wind 3G 37
Cookham Rise. Wind 3G 37
Cookhill. Worc 5E 61
Cookley. Suff 3F 67
Cookley. Worc 2C 60
Cookley Green. Oxon 2E 37
Cookney. Abers 4F 153
Cooksbridge. E Sus 4F 27
Cooksey Corner. Worc 4D 60
Cooksey Green. Worc 4D 60
Cookshill. Staf 1D 72
Cooksmill Green. Essx 5G 53
Coolham. W Sus 3C 26
Cooling. Medw 3B 40
Cooling Street. Medw 3B 40
Coombe. Corn 1C 10 (nr. Bude)
Coombe. Corn 3D 6 (nr. St Austell)
Coombe. Corn 4C 6 (nr. Truro)

Craigs, The—Crug-y-byddar

Craigs, The. High 4B 164
Craigton. Aber 3F 153
Craigton. Abers 3E 152
Craigton. Ang 5E 145
(nr. Carnoustie)
Craigton. Ang 3C 144
(nr. Kirriemuir)
Craigton. High 4A 158
Craigtown. High 3A 168
Craig-y-Duke. Neat 5H 45
Craigyloch. Ang 3B 144
Craig-y-nos. Powy 4B 46
Craik. Bord 4F 119
Crail. Fife 3H 137
Crailing. Bord 2A 120
Crailinghall. Bord 2A 120
Crakehill. N Yor 2G 99
Crakemarsh. Staf 2E 73
Crambe. N Yor 3B 100
Crambeck. N Yor 3B 100
Cramlington. Nmbd 2F 115
Cramond. Edin 2E 129
Cramond Bridge. Edin 2E 129
Cranage. Ches E 4B 84
Cranberry. Staf 2C 72
Cranborne. Dors 1F 15
Cranbourne. Brac 3A 38
Cranbrook. Kent 2B 28
Cranbrook Common. Kent 2B 28
Crane Moor. S Yor 4D 92
Crane's Corner. Norf 4B 78
Cranfield. C Beds 1H 51
Cranford. G Lon 3B 38
Cranford St Andrew. Nptn 3G 63
Cranford St John. Nptn 3G 63
Cranham. Glos 4D 49
Cranham. G Lon 2G 39
Crank. Mers 1H 83
Cranleigh. Surr 2B 26
Cranley. Suff 3D 66
Cranloch. Mor 3G 159
Cranmer Green. Suff 3C 66
Cranmore. IOW 3B 16
Cranmore. Linc 5A 76
Crannich. Arg 4G 139
Crannoch. Mor 3B 160
Cranoe. Leics 1E 63
Cransford. Suff 4F 67
Cranshaws. Bord 3C 130
Cranstal. IOM 1D 108
Crantock. Corn 2B 6
Cranwell. Linc 5H 87
Cranwich. Norf 1G 65
Cranworth. Norf 5B 78
Craobh Haven. Arg 3E 133
Craobhnaclag. High 4G 157
Crapstone. Devn 2B 8
Crarae. Arg 4G 133
Crask. High 2H 167
Crask Inn. High 1C 164
Crask of Aigas. High 4G 157
Craster. Nmbd 3G 121
Cratfield. Suff 3F 67
Crathes. Abers 4E 153
Crathie. Abers 4G 151
Crathie. High 4H 149
Crathorne. N Yor 4B 106
Craven Arms. Shrp 2G 59
Crawcrook. Tyne 3E 115
Crawford. Lanc 4D 90
Crawford. S Lan 2B 118
Crawforddyke. S Lan 4B 128
Crawfordjohn. S Lan 2A 118
Crawick. Dum 3G 117
Crawley. Devn 2F 13
Crawley. Hants 3C 24
Crawley. Oxon 4B 50
Crawley. W Sus 2D 26
Crawley Down. W Sus 2E 27
Crawley Side. Dur 5C 114
Crawshawbooth. Lanc 2G 91
Crawton. Abers 5F 153
Cray. N Yor 2B 98
Cray. Per 2A 144
Crayford. G Lon 3G 39
Crayke. N Yor 2H 99
Craymere Beck. Norf 2C 78
Crays Hill. Essx 1B 40
Cray's Pond. Oxon 3E 37
Crazies Hill. Wok 3F 37
Creacombe. Devn 1B 12
Creagan. Arg 4D 141
Creag Aoil. High 1F 141
Creag Ghoraidh. W Isl 4D 170
Creaguaineach Lodge. High 2H 141
Creamore Bank. Shrp 2H 71
Creaton. Nptn 3E 62
Creca. Dum 2D 112
Credenhill. Here 1H 47
Crediton. Devn 2B 12
Creebridge. Dum 3B 110
Creech. Dors 4E 15
Creech Heathfield. Som 4F 21
Creech St Michael. Som 4F 21
Creed. Corn 4D 6
Creekmoor. Pool 3E 15
Creekmouth. G Lon 2F 39
Creeting St Mary. Suff 5C 66
Creeting St Peter. Suff 5C 66
Creeton. Linc 3H 75
Creetown. Dum 4B 110
Creggans. Arg 3H 133
Cregneash. IOM 5A 108
Cregrina. Powy 5D 58
Creich. Arg 2B 132
Creighton. Staf 2E 73
Creigiau. Card 3D 32
Cremyll. Corn 3A 8
Crendell. Dors 1F 15
Crepkill. High 4D 154
Cressage. Shrp 5H 71
Cressbrook. Derbs 3F 85
Cresselly. Pemb 4E 43
Cressing. Essx 3A 54
Cresswell. Nmbd 5G 121
Cresswell. Staf 2D 73
Cresswell Quay. Pemb 4E 43
Creswell. Derbs 3C 86
Creswell Green. Staf 4E 73
Cretingham. Suff 4E 67
Crewe. Ches E 5B 84
Crewe-by-Farndon. Ches W 5G 83
Crewgreen. Powy 4F 71
Crewkerne. Som 2H 13
Crews Hill. G Lon 5D 52
Crewton. Derb 2A 74
Crianlarich. Stir 1C 134
Cribbs Causeway. S Glo 3A 34
Cribyn. Cdgn 5E 57
Criccieth. Gwyn 2D 69
Crich. Derbs 5A 86
Crichton. Midl 3G 129
Crick. Mon 2H 33
Crick. Nptn 3C 62
Crickadarn. Powy 1D 46
Cricket Hill. Hants 5G 37
Cricket Malherbie. Som 1G 13
Cricket St Thomas. Som 2G 13
Crickham. Som 2H 21
Crickheath. Shrp 3E 71
Crickhowell. Powy 4F 47
Cricklade. Wilts 2F 35
Cricklewood. G Lon 2D 38
Cridling Stubbs. N Yor 2F 93
Criech. Fife 1F 137
Crieff. Per 1A 136
Criftins. Shrp 2F 71
Criggion. Powy 4E 71
Crigglestone. W Yor 3D 92
Crimchard. Som 2G 13
Crimdon Park. Dur 1B 106
Crimond. Abers 3H 161
Crimonmogate. Abers 3H 161
Crimplesham. Norf 5F 77
Crimscote. Warw 1H 49
Crinan. Arg 4E 133
Cringleford. Norf 5D 78
Crinow. Pemb 3F 43
Cripplesease. Corn 3C 4
Cripplestyle. Dors 1F 15
Cripp's Corner. E Sus 3B 28
Croanford. Corn 5A 10
Crockenhill. Kent 4G 39
Crocker End. Oxon 3F 37
Crockerhill. Hants 2D 16
Crockernwell. Devn 3A 12
Crocker's Ash. Here 4A 48
Crockerton. Wilts 2D 22
Crocketford. Dum 2F 111
Crockey Hill. York 5A 100
Crockham Hill. Kent 5F 39
Crockhurst Street. Kent 1H 27
Crockleford Heath. Essx 3D 54
Croeserw. Neat 2B 32
Croes-Goch. Pemb 1C 42
Croes Hywel. Mon 4G 47
Croes-lan. Cdgn 1D 45
Croesor. Gwyn 1F 69
Croesoswallt. Shrp 3E 71
Croesyceiliog. Carm 4E 45
Croesyceiliog. Torf 2F 33
Croes-y-mwyalch. Torf 2G 33
Croesywaun. Gwyn 5E 81
Croford. Som 4E 20
Croft. Leics 1C 62
Croft. Linc 4E 89
Croft. Warr 1A 84
Croftamie. Stir 1F 127
Croftfoot. Glas 3G 127
Croftmill. Per 5F 143
Crofton. Cumb 4E 112
Crofton. W Yor 3D 93
Crofton. Wilts 5A 36
Croft-on-Tees. N Yor 4F 105
Crofts. Dum 2E 111
Crofts of Benachielt. High 5D 169
Crofts of Dipple. Mor 3H 159
Crofty. Swan 3E 31
Croggan. Arg 1E 132
Croglin. Cumb 5G 113
Croich. High 4B 164
Croick. High 3A 168
Croig. Arg 3E 139
Cromarty. High 2B 158
Crombie. Fife 1D 128
Cromdale. High 1E 151
Cromer. Herts 3C 52
Cromer. Norf 1E 79
Cromford. Derbs 5G 85
Cromhall. S Glo 2B 34
Cromhall Common. S Glo 3B 34
Cromor. W Isl 5G 171
Cromra. High 5H 149
Cromwell. Notts 4E 87
Cronberry. E Ayr 2F 117
Crondall. Hants 2F 25
Cronk, The. IOM 2C 108
Cronk-y-Voddy. IOM 3C 108
Cronton. Mers 2G 83
Crook. Cumb 5F 103
Crook. Dur 1E 105
Crookdake. Cumb 5C 112
Crooke. G Man 4D 90
Crookedholm. E Ayr 1D 116
Crooked Soley. Wilts 4B 36
Crookes. S Yor 2H 85
Crookgate Bank. Dur 4E 115
Crookhall. Dur 4E 115
Crookham. Nmbd 1D 120
Crookham. W Ber 5D 36
Crookham Village. Hants 1F 25
Crooklands. Cumb 1E 97
Crook of Devon. Per 3C 136
Crookston. Ren 3G 127
Cropredy. Oxon 1C 50
Cropston. Leics 4C 74
Cropthorne. Worc 1E 49
Cropton. N Yor 1B 100
Cropwell Bishop. Notts 2D 74
Cropwell Butler. Notts 2D 74
Cros. W Isl 1H 171
Crosbie. N Ayr 5D 126
Crosbost. W Isl 5F 171
Crosby. Cumb 1B 102
Crosby. IOM 4C 108
Crosby. Mers 1F 83
Crosby. N Lin 3B 94
Crosby Court. N Yor 5A 106
Crosby Garrett. Cumb 4A 104
Crosby Ravensworth. Cumb 3H 103
Crosby Villa. Cumb 1B 102
Croscombe. Som 2A 22
Crosland Moor. W Yor 3B 92
Cross. Som 1H 21
Crossaig. Arg 4G 125
Crossapol. Arg 4A 138
Cross Ash. Mon 4H 47
Cross-at-Hand. Kent 1B 28
Crossbush. W Sus 5B 26
Crosscanonby. Cumb 1B 102
Crossdale Street. Norf 2E 79
Cross End. Essx 2B 54
Crossens. Mers 3B 90
Crossford. Fife 1D 128
Crossford. S Lan 5B 128
Cross Foxes. Gwyn 4G 69
Crossgate. Orkn 6D 172
Crossgate. Staf 2D 72
Crossgatehall. E Lot 3G 129
Crossgates. Fife 1E 129
Crossgates. N Yor 1E 101
Crossgates. Powy 4C 58
Cross Gates. W Yor 1D 92
Crossgill. Lanc 3E 97
Cross Green. Devn 4D 11
Cross Green. Staf 5D 72
Cross Green. Suff 5A 66
(nr. Cockfield)
Cross Green. Suff 5B 66
(nr. Hitcham)
Cross Hands. Carm 4F 45
(nr. Ammanford)
Crosshands. Carm 2F 43
(nr. Whitland)
Crosshands. E Ayr 1D 117
Cross Hill. Derbs 1B 74
Crosshill. E Ayr 2D 117
Crosshill. Fife 4D 136
Cross Hill. Glos 2A 34
Crosshill. S Ayr 4C 116
Crosshills. High 1A 158
Cross Hills. N Yor 5C 98
Cross Holme. N Yor 5C 106
Crosshouse. E Ayr 1C 116
Cross Houses. Shrp 5H 71
Crossings. Cumb 2G 113
Cross in Hand. E Sus 3G 27
Cross Inn. Cdgn 4E 57
(nr. Aberaeron)
Cross Inn. Cdgn 5C 56
(nr. New Quay)
Cross Inn. Rhon 3D 32
Crosskeys. Cphy 2F 33
Crosskirk. High 2C 168
Crosslands. Cumb 1C 96
Cross Lane Head. Shrp 1B 60
Cross Lanes. Corn 4D 5
Cross Lanes. Dur 3D 104
Cross Lanes. N Yor 3H 99
Crosslanes. Shrp 4F 71
Cross Lanes. Wrex 1F 71
Crosslee. Ren 3F 127
Crossmichael. Dum 3E 111
Crossmoor. Lanc 1C 90
Cross Oak. Powy 3E 46
Cross of Jackston. Abers 5E 161
Cross o' th' Hands. Derbs 1G 73
Crossroads. Abers 3G 153
(nr. Aberdeen)
Crossroads. Abers 4E 153
(nr. Banchory)
Crossroads. E Ayr 1D 116
Cross Side. Devn 4B 20
Cross Street. Suff 3D 66
Crosston. Ang 3E 145
Cross Town. Ches E 3B 84
Crossway. Mon 4H 47
Crossway. Powy 5C 58
Crossway Green. Mon 2A 34
Crossway Green. Worc 4C 60
Crossways. Dors 4C 14
Crosswell. Pemb 1F 43
Crosswood. Cdgn 3F 57
Crosthwaite. Cumb 5F 103
Croston. Lanc 3C 90
Crostwick. Norf 4E 79
Crostwight. Norf 3F 79
Crothair. W Isl 4D 171
Crouch. Kent 5H 39
Croucheston. Wilts 4F 23
Crouch Hill. Dors 1C 14
Croughton. Nptn 2D 50
Crovie. Abers 2F 161
Crow. Hants 2G 15
Crowan. Corn 3D 4
Crowborough. E Sus 2G 27
Crowcombe. Som 3E 21
Crowcroft. Worc 5B 60
Crowdecote. Derbs 4F 85
Crowden. Derbs 1E 85
Crowden. Devn 3E 11
Crowdhill. Hants 1C 16
Crowdon. N Yor 5G 107
Crow Edge. S Yor 4B 92
Crow End. Cambs 5C 64
Crowfield. Nptn 1E 50
Crowfield. Suff 5D 66
Crow Green. Essx 1G 39
Crow Hill. Here 3B 48
Crowhurst. E Sus 4B 28
Crowhurst. Surr 1E 27
Crowhurst Lane End. Surr 1E 27
Crowland. Linc 4B 76
Crowland. Suff 3C 66
Crowlas. Corn 3C 4
Crowle. N Lin 3A 94
Crowle. Worc 5D 60
Crowle Green. Worc 5D 60
Crowmarsh Gifford. Oxon 3E 36
Crown Corner. Suff 3E 67
Crownthorpe. Norf 5C 78
Crowntown. Corn 3D 4
Crows-an-wra. Corn 4A 4
Crowshill. Norf 5B 78
Crowthorne. Brac 5G 37
Crowton. Ches W 3H 83
Croxall. Staf 4F 73
Croxby. Linc 1A 88
Croxdale. Dur 1F 105
Croxden. Staf 2E 73
Croxley Green. Herts 1B 38
Croxton. Cambs 4B 64
Croxton. Norf 2B 78
(nr. Fakenham)
Croxton. Norf 2A 66
(nr. Thetford)
Croxton. N Lin 3D 94
Croxton. Staf 2B 72
Croxtonbank. Staf 2B 72
Croxton Green. Ches E 5H 83
Croxton Kerrial. Leics 3F 75
Croy. High 4B 158
Croy. N Lan 2A 128
Croyde. Devn 3E 19
Croydon. Cambs 1D 52
Croydon. G Lon 4E 39
Crubenbeg. High 4A 150
Crubenmore Lodge. High 4A 150
Cruckmeore. Shrp 5G 71
Cruckton. Shrp 4G 71
Cruden Bay. Abers 5H 161
Crudgington. Telf 4A 72
Crudie. Abers 3E 161
Crudwell. Wilts 2E 35
Cruft. Devn 3F 11
Crug. Powy 3D 58
Crughywel. Powy 4F 47
Crugmeer. Corn 1D 6
Crugybar. Carm 2G 45
Crug-y-byddar. Powy 2D 58

Daw Cross—Doura

Daw Cross. *N Yor* 4E 99
Dawdon. *Dur* 5H 115
Dawesgreen. *Surr* 1D 26
Dawley. *Telf* 5A 72
Dawlish. *Devn* 5C 12
Dawlish Warren. *Devn* 5C 12
Dawn. *Cnwy* 3A 82
Daws Heath. *Essx* 2C 40
Dawshill. *Worc* 5C 60
Daw's House. *Corn* 4D 10
Dawsmere. *Linc* 2D 76
Dayhills. *Staf* 2D 72
Dayhouse Bank. *Worc* 3D 60
Daylesford. *Glos* 3H 49
Daywall. *Shrp* 2E 71
Ddol. *Flin* 3D 82
Ddol Cownwy. *Powy* 4C 70
Deadman's Cross. *C Beds* 1B 52
Deadwater. *Nmbd* 5A 120
Deaf Hill. *Dur* 1A 106
Deal. *Kent* 5H 41
Dean. *Cumb* 2B 102
Dean. *Devn* 2G 19
(nr. Combe Martin)
Dean. *Devn* 2H 19
(nr. Lynton)
Dean. *Dors* 1E 15
Dean. *Hants* 1D 16
(nr. Bishop's Waltham)
Dean. *Hants* 3C 24
(nr. Winchester)
Dean. *Som* 2B 22
Dean Bank. *Dur* 1F 105
Deanburnhaugh. *Bord* 3F 119
Dean Cross. *Devn* 2F 19
Deane. *Hants* 1D 24
Deanich Lodge. *High* 5A 164
Deanland. *Dors* 1E 15
Deanlane End. *W Sus* 1F 17
Dean Park. *Shrp* 4H 59
Dean Prior. *Devn* 2D 8
Dean Row. *Ches E* 2C 84
Deans. *W Lot* 3D 128
Deanscales. *Cumb* 2B 102
Deanshanger. *Nptn* 2F 51
Deanston. *Stir* 3G 135
Dearham. *Cumb* 1B 102
Dearne. *S Yor* 4E 93
Dearne Valley. *S Yor* 4D 93
Debach. *Suff* 5E 67
Debden. *Essx* 2F 53
Debden Green. *Essx* 1F 39
(nr. Loughton)
Debden Green. *Essx* 2F 53
(nr. Saffron Walden)
Debenham. *Suff* 4D 66
Dechmont. *W Lot* 2D 128
Deddington. *Oxon* 2C 50
Dedham. *Essx* 2D 54
Dedham Heath. *Essx* 2D 54
Deebank. *Abers* 4D 152
Deene. *Nptn* 1G 63
Deenethorpe. *Nptn* 1G 63
Deepcar. *S Yor* 1G 85
Deepcut. *Surr* 5A 38
Deepdale. *Cumb* 1G 97
Deepdale. *N Lin* 3D 94
Deepdale. *N Yor* 2A 98
Deeping Gate. *Pet* 5A 76
Deeping St James. *Linc* 5A 76
Deeping St Nicholas. *Linc* 4B 76
Deerhill. *Mor* 3B 160
Deerhurst. *Glos* 3D 48
Deerhurst Walton. *Glos* 3D 49
Deerness. *Orkn* 7E 172
Defford. *Worc* 1E 49
Defynnog. *Powy* 3C 46
Deganwy. *Cnwy* 3G 81
Deighton. *N Yor* 4A 106
Deighton. *W Yor* 3B 92
Deighton. *York* 5A 100
Deiniolen. *Gwyn* 4E 81
Delabole. *Corn* 4A 10
Delamere. *Ches W* 4H 83
Delfour. *High* 3C 150
Dellieture. *High* 5E 159
Dell, The. *Suff* 1G 67
Delly End. *Oxon* 4B 50
Delny. *High* 1B 158
Delph. *G Man* 4H 91
Delves. *Dur* 5E 115
Delves, The. *W Mid* 1E 61
Delvin End. *Essx* 2A 54
Dembleby. *Linc* 2H 75
Demelza. *Corn* 2D 6
Denaby Main. *S Yor* 1B 86
Denbeath. *Fife* 4F 137
Denbigh. *Den* 4C 82
Denbury. *Devn* 2E 9
Denby. *Derbs* 1A 74
Denby Common. *Derbs* 1B 74
Denby Dale. *W Yor* 4C 92
Denchworth. *Oxon* 2B 36
Dendron. *Cumb* 2B 96
Deneside. *Dur* 5H 115
Denford. *Nptn* 3G 63
Dengie. *Essx* 5C 54
Denham. *Buck* 2B 38
Denham. *Suff* 4G 65
(nr. Bury St Edmunds)
Denham. *Suff* 3D 66
(nr. Eye)
Denham Green. *Buck* 2B 38
Denham Street. *Suff* 3D 66
Denhead. *Abers* 5G 161
(nr. Ellon)
Denhead. *Abers* 3G 161
(nr. Strichen)
Denhead. *Fife* 2G 137
Denholm. *Bord* 3H 119
Denholme. *W Yor* 1A 92
Denholme Clough. *W Yor* 1A 92
Denholme Gate. *W Yor* 1A 92
Denio. *Gwyn* 2C 68
Denmead. *Hants* 1E 17
Dennington. *Suff* 4E 67
Denny. *Falk* 1B 128
Denny End. *Cambs* 4D 65
Dennyloanhead. *Falk* 1B 128
Den of Lindores. *Fife* 2E 137
Denshaw. *G Man* 3H 91
Denside. *Abers* 4F 153
Densole. *Kent* 1G 29
Denston. *Suff* 5G 65
Denstone. *Staf* 1F 73
Denstroude. *Kent* 4F 41
Dent. *Cumb* 1G 97
Den, The. *N Ayr* 4E 127
Denton. *Cambs* 2A 64
Denton. *Darl* 3F 105
Denton. *E Sus* 5F 27
Denton. *G Man* 1D 84
Denton. *Kent* 1G 29
Denton. *Linc* 2F 75
Denton. *Norf* 2E 67
Denton. *Nptn* 5F 63
Denton. *N Yor* 5D 98
Denton. *Oxon* 5D 50
Denver. *Norf* 5F 77
Denwick. *Nmbd* 3G 121
Deopham. *Norf* 5C 78
Deopham Green. *Norf* 1C 66
Depden. *Suff* 5G 65
Depden Green. *Suff* 5G 65
Deptford. *G Lon* 3E 39
Deptford. *Wilts* 3F 23
Derby. *Derb* 2A 74
Derbyhaven. *IOM* 5B 108
Derculich. *Per* 3F 143
Dereham. *Norf* 4B 78
Deri. *Cphy* 5E 47
Derril. *Devn* 2D 10
Derringstone. *Kent* 1G 29
Derrington. *Shrp* 1A 60
Derrington. *Staf* 3C 72
Derriton. *Devn* 2D 10
Derryguaig. *Arg* 5F 139
Derry Hill. *Wilts* 4E 35
Derrythorpe. *N Lin* 4B 94
Dersingham. *Norf* 2F 77
Dervaig. *Arg* 3F 139
Derwen. *Den* 5C 82
Derwen Gam. *Cdgn* 5D 56
Derwenlas. *Powy* 1G 57
Desborough. *Nptn* 2F 63
Desford. *Leics* 5B 74
Detchant. *Nmbd* 1E 121
Dethick. *Derbs* 5H 85
Detling. *Kent* 5B 40
Deuchar. *Ang* 2D 144
Deuddwr. *Powy* 4E 71
Devauden. *Mon* 2H 33
Devil's Bridge. *Cdgn* 3G 57
Devitts Green. *Warw* 1G 61
Devizes. *Wilts* 5F 35
Devonport. *Plym* 3A 8
Devonside. *Clac* 4B 136
Devoran. *Corn* 5B 6
Dewartown. *Midl* 3G 129
Dewlish. *Dors* 3C 14
Dewsbury. *W Yor* 2C 92
Dewshall Court. *Here* 2H 47
Dexbeer. *Devn* 2C 10
Dhoon. *IOM* 3D 108
Dhoor. *IOM* 2D 108
Dhowin. *IOM* 1D 108
Dial Green. *W Sus* 3A 26
Dial Post. *W Sus* 4C 26
Dibberford. *Dors* 2H 13
Dibden. *Hants* 2C 16
Dibden Purlieu. *Hants* 2C 16
Dickleburgh. *Norf* 2D 66
Didbrook. *Glos* 2F 49
Didcot. *Oxon* 2D 36
Diddington. *Cambs* 4A 64
Diddlebury. *Shrp* 2H 59
Didley. *Here* 2H 47
Didling. *W Sus* 1G 17
Didmarton. *Glos* 3D 34
Didsbury. *G Man* 1C 84
Didworthy. *Devn* 2C 8
Digby. *Linc* 5H 87
Digg. *High* 2D 154
Diggle. *G Man* 4A 92
Digmoor. *Lanc* 4C 90
Digswell. *Herts* 4C 52
Dihewyd. *Cdgn* 5D 57
Dilham. *Norf* 3F 79
Dilhorne. *Staf* 1D 72
Dillarburn. *S Lan* 5B 128
Dillington. *Cambs* 4A 64
Dilston. *Nmbd* 3C 114
Dilton Marsh. *Wilts* 2D 22
Dilwyn. *Here* 5G 59
Dimmer. *Som* 3B 22
Dimple. *G Man* 3F 91
Dinas. *Carm* 1G 43
Dinas. *Gwyn* 5D 81
(nr. Caernarfon)
Dinas. *Gwyn* 2B 68
(nr. Tudweiliog)
Dinas Cross. *Pemb* 1E 43
Dinas Dinlle. *Gwyn* 5D 80
Dinas Mawddwy. *Gwyn* 4A 70
Dinas Powys. *V Glam* 4E 33
Dinbych. *Den* 4C 82
Dinbych-y-Pysgod. *Pemb* 4F 43
Dinckley. *Lanc* 1E 91
Dinder. *Som* 2A 22
Dinedor. *Here* 2A 48
Dinedor Cross. *Here* 2A 48
Dingestow. *Mon* 4H 47
Dingle. *Mers* 2F 83
Dingleden. *Kent* 2C 28
Dingleton. *Bord* 1H 119
Dingley. *Nptn* 2E 63
Dingwall. *High* 3H 157
Dinmael. *Cnwy* 1C 70
Dinnet. *Abers* 4B 152
Dinnington. *Som* 1H 13
Dinnington. *S Yor* 2C 86
Dinnington. *Tyne* 2F 115
Dinorwic. *Gwyn* 4E 81
Dinton. *Buck* 4F 51
Dinton. *Wilts* 3F 23
Dinworthy. *Devn* 1D 10
Dipley. *Hants* 1F 25
Dippen. *Arg* 2B 122
Dippenhall. *Surr* 2G 25
Dippertown. *Devn* 4E 11
Dippin. *N Ayr* 3E 123
Dipple. *S Ayr* 4B 116
Diptford. *Devn* 3D 8
Dipton. *Dur* 4E 115
Dirleton. *E Lot* 1B 130
Dirt Pot. *Nmbd* 5B 114
Discoed. *Powy* 4E 59
Diseworth. *Leics* 3B 74
Dishforth. *N Yor* 2F 99
Disley. *Ches E* 2D 85
Diss. *Norf* 3D 66
Disserth. *Powy* 5C 58
Distington. *Cumb* 2B 102
Ditchampton. *Wilts* 3F 23
Ditcheat. *Som* 3B 22
Ditchingham. *Norf* 1F 67
Ditchling. *E Sus* 4E 27
Ditteridge. *Wilts* 5D 34
Dittisham. *Devn* 3E 9
Ditton. *Hal* 2G 83
Ditton. *Kent* 5B 40
Ditton Green. *Cambs* 5F 65
Ditton Priors. *Shrp* 2A 60
Divach. *High* 1G 149
Dixonfield. *High* 2D 168
Dixton. *Glos* 2E 49
Dixton. *Mon* 4A 48
Dizzard. *Corn* 3B 10
Dobcross. *G Man* 4H 91
Dobs Hill. *Flin* 4F 83
Dobson's Bridge. *Shrp* 2G 71
Dobwalls. *Corn* 2G 7
Doccombe. *Devn* 4A 12
Dochgarroch. *High* 4A 158
Docking. *Norf* 2G 77
Docklow. *Here* 5H 59
Dockray. *Cumb* 2E 103
Doc Penfro. *Pemb* 4D 42
Dodbrooke. *Devn* 4D 8
Doddenham. *Worc* 5B 60
Doddinghurst. *Essx* 1G 39
Doddington. *Cambs* 1C 64
Doddington. *Kent* 5D 40
Doddington. *Linc* 4G 87
Doddington. *Nmbd* 1D 121
Doddington. *Shrp* 3A 60
Doddiscombsleigh. *Devn* 4B 12
Doddshill. *Norf* 2G 77
Dodford. *Nptn* 4D 62
Dodford. *Worc* 3D 60
Dodington. *Som* 2E 21
Dodington. *S Glo* 4C 34
Dodleston. *Ches W* 4F 83
Dods Leigh. *Staf* 2E 73
Dodworth. *S Yor* 4D 92
Doe Lea. *Derbs* 4B 86
Dogdyke. *Linc* 5B 88
Dogmersfield. *Hants* 1F 25
Dogsthorpe. *Pet* 5B 76
Dog Village. *Devn* 3C 12
Dolanog. *Powy* 4C 70
Dolau. *Powy* 4D 58
Dolau. *Rhon* 3D 32
Dolbenmaen. *Gwyn* 1E 69
Doley. *Staf* 3B 72
Dol-fach. *Powy* 5B 70
(nr. Llanbrynmair)
Dolfach. *Powy* 3B 58
(nr. Llanidloes)
Dolfor. *Powy* 2D 58
Dolgarrog. *Cnwy* 4G 81
Dolgellau. *Gwyn* 4G 69
Dolgoch. *Gwyn* 5F 69
Dol-gran. *Carm* 2E 45
Dolhelfa. *Powy* 3B 58
Doll. *High* 3F 165
Dollar. *Clac* 4B 136
Dolley Green. *Powy* 4E 59
Dollwen. *Cdgn* 2F 57
Dolphin. *Flin* 3D 82
Dolphingstone. *E Lot* 2G 129
Dolphinholme. *Lanc* 4E 97
Dolphinton. *S Lan* 5E 129
Dolton. *Devn* 1F 11
Dolwen. *Cnwy* 3A 82
Dolwyddelan. *Cnwy* 5G 81
Dol-y-Bont. *Cdgn* 2F 57
Dolyhir. *Powy* 5E 59
Domgay. *Powy* 4E 71
Doncaster. *S Yor* 4F 93
Donhead St Andrew. *Wilts* 4E 23
Donhead St Mary. *Wilts* 4E 23
Doniford. *Som* 2D 20
Donington. *Linc* 2B 76
Donington. *Shrp* 5C 72
Donington Eaudike. *Linc* 2B 76
Donington le Heath. *Leics* 4B 74
Donington on Bain. *Linc* 2B 88
Donington South Ing. *Linc* 2B 76
Donisthorpe. *Leics* 4H 73
Donkey Street. *Kent* 2F 29
Donkey Town. *Surr* 4A 38
Donna Nook. *Linc* 1D 88
Donnington. *Glos* 3G 49
Donnington. *Here* 2C 48
Donnington. *Shrp* 5H 71
Donnington. *Telf* 4B 72
Donnington. *W Ber* 5C 36
Donnington. *W Sus* 2G 17
Donyatt. *Som* 1G 13
Doomsday Green. *W Sus* 2C 26
Doonfoot. *S Ayr* 3C 116
Doonholm. *S Ayr* 3C 116
Dorback Lodge. *High* 2E 151
Dorchester. *Dors* 3B 14
Dorchester on Thames. *Oxon* 2D 36
Dordon. *Warw* 5G 73
Dore. *S Yor* 2H 85
Dores. *High* 5H 157
Dorking. *Surr* 1C 26
Dorking Tye. *Suff* 2C 54
Dormansland. *Surr* 1F 27
Dormans Park. *Surr* 1E 27
Dormanstown. *Red C* 2C 106
Dormington. *Here* 1A 48
Dormston. *Worc* 5D 61
Dorn. *Glos* 2H 49
Dorney. *Buck* 3A 38
Dornie. *High* 1A 148
Dornoch. *High* 5E 165
Dornock. *Dum* 3D 112
Dorrery. *High* 3C 168
Dorridge. *W Mid* 3F 61
Dorrington. *Linc* 5H 87
Dorrington. *Shrp* 5G 71
Dorsington. *Warw* 1G 49
Dorstone. *Here* 1G 47
Dorton. *Buck* 4E 51
Dotham. *IOA* 3C 80
Dottery. *Dors* 3H 13
Doublebois. *Corn* 2F 7
Dougarie. *N Ayr* 2C 122
Doughton. *Glos* 2D 35
Douglas. *IOM* 4C 108
Douglas. *S Lan* 1H 117
Douglastown. *Ang* 4D 144
Douglas Water. *S Lan* 1A 118
Doulting. *Som* 2B 22
Dounby. *Orkn* 5B 172
Doune. *High* 3C 150
(nr. Kingussie)
Doune. *High* 3B 164
(nr. Lairg)
Doune. *Stir* 3G 135
Dounie. *High* 4C 164
(nr. Bonar Bridge)
Dounie. *High* 5D 164
(nr. Tain)
Dounreay. *High* 2B 168
Doura. *N Ayr* 5E 127

Dousland—Durrant Green

Dousland. *Devn* 2B 8
Dovaston. *Shrp* 3F 71
Dove Holes. *Derbs* 3E 85
Dovenby. *Cumb* 1B 102
Dover. *Kent* 1H 29
Dovercourt. *Essx* 2F 55
Doverdale. *Worc* 4C 60
Doveridge. *Derbs* 2F 73
Doversgreen. *Surr* 1D 26
Dowally. *Per* 4H 143
Dowbridge. *Lanc* 1C 90
Dowdeswell. *Glos* 4F 49
Dowlais. *Mer T* 5D 46
Dowland. *Devn* 1F 11
Dowlands. *Devn* 3F 13
Dowles. *Worc* 3B 60
Dowlesgreen. *Wok* 5G 37
Dowlish Wake. *Som* 1G 13
Downall Green. *Mers* 4D 90
Down Ampney. *Glos* 2F 35
Downderry. *Corn* 3H 7 (nr. Looe)
Downderry. *Corn* 3D 6 (nr. St Austell)
Downe. *G Lon* 4F 39
Downend. *IOW* 4D 16
Downend. *S Glo* 4B 34
Downend. *W Ber* 4C 36
Down Field. *Cambs* 3F 65
Downfield. *D'dee* 5C 144
Downgate. *Corn* 5D 10 (nr. Kelly Bray)
Downgate. *Corn* 5C 10 (nr. Upton Cross)
Downham. *Essx* 1B 40
Downham. *Lanc* 5G 97
Downham. *Nmbd* 1C 120
Downham Market. *Norf* 5F 77
Down Hatherley. *Glos* 3D 48
Downhead. *Som* 2B 22 (nr. Frome)
Downhead. *Som* 4A 22 (nr. Yeovil)
Downholland Cross. *Lanc* 4B 90
Downholme. *N Yor* 5E 105
Downies. *Abers* 4G 153
Downley. *Buck* 2G 37
Down St Mary. *Devn* 2H 11
Downside. *Som* 1B 22 (nr. Chilcompton)
Downside. *Som* 2B 22 (nr. Shepton Mallet)
Downside. *Surr* 5C 38
Down, The. *Shrp* 1A 60
Down Thomas. *Devn* 3B 8
Downton. *Hants* 3A 16
Downton. *Wilts* 4G 23
Downton on the Rock. *Here* 3G 59
Dowsby. *Linc* 3A 76
Dowsdale. *Linc* 4B 76
Dowthwaitehead. *Cumb* 2E 103
Doxey. *Staf* 3D 72
Doxford. *Nmbd* 2F 121
Doynton. *S Glo* 4C 34
Drabblegate. *Norf* 3E 78
Draethen. *Cphy* 3F 33
Draffan. *S Lan* 5A 128
Dragonby. *N Lin* 3C 94
Dragons Green. *W Sus* 3C 26
Drakelow. *Worc* 2C 60
Drakemyre. *N Ayr* 4D 126
Drakes Broughton. *Worc* 1E 49
Drakes Cross. *Worc* 3E 61
Drakewalls. *Corn* 5E 11
Draughton. *Nptn* 3E 63
Draughton. *N Yor* 4C 98
Drax. *N Yor* 2G 93
Draycot. *Oxon* 5E 51
Draycote. *Warw* 4B 62
Draycot Foliat. *Swin* 4G 35
Draycott. *Derbs* 2B 74
Draycott. *Glos* 2G 49
Draycott. *Shrp* 1C 60
Draycott. *Som* 1H 21 (nr. Cheddar)
Draycott. *Som* 4A 22 (nr. Yeovil)
Draycott. *Worc* 1D 48
Draycott in the Clay. *Staf* 3F 73
Draycott in the Moors. *Staf* 1D 73
Drayford. *Devn* 1A 12
Drayton. *Leics* 1F 63
Drayton. *Linc* 2B 76
Drayton. *Norf* 4D 78
Drayton. *Nptn* 4C 62
Drayton. *Oxon* 2C 36 (nr. Abingdon)
Drayton. *Oxon* 1C 50 (nr. Banbury)
Drayton. *Port* 2E 17
Drayton. *Som* 4H 21
Drayton. *Warw* 5F 61
Drayton. *Worc* 3D 60
Drayton Bassett. *Staf* 5F 73
Drayton Beauchamp. *Buck* 4H 51
Drayton Parslow. *Buck* 3G 51
Drayton St Leonard. *Oxon* 2D 36
Drebley. *N Yor* 4C 98
Dreenhill. *Pemb* 3D 42
Drefach. *Carm* 4F 45 (nr. Meidrim)
Drefach. *Carm* 2D 44 (nr. Newcastle Emlyn)
Drefach. *Carm* 2G 43 (nr. Tumble)
Drefach. *Cdgn* 1E 45
Dreghorn. *N Ayr* 1C 116
Drellingore. *Kent* 1G 29
Drem. *E Lot* 2B 130
Dreumasdal. *W Isl* 5C 170
Drewsteignton. *Devn* 3H 11
Drewston. *Devn* 4H 11
Driby. *Linc* 3C 88
Driffield. *E Yor* 4E 101
Driffield. *Glos* 2F 35
Drift. *Corn* 4B 4
Drigg. *Cumb* 5B 102
Drighlington. *W Yor* 2C 92
Drimnin. *High* 3G 139
Drimpton. *Dors* 2H 13
Dringhoe. *E Yor* 4F 101
Drinisiadar. *W Isl* 8D 171
Drinkstone. *Suff* 4B 66
Drinkstone Green. *Suff* 4B 66
Drointon. *Staf* 3E 73
Droitwich Spa. *Worc* 4C 60
Droman. *High* 3B 166
Dron. *Per* 2D 136
Dronfield. *Derbs* 3A 86
Dronfield Woodhouse. *Derbs* 3H 85
Drongan. *E Ayr* 3D 116
Dronley. *Ang* 5C 144
Droop. *Dors* 2C 14
Drope. *V Glam* 4E 32
Droxford. *Hants* 1E 16
Droylsden. *G Man* 1C 84
Druggers End. *Worc* 2C 48
Druid. *Den* 1C 70
Druid's Heath. *W Mid* 5E 73
Druidston. *Pemb* 3C 42
Druim. *High* 3D 158
Druimarbin. *High* 1E 141
Druim Fhearna. *High* 2E 147
Druimindarroch. *High* 5E 147
Drum. *Per* 3C 136
Drumbeg. *High* 5B 166
Drumblade. *Abers* 4C 160
Drumbuie. *Dum* 1C 110
Drumbuie. *High* 5G 155
Drumburgh. *Cumb* 4D 112
Drumburn. *Dum* 3A 112
Drumchapel. *Glas* 2G 127
Drumchardine. *High* 4H 157
Drumchork. *High* 5C 162
Drumclog. *S Lan* 1F 117
Drumeldrie. *Fife* 3G 137
Drumelzier. *Bord* 1D 118
Drumfearn. *High* 2E 147
Drumgask. *High* 4A 150
Drumgelloch. *N Lan* 3A 128
Drumgley. *Ang* 3D 144
Drumguish. *High* 4B 150
Drumin. *Mor* 5F 159
Drumindorsair. *High* 4G 157
Drumlamford House. *S Ayr* 2H 109
Drumlasie. *Abers* 3D 152
Drumlemble. *Arg* 4A 122
Drumlithie. *Abers* 5E 153
Drummoddie. *Dum* 5A 110
Drummond. *High* 2A 158
Drummore. *Dum* 5E 109
Drummuir. *Mor* 4A 160
Drumnadrochit. *High* 5H 157
Drumnagorrach. *Mor* 3C 160
Drumoak. *Abers* 4E 153
Drumrunie. *High* 3F 163
Drumry. *W Dun* 2G 127
Drums. *Abers* 1G 153
Drumsleet. *Dum* 2G 111
Drumsmittal. *High* 4A 158
Drums of Park. *Abers* 3C 160
Drumsturdy. *Ang* 5D 145
Drumtochty Castle. *Abers* 5D 152
Drumuie. *High* 4D 154
Drumuillie. *High* 1D 150
Drumvaich. *Stir* 3F 135
Drumwhindle. *Abers* 5G 161
Drunkendub. *Ang* 4F 145
Drury. *Flin* 4E 83
Drury Square. *Norf* 4B 78
Drybeck. *Cumb* 3H 103
Drybridge. *Mor* 2B 160
Drybridge. *N Ayr* 1C 116
Drybrook. *Glos* 4B 48
Drybrook. *Here* 4A 48
Dryburgh. *Bord* 1H 119
Dry Doddington. *Linc* 1F 75
Dry Drayton. *Cambs* 4C 64
Drym. *Corn* 3D 4
Drymen. *Stir* 1F 127
Drymuir. *Abers* 4G 161
Drynachan Lodge. *High* 5C 158
Drynie Park. *High* 3H 157
Drynoch. *High* 5D 154
Dry Sandford. *Oxon* 5C 50
Dryslwyn. *Carm* 3F 45
Dry Street. *Essx* 2A 40
Dryton. *Shrp* 5H 71
Dubford. *Abers* 2E 161
Dubiton. *Abers* 3D 160
Dubton. *Ang* 3E 145
Duchally. *High* 2A 164
Duck End. *Essx* 3G 53
Duckington. *Ches W* 5G 83
Ducklington. *Oxon* 5B 50
Duckmanton. *Derbs* 3B 86
Duck Street. *Hants* 2B 24
Dudbridge. *Glos* 5D 48
Duddenhoe End. *Essx* 2E 53
Duddingston. *Edin* 2F 129
Duddington. *Nptn* 5G 75
Duddleswell. *E Sus* 3F 27
Duddo. *Nmbd* 5F 131
Duddon. *Ches W* 4H 83
Duddon Bridge. *Cumb* 1A 96
Dudleston. *Shrp* 2F 71
Dudleston Heath. *Shrp* 2F 71
Dudley. *Tyne* 2F 115
Dudley. *W Mid* 2D 60
Dudston. *Shrp* 1E 59
Dudwells. *Pemb* 2D 42
Duffield. *Derbs* 1H 73
Duffryn. *Neat* 2B 32
Dufftown. *Mor* 4H 159
Duffus. *Mor* 2F 159
Dufton. *Cumb* 2H 103
Duggleby. *N Yor* 3C 100
Duirinish. *High* 5G 155
Duisdalemore. *High* 2E 147
Duisdeil Mòr. *High* 2E 147
Duisky. *High* 1E 141
Dukesfield. *Nmbd* 4C 114
Dukestown. *Blae* 5E 47
Dukinfield. *G Man* 1D 84
Dulas. *IOA* 2D 81
Dulcote. *Som* 2A 22
Dulford. *Devn* 2D 12
Dull. *Per* 4F 143
Dullatur. *N Lan* 2A 128
Dullingham. *Cambs* 5F 65
Dullingham Ley. *Cambs* 5F 65
Dulnain Bridge. *High* 1D 151
Duloe. *Bed* 4A 64
Duloe. *Corn* 3G 7
Dulverton. *Som* 4C 20
Dulwich. *G Lon* 3E 39
Dumbarton. *W Dun* 2F 127
Dumbleton. *Glos* 2F 49
Dumfin. *Arg* 1E 127
Dumfries. *Dum* 2A 112
Dumgoyne. *Stir* 1G 127
Dummer. *Hants* 2D 24
Dumpford. *W Sus* 4G 25
Dun. *Ang* 2F 145
Dunagoil. *Arg* 4B 126
Dunalastair. *Per* 3E 142
Dunan. *High* 1D 147
Dunball. *Som* 2G 21
Dunbar. *E Lot* 2C 130
Dunbeath. *High* 5D 168
Dunbeg. *Arg* 5C 140
Dunblane. *Stir* 3G 135
Dunbog. *Fife* 2E 137
Dunbridge. *Hants* 4B 24
Duncanston. *Abers* 1C 152
Duncanston. *High* 3H 157
Dun Charlabhaigh. *W Isl* 3D 171
Dunchideock. *Devn* 4B 12
Dunchurch. *Warw* 3B 62
Duncote. *Nptn* 5D 62
Duncow. *Dum* 1A 112
Duncrievie. *Per* 3D 136
Duncton. *W Sus* 4A 26
Dundee. *D'dee* 5D 144
Dundee Airport. *D'dee* 1F 137
Dundon. *Som* 3H 21
Dundonald. *S Ayr* 1C 116
Dundonnell. *High* 5E 163
Dundraw. *Cumb* 5D 112
Dundreggan. *High* 2F 149
Dundrennan. *Dum* 5E 111
Dundridge. *Hants* 1D 16
Dundry. *N Som* 5A 34
Dunecht. *Abers* 3E 153
Dunfermline. *Fife* 1D 129
Dunford Bridge. *S Yor* 4B 92
Dungate. *Kent* 5D 40
Dunge. *Wilts* 1D 23
Dungeness. *Kent* 4E 29
Dungworth. *S Yor* 2G 85
Dunham-on-the-Hill. *Ches W* 3G 83
Dunham-on-Trent. *Notts* 3F 87
Dunhampton. *Worc* 4C 60
Dunham Town. *G Man* 2B 84
Dunham Woodhouses. *G Man* 2B 84
Dunholme. *Linc* 3H 87
Dunino. *Fife* 2H 137
Dunipace. *Falk* 1B 128
Dunira. *Per* 1G 135
Dunkeld. *Per* 4H 143
Dunkerton. *Bath* 1C 22
Dunkeswell. *Devn* 2E 13
Dunkeswick. *N Yor* 5F 99
Dunkirk. *Kent* 5E 41
Dunkirk. *S Glo* 3C 34
Dunkirk. *Staf* 5C 84
Dunkirk. *Wilts* 5E 35
Dunk's Green. *Kent* 5H 39
Dunlappie. *Ang* 2E 145
Dunley. *Hants* 1C 24
Dunley. *Worc* 4B 60
Dunlichity Lodge. *High* 5A 158
Dunlop. *E Ayr* 5F 127
Dunmaglass Lodge. *High* 1H 149
Dunmore. *Arg* 3F 125
Dunmore. *Falk* 1B 128
Dunmore. *High* 4H 157
Dunnet. *High* 1E 169
Dunnichen. *Ang* 4E 145
Dunning. *Per* 2C 136
Dunnington. *E Yor* 4F 101
Dunnington. *Warw* 5E 61
Dunnington. *York* 4A 100
Dunnockshaw. *Lanc* 2G 91
Dunoon. *Arg* 2C 126
Dunphail. *Mor* 4E 159
Dunragit. *Dum* 4G 109
Dunrostan. *Arg* 1F 125
Duns. *Bord* 4D 130
Dunsby. *Linc* 3A 76
Dunscar. *G Man* 3F 91
Dunscore. *Dum* 1F 111
Dunscroft. *S Yor* 4G 93
Dunsdale. *Red C* 3D 106
Dunsden Green. *Oxon* 4F 37
Dunsfold. *Surr* 2B 26
Dunsford. *Devn* 4B 12
Dunshalt. *Fife* 2E 137
Dunshillock. *Abers* 4G 161
Dunsley. *N Yor* 3F 107
Dunsley. *Staf* 2C 60
Dunsmore. *Buck* 5G 51
Dunsop Bridge. *Lanc* 4F 97
Dunstable. *C Beds* 3A 52
Dunstal. *Staf* 3E 73
Dunstall. *Staf* 3F 73
Dunstall Green. *Suff* 4G 65
Dunstall Hill. *W Mid* 1D 60
Dunstan. *Nmbd* 3G 121
Dunster. *Som* 2C 20
Duns Tew. *Oxon* 3C 50
Dunston. *Linc* 4H 87
Dunston. *Norf* 5E 79
Dunston. *Staf* 4D 72
Dunston. *Tyne* 3F 115
Dunstone. *Devn* 3B 8
Dunston Heath. *Staf* 4D 72
Dunsville. *S Yor* 4G 93
Dunswell. *E Yor* 1D 94
Dunsyre. *S Lan* 5D 128
Dunterton. *Devn* 5D 11
Duntisbourne Abbots. *Glos* 5E 49
Duntisbourne Leer. *Glos* 5E 49
Duntisbourne Rouse. *Glos* 5E 49
Duntish. *Dors* 2B 14
Duntocher. *W Dun* 2F 127
Dunton. *Buck* 3G 51
Dunton. *C Beds* 1C 52
Dunton. *Norf* 2A 78
Dunton Bassett. *Leics* 1C 62
Dunton Green. *Kent* 5G 39
Dunton Patch. *Norf* 2A 78
Duntulm. *High* 1D 154
Dunure. *S Ayr* 3B 116
Dunvant. *Swan* 3E 31
Dunvegan. *High* 4B 154
Dunwich. *Suff* 3G 67
Dunwood. *Staf* 5D 84
Durdar. *Cumb* 4F 113
Durgates. *E Sus* 2H 27
Durham. *Dur* 5F 115
Durham Tees Valley Airport. *Darl* 3A 106
Durisdeer. *Dum* 4A 118
Durisdeermill. *Dum* 4A 118
Durkar. *W Yor* 3D 92
Durleigh. *Som* 3F 21
Durley. *Hants* 1D 16
Durley. *Wilts* 5H 35
Durley Street. *Hants* 1D 16
Durlow Common. *Here* 2B 48
Durnamuck. *High* 4E 163
Durness. *High* 2E 166
Durno. *Abers* 1E 152
Durns Town. *Hants* 3A 16
Duror. *High* 3D 141
Durran. *Arg* 3G 133
Durran. *High* 2D 169
Durrant Green. *Kent* 2C 28

Durrants—Easton-in-Gordano

Durrants. *Hants* . . . 1F **17**
Durrington. *W Sus* . . . 5C **26**
Durrington. *Wilts* . . . 2G **23**
Dursley. *Glos* . . . 2C **34**
Dursley Cross. *Glos* . . . 4B **48**
Durston. *Som* . . . 4F **21**
Durweston. *Dors* . . . 2D **14**
Duston. *Nptn* . . . 4E **62**
Duthil. *High* . . . 1D **150**
Dutlas. *Powy* . . . 3E **58**
Duton Hill. *Essx* . . . 3G **53**
Dutson. *Corn* . . . 4D **10**
Dutton. *Ches W* . . . 3H **83**
Duxford. *Cambs* . . . 1E **53**
Duxford. *Oxon* . . . 2B **36**
Dwygyfylchi. *Cnwy* . . . 3G **81**
Dwyran. *IOA* . . . 4D **80**
Dyce. *Aber* . . . 2F **153**
Dyffryn. *B'end* . . . 2B **32**
Dyffryn. *Carm* . . . 2H **43**
Dyffryn. *Pemb* . . . 1D **42**
Dyffryn. *V Glam* . . . 4D **32**
Dyffryn Ardudwy. *Gwyn* . . . 3E **69**
Dyffryn Castell. *Cdgn* . . . 2G **57**
Dyffryn Ceidrych. *Carm* . . . 3H **45**
Dyffryn Cellwen. *Neat* . . . 5B **46**
Dyke. *Linc* . . . 3A **76**
Dyke. *Mor* . . . 3D **159**
Dykehead. *Ang* . . . 2C **144**
Dykehead. *N Lan* . . . 3B **128**
Dykehead. *Stir* . . . 4E **135**
Dykend. *Ang* . . . 3B **144**
Dykesfield. *Cumb* . . . 4E **112**
Dylife. *Powy* . . . 1A **58**
Dymchurch. *Kent* . . . 3F **29**
Dymock. *Glos* . . . 2C **48**
Dyrham. *S Glo* . . . 4C **34**
Dysart. *Fife* . . . 4F **137**
Dyserth. *Den* . . . 3C **82**

E

Eachwick. *Nmbd* . . . 2E **115**
Eadar Dha Fhadhail. *W Isl* . . . 4C **171**
Eagland Hill. *Lanc* . . . 5D **96**
Eagle. *Linc* . . . 4F **87**
Eagle Barnsdale. *Linc* . . . 4F **87**
Eagle Moor. *Linc* . . . 4F **87**
Eaglescliffe. *Stoc T* . . . 3B **106**
Eaglesfield. *Cumb* . . . 2B **102**
Eaglesfield. *Dum* . . . 2D **112**
Eaglesham. *E Ren* . . . 4G **127**
Eaglethorpe. *Nptn* . . . 1H **63**
Eagley. *G Man* . . . 3F **91**
Eairy. *IOM* . . . 4B **108**
Eakley Lanes. *Mil* . . . 5F **63**
Eakring. *Notts* . . . 4D **86**
Ealand. *N Lin* . . . 3A **94**
Ealing. *G Lon* . . . 2C **38**
Eallabus. *Arg* . . . 3B **124**
Eals. *Nmbd* . . . 4H **113**
Eamont Bridge. *Cumb* . . . 2G **103**
Earby. *Lanc* . . . 5B **98**
Earcroft. *Bkbn* . . . 2E **91**
Eardington. *Shrp* . . . 1B **60**
Eardisland. *Here* . . . 5G **59**
Eardisley. *Here* . . . 1G **47**
Eardiston. *Shrp* . . . 3F **71**
Eardiston. *Worc* . . . 4A **60**
Earith. *Cambs* . . . 3C **64**
Earlais. *High* . . . 2C **154**
Earle. *Nmbd* . . . 2D **121**
Earlesfield. *Linc* . . . 2G **75**
Earlestown. *Mers* . . . 1H **83**
Earley. *Wok* . . . 4F **37**
Earlham. *Norf* . . . 5D **78**
Earlish. *High* . . . 2C **154**
Earls Barton. *Nptn* . . . 4F **63**
Earls Colne. *Essx* . . . 3B **54**
Earls Common. *Worc* . . . 5D **60**
Earl's Croome. *Worc* . . . 1D **48**
Earlsdon. *W Mid* . . . 3H **61**
Earlsferry. *Fife* . . . 3G **137**
Earlsford. *Abers* . . . 5F **161**
Earl's Green. *Suff* . . . 4C **66**
Earlsheaton. *W Yor* . . . 2C **92**
Earl Shilton. *Leics* . . . 1B **62**
Earl Soham. *Suff* . . . 4E **67**
Earl Sterndale. *Derbs* . . . 4E **85**
Earlston. *E Ayr* . . . 1D **116**
Earlston. *Bord* . . . 1H **119**
Earl Stonham. *Suff* . . . 5D **66**
Earlstoun. *Dum* . . . 1D **110**
Earlswood. *Mon* . . . 2H **33**
Earlswood. *Warw* . . . 3F **61**
Earlyvale. *Bord* . . . 4F **129**
Earnley. *W Sus* . . . 3G **17**
Earsairidh. *W Isl* . . . 9C **170**
Earsdon. *Tyne* . . . 2G **115**
Earsham. *Norf* . . . 2F **67**
Earsham Street. *Suff* . . . 3E **67**
Earswick. *York* . . . 4A **100**
Eartham. *W Sus* . . . 5A **26**
Earthcott Green. *S Glo* . . . 3B **34**
Easby. *N Yor* . . . 4C **106**
(nr. Great Ayton)
Easby. *N Yor* . . . 4E **105**
(nr. Richmond)
Easdale. *Arg* . . . 2E **133**
Easebourne. *W Sus* . . . 4G **25**
Easenhall. *Warw* . . . 3B **62**
Eashing. *Surr* . . . 1A **26**
Easington. *Buck* . . . 4E **51**
Easington. *Dur* . . . 5H **115**
Easington. *E Yor* . . . 3G **95**
Easington. *Nmbd* . . . 1F **121**
Easington. *Oxon* . . . 2C **50**
(nr. Banbury)
Easington. *Oxon* . . . 2E **37**
(nr. Watlington)
Easington. *Red C* . . . 3E **107**
Easington Colliery. *Dur* . . . 5H **115**
Easington Lane. *Tyne* . . . 5G **115**
Easingwold. *N Yor* . . . 3H **99**
Easole Street. *Kent* . . . 5G **41**
Eassie. *Ang* . . . 4C **144**
Eassie and Nevay. *Ang* . . . 4C **144**
East Aberthaw. *V Glam* . . . 5D **32**
Eastacombe. *Devn* . . . 4F **19**
Eastacott. *Devn* . . . 4G **19**
East Allington. *Devn* . . . 4D **8**
East Anstey. *Devn* . . . 4B **20**
East Anton. *Hants* . . . 2B **24**
East Appleton. *N Yor* . . . 5F **105**
East Ardsley. *W Yor* . . . 2D **92**
East Ashley. *Devn* . . . 1G **11**
East Ashling. *W Sus* . . . 2G **17**
East Aston. *Hants* . . . 2C **24**
East Ayton. *N Yor* . . . 1D **101**
East Barkwith. *Linc* . . . 2A **88**
East Barnby. *N Yor* . . . 3F **107**
East Barnet. *G Lon* . . . 1D **39**
East Barns. *E Lot* . . . 2D **130**
East Barsham. *Norf* . . . 2B **78**
East Beach. *W Sus* . . . 3G **17**
East Beckham. *Norf* . . . 1D **78**
East Bedfont. *G Lon* . . . 3B **38**
East Bennan. *N Ayr* . . . 3D **123**
East Bergholt. *Suff* . . . 2D **54**
East Bierley. *W Yor* . . . 2B **92**
East Blatchington.
E Sus . . . 5F **27**
East Bliney. *Norf* . . . 4B **78**
East Bloxworth. *Dors* . . . 3D **15**
East Boldre. *Hants* . . . 2B **16**
East Bolton. *Nmbd* . . . 3F **121**
Eastbourne. *Darl* . . . 3F **105**
Eastbourne. *E Sus* . . . 5H **27**
East Brent. *Som* . . . 1G **21**
East Bridge. *Suff* . . . 4G **67**
East Bridgford. *Notts* . . . 1D **74**
East Briscoe. *Dur* . . . 3C **104**
East Buckland. *Devn* . . . 3G **19**
(nr. Barnstaple)
East Buckland. *Devn* . . . 4C **8**
(nr. Thurlestone)
East Budleigh. *Devn* . . . 4D **12**
Eastburn. *W Yor* . . . 5C **98**
East Burnham. *Buck* . . . 2A **38**
East Burrafirth. *Shet* . . . 6E **173**
East Burton. *Dors* . . . 4D **14**
Eastbury. *Herts* . . . 1B **38**
Eastbury. *W Ber* . . . 4B **36**
East Butsfield. *Dur* . . . 5E **115**
East Butterleigh. *Devn* . . . 2C **12**
East Butterwick. *N Lin* . . . 4B **94**
Eastby. *N Yor* . . . 4C **98**
East Calder. *W Lot* . . . 3D **129**
East Carleton. *Norf* . . . 5D **78**
East Carlton. *Nptn* . . . 2F **63**
East Carlton. *W Yor* . . . 5E **98**
East Chaldon. *Dors* . . . 4C **14**
East Challow. *Oxon* . . . 3B **36**
East Charleton. *Devn* . . . 4D **8**
East Chelborough. *Dors* . . . 2A **14**
East Chiltington. *E Sus* . . . 4E **27**
East Chinnock. *Som* . . . 1H **13**
East Chisenbury. *Wilts* . . . 1G **23**
Eastchurch. *Kent* . . . 3D **40**
East Clandon. *Surr* . . . 5B **38**
East Claydon. *Buck* . . . 3F **51**
East Clevedon. *N Som* . . . 4H **33**
East Clyne. *High* . . . 3F **165**
East Clyth. *High* . . . 5E **169**
East Coker. *Som* . . . 1A **14**
Eastcombe. *Glos* . . . 5D **49**
East Combe. *Som* . . . 3E **21**
East Common. *N Yor* . . . 1G **93**
East Compton. *Som* . . . 2B **22**
East Cornworthy. *Devn* . . . 3E **9**
Eastcote. *G Lon* . . . 2C **38**
Eastcote. *Nptn* . . . 5D **62**
Eastcote. *W Mid* . . . 3F **61**
Eastcott. *Corn* . . . 1C **10**
Eastcott. *Wilts* . . . 1F **23**
East Cottingwith. *E Yor* . . . 5B **100**
East Coulston. *Wilts* . . . 1E **23**
Eastcourt. *Wilts* . . . 5H **35**
(nr. Pewsey)
Eastcourt. *Wilts* . . . 2E **35**
(nr. Tetbury)
East Cowes. *IOW* . . . 3D **16**
East Cowick. *E Yor* . . . 2G **93**
East Cowton. *N Yor* . . . 4A **106**
East Cramlington.
Nmbd . . . 2F **115**
East Cranmore. *Som* . . . 2B **22**
East Creech. *Dors* . . . 4E **15**
East Croachy. *High* . . . 1A **150**
East Dean. *E Sus* . . . 5G **27**
East Dean. *Glos* . . . 3B **48**
East Dean. *Hants* . . . 4A **24**
East Dean. *W Sus* . . . 4A **26**
East Down. *Devn* . . . 2G **19**
East Drayton. *Notts* . . . 3E **87**
East Dundry. *N Som* . . . 5A **34**
East Ella. *Hull* . . . 2D **94**
East End. *Cambs* . . . 3C **64**
East End. *Dors* . . . 3E **15**
East End. *E Yor* . . . 4F **101**
(nr. Ulrome)
East End. *E Yor* . . . 2F **95**
(nr. Withernsea)
East End. *Hants* . . . 3B **16**
(nr. Lymington)
East End. *Hants* . . . 5C **36**
(nr. Newbury)
East End. *Herts* . . . 3E **53**
East End. *Kent* . . . 3D **40**
(nr. Minster)
East End. *Kent* . . . 2C **28**
(nr. Tenterden)
East End. *N Som* . . . 4H **33**
East End. *Oxon* . . . 4B **50**
East End. *Som* . . . 1A **22**
East End. *Suff* . . . 2E **54**
Easter Ardross. *High* . . . 1A **158**
Easter Balgedie. *Per* . . . 3D **136**
Easter Balmoral. *Abers* . . . 4G **151**
Easter Brae. *High* . . . 2A **158**
Easter Buckieburn. *Stir* . . . 1A **128**
Easter Bush. *Midl* . . . 3F **129**
Easter Compton. *S Glo* . . . 3A **34**
Easter Fearn. *High* . . . 5D **164**
Easter Galcantray. *High* . . . 4C **158**
Eastergate. *W Sus* . . . 5A **26**
Easterhouse. *Glas* . . . 3H **127**
Easter Howgate. *Midl* . . . 3F **129**
Easter Kinkell. *High* . . . 3H **157**
Easter Lednathie. *Ang* . . . 2C **144**
Easter Ogil. *Ang* . . . 2D **144**
Easter Ord. *Abers* . . . 3F **153**
Easter Quarff. *Shet* . . . 8F **173**
Easter Rhynd. *Per* . . . 2D **136**
Easter Skeld. *Shet* . . . 7E **173**
Easter Suddie. *High* . . . 3A **158**
Easterton. *Wilts* . . . 1F **23**
Eastertown. *Som* . . . 1G **21**
Easter Tulloch. *Abers* . . . 1G **145**
East Everleigh. *Wilts* . . . 1H **23**
East Farleigh. *Kent* . . . 5B **40**
East Farndon. *Nptn* . . . 2E **62**
East Ferry. *Linc* . . . 1F **87**
Eastfield. *N Lan* . . . 3B **128**
(nr. Caldercruix)
Eastfield. *N Lan* . . . 3B **128**
(nr. Harthill)
Eastfield. *N Yor* . . . 1E **101**
Eastfield. *S Lan* . . . 3H **127**
Eastfield Hall. *Nmbd* . . . 4G **121**
East Fortune. *E Lot* . . . 2B **130**
East Garforth. *W Yor* . . . 1E **93**
East Garston. *W Ber* . . . 4B **36**
Eastgate. *Dur* . . . 1C **104**
Eastgate. *Norf* . . . 3D **78**
East Ginge. *Oxon* . . . 3C **36**
East Gores. *Essx* . . . 3B **54**
East Goscote. *Leics* . . . 4D **74**
East Grafton. *Wilts* . . . 5A **36**
East Green. *Suff* . . . 5F **65**
East Grimstead. *Wilts* . . . 4H **23**
East Grinstead. *W Sus* . . . 2E **27**
East Guldeford. *E Sus* . . . 3D **28**
East Haddon. *Nptn* . . . 4D **62**
East Hagbourne. *Oxon* . . . 3D **36**
East Halton. *N Lin* . . . 2E **95**
East Ham. *G Lon* . . . 2F **39**
Eastham. *Mers* . . . 2F **83**
Eastham. *Worc* . . . 4A **60**
Eastham Ferry. *Mers* . . . 2F **83**
Easthampstead. *Brac* . . . 5G **37**
Easthampton. *Here* . . . 4G **59**
East Hanney. *Oxon* . . . 2C **36**
East Hanningfield. *Essx* . . . 5A **54**
East Hardwick. *W Yor* . . . 3E **93**
East Harling. *Norf* . . . 2B **66**
East Harlsey. *N Yor* . . . 5B **106**
East Harnham. *Wilts* . . . 4G **23**
East Harptree. *Bath* . . . 1A **22**
East Hartford. *Nmbd* . . . 2F **115**
East Harting. *W Sus* . . . 1G **17**
East Hatch. *Wilts* . . . 4E **23**
East Hatley. *Cambs* . . . 5B **64**
Easthaugh. *Norf* . . . 4C **78**
East Hauxwell. *N Yor* . . . 5E **105**
East Haven. *Ang* . . . 5E **145**
Eastheath. *Wok* . . . 5G **37**
East Heckington. *Linc* . . . 1A **76**
East Hedleyhope. *Dur* . . . 5E **115**
East Helmsdale. *High* . . . 2H **165**
East Hendred. *Oxon* . . . 3C **36**
East Heslerton. *N Yor* . . . 2D **100**
East Hoathly. *E Sus* . . . 4G **27**
East Holme. *Dors* . . . 4D **15**
Easthope. *Shrp* . . . 1H **59**
Easthorpe. *Essx* . . . 3C **54**
Easthorpe. *Leics* . . . 2F **75**
East Horrington. *Som* . . . 2A **22**
East Horsley. *Surr* . . . 5B **38**
East Horton. *Nmbd* . . . 1E **121**
Easthouses. *Midl* . . . 3G **129**
East Howe. *Bour* . . . 3F **15**
East Huntspill. *Som* . . . 2G **21**
East Hyde. *C Beds* . . . 4B **52**
East Ilsley. *W Ber* . . . 3C **36**
Eastington. *Devn* . . . 2H **11**
Eastington. *Glos* . . . 4G **49**
(nr. Northleach)
Eastington. *Glos* . . . 5C **48**
(nr. Stonehouse)
East Keal. *Linc* . . . 4C **88**
East Kennett. *Wilts* . . . 5G **35**
East Keswick. *W Yor* . . . 5F **99**
East Kilbride. *S Lan* . . . 4H **127**
East Kirkby. *Linc* . . . 4C **88**
East Knapton. *N Yor* . . . 2C **100**
East Knighton. *Dors* . . . 4D **14**
East Knowstone. *Devn* . . . 4B **20**
East Knoyle. *Wilts* . . . 3D **23**
East Kyloe. *Nmbd* . . . 1E **121**
East Lambrook. *Som* . . . 1H **13**
East Langdon. *Kent* . . . 1H **29**
East Langton. *Leics* . . . 1E **63**
East Langwell. *High* . . . 3E **164**
East Lavant. *W Sus* . . . 2G **17**
East Lavington. *W Sus* . . . 4A **26**
East Layton. *N Yor* . . . 4E **105**
Eastleach Martin. *Glos* . . . 5H **49**
Eastleach Turville. *Glos* . . . 5G **49**
East Leake. *Notts* . . . 3C **74**
East Learmouth. *Nmbd* . . . 1C **120**
Eastleigh. *Devn* . . . 4E **19**
(nr. Bideford)
East Leigh. *Devn* . . . 2H **11**
(nr. Crediton)
East Leigh. *Devn* . . . 3C **8**
(nr. Modbury)
Eastleigh. *Hants* . . . 1C **16**
East Lexham. *Norf* . . . 4A **78**
East Lilburn. *Nmbd* . . . 2E **121**
Eastling. *Kent* . . . 5D **40**
East Linton. *E Lot* . . . 2B **130**
East Liss. *Hants* . . . 4F **25**
East Lockinge. *Oxon* . . . 3C **36**
East Looe. *Corn* . . . 3G **7**
East Lound. *N Lin* . . . 1E **87**
East Lulworth. *Dors* . . . 4D **14**
East Lutton. *N Yor* . . . 3D **100**
East Lydford. *Som* . . . 3A **22**
East Lyng. *Som* . . . 4G **21**
East Mains. *Abers* . . . 4D **152**
East Malling. *Kent* . . . 5B **40**
East Marden. *W Sus* . . . 1G **17**
East Markham. *Notts* . . . 3E **87**
East Marton. *N Yor* . . . 4B **98**
East Meon. *Hants* . . . 4E **25**
East Mersea. *Essx* . . . 4D **54**
East Mey. *High* . . . 1F **169**
East Midlands Airport.
Leics . . . 3B **74**
East Molesey. *Surr* . . . 4C **38**
Eastmoor. *Norf* . . . 5G **77**
East Morden. *Dors* . . . 3E **15**
East Morton. *W Yor* . . . 5D **98**
East Ness. *N Yor* . . . 2A **100**
East Newton. *E Yor* . . . 1F **95**
East Newton. *N Yor* . . . 2A **100**
Eastney. *Port* . . . 3E **17**
Eastnor. *Here* . . . 2C **48**
East Norton. *Leics* . . . 5E **75**
East Nynehead. *Som* . . . 4E **21**
East Oakley. *Hants* . . . 1D **24**
Eastoft. *N Lin* . . . 3B **94**
East Ogwell. *Devn* . . . 5B **12**
Easton. *Cambs* . . . 3A **64**
Easton. *Cumb* . . . 4D **112**
(nr. Burgh by Sands)
Easton. *Cumb* . . . 2F **113**
(nr. Longtown)
Easton. *Devn* . . . 4H **11**
Easton. *Dors* . . . 5B **14**
Easton. *Hants* . . . 3D **24**
Easton. *Linc* . . . 3G **75**
Easton. *Norf* . . . 4D **78**
Easton. *Som* . . . 2A **22**
Easton. *Suff* . . . 5E **67**
Easton. *Wilts* . . . 4D **35**
Easton Grey. *Wilts* . . . 3D **35**
Easton-in-Gordano. *N Som* . . . 4A **34**

Embo—Fawley

Embo. *High* 4F 165
Emborough. *Som* 1B 22
Embo Street. *High* 4F 165
Embsay. *N Yor* 4C 98
Emery Down. *Hants* 2A 16
Emley. *W Yor* 3C 92
Emmbrook. *Wok* 5F 37
Emmer Green. *Read* 4F 37
Emmington. *Oxon* 5F 51
Emneth. *Norf* 5D 77
Emneth Hungate. *Norf* 5E 77
Empingham. *Rut* 5G 75
Empshott. *Hants* 3F 25
Emsworth. *Hants* 2F 17
Enborne. *W Ber* 5C 36
Enborne Row. *W Ber* 5C 36
Enchmarsh. *Shrp* 1H 59
Enderby. *Leics* 1C 62
Endmoor. *Cumb* 1E 97
Endon. *Staf* 5D 84
Endon Bank. *Staf* 5D 84
Enfield. *G Lon* 1E 39
Enfield Wash. *G Lon* 1E 39
Enford. *Wilts* 1G 23
Engine Common. *S Glo* 3B 34
Englefield. *W Ber* 4E 36
Englefield Green. *Surr* 3A 38
Engleseabrook. *Ches E* 5B 84
English Bicknor. *Glos* 4A 48
Englishcombe. *Bath* 5C 34
English Frankton. *Shrp* 3G 71
Enham Alamein. *Hants* 2B 24
Enmore. *Som* 3F 21
Ennerdale Bridge. *Cumb* 3B 102
Enniscaven. *Corn* 3D 6
Enoch. *Dum* 4A 118
Enochdhu. *Per* 2H 143
Ensay. *Arg* 4E 139
Ensbury. *Bour* 3F 15
Ensdon. *Shrp* 4G 71
Ensis. *Devn* 4F 19
Enson. *Staf* 3D 72
Enstone. *Oxon* 3B 50
Enterkinfoot. *Dum* 4A 118
Enville. *Staf* 2C 60
Eolaigearraidh. *W Isl* 8C 170
Eorabus. *Arg* 1A 132
Eoropaidh. *W Isl* 1H 171
Epney. *Glos* 4C 48
Epperstone. *Notts* 1D 74
Epping. *Essx* 5E 53
Epping Green. *Essx* 5E 53
Epping Green. *Herts* 5C 52
Epping Upland. *Essx* 5E 53
Eppleby. *N Yor* 3E 105
Eppleworth. *E Yor* 1D 94
Epsom. *Surr* 4D 38
Epwell. *Oxon* 1B 50
Epworth. *N Lin* 4A 94
Epworth Turbary. *N Lin* 4A 94
Erbistock. *Wrex* 1F 71
Erbusaig. *High* 1F 147
Erchless Castle. *High* 4G 157
Erdington. *W Mid* 1F 61
Eredine. *Arg* 3G 133
Eriboll. *High* 3E 167
Ericstane. *Dum* 3C 118
Eridge Green. *E Sus* 2G 27
Erines. *Arg* 2G 125
Eriswell. *Suff* 3G 65
Erith. *G Lon* 3G 39
Erlestoke. *Wilts* 1E 23
Ermine. *Linc* 3G 87
Ermington. *Devn* 3C 8
Ernesettle. *Plym* 3A 8
Erpingham. *Norf* 2D 78
Erriottwood. *Kent* 5D 40
Errogie. *High* 1H 149
Errol. *Per* 1E 137
Errol Station. *Per* 1E 137
Erskine. *Ren* 2F 127
Erskine Bridge. *Ren* 2F 127
Ervie. *Dum* 3F 109
Erwarton. *Suff* 2F 55
Erwood. *Powy* 1D 46
Eryholme. *N Yor* 4A 106
Eryrys. *Den* 5E 82
Escalls. *Corn* 4A 4
Escomb. *Dur* 1E 105
Escrick. *N Yor* 5A 100
Esgair. *Carm* 3D 45
(nr. Carmarthen)
Esgair. *Carm* 3G 43
(nr. St Clears)
Esgairgeiliog. *Powy* 5G 69
Esh. *Dur* 5E 115
Esher. *Surr* 4C 38
Esholt. *W Yor* 5D 98
Eshott. *Nmbd* 5G 121
Eshton. *N Yor* 4B 98
Esh Winning. *Dur* 5E 115
Eskadale. *High* 5G 157
Eskbank. *Midl* 3G 129
Eskdale Green. *Cumb* 4C 102
Eskdalemuir. *Dum* 5E 119
Eskham. *Linc* 1C 88
Esknish. *Arg* 3B 124
Esk Valley. *N Yor* 4F 107
Eslington Hall. *Nmbd* 3E 121
Espley Hall. *Nmbd* 5F 121
Esprick. *Lanc* 1C 90
Essendine. *Rut* 4H 75
Essendon. *Herts* 5C 52
Essich. *High* 5A 158
Essington. *Staf* 5D 72
Eston. *Red C* 3C 106
Estover. *Plym* 3B 8
Eswick. *Shet* 6F 173
Etal. *Nmbd* 1D 120
Etchilhampton. *Wilts* 5F 35
Etchingham. *E Sus* 3B 28
Etchinghill. *Kent* 2F 29
Etchinghill. *Staf* 4E 73
Etherley Dene. *Dur* 2E 105
Ethie Haven. *Ang* 4F 145
Etling Green. *Norf* 4C 78
Etloe. *Glos* 5B 48
Eton. *Wind* 3A 38
Eton Wick. *Wind* 3A 38
Etteridge. *High* 4A 150
Ettersgill. *Dur* 2B 104
Ettiley Heath. *Ches E* 4B 84
Ettington. *Warw* 1A 50
Etton. *E Yor* 5D 101
Etton. *Pet* 5A 76
Ettrick. *Bord* 3E 119
Ettrickbridge. *Bord* 2F 119
Etwall. *Derbs* 2G 73
Eudon Burnell. *Shrp* 2B 60
Eudon George. *Shrp* 2A 60
Euston. *Suff* 3A 66
Euxton. *Lanc* 3D 90
Evanstown. *B'end* 3C 32
Evanton. *High* 2A 158
Evedon. *Linc* 1H 75
Evelix. *High* 4E 165
Evendine. *Here* 1C 48
Evenjobb. *Powy* 4E 59
Evenley. *Nptn* 2D 50
Evenlode. *Glos* 3H 49
Even Swindon. *Swin* 3G 35
Evenwood. *Dur* 2E 105
Evenwood Gate. *Dur* 2E 105
Everbay. *Orkn* 5F 172
Evercreech. *Som* 3B 22
Everdon. *Nptn* 5C 62
Everingham. *E Yor* 5C 100
Everleigh. *Wilts* 1H 23
Everley. *N Yor* 1D 100
Eversholt. *C Beds* 2H 51
Evershot. *Dors* 2A 14
Eversley. *Hants* 5F 37
Eversley Centre. *Hants* 5F 37
Eversley Cross. *Hants* 5F 37
Everthorpe. *E Yor* 1C 94
Everton. *C Beds* 5B 64
Everton. *Hants* 3A 16
Everton. *Mers* 1F 83
Everton. *Notts* 1D 86
Evertown. *Dum* 2E 113
Evesbatch. *Here* 1B 48
Evesham. *Worc* 1F 49
Evington. *Leic* 5D 74
Ewden Village. *S Yor* 1G 85
Ewdness. *Shrp* 1B 60
Ewell. *Surr* 4D 38
Ewell Minnis. *Kent* 1G 29
Ewelme. *Oxon* 2E 37
Ewen. *Glos* 2F 35
Ewenny. *V Glam* 4C 32
Ewerby. *Linc* 1A 76
Ewes. *Dum* 5F 119
Ewesley. *Nmbd* 5E 121
Ewhurst. *Surr* 1B 26
Ewhurst Green. *E Sus* 3B 28
Ewhurst Green. *Surr* 2B 26
Ewlo. *Flin* 4F 83
Ewloe. *Flin* 4F 83
Ewood Bridge. *Lanc* 2F 91
Eworthy. *Devn* 3E 11
Ewshot. *Hants* 1G 25
Ewyas Harold. *Here* 3G 47
Exbourne. *Devn* 2G 11
Exbury. *Hants* 2C 16
Exceat. *E Sus* 5G 27
Exebridge. *Som* 4C 20
Exelby. *N Yor* 1E 99
Exeter. *Devn* 3C 12
Exeter International Airport.
Devn 3D 12
Exford. *Som* 3B 20
Exfords Green. *Shrp* 5G 71
Exhall. *Warw* 5F 61
Exlade Street. *Oxon* 3E 37
Exminster. *Devn* 4C 12
Exmouth. *Devn* 4D 12
Exning. *Suff* 4F 65
Exton. *Devn* 4C 12
Exton. *Hants* 4E 24
Exton. *Rut* 4G 75
Exton. *Som* 3C 20
Exwick. *Devn* 3C 12
Eyam. *Derbs* 3G 85
Eydon. *Nptn* 5C 62
Eye. *Here* 4G 59
Eye. *Pet* 5B 76
Eye. *Suff* 3D 66
Eye Green. *Pet* 5B 76
Eyemouth. *Bord* 3F 131
Eyeworth. *C Beds* 1C 52
Eyhorne Street. *Kent* 5C 40
Eyke. *Suff* 5F 67
Eynesbury. *Cambs* 5A 64
Eynort. *High* 1B 146
Eynsford. *Kent* 4G 39
Eynsham. *Oxon* 5C 50
Eyre. *High* 3D 154
(on Isle of Skye)
Eyre. *High* 5E 155
(on Raasay)
Eythorne. *Kent* 1G 29
Eyton. *Here* 4G 59
Eyton. *Shrp* 2F 59
(nr. Bishop's Castle)
Eyton. *Shrp* 4F 71
(nr. Shrewsbury)
Eyton. *Wrex* 1F 71
Eyton on Severn. *Shrp* 5H 71
Eyton upon the Weald Moors.
Telf 4A 72

F

Faccombe. *Hants* 1B 24
Faceby. *N Yor* 4B 106
Faddiley. *Ches E* 5H 83
Fadmoor. *N Yor* 1A 100
Fagwyr. *Swan* 5G 45
Faichem. *High* 3E 149
Faifley. *W Dun* 2G 127
Fail. *S Ayr* 2D 116
Failand. *N Som* 4A 34
Failford. *S Ayr* 2D 116
Failsworth. *G Man* 4H 91
Fairbourne. *Gwyn* 4F 69
Fairbourne Heath. *Kent* 5C 40
Fairburn. *N Yor* 2E 93
Fairfield. *Derbs* 3E 85
Fairfield. *Kent* 3D 28
Fairfield. *Worc* 3D 60
(nr. Bromsgrove)
Fairfield. *Worc* 1F 49
(nr. Evesham)
Fairford. *Glos* 5G 49
Fair Green. *Norf* 4F 77
Fair Hill. *Cumb* 1G 103
Fairhill. *S Lan* 4A 128
Fair Isle Airport. *Shet* 1B 172
Fairlands. *Surr* 5A 38
Fairlie. *N Ayr* 4D 126
Fairlight. *E Sus* 4C 28
Fairlight Cove. *E Sus* 4C 28
Fairmile. *Devn* 3D 12
Fairmile. *Surr* 4C 38
Fairmilehead. *Edin* 3F 129
Fair Oak. *Devn* 1D 12
Fair Oak. *Hants* 1C 16
(nr. Eastleigh)
Fair Oak. *Hants* 5D 36
(nr. Kingsclere)
Fairoak. *Staf* 2B 72
Fair Oak Green. *Hants* 5E 37
Fairseat. *Kent* 4H 39
Fairstead. *Essx* 4A 54
Fairstead. *Norf* 4F 77
Fairwarp. *E Sus* 3F 27
Fairwater. *Card* 4E 33
Fairy Cross. *Devn* 4E 19
Fakenham. *Norf* 3B 78
Fakenham Magna. *Suff* 3B 66
Fala. *Midl* 3H 129
Fala Dam. *Midl* 3H 129
Falcon. *Here* 2B 48
Faldingworth. *Linc* 2H 87
Falfield. *S Glo* 2B 34
Falkenham. *Suff* 2F 55
Falkirk. *Falk* 2B 128
Falkland. *Fife* 3E 137
Fallin. *Stir* 4H 135
Fallowfield. *G Man* 1C 84
Falmer. *E Sus* 5E 27
Falmouth. *Corn* 5C 6
Falsgrave. *N Yor* 1E 101
Falstone. *Nmbd* 1A 114
Fanagmore. *High* 4B 166
Fancott. *C Beds* 3A 52
Fanellan. *High* 4G 157
Fangdale Beck. *N Yor* 5C 106
Fangfoss. *E Yor* 4B 100
Fankerton. *Falk* 1A 128
Fanmore. *Arg* 4F 139
Fanner's Green. *Essx* 4G 53
Fannich Lodge. *High* 2E 156
Fans. *Bord* 5C 130
Farcet. *Cambs* 1B 64
Far Cotton. *Nptn* 5E 63
Fareham. *Hants* 2D 16
Farewell. *Staf* 4E 73
Far Forest. *Worc* 3B 60
Farforth. *Linc* 3C 88
Far Green. *Glos* 5C 48
Far Hoarcross. *Staf* 3F 73
Faringdon. *Oxon* 2A 36
Farington. *Lanc* 2D 90
Farlam. *Cumb* 4G 113
Farleigh. *N Som* 5H 33
Farleigh. *Surr* 4E 39
Farleigh Hungerford. *Som* 1D 22
Farleigh Wallop. *Hants* 2E 24
Farleigh Wick. *Wilts* 5D 34
Farlesthorpe. *Linc* 3D 88
Farleton. *Cumb* 1E 97
Farleton. *Lanc* 3E 97
Farley. *High* 4G 157
Farley. *N Som* 4H 33
Farley. *Shrp* 5F 71
(nr. Shrewsbury)
Farley. *Shrp* 5A 72
(nr. Telford)
Farley. *Staf* 1E 73
Farley. *Wilts* 4H 23
Farley Green. *Suff* 5G 65
Farley Green. *Surr* 1B 26
Farley Hill. *Wok* 5F 37
Farley's End. *Glos* 4C 48
Farlington. *N Yor* 3A 100
Farlington. *Port* 2E 17
Farlow. *Shrp* 2A 60
Farmborough. *Bath* 5B 34
Farmcote. *Glos* 3F 49
Farmcote. *Shrp* 1B 60
Farmington. *Glos* 4G 49
Far Moor. *G Man* 4D 90
Farmoor. *Oxon* 5C 50
Farmtown. *Mor* 3C 160
Farnah Green. *Derbs* 1H 73
Farnborough. *G Lon* 4F 39
Farnborough. *Hants* 1G 25
Farnborough. *Warw* 1C 50
Farnborough. *W Ber* 3C 36
Farnborough Airport. *Surr* 1G 25
Farncombe. *Surr* 1A 26
Farndish. *Bed* 4G 63
Farndon. *Ches W* 5G 83
Farndon. *Notts* 5E 87
Farnell. *Ang* 3F 145
Farnham. *Dors* 1E 15
Farnham. *Essx* 3E 53
Farnham. *N Yor* 3F 99
Farnham. *Suff* 4F 67
Farnham. *Surr* 2G 25
Farnham Common. *Buck* 2A 38
Farnham Green. *Essx* 3E 53
Farnham Royal. *Buck* 2A 38
Farnhill. *N Yor* 5C 98
Farningham. *Kent* 4G 39
Farnley. *N Yor* 5E 98
Farnley Tyas. *W Yor* 3B 92
Farnsfield. *Notts* 5D 86
Farnworth. *G Man* 4F 91
Farnworth. *Hal* 2H 83
Far Oakridge. *Glos* 5E 49
Far Orrest. *Cumb* 4F 103
Farr. *High* 2H 167
(nr. Bettyhill)
Farr. *High* 5A 158
(nr. Inverness)
Farr. *High* 3C 150
(nr. Kingussie)
Farraline. *High* 1H 149
Farringdon. *Devn* 3D 12
Farrington. *Dors* 1D 14
Farrington Gurney. *Bath* 1B 22
Far Sawrey. *Cumb* 5E 103
Farsley. *W Yor* 1C 92
Farthinghoe. *Nptn* 2D 50
Farthingstone. *Nptn* 5D 62
Farthorpe. *Linc* 3B 88
Fartown. *W Yor* 3B 92
Farway. *Devn* 3E 13
Fasag. *High* 3A 156
Fascadale. *High* 1G 139
Fasnacloich. *Arg* 4E 141
Fassfern. *High* 1E 141
Fatfield. *Tyne* 4G 115
Faugh. *Cumb* 4G 113
Fauld. *Staf* 3F 73
Fauldhouse. *W Lot* 3C 128
Faulkbourne. *Essx* 4A 54
Faulkland. *Som* 1C 22
Fauls. *Shrp* 2H 71
Faverdale. *Darl* 3F 105
Faversham. *Kent* 4E 40
Fawdington. *N Yor* 2G 99
Fawfieldhead. *Staf* 4E 85
Fawkham Green. *Kent* 4G 39
Fawler. *Oxon* 4B 50
Fawley. *Buck* 3F 37
Fawley. *Hants* 2C 16

Fawley—Ford

Fawley. W Ber 3B 36
Fawley Chapel. Here 3A 48
Fawton. Corn 2F 7
Faxfleet. E Yor 2B 94
Faygate. W Sus 2D 26
Fazakerley. Mers 1F 83
Fazeley. Staf 5F 73
Feabuie. High 4B 158
Feagour. High 4H 149
Fearann Dhomhnaill. High 3E 147
Fearby. N Yor 1D 98
Fearn. High 1C 158
Fearnan. Per 4E 142
Fearnbeg. High 3G 155
Fearnhead. Warr 1A 84
Fearnmore. High 2G 155
Featherstone. Staf 5D 72
Featherstone. W Yor 2E 93
Featherstone Castle. Nmbd 3H 113
Feckenham. Worc 4E 61
Feering. Essx 3B 54
Feetham. N Yor 5C 104
Feizor. N Yor 3G 97
Felbridge. Surr 2E 27
Felbrigg. Norf 2E 78
Felcourt. Surr 1E 27
Felden. Herts 5A 52
Felhampton. Shrp 2G 59
Felindre. Carm 3F 45
(nr. Llandeilo)
Felindre. Carm 2G 45
(nr. Llandovery)
Felindre. Carm 2D 44
(nr. Newcastle Emlyn)
Felindre. Powy 2D 58
Felindre. Swan 5G 45
Felindre Farchog. Pemb 1F 43
Felinfach. Cdgn 5E 57
Felinfach. Powy 2D 46
Felinfoel. Carm 5F 45
Felingwmisaf. Carm 3F 45
Felingwmuchaf. Carm 3F 45
Felin Newydd. Powy 5C 70
(nr. Newtown)
Felin Newydd. Powy 3E 70
(nr. Oswestry)
Felin Wnda. Cdgn 1D 44
Felinwynt. Cdgn 5B 56
Felixkirk. N Yor 1G 99
Felixstowe. Suff 2F 55
Felixstowe Ferry. Suff 2G 55
Felkington. Nmbd 5F 131
Fell End. Cumb 5A 104
Felling. Tyne 3F 115
Fell Side. Cumb 1E 102
Felmersham. Bed 5G 63
Felmingham. Norf 3E 79
Felpham. W Sus 3H 17
Felsham. Suff 5B 66
Felsted. Essx 3G 53
Feltham. G Lon 3C 38
Felthamhill. Surr 3B 38
Felthorpe. Norf 4D 78
Felton. Here 1A 48
Felton. N Som 5A 34
Felton. Nmbd 4F 121
Felton Butler. Shrp 4F 71
Feltwell. Norf 1G 65
Fenay Bridge. W Yor 3B 92
Fence. Lanc 1G 91
Fence Houses. Tyne 4G 115
Fencott. Oxon 4D 50
Fen Ditton. Cambs 4D 65
Fen Drayton. Cambs 4C 64
Fen End. Linc 3B 76
Fen End. W Mid 3G 61
Fenham. Nmbd 5G 131
Fenham. Tyne 3F 115
Fenhouses. Linc 1B 76
Feniscowles. Bkbn 2E 91
Feniton. Devn 3D 12
Fenn Green. Shrp 2B 60
Fenn's Bank. Wrex 2H 71
Fenn Street. Medw 3B 40
Fenny Bentley. Derbs 5F 85
Fenny Bridges. Devn 3E 12
Fenny Compton. Warw 5B 62
Fenny Drayton. Leics 1A 62
Fenny Stratford. Mil 2G 51
Fenrother. Nmbd 5F 121
Fenstanton. Cambs 4C 64
Fen Street. Norf 1C 66
Fenton. Cambs 3C 64
Fenton. Cumb 4G 113
Fenton. Linc 5F 87
(nr. Caythorpe)
Fenton. Linc 3F 87
(nr. Saxilby)
Fenton. Nmbd 1D 120
Fenton. Notts 2E 87
Fenton. Stoke 1C 72
Fentonadle. Corn 5A 10
Fenton Barns. E Lot 1B 130
Fenwick. E Ayr 5F 127
Fenwick. Nmbd 5G 131
(nr. Berwick-upon-Tweed)
Fenwick. Nmbd 2D 114
(nr. Hexham)
Fenwick. S Yor 3F 93
Feochaig. Arg 4B 122
Feock. Corn 5C 6
Feolin Ferry. Arg 3C 124
Feorlan. Arg 5A 122
Ferindonald. High 3E 147
Feriniquarrie. High 3A 154
Fern. Ang 2D 145
Ferndale. Rhon 2C 32
Ferndown. Dors 2F 15
Ferness. High 4D 158
Fernham. Oxon 2A 36
Fernhill. W Sus 1D 27
Fernhill Heath. Worc 5C 60
Fernhurst. W Sus 4G 25
Fernieflatt. Abers 1H 145
Ferniegair. S Lan 4A 128
Fernilea. High 5C 154
Fernilee. Derbs 3E 85
Ferrensby. N Yor 3F 99
Ferriby Sluice. N Lin 2C 94
Ferring. W Sus 5C 26
Ferrybridge. W Yor 2E 93
Ferryden. Ang 3G 145
Ferryhill. Aber 3G 153
Ferry Hill. Cambs 2C 64
Ferryhill. Dur 1F 105
Ferryhill Station. Dur 1F 105
Ferryside. Carm 4D 44
Ferryton. High 2A 158
Fersfield. Norf 2C 66
Fersit. High 1A 142
Feshiebridge. High 3C 150
Fetcham. Surr 5C 38
Fetterangus. Abers 3G 161
Fettercairn. Abers 1F 145
Fewcott. Oxon 3D 50
Fewston. N Yor 4D 98
Ffairfach. Carm 3G 45
Ffair Rhos. Cdgn 4G 57
Ffaldybrenin. Carm 1G 45
Ffarmers. Carm 1G 45
Ffawyddog. Powy 4F 47
Ffodun. Powy 5E 71
Ffont-y-gari. V Glam 5D 32
Fforest. Carm 5F 45
Fforest-fach. Swan 3F 31
Fforest Goch. Neat 5H 45
Ffostrasol. Cdgn 1D 44
Ffos-y-ffin. Cdgn 4D 56
Ffrith. Flin 5E 83
Ffrwdgrech. Powy 3D 46
Ffwl-y-mwn. V Glam 5D 32
Ffynnon-ddrain. Carm 3E 45
Ffynnongroyw. Flin 2D 82
Ffynnon Gynydd. Powy 1E 47
Ffynnonoer. Cdgn 5E 57
Fiag Lodge. High 1B 164
Fidden. Arg 2B 132
Fiddington. Glos 2E 49
Fiddington. Som 2F 21
Fiddleford. Dors 1D 14
Fiddlers Hamlet. Essx 5E 53
Field. Staf 2E 73
Field Assarts. Oxon 4B 50
Field Broughton. Cumb 1C 96
Field Dalling. Norf 2C 78
Fieldhead. Cumb 1F 103
Field Head. Leics 5B 74
Fifehead Magdalen. Dors 4C 22
Fifehead Neville. Dors 1C 14
Fifehead St Quintin. Dors 1C 14
Fife Keith. Mor 3B 160
Fifield. Oxon 4H 49
Fifield. Wilts 1G 23
Fifield. Wind 3A 38
Fifield Bavant. Wilts 4F 23
Figheldean. Wilts 2G 23
Filby. Norf 4G 79
Filey. N Yor 1F 101
Filford. Dors 3H 13
Filgrave. Mil 1G 51
Filkins. Oxon 5H 49
Filleigh. Devn 1H 11
(nr. Crediton)
Filleigh. Devn 4G 19
(nr. South Molton)
Fillingham. Linc 2G 87
Fillongley. Warw 2G 61
Filton. S Glo 4B 34
Fimber. E Yor 3C 100
Finavon. Ang 3D 145
Fincham. Norf 5F 77
Finchampstead. Wok 5F 37
Fincharn. Arg 3G 133
Finchdean. Hants 1F 17
Finchingfield. Essx 2G 53
Finchley. G Lon 1D 38
Findern. Derbs 2H 73
Findhorn. Mor 2E 159
Findhorn Bridge. High 1C 150
Findochty. Mor 2B 160
Findo Gask. Per 1C 136
Findon. Abers 4G 153
Findon. W Sus 5C 26
Findon Mains. High 2A 158
Findon Valley. W Sus 5C 26
Finedon. Nptn 3G 63
Fingal Street. Suff 3E 66
Fingest. Buck 2F 37
Finghall. N Yor 1D 98
Fingland. Cumb 4D 112
Fingland. Dum 3G 117
Finglesham. Kent 5H 41
Fingringhoe. Essx 3D 54
Finiskaig. High 4A 148
Finmere. Oxon 2E 51
Finnart. Per 3C 142
Finningham. Suff 4C 66
Finningley. S Yor 1D 86
Finnyguad. Abers 3D 160
Finsbury. G Lon 2E 39
Finstall. Worc 3D 61
Finsthwaite. Cumb 1C 96
Finstock. Oxon 4B 50
Finstown. Orkn 6C 172
Fintry. Abers 3E 161
Fintry. D'dee 5D 144
Fintry. Stir 1H 127
Finwood. Warw 4F 61
Finzean. Abers 4D 152
Fionnphort. Arg 2B 132
Fionnsabhagh. W Isl 9C 171
Firbeck. S Yor 2C 86
Firby. N Yor 1E 99
(nr. Bedale)
Firby. N Yor 3B 100
(nr. Malton)
Firgrove. G Man 3H 91
Firsdown. Wilts 3H 23
First Coast. High 4D 162
Firth. Shet 4F 173
Fir Tree. Dur 1E 105
Fishbourne. IOW 3D 16
Fishbourne. W Sus 2G 17
Fishburn. Dur 1A 106
Fishcross. Clac 4B 136
Fisherford. Abers 5D 160
Fisherrow. E Lot 2G 129
Fisher's Pond. Hants 4C 24
Fisher's Row. Lanc 5D 96
Fisherstreet. W Sus 2A 26
Fisherton. High 3B 158
Fisherton. S Ayr 3B 116
Fisherton de la Mere. Wilts 3E 23
Fishguard. Pemb 1D 42
Fishlake. S Yor 3G 93
Fishley. Norf 4G 79
Fishnish. Arg 4A 140
Fishpond Bottom. Dors 3G 13
Fishponds. Bris 4B 34
Fishpool. Glos 3B 48
Fishpool. G Man 4G 91
Fishpools. Powy 4D 58
Fishtoft. Linc 1C 76
Fishtoft Drove. Linc 1C 76
Fishwick. Bord 4F 131
Fiskavaig. High 5C 154
Fiskerton. Linc 3H 87
Fiskerton. Notts 5E 87
Fitling. E Yor 1F 95
Fittleton. Wilts 2G 23
Fittleworth. W Sus 4B 26
Fitton End. Cambs 4D 76
Fitz. Shrp 4G 71
Fitzhead. Som 4E 20
Fitzwilliam. W Yor 3E 93
Fiunary. High 4A 140
Five Ash Down. E Sus 3F 27
Five Ashes. E Sus 3G 27
Five Bells. Som 2D 20
Five Bridges. Here 1B 48
Fivehead. Som 4G 21
Five Lane Ends. Lanc 4E 97
Fivelanes. Corn 4C 10
Five Oak Green. Kent 1H 27
Five Oaks. W Sus 3B 26
Five Roads. Carm 5E 45
Five Ways. Warw 3G 61
Flack's Green. Essx 4A 54
Flackwell Heath. Buck 3G 37
Fladbury. Worc 1E 49
Fladdabister. Shet 8F 173
Flagg. Derbs 4F 85
Flamborough. E Yor 2G 101
Flamstead. Herts 4A 52
Flansham. W Sus 5A 26
Flasby. N Yor 4B 98
Flash. Staf 4E 85
Flashader. High 3C 154
Flatt, The. Cumb 2G 113
Flaunden. Herts 5A 52
Flawborough. Notts 1E 75
Flawith. N Yor 3G 99
Flax Bourton. N Som 5A 34
Flaxby. N Yor 4F 99
Flaxholme. Derbs 1H 73
Flaxley. Glos 4B 48
Flaxley Green. Staf 4E 73
Flaxpool. Som 3E 21
Flaxton. N Yor 3A 100
Fleckney. Leics 1D 62
Flecknoe. Warw 4C 62
Fledborough. Notts 3F 87
Fleet. Dors 4B 14
Fleet. Hants 1G 25
(nr. Farnborough)
Fleet. Hants 2F 17
(nr. South Hayling)
Fleet. Linc 3C 76
Fleet Hargate. Linc 3C 76
Fleetville. Herts 5B 52
Fleetwood. Lanc 5C 96
Fleggburgh. Norf 4G 79
Fleisirin. W Isl 4H 171
Flemingston. V Glam 4D 32
Flemington. S Lan 3H 127
(nr. Glasgow)
Flemington. S Lan 5A 128
(nr. Strathaven)
Flempton. Suff 4H 65
Fleoideabhagh. W Isl 9C 171
Fletcher's Green. Kent 1G 27
Fletchertown. Cumb 5D 112
Fletching. E Sus 3F 27
Fleuchary. High 4E 165
Flexbury. Corn 2C 10
Flexford. Surr 5A 38
Flimby. Cumb 1B 102
Flimwell. E Sus 2B 28
Flint. Flin 3E 83
Flintham. Notts 1E 75
Flint Mountain. Flin 3E 83
Flinton. E Yor 1F 95
Flintsham. Here 5F 59
Flishinghurst. Kent 2B 28
Flitcham. Norf 3G 77
Flitton. C Beds 2A 52
Flitwick. C Beds 2A 52
Flixborough. N Lin 3B 94
Flixton. G Man 1B 84
Flixton. N Yor 2E 101
Flixton. Suff 2F 67
Flockton. W Yor 3C 92
Flodden. Nmbd 1D 120
Flodigarry. High 1D 154
Flood's Ferry. Cambs 1C 64
Flookburgh. Cumb 2C 96
Flordon. Norf 1D 66
Flore. Nptn 4D 62
Flotterton. Nmbd 4E 121
Flowton. Suff 1D 54
Flushing. Abers 4H 161
Flushing. Corn 5C 6
Fluxton. Devn 3D 12
Flyford Flavell. Worc 5D 61
Fobbing. Thur 2B 40
Fochabers. Mor 3H 159
Fochriw. Cphy 5E 46
Fockerby. N Lin 3B 94
Fodderty. High 3H 157
Foddington. Som 4A 22
Foel. Powy 4B 70
Foffarty. Ang 4D 144
Foggathorpe. E Yor 1A 94
Fogo. Bord 5D 130
Fogorig. Bord 5D 130
Foindle. High 4B 166
Folda. Ang 2A 144
Fole. Staf 2E 73
Foleshill. W Mid 2A 62
Foley Park. Worc 3C 60
Folke. Dors 1B 14
Folkestone. Kent 2G 29
Folkingham. Linc 2H 75
Folkington. E Sus 5G 27
Folksworth. Cambs 1A 64
Folkton. N Yor 2E 101
Folla Rule. Abers 5E 161
Follifoot. N Yor 4F 99
Folly Cross. Devn 2E 11
Folly Gate. Devn 3F 11
Folly, The. Herts 4B 52
Folly, The. W Ber 5C 36
Fonmon. V Glam 5D 32
Fonthill Bishop. Wilts 3E 23
Fonthill Gifford. Wilts 3E 23
Fontmell Magna. Dors 1D 14
Fontwell. W Sus 5A 26
Font-y-gary. V Glam 5D 32
Foodieash. Fife 2F 137
Foolow. Derbs 3F 85
Footdee. Aber 3G 153
Footherley. Staf 5F 73
Foots Cray. G Lon 3F 39
Forbestown. Abers 2A 152
Force Forge. Cumb 5E 103
Force Mills. Cumb 5E 103
Forcett. N Yor 3E 105
Ford. Arg 3F 133

Gairletter—Glen Bernisdale

Gairletter. *Arg* 1C **126**
Gairloch. *Abers* 3E **153**
Gairloch. *High* 1H **155**
Gairlochy. *High* 5D **148**
Gairney Bank. *Per* 4D **136**
Gairnshiel Lodge. *Abers* 3G **151**
Gaisgill. *Cumb* 4H **103**
Gaitsgill. *Cumb* 5E **113**
Galashiels. *Bord* 1G **119**
Galgate. *Lanc* 4D **97**
Galhampton. *Som* 4B **22**
Gallatown. *Fife* 4E **137**
Galley Common. *Warw* 1H **61**
Galleyend. *Essx* 5H **53**
Galleywood. *Essx* 5H **53**
Gallin. *Per* 4C **142**
Gallowfauld. *Ang* 4D **144**
Gallowhill. *E Dun* 2H **127**
Gallowhill. *Per* 5A **144**
Gallowhill. *Ren* 3F **127**
Gallowhills. *Abers* 3H **161**
Gallows Green. *Staf* 1E **73**
Gallows Green. *Worc* 4D **60**
Gallowstree Common. *Oxon* 3E **37**
Galltair. *High* 1G **147**
Gallt Melyd. *Den* 2C **82**
Galmington. *Som* 4F **21**
Galmisdale. *High* 5C **146**
Galmpton. *Devn* 4C **8**
Galmpton. *Torb* 3E **9**
Galmpton Warborough. *Torb* 3E **9**
Galphay. *N Yor* 2E **99**
Galston. *E Ayr* 1D **117**
Galton. *Dors* 4C **14**
Galtrigill. *High* 3A **154**
Gamblesby. *Cumb* 1H **103**
Gamelsby. *Cumb* 4D **112**
Gamesley. *Derbs* 1E **85**
Gamlingay. *Cambs* 5B **64**
Gamlingay Cinques. *Cambs* 5B **64**
Gamlingay Great Heath. *C Beds* 5B **64**
Gammaton. *Devn* 4E **19**
Gammersgill. *N Yor* 1C **98**
Gamston. *Notts* 2D **74** (nr. Nottingham)
Gamston. *Notts* 3E **86** (nr. Retford)
Ganarew. *Here* 4A **48**
Ganavan. *Arg* 5C **140**
Ganborough. *Glos* 3G **49**
Gang. *Corn* 2H **7**
Ganllwyd. *Gwyn* 3G **69**
Gannochy. *Ang* 1E **145**
Gannochy. *Per* 1D **136**
Gansclet. *High* 4F **169**
Ganstead. *E Yor* 1E **95**
Ganthorpe. *N Yor* 2A **100**
Ganton. *N Yor* 2D **101**
Gants Hill. *G Lon* 2F **39**
Gappah. *Devn* 5B **12**
Garafad. *High* 2D **155**
Garboldisham. *Norf* 2C **66**
Garden City. *Flin* 4F **83**
Gardeners Green. *Wok* 5G **37**
Gardenstown. *Abers* 2F **161**
Garden Village. *S Yor* 1G **85**
Garden Village. *Swan* 3E **31**
Garderhouse. *Shet* 7E **173**
Gardham. *E Yor* 5D **100**
Gare Hill. *Som* 2C **22**
Garelochhead. *Arg* 4B **134**
Garford. *Oxon* 2C **36**
Garforth. *W Yor* 1E **93**
Gargrave. *N Yor* 4B **98**
Gargunnock. *Stir* 4G **135**
Garleffin. *S Ayr* 1F **109**
Garlieston. *Dum* 5B **110**
Garlinge Green. *Kent* 5F **41**
Garlogie. *Abers* 3E **153**
Garmelow. *Staf* 3B **72**
Garmond. *Abers* 3F **161**
Garmondsway. *Dur* 1A **106**
Garmony. *Arg* 4A **140**
Garmouth. *Mor* 2H **159**
Garmston. *Shrp* 5A **72**
Garnant. *Carm* 4G **45**
Garndiffaith. *Torf* 5F **47**
Garndolbenmaen. *Gwyn* 1D **69**
Garnett Bridge. *Cumb* 5G **103**
Garnfadryn. *Gwyn* 2B **68**
Garnkirk. *N Lan* 3H **127**
Garnlydan. *Blae* 4E **47**
Garnsgate. *Linc* 3D **76**
Garnswllt. *Swan* 5G **45**
Garn-yr-erw. *Torf* 4F **47**
Garrabost. *W Isl* 4H **171**
Garrallan. *E Ayr* 3E **117**
Garras. *Corn* 4E **5**
Garreg. *Gwyn* 1F **69**
Garrigill. *Cumb* 5A **114**
Garriston. *N Yor* 5E **105**
Garrogie Lodge. *High* 2H **149**
Garros. *High* 2D **155**
Garrow. *Per* 4F **143**
Garsdale. *Cumb* 1G **97**
Garsdale Head. *Cumb* 5A **104**
Garsdon. *Wilts* 3E **35**
Garshall Green. *Staf* 2D **72**
Garsington. *Oxon* 5D **50**
Garstang. *Lanc* 5D **97**
Garston. *Mers* 2G **83**
Garswood. *Mers* 1H **83**
Gartcosh. *N Lan* 3H **127**
Garth. *B'end* 2B **32**
Garth. *Cdgn* 2F **57**
Garth. *Gwyn* 2E **69**
Garth. *IOM* 4C **108**
Garth. *Powy* 1C **46** (nr. Builth Wells)
Garth. *Powy* 3E **59** (nr. Knighton)
Garth. *Wrex* 1E **71**
Garthamlock. *Glas* 3H **127**
Garthbrengy. *Powy* 2D **46**
Gartheli. *Cdgn* 5E **57**
Garthmyl. *Powy* 1D **58**
Garthorpe. *Leics* 3F **75**
Garthorpe. *N Lin* 3B **94**
Garth Owen. *Powy* 1D **58**
Garth Row. *Cumb* 5G **103**
Gartly. *Abers* 5C **160**
Gartmore. *Stir* 4E **135**
Gartness. *N Lan* 3A **128**
Gartness. *Stir* 1G **127**
Gartocharn. *W Dun* 1F **127**
Garton. *E Yor* 1F **95**
Garton-on-the-Wolds. *E Yor* 4D **101**
Gartsherrie. *N Lan* 3A **128**
Gartymore. *High* 2H **165**
Garvald. *E Lot* 2B **130**
Garvamore. *High* 4H **149**
Garvard. *Arg* 4A **132**
Garvault. *High* 5H **167**
Garve. *High* 2F **157**
Garvestone. *Norf* 5C **78**
Garvie. *Arg* 4H **133**
Garvock. *Abers* 1G **145**
Garvock. *Inv* 2D **126**
Garway. *Here* 3H **47**
Garway Common. *Here* 3H **47**
Garway Hill. *Here* 3H **47**
Garwick. *Linc* 1A **76**
Gaskan. *High* 1C **140**
Gasper. *Wilts* 3C **22**
Gastard. *Wilts* 5D **35**
Gasthorpe. *Norf* 2B **66**
Gatcombe. *IOW* 4C **16**
Gateacre. *Mers* 2G **83**
Gatebeck. *Cumb* 1E **97**
Gate Burton. *Linc* 2F **87**
Gateforth. *N Yor* 2F **93**
Gatehead. *E Ayr* 1C **116**
Gate Helmsley. *N Yor* 4A **100**
Gatehouse. *Nmbd* 1A **114**
Gatehouse of Fleet. *Dum* 4D **110**
Gatelawbridge. *Dum* 5B **118**
Gateley. *Norf* 3B **78**
Gatenby. *N Yor* 1F **99**
Gatesgarth. *Cumb* 3C **102**
Gateshead. *Tyne* 3F **115**
Gatesheath. *Ches W* 4G **83**
Gateside. *Ang* 4D **144** (nr. Forfar)
Gateside. *Ang* 4C **144** (nr. Kirriemuir)
Gateside. *Fife* 3D **136**
Gateside. *N Ayr* 4E **127**
Gathurst. *G Man* 4D **90**
Gatley. *G Man* 2C **84**
Gatton. *Surr* 5D **39**
Gattonside. *Bord* 1H **119**
Gatwick (London) Airport. *W Sus* 1D **27**
Gaufron. *Powy* 4B **58**
Gaulby. *Leics* 5D **74**
Gauldry. *Fife* 1F **137**
Gaultree. *Norf* 5D **77**
Gaunt's Common. *Dors* 2F **15**
Gaunt's Earthcott. *S Glo* 3B **34**
Gautby. *Linc* 3A **88**
Gavinton. *Bord* 4D **130**
Gawber. *S Yor* 4D **92**
Gawcott. *Buck* 2E **51**
Gawsworth. *Ches E* 4C **84**
Gawthorpe. *W Yor* 2C **92**
Gawthrop. *Cumb* 1F **97**
Gawthwaite. *Cumb* 1B **96**
Gay Bowers. *Essx* 5A **54**
Gaydon. *Warw* 5A **62**
Gayhurst. *Mil* 1G **51**
Gayle. *N Yor* 1A **98**
Gayles. *N Yor* 4E **105**
Gay Street. *W Sus* 3B **26**
Gayton. *Mers* 2E **83**
Gayton. *Norf* 4G **77**
Gayton. *Nptn* 5E **62**
Gayton. *Staf* 3D **73**
Gayton le Marsh. *Linc* 2D **88**
Gayton le Wold. *Linc* 2B **88**
Gayton Thorpe. *Norf* 4G **77**
Gaywood. *Norf* 3F **77**
Gazeley. *Suff* 4G **65**
Geanies. *High* 1C **158**
Gearraidh Bhailteas. *W Isl* 6C **170**
Gearraidh Bhaird. *W Isl* 6F **171**
Gearraidh ma Monadh. *W Isl* 7C **170**
Geary. *High* 2B **154**
Geddes. *High* 3C **158**
Gedding. *Suff* 5B **66**
Geddington. *Nptn* 2F **63**
Gedintailor. *High* 5E **155**
Gedling. *Notts* 1D **74**
Gedney. *Linc* 3D **76**
Gedney Broadgate. *Linc* 3D **76**
Gedney Drove End. *Linc* 3D **76**
Gedney Dyke. *Linc* 3D **76**
Gedney Hill. *Linc* 4C **76**
Gee Cross. *G Man* 1D **84**
Geeston. *Rut* 5G **75**
Geilston. *Arg* 2E **127**
Geirinis. *W Isl* 4C **170**
Geise. *High* 2D **168**
Geisiadar. *W Isl* 4D **171**
Gelder Shiel. *Abers* 5G **151**
Geldeston. *Norf* 1F **67**
Gell. *Cnwy* 4A **82**
Gelli. *Pemb* 3E **43**
Gelli. *Rhon* 2C **32**
Gellifor. *Den* 4D **82**
Gelligaer. *Cphy* 2E **33**
Gellilydan. *Gwyn* 2F **69**
Gellinudd. *Neat* 5H **45**
Gellyburn. *Per* 5H **143**
Gellywen. *Carm* 2G **43**
Gelston. *Dum* 4E **111**
Gelston. *Linc* 1G **75**
Gembling. *E Yor* 4F **101**
Geneva. *Cdgn* 5D **56**
Gentleshaw. *Staf* 4E **73**
Geocrab. *W Isl* 8D **171**
George Green. *Buck* 2A **38**
Georgeham. *Devn* 3E **19**
George Nympton. *Devn* 4H **19**
Georgetown. *Blae* 5E **47**
Georgetown. *Ren* 3F **127**
Georth. *Orkn* 5C **172**
Gerlan. *Gwyn* 4F **81**
Germansweek. *Devn* 3E **11**
Germoe. *Corn* 4C **4**
Gerrans. *Corn* 5C **6**
Gerrard's Bromley. *Staf* 2B **72**
Gerrards Cross. *Buck* 2A **38**
Gerston. *High* 3D **168**
Gestingthorpe. *Essx* 2B **54**
Gethsemane. *Pemb* 1A **44**
Geuffordd. *Powy* 4E **70**
Gibraltar. *Buck* 4F **51**
Gibraltar. *Linc* 5E **89**
Gibraltar. *Suff* 5D **66**
Gibsmere. *Notts* 1E **74**
Giddeahall. *Wilts* 4D **34**
Gidea Park. *G Lon* 2G **39**
Gidleigh. *Devn* 4G **11**
Giffnock. *E Ren* 4G **127**
Gifford. *E Lot* 3B **130**
Giffordtown. *Fife* 2E **137**
Giggetty. *Staf* 1C **60**
Giggleswick. *N Yor* 3H **97**
Gignog. *Pemb* 2C **42**
Gilberdyke. *E Yor* 2B **94**
Gilbert's End. *Worc* 1D **48**
Gilbert's Green. *Warw* 3F **61**
Gilchriston. *E Lot* 3A **130**
Gilcrux. *Cumb* 1C **102**
Gildersome. *W Yor* 2C **92**
Gildingwells. *S Yor* 2C **86**
Gilesgate Moor. *Dur* 5F **115**
Gileston. *V Glam* 5D **32**
Gilfach. *Cphy* 2E **33**
Gilfach Goch. *Rhon* 3C **32**
Gilfachreda. *Cdgn* 5D **56**
Gillamoor. *N Yor* 5D **107**
Gillan. *Corn* 4E **5**
Gillar's Green. *Mers* 1G **83**
Gillen. *High* 3B **154**
Gilling East. *N Yor* 2A **100**
Gillingham. *Dors* 4D **22**
Gillingham. *Medw* 4B **40**
Gillingham. *Norf* 1G **67**
Gilling West. *N Yor* 4E **105**
Gillock. *High* 3E **169**
Gillow Heath. *Staf* 5C **84**
Gills. *High* 1F **169**
Gill's Green. *Kent* 2B **28**
Gilmanscleuch. *Bord* 2F **119**
Gilmerton. *Edin* 3F **129**
Gilmerton. *Per* 1A **136**
Gilmonby. *Dur* 3C **104**
Gilmorton. *Leics* 2C **62**
Gilsland. *Nmbd* 3H **113**
Gilsland Spa. *Cumb* 3H **113**
Gilston. *Midl* 4H **129**
Giltbrook. *Notts* 1B **74**
Gilwern. *Mon* 4F **47**
Gimingham. *Norf* 2E **79**
Giosla. *W Isl* 5D **171**
Gipping. *Suff* 4C **66**
Gipsey Bridge. *Linc* 1B **76**
Gipton. *W Yor* 1D **92**
Girdle Toll. *N Ayr* 5E **127**
Girlsta. *Shet* 6F **173**
Girsby. *N Yor* 4A **106**
Girthon. *Dum* 4D **110**
Girton. *Cambs* 4D **64**
Girton. *Notts* 4F **87**
Girvan. *S Ayr* 5A **116**
Gisburn. *Lanc* 5H **97**
Gisleham. *Suff* 2H **67**
Gislingham. *Suff* 3C **66**
Gissing. *Norf* 2D **66**
Gittisham. *Devn* 3E **13**
Gladestry. *Powy* 5E **59**
Gladsmuir. *E Lot* 2A **130**
Glaichbea. *High* 5H **157**
Glais. *Swan* 5H **45**
Glaisdale. *N Yor* 4E **107**
Glame. *High* 4E **155**
Glamis. *Ang* 4C **144**
Glamisdale. *High* 5C **146**
Glanaman. *Carm* 4G **45**
Glan-Conwy. *Cnwy* 5H **81**
Glandford. *Norf* 1C **78**
Glan Duar. *Carm* 1F **45**
Glandwr. *Blae* 5F **47**
Glandwr. *Pemb* 2F **43**
Glan-Dwyfach. *Gwyn* 1D **69**
Glandy Cross. *Carm* 2F **43**
Glandyfi. *Cdgn* 1F **57**
Glangrwyney. *Powy* 4F **47**
Glanmule. *Powy* 1D **58**
Glanrhyd. *Gwyn* 2B **68**
Glanrhyd. *Pemb* 1B **44** (nr. Cardigan)
Glan-rhyd. *Pemb* 1F **43** (nr. Crymych)
Glan-rhyd. *Powy* 5A **46**
Glanton. *Nmbd* 3E **121**
Glanton Pyke. *Nmbd* 3E **121**
Glanvilles Wootton. *Dors* 2B **14**
Glan-y-don. *Flin* 3D **82**
Glan-y-nant. *Powy* 2B **58**
Glan-yr-afon. *Gwyn* 1C **70**
Glan-yr-afon. *IOA* 2F **81**
Glan-yr-afon. *Powy* 5C **70**
Glan-y-wern. *Gwyn* 2F **69**
Glapthorn. *Nptn* 1H **63**
Glapwell. *Derbs* 4B **86**
Glas Aird. *Arg* 4A **132**
Glas-allt Shiel. *Abers* 5G **151**
Glasbury. *Powy* 2E **47**
Glaschoil. *Mor* 5E **159**
Glascoed. *Den* 3B **82**
Glascoed. *Mon* 5G **47**
Glascote. *Staf* 5G **73**
Glascwm. *Powy* 5D **58**
Glasfryn. *Cnwy* 5B **82**
Glasgow. *Glas* 3G **127**
Glasgow Airport. *Ren* 3F **127**
Glasgow Prestwick International Airport. *S Ayr* 2C **116**
Glashvin. *High* 2D **154**
Glasinfryn. *Gwyn* 4E **81**
Glas na Cardaich. *High* 4E **147**
Glasnacardoch. *High* 4E **147**
Glasnakille. *High* 2D **146**
Glaspwll. *Cdgn* 1G **57**
Glassburn. *High* 5F **157**
Glassenbury. *Kent* 2B **28**
Glasserton. *Dum* 5B **110**
Glassford. *S Lan* 5A **128**
Glassgreen. *Mor* 2G **159**
Glasshouse. *Glos* 3C **48**
Glasshouses. *N Yor* 3D **98**
Glasson. *Cumb* 3D **112**
Glasson. *Lanc* 4D **96**
Glassonby. *Cumb* 1G **103**
Glasterlaw. *Ang* 3E **145**
Glaston. *Rut* 5F **75**
Glastonbury. *Som* 3H **21**
Glatton. *Cambs* 2A **64**
Glazebrook. *Warr* 1A **84**
Glazebury. *Warr* 1A **84**
Glazeley. *Shrp* 2B **60**
Gleadless. *S Yor* 2A **86**
Gleadsmoss. *Ches E* 4C **84**
Gleann Dail bho Dheas. *W Isl* 7C **170**
Gleann Tholastaidh. *W Isl* 3H **171**
Gleann Uige. *High* 1A **140**
Gleaston. *Cumb* 2B **96**
Glecknabae. *Arg* 3B **126**
Gledrid. *Shrp* 2E **71**
Gleiniant. *Powy* 1B **58**
Glemsford. *Suff* 1B **54**
Glen. *Dum* 4C **110**
Glenancross. *High* 4E **147**
Glen Audlyn. *IOM* 2D **108**
Glenbarr. *Arg* 2A **122**
Glenbeg. *High* 2G **139**
Glen Bernisdale. *High* 4D **154**

Glenbervie—Great Bardfield

Glenbervie. *Abers* 5E **153**
Glenboig. *N Lan* 3A **128**
Glenborrodale. *High* 2A **140**
Glenbranter. *Arg* 4A **134**
Glenbreck. *Bord* 2C **118**
Glenbrein Lodge. *High* 2G **149**
Glenbrittle. *High* 1C **146**
Glenbuchat Lodge. *Abers* 2H **151**
Glenbuck. *E Ayr* 2G **117**
Glenburn. *Ren* 3F **127**
Glencalvie Lodge. *High* 5B **164**
Glencaple. *Dum* 3A **112**
Glencarron Lodge. *High* 3C **156**
Glencarse. *Per* 1D **136**
Glencassley Castle. *High* 3B **164**
Glencat. *Abers* 4C **152**
Glencoe. *High* 3F **141**
Glen Cottage. *High* 5E **147**
Glencraig. *Fife* 4D **136**
Glendale. *High* 4A **154**
Glendevon. *Per* 3B **136**
Glendoebeg. *High* 3G **149**
Glendoick. *Per* 1E **136**
Glendoune. *S Ayr* 5A **116**
Glenduckie. *Fife* 2E **137**
Gleneagles. *Per* 3B **136**
Glenegedale. *Arg* 4B **124**
Glenegedale Lots. *Arg* 4B **124**
Glenelg. *High* 2G **147**
Glenernie. *Mor* 4E **159**
Glenesslin. *Dum* 1F **111**
Glenfarg. *Per* 2D **136**
Glenfarquhar Lodge. *Abers* 5E **152**
Glenferness Mains. *High* 4D **158**
Glenfeshie Lodge. *High* 4C **150**
Glenfiddich Lodge. *Mor* 5H **159**
Glenfield. *Leics* 5C **74**
Glenfinnan. *High* 5B **148**
Glenfintaig Lodge. *High* 5E **149**
Glenfoot. *Per* 2D **136**
Glenfyne Lodge. *Arg* 2B **134**
Glengap. *Dum* 4D **110**
Glengarnock. *N Ayr* 4E **126**
Glengolly. *High* 2D **168**
Glengorm Castle. *Arg* 3F **139**
Glengrasco. *High* 4D **154**
Glenhead Farm. *Ang* 2B **144**
Glenholm. *Bord* 1D **118**
Glen House. *Bord* 1E **119**
Glenhurich. *High* 2C **140**
Glenkerry. *Bord* 3E **119**
Glenkiln. *Dum* 2F **111**
Glenkindle. *Abers* 2B **152**
Glenkinglass Lodge. *Arg* 5F **141**
Glenkirk. *Bord* 2C **118**
Glenlean. *Arg* 1B **126**
Glenlee. *Dum* 1D **110**
Glenleraig. *High* 5B **166**
Glenlichorn. *Per* 2G **135**
Glenlivet. *Mor* 1F **151**
Glenlochar. *Dum* 3E **111**
Glenlochsie Lodge. *Per* 1H **143**
Glenluce. *Dum* 4G **109**
Glenmarskie. *High* 3F **157**
Glenmassan. *Arg* 1C **126**
Glenmavis. *N Lan* 3A **128**
Glen Maye. *IOM* 4B **108**
Glenmazeran Lodge. *High* 1B **150**
Glenmidge. *Dum* 1F **111**
Glen Mona. *IOM* 3D **108**
Glenmore. *High* 2G **139** (nr. Glenborrodale)
Glenmore. *High* 3D **151** (nr. Kingussie)
Glenmore. *High* 4D **154** (on Isle of Skye)
Glenmoy. *Ang* 2D **144**
Glennoe. *Arg* 5E **141**
Glen of Coachford. *Abers* 4B **160**
Glenogil. *Ang* 2D **144**
Glen Parva. *Leics* 1C **62**
Glenprosen Village. *Ang* 2C **144**
Glenree. *N Ayr* 3D **122**
Glenridding. *Cumb* 3E **103**
Glenrosa. *N Ayr* 2E **123**
Glenrothes. *Fife* 3E **137**
Glensanda. *High* 4C **140**
Glensaugh. *Abers* 1F **145**
Glenshero Lodge. *High* 4H **149**
Glensluain. *Arg* 4H **133**
Glenstockadale. *Dum* 3F **109**
Glenstriven. *Arg* 2B **126**
Glen Tanar House. *Abers* 4B **152**
Glentham. *Linc* 1H **87**
Glenton. *Abers* 1D **152**
Glentress. *Bord* 1E **119**
Glentromie Lodge. *High* 4B **150**
Glentrool Lodge. *Dum* 1B **110**
Glentrool Village. *Dum* 2A **110**
Glentruim House. *High* 4A **150**
Glentworth. *Linc* 2G **87**
Glenuig. *High* 1A **140**
Glen Village. *Falk* 2B **128**
Glen Vine. *IOM* 4C **108**
Glenwhilly. *Dum* 2G **109**
Glenzierfoot. *Dum* 2E **113**
Glespin. *S Lan* 2H **117**
Gletness. *Shet* 6F **173**
Glewstone. *Here* 3A **48**
Glib Cheois. *W Isl* 5F **171**
Glinton. *Pet* 5A **76**
Glooston. *Leics* 1E **63**
Glossop. *Derbs* 1E **85**
Gloster Hill. *Nmbd* 4G **121**
Gloucester. *Glos* 4D **48**
Gloucestershire Airport. *Glos* 3D **49**
Gloup. *Shet* 1G **173**
Glusburn. *N Yor* 5C **98**
Glutt Lodge. *High* 5B **168**
Glutton Bridge. *Staf* 4E **85**
Gluvian. *Corn* 2D **6**
Glympton. *Oxon* 3C **50**
Glyn. *Cnwy* 3A **82**
Glynarthen. *Cdgn* 1D **44**
Glynbrochan. *Powy* 2B **58**
Glyn Ceiriog. *Wrex* 2E **70**
Glyncoch. *Rhon* 2D **32**
Glyncorrwg. *Neat* 2B **32**
Glynde. *E Sus* 5F **27**
Glyndebourne. *E Sus* 4F **27**
Glyndyfrdwy. *Den* 1D **70**
Glyn Ebwy. *Blae* 5E **47**
Glynllan. *B'end* 3C **32**
Glyn-neath. *Neat* 5B **46**
Glynogwr. *B'end* 3C **32**
Glyntaff. *Rhon* 3D **32**
Glyntawe. *Powy* 4B **46**
Glynteg. *Carm* 2D **44**
Gnosall. *Staf* 3C **72**
Gnosall Heath. *Staf* 3C **72**
Goadby. *Leics* 1E **63**
Goadby Marwood. *Leics* 3E **75**
Goatacre. *Wilts* 4F **35**
Goathill. *Dors* 1B **14**
Goathland. *N Yor* 4F **107**
Goathurst. *Som* 3F **21**
Goathurst Common. *Kent* 5F **39**
Goat Lees. *Kent* 1E **28**
Gobernuisgach Lodge. *High* 4E **167**
Gobernuisgeach. *High* 5B **168**
Gobhaig. *W Isl* 7C **171**
Gobowen. *Shrp* 2F **71**
Godalming. *Surr* 1A **26**
Goddard's Corner. *Suff* 4E **67**
Goddard's Green. *Kent* 2C **28** (nr. Benenden)
Goddard's Green. *Kent* 2B **28** (nr. Cranbrook)
Goddards Green. *W Sus* 3D **27**
Godford Cross. *Devn* 2E **13**
Godleybrook. *Staf* 1D **73**
Godmanchester. *Cambs* 3B **64**
Godmanstone. *Dors* 3B **14**
Godmersham. *Kent* 5E **41**
Godolphin Cross. *Corn* 3D **4**
Godre'r-graig. *Neat* 5A **46**
Godshill. *Hants* 1G **15**
Godshill. *IOW* 4D **16**
Godstone. *Staf* 2E **73**
Godstone. *Surr* 5E **39**
Goetre. *Mon* 5G **47**
Goff's Oak. *Herts* 5D **52**
Gogar. *Edin* 2E **129**
Goginan. *Cdgn* 2F **57**
Golan. *Gwyn* 1E **69**
Golant. *Corn* 3F **7**
Golberdon. *Corn* 5D **10**
Golborne. *G Man* 1A **84**
Golcar. *W Yor* 3A **92**
Goldcliff. *Newp* 3G **33**
Golden Cross. *E Sus* 4G **27**
Golden Green. *Kent* 1H **27**
Golden Grove. *Carm* 4F **45**
Golden Grove. *N Yor* 4F **107**
Golden Hill. *Pemb* 2D **43**
Goldenhill. *Stoke* 5C **84**
Golden Pot. *Hants* 2F **25**
Golden Valley. *Glos* 3E **49**
Golders Green. *G Lon* 2D **38**
Goldhanger. *Essx* 5C **54**
Gold Hill. *Norf* 1E **65**
Golding. *Shrp* 5H **71**
Goldington. *Bed* 5H **63**
Goldsborough. *N Yor* 4F **99** (nr. Harrogate)
Goldsborough. *N Yor* 3F **107** (nr. Whitby)
Goldsithney. *Corn* 3C **4**
Goldstone. *Kent* 4G **41**
Goldstone. *Shrp* 3B **72**
Goldthorpe. *S Yor* 4E **93**
Goldworthy. *Devn* 4D **19**
Golfa. *Powy* 3D **70**
Gollanfield. *High* 3C **158**
Gollinglith Foot. *N Yor* 1D **98**
Golsoncott. *Som* 3D **20**
Golspie. *High* 4F **165**
Gomeldon. *Wilts* 3G **23**
Gomersal. *W Yor* 2C **92**
Gometra House. *Arg* 4E **139**
Gomshall. *Surr* 1B **26**
Gonalston. *Notts* 1D **74**
Gonerby Hill Foot. *Linc* 2G **75**
Gonnabarn. *Corn* 3D **6**
Good Easter. *Essx* 4G **53**
Gooderstone. *Norf* 5G **77**
Goodleigh. *Devn* 3G **19**
Goodmanham. *E Yor* 5C **100**
Goodmayes. *G Lon* 2F **39**
Goodnestone. *Kent* 5G **41** (nr. Aylesham)
Goodnestone. *Kent* 4E **41** (nr. Faversham)
Goodrich. *Here* 4A **48**
Goodrington. *Torb* 3E **9**
Goodshaw. *Lanc* 2G **91**
Goodshaw Fold. *Lanc* 2G **91**
Goodstone. *Devn* 5A **12**
Goodwick. *Pemb* 1D **42**
Goodworth Clatford. *Hants* 2B **24**
Goole. *E Yor* 2H **93**
Goom's Hill. *Worc* 5E **61**
Goonbell. *Corn* 4B **6**
Goonhavern. *Corn* 3B **6**
Goonvrea. *Corn* 4B **6**
Goose Green. *Cumb* 1E **97**
Goose Green. *S Glo* 3C **34**
Gooseham. *Corn* 1C **10**
Goosewell. *Plym* 3B **8**
Goosey. *Oxon* 2B **36**
Goosnargh. *Lanc* 1D **90**
Goostrey. *Ches E* 3B **84**
Gorcott Hill. *Warw* 4E **61**
Gordon. *Bord* 5C **130**
Gordonbush. *High* 3F **165**
Gordonstown. *Abers* 3C **160** (nr. Cornhill)
Gordonstown. *Abers* 5E **160** (nr. Fyvie)
Gorebridge. *Midl* 3G **129**
Gorefield. *Cambs* 4D **76**
Gores. *Wilts* 1G **23**
Gorgie. *Edin* 2F **129**
Goring. *Oxon* 3E **36**
Goring-by-Sea. *W Sus* 5C **26**
Goring Heath. *Oxon* 4E **37**
Gorleston-on-Sea. *Norf* 5H **79**
Gornalwood. *W Mid* 1D **60**
Gorran Churchtown. *Corn* 4D **6**
Gorran Haven. *Corn* 4E **6**
Gorran High Lanes. *Corn* 4D **6**
Gors. *Cdgn* 3F **57**
Gorsedd. *Flin* 3D **82**
Gorseinon. *Swan* 3E **31**
Gorseness. *Orkn* 6D **172**
Gorseybank. *Derbs* 5G **85**
Gorsgoch. *Cdgn* 5D **57**
Gorslas. *Carm* 4F **45**
Gorsley. *Glos* 3B **48**
Gorsley Common. *Here* 3B **48**
Gorstan. *High* 2F **157**
Gorstella. *Ches W* 4F **83**
Gorsty Common. *Here* 2H **47**
Gorsty Hill. *Staf* 3E **73**
Gortantaoid. *Arg* 2B **124**
Gorteneorn. *High* 2A **140**
Gortenfern. *High* 2A **140**
Gorton. *G Man* 1C **84**
Gosbeck. *Suff* 5D **66**
Gosberton. *Linc* 2B **76**
Gosberton Clough. *Linc* 3A **76**
Goseley Dale. *Derbs* 3H **73**
Gosfield. *Essx* 3A **54**
Gosford. *Oxon* 4D **50**
Gosforth. *Cumb* 4B **102**
Gosforth. *Tyne* 3F **115**
Gosmore. *Herts* 3B **52**
Gospel End Village. *Staf* 1C **60**
Gosport. *Hants* 2E **16**
Gossabrough. *Shet* 3G **173**
Gossington. *Glos* 5C **48**
Gossops Green. *W Sus* 2D **26**
Goswick. *Nmbd* 5G **131**
Gotham. *Notts* 2C **74**
Gotherington. *Glos* 3E **49**
Gott. *Arg* 4B **138**
Goudhurst. *Kent* 2B **28**
Goulceby. *Linc* 3B **88**
Gourdon. *Abers* 1H **145**
Gourock. *Inv* 2D **126**
Govan. *Glas* 3G **127**
Govanhill. *Glas* 3G **127**
Goverton. *Notts* 1E **74**
Goveton. *Devn* 4D **8**
Govilon. *Mon* 4F **47**
Gowanhill. *Abers* 2H **161**
Gowdall. *E Yor* 2G **93**
Gowerton. *Swan* 3E **31**
Gowkhall. *Fife* 1D **128**
Gowthorpe. *E Yor* 4B **100**
Goxhill. *E Yor* 5F **101**
Goxhill. *N Lin* 2E **94**
Goxhill Haven. *N Lin* 2E **94**
Goytre. *Neat* 3A **32**
Grabhair. *W Isl* 6F **171**
Graby. *Linc* 3H **75**
Graffham. *W Sus* 4A **26**
Grafham. *Cambs* 4A **64**
Grafham. *Surr* 1B **26**
Grafton. *Here* 2H **47**
Grafton. *N Yor* 3G **99**
Grafton. *Oxon* 5A **50**
Grafton. *Shrp* 4G **71**
Grafton. *Worc* 2E **49** (nr. Evesham)
Grafton. *Worc* 4H **59** (nr. Leominster)
Grafton Flyford. *Worc* 5D **60**
Grafton Regis. *Nptn* 1F **51**
Grafton Underwood. *Nptn* 2G **63**
Grafty Green. *Kent* 1C **28**
Graianrhyd. *Den* 5E **82**
Graig. *Carm* 5E **45**
Graig. *Cnwy* 3H **81**
Graig. *Den* 3C **82**
Graig-fechan. *Den* 5D **82**
Graig Penllyn. *V Glam* 4C **32**
Grain. *Medw* 3C **40**
Grainsby. *Linc* 1B **88**
Grainthorpe. *Linc* 1C **88**
Grainthorpe Fen. *Linc* 1C **88**
Graiselound. *N Lin* 1E **87**
Gramasdail. *W Isl* 3D **170**
Grampound. *Corn* 4D **6**
Grampound Road. *Corn* 3D **6**
Granborough. *Buck* 3F **51**
Granby. *Notts* 2E **75**
Grandborough. *Warw* 4B **62**
Grandpont. *Oxon* 5D **50**
Grandtully. *Per* 3G **143**
Grange. *Cumb* 3D **102**
Grange. *E Ayr* 1D **116**
Grange. *Here* 3G **59**
Grange. *Mers* 2E **83**
Grange. *Per* 1E **137**
Grange Crossroads. *Mor* 3B **160**
Grange Hill. *G Lon* 1F **39**
Grangemill. *Derbs* 5G **85**
Grange Moor. *W Yor* 3C **92**
Grangemouth. *Falk* 1C **128**
Grange of Lindores. *Fife* 2E **137**
Grange-over-Sands. *Cumb* 2D **96**
Grangepans. *Falk* 1D **128**
Grange, The. *N Yor* 5C **106**
Grangetown. *Card* 4E **33**
Grangetown. *Red C* 2C **106**
Grange Villa. *Dur* 4F **115**
Granish. *High* 2C **150**
Gransmoor. *E Yor* 4F **101**
Granston. *Pemb* 1C **42**
Grantchester. *Cambs* 5D **64**
Grantham. *Linc* 2G **75**
Grantley. *N Yor* 3E **99**
Grantlodge. *Abers* 2E **152**
Granton. *Edin* 2F **129**
Grantown-on-Spey. *High* 1E **151**
Grantshouse. *Bord* 3E **130**
Grappenhall. *Warr* 2A **84**
Grasby. *Linc* 4D **94**
Grasmere. *Cumb* 4E **103**
Grasscroft. *G Man* 4H **91**
Grassendale. *Mers* 2F **83**
Grassgarth. *Cumb* 5E **113**
Grassholme. *Dur* 2C **104**
Grassington. *N Yor* 3C **98**
Grassmoor. *Derbs* 4B **86**
Grassthorpe. *Notts* 4E **87**
Grateley. *Hants* 2A **24**
Gratton. *Devn* 1D **11**
Gratton. *Staf* 5D **84**
Gratwich. *Staf* 2E **73**
Graveley. *Cambs* 4B **64**
Graveley. *Herts* 3C **52**
Gravelhill. *Shrp* 4G **71**
Gravel Hole. *G Man* 4H **91**
Gravelly Hill. *W Mid* 1F **61**
Graven. *Shet* 4F **173**
Graveney. *Kent* 4E **41**
Gravesend. *Kent* 3H **39**
Grayingham. *Linc* 1G **87**
Grayrigg. *Cumb* 5G **103**
Grays. *Thur* 3H **39**
Grayshott. *Hants* 3G **25**
Grayson Green. *Cumb* 2A **102**
Grayswood. *Surr* 2A **26**
Graythorp. *Hart* 2C **106**
Grazeley. *Wok* 5E **37**
Grealin. *High* 2E **155**
Greasbrough. *S Yor* 1B **86**
Greasby. *Mers* 2E **83**
Great Abington. *Cambs* 1F **53**
Great Addington. *Nptn* 3G **63**
Great Alne. *Warw* 5F **61**
Great Altcar. *Lanc* 4B **90**
Great Amwell. *Herts* 4D **52**
Great Asby. *Cumb* 3H **103**
Great Ashfield. *Suff* 4B **66**
Great Ayton. *N Yor* 3C **106**
Great Baddow. *Essx* 5H **53**
Great Bardfield. *Essx* 2G **53**

Great Barford—Grove

Great Barford. *Bed* 5A **64**
Great Barr. *W Mid* 1E **61**
Great Barrington. *Glos* 4H **49**
Great Barrow. *Ches W* 4G **83**
Great Barton. *Suff* 4A **66**
Great Barugh. *N Yor* 2B **100**
Great Bavington. *Nmbd* 1C **114**
Great Bealings. *Suff* 1F **55**
Great Bedwyn. *Wilts* 5A **36**
Great Bentley. *Essx* 3E **54**
Great Billing. *Nptn* 4F **63**
Great Bircham. *Norf* 2G **77**
Great Blakenham. *Suff* 5D **66**
Great Blencow. *Cumb* 1F **103**
Great Bolas. *Telf* 3A **72**
Great Bookham. *Surr* 5C **38**
Great Bosullow. *Corn* 3B **4**
Great Bourton. *Oxon* 1C **50**
Great Bowden. *Leics* 2E **63**
Great Bradley. *Suff* 5F **65**
Great Braxted. *Essx* 4B **54**
Great Bricett. *Suff* 5C **66**
Great Brickhill. *Buck* 2H **51**
Great Bridgeford. *Staf* 3C **72**
Great Brington. *Nptn* 4D **62**
Great Bromley. *Essx* 3D **54**
Great Broughton. *Cumb* 1B **102**
Great Broughton. *N Yor* 4C **106**
Great Budworth. *Ches W* 3A **84**
Great Burdon. *Darl* 3A **106**
Great Burstead. *Essx* 1A **40**
Great Busby. *N Yor* 4C **106**
Great Canfield. *Essx* 4F **53**
Great Carlton. *Linc* 2D **88**
Great Casterton. *Rut* 5H **75**
Great Chalfield. *Wilts* 5D **34**
Great Chart. *Kent* 1D **28**
Great Chatwell. *Staf* 4B **72**
Great Chesterford. *Essx* 1F **53**
Great Cheverell. *Wilts* 1E **23**
Great Chilton. *Dur* 1F **105**
Great Chishill. *Cambs* 2E **53**
Great Clacton. *Essx* 4E **55**
Great Cliff. *W Yor* 3D **92**
Great Clifton. *Cumb* 2B **102**
Great Coates. *NE Lin* 3F **95**
Great Comberton. *Worc* 1E **49**
Great Corby. *Cumb* 4F **113**
Great Cornard. *Suff* 1B **54**
Great Cowden. *E Yor* 5G **101**
Great Coxwell. *Oxon* 2A **36**
Great Crakehall. *N Yor* 1E **99**
Great Cransley. *Nptn* 3F **63**
Great Cressingham. *Norf* 5H **77**
Great Crosby. *Mers* 1F **83**
Great Cubley. *Derbs* 2F **73**
Great Dalby. *Leics* 4E **75**
Great Doddington. *Nptn* 4F **63**
Great Doward. *Here* 4A **48**
Great Dunham. *Norf* 4A **78**
Great Dunmow. *Essx* 3G **53**
Great Durnford. *Wilts* 3G **23**
Great Easton. *Essx* 3G **53**
Great Easton. *Leics* 1F **63**
Great Eccleston. *Lanc* 5D **96**
Great Edstone. *N Yor* 1B **100**
Great Ellingham. *Norf* 1C **66**
Great Elm. *Som* 2C **22**
Great Eppleton. *Tyne* 5G **115**
Great Eversden. *Cambs* 5C **64**
Great Fencote. *N Yor* 5F **105**
Great Finborough. *Suff* 5C **66**
Greatford. *Linc* 4H **75**
Great Fransham. *Norf* 4A **78**
Great Gaddesden. *Herts* 4A **52**
Great Gate. *Staf* 1E **73**
Great Gidding. *Cambs* 2A **64**
Great Givendale. *E Yor* 4C **100**
Great Glemham. *Suff* 4F **67**
Great Glen. *Leics* 1D **62**
Great Gonerby. *Linc* 2G **75**
Great Gransden. *Cambs* 5B **64**
Great Green. *Norf* 2E **67**
Great Green. *Suff* 5B **66** (nr. Lavenham)
Great Green. *Suff* 3D **66** (nr. Palgrave)
Great Habton. *N Yor* 2B **100**
Great Hale. *Linc* 1A **76**
Great Hallingbury. *Essx* 4F **53**
Greatham. *Hants* 3F **25**
Greatham. *Hart* 2B **106**
Greatham. *W Sus* 4B **26**
Great Hampden. *Buck* 5G **51**
Great Harrowden. *Nptn* 3F **63**
Great Harwood. *Lanc* 1F **91**
Great Haseley. *Oxon* 5E **51**
Great Hatfield. *E Yor* 5F **101**
Great Haywood. *Staf* 3D **73**
Great Heath. *W Mid* 2H **61**
Great Heck. *N Yor* 2F **93**
Great Henny. *Essx* 2B **54**
Great Hinton. *Wilts* 1E **23**
Great Hockham. *Norf* 1B **66**
Great Holland. *Essx* 4F **55**
Great Horkesley. *Essx* 2C **54**
Great Hormead. *Herts* 2E **53**
Great Horton. *W Yor* 1B **92**
Great Horwood. *Buck* 2F **51**
Great Houghton. *Nptn* 5E **63**
Great Houghton. *S Yor* 4E **93**
Great Hucklow. *Derbs* 3F **85**
Great Kelk. *E Yor* 4F **101**
Great Kendale. *E Yor* 3E **101**
Great Kimble. *Buck* 5G **51**
Great Kingshill. *Buck* 2G **37**
Great Langdale. *Cumb* 4D **102**
Great Langton. *N Yor* 5F **105**
Great Leighs. *Essx* 4H **53**
Great Limber. *Linc* 4E **95**
Great Linford. *Mil* 1G **51**
Great Livermere. *Suff* 3A **66**
Great Longstone. *Derbs* 3G **85**
Great Lumley. *Dur* 5F **115**
Great Lyth. *Shrp* 5G **71**
Great Malvern. *Worc* 1C **48**
Great Maplestead. *Essx* 2B **54**
Great Marton. *Bkpl* 1B **90**
Great Massingham. *Norf* 3G **77**
Great Melton. *Norf* 5D **78**
Great Milton. *Oxon* 5E **51**
Great Missenden. *Buck* 5G **51**
Great Mitton. *Lanc* 1F **91**
Great Mongeham. *Kent* 5H **41**
Great Moulton. *Norf* 1D **66**
Great Munden. *Herts* 3D **52**
Great Musgrave. *Cumb* 3A **104**
Great Ness. *Shrp* 4F **71**
Great Notley. *Essx* 3H **53**
Great Oak. *Mon* 5G **47**
Great Oakley. *Essx* 3E **55**
Great Oakley. *Nptn* 2F **63**
Great Offley. *Herts* 3B **52**
Great Ormside. *Cumb* 3A **104**
Great Orton. *Cumb* 4E **113**
Great Ouseburn. *N Yor* 3G **99**
Great Oxendon. *Nptn* 2E **63**
Great Oxney Green. *Essx* 5G **53**
Great Parndon. *Essx* 5E **53**
Great Paxton. *Cambs* 4B **64**
Great Plumpton. *Lanc* 1B **90**
Great Plumstead. *Norf* 4F **79**
Great Ponton. *Linc* 2G **75**
Great Potheridge. *Devn* 1F **11**
Great Preston. *W Yor* 2E **93**
Great Raveley. *Cambs* 2B **64**
Great Rissington. *Glos* 4G **49**
Great Rollright. *Oxon* 2B **50**
Great Ryburgh. *Norf* 3B **78**
Great Ryle. *Nmbd* 3E **121**
Great Ryton. *Shrp* 5G **71**
Great Saling. *Essx* 3G **53**
Great Salkeld. *Cumb* 1G **103**
Great Sampford. *Essx* 2G **53**
Great Sankey. *Warr* 2H **83**
Great Saredon. *Staf* 5D **72**
Great Saxham. *Suff* 4G **65**
Great Shefford. *W Ber* 4B **36**
Great Shelford. *Cambs* 5D **64**
Great Shoddesden. *Hants* 2A **24**
Great Smeaton. *N Yor* 4A **106**
Great Snoring. *Norf* 2B **78**
Great Somerford. *Wilts* 3E **35**
Great Stainton. *Darl* 2A **106**
Great Stambridge. *Essx* 1C **40**
Great Staughton. *Cambs* 4A **64**
Great Steeping. *Linc* 4D **88**
Great Stonar. *Kent* 5H **41**
Greatstone-on-Sea. *Kent* 3E **29**
Great Strickland. *Cumb* 2G **103**
Great Stukeley. *Cambs* 3B **64**
Great Sturton. *Linc* 3B **88**
Great Sutton. *Ches W* 3F **83**
Great Sutton. *Shrp* 2H **59**
Great Swinburne. *Nmbd* 2C **114**
Great Tew. *Oxon* 3B **50**
Great Tey. *Essx* 3B **54**
Great Thirkleby. *N Yor* 2G **99**
Great Thorness. *IOW* 3C **16**
Great Thurlow. *Suff* 5F **65**
Great Torr. *Devn* 4C **8**
Great Torrington. *Devn* 1E **11**
Great Tosson. *Nmbd* 4E **121**
Great Totham North. *Essx* 4B **54**
Great Totham South. *Essx* 4B **54**
Great Tows. *Linc* 1B **88**
Great Urswick. *Cumb* 2B **96**
Great Wakering. *Essx* 2D **40**
Great Waldingfield. *Suff* 1C **54**
Great Walsingham. *Norf* 2B **78**
Great Waltham. *Essx* 4G **53**
Great Warley. *Essx* 1G **39**
Great Washbourne. *Glos* 2E **49**
Great Wenham. *Suff* 2D **54**
Great Whelnetham. *Suff* 5A **66**
Great Whittington. *Nmbd* 2D **114**
Great Wigborough. *Essx* 4C **54**
Great Wilbraham. *Cambs* 5E **65**
Great Wilne. *Derbs* 2B **74**
Great Wishford. *Wilts* 3F **23**
Great Witchingham. *Norf* 3D **78**
Great Witcombe. *Glos* 4E **49**
Great Witley. *Worc* 4B **60**
Great Wolford. *Warw* 2H **49**
Greatworth. *Nptn* 1D **50**
Great Wratting. *Suff* 1G **53**
Great Wymondley. *Herts* 3C **52**
Great Wyrley. *Staf* 5D **73**
Great Wytheford. *Shrp* 4H **71**
Great Yarmouth. *Norf* 5H **79**
Great Yeldham. *Essx* 2A **54**
Grebby. *Linc* 4D **88**
Greeba Castle. *IOM* 3C **108**
Greenbank. *Shet* 1G **173**
Greenbottom. *Corn* 4B **6**
Greenburn. *W Lot* 3C **128**
Greencroft. *Dur* 4E **115**
Greencroft Park. *Dur* 5E **115**
Greendown. *Som* 1A **22**
Greendykes. *Nmbd* 2E **121**
Green End. *Bed* 1A **52** (nr. Bedford)
Green End. *Bed* 4A **64** (nr. St Neots)
Green End. *Herts* 2D **52** (nr. Buntingford)
Green End. *Herts* 3D **52** (nr. Stevenage)
Green End. *N Yor* 4F **107**
Green End. *Warw* 2G **61**
Greenfield. *Arg* 4B **134**
Greenfield. *C Beds* 2A **52**
Greenfield. *Flin* 3D **82**
Greenfield. *G Man* 4H **91**
Greenfield. *Oxon* 2F **37**
Greenfoot. *N Lan* 3A **128**
Greenford. *G Lon* 2C **38**
Greengairs. *N Lan* 2A **128**
Greengate. *Norf* 4C **78**
Greengill. *Cumb* 1C **102**
Greenhalgh. *Lanc* 1C **90**
Greenham. *Dors* 2H **13**
Greenham. *Som* 4D **20**
Greenham. *W Ber* 5C **36**
Green Hammerton. *N Yor* 4G **99**
Greenhaugh. *Nmbd* 1A **114**
Greenhead. *Nmbd* 3H **113**
Green Heath. *Staf* 4D **73**
Greenhill. *Dum* 2C **112**
Greenhill. *Falk* 2B **128**
Greenhill. *Kent* 4F **41**
Greenhill. *S Yor* 2H **85**
Greenhill. *Worc* 3C **60**
Greenhills. *N Ayr* 4E **127**
Greenhithe. *Kent* 3G **39**
Greenholm. *E Ayr* 1E **117**
Greenhow Hill. *N Yor* 3D **98**
Greenigoe. *Orkn* 7D **172**
Greenland. *High* 2E **169**
Greenland Mains. *High* 2E **169**
Greenlands. *Worc* 4E **61**
Green Lane. *Shrp* 3A **72**
Green Lane. *Warw* 4E **61**
Greenlaw. *Bord* 5D **130**
Greenlea. *Dum* 2B **112**
Greenloaning. *Per* 3H **135**
Greenmount. *G Man* 3F **91**
Greenock. *Inv* 2D **126**
Greenock Mains. *E Ayr* 2F **117**
Greenodd. *Cumb* 1C **96**
Green Ore. *Som* 1A **22**
Greenrow. *Cumb* 4C **112**
Greens. *Abers* 4F **161**
Greensgate. *Norf* 4D **78**
Greenside. *Tyne* 3E **115**
Greensidehill. *Nmbd* 3D **121**
Greens Norton. *Nptn* 1E **51**
Greenstead Green. *Essx* 3B **54**
Greensted Green. *Essx* 5F **53**
Green Street. *Herts* 1C **38**
Green Street. *Suff* 3D **66**
Green Street Green. *G Lon* 4F **39**
Green Street Green. *Kent* 3G **39**
Greenstreet Green. *Suff* 1D **54**
Green, The. *Cumb* 1A **96**
Green, The. *Wilts* 3D **22**
Green Tye. *Herts* 4E **53**
Greenway. *Pemb* 2E **43**
Greenway. *V Glam* 4D **32**
Greenwell. *Cumb* 4G **113**
Greenwich. *G Lon* 3E **39**
Greet. *Glos* 2F **49**
Greete. *Shrp* 3H **59**
Greetham. *Linc* 3C **88**
Greetham. *Rut* 4G **75**
Greetland. *W Yor* 2A **92**
Gregson Lane. *Lanc* 2D **90**
Grein. *W Isl* 8B **170**
Greinetobht. *W Isl* 1D **170**
Greinton. *Som* 3H **21**
Grenaby. *IOM* 4B **108**
Grendon. *Nptn* 4F **63**
Grendon. *Warw* 1G **61**
Grendon Common. *Warw* 1G **61**
Grendon Green. *Here* 5H **59**
Grendon Underwood. *Buck* 3E **51**
Grenofen. *Devn* 5E **11**
Grenoside. *S Yor* 1H **85**
Greosabhagh. *W Isl* 8D **171**
Gresford. *Wrex* 5F **83**
Gresham. *Norf* 2D **78**
Greshornish. *High* 3C **154**
Gressenhall. *Norf* 4B **78**
Gressingham. *Lanc* 2E **97**
Greta Bridge. *Dur* 3D **105**
Gretna. *Dum* 3E **112**
Gretna Green. *Dum* 3E **112**
Gretton. *Glos* 2F **49**
Gretton. *Nptn* 1G **63**
Gretton. *Shrp* 1H **59**
Grewelthorpe. *N Yor* 2E **99**
Greygarth. *N Yor* 2D **98**
Grey Green. *N Lin* 4A **94**
Greylake. *Som* 3G **21**
Greysouthen. *Cumb* 2B **102**
Greystoke. *Cumb* 1F **103**
Greystoke Gill. *Cumb* 2F **103**
Greystone. *Ang* 4E **145**
Greystones. *S Yor* 2H **85**
Greywell. *Hants* 1F **25**
Griais. *W Isl* 3G **171**
Grianan. *W Isl* 4G **171**
Gribthorpe. *E Yor* 1A **94**
Gribun. *Arg* 5F **139**
Griff. *Warw* 2A **62**
Griffithstown. *Torf* 2F **33**
Griffydam. *Leics* 4B **74**
Griggs Green. *Hants* 3G **25**
Grimbister. *Orkn* 6C **172**
Grimeford Village. *Lanc* 3E **90**
Grimethorpe. *S Yor* 4E **93**
Griminis. *W Isl* 3C **170** (on Benbecula)
Griminis. *W Isl* 1C **170** (on North Uist)
Grimister. *Shet* 2F **173**
Grimley. *Worc* 4C **60**
Grimoldby. *Linc* 2C **88**
Grimpo. *Shrp* 3F **71**
Grimsargh. *Lanc* 1D **90**
Grimsbury. *Oxon* 1C **50**
Grimsby. *NE Lin* 3F **95**
Grimscote. *Nptn* 5D **62**
Grimscott. *Corn* 2C **10**
Grimshaw. *Bkbn* 2F **91**
Grimshaw Green. *Lanc* 3C **90**
Grimsthorpe. *Linc* 3H **75**
Grimston. *E Yor* 1F **95**
Grimston. *Leics* 3D **74**
Grimston. *Norf* 3G **77**
Grimston. *York* 4A **100**
Grimstone. *Dors* 3B **14**
Grimstone End. *Suff* 4B **66**
Grinacombe Moor. *Devn* 3E **11**
Grindale. *E Yor* 2F **101**
Grindhill. *Devn* 3E **11**
Grindiscol. *Shet* 8F **173**
Grindle. *Shrp* 5B **72**
Grindleford. *Derbs* 3G **85**
Grindleton. *Lanc* 5G **97**
Grindley. *Staf* 3E **73**
Grindley Brook. *Shrp* 1H **71**
Grindlow. *Derbs* 3F **85**
Grindon. *Nmbd* 5F **131**
Grindon. *Staf* 5E **85**
Gringley on the Hill. *Notts* 1E **87**
Grinsdale. *Cumb* 4E **113**
Grinshill. *Shrp* 3H **71**
Grinton. *N Yor* 5D **104**
Griomsidar. *W Isl* 5G **171**
Grishipoll. *Arg* 3C **138**
Grisling Common. *E Sus* 3F **27**
Gristhorpe. *N Yor* 1E **101**
Griston. *Norf* 1B **66**
Gritley. *Orkn* 7E **172**
Grittenham. *Wilts* 3F **35**
Grittleton. *Wilts* 4D **34**
Grizebeck. *Cumb* 1B **96**
Grizedale. *Cumb* 5E **103**
Grobister. *Orkn* 5F **172**
Groby. *Leics* 5C **74**
Groes. *Cnwy* 4C **82**
Groes. *Neat* 3A **32**
Groes-faen. *Rhon* 3D **32**
Groesffordd. *Gwyn* 2B **68**
Groesffordd. *Powy* 3D **46**
Groeslon. *Gwyn* 5D **81**
Groes-lwyd. *Powy* 4E **70**
Groes-wen. *Cphy* 3E **33**
Grogport. *Arg* 5G **125**
Groigearraidh. *W Isl* 4C **170**
Gromford. *Suff* 5F **67**
Gronant. *Flin* 2C **82**
Groombridge. *E Sus* 2G **27**
Grosmont. *Mon* 3H **47**
Grosmont. *N Yor* 4F **107**
Groton. *Suff* 1C **54**
Grove. *Dors* 5C **14**
Grove. *Kent* 4G **41**

Grove—Hannaborough

Grove. *Notts* 3E **87**
Grove. *Oxon* 2B **36**
Grovehill. *E Yor* 1D **94**
Grove Park. *G Lon* 3F **39**
Grovesend. *Swan* 5F **45**
Grove, The. *Dum* 2A **112**
Grove, The. *Worc* 1D **48**
Grub Street. *Staf* 3B **72**
Grudie. *High* 2F **157**
Gruids. *High* 3C **164**
Gruinard House. *High* 4D **162**
Gruinart. *Arg* 3A **124**
Grulinbeg. *Arg* 3A **124**
Gruline. *Arg* 4G **139**
Grummore. *High* 5G **167**
Grundisburgh. *Suff* 5E **66**
Gruting. *Shet* 7D **173**
Grutness. *Shet* 10F **173**
Gualachulain. *High* 4F **141**
Gualin House. *High* 3D **166**
Guardbridge. *Fife* 2G **137**
Guarlford. *Worc* 1D **48**
Guay. *Per* 4H **143**
Gubblecote. *Herts* 4H **51**
Guestling Green. *E Sus* 4C **28**
Guestling Thorn. *E Sus* 4C **28**
Guestwick. *Norf* 3C **78**
Guestwick Green. *Norf* 3C **78**
Guide. *Bkbn* 2F **91**
Guide Post. *Nmbd* 1F **115**
Guilden Down. *Shrp* 2F **59**
Guilden Morden. *Cambs* 1C **52**
Guilden Sutton. *Ches W* 4G **83**
Guildford. *Surr* 1A **26**
Guildtown. *Per* 5A **144**
Guilsborough. *Nptn* 3D **62**
Guilsfield. *Powy* 4E **70**
Guineaford. *Devn* 3F **19**
Guisborough. *Red C* 3D **106**
Guiseley. *W Yor* 5D **98**
Guist. *Norf* 3B **78**
Guiting Power. *Glos* 3F **49**
Gulberwick. *Shet* 8F **173**
Gullane. *E Lot* 1A **130**
Gulling Green. *Suff* 5H **65**
Gulval. *Corn* 3B **4**
Gumfreston. *Pemb* 4F **43**
Gumley. *Leics* 1D **62**
Gunby. *E Yor* 1H **93**
Gunby. *Linc* 3G **75**
Gundleton. *Hants* 3E **24**
Gun Green. *Kent* 2B **28**
Gun Hill. *E Sus* 4G **27**
Gunn. *Devn* 3G **19**
Gunnerside. *N Yor* 5C **104**
Gunnerton. *Nmbd* 2C **114**
Gunness. *N Lin* 3B **94**
Gunnislake. *Corn* 5E **11**
Gunsgreenhill. *Bord* 3F **131**
Gunstone. *Staf* 5C **72**
Gunthorpe. *Norf* 2C **78**
Gunthorpe. *N Lin* 1F **87**
Gunthorpe. *Notts* 1D **74**
Gunthorpe. *Pet* 5A **76**
Gunville. *IOW* 4C **16**
Gupworthy. *Som* 3C **20**
Gurnard. *IOW* 3C **16**
Gurney Slade. *Som* 2B **22**
Gurnos. *Powy* 5A **46**
Gussage All Saints. *Dors* 1F **15**
Gussage St Andrew. *Dors* 1E **15**
Gussage St Michael. *Dors* 1E **15**
Guston. *Kent* 1H **29**
Gutcher. *Shet* 2G **173**
Guthram Gowt. *Linc* 3A **76**
Guthrie. *Ang* 3E **145**
Guyhirn. *Cambs* 5D **76**
Guyhirn Gull. *Cambs* 5C **76**
Guy's Head. *Linc* 3D **77**
Guy's Marsh. *Dors* 4D **22**
Guyzance. *Nmbd* 4G **121**
Gwaelod-y-garth. *Card* 3E **32**
Gwaenynog Bach. *Den* 4C **82**
Gwaenysgor. *Flin* 2C **82**
Gwalchmai. *IOA* 3C **80**
Gwastad. *Pemb* 2E **43**
Gwaun-Cae-Gurwen. *Neat* 4H **45**
Gwaun-y-bara. *Cphy* 3E **33**
Gwbert. *Cdgn* 1B **44**
Gweek. *Corn* 4E **5**
Gwehelog. *Mon* 5G **47**
Gwenddwr. *Powy* 1D **46**
Gwennap. *Corn* 4B **6**
Gwenter. *Corn* 5E **5**
Gwernaffield. *Flin* 4E **82**
Gwernesney. *Mon* 5H **47**
Gwernogle. *Carm* 2F **45**
Gwern-y-go. *Powy* 1E **58**
Gwernymynydd. *Flin* 4E **82**
Gwersyllt. *Wrex* 5F **83**
Gwespyr. *Flin* 2D **82**
Gwinear. *Corn* 3C **4**
Gwithian. *Corn* 2C **4**
Gwredog. *IOA* 2D **80**
Gwyddelwern. *Den* 1C **70**
Gwyddgrug. *Carm* 2E **45**
Gwynfryn. *Wrex* 5E **83**
Gwystre. *Powy* 4C **58**
Gwytherin. *Cnwy* 4A **82**
Gyfelia. *Wrex* 1F **71**
Gyffin. *Cnwy* 3G **81**

H

Habberley. *Shrp* 5F **71**
Habblesthorpe. *Notts* 2E **87**
Habergham. *Lanc* 1G **91**
Habin. *W Sus* 4G **25**
Habrough. *NE Lin* 3E **95**
Haceby. *Linc* 2H **75**
Hacheston. *Suff* 5F **67**
Hackenthorpe. *S Yor* 2B **86**
Hackford. *Norf* 5C **78**
Hackforth. *N Yor* 5F **105**
Hackleton. *Nptn* 5F **63**
Hackness. *N Yor* 5G **107**
Hackness. *Orkn* 8C **172**
Hackney. *G Lon* 2E **39**
Hackthorn. *Linc* 2G **87**
Hackthorpe. *Cumb* 2G **103**
Haclait. *W Isl* 4D **170**
Haconby. *Linc* 3A **76**
Hadden. *Bord* 1B **120**
Haddenham. *Buck* 5F **51**
Haddenham. *Cambs* 3D **64**
Haddenham End. *Cambs* 3D **64**
Haddington. *E Lot* 2B **130**
Haddington. *Linc* 4G **87**
Haddiscoe. *Norf* 1G **67**
Haddo. *Abers* 5F **161**
Haddon. *Cambs* 1A **64**
Hademore. *Staf* 5F **73**
Hadfield. *Derbs* 1E **85**
Hadham Cross. *Herts* 4E **53**
Hadham Ford. *Herts* 3E **53**
Hadleigh. *Essx* 2C **40**
Hadleigh. *Suff* 1D **54**
Hadleigh Heath. *Suff* 1C **54**
Hadley. *Telf* 4A **72**
Hadley. *Worc* 4C **60**
Hadley End. *Staf* 3F **73**
Hadley Wood. *G Lon* 1D **38**
Hadlow. *Kent* 1H **27**
Hadlow Down. *E Sus* 3G **27**
Hadnall. *Shrp* 3H **71**
Hadstock. *Essx* 1F **53**
Hadston. *Nmbd* 5G **121**
Hady. *Derbs* 3A **86**
Hadzor. *Worc* 4D **60**
Haffenden Quarter. *Kent* 1C **28**
Haggate. *Lanc* 1G **91**
Haggbeck. *Cumb* 2F **113**
Haggerston. *Nmbd* 5G **131**
Haggrister. *Shet* 4E **173**
Hagley. *Here* 1A **48**
Hagley. *Worc* 2D **60**
Hagnaby. *Linc* 4C **88**
Hagworthingham. *Linc* 4C **88**
Haigh. *G Man* 4E **90**
Haigh Moor. *W Yor* 2C **92**
Haighton Green. *Lanc* 1D **90**
Haile. *Cumb* 4B **102**
Hailes. *Glos* 2F **49**
Hailey. *Herts* 4D **52**
Hailey. *Oxon* 4B **50**
Hailsham. *E Sus* 5G **27**
Hail Weston. *Cambs* 4A **64**
Hainault. *G Lon* 1F **39**
Hainford. *Norf* 4E **78**
Hainton. *Linc* 2A **88**
Hainworth. *W Yor* 1A **92**
Haisthorpe. *E Yor* 3F **101**
Hakin. *Pemb* 4C **42**
Halam. *Notts* 5D **86**
Halbeath. *Fife* 1E **129**
Halberton. *Devn* 1D **12**
Halcro. *High* 2E **169**
Hale. *Cumb* 2E **97**
Hale. *G Man* 2B **84**
Hale. *Hal* 2G **83**
Hale. *Hants* 1G **15**
Hale. *Surr* 2G **25**
Hale Bank. *Hal* 2G **83**
Halebarns. *G Man* 2B **84**
Hales. *Norf* 1F **67**
Hales. *Staf* 2B **72**
Halesgate. *Linc* 3C **76**
Hales Green. *Derbs* 1F **73**
Halesowen. *W Mid* 2D **60**
Hale Street. *Kent* 1A **28**
Halesworth. *Suff* 3F **67**
Halewood. *Mers* 2G **83**
Halford. *Devn* 5B **12**
Halford. *Shrp* 2G **59**
Halford. *Warw* 1A **50**
Halfpenny. *Cumb* 1E **97**
Halfpenny Furze. *Carm* 3G **43**
Halfpenny Green. *Shrp* 1C **60**
Halfway. *Carm* 2G **45**
Halfway. *Powy* 2B **46**
Halfway. *S Yor* 2B **86**
Halfway. *W Ber* 5C **36**
Halfway House. *Shrp* 4F **71**
Halfway Houses. *Kent* 3D **40**
Halgabron. *Corn* 4A **10**
Halifax. *W Yor* 2A **92**
Halistra. *High* 3B **154**
Halket. *E Ayr* 4F **127**
Halkirk. *High* 3D **168**
Halkyn. *Flin* 3E **82**
Hall. *E Ren* 4F **127**
Hallam Fields. *Derbs* 1B **74**
Halland. *E Sus* 4G **27**
Hallands, The. *N Lin* 2D **94**
Hallaton. *Leics* 1E **63**
Hallatrow. *Bath* 1B **22**
Hallbank. *Cumb* 5H **103**
Hallbankgate. *Cumb* 4G **113**
Hall Dunnerdale. *Cumb* 5D **102**
Hallen. *S Glo* 3A **34**
Hall End. *Bed* 1A **52**
Hallgarth. *Dur* 5G **115**
Hall Green. *Ches E* 5C **84**
Hall Green. *Norf* 2D **66**
Hall Green. *W Mid* 2F **61**
Hall Green. *W Yor* 3D **92**
Hall Green. *Wrex* 1G **71**
Halliburton. *Bord* 5C **130**
Hallin. *High* 3B **154**
Halling. *Medw* 4B **40**
Hallington. *Linc* 2C **88**
Hallington. *Nmbd* 2C **114**
Halloughton. *Notts* 5D **86**
Hallow. *Worc* 5C **60**
Hallow Heath. *Worc* 5C **60**
Hallowsgate. *Ches W* 4H **83**
Hallsands. *Devn* 5E **9**
Hall's Green. *Herts* 3C **52**
Hallspill. *Devn* 4E **19**
Hallthwaites. *Cumb* 1A **96**
Hall Waberthwaite. *Cumb* 5C **102**
Hallwood Green. *Glos* 2B **48**
Hallworthy. *Corn* 4B **10**
Hallyne. *Bord* 5E **129**
Halmer End. *Staf* 1C **72**
Halmond's Frome. *Here* 1B **48**
Halmore. *Glos* 5B **48**
Halnaker. *W Sus* 5A **26**
Halsall. *Lanc* 3B **90**
Halse. *Nptn* 1D **50**
Halse. *Som* 4E **21**
Halsetown. *Corn* 3C **4**
Halsham. *E Yor* 2F **95**
Halsinger. *Devn* 3F **19**
Halstead. *Essx* 2B **54**
Halstead. *Kent* 4F **39**
Halstead. *Leics* 5E **75**
Halstock. *Dors* 2A **14**
Halstow. *Devn* 3B **12**
Halsway. *Som* 3E **21**
Haltcliff Bridge. *Cumb* 1E **103**
Haltham. *Linc* 4B **88**
Haltoft End. *Linc* 1C **76**
Halton. *Buck* 5G **51**
Halton. *Hal* 2H **83**
Halton. *Lanc* 3E **97**
Halton. *Nmbd* 3C **114**
Halton. *W Yor* 1D **92**
Halton. *Wrex* 2F **71**
Halton East. *N Yor* 4C **98**
Halton Fenside. *Linc* 4D **88**
Halton Gill. *N Yor* 2A **98**
Halton Holegate. *Linc* 4D **88**
Halton Lea Gate. *Nmbd* 4H **113**
Halton Moor. *W Yor* 1D **92**
Halton Shields. *Nmbd* 3D **114**
Halton West. *N Yor* 4H **97**
Haltwhistle. *Nmbd* 3A **114**
Halvergate. *Norf* 5G **79**
Halwell. *Devn* 3D **9**
Halwill. *Devn* 3E **11**
Halwill Junction. *Devn* 3E **11**
Ham. *Devn* 2F **13**
Ham. *Glos* 2B **34**
Ham. *G Lon* 3C **38**
Ham. *High* 1E **169**
Ham. *Kent* 5H **41**
Ham. *Plym* 3A **8**
Ham. *Shet* 8A **173**
Ham. *Som* 1F **13** (nr. Ilminster)
Ham. *Som* 4F **21** (nr. Taunton)
Ham. *Som* 4E **21** (nr. Wellington)
Ham. *Wilts* 5B **36**
Hambleden. *Buck* 3F **37**
Hambledon. *Hants* 1E **17**
Hambledon. *Surr* 2A **26**
Hamble-le-Rice. *Hants* 2C **16**
Hambleton. *Lanc* 5C **96**
Hambleton. *N Yor* 1F **93**
Hambridge. *Som* 4G **21**
Hambrook. *S Glo* 4B **34**
Hambrook. *W Sus* 2F **17**
Ham Common. *Dors* 4D **22**
Hameringham. *Linc* 4C **88**
Hamerton. *Cambs* 3A **64**
Ham Green. *Here* 1C **48**
Ham Green. *Kent* 4C **40**
Ham Green. *N Som* 4A **34**
Ham Green. *Worc* 4E **61**
Ham Hill. *Kent* 4A **40**
Hamilton. *Leics* 5D **74**
Hamilton. *S Lan* 4A **128**
Hammer. *W Sus* 3G **25**
Hammersmith. *G Lon* 3D **38**
Hammerwich. *Staf* 5E **73**
Hammerwood. *E Sus* 2F **27**
Hammill. *Kent* 5G **41**
Hammond Street. *Herts* 5D **52**
Hammoon. *Dors* 1D **14**
Hamnavoe. *Shet* 8E **173** (nr. Burland)
Hamnavoe. *Shet* 3F **173** (on Yell)
Hamp. *Som* 3G **21**
Hampden Park. *E Sus* 5H **27**
Hampen. *Glos* 3F **49**
Hamperden End. *Essx* 2F **53**
Hamperley. *Shrp* 2G **59**
Hampnett. *Glos* 4F **49**
Hampole. *S Yor* 3F **93**
Hampreston. *Dors* 3F **15**
Hampstead. *G Lon* 2D **38**
Hampstead Norreys. *W Ber* 4D **36**
Hampsthwaite. *N Yor* 4E **99**
Hampton. *Devn* 3F **13**
Hampton. *G Lon* 3C **38**
Hampton. *Kent* 4F **41**
Hampton. *Shrp* 2B **60**
Hampton. *Swin* 2G **35**
Hampton. *Worc* 1F **49**
Hampton Bishop. *Here* 2A **48**
Hampton Fields. *Glos* 2D **35**
Hampton Hargate. *Pet* 1A **64**
Hampton Heath. *Ches W* 1H **71**
Hampton in Arden. *W Mid* 2G **61**
Hampton Loade. *Shrp* 2B **60**
Hampton Lovett. *Worc* 4C **60**
Hampton Lucy. *Warw* 5G **61**
Hampton Magna. *Warw* 4G **61**
Hampton on the Hill. *Warw* 4G **61**
Hampton Poyle. *Oxon* 4D **50**
Hampton Wick. *G Lon* 4C **38**
Hamptworth. *Wilts* 1H **15**
Hamrow. *Norf* 3B **78**
Hamsey. *E Sus* 4F **27**
Hamsey Green. *Surr* 5E **39**
Hamstall Ridware. *Staf* 4F **73**
Hamstead. *IOW* 3C **16**
Hamstead. *W Mid* 1E **61**
Hamstead Marshall. *W Ber* 5C **36**
Hamsterley. *Dur* 4E **115** (nr. Consett)
Hamsterley. *Dur* 1E **105** (nr. Wolsingham)
Hamsterley Mill. *Dur* 4E **115**
Hamstreet. *Kent* 2E **28**
Ham Street. *Som* 3A **22**
Hamworthy. *Pool* 3E **15**
Hanbury. *Staf* 3F **73**
Hanbury. *Worc* 4D **60**
Hanbury Woodend. *Staf* 3F **73**
Hanby. *Linc* 2H **75**
Hanchurch. *Staf* 1C **72**
Hand and Pen. *Devn* 3D **12**
Handbridge. *Ches W* 4G **83**
Handcross. *W Sus* 3D **26**
Handforth. *Ches E* 2C **84**
Handley. *Ches W* 5G **83**
Handley. *Derbs* 4A **86**
Handsacre. *Staf* 4E **73**
Handsworth. *S Yor* 2B **86**
Handsworth. *W Mid* 1E **61**
Handy Cross. *Buck* 2G **37**
Hanford. *Dors* 1D **14**
Hanford. *Stoke* 1C **72**
Hangersley. *Hants* 2G **15**
Hanging Houghton. *Nptn* 3E **63**
Hanging Langford. *Wilts* 3F **23**
Hangleton. *Brig* 5D **26**
Hangleton. *W Sus* 5B **26**
Hanham. *S Glo* 4B **34**
Hanham Green. *S Glo* 4B **34**
Hankelow. *Ches E* 1A **72**
Hankerton. *Wilts* 2E **35**
Hankham. *E Sus* 5H **27**
Hanley. *Stoke* 1C **72**
Hanley Castle. *Worc* 1D **48**
Hanley Childe. *Worc* 4A **60**
Hanley Swan. *Worc* 1D **48**
Hanley William. *Worc* 4A **60**
Hanlith. *N Yor* 3B **98**
Hanmer. *Wrex* 2G **71**
Hannaborough. *Devn* 2F **11**

Hannaford. Devn 4G 19
Hannah. Linc 3E 89
Hannington. Hants 1D 24
Hannington. Nptn 3F 63
Hannington. Swin 2G 35
Hannington Wick. Swin 2G 35
Hanscombe End. C Beds 2B 52
Hanslope. Mil 1G 51
Hanthorpe. Linc 3H 75
Hanwell. G Lon 2C 38
Hanwood. Shrp 5G 71
Hanworth. G Lon 3C 38
Hanworth. Norf 2D 78
Happas. Ang 4D 144
Happendon. S Lan 1A 118
Happisburgh. Norf 2F 79
Happisburgh Common. Norf 3F 79
Hapsford. Ches W 3G 83
Hapton. Lanc 1F 91
Hapton. Norf 1D 66
Harberton. Devn 3D 9
Harbertonford. Devn 3D 9
Harbledown. Kent 5F 41
Harborne. W Mid 2E 61
Harborough Magna. Warw 3B 62
Harbottle. Nmbd 4D 120
Harbourneford. Devn 2D 8
Harbours Hill. Worc 4D 60
Harbridge. Hants 1G 15
Harbury. Warw 4A 62
Harby. Leics 2E 75
Harby. Notts 3F 87
Harcombe. Devn 3E 13
Harcombe Bottom. Devn 3G 13
Harcourt. Corn 5C 6
Harden. W Yor 1A 92
Hardenhuish. Wilts 4E 35
Hardgate. Abers 3E 153
Hardgate. Dum 3F 111
Hardham. W Sus 4B 26
Hardingham. Norf 5C 78
Hardingstone. Nptn 5E 63
Hardings Wood. Ches E 5C 84
Hardington. Som 1C 22
Hardington Mandeville. Som 1A 14
Hardington Marsh. Som 2A 14
Hardington Moor. Som 1A 14
Hardley. Hants 2C 16
Hardley Street. Norf 5F 79
Hardmead. Mil 1H 51
Hardraw. N Yor 5B 104
Hardstoft. Derbs 4B 86
Hardway. Hants 2E 16
Hardway. Som 3C 22
Hardwick. Buck 4G 51
Hardwick. Cambs 5C 64
Hardwick. Norf 2E 66
Hardwick. Nptn 4F 63
Hardwick. Oxon 3D 50
(nr. Bicester)
Hardwick. Oxon 5B 50
(nr. Witney)
Hardwick. Shrp 1F 59
Hardwick. S Yor 2B 86
Hardwick. Stoc T 2B 106
Hardwick. W Mid 1E 61
Hardwicke. Glos 3E 49
(nr. Cheltenham)
Hardwicke. Glos 4C 48
(nr. Gloucester)
Hardwicke. Here 1F 47
Hardwick Village. Notts 3D 86
Hardy's Green. Essx 3C 54
Hare. Som 1F 13
Hareby. Linc 4C 88
Hareden. Lanc 4F 97
Harefield. G Lon 1B 38
Hare Green. Essx 3D 54
Hare Hatch. Wok 4G 37
Harehill. Derbs 2F 73
Harehills. W Yor 1D 92
Harehope. Nmbd 2E 121
Harelaw. Dum 2F 113

Harelaw. Dur 4E 115
Hareplain. Kent 2C 28
Haresceugh. Cumb 5H 113
Harescombe. Glos 4D 48
Haresfield. Glos 4D 48
Harefinch. Mers 1H 83
Hareshaw. N Lan 3B 128
Hare Street. Essx 5E 53
Hare Street. Herts 3D 53
Harewood. W Yor 5F 99
Harewood End. Here 3A 48
Harford. Devn 3C 8
Harford. Devn 1D 66
Hargatewall. Derbs 3F 85
Hargrave. Ches W 4G 83
Hargrave. Nptn 3H 63
Hargrave. Suff 5G 65
Harker. Cumb 3E 113
Harkstead. Suff 2E 55
Harlaston. Staf 4G 73
Harlaxton. Linc 2F 75
Harlech. Gwyn 2E 69
Harlequin. Notts 2D 74
Harlescott. Shrp 4H 71
Harleston. Devn 4D 9
Harleston. Norf 2E 67
Harleston. Suff 4C 66
Harleston. Nptn 4E 62
Harley. Shrp 5H 71
Harley. S Yor 1A 86
Harling Road. Norf 2B 66
Harlington. C Beds 2A 52
Harlington. G Lon 3B 38
Harlington. S Yor 4E 93
Harlosh. High 4B 154
Harlow. Essx 4E 53
Harlow Hill. Nmbd 3D 115
Harlsey Castle. N Yor 5B 106
Harlthorpe. E Yor 1H 93
Harlton. Cambs 5C 64
Harlyn. Corn 1C 6
Harman's Cross. Dors 4E 15
Harmby. N Yor 1D 98
Harmer Green. Herts 4C 52
Harmer Hill. Shrp 3G 71
Harmondsworth. G Lon 3B 38
Harmston. Linc 4G 87
Harnage. Shrp 5H 71
Harnham. Nmbd 1D 115
Harnhill. Glos 5F 49
Harold Hill. G Lon 1G 39
Haroldston West. Pemb 3C 42
Haroldswick. Shet 1H 173
Harold Wood. G Lon 1G 39
Harome. N Yor 1A 100
Harpenden. Herts 4B 52
Harpford. Devn 3D 12
Harpham. E Yor 3E 101
Harpley. Norf 3G 77
Harpley. Worc 4A 60
Harpole. Nptn 4D 62
Harpsdale. High 3D 168
Harpsden. Oxon 3F 37
Harpswell. Linc 2G 87
Harpurhey. G Man 4G 91
Harpur Hill. Derbs 3E 85
Harraby. Cumb 4F 113
Harracott. Devn 4F 19
Harrapool. High 1E 147
Harrapul. High 1E 147
Harrietfield. Per 1B 136
Harrietsham. Kent 5C 40
Harrington. Cumb 2A 102
Harrington. Linc 3C 88
Harrington. Nptn 2E 63
Harringworth. Nptn 1G 63
Harriseahead. Staf 5C 84
Harriston. Cumb 5C 112
Harrogate. N Yor 4F 99
Harrold. Bed 5G 63
Harrop Dale. G Man 4A 92
Harrow. G Lon 2C 38
Harrowbarrow. Corn 2H 7
Harrowden. Bed 1A 52

Harrowgate Hill. Darl 3F 105
Harrow on the Hill. G Lon 2C 38
Harrow Weald. G Lon 1C 38
Harry Stoke. S Glo 4B 34
Harston. Cambs 5D 64
Harston. Leics 2F 75
Harswell. E Yor 5C 100
Hart. Hart 1B 106
Hartburn. Nmbd 1D 115
Hartburn. Stoc T 3B 106
Hartest. Suff 5H 65
Hartfield. E Sus 2F 27
Hartford. Cambs 3B 64
Hartford. Ches W 3A 84
Hartford. Som 4C 20
Hartfordbridge. Hants 1F 25
Hartford End. Essx 4G 53
Harthill. Ches W 5H 83
Harthill. N Lan 3C 128
Harthill. S Yor 2B 86
Hartington. Derbs 4F 85
Hartland. Devn 4C 18
Hartland Quay. Devn 4C 18
Hartle. Worc 3D 60
Hartlebury. Worc 3C 60
Hartlepool. Hart 1C 106
Hartley. Cumb 4A 104
Hartley. Kent 2B 28
(nr. Cranbrook)
Hartley. Kent 4H 39
(nr. Dartford)
Hartley. Nmbd 2G 115
Hartley Green. Staf 2D 73
Hartley Mauditt. Hants 3F 25
Hartley Wespall. Hants 1E 25
Hartley Wintney. Hants 1F 25
Hartlip. Kent 4C 40
Hartmount. High 1B 158
Hartoft End. N Yor 5E 107
Harton. N Yor 3B 100
Harton. Shrp 2G 59
Harton. Tyne 3G 115
Hartpury. Glos 3C 48
Hartshead. W Yor 2B 92
Hartshill. Warw 1H 61
Hartshorne. Derbs 3H 73
Hartsop. Cumb 3F 103
Hart Station. Hart 1B 106
Hartswell. Som 4D 20
Hartwell. Nptn 5E 63
Hartwood. Lanc 3D 90
Hartwood. N Lan 4B 128
Harvel. Kent 4A 40
Harvington. Worc 1F 49
(nr. Evesham)
Harvington. Worc 3C 60
(nr. Kidderminster)
Harwell. Oxon 3C 36
Harwich. Essx 2F 55
Harwood. Dur 1B 104
Harwood. G Man 3F 91
Harwood Dale. N Yor 5G 107
Harworth. Notts 1D 86
Hascombe. Surr 2A 26
Haselbech. Nptn 3E 62
Haselbury Plucknett. Som 1H 13
Haseley. Warw 4G 61
Haselor. Warw 5F 61
Hasfield. Glos 3D 48
Hasguard. Pemb 4C 42
Haskayne. Lanc 4B 90
Hasketon. Suff 5E 67
Hasland. Derbs 4A 86
Haslemere. Surr 2A 26
Haslingden. Lanc 2F 91
Haslingden Grane. Lanc 2F 91
Haslingfield. Cambs 5D 64
Haslington. Ches E 5B 84
Hassall. Ches E 5B 84
Hassall Green. Ches E 5B 84
Hassall Street. Kent 1E 29
Hassendean. Bord 2H 119
Hassingham. Norf 5F 79
Hassness. Cumb 3C 102

Hassocks. W Sus 4E 27
Hassop. Derbs 3G 85
Haste Hill. Surr 2A 26
Haster. High 3F 169
Hasthorpe. Linc 4D 89
Hastigrow. High 2E 169
Hastingleigh. Kent 1E 29
Hastings. E Sus 5C 28
Hastingwood. Essx 5E 53
Hastoe. Herts 5H 51
Haston. Shrp 3H 71
Haswell. Dur 5G 115
Haswell Plough. Dur 5G 115
Hatch. C Beds 1B 52
Hatch Beauchamp. Som 4G 21
Hatch End. G Lon 1C 38
Hatch Green. Som 1G 13
Hatching Green. Herts 4B 52
Hatchmere. Ches W 3H 83
Hatch Warren. Hants 2E 24
Hatcliffe. NE Lin 4F 95
Hatfield. Here 5H 59
Hatfield. Herts 5C 52
Hatfield. S Yor 4G 93
Hatfield. Worc 5C 60
Hatfield Broad Oak. Essx 4F 53
Hatfield Garden Village. Herts 5C 52
Hatfield Heath. Essx 4F 53
Hatfield Hyde. Herts 4C 52
Hatfield Peverel. Essx 4A 54
Hatfield Woodhouse. S Yor 4G 93
Hatford. Oxon 2B 36
Hatherden. Hants 1B 24
Hatherleigh. Devn 2F 11
Hathern. Leics 3C 74
Hatherop. Glos 5G 49
Hathersage. Derbs 2G 85
Hathersage Booths. Derbs 2G 85
Hatherton. Ches E 1A 72
Hatherton. Staf 4D 72
Hatley St George. Cambs 5B 64
Hatt. Corn 2H 7
Hattersley. G Man 1D 85
Hattingley. Hants 3E 25
Hatton. Abers 5H 161
Hatton. Derbs 2G 73
Hatton. G Lon 3B 38
Hatton. Linc 3A 88
Hatton. Shrp 1G 59
Hatton. Warw 4G 61
Hattoncrook. Abers 1F 153
Hatton Heath. Ches W 4G 83
Hatton of Fintray. Abers 2F 153
Haugh. E Ayr 2D 117
Haugh. Linc 3D 88
Haugham. Linc 2C 88
Haugh Head. Nmbd 2E 121
Haughley. Suff 4C 66
Haughley Green. Suff 4C 66
Haugh of Ballechin. Per 3G 143
Haugh of Glass. Mor 5B 160
Haugh of Urr. Dum 3F 111
Haughton. Notts 3D 86
Haughton. Shrp 1A 60
(nr. Bridgnorth)
Haughton. Shrp 3F 71
(nr. Oswestry)
Haughton. Shrp 5B 72
(nr. Shifnal)
Haughton. Shrp 4H 71
(nr. Shrewsbury)
Haughton. Staf 3C 72
Haughton Green. G Man 1D 84
Haughton le Skerne. Darl 3A 106
Haughton Moss. Ches E 5H 83
Haultwick. Herts 3D 52
Haunn. Arg 4E 139
Haunn. W Isl 7C 170
Haunton. Staf 4G 73
Hauxton. Cambs 5D 64
Havannah. Ches E 4C 84
Havant. Hants 2F 17
Haven. Here 5G 59

Haven Bank. Linc 5B 88
Havenside. E Yor 2E 95
Havenstreet. IOW 3D 16
Haven, The. W Sus 2B 26
Havercroft. W Yor 3D 93
Haverfordwest. Pemb 3D 42
Haverhill. Suff 1G 53
Haverigg. Cumb 2A 96
Havering-atte-Bower. G Lon 1G 39
Havering's Grove. Essx 1A 40
Haversham. Mil 1G 51
Haverthwaite. Cumb 1C 96
Haverton Hill. Stoc T 2B 106
Havyatt. Som 3A 22
Hawarden. Flin 4F 83
Hawcoat. Cumb 2B 96
Hawcross. Glos 2C 48
Hawen. Cdgn 1D 44
Hawes. N Yor 1A 98
Hawes Green. Norf 1E 67
Hawick. Bord 3H 119
Hawkchurch. Devn 2G 13
Hawkedon. Suff 5G 65
Hawkenbury. Kent 1C 28
Hawkeridge. Wilts 1D 22
Hawkerland. Devn 4D 12
Hawkesbury. S Glo 3C 34
Hawkesbury Upton. S Glo 3C 34
Hawkes End. W Mid 2G 61
Hawk Green. G Man 2D 84
Hawkhurst. Kent 2B 28
Hawkhurst Common. E Sus 4G 27
Hawkinge. Kent 1G 29
Hawkley. Hants 4F 25
Hawksdale. Cumb 5E 113
Hawkshaw. G Man 3F 91
Hawkshead. Cumb 5E 103
Hawkshead Hill. Cumb 5E 103
Hawkswick. N Yor 2B 98
Hawksworth. Notts 1E 75
Hawksworth. W Yor 5D 98
Hawkwell. Essx 1C 40
Hawley. Hants 1G 25
Hawley. Kent 3G 39
Hawling. Glos 3F 49
Hawnby. N Yor 1H 99
Haworth. W Yor 1A 92
Hawstead. Suff 5A 66
Hawthorn. Dur 5H 115
Hawthorn. Brac 4G 37
Hawthorn Hill. Linc 5B 88
Hawthorpe. Linc 3H 75
Hawton. Notts 5E 87
Haxby. York 4A 100
Haxey. N Lin 1E 87
Haybridge. Shrp 3A 60
Haybridge. Som 2A 22
Haydock. Mers 1H 83
Haydon. Bath 1B 22
Haydon. Dors 1B 14
Haydon. Som 4F 21
Haydon Bridge. Nmbd 3B 114
Haydon Wick. Swin 3G 35
Haye. Corn 2H 7
Hayes. G Lon 2E 39
(nr. Bromley)
Hayes. G Lon 2B 38
(nr. Uxbridge)
Hayfield. Derbs 2E 85
Hay Green. Norf 4E 77
Hayhill. E Ayr 3D 116
Haylands. IOW 3D 16
Hayle. Corn 3C 4
Hayley Green. W Mid 2D 60
Hayling Island. Hants 3F 17
Haynes. C Beds 1A 52
Haynes West End. C Beds 1A 52
Hay-on-Wye. Powy 1F 47
Hayscastle. Pemb 2C 42
Hayscastle Cross. Pemb 2D 42
Haysden. Kent 1G 27
Hayshead. Ang 4F 145

Holbeck Woodhouse—Houston

Holbeck Woodhouse. Notts 3C 86
Holberrow Green. Worc 5E 61
Holbeton. Devn 3C 8
Holborn. G Lon 2E 39
Holbrook. Derbs 1A 74
Holbrook. S Yor 2B 86
Holbrook. Suff 2E 55
Holburn. Nmbd 1E 121
Holbury. Hants 2C 16
Holcombe. Devn 5C 12
Holcombe. G Man 3F 91
Holcombe. Som 2B 22
Holcombe Brook. G Man 3F 91
Holcombe Rogus. Devn 1D 12
Holcot. Nptn 4E 63
Holden. Lanc 5G 97
Holdenby. Nptn 4D 62
Holder's Green. Essx 3G 53
Holdgate. Shrp 2H 59
Holdingham. Linc 1H 75
Holditch. Dors 2G 13
Holemoor. Devn 2E 11
Hole Street. W Sus 4C 26
Holford. Som 2E 21
Holker. Cumb 2C 96
Holkham. Norf 1A 78
Hollacombe. Devn 2D 11
Holland. Orkn 2D 172
Holland Fen. Linc 1B 76
Holland Lees. Lanc 4D 90
Holland-on-Sea. Essx 4F 55
Holland Park. W Mid 5E 73
Hollandstoun. Orkn 2G 172
Hollesley. Suff 1G 55
Hollinfare. Warr 1A 84
Hollingbourne. Kent 5C 40
Hollingbury. Brig 5E 27
Hollingdon. Buck 3G 51
Hollingrove. E Sus 3A 28
Hollington. Derbs 1G 73
Hollington. E Sus 4B 28
Hollington. Staf 2E 73
Hollington Grove. Derbs 2G 73
Hollingworth. G Man 1E 85
Hollins. Derbs 3H 85
Hollins. G Man 4G 91
(nr. Bury)
Hollins. G Man 4G 91
(nr. Middleton)
Hollinsclough. Staf 4E 85
Hollinswood. Telf 5A 72
Hollinthorpe. W Yor 1D 93
Hollinwood. G Man 4H 91
Hollinwood. Shrp 2H 71
Hollocombe. Devn 1G 11
Holloway. Derbs 5H 85
Hollow Court. Worc 5D 61
Hollowell. Nptn 3D 62
Hollow Meadows. S Yor 2G 85
Hollows. Dum 2E 113
Hollybush. Cphy 5E 47
Hollybush. E Ayr 3C 116
Hollybush. Worc 2C 48
Holly End. Norf 5D 77
Holly Hill. N Yor 4E 105
Hollyhurst. Ches E 1H 71
Hollym. E Yor 2G 95
Hollywood. Staf 2D 72
Hollywood. Worc 3E 61
Holmacott. Devn 4F 19
Holmbridge. W Yor 4B 92
Holmbury St Mary. Surr 1C 26
Holmbush. Corn 3E 7
Holmcroft. Staf 3D 72
Holme. Cambs 2A 64
Holme. Cumb 2E 97
Holme. N Lin 4C 94
Holme. N Yor 1F 99
Holme. Notts 5F 87
Holme. W Yor 4B 92
Holmebridge. Dors 4D 15
Holme Chapel. Lanc 2G 91
Holme Hale. Norf 5A 78
Holme Lacy. Here 2A 48
Holme Marsh. Here 5F 59
Holmend. Dum 4C 118
Holme next the Sea. Norf 1G 77
Holme-on-Spalding-Moor. E Yor 1B 94
Holme on the Wolds. E Yor 5D 100
Holme Pierrepont. Notts 2D 74
Holmer. Here 1A 48
Holmer Green. Buck 1A 38
Holmes. Lanc 3C 90
Holme St Cuthbert. Cumb 5C 112
Holmes Chapel. Ches E 4B 84
Holmesfield. Derbs 3H 85
Holmeswood. Lanc 3C 90
Holmewood. Derbs 4B 86
Holmfirth. W Yor 4B 92
Holmhead. E Ayr 2E 117
Holmisdale. High 4A 154
Holm of Drumlanrig. Dum 5H 117
Holmpton. E Yor 2G 95
Holmrook. Cumb 5B 102
Holmside. Dur 5F 115
Holmwrangle. Cumb 5G 113
Holne. Devn 2D 8
Holsworthy. Devn 2D 10
Holsworthy Beacon. Devn 2D 10
Holt. Dors 2F 15
Holt. Norf 2C 78
Holt. Wilts 5D 34
Holt. Worc 4C 60
Holt. Wrex 5G 83
Holtby. York 4A 100
Holt End. Hants 3E 25
Holt End. Worc 4E 61
Holt Fleet. Worc 4C 60
Holt Green. Lanc 4B 90
Holt Heath. Dors 2F 15
Holt Heath. Worc 4C 60
Holton. Oxon 5E 50
Holton. Som 4B 22
Holton. Suff 3F 67
Holton cum Beckering. Linc 2A 88
Holton Heath. Dors 3E 15
Holton le Clay. Linc 4F 95
Holton le Moor. Linc 1H 87
Holton St Mary. Suff 2D 54
Holt Pound. Hants 2G 25
Holtsmere End. Herts 4A 52
Holtye. E Sus 2F 27
Holwell. Dors 1C 14
Holwell. Herts 2B 52
Holwell. Leics 3E 75
Holwell. Oxon 5H 49
Holwell. Som 2C 22
Holwick. Dur 2C 104
Holworth. Dors 4C 14
Holybourne. Hants 2F 25
Holy City. Devn 2G 13
Holy Cross. Worc 3D 60
Holyfield. Essx 5D 53
Holyhead. IOA 2B 80
Holy Island. Nmbd 5H 131
Holymoorside. Derbs 4H 85
Holyport. Wind 4G 37
Holystone. Nmbd 4D 120
Holytown. N Lan 3A 128
Holywell. Cambs 3C 64
Holywell. Corn 3B 6
Holywell. Dors 2A 14
Holywell. Flin 3D 82
Holywell. Glos 2C 34
Holywell. Nmbd 2G 115
Holywell. Warw 4F 61
Holywell Green. W Yor 3A 92
Holywell Lake. Som 4E 20
Holywell Row. Suff 3G 65
Holywood. Dum 1G 111
Homer. Shrp 5A 72
Homer Green. Mers 4B 90
Homersfield. Suff 2E 67
Hom Green. Here 3A 48
Homington. Wilts 4G 23
Honeyborough. Pemb 4D 42
Honeybourne. Worc 1G 49
Honeychurch. Devn 2G 11
Honeydon. Bed 5A 64
Honey Hill. Kent 4F 41
Honey Street. Wilts 5G 35
Honey Tye. Suff 2C 54
Honeywick. C Beds 3H 51
Honiley. Warw 3G 61
Honing. Norf 3F 79
Honingham. Norf 4D 78
Honington. Linc 1G 75
Honington. Suff 3B 66
Honington. Warw 1A 50
Honiton. Devn 2E 13
Honley. W Yor 3B 92
Honnington. Telf 4B 72
Hoo. Suff 5E 67
Hoobrook. Worc 3C 60
Hood Green. S Yor 4D 92
Hooe. E Sus 5A 28
Hooe. Plym 3B 8
Hooe Common. E Sus 4A 28
Hoohill. Bkpl 1B 90
Hook. Cambs 1D 64
Hook. E Yor 2A 94
Hook. G Lon 4C 38
Hook. Hants 1F 25
(nr. Basingstoke)
Hook. Hants 2D 16
(nr. Fareham)
Hook. Pemb 3D 43
Hook. Wilts 3F 35
Hook-a-Gate. Shrp 5G 71
Hook Bank. Worc 1D 48
Hooke. Dors 2A 14
Hooker Gate. Tyne 4E 115
Hookgate. Staf 2B 72
Hook Green. Kent 2A 28
(nr. Lamberhurst)
Hook Green. Kent 3H 39
(nr. Longfield)
Hook Green. Kent 4H 39
(nr. Meopham)
Hook Norton. Oxon 2B 50
Hook's Cross. Herts 3C 52
Hook Street. Glos 2B 34
Hookway. Devn 3B 12
Hookwood. Surr 1D 26
Hoole. Ches W 4G 83
Hooley. Surr 5D 39
Hooley Bridge. G Man 3G 91
Hooley Brow. G Man 3G 91
Hoo St Werburgh. Medw 3B 40
Hooton. Ches W 3F 83
Hooton Levitt. S Yor 1C 86
Hooton Pagnell. S Yor 4E 93
Hooton Roberts. S Yor 1B 86
Hope. Derbs 2F 85
Hope. Flin 5F 83
Hope. High 2E 167
Hope. Powy 5E 71
Hope. Shrp 5F 71
Hope. Staf 5F 85
Hope Bagot. Shrp 3H 59
Hope Bowdler. Shrp 1G 59
Hopedale. Staf 5F 85
Hope Green. Ches E 2D 84
Hopeman. Mor 2F 159
Hope Mansell. Here 4B 48
Hopesay. Shrp 2F 59
Hope's Green. Essx 2B 40
Hopetown. W Yor 2D 93
Hope under Dinmore. Here 5H 59
Hopley's Green. Here 5F 59
Hopperton. N Yor 4G 99
Hop Pole. Linc 4A 76
Hopstone. Shrp 1B 60
Hopton. Derbs 5G 85
Hopton. Powy 1E 59
Hopton. Shrp 3F 71
(nr. Oswestry)
Hopton. Shrp 3H 71
(nr. Wem)
Hopton. Staf 3D 72
Hopton. Suff 3B 66
Hopton Cangeford. Shrp 2H 59
Hopton Castle. Shrp 3F 59
Hoptonheath. Shrp 3F 59
Hopton Heath. Staf 3D 72
Hopton on Sea. Norf 5H 79
Hopton Wafers. Shrp 3A 60
Hopwas. Staf 5F 73
Hopwood. Worc 3E 61
Horam. E Sus 4G 27
Horbling. Linc 2A 76
Horbury. W Yor 3C 92
Horcott. Glos 5G 49
Horden. Dur 5H 115
Horderley. Shrp 2G 59
Hordle. Hants 3A 16
Hordley. Shrp 2F 71
Horeb. Carm 3F 45
(nr. Brechfa)
Horeb. Carm 5E 45
(nr. Llanelli)
Horeb. Cdgn 1D 45
Horfield. Bris 4B 34
Horgabost. W Isl 8C 171
Horham. Suff 3E 66
Horkesley Heath. Essx 3C 54
Horkstow. N Lin 3C 94
Horley. Oxon 1C 50
Horley. Surr 1D 27
Horn Ash. Dors 2G 13
Hornblotton Green. Som 3A 22
Hornby. Lanc 3E 97
Hornby. N Yor 4A 106
(nr. Appleton Wiske)
Hornby. N Yor 5F 105
(nr. Catterick Garrison)
Horncastle. Linc 4B 88
Hornchurch. G Lon 2G 39
Horncliffe. Nmbd 5F 131
Horndean. Hants 1E 17
Horndean. Bord 5E 131
Horndon. Devn 4F 11
Horndon on the Hill. Thur 2A 40
Horne. Surr 1E 27
Horner. Som 2C 20
Horning. Norf 4F 79
Horninghold. Leics 1F 63
Horninglow. Staf 3G 73
Horningsea. Cambs 4D 65
Horningsham. Wilts 2D 22
Horningtoft. Norf 3B 78
Hornsbury. Som 1G 13
Hornsby. Cumb 4G 113
Hornsbygate. Cumb 4G 113
Horns Corner. Kent 3B 28
Horns Cross. Devn 4D 19
Hornsea. E Yor 5G 101
Hornsea Burton. E Yor 5G 101
Hornsey. G Lon 2E 39
Hornton. Oxon 1B 50
Horpit. Swin 3H 35
Horrabridge. Devn 2B 8
Horringer. Suff 4H 65
Horringford. IOW 4D 16
Horrocks Fold. G Man 3F 91
Horrocksford. Lanc 5G 97
Horsbrugh Ford. Bord 1E 119
Horsebridge. Devn 5E 11
Horsebridge. Hants 3B 24
Horse Bridge. Staf 5D 84
Horsebrook. Staf 4C 72
Horsecastle. N Som 5H 33
Horsehay. Telf 5A 72
Horseheath. Cambs 1G 53
Horsehouse. N Yor 1C 98
Horsell. Surr 5A 38
Horseman's Green. Wrex 1G 71
Horsenden. Buck 5F 51
Horseway. Cambs 2D 64
Horsey. Norf 3G 79
Horsey. Som 3G 21
Horsford. Norf 4D 78
Horsforth. W Yor 1C 92
Horsham. W Sus 2C 26
Horsham. Worc 5B 60
Horsham St Faith. Norf 4E 78
Horsington. Linc 4A 88
Horsington. Som 4C 22
Horsley. Derbs 1A 74
Horsley. Glos 2D 34
Horsley. Nmbd 3D 115
(nr. Prudhoe)
Horsley. Nmbd 5C 120
(nr. Rochester)
Horsley Cross. Essx 3E 54
Horsleycross Street. Essx 3E 54
Horsleyhill. Bord 3H 119
Horsleyhope. Dur 5D 114
Horsley Woodhouse. Derbs 1A 74
Horsmonden. Kent 1A 28
Horspath. Oxon 5D 50
Horstead. Norf 4E 79
Horsted Keynes. W Sus 3E 27
Horton. Buck 4H 51
Horton. Dors 2F 15
Horton. Lanc 4A 98
Horton. Nptn 5F 63
Horton. Shrp 2G 71
Horton. Som 1G 13
Horton. S Glo 3C 34
Horton. Staf 5D 84
Horton. Swan 4D 30
Horton. Wilts 5F 35
Horton. Wind 3B 38
Horton Cross. Som 1G 13
Horton-cum-Studley. Oxon 4D 50
Horton Grange. Nmbd 2F 115
Horton Green. Ches W 1G 71
Horton Heath. Hants 1C 16
Horton in Ribblesdale. N Yor 2H 97
Horton Kirby. Kent 4G 39
Hortonwood. Telf 4A 72
Horwich. G Man 3E 91
Horwich End. Derbs 2E 85
Horwood. Devn 4F 19
Hoscar. Lanc 3C 90
Hose. Leics 3E 75
Hosh. Per 1A 136
Hosta. W Isl 1C 170
Hoswick. Shet 9F 173
Hotham. E Yor 1B 94
Hothfield. Kent 1D 28
Hoton. Leics 3C 74
Houbie. Shet 2H 173
Hough. Arg 4A 138
Hough. Ches E 5B 84
(nr. Crewe)
Hough. Ches E 3C 84
(nr. Wilmslow)
Hougham. Linc 1F 75
Hough Green. Hal 2G 83
Hough-on-the-Hill. Linc 1G 75
Houghton. Cambs 3B 64
Houghton. Cumb 4F 113
Houghton. Hants 3B 24
Houghton. Nmbd 3E 115
Houghton. Pemb 4D 43
Houghton. W Sus 4B 26
Houghton Bank. Darl 2F 105
Houghton Conquest. C Beds 1A 52
Houghton Green. E Sus 3D 28
Houghton-le-Side. Darl 2F 105
Houghton-le-Spring. Tyne 5G 115
Houghton on the Hill. Leics 5D 74
Houghton Regis. C Beds 3A 52
Houghton St Giles. Norf 2B 78
Houlsyke. N Yor 4E 107
Hound. Hants 2C 16
Hound Green. Hants 1F 25
Houndslow. Bord 5C 130
Houndsmoor. Som 4E 21
Houndwood. Bord 3E 131
Hounsdown. Hants 1B 16
Hounslow. G Lon 3C 38
Housay. Shet 4H 173
Househill. High 3C 158
Housetter. Shet 3E 173
Houss. Shet 8E 173
Houston. Ren 3F 127

Insch—Keswick

Insch. *Abers* 1D **152**
Insh. *High* 3C **150**
Inshegra. *High* 3C **166**
Inshore. *High* 1D **166**
Inskip. *Lanc* 1C **90**
Instow. *Devn* 3E **19**
Intwood. *Norf* 5D **78**
Inver. *Abers* 4G **151**
Inver. *High* 5F **165**
Inver. *Per* 4H **143**
Inverailort. *High* 5F **147**
Inveralligin. *High* 3H **155**
Inverallochy. *Abers* 2H **161**
Inveramsay. *Abers* 1E **153**
Inveran. *High* 4C **164**
Inveraray. *Arg* 3H **133**
Inverarish. *High* 5E **155**
Inverarity. *Ang* 4D **144**
Inverarnan. *Arg* 2C **134**
Inverarnie. *High* 5A **158**
Inverbeg. *Arg* 4C **134**
Inverbervie. *Abers* 1H **145**
Inverboyndie. *Abers* 2D **160**
Invercassley. *High* 3B **164**
Invercharnan. *High* 4F **141**
Inverchoran. *High* 3E **157**
Invercreran. *Arg* 4E **141**
Inverdruie. *High* 2D **150**
Inverebrie. *Abers* 5G **161**
Invereck. *Arg* 1C **126**
Inveresk. *E Lot* 2G **129**
Inveresragan. *Arg* 5D **141**
Inverey. *Abers* 5E **151**
Inverfarigaig. *High* 1H **149**
Invergarry. *High* 3F **149**
Invergeldie. *Per* 1G **135**
Invergordon. *High* 2B **158**
Invergowrie. *Per* 5C **144**
Inverguseran. *High* 3F **147**
Inverharroch. *Mor* 5A **160**
Inverie. *High* 3F **147**
Inverinan. *Arg* 2G **133**
Inverinate. *High* 1B **148**
Inverkeilor. *Ang* 4F **145**
Inverkeithing. *Fife* 1E **129**
Inverkeithny. *Abers* 4D **160**
Inverkip. *Inv* 2D **126**
Inverkirkaig. *High* 2E **163**
Inverlael. *High* 5F **163**
Inverliever Lodge. *Arg* 3F **133**
Inverliver. *Arg* 5E **141**
Inverloch. *High* 1F **141**
Inverlochlarig. *Stir* 2D **134**
Inverlussa. *Arg* 1E **125**
Inver Mallie. *High* 5D **148**
Invermarkie. *Abers* 5B **160**
Invermoriston. *High* 2G **149**
Invernaver. *High* 2H **167**
Inverneil House. *Arg* 1G **125**
Inverness. *High* 4A **158**
Inverness Airport. *High* 3B **158**
Invernettie. *Abers* 4H **161**
Inverpolly Lodge. *High* 2E **163**
Inverquhomery. *Abers* 4H **161**
Inverroy. *High* 5E **149**
Inversanda. *High* 3D **140**
Invershiel. *High* 2B **148**
Invershin. *High* 4C **164**
Invershore. *High* 5E **169**
Inversnaid. *Stir* 3C **134**
Inverugie. *Abers* 4H **161**
Inveruglas. *Arg* 3C **134**
Inverurie. *Abers* 1E **153**
Invervar. *Per* 4D **142**
Inverythan. *Abers* 4E **161**
Inwardleigh. *Devn* 3F **11**
Inworth. *Essx* 4B **54**
Iochdar. *W Isl* 4C **170**
Iping. *W Sus* 4G **25**
Ipplepen. *Devn* 2E **9**
Ipsden. *Oxon* 3E **37**
Ipstones. *Staf* 1E **73**
Ipswich. *Suff* 1E **55**
Irby. *Mers* 2E **83**
Irby in the Marsh. *Linc* 4D **88**
Irby upon Humber. *NE Lin* 4E **95**
Irchester. *Nptn* 4G **63**
Ireby. *Cumb* 1D **102**
Ireby. *Lanc* 2F **97**
Ireland. *Shet* 9E **173**
Ireleth. *Cumb* 2B **96**
Ireshopeburn. *Dur* 1B **104**
Ireton Wood. *Derbs* 1G **73**
Irlam. *G Man* 1B **84**
Irnham. *Linc* 3H **75**
Iron Acton. *S Glo* 3B **34**
Iron Bridge. *Cambs* 1D **65**
Ironbridge. *Telf* 5A **72**
Iron Cross. *Warw* 5E **61**
Ironville. *Derbs* 5B **86**
Irstead. *Norf* 3F **79**
Irthington. *Cumb* 3F **113**
Irthlingborough. *Nptn* 3G **63**
Irton. *N Yor* 1E **101**
Irvine. *N Ayr* 1C **116**
Irvine Mains. *N Ayr* 1C **116**
Isabella Pit. *Nmbd* 1G **115**
Isauld. *High* 2B **168**
Isbister. *Orkn* 6D **172**
Isbister. *Shet* 5G **173**
Isfield. *E Sus* 4F **27**
Isham. *Nptn* 3F **63**
Island Carr. *N Lin* 4C **94**
Islay Airport. *Arg* 4B **124**
Isle Abbotts. *Som* 4G **21**
Isle Brewers. *Som* 4G **21**
Isleham. *Cambs* 3F **65**
Isle of Man Airport. *IOM* 5B **108**
Isle of Thanet. *Kent* 4H **41**
Isle of Whithorn. *Dum* 5B **110**
Isleornsay. *High* 2F **147**
Isles of Scilly (St Mary's) Airport. *IOS* 1B **4**
Islesteps. *Dum* 2A **112**
Isleworth. *G Lon* 3C **38**
Isley Walton. *Leics* 3B **74**
Islibhig. *W Isl* 5B **171**
Islington. *G Lon* 2E **39**
Islington. *Telf* 3B **72**
Islip. *Nptn* 3G **63**
Islip. *Oxon* 4D **50**
Islwyn. *Cphy* 2F **33**
Istead Rise. *Kent* 4H **39**
Itchen. *Sotn* 1C **16**
Itchen Abbas. *Hants* 3D **24**
Itchen Stoke. *Hants* 3D **24**
Itchingfield. *W Sus* 3C **26**
Itchington. *S Glo* 3B **34**
Itlaw. *Abers* 3D **160**
Itteringham. *Norf* 2D **78**
Itteringham Common. *Norf* 3D **78**
Itton. *Devn* 3G **11**
Itton Common. *Mon* 2H **33**
Ivegill. *Cumb* 5F **113**
Ivelet. *N Yor* 5C **104**
Iverchaolain. *Arg* 2B **126**
Iver Heath. *Buck* 2B **38**
Iveston. *Dur* 4E **115**
Ivetsey Bank. *Staf* 4C **72**
Ivinghoe. *Buck* 4H **51**
Ivinghoe Aston. *Buck* 4H **51**
Ivington. *Here* 5G **59**
Ivington Green. *Here* 5G **59**
Ivybridge. *Devn* 3C **8**
Ivychurch. *Kent* 3E **29**
Ivy Hatch. *Kent* 5G **39**
Ivy Todd. *Norf* 5A **78**
Iwade. *Kent* 4D **40**
Iwerne Courtney. *Dors* 1D **14**
Iwerne Minster. *Dors* 1D **14**
Ixworth. *Suff* 3B **66**
Ixworth Thorpe. *Suff* 3B **66**

J

Jackfield. *Shrp* 5A **72**
Jack Hill. *N Yor* 4E **98**
Jacksdale. *Notts* 5B **86**
Jackton. *S Lan* 4G **127**
Jacobstow. *Corn* 3B **10**
Jacobstowe. *Devn* 2F **11**
Jacobswell. *Surr* 5A **38**
Jameston. *Pemb* 5E **43**
Jamestown. *Dum* 5F **119**
Jamestown. *Fife* 1E **129**
Jamestown. *High* 3G **157**
Jamestown. *W Dun* 1E **127**
Janetstown. *High* 2C **168** (nr. Thurso)
Janetstown. *High* 3F **169** (nr. Wick)
Jarrow. *Tyne* 3G **115**
Jarvis Brook. *E Sus* 3G **27**
Jasper's Green. *Essx* 3H **53**
Jaywick. *Essx* 4E **55**
Jedburgh. *Bord* 2A **120**
Jeffreyston. *Pemb* 4E **43**
Jemimaville. *High* 2B **158**
Jenkins Park. *High* 3F **149**
Jersey Marine. *Neat* 3G **31**
Jesmond. *Tyne* 3F **115**
Jevington. *E Sus* 5G **27**
Jingle Street. *Mon* 4H **47**
Jockey End. *Herts* 4A **52**
Jodrell Bank. *Ches E* 3B **84**
Johnby. *Cumb* 1F **103**
John o' Gaunts. *W Yor* 2D **92**
John o' Groats. *High* 1F **169**
John's Cross. *E Sus* 3B **28**
Johnshaven. *Abers* 2G **145**
Johnson Street. *Norf* 4F **79**
Johnston. *Pemb* 3D **42**
Johnstone. *Ren* 3F **127**
Johnstonebridge. *Dum* 5C **118**
Johnstown. *Carm* 4D **45**
Johnstown. *Wrex* 1F **71**
Joppa. *Edin* 2G **129**
Joppa. *S Ayr* 3D **116**
Jordan Green. *Norf* 3C **78**
Jordans. *Buck* 1A **38**
Jordanston. *Pemb* 1D **42**
Jump. *S Yor* 4D **93**
Jumpers Common. *Dors* 3G **15**
Juniper. *Nmbd* 4C **114**
Juniper Green. *Edin* 3E **129**
Jurby East. *IOM* 2C **108**
Jurby West. *IOM* 2C **108**
Jury's Gap. *E Sus* 4D **28**

K

Kaber. *Cumb* 3A **104**
Kaimend. *S Lan* 5C **128**
Kaimes. *Edin* 3F **129**
Kaimrig End. *Bord* 5D **129**
Kames. *Arg* 2A **126**
Kames. *E Ayr* 2F **117**
Kea. *Corn* 4C **6**
Keadby. *N Lin* 3B **94**
Keal Cotes. *Linc* 4C **88**
Kearsley. *G Man* 4F **91**
Kearsney. *Kent* 1G **29**
Kearstwick. *Cumb* 1F **97**
Kearton. *N Yor* 5C **104**
Kearvaig. *High* 1C **166**
Keasden. *N Yor* 3G **97**
Keason. *Corn* 2H **7**
Keckwick. *Hal* 2H **83**
Keddington. *Linc* 2C **88**
Keddington Corner. *Linc* 2C **88**
Kedington. *Suff* 1H **53**
Kedleston. *Derbs* 1H **73**
Kedlock Feus. *Fife* 2F **137**
Keelby. *Linc* 3E **95**
Keele. *Staf* 1C **72**
Keeley Green. *Bed* 1A **52**
Keeston. *Pemb* 3D **42**
Keevil. *Wilts* 1E **23**
Kegworth. *Leics* 3B **74**
Kehelland. *Corn* 2D **4**
Keig. *Abers* 2D **152**
Keighley. *W Yor* 5C **98**
Keilarsbrae. *Clac* 4A **136**
Keillmore. *Arg* 1E **125**
Keillor. *Per* 4B **144**
Keillour. *Per* 1B **136**
Keills. *Arg* 3C **124**
Keiloch. *Abers* 4F **151**
Keils. *Arg* 3D **124**
Keinton Mandeville. *Som* 3A **22**
Keir Mill. *Dum* 5A **118**
Keirsleywell Row. *Nmbd* 4A **114**
Keisby. *Linc* 3H **75**
Keisley. *Cumb* 2A **104**
Keiss. *High* 2F **169**
Keith. *Mor* 3B **160**
Keith Inch. *Abers* 4H **161**
Kelbrook. *Lanc* 5B **98**
Kelby. *Linc* 1H **75**
Keld. *Cumb* 3G **103**
Keld. *N Yor* 4B **104**
Keldholme. *N Yor* 1B **100**
Kelfield. *N Lin* 4B **94**
Kelfield. *N Yor* 1F **93**
Kelham. *Notts* 5E **87**
Kellacott. *Devn* 4E **11**
Kellan. *Arg* 4G **139**
Kellas. *Ang* 5D **144**
Kellas. *Mor* 3F **159**
Kellaton. *Devn* 5E **9**
Kelleth. *Cumb* 4H **103**
Kelling. *Norf* 1C **78**
Kellingley. *N Yor* 2F **93**
Kellington. *N Yor* 2F **93**
Kelloe. *Dur* 1A **106**
Kelloholm. *Dum* 3G **117**
Kells. *Cumb* 3A **102**
Kelly. *Devn* 4D **11**
Kelly Bray. *Corn* 5D **10**
Kelmarsh. *Nptn* 3E **63**
Kelmscott. *Oxon* 2A **36**
Kelsale. *Suff* 4F **67**
Kelsall. *Ches W* 4H **83**
Kelshall. *Herts* 2D **52**
Kelsick. *Cumb* 4C **112**
Kelso. *Bord* 1B **120**
Kelstedge. *Derbs* 4H **85**
Kelstern. *Linc* 1B **88**
Kelsterton. *Flin* 3E **83**
Kelston. *Bath* 5C **34**
Keltneyburn. *Per* 4E **143**
Kelton. *Dum* 2A **112**
Kelton Hill. *Dum* 4E **111**
Kelty. *Fife* 4D **136**
Kelvedon. *Essx* 4B **54**
Kelvedon Hatch. *Essx* 1G **39**
Kelvinside. *Glas* 3G **127**
Kelynack. *Corn* 3A **4**
Kemback. *Fife* 2G **137**
Kemberton. *Shrp* 5B **72**
Kemble. *Glos* 2E **35**
Kemerton. *Worc* 2E **49**
Kemeys Commander. *Mon* 5G **47**
Kemnay. *Abers* 2E **153**
Kempe's Corner. *Kent* 1E **29**
Kempley. *Glos* 3B **48**
Kempley Green. *Glos* 3B **48**
Kempsey. *Worc* 1D **48**
Kempsford. *Glos* 2G **35**
Kemps Green. *Warw* 3F **61**
Kempshott. *Hants* 1E **24**
Kempston. *Bed* 1A **52**
Kempston Hardwick. *Bed* 1A **52**
Kempton. *Shrp* 2F **59**
Kemp Town. *Brig* 5E **27**
Kemsing. *Kent* 5G **39**
Kemsley. *Kent* 4D **40**
Kenardington. *Kent* 2D **28**
Kenchester. *Here* 1H **47**
Kencot. *Oxon* 5A **50**
Kendal. *Cumb* 5G **103**
Kendleshire. *S Glo* 4B **34**
Kendray. *S Yor* 4D **92**
Kenfig. *B'end* 3B **32**
Kenfig Hill. *B'end* 3B **32**
Kengharair. *Arg* 4F **139**
Kenidjack. *Corn* 3A **4**
Kenilworth. *Warw* 3G **61**
Kenknock. *Stir* 5B **142**
Kenley. *G Lon* 5E **39**
Kenley. *Shrp* 5H **71**
Kenmore. *High* 3G **155**
Kenmore. *Per* 4E **143**
Kenn. *Devn* 4C **12**
Kenn. *N Som* 5H **33**
Kennacraig. *Arg* 3G **125**
Kenneggy Downs. *Corn* 4C **4**
Kennerleigh. *Devn* 2B **12**
Kennet. *Clac* 4B **136**
Kennethmont. *Abers* 1C **152**
Kennett. *Cambs* 4G **65**
Kennford. *Devn* 4C **12**
Kenninghall. *Norf* 2C **66**
Kennington. *Kent* 1E **29**
Kennington. *Oxon* 5D **50**
Kennoway. *Fife* 3F **137**
Kennyhill. *Suff* 3F **65**
Kennythorpe. *N Yor* 3B **100**
Kenovay. *Arg* 4A **138**
Kensaleyre. *High* 3D **154**
Kensington. *G Lon* 3D **38**
Kenstone. *Shrp* 3H **71**
Kensworth. *C Beds* 4A **52**
Kensworth Common. *C Beds* 4A **52**
Kentallen. *High* 3E **141**
Kentchurch. *Here* 3H **47**
Kentford. *Suff* 4G **65**
Kent International Airport. *Kent* 4H **41**
Kentisbeare. *Devn* 2D **12**
Kentisbury. *Devn* 2G **19**
Kentisbury Ford. *Devn* 2G **19**
Kentmere. *Cumb* 4F **103**
Kenton. *Devn* 4C **12**
Kenton. *G Lon* 2C **38**
Kenton. *Suff* 4D **66**
Kenton Bankfoot. *Tyne* 3F **115**
Kentra. *High* 2A **140**
Kentrigg. *Cumb* 5G **103**
Kents Bank. *Cumb* 2C **96**
Kent's Green. *Glos* 3C **48**
Kent's Oak. *Hants* 4B **24**
Kent Street. *E Sus* 4B **28**
Kent Street. *Kent* 5A **40**
Kent Street. *W Sus* 3D **26**
Kenwick. *Shrp* 2G **71**
Kenwyn. *Corn* 4C **6**
Kenyon. *Warr* 1A **84**
Keoldale. *High* 2D **166**
Keppoch. *High* 1B **148**
Kepwick. *N Yor* 5B **106**
Keresley. *W Mid* 2H **61**
Keresley Newland. *Warw* 2H **61**
Keristal. *IOM* 4C **108**
Kerne Bridge. *Here* 4A **48**
Kerridge. *Ches E* 3D **84**
Kerris. *Corn* 4B **4**
Kerrow. *High* 5F **157**
Kerry. *Powy* 2D **58**
Kerrycroy. *Arg* 3C **126**
Kerry's Gate. *Here* 2G **47**
Kersall. *Notts* 4E **86**
Kersbrook. *Devn* 4D **12**
Kerse. *Ren* 4E **127**
Kersey. *Suff* 1D **54**
Kershopefoot. *Cumb* 1F **113**
Kersoe. *Worc* 2E **49**
Kerswell. *Devn* 2D **12**
Kerswell Green. *Worc* 1D **48**
Kesgrave. *Suff* 1F **55**
Kessingland. *Suff* 2H **67**
Kessingland Beach. *Suff* 2H **67**
Kestle. *Corn* 4D **6**
Kestle Mill. *Corn* 3C **6**
Keston. *G Lon* 4F **39**
Keswick. *Cumb* 2D **102**

Keswick—Kinross

Keswick. Norf 2F 79 (nr. North Walsham)
Keswick. Norf 5E 78 (nr. Norwich)
Ketsby. Linc 3C 88
Kettering. Nptn 3F 63
Ketteringham. Norf 5D 78
Kettins. Per 5B 144
Kettlebaston. Suff 5B 66
Kettlebridge. Fife 3F 137
Kettlebrook. Staf 5G 73
Kettleburgh. Suff 4E 67
Kettleholm. Dum 2C 112
Kettleness. N Yor 3F 107
Kettleshulme. Ches E 3D 85
Kettlesing. N Yor 4E 99
Kettlesing Bottom. N Yor 4E 99
Kettlestone. Norf 2B 78
Kettlethorpe. Linc 3F 87
Kettletoft. Orkn 4F 172
Kettlewell. N Yor 2B 98
Ketton. Rut 5G 75
Kew. G Lon 3C 38
Kewaigue. IOM 4C 108
Kewstoke. N Som 5G 33
Kexbrough. S Yor 4D 92
Kexby. Linc 2F 87
Kexby. York 4B 100
Keyford. Som 2C 22
Key Green. Ches E 4C 84
Key Green. N Yor 4F 107
Keyham. Leics 5D 74
Keyhaven. Hants 3B 16
Keyhead. Abers 3H 161
Keyingham. E Yor 2F 95
Keymer. W Sus 4E 27
Keynsham. Bath 5B 34
Keysoe. Bed 4H 63
Keysoe Row. Bed 4H 63
Key's Toft. Linc 5D 89
Keyston. Cambs 3H 63
Key Street. Kent 4C 40
Keyworth. Notts 2D 74
Kibblesworth. Tyne 4F 115
Kibworth Beauchamp. Leics 1D 62
Kibworth Harcourt. Leics 1D 62
Kidbrooke. G Lon 3F 39
Kidburngill. Cumb 2B 102
Kiddemore Green. Staf 5C 72
Kidderminster. Worc 3C 60
Kiddington. Oxon 3C 50
Kidd's Moor. Norf 5D 78
Kidlington. Oxon 4C 50
Kidmore End. Oxon 4E 37
Kidnal. Ches W 1G 71
Kidsgrove. Staf 5C 84
Kidstones. N Yor 1B 98
Kidwelly. Carm 5E 45
Kiel Crofts. Arg 5D 140
Kielder. Nmbd 5A 120
Kilbagie. Fife 4B 136
Kilbarchan. Ren 3F 127
Kilbeg. High 3E 147
Kilberry. Arg 3F 125
Kilbirnie. N Ayr 4E 126
Kilbride. Arg 1F 133
Kilbride. High 1D 147
Kilbucho Place. Bord 1C 118
Kilburn. Derbs 1A 74
Kilburn. G Lon 2D 38
Kilburn. N Yor 2H 99
Kilby. Leics 1D 62
Kilchattan. Arg 4A 132 (on Colonsay)
Kilchattan. Arg 4C 126 (on Isle of Bute)
Kilchattan Bay. Arg 4B 126
Kilchenzie. Arg 3A 122
Kilcheran. Arg 5C 140
Kilchiaran. Arg 3A 124
Kilchoan. High 4F 147 (nr. Inverie)
Kilchoan. High 2F 139 (nr. Tobermory)
Kilchoman. Arg 3A 124
Kilchrenan. Arg 1H 133
Kilconquhar. Fife 3G 137
Kilcot. Glos 3B 48
Kilcoy. High 3H 157
Kilcreggan. Arg 1D 126
Kildale. N Yor 4D 106
Kildary. High 1B 158
Kildermorie Lodge. High 1H 157
Kildonan. Dum 4F 109
Kildonan. High 1G 165 (nr. Helmsdale)
Kildonan. High 3C 154 (on Isle of Skye)
Kildonan. N Ayr 3E 123
Kildonnan. High 5C 146
Kildrummy. Abers 2B 152
Kildwick. N Yor 5C 98
Kilfillan. Dum 4H 109
Kilfinan. Arg 2H 125
Kilfinnan. High 4E 149
Kilgetty. Pemb 4F 43
Kilgour. Fife 3E 136
Kilgrammie. S Ayr 4B 116
Kilham. E Yor 3E 101
Kilham. Nmbd 1C 120
Kilkenneth. Arg 4A 138
Kilkhampton. Corn 1C 10
Killamarsh. Derbs 2B 86
Killandrist. Arg 4C 140
Killay. Swan 3F 31
Killean. Arg 5E 125
Killearn. Stir 1G 127
Killellan. Arg 4A 122
Killen. High 3A 158
Killerby. Darl 3E 105
Killichonan. Per 3C 142
Killiechronan. Arg 4G 139
Killiecrankie. Per 2G 143
Killilan. High 5B 156
Killimster. High 3F 169
Killin. Stir 5C 142
Killinghall. N Yor 4E 99
Killinghurst. Surr 2A 26
Killington. Cumb 1F 97
Killingworth. Tyne 2F 115
Killin Lodge. High 3H 149
Killinochonoch. Arg 4F 133
Killochyett. Bord 5A 130
Killundine. High 4G 139
Kilmacolm. Inv 3E 127
Kilmahog. Stir 3F 135
Kilmahumaig. Arg 4E 133
Kilmalieu. High 3C 140
Kilmaluag. High 1D 154
Kilmany. Fife 1F 137
Kilmarie. High 2D 146
Kilmarnock. E Ayr 1D 116
Kilmaron. Fife 2F 137
Kilmartin. Arg 4F 133
Kilmaurs. E Ayr 5F 127
Kilmelford. Arg 2F 133
Kilmeny. Arg 3B 124
Kilmersdon. Som 1B 22
Kilmeston. Hants 4D 24
Kilmichael Glassary. Arg 4F 133
Kilmichael of Inverlussa. Arg 1F 125
Kilmington. Devn 3F 13
Kilmington. Wilts 3C 22
Kilmoluag. Arg 4A 138
Kilmorack. High 4G 157
Kilmore. Arg 1F 133
Kilmore. High 3E 147
Kilmory. Arg 2F 125
Kilmory. High 1G 139 (nr. Kilchoan)
Kilmory. High 3B 146 (on Rùm)
Kilmory. N Ayr 3D 122
Kilmory Lodge. Arg 3E 132
Kilmote. High 2G 165
Kilmuir. High 4B 154 (nr. Dunvegan)
Kilmuir. High 1B 158 (nr. Invergordon)
Kilmuir. High 4A 158 (nr. Inverness)
Kilmuir. High 1C 154 (nr. Uig)
Kilmun. Arg 1C 126
Kilnave. Arg 2A 124
Kilncadzow. S Lan 5B 128
Kilndown. Kent 2B 28
Kiln Green. Here 4B 48
Kiln Green. Wind 4G 37
Kilnhill. Cumb 1D 102
Kilnhurst. S Yor 1B 86
Kilninian. Arg 4E 139
Kilninver. Arg 1F 133
Kiln Pit Hill. Nmbd 4D 114
Kilnsea. E Yor 3H 95
Kilnsey. N Yor 3B 98
Kilnwick. E Yor 5D 101
Kiloran. Arg 4A 132
Kilpatrick. N Ayr 3D 122
Kilpeck. Here 2H 47
Kilpin. E Yor 2A 94
Kilpin Pike. E Yor 2A 94
Kilrenny. Fife 3H 137
Kilsby. Nptn 3C 62
Kilspindie. Per 1E 136
Kilsyth. N Lan 2A 128
Kiltarlity. High 4H 157
Kilton. Som 2E 21
Kilton Thorpe. Red C 3D 107
Kilvaxter. High 2C 154
Kilve. Som 2E 21
Kilvington. Notts 1F 75
Kilwinning. N Ayr 5D 126
Kimberley. Norf 5C 78
Kimberley. Notts 1B 74
Kimblesworth. Dur 5F 115
Kimble Wick. Buck 5G 51
Kimbolton. Cambs 4H 63
Kimbolton. Here 4H 59
Kimcote. Leics 2C 62
Kimmeridge. Dors 5E 15
Kimmerston. Nmbd 1D 120
Kimpton. Hants 2A 24
Kimpton. Herts 4B 52
Kinbeachie. High 2A 158
Kinbrace. High 5A 168
Kinbuck. Stir 3G 135
Kincaple. Fife 2G 137
Kincardine. Fife 1C 128
Kincardine. High 5D 164
Kincardine Bridge. Fife 1C 128
Kincardine O'Neil. Abers 4C 152
Kinchrackine. Arg 1A 134
Kincorth. Aber 3G 153
Kincraig. High 3C 150
Kincraigie. Per 4G 143
Kindallachan. Per 3G 143
Kineton. Glos 3F 49
Kineton. Warw 5H 61
Kinfauns. Per 1D 136
Kingairloch. High 3C 140
Kingarth. Arg 4B 126
Kingcoed. Mon 5H 47
Kingerby. Linc 1H 87
Kingham. Oxon 3A 50
Kingholm Quay. Dum 2A 112
Kinghorn. Fife 1F 129
Kingie. High 3D 148
Kinglassie. Fife 4E 137
Kingledores. Bord 2D 118
Kingodie. Per 1F 137
King o' Muirs. Clac 4A 136
King's Acre. Here 1H 47
Kingsand. Corn 3A 8
Kingsash. Buck 5G 51
Kingsbarns. Fife 2H 137
Kingsbridge. Devn 4D 8
Kingsbridge. Som 3C 20
King's Bromley. Staf 4F 73
Kingsburgh. High 3C 154
Kingsbury. G Lon 2C 38
Kingsbury. Warw 1G 61
Kingsbury Episcopi. Som 4H 21
Kings Caple. Here 3A 48
Kingscavil. W Lot 2D 128
Kingsclere. Hants 1D 24
King's Cliffe. Nptn 1H 63
Kingscote. Glos 2D 34
Kingscott. Devn 1F 11
Kings Coughton. Warw 5E 61
Kingscross. N Ayr 3E 123
Kingsdon. Som 4A 22
Kingsdown. Kent 1H 29
Kingsdown. Swin 3G 35
Kingsdown. Wilts 5D 34
Kingseat. Fife 4D 136
Kingsey. Buck 5F 51
Kingsfold. Lanc 2D 90
Kingsfold. W Sus 2C 26
Kingsford. E Ayr 5F 127
Kingsford. Worc 2C 60
Kingsforth. N Lin 3D 94
Kingsgate. Kent 3H 41
King's Green. Glos 2C 48
Kingshall Street. Suff 4B 66
Kingsheanton. Devn 3F 19
King's Heath. W Mid 2E 61
Kings Hill. Kent 5A 40
Kingsholm. Glos 4D 48
Kingshouse. High 3G 141
Kingshouse. Stir 1E 135
Kingshurst. W Mid 2F 61
Kingskerswell. Devn 2E 9
Kingskettle. Fife 3F 137
Kingsland. Here 4G 59
Kingsland. IOA 2B 80
Kings Langley. Herts 5A 52
Kingsley. Ches W 3H 83
Kingsley. Hants 3F 25
Kingsley. Staf 1E 73
Kingsley Green. W Sus 3G 25
Kingsley Holt. Staf 1E 73
King's Lynn. Norf 3F 77
King's Meaburn. Cumb 2H 103
Kings Moss. Mers 4D 90
Kingsmuir. Ang 4D 145
Kingsmuir. Fife 3H 137
Kings Muir. Bord 1E 119
King's Newnham. Warw 3B 62
Kings Newton. Derbs 3A 74
Kingsnorth. Kent 2E 28
Kingsnorth. Medw 3C 40
King's Norton. Leics 5D 74
King's Norton. W Mid 3E 61
King's Nympton. Devn 1G 11
King's Pyon. Here 5G 59
Kings Ripton. Cambs 3B 64
King's Somborne. Hants 3B 24
King's Stag. Dors 1C 14
King's Stanley. Glos 5D 48
King's Sutton. Nptn 2C 50
Kingstanding. W Mid 1E 61
Kingsteignton. Devn 5B 12
Kingsteps. High 3D 158
King Sterndale. Derbs 3E 85
King's Thorn. Here 2A 48
Kingsthorpe. Nptn 4E 63
Kingston. Cambs 5C 64
Kingston. Devn 4C 8
Kingston. Dors 2C 14 (nr. Sturminster Newton)
Kingston. Dors 5E 15 (nr. Swanage)
Kingston. E Lot 1B 130
Kingston. Hants 2G 15
Kingston. IOW 4C 16
Kingston. Kent 5F 41
Kingston. Mor 2H 159
Kingston. W Sus 5B 26
Kingston Bagpuize. Oxon 2C 36
Kingston Blount. Oxon 2F 37
Kingston by Sea. W Sus 5D 26
Kingston Deverill. Wilts 3D 22
Kingstone. Here 2H 47
Kingstone. Som 1G 13
Kingstone. Staf 3E 73
Kingston Lisle. Oxon 3B 36
Kingston Maurward. Dors 3C 14
Kingston near Lewes. E Sus 5E 27
Kingston on Soar. Notts 3C 74
Kingston Russell. Dors 3A 14
Kingston St Mary. Som 4F 21
Kingston Seymour. N Som 5H 33
Kingston Stert. Oxon 5F 51
Kingston upon Hull. Hull 2D 94
Kingston upon Thames. G Lon 4C 38
King's Walden. Herts 3B 52
Kingswear. Devn 3E 9
Kingswells. Aber 3F 153
Kingswinford. W Mid 2C 60
Kingswood. Buck 4E 51
Kingswood. Glos 2C 34
Kingswood. Here 5E 59
Kingswood. Kent 5C 40
Kingswood. Per 5H 143
Kingswood. Powy 5E 71
Kingswood. Som 3E 20
Kingswood. S Glo 4B 34
Kingswood. Surr 5D 38
Kingswood. Warw 3F 61
Kingswood Common. Staf 5C 72
Kings Worthy. Hants 3C 24
Kingthorpe. Linc 3A 88
Kington. Here 5F 59
Kington. S Glo 2B 34
Kington. Worc 5D 61
Kington Langley. Wilts 4E 35
Kington Magna. Dors 4C 22
Kington St Michael. Wilts 4E 35
Kingussie. High 3B 150
Kingweston. Som 3A 22
Kinharrachie. Abers 5G 161
Kinhrive. High 1B 158
Kinkell Bridge. Per 2B 136
Kinknockie. Abers 4H 161
Kinkry Hill. Cumb 2G 113
Kinlet. Shrp 2B 60
Kinloch. High 5D 166 (nr. Loch More)
Kinloch. High 3A 140 (nr. Lochaline)
Kinloch. High 4C 146 (on Rùm)
Kinloch. Per 4A 144
Kinlochard. Stir 3D 134
Kinlochbervie. High 3C 166
Kinlocheil. High 1D 141
Kinlochewe. High 2C 156
Kinloch Hourn. High 3B 148
Kinloch Laggan. High 5H 149
Kinlochleven. High 2F 141
Kinloch Lodge. High 3F 167
Kinlochmoidart. High 1B 140
Kinlochmore. High 2F 141
Kinloch Rannoch. Per 3D 142
Kinlochspelve. Arg 1D 132
Kinloid. High 5E 147
Kinloss. Mor 2E 159
Kinmel Bay. Cnwy 2B 82
Kinmuck. Abers 2F 153
Kinnadie. Abers 4G 161
Kinnaird. Per 1E 137
Kinneff. Abers 1H 145
Kinnelhead. Dum 4C 118
Kinnell. Ang 3F 145
Kinnerley. Shrp 3F 71
Kinnernie. Abers 2E 152
Kinnersley. Here 1G 47
Kinnersley. Worc 1D 48
Kinnerton. Powy 4E 59
Kinnerton. Shrp 1F 59
Kinnesswood. Per 3D 136
Kinninvie. Dur 2D 104
Kinnordy. Ang 3C 144
Kinoulton. Notts 2D 74
Kinross. Per 3D 136

Lees, The—Little Driffield

Lees, The. *Kent* 5E **40**
Leeswood. *Flin* 4E **83**
Lee, The. *Buck* 5H **51**
Leetown. *Per* 1E **136**
Leftwich. *Ches W* 3A **84**
Legbourne. *Linc* 2C **88**
Legburthwaite. *Cumb* 3E **102**
Legerwood. *Bord* 5B **130**
Legsby. *Linc* 2A **88**
Leicester. *Leic* 5C **74**
Leicester Forest East. *Leics* 5C **74**
Leigh. *Dors* 2B **14**
Leigh. *G Man* 4E **91**
Leigh. *Kent* 1G **27**
Leigh. *Shrp* 5F **71**
Leigh. *Surr* 1D **26**
Leigh. *Wilts* 2F **35**
Leigh. *Worc* 5B **60**
Leigham. *Plym* 3B **8**
Leigh Beck. *Essx* 2C **40**
Leigh Common. *Som* 4C **22**
Leigh Delamere. *Wilts* 4D **35**
Leigh Green. *Kent* 2D **28**
Leighland Chapel. *Som* 3D **20**
Leigh-on-Sea. *S'end* 2C **40**
Leigh Park. *Hants* 2F **17**
Leigh Sinton. *Worc* 5B **60**
Leighterton. *Glos* 2D **34**
Leigh, The. *Glos* 3D **48**
Leighton. *N Yor* 2D **98**
Leighton. *Powy* 5E **71**
Leighton. *Shrp* 5A **72**
Leighton. *Som* 2C **22**
Leighton Bromswold. *Cambs* 3A **64**
Leighton Buzzard. *C Beds* 3H **51**
Leigh-upon-Mendip. *Som* 2B **22**
Leinthall Earls. *Here* 4G **59**
Leinthall Starkes. *Here* 4G **59**
Leintwardine. *Here* 3G **59**
Leire. *Leics* 1C **62**
Leirinmore. *High* 2E **166**
Leishmore. *High* 4G **157**
Leiston. *Suff* 4G **67**
Leitfie. *Per* 4B **144**
Leith. *Edin* 2F **129**
Leitholm. *Bord* 5D **130**
Lelant. *Corn* 3C **4**
Lelant Downs. *Corn* 3C **4**
Lelley. *E Yor* 1F **95**
Lem Hill. *Worc* 3B **60**
Lemington. *Tyne* 3E **115**
Lemmington Hall. *Nmbd* 3F **121**
Lempitlaw. *Bord* 1B **120**
Lemsford. *Herts* 4C **52**
Lenacre. *Cumb* 1F **97**
Lenchie. *Abers* 5C **160**
Lenchwick. *Worc* 1F **49**
Lendalfoot. *S Ayr* 5A **116**
Lendrick. *Stir* 3E **135**
Lenham. *Kent* 5C **40**
Lenham Heath. *Kent* 1D **28**
Lenimore. *N Ayr* 5G **125**
Lennel. *Bord* 5E **131**
Lennoxtown. *E Dun* 2H **127**
Lenton. *Linc* 2H **75**
Lentran. *High* 4H **157**
Lenwade. *Norf* 4C **78**
Lenzie. *E Dun* 2H **127**
Leochel Cushnie. *Abers* 2C **152**
Leominster. *Here* 5G **59**
Leonard Stanley. *Glos* 5D **48**
Lepe. *Hants* 3C **16**
Lephenstrath. *Arg* 5A **122**
Lephin. *High* 4A **154**
Lephinchapel. *Arg* 4G **133**
Lephinmore. *Arg* 4G **133**
Leppington. *N Yor* 3B **100**
Lepton. *W Yor* 3C **92**
Lerryn. *Corn* 3F **7**
Lerwick. *Shet* 7F **173**
Lerwick (Tingwall) Airport. *Shet* 7F **173**
Lesbury. *Nmbd* 3G **121**
Leslie. *Abers* 1C **152**
Leslie. *Fife* 3E **137**
Lesmahagow. *S Lan* 1H **117**
Lesnewth. *Corn* 3B **10**
Lessingham. *Norf* 3F **79**
Lessonhall. *Cumb* 4D **112**
Leswalt. *Dum* 3F **109**
Letchmore Heath. *Herts* 1C **38**
Letchworth Garden City. *Herts* 2C **52**
Letcombe Bassett. *Oxon* 3B **36**
Letcombe Regis. *Oxon* 3B **36**
Letham. *Ang* 4E **145**
Letham. *Falk* 1B **128**
Letham. *Fife* 2F **137**
Lethanhill. *E Ayr* 3D **116**
Lethenty. *Abers* 4F **161**
Letheringham. *Suff* 5E **67**
Letheringsett. *Norf* 2C **78**
Lettaford. *Devn* 4H **11**
Lettan. *Orkn* 3G **172**
Letter. *Abers* 2E **153**
Letterewe. *High* 1B **156**
Letterfearn. *High* 1A **148**
Lettermore. *Arg* 4F **139**
Letters. *High* 5F **163**
Letterston. *Pemb* 2D **42**
Letton. *Here* 1G **47** (nr. Kington)
Letton. *Here* 3F **59** (nr. Leintwardine)
Letty Green. *Herts* 4C **52**
Letwell. *S Yor* 2C **86**
Leuchars. *Fife* 1G **137**
Leumrabhagh. *W Isl* 6F **171**
Leusdon. *Devn* 5H **11**
Levedale. *Staf* 4C **72**
Leven. *E Yor* 5F **101**
Leven. *Fife* 3F **137**
Levencorroch. *N Ayr* 3E **123**
Levenhall. *E Lot* 2G **129**
Levens. *Cumb* 1D **97**
Levens Green. *Herts* 3D **52**
Levenshulme. *G Man* 1C **84**
Levenwick. *Shet* 9F **173**
Leverburgh. *W Isl* 9C **171**
Leverington. *Cambs* 4D **76**
Leverton. *Linc* 1C **76**
Leverton. *W Ber* 4B **36**
Leverton Lucasgate. *Linc* 1D **76**
Leverton Outgate. *Linc* 1D **76**
Levington. *Suff* 2F **55**
Levisham. *N Yor* 5F **107**
Levishie. *High* 2G **149**
Lew. *Oxon* 5B **50**
Lewaigue. *IOM* 2D **108**
Lewannick. *Corn* 4C **10**
Lewdown. *Devn* 4E **11**
Lewes. *E Sus* 4F **27**
Leweston. *Pemb* 2D **42**
Lewisham. *G Lon* 3E **39**
Lewiston. *High* 1H **149**
Lewistown. *B'end* 3C **32**
Lewknor. *Oxon* 2F **37**
Leworthy. *Devn* 3G **19** (nr. Barnstaple)
Leworthy. *Devn* 2D **10** (nr. Holsworthy)
Lewson Street. *Kent* 4D **40**
Lewthorn Cross. *Devn* 5A **12**
Lewtrenchard. *Devn* 4E **11**
Ley. *Corn* 2F **7**
Leybourne. *Kent* 5A **40**
Leyburn. *N Yor* 5E **105**
Leycett. *Staf* 1B **72**
Leyfields. *Staf* 5G **73**
Ley Green. *Herts* 3B **52**
Ley Hill. *Buck* 5H **51**
Leyland. *Lanc* 2D **90**
Leylodge. *Abers* 2E **153**
Leymoor. *W Yor* 3B **92**
Leys. *Per* 5B **144**
Leysdown-on-Sea. *Kent* 3E **41**
Leysmill. *Ang* 4F **145**
Leyton. *G Lon* 2E **39**
Leytonstone. *G Lon* 2F **39**
Lezant. *Corn* 5D **10**
Leziate. *Norf* 4F **77**
Lhanbryde. *Mor* 2G **159**
Lhen, The. *IOM* 1C **108**
Liatrie. *High* 5E **157**
Libanus. *Powy* 3C **46**
Libberton. *S Lan* 5C **128**
Libbery. *Worc* 5D **60**
Liberton. *Edin* 3F **129**
Lichfield. *Staf* 5F **73**
Lickey. *Worc* 3D **61**
Lickey End. *Worc* 3D **61**
Lickfold. *W Sus* 3A **26**
Liddaton. *Devn* 4E **11**
Liddington. *Swin* 3H **35**
Lidgate. *Suff* 5G **65**
Lidgett. *Notts* 4D **86**
Lidham Hill. *E Sus* 4C **28**
Lidlington. *C Beds* 2H **51**
Lidsey. *W Sus* 5A **26**
Lidstone. *Oxon* 3B **50**
Lienassie. *High* 1B **148**
Liff. *Ang* 5C **144**
Lifford. *W Mid* 2E **61**
Lifton. *Devn* 4D **11**
Liftondown. *Devn* 4D **10**
Lighthorne. *Warw* 5H **61**
Light Oaks. *Staf* 5D **84**
Lightwater. *Surr* 4A **38**
Lightwood. *Staf* 1E **73**
Lightwood. *Stoke* 1D **72**
Lightwood Green. *Ches E* 1A **72**
Lightwood Green. *Wrex* 1F **71**
Lilbourne. *Nptn* 3C **62**
Lilburn Tower. *Nmbd* 2E **121**
Lillesdon. *Som* 4G **21**
Lilleshall. *Telf* 4B **72**
Lilley. *Herts* 3B **52**
Lilliesleaf. *Bord* 2H **119**
Lillingstone Dayrell. *Buck* 2F **51**
Lillingstone Lovell. *Buck* 1F **51**
Lillington. *Dors* 1B **14**
Lilstock. *Som* 2E **21**
Lilybank. *Inv* 2E **126**
Lilyhurst. *Shrp* 4B **72**
Limbrick. *Lanc* 3E **90**
Limbury. *Lutn* 3A **52**
Limekilnburn. *S Lan* 4A **128**
Lime Kiln Nook. *Cumb* 5E **113**
Limekilns. *Fife* 1D **129**
Limerigg. *Falk* 2B **128**
Limestone Brae. *Nmbd* 5A **114**
Lime Street. *Worc* 2D **48**
Limington. *Som* 4A **22**
Limpenhoe. *Norf* 5F **79**
Limpley Stoke. *Wilts* 5C **34**
Limpsfield. *Surr* 5E **39**
Linburn. *W Lot* 3E **129**
Linby. *Notts* 5C **86**
Linchmere. *W Sus* 3G **25**
Lincluden. *Dum* 2A **112**
Lincoln. *Linc* 3G **87**
Lincomb. *Worc* 4C **60**
Lindale. *Cumb* 1D **96**
Lindal in Furness. *Cumb* 2B **96**
Lindean. *Bord* 1G **119**
Linden. *Glos* 4D **48**
Lindfield. *W Sus* 3E **27**
Lindford. *Hants* 3G **25**
Lindores. *Fife* 2E **137**
Lindridge. *Worc* 4A **60**
Lindsell. *Essx* 3G **53**
Lindsey. *Suff* 1C **54**
Lindsey Tye. *Suff* 1C **54**
Linford. *Hants* 2G **15**
Linford. *Thur* 3A **40**
Lingague. *IOM* 4B **108**
Lingdale. *Red C* 3D **106**
Lingen. *Here* 4F **59**
Lingfield. *Surr* 1E **27**
Lingoed. *Mon* 3G **47**
Lingreabhagh. *W Isl* 9C **171**
Ling, The. *Norf* 1F **67**
Lingwood. *Norf* 5F **79**
Lingyclose Head. *Cumb* 4E **113**
Linicro. *High* 2C **154**
Linkend. *Worc* 2D **48**
Linkenholt. *Hants* 1B **24**
Linkinhorne. *Corn* 5D **10**
Linklater. *Orkn* 9D **172**
Linktown. *Fife* 4E **137**
Linkwood. *Mor* 2G **159**
Linley. *Shrp* 1F **59** (nr. Bishop's Castle)
Linley. *Shrp* 1A **60** (nr. Bridgnorth)
Linley Green. *Here* 5A **60**
Linlithgow. *W Lot* 2C **128**
Linlithgow Bridge. *Falk* 2C **128**
Linneraineach. *High* 3F **163**
Linshiels. *Nmbd* 4C **120**
Linsiadar. *W Isl* 4E **171**
Linsidemore. *High* 4C **164**
Linslade. *C Beds* 3H **51**
Linstead Parva. *Suff* 3F **67**
Linstock. *Cumb* 4F **113**
Linthwaite. *W Yor* 3B **92**
Lintlaw. *Bord* 4E **131**
Lintmill. *Mor* 2C **160**
Linton. *Cambs* 1F **53**
Linton. *Derbs* 4G **73**
Linton. *Here* 3B **48**
Linton. *Kent* 5B **40**
Linton. *N Yor* 3B **98**
Linton. *Bord* 2B **120**
Linton. *W Yor* 5F **99**
Linton Colliery. *Nmbd* 5G **121**
Linton Hill. *Here* 3B **48**
Linton-on-Ouse. *N Yor* 3G **99**
Lintzford. *Tyne* 4E **115**
Lintzgarth. *Dur* 5C **114**
Linwood. *Hants* 2G **15**
Linwood. *Linc* 2A **88**
Linwood. *Ren* 3F **127**
Lionacleit. *W Isl* 4C **170**
Lionacro. *High* 2C **154**
Lionacuidhe. *W Isl* 4C **170**
Lional. *W Isl* 1H **171**
Liphook. *Hants* 3G **25**
Lipley. *Shrp* 2B **72**
Lipyeate. *Som* 1B **22**
Liquo. *N Lan* 4B **128**
Liscard. *Mers* 1F **83**
Liscombe. *Som* 3B **20**
Liskeard. *Corn* 2G **7**
Lisle Court. *Hants* 3B **16**
Liss. *Hants* 4F **25**
Lissett. *E Yor* 4F **101**
Liss Forest. *Hants* 4F **25**
Lissington. *Linc* 2A **88**
Liston. *Essx* 1B **54**
Lisvane. *Card* 3E **33**
Liswerry. *Newp* 3G **33**
Litcham. *Norf* 4A **78**
Litchard. *B'end* 3C **32**
Litchborough. *Nptn* 5D **62**
Litchfield. *Hants* 1C **24**
Litherland. *Mers* 1F **83**
Litlington. *Cambs* 1D **52**
Litlington. *E Sus* 5G **27**
Littemill. *Nmbd* 3G **121**
Litterty. *Abers* 3E **161**
Little Abington. *Cambs* 1F **53**
Little Addington. *Nptn* 3G **63**
Little Airmyn. *N Yor* 2H **93**
Little Alne. *Warw* 4F **61**
Little Ardo. *Abers* 5F **161**
Little Asby. *Cumb* 4H **103**
Little Aston. *Staf* 5E **73**
Little Atherfield. *IOW* 4C **16**
Little Ayton. *N Yor* 3C **106**
Little Baddow. *Essx* 5A **54**
Little Badminton. *S Glo* 3D **34**
Little Ballinluig. *Per* 3G **143**
Little Bampton. *Cumb* 4D **112**
Little Bardfield. *Essx* 2G **53**
Little Barford. *Bed* 5A **64**
Little Barningham. *Norf* 2D **78**
Little Barrington. *Glos* 4H **49**
Little Barrow. *Ches W* 4G **83**
Little Barugh. *N Yor* 2B **100**
Little Bavington. *Nmbd* 2C **114**
Little Bealings. *Suff* 1F **55**
Littlebeck. *Cumb* 3H **103**
Little Bedwyn. *Wilts* 5A **36**
Little Bentley. *Essx* 3E **54**
Little Berkhamsted. *Herts* 5C **52**
Little Billing. *Nptn* 4F **63**
Little Billington. *C Beds* 3H **51**
Little Birch. *Here* 2A **48**
Little Bispham. *Bkpl* 5C **96**
Little Blakenham. *Suff* 1E **54**
Little Blencow. *Cumb* 1F **103**
Little Bognor. *W Sus* 3B **26**
Little Bolas. *Shrp* 3A **72**
Little Bollington. *Ches E* 2B **84**
Little Bookham. *Surr* 5C **38**
Littleborough. *Devn* 1B **12**
Littleborough. *G Man* 3H **91**
Littleborough. *Notts* 2F **87**
Littlebourne. *Kent* 5G **41**
Little Bourton. *Oxon* 1C **50**
Little Bowden. *Leics* 2E **63**
Little Bradley. *Suff* 5F **65**
Little Brampton. *Shrp* 2F **59**
Little Brechin. *Ang* 2E **145**
Littlebredy. *Dors* 4A **14**
Little Brickhill. *Mil* 2H **51**
Little Bridgeford. *Staf* 3C **72**
Little Brington. *Nptn* 4D **62**
Little Bromley. *Essx* 3D **54**
Little Broughton. *Cumb* 1B **102**
Little Budworth. *Ches W* 4H **83**
Little Burstead. *Essx* 1A **40**
Little Burton. *E Yor* 5F **101**
Littlebury. *Essx* 2F **53**
Littlebury Green. *Essx* 2E **53**
Little Bytham. *Linc* 4H **75**
Little Canfield. *Essx* 3F **53**
Little Canford. *Dors* 3F **15**
Little Carlton. *Linc* 2C **88**
Little Carlton. *Notts* 5E **87**
Little Casterton. *Rut* 5H **75**
Little Catwick. *E Yor* 5F **101**
Little Catworth. *Cambs* 3A **64**
Little Cawthorpe. *Linc* 2C **88**
Little Chalfont. *Buck* 1A **38**
Little Chart. *Kent* 1D **28**
Little Chesterford. *Essx* 1F **53**
Little Cheverell. *Wilts* 1E **23**
Little Chishill. *Cambs* 2E **53**
Little Clacton. *Essx* 4E **55**
Little Clanfield. *Oxon* 5A **50**
Little Clifton. *Cumb* 2B **102**
Little Coates. *NE Lin* 4F **95**
Little Comberton. *Worc* 1E **49**
Little Common. *E Sus* 5B **28**
Little Compton. *Warw* 2A **50**
Little Cornard. *Suff* 2B **54**
Littlecote. *Buck* 3G **51**
Littlecott. *Wilts* 1G **23**
Little Cowarne. *Here* 5A **60**
Little Coxwell. *Oxon* 2A **36**
Little Crakehall. *N Yor* 5F **105**
Little Crawley. *Mil* 1H **51**
Little Creich. *High* 5D **164**
Little Cressingham. *Norf* 5A **78**
Little Crosby. *Mers* 4B **90**
Little Crosthwaite. *Cumb* 2D **102**
Little Cubley. *Derbs* 2F **73**
Little Dalby. *Leics* 4E **75**
Little Dawley. *Telf* 5A **72**
Littledean. *Glos* 4B **48**
Little Dens. *Abers* 4H **161**
Little Dewchurch. *Here* 2A **48**
Little Ditton. *Cambs* 5F **65**
Little Down. *Hants* 1B **24**
Little Downham. *Cambs* 2E **65**
Little Drayton. *Shrp* 2A **72**
Little Driffield. *E Yor* 4E **101**

Little Dunham—Llanfair Clydogau

Little Dunham. Norf 4A 78
Little Dunkeld. Per 4H 143
Little Dunmow. Essx 3G 53
Little Easton. Essx 3G 53
Little Eaton. Derbs 1A 74
Little Eccleston. Lanc 5D 96
Little Ellingham. Norf 1C 66
Little Elm. Som 2C 22
Little End. Essx 5F 53
Little Everdon. Nptn 5C 62
Little Eversden. Cambs 5C 64
Little Faringdon. Oxon 5H 49
Little Fencote. N Yor 5F 105
Little Fenton. N Yor 1F 93
Littleferry. High 4F 165
Little Fransham. Norf 4B 78
Little Gaddesden. Herts 4H 51
Little Garway. Here 3H 47
Little Gidding. Cambs 2A 64
Little Glemham. Suff 5F 67
Little Glenshee. Per 5G 143
Little Gransden. Cambs 5B 64
Little Green. Suff 3C 66
Little Green. Wrex 1G 71
Little Grimsby. Linc 1C 88
Little Habton. N Yor 2B 100
Little Hadham. Herts 3E 53
Little Hale. Linc 1A 76
Little Hallingbury. Essx 4E 53
Littleham. Devn 4E 19
(nr. Bideford)
Littleham. Devn 4D 12
(nr. Exmouth)
Little Hampden. Buck 5G 51
Littlehampton. W Sus 5B 26
Little Haresfield. Glos 5D 48
Little Harrowden. Nptn 3F 63
Little Haseley. Oxon 5E 51
Little Hatfield. E Yor 5F 101
Little Hautbois. Norf 3E 79
Little Haven. Pemb 3C 42
Little Hay. Staf 5F 73
Little Hayfield. Derbs 2E 85
Little Haywood. Staf 3E 73
Little Heath. W Mid 2H 61
Little Heck. N Yor 2F 93
Littlehempston. Devn 2E 9
Little Herbert's. Glos 3E 49
Little Hereford. Here 4H 59
Little Horkesley. Essx 2C 54
Little Hormead. Herts 3E 53
Little Horsted. E Sus 4F 27
Little Horton. W Yor 1B 92
Little Horwood. Buck 2F 51
Little Houghton. Nptn 5F 63
Littlehoughton. Nmbd 3G 121
Little Houghton. S Yor 4E 93
Little Hucklow. Derbs 3F 85
Little Hulton. G Man 4F 91
Little Ingestre. Staf 3D 73
Little Irchester. Nptn 4G 63
Little Kelk. E Yor 3E 101
Little Kimble. Buck 5G 51
Little Kineton. Warw 5H 61
Little Kingshill. Buck 2G 37
Little Langdale. Cumb 4E 102
Little Langford. Wilts 3F 23
Little Laver. Essx 5F 53
Little Lawford. Warw 3B 62
Little Leigh. Ches W 3A 84
Little Leighs. Essx 4H 53
Little Leven. E Yor 5E 101
Little Lever. G Man 4F 91
Little Linford. Mil 1G 51
Little London. Buck 4E 51
Little London. E Sus 4G 27
Little London. Hants 2B 24
(nr. Andover)
Little London. Hants 1E 24
(nr. Basingstoke)
Little London. Linc 3D 76
(nr. Long Sutton)
Little London. Linc 3B 76
(nr. Spalding)
Little London. Norf 2E 79
(nr. North Walsham)
Little London. Norf 1G 65
(nr. Northwold)
Little London. Norf 2D 78
(nr. Saxthorpe)
Little London. Norf 1F 65
(nr. Southery)
Little London. Powy 2C 58
Little Longstone. Derbs 3F 85
Little Malvern. Worc 1C 48
Little Maplestead. Essx 2B 54
Little Marcle. Here 2B 48
Little Marlow. Buck 3G 37
Little Massingham. Norf 3G 77
Little Melton. Norf 5D 78
Littlemill. Abers 4H 151
Littlemill. E Ayr 3D 116
Littlemill. High 4D 158
Little Mill. Mon 5G 47
Little Milton. Oxon 5E 50
Little Missenden. Buck 1A 38
Littlemoor. Derbs 4A 86
Littlemoor. Dors 4B 14
Littlemore. Oxon 5D 50
Little Mountain. Flin 4E 83
Little Musgrave. Cumb 3A 104
Little Ness. Shrp 4G 71
Little Neston. Ches W 3F 83
Little Newcastle. Pemb 2D 43
Little Newsham. Dur 3E 105
Little Oakley. Essx 3F 55
Little Oakley. Nptn 2F 63
Little Onn. Staf 4C 72
Little Ormside. Cumb 3A 104
Little Orton. Cumb 4E 113
Little Orton. Leics 5H 73
Little Ouse. Norf 2F 65
Little Ouseburn. N Yor 3G 99
Littleover. Derb 2H 73
Little Packington. Warw 2G 61
Little Paxton. Cambs 4A 64
Little Petherick. Corn 1D 6
Little Plumpton. Lanc 1B 90
Little Plumstead. Norf 4F 79
Little Ponton. Linc 2G 75
Littleport. Cambs 2E 65
Little Posbrook. Hants 2D 16
Little Potheridge. Devn 1F 11
Little Preston. Nptn 5C 62
Little Raveley. Cambs 3B 64
Little Reynoldston. Swan 4D 31
Little Ribston. N Yor 4F 99
Little Rissington. Glos 4G 49
Little Rogart. High 3E 165
Little Rollright. Oxon 2A 50
Little Ryburgh. Norf 3B 78
Little Ryle. Nmbd 3E 121
Little Ryton. Shrp 5G 71
Little Salkeld. Cumb 1G 103
Little Sampford. Essx 2G 53
Little Sandhurst. Brac 5G 37
Little Saredon. Staf 5D 72
Little Saxham. Suff 4G 65
Little Scatwell. High 3F 157
Little Shelford. Cambs 5D 64
Little Shoddesden. Hants 2A 24
Little Singleton. Lanc 1B 90
Little Smeaton. N Yor 3F 93
Little Snoring. Norf 2B 78
Little Sodbury. S Glo 3C 34
Little Somborne. Hants 3B 24
Little Somerford. Wilts 3E 35
Little Soudley. Shrp 3B 72
Little Stainforth. N Yor 3H 97
Little Stainton. Darl 2A 106
Little Stanney. Ches W 3G 83
Little Staughton. Bed 4A 64
Little Steeping. Linc 4D 88
Littlester. Shet 4G 173
Little Stoke. Staf 2D 72
Littlestone-on-Sea. Kent 3E 29
Little Stonham. Suff 4D 66
Little Stretton. Leics 5D 74
Little Stretton. Shrp 1G 59
Little Strickland. Cumb 3G 103
Little Stukeley. Cambs 3B 64
Little Sugnall. Staf 2C 72
Little Sutton. Ches W 3F 83
Little Sutton. Linc 3D 76
Little Swinburne. Nmbd 2C 114
Little Tew. Oxon 3B 50
Little Tey. Essx 3B 54
Little Thetford. Cambs 3E 65
Little Thirkleby. N Yor 2G 99
Little Thornton. Lanc 5C 96
Littlethorpe. Leics 1C 62
Littlethorpe. N Yor 3F 99
Little Thorpe. W Yor 2B 92
Little Thurlow. Suff 5F 65
Little Thurrock. Thur 3H 39
Littleton. Ches W 4G 83
Littleton. Hants 3C 24
Littleton. Som 3H 21
Littleton. Surr 1A 26
(nr. Guildford)
Littleton. Surr 4B 38
(nr. Staines)
Littleton Drew. Wilts 3D 34
Littleton Pannell. Wilts 1E 23
Littleton-upon-Severn. S Glo 3A 34
Little Torboll. High 4E 165
Little Torrington. Devn 1E 11
Little Totham. Essx 4B 54
Little Town. Cumb 3D 102
Littletown. Dur 5G 115
Littletown. High 5E 165
Little Town. Lanc 1E 91
Little Twycross. Leics 5H 73
Little Urswick. Cumb 2B 96
Little Wakering. Essx 2D 40
Little Walden. Essx 1F 53
Little Waldingfield. Suff 1C 54
Little Walsingham. Norf 2B 78
Little Waltham. Essx 4H 53
Little Warley. Essx 1H 39
Little Washbourne. Glos 2E 49
Little Weighton. E Yor 1C 94
Little Wenham. Suff 2D 54
Little Wenlock. Telf 5A 72
Little Whelnetham. Suff 5A 66
Little Whittingham Green. Suff 3E 67
Littlewick Green. Wind 4G 37
Little Wilbraham. Cambs 5E 65
Littlewindsor. Dors 2H 13
Little Wisbeach. Linc 2A 76
Little Witcombe. Glos 4E 49
Little Witley. Worc 4B 60
Little Wittenham. Oxon 2D 36
Little Wolford. Warw 2A 50
Littleworth. Bed 1A 52
Littleworth. Glos 2G 49
Littleworth. Oxon 2B 36
Littleworth. Staf 4E 73
(nr. Cannock)
Littleworth. Staf 3B 72
(nr. Eccleshall)
Littleworth. Staf 3D 72
(nr. Stafford)
Littleworth. W Sus 3C 26
Littleworth. Worc 4D 61
(nr. Redditch)
Littleworth. Worc 1D 49
(nr. Worcester)
Little Wratting. Suff 1G 53
Little Wymington. Nptn 4G 63
Little Wymondley. Herts 3C 52
Little Wyrley. Staf 5E 73
Little Yeldham. Essx 2A 54
Littley Green. Essx 4G 53
Litton. Derbs 3F 85
Litton. N Yor 2B 98
Litton. Som 1A 22
Litton Cheney. Dors 3A 14
Liurbost. W Isl 5F 171
Liverpool. Mers 1F 83
Liverpool John Lennon Airport. Mers 2G 83
Liversedge. W Yor 2B 92
Liverton. Devn 5B 12
Liverton. Red C 3E 107
Liverton Mines. Red C 3E 107
Livingston. W Lot 3D 128
Livingston Village. W Lot 3D 128
Lixwm. Flin 3D 82
Lizard. Corn 5E 5
Llaingoch. IOA 2B 80
Llaithddu. Powy 2C 58
Llampha. V Glam 4C 32
Llan. Powy 5A 70
Llanaber. Gwyn 4F 69
Llanaelhaearn. Gwyn 1C 68
Llanaeron. Cdgn 4D 57
Llanafan. Cdgn 3F 57
Llanafan-fawr. Powy 5B 58
Llanafan-fechan. Powy 5B 58
Llanallgo. IOA 2D 81
Llanandras. Powy 4F 59
Llananno. Powy 3C 58
Llanarmon. Gwyn 2D 68
Llanarmon Dyffryn Ceiriog. Wrex 2D 70
Llanarmon-yn-Ial. Den 5D 82
Llanarth. Cdgn 5D 56
Llanarth. Mon 4G 47
Llanarthne. Carm 3F 45
Llanasa. Flin 2D 82
Llanbabo. IOA 2C 80
Llanbadarn Fawr. Cdgn 2F 57
Llanbadarn Fynydd. Powy 3C 58
Llanbadarn-y-garreg. Powy 1E 46
Llanbadoc. Mon 5G 47
Llanbadrig. IOA 1C 80
Llanbeder. Newp 2G 33
Llanbedr. Gwyn 3E 69
Llanbedr. Powy 3F 47
(nr. Crickhowell)
Llanbedr. Powy 1E 47
(nr. Hay-on-Wye)
Llanbedr-Dyffryn-Clwyd. Den 5D 82
Llanbedrgoch. IOA 2E 81
Llanbedrog. Gwyn 2C 68
Llanbedr Pont Steffan. Cdgn 1F 45
Llanbedr-y-cennin. Cnwy 4G 81
Llanberis. Gwyn 4E 81
Llanbethery. V Glam 5D 32
Llanbister. Powy 3D 58
Llanblethian. V Glam 4C 32
Llanboidy. Carm 2G 43
Llanbradach. Cphy 2E 33
Llanbrynmair. Powy 5A 70
Llanbydderi. V Glam 5D 32
Llancadle. V Glam 5D 32
Llancarfan. V Glam 4D 32
Llancatal. V Glam 5D 32
Llancayo. Mon 5G 47
Llancloudy. Here 3H 47
Llancoch. Powy 3E 58
Llancynfelyn. Cdgn 1F 57
Llandaff. Card 4E 33
Llandanwg. Gwyn 3E 69
Llandarcy. Neat 3G 31
Llandawke. Carm 3G 43
Llanddaniel-Fab. IOA 3D 81
Llanddarog. Carm 4F 45
Llanddeiniol. Cdgn 3E 57
Llanddeiniolen. Gwyn 4E 81
Llandderfel. Gwyn 2B 70
Llanddeusant. Carm 3A 46
Llanddeusant. IOA 2C 80
Llanddew. Powy 2D 46
Llanddewi. Swan 4D 30
Llanddewi Brefi. Cdgn 5F 57
Llanddewi'r Cwm. Powy 1D 46
Llanddewi Rhydderch. Mon 4G 47
Llanddewi Velfrey. Pemb 3F 43
Llanddewi Ystradenni. Powy 4D 58
Llanddoged. Cnwy 4H 81
Llanddona. IOA 3E 81
Llanddowror. Carm 3G 43
Llanddulas. Cnwy 3B 82
Llanddwywe. Gwyn 3E 69
Llanddyfnan. IOA 3E 81
Llandecwyn. Gwyn 2F 69
Llandefaelog Fach. Powy 2D 46
Llandefaelog-tre'r-graig. Powy 2E 47
Llandefalle. Powy 2E 46
Llandegai. Gwyn 3E 81
Llandegfan. IOA 3E 81
Llandegla. Den 5D 82
Llandegley. Powy 4D 58
Llandegveth. Mon 2G 33
Llandeilo. Carm 3G 45
Llandeilo Graban. Powy 1D 46
Llandeilo'r Fan. Powy 2B 46
Llandeloy. Pemb 2C 42
Llandenny. Mon 5H 47
Llandevaud. Newp 2H 33
Llandevenny. Mon 3G 33
Llandilo. Pemb 2F 43
Llandinabo. Here 3A 48
Llandinam. Powy 2C 58
Llandissilio. Pemb 2F 43
Llandogo. Mon 5A 48
Llandough. V Glam 4C 32
(nr. Cowbridge)
Llandough. V Glam 4E 33
(nr. Penarth)
Llandovery. Carm 2A 46
Llandow. V Glam 4C 32
Llandre. Cdgn 2F 57
Llandrillo. Den 2C 70
Llandrillo-yn-Rhos. Cnwy 2H 81
Llandrindod. Powy 4C 58
Llandrindod Wells. Powy 4C 58
Llandrinio. Powy 4E 71
Llandsadwrn. Carm 2G 45
Llandudno. Cnwy 2G 81
Llandudno Junction. Cnwy 3G 81
Llandudoch. Pemb 1B 44
Llandw. V Glam 4C 32
Llandwrog. Gwyn 5D 80
Llandybie. Carm 4G 45
Llandyfaelog. Carm 4E 45
Llandyfan. Carm 4G 45
Llandyfriog. Cdgn 1D 44
Llandyfrydog. IOA 2D 80
Llandygwydd. Cdgn 1C 44
Llandynan. Den 1D 70
Llandyrnog. Den 4D 82
Llandysilio. Powy 4E 71
Llandyssil. Powy 1D 58
Llandysul. Cdgn 1E 45
Llanedeyrn. Card 3F 33
Llaneglwys. Powy 2D 46
Llanegryn. Gwyn 5F 69
Llanegwad. Carm 3F 45
Llaneilian. IOA 1D 80
Llanelian-yn-Rhos. Cnwy 3A 82
Llanelidan. Den 5D 82
Llanelieu. Powy 2E 47
Llanellen. Mon 4G 47
Llanelli. Carm 3E 31
Llanelltyd. Gwyn 4G 69
Llanelly. Mon 4F 47
Llanelly Hill. Mon 4F 47
Llanelwedd. Powy 5C 58
Llanelwy. Den 3C 82
Llanenddwyn. Gwyn 3E 69
Llanengan. Gwyn 3B 68
Llanerch. Powy 1F 59
Llanerchymedd. IOA 2D 80
Llanerfyl. Powy 5C 70
Llaneuddog. IOA 2D 80
Llanfachraeth. IOA 2C 80
Llanfaelog. IOA 3C 80
Llanfaelrhys. Gwyn 3B 68
Llanfaenor. Mon 4H 47
Llanfaes. IOA 3F 81
Llanfaes. Powy 3D 46
Llanfaethlu. IOA 2C 80
Llanfaglan. Gwyn 4D 80
Llanfair. Gwyn 3E 69
Llanfair. Here 1F 47
Llanfair Caereinion. Powy 5D 70
Llanfair Clydogau. Cdgn 5F 57

Llanfair Dyffryn Clwyd—Longbridge

Llanfair Dyffryn Clwyd. *Den* 5D **82**
Llanfairfechan. *Cnwy* 3F **81**
Llanfair-Nant-Gwyn. *Pemb* 1F **43**
Llanfair Pwllgwyngyll. *IOA* 3E **81**
Llanfair Talhaiarn. *Cnwy* 3B **82**
Llanfair Waterdine. *Shrp* 3E **59**
Llanfair-ym-Muallt. *Powy* 5C **58**
Llanfairyneubwll. *IOA* 3C **80**
Llanfairynghornwy. *IOA* 1C **80**
Llanfallteg. *Carm* 3F **43**
Llanfallteg West. *Carm* 3F **43**
Llanfaredd. *Powy* 5C **58**
Llanfarian. *Cdgn* 3E **57**
Llanfechain. *Powy* 3D **70**
Llanfechell. *IOA* 1C **80**
Llanfechreth. *Gwyn* 3G **69**
Llanfendigaid. *Gwyn* 5E **69**
Llanferres. *Den* 4D **82**
Llan Ffestiniog. *Gwyn* 1G **69**
Llanfflewyn. *IOA* 2C **80**
Llanfihangel Glyn Myfyr. *Cnwy* 1B **70**
Llanfihangel Nant Bran. *Powy* 2C **46**
Llanfihangel-Nant-Melan. *Powy* 5D **58**
Llanfihangel Rhydithon. *Powy* 4D **58**
Llanfihangel Rogiet. *Mon* 3H **33**
Llanfihangel Tal-y-llyn. *Powy* 3E **46**
Llanfihangel-uwch-Gwili. *Carm* 3E **45**
Llanfihangel-yng-Ngwynfa. *Powy* 4C **70**
Llanfihangel yn Nhowyn. *IOA* 3C **80**
Llanfihangel-y-pennant. *Gwyn* 1E **69** (nr. Golan)
Llanfihangel-y-pennant. *Gwyn* 5F **69** (nr. Tywyn)
Llanfilo. *Powy* 2E **46**
Llanfinhangel-ar-Arth. *Carm* 2E **45**
Llanfinhangel-y-Creuddyn. *Cdgn* 3F **57**
Llanfinhangel-y-traethau. *Gwyn* 2E **69**
Llanfleiddan. *V Glam* 4C **32**
Llanfoist. *Mon* 4F **47**
Llanfor. *Gwyn* 2B **70**
Llanfrechfa. *Torf* 2G **33**
Llanfrothen. *Gwyn* 1F **69**
Llanfrynach. *Powy* 3D **46**
Llanfwrog. *Den* 5D **82**
Llanfwrog. *IOA* 2C **80**
Llanfyllin. *Powy* 4D **70**
Llanfynydd. *Carm* 3F **45**
Llanfynydd. *Flin* 5E **83**
Llanfyrnach. *Pemb* 1G **43**
Llangadfan. *Powy* 4C **70**
Llangadog. *Carm* 3H **45** (nr. Llandovery)
Llangadog. *Carm* 5E **45** (nr. Llanelli)
Llangadwaladr. *IOA* 4C **80**
Llangadwaladr. *Powy* 2D **70**
Llangaffo. *IOA* 4D **80**
Llangain. *Carm* 4D **45**
Llangammarch Wells. *Powy* 1C **46**
Llangan. *V Glam* 4C **32**
Llangarron. *Here* 3A **48**
Llangasty-Talyllyn. *Powy* 3E **47**
Llangathen. *Carm* 3F **45**
Llangattock. *Powy* 4F **47**
Llangattock Lingoed. *Mon* 3G **47**
Llangattock-Vibon-Avel. *Mon* 4H **47**
Llangedwyn. *Powy* 3D **70**
Llangefni. *IOA* 3D **80**
Llangeinor. *B'end* 3C **32**
Llangeitho. *Cdgn* 5F **57**
Llangeler. *Carm* 2D **44**
Llangelynin. *Gwyn* 5E **69**
Llangendeirne. *Carm* 4E **45**
Llangennech. *Carm* 5F **45**
Llangennith. *Swan* 3D **30**
Llangenny. *Powy* 4F **47**
Llangernyw. *Cnwy* 4A **82**
Llangian. *Gwyn* 3B **68**
Llangiwg. *Neat* 5H **45**
Llangloffan. *Pemb* 1D **42**
Llanglydwen. *Carm* 2F **43**
Llangoed. *IOA* 3F **81**
Llangoedmor. *Cdgn* 1B **44**
Llangollen. *Den* 1E **70**
Llangolman. *Pemb* 2F **43**
Llangorse. *Powy* 3E **47**
Llangorwen. *Cdgn* 2F **57**
Llangovan. *Mon* 5H **47**
Llangower. *Gwyn* 2B **70**
Llangranog. *Cdgn* 5C **56**
Llangristiolus. *IOA* 3D **80**
Llangrove. *Here* 4A **48**
Llangua. *Mon* 3G **47**
Llangunllo. *Powy* 3E **58**
Llangunnor. *Carm* 3E **45**
Llangurig. *Powy* 3B **58**
Llangwm. *Cnwy* 1B **70**
Llangwm. *Mon* 5H **47**
Llangwm. *Pemb* 4D **43**
Llangwm-isaf. *Mon* 5H **47**
Llangwnnadl. *Gwyn* 2B **68**
Llangwyfan. *Den* 4D **82**
Llangwyfan-isaf. *IOA* 4C **80**
Llangwyllog. *IOA* 3D **80**
Llangwyryfon. *Cdgn* 3E **57**
Llangybi. *Cdgn* 5F **57**
Llangybi. *Gwyn* 1D **68**
Llangybi. *Mon* 2G **33**
Llangyfelach. *Swan* 3F **31**
Llangynhafal. *Den* 4D **82**
Llangynidr. *Powy* 4E **47**
Llangynin. *Carm* 3G **43**
Llangynog. *Carm* 3H **43**
Llangynog. *Powy* 3C **70**
Llangynwyd. *B'end* 3B **32**
Llanhamlach. *Powy* 3D **46**
Llanharan. *Rhon* 3D **32**
Llanharry. *Rhon* 3D **32**
Llanhennock. *Mon* 2G **33**
Llanhilleth. *Blae* 5F **47**
Llanidloes. *Powy* 2B **58**
Llaniestyn. *Gwyn* 2B **68**
Llanigon. *Powy* 1F **47**
Llanilar. *Cdgn* 3F **57**
Llanilid. *Rhon* 3C **32**
Llanilltud Fawr. *V Glam* 5C **32**
Llanishen. *Card* 3E **33**
Llanishen. *Mon* 5H **47**
Llanllawddog. *Carm* 3E **45**
Llanllechid. *Gwyn* 4F **81**
Llanllowell. *Mon* 2G **33**
Llanllugan. *Powy* 5C **70**
Llanllwch. *Carm* 4D **45**
Llanllwchaiarn. *Powy* 1D **58**
Llanllwni. *Carm* 2E **45**
Llanllyfni. *Gwyn* 5D **80**
Llanmadoc. *Swan* 3D **30**
Llanmaes. *V Glam* 5C **32**
Llanmartin. *Newp* 3G **33**
Llanmerwig. *Powy* 1D **58**
Llanmihangel. *V Glam* 4C **32**
Llan-mill. *Pemb* 3F **43**
Llanmiloe. *Carm* 4G **43**
Llanmorlais. *Swan* 3E **31**
Llannefydd. *Cnwy* 3B **82**
Llannon. *Carm* 5F **45**
Llan-non. *Cdgn* 4E **57**
Llannor. *Gwyn* 2C **68**
Llanpumsaint. *Carm* 3E **45**
Llanrhaeadr. *Den* 4C **82**
Llanrhaeadr-ym-Mochnant. *Powy* 3D **70**
Llanrhidian. *Swan* 3D **31**
Llanrhos. *Cnwy* 2G **81**
Llanrhyddlad. *IOA* 2C **80**
Llanrhystud. *Cdgn* 4E **57**
Llanrian. *Pemb* 1C **42**
Llanrothal. *Here* 4H **47**
Llanrug. *Gwyn* 4E **81**
Llanrumney. *Card* 3F **33**
Llanrwst. *Cnwy* 4G **81**
Llansadurnen. *Carm* 3G **43**
Llansadwrn. *IOA* 3E **81**
Llansaint. *Carm* 5D **45**
Llansamlet. *Swan* 3F **31**
Llansanffraid Glan Conwy. *Cnwy* 3H **81**
Llansannan. *Cnwy* 4B **82**
Llansannor. *V Glam* 4C **32**
Llansantffraed. *Cdgn* 4E **57**
Llansantffraed. *Powy* 3E **46**
Llansantffraed Cwmdeuddwr. *Powy* 4B **58**
Llansantffraed in Elwel. *Powy* 5C **58**
Llansantffraid-ym-Mechain. *Powy* 3E **70**
Llansawel. *Carm* 2G **45**
Llansawel. *Neat* 3G **31**
Llansilin. *Powy* 3E **70**
Llansoy. *Mon* 5H **47**
Llanspyddid. *Powy* 3D **46**
Llanstadwell. *Pemb* 4D **42**
Llansteffan. *Carm* 3H **43**
Llanstephan. *Powy* 1E **46**
Llantarnam. *Torf* 2F **33**
Llanteg. *Pemb* 3F **43**
Llanthony. *Mon* 3F **47**
Llantilio Crossenny. *Mon* 4G **47**
Llantilio Pertholey. *Mon* 4G **47**
Llantood. *Pemb* 1B **44**
Llantrisant. *Mon* 2G **33**
Llantrisant. *Rhon* 3D **32**
Llantrithyd. *V Glam* 4D **32**
Llantwit Fardre. *Rhon* 3D **32**
Llantwit Major. *V Glam* 5C **32**
Llanuwchllyn. *Gwyn* 2A **70**
Llanvaches. *Newp* 2H **33**
Llanvair Discoed. *Mon* 2H **33**
Llanvapley. *Mon* 4G **47**
Llanvetherine. *Mon* 4G **47**
Llanveynoe. *Here* 2G **47**
Llanvihangel Crucorney. *Mon* 3G **47**
Llanvihangel Gobion. *Mon* 5G **47**
Llanvihangel Ystern-Llewern. *Mon* 4H **47**
Llanwarne. *Here* 3A **48**
Llanwddyn. *Powy* 4C **70**
Llanwenarth. *Mon* 4F **47**
Llanwenog. *Cdgn* 1E **45**
Llanwern. *Newp* 3G **33**
Llanwinio. *Carm* 2G **43**
Llanwnda. *Gwyn* 5D **81**
Llanwnda. *Pemb* 1D **42**
Llanwnnen. *Cdgn* 1F **45**
Llanwnog. *Powy* 1C **58**
Llanwrda. *Carm* 2H **45**
Llanwrin. *Powy* 5G **69**
Llanwrthwl. *Powy* 4B **58**
Llanwrtud. *Powy* 1B **46**
Llanwrtyd. *Powy* 1B **46**
Llanwrtyd Wells. *Powy* 1B **46**
Llanwyddelan. *Powy* 5C **70**
Llanyblodwel. *Shrp* 3E **71**
Llanybri. *Carm* 3H **43**
Llanybydder. *Carm* 1F **45**
Llanycefn. *Pemb* 2E **43**
Llanychaer. *Pemb* 1D **43**
Llanycil. *Gwyn* 2B **70**
Llanymawddwy. *Gwyn* 4B **70**
Llanymddyfri. *Carm* 2A **46**
Llanymynech. *Shrp* 3E **71**
Llanynghenedl. *IOA* 2C **80**
Llanynys. *Den* 4D **82**
Llan-y-pwll. *Wrex* 5F **83**
Llanyrafon. *Torf* 2G **33**
Llanyre. *Powy* 4C **58**
Llanystumdwy. *Gwyn* 2D **68**
Llanywern. *Powy* 3E **46**
Llawhaden. *Pemb* 3E **43**
Llawndy. *Flin* 2D **82**
Llawnt. *Shrp* 2E **71**
Llawr Dref. *Gwyn* 3B **68**
Llawryglyn. *Powy* 1B **58**
Llay. *Wrex* 5F **83**
Llechfaen. *Powy* 3D **46**
Llechryd. *Cphy* 5E **46**
Llechryd. *Cdgn* 1C **44**
Llechrydau. *Wrex* 2E **71**
Lledrod. *Cdgn* 3F **57**
Llethrid. *Swan* 3E **31**
Llidiad-Nenog. *Carm* 2F **45**
Llidiardau. *Gwyn* 2A **70**
Llidiart y Parc. *Den* 1D **70**
Llithfaen. *Gwyn* 1C **68**
Lloc. *Flin* 3D **82**
Llong. *Flin* 4E **83**
Llowes. *Powy* 1E **47**
Lloyney. *Powy* 3E **59**
Llundain-fach. *Cdgn* 5E **57**
Llwydcoed. *Rhon* 5C **46**
Llwyncelyn. *Cdgn* 5D **56**
Llwyncelyn. *Swan* 5G **45**
Llwyndaffydd. *Cdgn* 5C **56**
Llwynderw. *Powy* 5E **70**
Llwyn-du. *Mon* 4F **47**
Llwyngwril. *Gwyn* 5E **69**
Llwynhendy. *Carm* 3E **31**
Llwynmawr. *Wrex* 2E **71**
Llwyn-on Village. *Mer T* 4D **46**
Llwyn-teg. *Carm* 5F **45**
Llwyn-y-brain. *Carm* 3F **43**
Llwynygog. *Powy* 1A **58**
Llwyn-y-groes. *Cdgn* 5E **57**
Llwynypia. *Rhon* 2C **32**
Llynclys. *Shrp* 3E **71**
Llynfaes. *IOA* 3D **80**
Llysfaen. *Cnwy* 3A **82**
Llyswen. *Powy* 2E **47**
Llysworney. *V Glam* 4C **32**
Llys-y-fran. *Pemb* 2E **43**
Llywel. *Powy* 2B **46**
Llywernog. *Cdgn* 2G **57**
Loan. *Falk* 2C **128**
Loanend. *Nmbd* 4F **131**
Loanhead. *Midl* 3F **129**
Loaningfoot. *Dum* 4A **112**
Loanreoch. *High* 1A **158**
Loans. *S Ayr* 1C **116**
Loansdean. *Nmbd* 1F **115**
Lobb. *Devn* 3E **19**
Lobhillcross. *Devn* 4E **11**
Lochaber. *Mor* 3E **159**
Loch a Charnain. *W Isl* 4D **170**
Lochailort. *High* 5F **147**
Lochaline. *High* 4A **140**
Lochans. *Dum* 4F **109**
Locharbriggs. *Dum* 1A **112**
Lochardil. *High* 4A **158**
Lochassynt Lodge. *High* 1F **163**
Lochavich. *Arg* 2G **133**
Lochawe. *Arg* 1A **134**
Loch Baghasdail. *W Isl* 7C **170**
Lochboisdale. *W Isl* 7C **170**
Lochbuie. *Arg* 1D **132**
Lochcarron. *High* 5A **156**
Loch Choire Lodge. *High* 5G **167**
Lochdochart House. *Stir* 1D **134**
Lochdon. *Arg* 5B **140**
Lochearnhead. *Stir* 1E **135**
Lochee. *D'dee* 5C **144**
Lochend. *High* 5H **157** (nr. Inverness)
Lochend. *High* 2E **169** (nr. Thurso)
Locherben. *Dum* 5B **118**
Loch Euphort. *W Isl* 2D **170**
Lochfoot. *Dum* 2F **111**
Lochgair. *Arg* 4G **133**
Lochgarthside. *High* 2H **149**
Lochgelly. *Fife* 4D **136**
Lochgilphead. *Arg* 1G **125**
Lochgoilhead. *Arg* 3A **134**
Loch Head. *Dum* 5A **110**
Lochhill. *Mor* 2G **159**
Lochindorb Lodge. *High* 5D **158**
Lochinver. *High* 1E **163**
Lochlane. *Per* 1H **135**
Loch Loyal Lodge. *High* 4G **167**
Lochluichart. *High* 2F **157**
Lochmaben. *Dum* 1B **112**
Lochmaddy. *W Isl* 2E **170**
Loch nam Madadh. *W Isl* 2E **170**
Lochore. *Fife* 4D **136**
Lochportain. *W Isl* 1E **170**
Lochranza. *N Ayr* 4H **125**
Loch Sgioport. *W Isl* 5D **170**
Lochside. *Abers* 2G **145**
Lochside. *High* 5A **168** (nr. Achentoul)
Lochside. *High* 3C **158** (nr. Nairn)
Lochslin. *High* 5F **165**
Lochstack Lodge. *High* 4C **166**
Lochton. *Abers* 4E **153**
Lochty. *Fife* 3H **137**
Lochuisge. *High* 3B **140**
Lochussie. *High* 3G **157**
Lochwinnoch. *Ren* 4E **127**
Lochyside. *High* 1F **141**
Lockengate. *Corn* 2E **7**
Lockerbie. *Dum* 1C **112**
Lockeridge. *Wilts* 5G **35**
Lockerley. *Hants* 4A **24**
Lockhills. *Cumb* 5G **113**
Locking. *N Som* 1G **21**
Lockington. *E Yor* 5D **101**
Lockington. *Leics* 3B **74**
Lockleywood. *Shrp* 3A **72**
Locksgreen. *IOW* 3C **16**
Locks Heath. *Hants* 2D **16**
Lockton. *N Yor* 5F **107**
Loddington. *Leics* 5E **75**
Loddington. *Nptn* 3F **63**
Loddiswell. *Devn* 4D **8**
Loddon. *Norf* 1F **67**
Lode. *Cambs* 4E **65**
Loders. *Dors* 3H **13**
Lodsworth. *W Sus* 3A **26**
Lofthouse. *N Yor* 2D **98**
Lofthouse. *W Yor* 2D **92**
Lofthouse Gate. *W Yor* 2D **92**
Loftus. *Red C* 3E **107**
Logan. *E Ayr* 2E **117**
Loganlea. *W Lot* 3C **128**
Logaston. *Here* 5F **59**
Loggerheads. *Staf* 2B **72**
Loggie. *High* 4F **163**
Logie. *Ang* 2F **145**
Logie. *Fife* 1G **137**
Logie. *Mor* 3E **159**
Logie Coldstone. *Abers* 3B **152**
Logie Pert. *Ang* 2F **145**
Logierait. *Per* 3G **143**
Login. *Carm* 2F **43**
Lolworth. *Cambs* 4C **64**
Lonbain. *High* 3F **155**
Londesborough. *E Yor* 5C **100**
London. *G Lon* 2E **39**
London Apprentice. *Corn* 3E **6**
London Ashford (Lydd) Airport. *Kent* 3E **29**
London City Airport. *G Lon* 2F **39**
London Colney. *Herts* 5B **52**
Londonderry. *N Yor* 1F **99**
London Gatwick Airport. *W Sus* 1D **27**
London Heathrow Airport. *G Lon* 3B **38**
London Luton Airport. *Lutn* 3B **52**
London Southend Airport. *Essx* 2C **40**
London Stansted Airport. *Essx* 3F **53**
Londonthorpe. *Linc* 2G **75**
Londubh. *High* 5C **162**
Lone. *High* 4D **166**
Lonemore. *High* 5E **165** (nr. Dornoch)
Lonemore. *High* 1G **155** (nr. Gairloch)
Long Ashton. *N Som* 4A **34**
Long Bank. *Worc* 3B **60**
Longbar. *N Ayr* 4E **127**
Long Bennington. *Linc* 1F **75**
Longbenton. *Tyne* 3F **115**
Longborough. *Glos* 3G **49**
Long Bredy. *Dors* 3A **14**
Longbridge. *Warw* 4G **61**
Longbridge. *W Mid* 3E **61**

Longbridge Deverill—Lubcroy

Longbridge Deverill. Wilts 2D 22
Long Buckby. Nptn 4D 62
Long Buckby Wharf. Nptn 4D 62
Longburgh. Cumb 4E 112
Longburton. Dors 1B 14
Long Clawson. Leics 3E 74
Longcliffe. Derbs 5G 85
Long Common. Hants 1D 16
Long Compton. Staf 3C 72
Long Compton. Warw 2A 50
Longcot. Oxon 2A 36
Long Crendon. Buck 5E 51
Long Crichel. Dors 1E 15
Longcroft. Cumb 4D 112
Longcroft. Falk 2A 128
Longcross. Surr 4A 38
Longdale. Cumb 4H 103
Longdales. Cumb 5G 113
Longden. Shrp 5G 71
Longden Common. Shrp 5G 71
Long Ditton. Surr 4C 38
Longdon. Staf 4E 73
Longdon. Worc 2D 48
Longdon Green. Staf 4E 73
Longdon on Tern. Telf 4A 72
Longdown. Devn 3B 12
Longdowns. Corn 5B 6
Long Drax. N Yor 2G 93
Long Duckmanton. Derbs 3B 86
Long Eaton. Derbs 2B 74
Longfield. Kent 4H 39
Longfield Hill. Kent 4H 39
Longford. Derbs 2G 73
Longford. Glos 3D 48
Longford. G Lon 3B 38
Longford. Shrp 2A 72
Longford. Telf 4B 72
Longford. W Mid 2H 61
Longforgan. Per 1F 137
Longformacus. Bord 4C 130
Longframlington. Nmbd 4F 121
Long Gardens. Essx 2B 54
Long Green. Ches W 3G 83
Long Green. Worc 2D 48
Longham. Dors 3F 15
Longham. Norf 4B 78
Long Hanborough. Oxon 4C 50
Longhedge. Wilts 2D 22
Longhill. Abers 3H 161
Longhirst. Nmbd 1F 115
Longhope. Glos 4B 48
Longhope. Orkn 8C 172
Longhorsley. Nmbd 5F 121
Longhoughton. Nmbd 3G 121
Long Itchington. Warw 4B 62
Longlands. Cumb 1D 102
Longlane. Derbs 2G 73
Long Lane. Telf 4A 72
Longlane. W Ber 4C 36
Long Lawford. Warw 3B 62
Long Lease. N Yor 4G 107
Longley Green. Worc 5B 60
Long Load. Som 4H 21
Longmanhill. Abers 2E 161
Long Marston. Herts 4G 51
Long Marston. N Yor 4H 99
Long Marston. Warw 1G 49
Long Marton. Cumb 2H 103
Long Meadow. Cambs 4E 65
Long Meadowend. Shrp 2G 59
Long Melford. Suff 1B 54
Longmoor Camp. Hants 3F 25
Longmorn. Mor 3G 159
Longmoss. Ches E 3C 84
Long Newnton. Glos 2E 35
Longnewton. Bord 2H 119
Long Newton. Stoc T 3A 106
Longney. Glos 4C 48
Longniddry. E Lot 2H 129
Longnor. Shrp 5G 71
Longnor. Staf 4E 85
(nr. Leek)
Longnor. Staf 4C 72
(nr. Stafford)
Longparish. Hants 2C 24
Longpark. Cumb 3F 113
Long Preston. N Yor 4H 97
Longridge. Lanc 1E 90
Longridge. Staf 4D 72
Longridge. W Lot 3C 128
Longriggend. N Lan 2B 128
Long Riston. E Yor 5F 101
Long Rock. Corn 3C 4
Longsdon. Staf 5D 84
Longshaw. G Man 4D 90
Longshaw. Staf 1E 73
Longside. Abers 4H 161
Longslow. Shrp 2A 72
Longstanton. Cambs 4C 64
Longstock. Hants 3B 24
Longstowe. Cambs 5C 64
Long Stratton. Norf 1D 66
Long Street. Mil 1F 51
Longstreet. Wilts 1G 23
Long Sutton. Hants 2F 25
Long Sutton. Linc 3D 76
Long Sutton. Som 4H 21
Longthorpe. Pet 1A 64
Long Thurlow. Suff 4C 66
Longthwaite. Cumb 2F 103
Longton. Lanc 2C 90
Longton. Stoke 1D 72
Longtown. Cumb 3E 113
Longtown. Here 3G 47
Longville in the Dale. Shrp 1H 59
Long Whatton. Leics 3B 74
Longwick. Buck 5F 51
Long Wittenham. Oxon 2D 36
Longwitton. Nmbd 1D 115
Longworth. Oxon 2B 36
Longyester. E Lot 3B 130
Lonmore. High 4B 154
Looe. Corn 3G 7
Loose. Kent 5B 40
Loosegate. Linc 3C 76
Loosley Row. Buck 5G 51
Lopcombe Corner. Wilts 3A 24
Lopen. Som 1H 13
Loppington. Shrp 3G 71
Lorbottle. Nmbd 4E 121
Lorbottle Hall. Nmbd 4E 121
Lordington. W Sus 2F 17
Loscoe. Derbs 1B 74
Loscombe. Dors 3A 14
Losgaintir. W Isl 8C 171
Lossiemouth. Mor 2G 159
Lossit. Arg 4A 124
Lostock Gralam. Ches W 3A 84
Lostock Green. Ches W 3A 84
Lostock Hall. Lanc 2D 90
Lostock Junction. G Man 4E 91
Lostwithiel. Corn 3F 7
Lothbeg. High 2G 165
Lothersdale. N Yor 5B 98
Lothianbridge. Midl 3G 129
Lothianburn. Edin 3F 129
Lothmore. High 2G 165
Lottisham. Som 3A 22
Loudwater. Buck 1A 38
Loughborough. Leics 4C 74
Loughor. Swan 3E 31
Loughton. Essx 1F 39
Loughton. Mil 2G 51
Loughton. Shrp 2A 60
Lound. Linc 4H 75
Lound. Notts 2D 86
Lound. Suff 1H 67
Lount. Leics 4A 74
Louth. Linc 2C 88
Love Clough. Lanc 2G 91
Lovedean. Hants 1E 17
Lover. Wilts 4H 23
Loversall. S Yor 1C 86
Loves Green. Essx 5G 53
Loveston. Pemb 4E 43
Lovington. Som 3A 22
Low Ackworth. W Yor 3E 93
Low Angerton. Nmbd 1D 115
Low Ardwell. Dum 5F 109
Low Ballochdoan. S Ayr 2F 109
Lowbands. Glos 2C 48
Low Barlings. Linc 3H 87
Low Bell End. N Yor 5E 107
Low Bentham. N Yor 3F 97
Low Borrowbridge. Cumb 4H 103
Low Bradfield. S Yor 1G 85
Low Bradley. N Yor 5C 98
Low Braithwaite. Cumb 5F 113
Low Brunton. Nmbd 2C 114
Low Burnham. N Lin 4A 94
Lowca. Cumb 2A 102
Low Catton. E Yor 4B 100
Low Coniscliffe. Darl 3F 105
Low Coylton. S Ayr 3D 116
Low Crosby. Cumb 4F 113
Low Dalby. N Yor 1C 100
Lowdham. Notts 1D 74
Low Dinsdale. Darl 3A 106
Lowe. Shrp 2G 71
Low Ellington. N Yor 1E 98
Lower Amble. Corn 1D 6
Lower Ansty. Dors 2C 14
Lower Arboll. High 5F 165
Lower Arncott. Oxon 4E 50
Lower Ashton. Devn 4B 12
Lower Assendon. Oxon 3F 37
Lower Auchenreath. Mor 2A 160
Lower Badcall. High 4B 166
Lower Ballam. Lanc 1B 90
Lower Basildon. W Ber 4E 36
Lower Beeding. W Sus 3D 26
Lower Benefield. Nptn 2G 63
Lower Bentley. Worc 4D 61
Lower Beobridge. Shrp 1B 60
Lower Bockhampton. Dors 3C 14
Lower Boddington. Nptn 5B 62
Lower Bordean. Hants 4E 25
Lower Brailes. Warw 2B 50
Lower Breakish. High 1E 147
Lower Broadheath. Worc 5C 60
Lower Brynamman. Neat 4H 45
Lower Bullingham. Here 2A 48
Lower Bullington. Hants 2C 24
Lower Burgate. Hants 1G 15
Lower Cam. Glos 5C 48
Lower Catesby. Nptn 5C 62
Lower Chapel. Powy 2D 46
Lower Cheriton. Devn 2E 12
Lower Chicksgrove. Wilts 3E 23
Lower Chute. Wilts 1B 24
Lower Clopton. Warw 5F 61
Lower Common. Hants 2E 25
Lower Cumberworth. W Yor 4C 92
Lower Darwen. Bkbn 2E 91
Lower Dean. Bed 4H 63
Lower Dean. Devn 2D 8
Lower Diabaig. High 2G 155
Lower Dicker. E Sus 4G 27
Lower Dounreay. High 2B 168
Lower Down. Shrp 2F 59
Lower Dunsforth. N Yor 3G 99
Lower East Carleton. Norf 5D 78
Lower Egleton. Here 1B 48
Lower Ellastone. Derbs 1F 73
Lower End. Nptn 4F 63
Lower Everleigh. Wilts 1G 23
Lower Eype. Dors 3H 13
Lower Failand. N Som 4A 34
Lower Faintree. Shrp 2A 60
Lower Farringdon. Hants 3F 25
Lower Foxdale. IOM 4B 108
Lower Frankton. Shrp 2F 71
Lower Froyle. Hants 2F 25
Lower Gabwell. Devn 2F 9
Lower Gledfield. High 4C 164
Lower Godney. Som 2H 21
Lower Gravenhurst. C Beds 2B 52
Lower Green. Essx 2E 53
Lower Green. Norf 2B 78
Lower Green. Staf 5D 72
Lower Green. W Ber 5B 36
Lower Halstow. Kent 4C 40
Lower Hardres. Kent 5F 41
Lower Hardwick. Here 5G 59
Lower Hartshay. Derbs 5A 86
Lower Hawthwaite. Cumb 1B 96
Lower Hayton. Shrp 2H 59
Lower Hergest. Here 5E 59
Lower Heyford. Oxon 3C 50
Lower Heysham. Lanc 3D 96
Lower Higham. Kent 3B 40
Lower Holbrook. Suff 2E 55
Lower Holditch. Dors 2G 13
Lower Hordley. Shrp 3F 71
Lower Horncroft. W Sus 4B 26
Lower Horsebridge. E Sus 4G 27
Lower Kilcott. Glos 3C 34
Lower Killeyan. Arg 5A 124
Lower Kingcombe. Dors 3A 14
Lower Kingswood. Surr 5D 38
Lower Kinnerton. Ches W 4F 83
Lower Langford. N Som 5H 33
Lower Largo. Fife 3G 137
Lower Layham. Suff 1D 54
Lower Ledwyche. Shrp 3H 59
Lower Leigh. Staf 2E 73
Lower Lemington. Glos 2H 49
Lower Lenie. High 1H 149
Lower Ley. Glos 4C 48
Lower Llanfadog. Powy 4B 58
Lower Lode. Glos 2D 49
Lower Lovacott. Devn 4F 19
Lower Loxhore. Devn 3G 19
Lower Loxley. Staf 2E 73
Lower Lydbrook. Glos 4A 48
Lower Lye. Here 4G 59
Lower Machen. Newp 3F 33
Lower Maes-coed. Here 2G 47
Lower Meend. Glos 5A 48
Lower Milovaig. High 3A 154
Lower Moor. Worc 1E 49
Lower Morton. S Glo 2B 34
Lower Mountain. Flin 5F 83
Lower Nazeing. Essx 5D 53
Lower Nyland. Dors 4C 22
Lower Oakfield. Fife 4D 136
Lower Oddington. Glos 3H 49
Lower Ollach. High 5E 155
Lower Penarth. V Glam 5E 33
Lower Penn. Staf 1C 60
Lower Pennington. Hants 3B 16
Lower Peover. Ches W 3B 84
Lower Pitkerrie. High 1C 158
Lower Place. G Man 3H 91
Lower Quinton. Warw 1G 49
Lower Rainham. Medw 4C 40
Lower Raydon. Suff 2D 54
Lower Seagry. Wilts 3E 35
Lower Shelton. C Beds 1H 51
Lower Shiplake. Oxon 4F 37
Lower Shuckburgh. Warw 4B 62
Lower Sketty. Swan 3F 31
Lower Slade. Devn 2F 19
Lower Slaughter. Glos 3G 49
Lower Soudley. Glos 4B 48
Lower Stanton St Quintin. Wilts 3E 35
Lower Stoke. Medw 3C 40
Lower Stondon. C Beds 2B 52
Lower Stonnall. Staf 5E 73
Lower Stow Bedon. Norf 1B 66
Lower Street. Norf 2E 79
Lower Strensham. Worc 1E 49
Lower Sundon. C Beds 3A 52
Lower Swanwick. Hants 2C 16
Lower Swell. Glos 3G 49
Lower Tale. Devn 2D 12
Lower Tean. Staf 2E 73
Lower Thurlton. Norf 1G 67
Lower Thurnham. Lanc 4D 96
Lower Thurvaston. Derbs 2G 73
Lowertown. Corn 4D 4
Lower Town. Devn 5H 11
Lower Town. Here 1B 48
Lower Town. IOS 1B 4
Lower Town. Pemb 1D 42
Lower Tysoe. Warw 1B 50
Lower Upham. Hants 1D 16
Lower Upnor. Medw 3B 40
Lower Vexford. Som 3E 20
Lower Walton. Warr 2A 84
Lower Wear. Devn 4C 12
Lower Weare. Som 1H 21
Lower Welson. Here 5E 59
Lower Whatcombe. Dors 2D 14
Lower Whitley. Ches W 3A 84
Lower Wield. Hants 2E 25
Lower Winchendon. Buck 4F 51
Lower Withington. Ches E 4C 84
Lower Woodend. Buck 3G 37
Lower Woodford. Wilts 3G 23
Lower Wraxall. Dors 2A 14
Lower Wych. Ches W 1G 71
Lower Wyche. Worc 1C 48
Lowesby. Leics 5E 74
Lowestoft. Suff 1H 67
Loweswater. Cumb 2C 102
Low Etherley. Dur 2E 105
Lowfield Heath. W Sus 1D 26
Lowford. Hants 1C 16
Low Fulney. Linc 3B 76
Low Gate. Nmbd 3C 114
Lowgill. Cumb 5H 103
Lowgill. Lanc 3F 97
Low Grantley. N Yor 2E 99
Low Green. N Yor 4E 98
Low Habberley. Worc 3C 60
Low Ham. Som 4H 21
Low Hameringham. Linc 4C 88
Low Hawkser. N Yor 4G 107
Low Hesket. Cumb 5F 113
Low Hesleyhurst. Nmbd 5E 121
Lowick. Cumb 1B 96
Lowick. Nptn 2G 63
Lowick. Nmbd 1E 121
Lowick Bridge. Cumb 1B 96
Lowick Green. Cumb 1B 96
Low Knipe. Cumb 3G 103
Low Leighton. Derbs 2E 85
Low Lorton. Cumb 2C 102
Low Marishes. N Yor 2C 100
Low Marnham. Notts 4F 87
Low Mill. N Yor 5D 106
Low Moor. Lanc 5G 97
Low Moor. W Yor 2B 92
Low Moorsley. Tyne 5G 115
Low Newton-by-the-Sea. Nmbd 2G 121
Lownie Moor. Ang 4D 145
Lowood. Bord 1H 119
Low Row. Cumb 3G 113
(nr. Brampton)
Low Row. Cumb 5C 112
(nr. Wigton)
Low Row. N Yor 5C 104
Lowsonford. Warw 4F 61
Low Street. Norf 5C 78
Lowther. Cumb 2G 103
Lowthorpe. E Yor 3E 101
Lowton. Devn 2G 11
Lowton. G Man 1A 84
Lowton. Som 1E 13
Lowton Common. G Man 1A 84
Low Torry. Fife 1D 128
Low Toynton. Linc 3B 88
Low Valleyfield. Fife 1C 128
Low Westwood. Dur 4E 115
Low Whinnow. Cumb 4E 112
Low Wood. Cumb 1C 96
Low Worsall. N Yor 4A 106
Low Wray. Cumb 4E 103
Loxbeare. Devn 1C 12
Loxhill. Surr 2B 26
Loxhore. Devn 3G 19
Loxley. S Yor 2H 85
Loxley. Warw 5G 61
Loxley Green. Staf 2E 73
Loxton. N Som 1G 21
Loxwood. W Sus 2B 26
Lubcroy. High 3A 164

Lubenham—Margaretting Tye

Lubenham. Leics 2E 62
Lubinvullin. High 2F 167
Luccombe. Som 2C 20
Luccombe Village. IOW 4D 16
Lucker. Nmbd 1F 121
Luckett. Corn 5D 11
Luckington. Wilts 3D 34
Lucklawhill. Fife 1G 137
Luckwell Bridge. Som 3C 20
Lucton. Here 4G 59
Ludag. W Isl 7C 170
Ludborough. Linc 1B 88
Ludchurch. Pemb 3F 43
Luddenden. W Yor 2A 92
Luddenden Foot. W Yor 2A 92
Luddenham. Kent 4D 40
Ludderburn. Cumb 5F 103
Luddesdown. Kent 4A 40
Luddington. N Lin 3B 94
Luddington. Warw 5F 61
Luddington in the Brook. Nptn 2A 64
Ludford. Linc 2A 88
Ludford. Shrp 3H 59
Ludgershall. Buck 4E 51
Ludgershall. Wilts 1A 24
Ludgvan. Corn 3C 4
Ludham. Norf 4F 79
Ludlow. Shrp 3H 59
Ludstone. Shrp 1C 60
Ludwell. Wilts 4E 23
Ludworth. Dur 5G 115
Luffenhall. Herts 3C 52
Luffincott. Devn 3D 10
Lugar. E Ayr 2E 117
Luggate Burn. E Lot 2C 130
Lugg Green. Here 4G 59
Luggiebank. N Lan 2A 128
Lugton. E Ayr 4F 127
Lugwardine. Here 1A 48
Luib. High 1D 146
Luib. Stir 1D 135
Lulham. Here 1H 47
Lullington. Derbs 4G 73
Lullington. Som 1C 22
Lulsgate Bottom. N Som 5A 34
Lulsley. Worc 5B 60
Lulworth Camp. Dors 4D 14
Lumb. Lanc 2G 91
Lumb. W Yor 2A 92
Lumby. N Yor 1E 93
Lumphanan. Abers 3C 152
Lumphinnans. Fife 4D 136
Lumsdaine. Bord 3E 131
Lumsden. Abers 1B 152
Lunan. Ang 3F 145
Lunanhead. Ang 3D 145
Luncarty. Per 1C 136
Lund. E Yor 5D 100
Lund. N Yor 1G 93
Lundie. Ang 5B 144
Lundin Links. Fife 3G 137
Lundy Green. Norf 1E 67
Lunna. Shet 5F 173
Lunning. Shet 5G 173
Lunnon. Swan 4E 31
Lunsford. Kent 5B 40
Lunsford's Cross. E Sus 4B 28
Lunt. Mers 4B 90
Luppitt. Devn 2E 13
Lupridge. Devn 3D 8
Lupset. W Yor 3D 92
Lupton. Cumb 1E 97
Lurgashall. W Sus 3A 26
Lurley. Devn 1C 12
Lusby. Linc 4C 88
Luscombe. Devn 3D 9
Luson. Devn 4C 8
Luss. Arg 4C 134
Lussagiven. Arg 1E 125
Lusta. High 3B 154
Lustleigh. Devn 4A 12
Luston. Here 4G 59
Luthermuir. Abers 2F 145
Luthrie. Fife 2F 137
Lutley. Staf 2C 60
Luton. Devn 2D 12
(nr. Honiton)
Luton. Devn 5C 12
(nr. Teignmouth)
Luton. Lutn 3A 52
Luton (London) Airport. Lutn 3B 52
Lutterworth. Leics 2C 62
Lutton. Devn 3B 8
(nr. Ivybridge)
Lutton. Devn 2C 8
(nr. South Brent)
Lutton. Linc 3D 76
Lutton. Nptn 2A 64
Lutton Gowts. Linc 3D 76
Lutworthy. Devn 1A 12
Luxborough. Som 3C 20
Luxley. Glos 3B 48
Luxulyan. Corn 3E 7
Lybster. High 5E 169
Lydbury North. Shrp 2F 59
Lydcott. Devn 3G 19
Lydd. Kent 3E 29
Lydden. Kent 1G 29
(nr. Dover)
Lydden. Kent 4H 41
(nr. Margate)
Lyddington. Rut 1F 63
Lydd (London Ashford) Airport. Kent 3E 29
Lydd-on-Sea. Kent 3E 29
Lydeard St Lawrence. Som 3E 21
Lyde Green. Hants 1F 25
Lydford. Devn 4F 11
Lydford Fair Place. Som 3A 22
Lydgate. G Man 4H 91
Lydgate. W Yor 2H 91
Lydham. Shrp 1F 59
Lydiard Millicent. Wilts 3F 35
Lydiate. Mers 4B 90
Lydiate Ash. Worc 3D 61
Lydlinch. Dors 1C 14
Lydmarsh. Som 2G 13
Lydney. Glos 5B 48
Lydstep. Pemb 5E 43
Lye. W Mid 2D 60
Lye Green. Buck 5H 51
Lye Green. E Sus 2G 27
Lye Head. Worc 3B 60
Lye, The. Shrp 1A 60
Lyford. Oxon 2B 36
Lyham. Nmbd 1E 121
Lylestone. N Ayr 5E 127
Lymbridge Green. Kent 1F 29
Lyme Regis. Dors 3G 13
Lyminge. Kent 1F 29
Lymington. Hants 3B 16
Lyminster. W Sus 5B 26
Lymm. Warr 2A 84
Lymore. Hants 3A 16
Lympne. Kent 2F 29
Lympsham. Som 1G 21
Lympstone. Devn 4C 12
Lynaberack Lodge. High 4B 150
Lynbridge. Devn 2H 19
Lynch. Som 2C 20
Lynchat. High 3B 150
Lynch Green. Norf 5D 78
Lyndhurst. Hants 2B 16
Lyndon. Rut 5G 75
Lyne. Bord 5F 129
Lyne. Surr 4B 38
Lyneal. Shrp 2G 71
Lyne Down. Here 2B 48
Lyneham. Oxon 3A 50
Lyneham. Wilts 4F 35
Lyneholmeford. Cumb 2G 113
Lynemouth. Nmbd 5G 121
Lyne of Gorthleck. High 1H 149
Lyne of Skene. Abers 2E 153
Lynesack. Dur 2D 105
Lyness. Orkn 8C 172
Lyng. Norf 4C 78
Lyngate. Norf 2E 79
(nr. North Walsham)
Lyngate. Norf 3F 79
(nr. Worstead)
Lynmouth. Devn 2H 19
Lynn. Staf 5E 73
Lynn. Telf 4B 72
Lynsted. Kent 4D 40
Lynstone. Corn 2C 10
Lynton. Devn 2H 19
Lynwilg. High 2C 150
Lyon's Gate. Dors 2B 14
Lyonshall. Here 5F 59
Lytchett Matravers. Dors 3E 15
Lytchett Minster. Dors 3E 15
Lyth. High 2E 169
Lytham. Lanc 2B 90
Lytham St Anne's. Lanc 2B 90
Lythe. N Yor 3F 107
Lythes. Orkn 9D 172
Lythmore. High 2C 168

M

Mabe Burnthouse. Corn 5B 6
Mabie. Dum 2A 112
Mablethorpe. Linc 2E 89
Macbiehill. Bord 4E 129
Macclesfield. Ches E 3D 84
Macclesfield Forest. Ches E 3D 85
Macduff. Abers 2E 160
Machan. S Lan 4A 128
Macharioch. Arg 5B 122
Machen. Cphy 3F 33
Machrie. N Ayr 2C 122
Machrihanish. Arg 3A 122
Machroes. Gwyn 3C 68
Machynlleth. Powy 5G 69
Mackerye End. Herts 4B 52
Mackworth. Derb 2H 73
Macmerry. E Lot 2H 129
Maddaford. Devn 3F 11
Madderty. Per 1B 136
Maddington. Wilts 2F 23
Maddiston. Falk 2C 128
Madehurst. W Sus 4A 26
Madeley. Staf 1B 72
Madeley. Telf 5A 72
Madeley Heath. Staf 1B 72
Madeley Heath. Worc 3D 60
Madford. Devn 1E 13
Madingley. Cambs 4C 64
Madley. Here 2H 47
Madresfield. Worc 1D 48
Madron. Corn 3B 4
Maenaddwyn. IOA 2D 80
Maenclochog. Pemb 2E 43
Maendy. V Glam 4D 32
Maenporth. Corn 4E 5
Maentwrog. Gwyn 1F 69
Maen-y-groes. Cdgn 5C 56
Maer. Staf 2B 72
Maerdy. Carm 3G 45
Maerdy. Cnwy 1C 70
Maerdy. Rhon 2C 32
Maesbrook. Shrp 3F 71
Maesbury. Shrp 3F 71
Maesbury Marsh. Shrp 3F 71
Maes-glas. Flin 3D 82
Maesgwyn-Isaf. Powy 4D 70
Maeshafn. Den 4E 82
Maes Llyn. Cdgn 1D 44
Maesmynis. Powy 1D 46
Maesteg. B'end 2B 32
Maestir. Cdgn 1F 45
Maesybont. Carm 4F 45
Maesycrugiau. Carm 1E 45
Maesycwmmer. Cphy 2E 33
Maesyrhandir. Powy 1C 58
Magdalen Laver. Essx 5F 53
Maggieknockater. Mor 4H 159
Magham Down. E Sus 4H 27
Maghull. Mers 4B 90
Magna Park. Leics 2C 62
Magor. Mon 3H 33
Magpie Green. Suff 3C 66
Magwyr. Mon 3H 33
Maidenbower. W Sus 2D 27
Maiden Bradley. Wilts 3D 22
Maidencombe. Torb 2F 9
Maidenhayne. Devn 3F 13
Maidenhead. Wind 3G 37
Maiden Law. Dur 5E 115
Maiden Newton. Dors 3A 14
Maidens. S Ayr 4B 116
Maiden's Green. Brac 4G 37
Maidensgrove. Oxon 3F 37
Maidenwell. Corn 5B 10
Maidenwell. Linc 3C 88
Maiden Wells. Pemb 5D 42
Maidford. Nptn 5D 62
Maids Moreton. Buck 2F 51
Maidstone. Kent 5B 40
Maidwell. Nptn 3E 63
Mail. Shet 9F 173
Maindee. Newp 3G 33
Mainsforth. Dur 1A 106
Mains of Auchindachy. Mor 4B 160
Mains of Auchnagatt. Abers 4G 161
Mains of Drum. Abers 4F 153
Mains of Edingight. Mor 3C 160
Mainsriddle. Dum 4G 111
Mainstone. Shrp 2E 59
Maisemore. Glos 3D 48
Major's Green. Worc 3F 61
Makeney. Derbs 1A 74
Makerstoun. Bord 1A 120
Malacleit. W Isl 1C 170
Malaig. High 4E 147
Malaig Bheag. High 4E 147
Malborough. Devn 5D 8
Malcoff. Derbs 2E 85
Malcolmburn. Mor 3A 160
Malden Rushett. G Lon 4C 38
Maldon. Essx 5B 54
Malham. N Yor 3B 98
Maligar. High 2D 155
Malinslee. Telf 5A 72
Mallaig. High 4E 147
Malleny Mills. Edin 3E 129
Mallows Green. Essx 3E 53
Malltraeth. IOA 4D 80
Mallwyd. Gwyn 4A 70
Malmesbury. Wilts 3E 35
Malmsmead. Devn 2A 20
Malpas. Ches W 1G 71
Malpas. Corn 4C 6
Malpas. Newp 2F 33
Malswick. Glos 3C 48
Maltby. S Yor 1C 86
Maltby. Stoc T 3B 106
Maltby le Marsh. Linc 2D 88
Malt Lane. Arg 3H 133
Maltman's Hill. Kent 1D 28
Malton. N Yor 2B 100
Malvern Link. Worc 1C 48
Malvern Wells. Worc 1C 48
Mamble. Worc 3A 60
Mamhilad. Mon 5G 47
Manaccan. Corn 4E 5
Manafon. Powy 5D 70
Manaton. Devn 4A 12
Manby. Linc 2C 88
Mancetter. Warw 1H 61
Manchester. G Man 1C 84
Manchester International Airport. G Man 2C 84
Mancot. Flin 4F 83
Manea. Cambs 2D 65
Maney. W Mid 1F 61
Manfield. N Yor 3F 105
Mangotsfield. S Glo 4B 34
Mangurstadh. W Isl 4C 171
Mankinholes. W Yor 2H 91
Manley. Ches W 3H 83
Manmoel. Cphy 5E 47
Mannal. Arg 4A 138
Mannerston. Falk 2D 128
Manningford Bohune. Wilts 1G 23
Manningford Bruce. Wilts 1G 23
Manningham. W Yor 1B 92
Mannings Heath. W Sus 3D 26
Mannington. Dors 2F 15
Manningtree. Essx 2E 54
Mannofield. Aber 3G 153
Manorbier. Pemb 5E 43
Manorbier Newton. Pemb 5E 43
Manorowen. Pemb 1D 42
Manor Park. G Lon 2F 39
Mansell Gamage. Here 1G 47
Mansell Lacy. Here 1H 47
Mansergh. Cumb 1F 97
Mansewood. Glas 3G 127
Mansfield. E Ayr 3F 117
Mansfield. Notts 4C 86
Mansfield Woodhouse. Notts 4C 86
Mansriggs. Cumb 1B 96
Manston. Dors 1D 14
Manston. Kent 4H 41
Manston. W Yor 1D 92
Manswood. Dors 2E 15
Manthorpe. Linc 4H 75
(nr. Bourne)
Manthorpe. Linc 2G 75
(nr. Grantham)
Manton. N Lin 4C 94
Manton. Notts 3C 86
Manton. Rut 5F 75
Manton. Wilts 5G 35
Manuden. Essx 3E 53
Maperton. Som 4B 22
Maplebeck. Notts 4E 86
Maple Cross. Herts 1B 38
Mapledurham. Oxon 4E 37
Mapledurwell. Hants 1E 25
Maplehurst. W Sus 3C 26
Maplescombe. Kent 4G 39
Mapperley. Derbs 1B 74
Mapperley. Notts 1C 74
Mapperley Park. Notts 1C 74
Mapperton. Dors 3A 14
(nr. Beaminster)
Mapperton. Dors 3E 15
(nr. Poole)
Mappleborough Green. Warw 4E 61
Mappleton. Derbs 1F 73
Mappleton. E Yor 5G 101
Mapplewell. S Yor 4D 92
Mappowder. Dors 2C 14
Maraig. W Isl 7E 171
Marazion. Corn 3C 4
Marbhig. W Isl 6G 171
Marbury. Ches E 1H 71
March. Cambs 1D 64
Marcham. Oxon 2C 36
Marchamley. Shrp 3H 71
Marchington. Staf 2F 73
Marchington Woodlands. Staf 3F 73
Marchwiel. Wrex 1F 71
Marchwood. Hants 1B 16
Marcross. V Glam 5C 32
Marden. Here 1A 48
Marden. Kent 1B 28
Marden. Wilts 1F 23
Marden Beech. Kent 1B 28
Marden Thorn. Kent 1B 28
Mardu. Shrp 2E 59
Mardy. Mon 4G 47
Marefield. Leics 5E 75
Mareham le Fen. Linc 4B 88
Mareham on the Hill. Linc 4B 88
Marehay. Derbs 1A 74
Marehill. W Sus 4B 26
Maresfield. E Sus 3F 27
Marfleet. Hull 2E 95
Marford. Wrex 5F 83
Margam. Neat 3A 32
Margaret Marsh. Dors 1D 14
Margaret Roding. Essx 4F 53
Margaretting. Essx 5G 53
Margaretting Tye. Essx 5G 53

Margate—Mere Green

Margate. Kent 3H 41
Margery. Surr 5D 38
Margnaheglish. N Ayr 2E 123
Marham. Norf 5G 77
Marhamchurch. Corn 2C 10
Marholm. Pet 5A 76
Marian Cwm. Den 3C 82
Mariandyrys. IOA 2F 81
Marian-glas. IOA 2E 81
Mariansleigh. Devn 4H 19
Marian-y-de. Gwyn 2C 68
Marine Town. Kent 3D 40
Marion-y-mor. Gwyn 2C 68
Marishader. High 2D 155
Marjoriebanks. Dum 1B 112
Mark. Dum 4G 109
Mark. Som 2G 21
Markbeech. Kent 1F 27
Markby. Linc 3D 89
Mark Causeway. Som 2G 21
Mark Cross. E Sus 2G 27
Markeaton. Derb 2H 73
Market Bosworth. Leics 5B 74
Market Deeping. Linc 4A 76
Market Drayton. Shrp 2A 72
Market End. Warw 2H 61
Market Harborough. Leics 2E 63
Markethill. Per 5B 144
Market Lavington. Wilts 1F 23
Market Overton. Rut 4F 75
Market Rasen. Linc 2A 88
Market Stainton. Linc 2B 88
Market Weighton. E Yor 5C 100
Market Weston. Suff 3B 66
Markfield. Leics 4B 74
Markham. Cphy 5E 47
Markinch. Fife 3E 137
Markington. N Yor 3E 99
Marksbury. Bath 5B 34
Mark's Corner. IOW 3C 16
Marks Tey. Essx 3C 54
Markwell. Corn 3H 7
Markyate. Herts 4A 52
Marlborough. Wilts 5G 35
Marlcliff. Warw 5E 61
Marldon. Devn 2E 9
Marle Green. E Sus 4G 27
Marlesford. Suff 5F 67
Marley Green. Ches E 1H 71
Marley Hill. Tyne 4F 115
Marlingford. Norf 5D 78
Marloes. Pemb 4B 42
Marlow. Buck 3G 37
Marlow. Here 3G 59
Marlow Bottom. Buck 3G 37
Marlow Common. Buck 3G 37
Marlpit Hill. Kent 1F 27
Marlpits. E Sus 3F 27
Marlpool. Derbs 1B 74
Marnhull. Dors 1C 14
Marnoch. Abers 3C 160
Marnock. N Lan 3A 128
Marple. G Man 2D 84
Marr. S Yor 4F 93
Marrel. High 2H 165
Marrick. N Yor 5D 105
Marros. Carm 4G 43
Marsden. Tyne 3G 115
Marsden. W Yor 3A 92
Marsett. N Yor 1B 98
Marsh. Buck 5G 51
Marsh. Devn 1F 13
Marshall Meadows. Nmbd 4F 131
Marshalsea. Dors 2G 13
Marshalswick. Herts 5B 52
Marsham. Norf 3D 78
Marshaw. Lanc 4E 97
Marsh Baldon. Oxon 2D 36
Marsh Benham. W Ber 5C 36
Marshborough. Kent 5H 41
Marshbrook. Shrp 2G 59
Marshbury. Essx 4G 53
Marshchapel. Linc 1C 88
Marshfield. Newp 3F 33
Marshfield. S Glo 4C 34
Marshgate. Corn 3B 10
Marsh Gibbon. Buck 3E 51
Marsh Green. Devn 3D 12
Marsh Green. Kent 1F 27
Marsh Green. Staf 5C 84
Marsh Green. Telf 4A 72
Marsh Lane. Derbs 3B 86
Marshside. Kent 4G 41
Marshside. Mers 3B 90
Marsh Side. Norf 1G 77
Marsh Street. Som 2C 20
Marsh, The. Powy 1F 59
Marsh, The. Shrp 3A 72
Marshwood. Dors 3G 13
Marske. N Yor 4E 105
Marske-by-the-Sea. Red C 2D 106
Marston. Ches W 3A 84
Marston. Here 5F 59
Marston. Linc 1F 75
Marston. Oxon 5D 50
Marston. Staf 3D 72
(nr. Stafford)
Marston. Staf 4C 72
(nr. Wheaton Aston)
Marston. Warw 1G 61
Marston. Wilts 1E 23
Marston Doles. Warw 5B 62
Marston Green. W Mid 2F 61
Marston Hill. Glos 2G 35
Marston Jabbett. Warw 2A 62
Marston Magna. Som 4A 22
Marston Meysey. Wilts 2G 35
Marston Montgomery. Derbs 2F 73
Marston Moretaine. C Beds 1H 51
Marston on Dove. Derbs 3G 73
Marston St Lawrence. Nptn 1D 50
Marston Stannett. Here 5H 59
Marston Trussell. Nptn 2D 62
Marstow. Here 4A 48
Marsworth. Buck 4H 51
Marten. Wilts 5A 36
Marthall. Ches E 3C 84
Martham. Norf 4G 79
Marthwaite. Cumb 5H 103
Martin. Hants 1F 15
Martin. Kent 1H 29
Martin. Linc 4B 88
(nr. Horncastle)
Martin. Linc 5A 88
(nr. Metheringham)
Martindale. Cumb 3F 103
Martin Dales. Linc 4A 88
Martin Drove End. Hants 4F 23
Martinhoe. Devn 2G 19
Martinhoe Cross. Devn 2G 19
Martin Hussingtree. Worc 4C 60
Martin Mill. Kent 1H 29
Martinscroft. Warr 2A 84
Martin's Moss. Ches E 4C 84
Martinstown. Dors 4B 14
Martlesham. Suff 1F 55
Martlesham Heath. Suff 1F 55
Martletwy. Pemb 3E 43
Martley. Worc 5B 60
Martock. Som 1H 13
Marton. Ches E 4C 84
Marton. Cumb 2B 96
Marton. E Yor 3G 101
(nr. Bridlington)
Marton. E Yor 1E 95
(nr. Hull)
Marton. Linc 2F 87
Marton. Midd 3C 106
Marton. N Yor 3G 99
(nr. Boroughbridge)
Marton. N Yor 1B 100
(nr. Pickering)
Marton. Shrp 3G 71
(nr. Myddle)
Marton. Shrp 5E 71
(nr. Worthen)
Marton. Warw 4B 62
Marton Abbey. N Yor 3H 99
Marton-le-Moor. N Yor 2F 99
Martyr's Green. Surr 5B 38
Martyr Worthy. Hants 3D 24
Marwood. Devn 3F 19
Marybank. High 3G 157
(nr. Dingwall)
Marybank. High 1B 158
(nr. Invergordon)
Maryburgh. High 3H 157
Maryfield. Corn 3A 8
Maryhill. Glas 3G 127
Marykirk. Abers 2F 145
Marylebone. G Lon 2D 39
Marylebone. G Man 4D 90
Marypark. Mor 5F 159
Maryport. Cumb 1B 102
Maryport. Dum 5E 109
Marystow. Devn 4E 11
Mary Tavy. Devn 5F 11
Maryton. Ang 3C 144
(nr. Kirriemuir)
Maryton. Ang 3F 145
(nr. Montrose)
Marywell. Abers 4C 152
Marywell. Ang 4F 145
Masham. N Yor 1E 98
Mashbury. Essx 4G 53
Masongill. N Yor 2F 97
Masons Lodge. Abers 3F 153
Mastin Moor. Derbs 3B 86
Mastrick. Aber 3G 153
Matching. Essx 4F 53
Matching Green. Essx 4F 53
Matching Tye. Essx 4F 53
Matfen. Nmbd 2D 114
Matfield. Kent 1A 28
Mathern. Mon 2A 34
Mathon. Here 1C 48
Mathry. Pemb 1C 42
Matlaske. Norf 2D 78
Matlock. Derbs 4G 85
Matlock Bath. Derbs 5G 85
Matterdale End. Cumb 2E 103
Mattersey. Notts 2D 86
Mattersey Thorpe. Notts 2D 86
Mattingley. Hants 1F 25
Mattishall. Norf 4C 78
Mattishall Burgh. Norf 4C 78
Mauchline. E Ayr 2D 117
Maud. Abers 4G 161
Maudlin. Corn 2E 7
Maugersbury. Glos 3G 49
Maughold. IOM 2D 108
Maulden. C Beds 2A 52
Maulds Meaburn. Cumb 3H 103
Maunby. N Yor 1F 99
Maund Bryan. Here 5H 59
Mautby. Norf 4G 79
Mavesyn Ridware. Staf 4E 73
Mavis Enderby. Linc 4C 88
Mawbray. Cumb 5B 112
Mawdesley. Lanc 3C 90
Mawdlam. B'end 3B 32
Mawgan. Corn 4E 5
Mawgan Porth. Corn 2C 6
Maw Green. Ches E 5B 84
Mawla. Corn 4B 6
Mawnan. Corn 4E 5
Mawnan Smith. Corn 4E 5
Mawsley Village. Nptn 3F 63
Mawthorpe. Linc 3D 88
Maxey. Pet 5A 76
Maxstoke. Warw 2G 61
Maxted Street. Kent 1F 29
Maxton. Kent 1G 29
Maxton. Bord 1A 120
Maxwellheugh. Bord 1B 120
Maxwelltown. Dum 2A 112
Maxworthy. Corn 3C 10
Mayals. Swan 4F 31
Maybole. S Ayr 4C 116
Maybush. Sotn 1B 16
Mayes Green. Surr 2C 26
Mayfield. E Sus 3G 27
Mayfield. Midl 3G 129
Mayfield. Per 1C 136
Mayfield. Staf 1F 73
Mayford. Surr 5A 38
Mayhill. Swan 3F 31
Mayland. Essx 5C 54
Maylandsea. Essx 5C 54
Maynard's Green. E Sus 4G 27
Maypole. IOS 1B 4
Maypole. Kent 4G 41
Maypole. Mon 4H 47
Maypole Green. Norf 1G 67
Maypole Green. Suff 5B 66
Mayshill. S Glo 3B 34
Maywick. Shet 9E 173
Mead. Devn 1C 10
Meadgate. Bath 1B 22
Meadle. Buck 5G 51
Meadowbank. Ches W 4A 84
Meadowfield. Dur 1F 105
Meadow Green. Here 5B 60
Meadowmill. E Lot 2H 129
Meadows. Nott 2C 74
Meadowtown. Shrp 5F 71
Meadwell. Devn 4E 11
Mealabost. W Isl 2G 171
(nr. Borgh)
Mealabost. W Isl 4G 171
(nr. Stornoway)
Meal Bank. Cumb 5G 103
Mealrigg. Cumb 5C 112
Mealsgate. Cumb 5D 112
Meanwood. W Yor 1C 92
Mearbeck. N Yor 3H 97
Meare. Som 2H 21
Meare Green. Som 4F 21
(nr. Curry Mallet)
Meare Green. Som 4G 21
(nr. Stoke St Gregory)
Mears Ashby. Nptn 4F 63
Measham. Leics 4H 73
Meath Green. Surr 1D 27
Meathop. Cumb 1D 96
Meaux. E Yor 1D 94
Meavy. Devn 2B 8
Medbourne. Leics 1E 63
Medburn. Nmbd 2E 115
Meddon. Devn 1C 10
Meden Vale. Notts 4C 86
Medlam. Linc 5C 88
Medlicott. Shrp 1G 59
Medmenham. Buck 3G 37
Medomsley. Dur 4E 115
Medstead. Hants 3E 25
Medway Towns. Medw 4B 40
Meerbrook. Staf 4D 85
Meer End. W Mid 3G 61
Meers Bridge. Linc 2D 89
Meesden. Herts 2E 53
Meeson. Telf 3A 72
Meeth. Devn 2F 11
Meeting Green. Suff 5G 65
Meeting House Hill. Norf 3F 79
Meidrim. Carm 2G 43
Meifod. Powy 4D 70
Meigle. Per 4B 144
Meikle Earnock. S Lan 4A 128
Meikle Kilchattan Butts. Arg 4B 126
Meikleour. Per 5A 144
Meikle Tarty. Abers 1G 153
Meikle Wartle. Abers 5E 160
Meinciau. Carm 4E 45
Meir. Stoke 1D 72
Meir Heath. Staf 1D 72
Melbourn. Cambs 1D 53
Melbourne. Derbs 3A 74
Melbourne. E Yor 5B 100
Melbury Abbas. Dors 4D 23
Melbury Bubb. Dors 2A 14
Melbury Osmond. Dors 2A 14
Melbury Sampford. Dors 2A 14
Melby. Shet 6C 173
Melchbourne. Bed 4H 63
Melcombe Bingham. Dors 2C 14
Melcombe Regis. Dors 4B 14
Meldon. Devn 3F 11
Meldon. Nmbd 1E 115
Meldreth. Cambs 1D 53
Melfort. Arg 2F 133
Melgarve. High 4G 149
Meliden. Den 2C 82
Melinbyrhedyn. Powy 1H 57
Melincourt. Neat 5B 46
Melin-y-coed. Cnwy 4H 81
Melin-y-ddol. Powy 5C 70
Melin-y-wig. Den 1C 70
Melkington. Nmbd 5E 131
Melkinthorpe. Cumb 2G 103
Melkridge. Nmbd 3A 114
Melksham. Wilts 5E 35
Mellangaun. High 5C 162
Melldalloch. Arg 2H 125
Mellguards. Cumb 5F 113
Melling. Lanc 2E 97
Melling. Mers 4B 90
Melling Mount. Mers 4C 90
Mellis. Suff 3C 66
Mellon Charles. High 4C 162
Mellon Udrigle. High 4C 162
Mellor. G Man 2D 85
Mellor. Lanc 1E 91
Mellor Brook. Lanc 1E 91
Mells. Som 2C 22
Melmerby. Cumb 1H 103
Melmerby. N Yor 1C 98
(nr. Middleham)
Melmerby. N Yor 2F 99
(nr. Ripon)
Melplash. Dors 3H 13
Melrose. Bord 1H 119
Melsonby. N Yor 4E 105
Meltham. W Yor 3A 92
Meltham Mills. W Yor 3B 92
Melton. E Yor 2C 94
Melton. Suff 5E 67
Meltonby. E Yor 4B 100
Melton Constable. Norf 2C 78
Melton Mowbray. Leics 4E 75
Melton Ross. N Lin 3D 94
Melvaig. High 5B 162
Melverley. Shrp 4F 71
Melverley Green. Shrp 4F 71
Melvich. High 2A 168
Membury. Devn 2F 13
Memsie. Abers 2G 161
Memus. Ang 3D 144
Menabilly. Corn 3E 7
Menai Bridge. IOA 3E 81
Mendham. Suff 2E 67
Mendlesham. Suff 4D 66
Mendlesham Green. Suff 4C 66
Menethorpe. N Yor 3B 100
Menheniot. Corn 2G 7
Menithwood. Worc 4B 60
Menna. Corn 3D 6
Mennock. Dum 4H 117
Menston. W Yor 5D 98
Menstrie. Clac 4H 135
Menthorpe. N Yor 1H 93
Mentmore. Buck 4H 51
Meole Brace. Shrp 4G 71
Meols. Mers 2E 83
Meon. Hants 2D 16
Meonstoke. Hants 4E 24
Meopham. Kent 4H 39
Meopham Green. Kent 4H 39
Meopham Station. Kent 4H 39
Mepal. Cambs 2D 64
Meppershall. C Beds 2B 52
Merbach. Here 1G 47
Mercaston. Derbs 1G 73
Merchiston. Edin 2F 129
Mere. Ches E 2B 84
Mere. Wilts 3D 22
Mere Brow. Lanc 3C 90
Mereclough. Lanc 1G 91
Mere Green. W Mid 1F 61
Mere Green. Worc 4D 60

A-Z Great Britain Handy Road Atlas 225

Mere Heath—Milton of Balgonie

Mere Heath. *Ches W* 3A **84**
Mereside. *Bkpl* 1B **90**
Meretown. *Staf* 3B **72**
Mereworth. *Kent* 5A **40**
Meriden. *W Mid* 2G **61**
Merkadale. *High* 5C **154**
Merkland. *S Ayr* 5B **116**
Merkland Lodge. *High* 1A **164**
Merley. *Pool* 3F **15**
Merlin's Bridge. *Pemb* 3D **42**
Merridge. *Som* 3F **21**
Merrington. *Shrp* 3G **71**
Merrion. *Pemb* 5D **42**
Merriott. *Som* 1H **13**
Merrivale. *Devn* 5F **11**
Merrow. *Surr* 5B **38**
Merrybent. *Darl* 3F **105**
Merry Lees. *Leics* 5B **74**
Merrymeet. *Corn* 2G **7**
Mersham. *Kent* 2E **29**
Merstham. *Surr* 5D **39**
Merston. *W Sus* 2G **17**
Merstone. *IOW* 4D **16**
Merther. *Corn* 4C **6**
Merthyr. *Carm* 3D **44**
Merthyr Cynog. *Powy* 2C **46**
Merthyr Dyfan. *V Glam* 4E **32**
Merthyr Mawr. *B'end* 4B **32**
Merthyr Tudful. *Mer T* 5D **46**
Merthyr Tydfil. *Mer T* 5D **46**
Merthyr Vale. *Mer T* 5D **46**
Merton. *Devn* 1F **11**
Merton. *G Lon* 4D **38**
Merton. *Norf* 1B **66**
Merton. *Oxon* 4D **50**
Meshaw. *Devn* 1A **12**
Messing. *Essx* 4B **54**
Messingham. *N Lin* 4B **94**
Metcombe. *Devn* 3D **12**
Metfield. *Suff* 2E **67**
Metherell. *Corn* 2A **8**
Metheringham. *Linc* 4H **87**
Methil. *Fife* 4F **137**
Methilhill. *Fife* 4F **137**
Methley. *W Yor* 2D **93**
Methley Junction. *W Yor* 2D **93**
Methlick. *Abers* 5F **161**
Methven. *Per* 1C **136**
Methwold. *Norf* 1G **65**
Methwold Hythe. *Norf* 1G **65**
Mettingham. *Suff* 1F **67**
Metton. *Norf* 2D **78**
Mevagissey. *Corn* 4E **6**
Mexborough. *S Yor* 4E **93**
Mey. *High* 1E **169**
Meysey Hampton. *Glos* 2G **35**
Miabhag. *W Isl* 8D **171**
Miabhaig. *W Isl* 7C **171**
(nr. Cliasmol)
Miabhaig. *W Isl* 4C **171**
(nr. Timsgearraidh)
Mial. *High* 1G **155**
Michaelchurch. *Here* 3A **48**
Michaelchurch Escley. *Here* 2G **47**
Michaelchurch-on-Arrow. *Powy* 5E **59**
Michaelston-le-Pit. *V Glam* 4E **33**
Michaelston-y-Fedw. *Newp* 3F **33**
Michaelstow. *Corn* 5A **10**
Michelcombe. *Devn* 2C **8**
Micheldever. *Hants* 3D **24**
Micheldever Station. *Hants* 2D **24**
Michelmersh. *Hants* 4B **24**
Mickfield. *Suff* 4D **66**
Micklebring. *S Yor* 1C **86**
Mickleby. *N Yor* 3F **107**
Micklefield. *W Yor* 1E **93**
Micklefield Green. *Herts* 1B **38**
Mickleham. *Surr* 5C **38**
Mickleover. *Derb* 2H **73**
Micklethwaite. *Cumb* 4D **112**
Micklethwaite. *W Yor* 5D **98**
Mickleton. *Dur* 2C **104**
Mickleton. *Glos* 1G **49**
Mickletown. *W Yor* 2D **93**
Mickle Trafford. *Ches W* 4G **83**
Mickley. *N Yor* 2E **99**
Mickley Green. *Suff* 5H **65**
Mickley Square. *Nmbd* 3D **115**
Mid Ardlaw. *Abers* 2G **161**
Midbea. *Orkn* 3D **172**
Mid Beltie. *Abers* 3D **152**
Mid Calder. *W Lot* 3D **129**
Mid Clyth. *High* 5E **169**
Middle Assendon. *Oxon* 3F **37**
Middle Aston. *Oxon* 3C **50**
Middle Barton. *Oxon* 3C **50**
Middlebie. *Dum* 2D **112**
Middle Chinnock. *Som* 1H **13**
Middle Claydon. *Buck* 3F **51**
Middlecliffe. *S Yor* 4E **93**
Middlecott. *Devn* 4H **11**
Middle Drums. *Ang* 3E **145**
Middle Duntisbourne. *Glos* 5E **49**
Middle Essie. *Abers* 3H **161**
Middleforth Green. *Lanc* 2D **90**
Middleham. *N Yor* 1D **98**
Middle Handley. *Derbs* 3B **86**
Middle Harling. *Norf* 2B **66**
Middlehope. *Shrp* 2G **59**
Middle Littleton. *Worc* 1F **49**
Middle Maes-coed. *Here* 2G **47**
Middlemarsh. *Dors* 2B **14**
Middle Marwood. *Devn* 3F **19**
Middle Mayfield. *Staf* 1F **73**
Middlemoor. *Devn* 5E **11**
Middlemuir. *Abers* 4F **161**
(nr. New Deer)
Middlemuir. *Abers* 3G **161**
(nr. Strichen)
Middle Rainton. *Tyne* 5G **115**
Middle Rasen. *Linc* 2H **87**
Middlesbrough. *Midd* 3B **106**
Middlesceugh. *Cumb* 5E **113**
Middleshaw. *Cumb* 1E **97**
Middlesmoor. *N Yor* 2C **98**
Middles, The. *Dur* 4F **115**
Middlestone. *Dur* 1F **105**
Middlestone Moor. *Dur* 1F **105**
Middle Stoughton. *Som* 2H **21**
Middlestown. *W Yor* 3C **92**
Middle Street. *Glos* 5C **48**
Middle Taphouse. *Corn* 2F **7**
Middleton. *Ang* 4E **145**
Middleton. *Arg* 4A **138**
Middleton. *Cumb* 1F **97**
Middleton. *Derbs* 4F **85**
(nr. Bakewell)
Middleton. *Derbs* 5G **85**
(nr. Wirksworth)
Middleton. *Essx* 2B **54**
Middleton. *G Man* 4G **91**
Middleton. *Hants* 2C **24**
Middleton. *Hart* 1C **106**
Middleton. *Here* 4H **59**
Middleton. *IOW* 4B **16**
Middleton. *Lanc* 4D **96**
Middleton. *Midl* 4G **129**
Middleton. *Norf* 4F **77**
Middleton. *Nptn* 1F **63**
Middleton. *Nmbd* 1F **121**
(nr. Belford)
Middleton. *Nmbd* 1D **114**
(nr. Morpeth)
Middleton. *N Yor* 5D **98**
(nr. Ilkley)
Middleton. *N Yor* 1B **100**
(nr. Pickering)
Middleton. *Per* 3D **136**
Middleton. *Shrp* 3H **59**
(nr. Ludlow)
Middleton. *Shrp* 3F **71**
(nr. Oswestry)
Middleton. *Suff* 4G **67**
Middleton. *Swan* 4D **30**
Middleton. *Warw* 1F **61**
Middleton. *W Yor* 2D **92**
Middleton Cheney. *Nptn* 1D **50**
Middleton Green. *Staf* 2D **73**
Middleton Hall. *Nmbd* 2D **121**
Middleton-in-Teesdale. *Dur* 2C **104**
Middleton One Row. *Darl* 3A **106**
Middleton-on-Leven. *N Yor* 4B **106**
Middleton-on-Sea. *W Sus* 5A **26**
Middleton on the Hill. *Here* 4H **59**
Middleton-on-the-Wolds. *E Yor* 5D **100**
Middleton Priors. *Shrp* 1A **60**
Middleton Quernhow. *N Yor* 2F **99**
Middleton St George. *Darl* 3A **106**
Middleton Scriven. *Shrp* 2A **60**
Middleton Stoney. *Oxon* 3D **50**
Middleton Tyas. *N Yor* 4F **105**
Middletown. *Cumb* 4A **102**
Middle Town. *IOS* 1B **4**
Middletown. *Powy* 4F **71**
Middle Tysoe. *Warw* 1B **50**
Middle Wallop. *Hants* 3A **24**
Middlewich. *Ches E* 4B **84**
Middle Winterslow. *Wilts* 3H **23**
Middlewood. *Corn* 5C **10**
Middlewood. *S Yor* 1H **85**
Middle Woodford. *Wilts* 3G **23**
Middlewood Green. *Suff* 4C **66**
Middleyard. *Glos* 5D **48**
Middlezoy. *Som* 3G **21**
Middridge. *Dur* 2F **105**
Midelney. *Som* 4H **21**
Midfield. *High* 2F **167**
Midford. *Bath* 5C **34**
Mid Garrary. *Dum* 2C **110**
Midge Hall. *Lanc* 2D **90**
Midgeholme. *Cumb* 4H **113**
Midgham. *W Ber* 5D **36**
Midgley. *W Yor* 2A **92**
(nr. Halifax)
Midgley. *W Yor* 3C **92**
(nr. Horbury)
Midhopestones. *S Yor* 1G **85**
Midhurst. *W Sus* 4G **25**
Mid Kirkton. *N Ayr* 4C **126**
Mid Lambrook. *Som* 1H **13**
Midland. *Orkn* 7C **172**
Mid Lavant. *W Sus* 2G **17**
Midlem. *Bord* 2H **119**
Midney. *Som* 4A **22**
Midsomer Norton. *Bath* 1B **22**
Midton. *Inv* 2D **126**
Midtown. *High* 5C **162**
(nr. Poolewe)
Midtown. *High* 2F **167**
(nr. Tongue)
Midville. *Linc* 5C **88**
Midway. *Derbs* 3H **73**
Mid Yell. *Shet* 2G **173**
Migdale. *High* 4D **164**
Migvie. *Abers* 3B **152**
Milborne Port. *Som* 1B **14**
Milborne St Andrew. *Dors* 3D **14**
Milborne Wick. *Som* 4B **22**
Milbourne. *Nmbd* 2E **115**
Milbourne. *Wilts* 3E **35**
Milburn. *Cumb* 2H **103**
Milbury Heath. *S Glo* 2B **34**
Milby. *N Yor* 3G **99**
Milcombe. *Oxon* 2C **50**
Milden. *Suff* 1C **54**
Mildenhall. *Suff* 3G **65**
Mildenhall. *Wilts* 5H **35**
Milebrook. *Powy* 3F **59**
Milebush. *Kent* 1B **28**
Mile End. *Cambs* 2F **65**
Mile End. *Essx* 3C **54**
Mileham. *Norf* 4B **78**
Mile Oak. *Brig* 5D **26**
Miles Green. *Staf* 5C **84**
Miles Hope. *Here* 4H **59**
Milesmark. *Fife* 1D **128**
Mile Town. *Kent* 3D **40**
Milfield. *Nmbd* 1D **120**
Milford. *Derbs* 1A **74**
Milford. *Devn* 4C **18**
Milford. *Powy* 1C **58**
Milford. *Staf* 3D **72**
Milford. *Surr* 1A **26**
Milford Haven. *Pemb* 4D **42**
Milford on Sea. *Hants* 3A **16**
Milkwall. *Glos* 5A **48**
Milkwell. *Wilts* 4E **23**
Milland. *W Sus* 4G **25**
Millbank. *High* 2D **168**
Mill Bank. *W Yor* 2A **92**
Millbeck. *Cumb* 2D **102**
Millbounds. *Orkn* 4E **172**
Millbreck. *Abers* 4H **161**
Millbridge. *Surr* 2G **25**
Millbrook. *C Beds* 2A **52**
Millbrook. *Corn* 3A **8**
Millbrook. *G Man* 1D **85**
Millbrook. *Sotn* 1B **16**
Mill Common. *Suff* 2G **67**
Mill Corner. *E Sus* 3C **28**
Milldale. *Staf* 5F **85**
Millden Lodge. *Ang* 1E **145**
Milldens. *Ang* 3E **145**
Millearn. *Per* 2B **136**
Mill End. *Buck* 3F **37**
Mill End. *Cambs* 5F **65**
Millend. *Glos* 2C **34**
(nr. Dursley)
Mill End. *Glos* 4G **49**
(nr. Northleach)
Mill End. *Herts* 2D **52**
Millerhill. *Midl* 3G **129**
Miller's Dale. *Derbs* 3F **85**
Millers Green. *Derbs* 5G **85**
Millerston. *N Lan* 3H **127**
Millfield. *Abers* 4B **152**
Millfield. *Pet* 1A **64**
Millgate. *Lanc* 3G **91**
Mill Green. *Essx* 5G **53**
Mill Green. *Norf* 2D **66**
Mill Green. *Shrp* 3A **72**
Mill Green. *Staf* 3E **73**
Mill Green. *Suff* 1C **54**
Millhalf. *Here* 1F **47**
Millhall. *E Ren* 4G **127**
Millhayes. *Devn* 2F **13**
(nr. Honiton)
Millhayes. *Devn* 1E **13**
(nr. Wellington)
Millhead. *Lanc* 2D **97**
Millheugh. *S Lan* 4A **128**
Mill Hill. *Bkbn* 2E **91**
Mill Hill. *G Lon* 1D **38**
Millholme. *Cumb* 5G **103**
Millhouse. *Arg* 2A **126**
Millhousebridge. *Dum* 1C **112**
Millhouses. *S Yor* 2H **85**
Millikenpark. *Ren* 3F **127**
Millington. *E Yor* 4C **100**
Millington Green. *Derbs* 1G **73**
Mill Knowe. *Arg* 3B **122**
Mill Lane. *Hants* 1F **25**
Millmeece. *Staf* 2C **72**
Mill of Craigievar. *Abers* 2C **152**
Mill of Fintray. *Abers* 2F **153**
Mill of Haldane. *W Dun* 1F **127**
Millom. *Cumb* 1A **96**
Millow. *C Beds* 1C **52**
Millpool. *Corn* 5B **10**
Millport. *N Ayr* 4C **126**
Mill Side. *Cumb* 1D **96**
Mill Street. *Norf* 4C **78**
(nr. Lyng)
Mill Street. *Norf* 4C **78**
(nr. Swanton Morley)
Millthorpe. *Derbs* 3H **85**
Millthorpe. *Linc* 2A **76**
Millthrop. *Cumb* 5H **103**
Milltimber. *Aber* 3F **153**
Milltown. *Abers* 3G **151**
(nr. Corgarff)
Milltown. *Abers* 2B **152**
(nr. Lumsden)
Milltown. *Corn* 3F **7**
Milltown. *Derbs* 4A **86**
Milltown. *Devn* 3F **19**
Milltown. *Dum* 2E **113**
Milltown. *Mor* 4C **160**
Milltown of Aberdalgie. *Per* 1C **136**
Milltown of Auchindoun. *Mor* 4A **160**
Milltown of Campfield. *Abers* 3D **152**
Milltown of Edinville. *Mor* 4G **159**
Milltown of Towie. *Abers* 2B **152**
Milnacraig. *Ang* 3B **144**
Milnathort. *Per* 3D **136**
Milngavie. *E Dun* 2G **127**
Milnholm. *Stir* 1A **128**
Milnrow. *G Man* 3H **91**
Milnthorpe. *Cumb* 1D **97**
Milnthorpe. *W Yor* 3D **92**
Milson. *Shrp* 3A **60**
Milstead. *Kent* 5D **40**
Milston. *Wilts* 2G **23**
Milthorpe. *Nptn* 1D **50**
Milton. *Ang* 4C **144**
Milton. *Cambs* 4D **65**
Milton. *Cumb* 3G **113**
Milton. *Derbs* 3H **73**
Milton. *Dum* 2F **111**
(nr. Crocketford)
Milton. *Dum* 4H **109**
(nr. Glenluce)
Milton. *E Ayr* 2D **116**
Milton. *Glas* 2G **127**
Milton. *High* 3F **157**
(nr. Achnasheen)
Milton. *High* 4G **155**
(nr. Applecross)
Milton. *High* 5G **157**
(nr. Drumnadrochit)
Milton. *High* 1B **158**
(nr. Invergordon)
Milton. *High* 4H **157**
(nr. Inverness)
Milton. *High* 3F **169**
(nr. Wick)
Milton. *Mor* 2C **160**
(nr. Cullen)
Milton. *Mor* 2F **151**
(nr. Tomintoul)
Milton. *N Som* 5G **33**
Milton. *Notts* 3E **86**
Milton. *Oxon* 2C **50**
(nr. Banbury)
Milton. *Oxon* 2C **36**
(nr. Didcot)
Milton. *Pemb* 4E **43**
Milton. *Port* 3E **17**
Milton. *Som* 4H **21**
Milton. *Stir* 3E **135**
(nr. Aberfoyle)
Milton. *Stir* 4D **134**
(nr. Drymen)
Milton. *Stoke* 5D **84**
Milton. *W Dun* 2F **127**
Milton Abbas. *Dors* 2D **14**
Milton Abbot. *Devn* 5E **11**
Milton Auchlossan. *Abers* 3C **152**
Milton Bridge. *Midl* 3F **129**
Milton Bryan. *C Beds* 2H **51**
Milton Clevedon. *Som* 3B **22**
Milton Coldwells. *Abers* 5G **161**
Milton Combe. *Devn* 2A **8**
Milton Common. *Oxon* 5E **51**
Milton Damerel. *Devn* 1D **11**
Miltonduff. *Mor* 2F **159**
Milton End. *Glos* 5G **49**
Milton Ernest. *Bed* 5H **63**
Milton Green. *Ches W* 5G **83**
Milton Hill. *Devn* 5C **12**
Milton Hill. *Oxon* 2C **36**
Milton Keynes. *Mil* 2G **51**
Milton Keynes Village. *Mil* 2G **51**
Milton Lilbourne. *Wilts* 5G **35**
Milton Malsor. *Nptn* 5E **63**
Milton Morenish. *Per* 5D **142**
Milton of Auchinhove. *Abers* 3C **152**
Milton of Balgonie. *Fife* 3F **137**

Milton of Barras—Mount Pleasant

Milton of Barras. *Abers* 1H 145
Milton of Campsie. *E Dun* 2H 127
Milton of Cultoquhey. *Per* 1A 136
Milton of Cushnie. *Abers* 2C 152
Milton of Finavon. *Ang* 3D 145
Milton of Gollanfield. *High* 3B 158
Milton of Lesmore. *Abers* 1B 152
Milton of Tullich. *Abers* 4A 152
Milton on Stour. *Dors* 4C 22
Milton Regis. *Kent* 4C 40
Milton Street. *E Sus* 5G 27
Milton-under-Wychwood. *Oxon* 4A 50
Milverton. *Som* 4E 20
Milverton. *Warw* 4H 61
Milwich. *Staf* 2D 72
Mimbridge. *Surr* 4A 38
Minard. *Arg* 4G 133
Minchington. *Dors* 1E 15
Minchinhampton. *Glos* 5D 49
Mindrum. *Nmbd* 1C 120
Minehead. *Som* 2C 20
Minera. *Wrex* 5E 83
Minety. *Wilts* 2F 35
Minffordd. *Gwyn* 2E 69
Mingarrypark. *High* 2A 140
Mingary. *High* 2G 139
Mingearraidh. *W Isl* 6C 170
Miningsby. *Linc* 4C 88
Minions. *Corn* 5C 10
Minishant. *S Ayr* 3C 116
Minllyn. *Gwyn* 4A 70
Minnigaff. *Dum* 3B 110
Minorca. *IOM* 3D 108
Minskip. *N Yor* 3F 99
Minstead. *Hants* 1A 16
Minsted. *W Sus* 4G 25
Minster. *Kent* 4H 41 (nr. Ramsgate)
Minster. *Kent* 3D 40 (nr. Sheerness)
Minsteracres. *Nmbd* 4D 114
Minsterley. *Shrp* 5F 71
Minster Lovell. *Oxon* 4B 50
Minsterworth. *Glos* 4C 48
Minterne Magna. *Dors* 2B 14
Minterne Parva. *Dors* 2B 14
Minting. *Linc* 3A 88
Mintlaw. *Abers* 4H 161
Minto. *Bord* 2H 119
Minton. *Shrp* 1G 59
Minwear. *Pemb* 3E 43
Minworth. *W Mid* 1F 61
Miodar. *Arg* 4B 138
Mirehouse. *Cumb* 3A 102
Mireland. *High* 2F 169
Mirfield. *W Yor* 3C 92
Miserden. *Glos* 5E 49
Miskin. *Rhon* 3D 32
Misson. *Notts* 1D 86
Misterton. *Leics* 2C 62
Misterton. *Notts* 1E 87
Misterton. *Som* 2H 13
Mistley. *Essx* 2E 54
Mistley Heath. *Essx* 2E 55
Mitcham. *G Lon* 4D 39
Mitcheldean. *Glos* 4B 48
Mitchell. *Corn* 3C 6
Mitchel Troy. *Mon* 4H 47
Mitcheltroy Common. *Mon* 5H 47
Mitford. *Nmbd* 1E 115
Mithian. *Corn* 3B 6
Mitton. *Staf* 4C 72
Mixbury. *Oxon* 2E 50
Mixenden. *W Yor* 2A 92
Mixon. *Staf* 5E 85
Moat. *Cumb* 2F 113
Moats Tye. *Suff* 5C 66
Mobberley. *Ches E* 3B 84
Mobberley. *Staf* 1E 73
Moccas. *Here* 1G 47
Mochdre. *Cnwy* 3H 81
Mochdre. *Powy* 2C 58
Mochrum. *Dum* 5A 110
Mockbeggar. *Hants* 2G 15
Mockerkin. *Cumb* 2B 102
Modbury. *Devn* 3C 8
Moddershall. *Staf* 2D 72
Modsarie. *High* 2G 167
Moelfre. *Cnwy* 3B 82
Moelfre. *IOA* 2E 81
Moelfre. *Powy* 3D 70
Moffat. *Dum* 4C 118
Moggerhanger. *C Beds* 1B 52
Mogworthy. *Devn* 1B 12
Moira. *Leics* 4H 73
Molash. *Kent* 5E 41
Mol-chlach. *High* 2C 146
Mold. *Flin* 4E 83
Molehill Green. *Essx* 3F 53
Molescroft. *E Yor* 5E 101
Molesden. *Nmbd* 1E 115
Molesworth. *Cambs* 3H 63
Moll. *High* 5E 155
Molland. *Devn* 4B 20
Mollington. *Ches W* 3F 83
Mollington. *Oxon* 1C 50
Mollinsburn. *N Lan* 2A 128
Monachty. *Cdgn* 4E 57
Monachyle. *Stir* 2D 134
Monar Lodge. *High* 4E 156
Monaughty. *Powy* 4E 59
Monewden. *Suff* 5E 67
Moneydie. *Per* 1C 136
Moneyrow Green. *Wind* 4G 37
Moniaive. *Dum* 5G 117
Monifieth. *Ang* 5E 145
Monikie. *Ang* 5E 145
Monimail. *Fife* 2E 137
Monington. *Pemb* 1B 44
Monk Bretton. *S Yor* 4D 92
Monken Hadley. *G Lon* 1D 38
Monk Fryston. *N Yor* 2F 93
Monk Hesleden. *Dur* 1B 106
Monkhide. *Here* 1B 48
Monkhill. *Cumb* 4E 113
Monkhopton. *Shrp* 1A 60
Monkland. *Here* 5G 59
Monkleigh. *Devn* 4E 19
Monknash. *V Glam* 4C 32
Monkokehampton. *Devn* 2F 11
Monkseaton. *Tyne* 2G 115
Monks Eleigh. *Suff* 1C 54
Monk's Gate. *W Sus* 3D 26
Monk's Heath. *Ches E* 3C 84
Monk Sherborne. *Hants* 1E 24
Monkshill. *Abers* 4E 161
Monksilver. *Som* 3D 20
Monks Kirby. *Warw* 2B 62
Monk Soham. *Suff* 4E 66
Monk Soham Green. *Suff* 4E 66
Monkspath. *W Mid* 3F 61
Monks Risborough. *Buck* 5G 51
Monksthorpe. *Linc* 4D 88
Monk Street. *Essx* 3G 53
Monkswood. *Mon* 5G 47
Monkton. *Devn* 2E 13
Monkton. *Kent* 4G 41
Monkton. *Pemb* 4D 42
Monkton. *S Ayr* 2C 116
Monkton Combe. *Bath* 5C 34
Monkton Deverill. *Wilts* 3D 22
Monkton Farleigh. *Wilts* 5D 34
Monkton Heathfield. *Som* 4F 21
Monktonhill. *S Ayr* 2C 116
Monkton Up Wimborne. *Dors* 1F 15
Monkton Wyld. *Dors* 3G 13
Monkwearmouth. *Tyne* 4H 115
Monkwood. *Dors* 3H 13
Monkwood. *Hants* 3E 25
Monmarsh. *Here* 1A 48
Monmouth. *Mon* 4A 48
Monnington on Wye. *Here* 1G 47
Monreith. *Dum* 5A 110
Montacute. *Som* 1H 13
Montford. *Arg* 3C 126
Montford. *Shrp* 4G 71
Montford Bridge. *Shrp* 4G 71
Montgarrie. *Abers* 2C 152
Montgarswood. *E Ayr* 2E 117
Montgomery. *Powy* 1E 58
Montgreenan. *N Ayr* 5E 127
Montrave. *Fife* 3F 137
Montrose. *Ang* 3G 145
Monxton. *Hants* 2B 24
Monyash. *Derbs* 4F 85
Monymusk. *Abers* 2D 152
Monzie. *Per* 1A 136
Moodiesburn. *N Lan* 2H 127
Moon's Green. *Kent* 3C 28
Moonzie. *Fife* 2F 137
Moor. *Som* 1H 13
Moor Allerton. *W Yor* 1C 92
Moorbath. *Dors* 3H 13
Moorby. *Linc* 4B 88
Moorcot. *Here* 5F 59
Moor Crichel. *Dors* 2E 15
Moor Cross. *Devn* 3C 8
Moordown. *Bour* 3F 15
Moore. *Hal* 2H 83
Moorend. *Dum* 2D 112
Moor End. *E Yor* 1B 94
Moorend. *Glos* 5C 48 (nr. Dursley)
Moorend. *Glos* 4D 48 (nr. Gloucester)
Moorends. *S Yor* 3G 93
Moorgate. *S Yor* 1B 86
Moorgreen. *Hants* 1C 16
Moorgreen. *Notts* 1B 74
Moor Green. *Wilts* 5D 34
Moorhaigh. *Notts* 4C 86
Moorhall. *Derbs* 3H 85
Moorhampton. *Here* 1G 47
Moorhouse. *Cumb* 4E 113 (nr. Carlisle)
Moorhouse. *Cumb* 4D 112 (nr. Wigton)
Moorhouse. *Notts* 4E 87
Moorhouse. *Surr* 5F 39
Moorhouses. *Linc* 5B 88
Moorland. *Som* 3G 21
Moorlinch. *Som* 3H 21
Moor Monkton. *N Yor* 4H 99
Moor of Granary. *Mor* 3E 159
Moor Row. *Cumb* 3B 102 (nr. Whitehaven)
Moor Row. *Cumb* 5D 112 (nr. Wigton)
Moorsholm. *Red C* 3D 107
Moorside. *Dors* 1C 14
Moorside. *G Man* 4H 91
Moor, The. *Kent* 3B 28
Moortown. *Devn* 3D 10
Moortown. *Hants* 2G 15
Moortown. *IOW* 4C 16
Moortown. *Linc* 1H 87
Moortown. *Telf* 4A 72
Moortown. *W Yor* 1D 92
Morangie. *High* 5E 165
Morar. *High* 4E 147
Morborne. *Cambs* 1A 64
Morchard Bishop. *Devn* 2A 12
Morcombelake. *Dors* 3H 13
Morcott. *Rut* 5G 75
Morda. *Shrp* 3E 71
Morden. *G Lon* 4D 38
Mordiford. *Here* 2A 48
Mordon. *Dur* 2A 106
More. *Shrp* 1F 59
Morebath. *Devn* 4C 20
Morebattle. *Bord* 2B 120
Morecambe. *Lanc* 3D 96
Morefield. *High* 4F 163
Morehouse, The. *Shrp* 1H 59
Moreleigh. *Devn* 3D 8
Morenish. *Per* 5C 142
Moresby Parks. *Cumb* 3A 102
Morestead. *Hants* 4D 24
Moreton. *Dors* 4D 14
Moreton. *Essx* 5F 53
Moreton. *Here* 4H 59
Moreton. *Mers* 1E 83
Moreton. *Oxon* 5E 51
Moreton. *Staf* 4B 72
Moreton Corbet. *Shrp* 3H 71
Moretonhampstead. *Devn* 4A 12
Moreton-in-Marsh. *Glos* 2H 49
Moreton Jeffries. *Here* 1B 48
Moreton Morrell. *Warw* 5H 61
Moreton on Lugg. *Here* 1A 48
Moreton Pinkney. *Nptn* 1D 50
Moreton Say. *Shrp* 2A 72
Moreton Valence. *Glos* 5C 48
Morfa. *Cdgn* 5C 56
Morfa Bach. *Carm* 4D 44
Morfa Bychan. *Gwyn* 2E 69
Morfa Glas. *Neat* 5B 46
Morfa Nefyn. *Gwyn* 1B 68
Morganstown. *Card* 3E 33
Morgan's Vale. *Wilts* 4G 23
Morham. *E Lot* 2B 130
Moriah. *Cdgn* 3F 57
Morland. *Cumb* 2G 103
Morley. *Ches E* 2C 84
Morley. *Derbs* 1A 74
Morley. *Dur* 2E 105
Morley. *W Yor* 2C 92
Morley St Botolph. *Norf* 1C 66
Morningside. *Edin* 2F 129
Morningside. *N Lan* 4B 128
Morningthorpe. *Norf* 1E 66
Morpeth. *Nmbd* 1F 115
Morrey. *Staf* 4F 73
Morridge Side. *Staf* 5E 85
Morridge Top. *Staf* 4E 85
Morrington. *Dum* 1F 111
Morris Green. *Essx* 2H 53
Morriston. *Swan* 3F 31
Morston. *Norf* 1C 78
Mortehoe. *Devn* 2E 19
Morthen. *S Yor* 2B 86
Mortimer. *W Ber* 5E 37
Mortimer's Cross. *Here* 4G 59
Mortimer West End. *Hants* 5E 37
Mortomley. *S Yor* 1H 85
Morton. *Cumb* 1F 103 (nr. Calthwaite)
Morton. *Cumb* 4E 113 (nr. Carlisle)
Morton. *Derbs* 4B 86
Morton. *Linc* 3H 75 (nr. Bourne)
Morton. *Linc* 1F 87 (nr. Gainsborough)
Morton. *Linc* 4F 87 (nr. Lincoln)
Morton. *Norf* 4D 78
Morton. *Notts* 5E 87
Morton. *Shrp* 3E 71
Morton. *S Glo* 2B 34
Morton Bagot. *Warw* 4F 61
Morton Mill. *Shrp* 3H 71
Morton-on-Swale. *N Yor* 5A 106
Morton Tinmouth. *Dur* 2E 105
Morvah. *Corn* 3B 4
Morval. *Corn* 3G 7
Morvich. *High* 3E 165 (nr. Golspie)
Morvich. *High* 1B 148 (nr. Shiel Bridge)
Morvil. *Pemb* 1E 43
Morville. *Shrp* 1A 60
Morwenstow. *Corn* 1C 10
Morwick Hall. *Nmbd* 4G 121
Mosborough. *S Yor* 2B 86
Moscow. *E Ayr* 5F 127
Mose. *Shrp* 1B 60
Mosedale. *Cumb* 1E 103
Moseley. *W Mid* 2E 61 (nr. Birmingham)
Moseley. *W Mid* 5D 72 (nr. Wolverhampton)
Moseley. *Worc* 5C 60
Moss. *Arg* 4A 138
Moss. *High* 2A 140
Moss. *S Yor* 3F 93
Moss. *Wrex* 5F 83
Mossatt. *Abers* 2B 152
Moss Bank. *Mers* 1H 83
Mossbank. *Shet* 4F 173
Mossblown. *S Ayr* 2D 116
Mossbrow. *G Man* 2B 84
Mossburnford. *Bord* 3A 120
Mossdale. *Dum* 2D 110
Mossedge. *Cumb* 3F 113
Mossend. *N Lan* 3A 128
Mossgate. *Staf* 2D 72
Moss Lane. *Ches E* 3D 84
Mossley. *Ches E* 4C 84
Mossley. *G Man* 4H 91
Mossley Hill. *Mers* 2F 83
Moss of Barmuckity. *Mor* 2G 159
Mosspark. *Glas* 3G 127
Mosspaul. *Bord* 5G 119
Moss Side. *Cumb* 4C 112
Moss Side. *G Man* 1C 84
Moss-side. *High* 3C 158
Moss Side. *Lanc* 1B 90 (nr. Blackpool)
Moss Side. *Lanc* 2D 90 (nr. Preston)
Moss Side. *Mers* 4B 90
Moss-side of Cairness. *Abers* 2H 161
Mosstodloch. *Mor* 2H 159
Mosswood. *Nmbd* 4D 114
Mossy Lea. *Lanc* 3D 90
Mosterton. *Dors* 2H 13
Moston. *Shrp* 3H 71
Moston Green. *Ches E* 4B 84
Mostyn. *Flin* 2D 82
Mostyn Quay. *Flin* 2D 82
Motcombe. *Dors* 4D 22
Mothecombe. *Devn* 4C 8
Motherby. *Cumb* 2F 103
Motherwell. *N Lan* 4A 128
Mottingham. *G Lon* 3F 39
Mottisfont. *Hants* 4B 24
Mottistone. *IOW* 4C 16
Mottram in Longdendale. *G Man* 1D 85
Mottram St Andrew. *Ches E* 3C 84
Mott's Mill. *E Sus* 2G 27
Mouldsworth. *Ches W* 3H 83
Moulin. *Per* 3G 143
Moulsecoomb. *Brig* 5E 27
Moulsford. *Oxon* 3D 36
Moulsoe. *Mil* 1H 51
Moulton. *Ches W* 4A 84
Moulton. *Linc* 3C 76
Moulton. *Nptn* 4E 63
Moulton. *N Yor* 4F 105
Moulton. *Suff* 4F 65
Moulton. *V Glam* 4D 32
Moulton Chapel. *Linc* 4B 76
Moulton Eugate. *Linc* 4B 76
Moulton St Mary. *Norf* 5F 79
Moulton Seas End. *Linc* 3C 76
Mount. *Corn* 2F 7 (nr. Bodmin)
Mount. *Corn* 3B 6 (nr. Newquay)
Mountain Ash. *Rhon* 2D 32
Mountain Cross. *Bord* 5E 129
Mountain Street. *Kent* 5E 41
Mountain Water. *Pemb* 2D 42
Mount Ambrose. *Corn* 4B 6
Mountbenger. *Bord* 2F 119
Mountblow. *W Dun* 2F 127
Mount Bures. *Essx* 2C 54
Mountfield. *E Sus* 3B 28
Mountgerald. *High* 2H 157
Mount Hawke. *Corn* 4B 6
Mount High. *High* 2A 158
Mountjoy. *Corn* 2C 6
Mount Lothian. *Midl* 4F 129
Mountnessing. *Essx* 1H 39
Mounton. *Mon* 2A 34
Mount Pleasant. *Buck* 2E 51
Mount Pleasant. *Ches E* 5C 84

Mount Pleasant—Newbiggin

Mount Pleasant. Derbs 1H 73 (nr. Derby)
Mount Pleasant. Derbs 4G 73 (nr. Swadlincote)
Mount Pleasant. E Sus 4F 27
Mount Pleasant. Fife 2E 137
Mount Pleasant. Hants 3A 16
Mount Pleasant. Norf 1B 66
Mount Skippett. Oxon 4B 50
Mountsorrel. Leics 4C 74
Mount Stuart. Arg 4C 126
Mousehole. Corn 4B 4
Mouswald. Dum 2B 112
Mow Cop. Ches E 5C 84
Mowden. Darl 3F 105
Mowhaugh. Bord 2C 120
Mowmacre Hill. Leic 5C 74
Mowsley. Leics 2D 62
Moy. High 5B 158
Moylgrove. Pemb 1B 44
Moy Lodge. High 5G 149
Muasdale. Arg 5E 125
Muchalls. Abers 4G 153
Much Birch. Here 2A 48
Much Cowarne. Here 1B 48
Much Dewchurch. Here 2H 47
Muchelney. Som 4H 21
Muchelney Ham. Som 4H 21
Much Hadham. Herts 4E 53
Much Hoole. Lanc 2C 90
Muchlarnick. Corn 3G 7
Much Marcle. Here 2B 48
Muchrachd. High 5E 157
Much Wenlock. Shrp 1A 60
Mucking. Thur 2A 40
Muckleford. Dors 3B 14
Mucklestone. Staf 2B 72
Muckleton. Norf 2H 77
Muckleton. Shrp 3H 71
Muckley. Shrp 1A 60
Muckley Corner. Staf 5E 73
Muckton. Linc 2C 88
Mudale. High 5F 167
Muddiford. Devn 3F 19
Mudeford. Dors 3G 15
Mudford. Som 1A 14
Mudgley. Som 2H 21
Mugdock. Stir 2G 127
Mugeary. High 5D 154
Muggington. Derbs 1G 73
Muggintonlane End. Derbs 1G 73
Muggleswick. Dur 4D 114
Mugswell. Surr 5D 38
Muie. High 3D 164
Muirden. Abers 3E 160
Muirdrum. Ang 5E 145
Muiredge. Per 1E 137
Muirend. Glas 3G 127
Muirhead. Ang 5C 144
Muirhead. Fife 3E 137
Muirhead. N Lan 3H 127
Muirhouses. Falk 1D 128
Muirkirk. E Ayr 2F 117
Muir of Alford. Abers 2C 152
Muir of Fairburn. High 3G 157
Muir of Fowlis. Abers 2C 152
Muir of Miltonduff. Mor 3F 159
Muir of Ord. High 3H 157
Muir of Tarradale. High 3H 157
Muirshearlich. High 5D 148
Muirtack. Abers 5G 161
Muirton. High 2B 158
Muirton. Per 1D 136
Muirton of Ardblair. Per 4A 144
Muirtown. Per 2B 136
Muiryfold. Abers 3E 161
Muker. N Yor 5C 104
Mulbarton. Norf 5D 78
Mulben. Mor 3A 160
Mulindry. Arg 4B 124
Mullach Charlabhaigh. W Isl 3E 171
Mullacott. Devn 2F 19
Mullion. Corn 5D 5
Mullion Cove. Corn 5D 4
Mumbles. Swan 4F 31
Mumby. Linc 3E 89
Munderfield Row. Here 5A 60
Munderfield Stocks. Here 5A 60
Mundesley. Norf 2F 79
Mundford. Norf 1H 65
Mundham. Norf 1F 67
Mundon. Essx 5B 54
Munerigie. High 3E 149
Muness. Shet 1H 173
Mungasdale. High 4D 162
Mungrisdale. Cumb 1E 103
Munlochy. High 3A 158
Munsley. Here 1B 48
Munslow. Shrp 2H 59
Murchington. Devn 4G 11
Murcot. Worc 1F 49
Murcott. Oxon 4D 50
Murdishaw. Hal 2H 83
Murieston. W Lot 3D 128
Murkle. High 2D 168
Murlaggan. High 4C 148
Murra. Orkn 7B 172
Murrayfield. Edin 2F 129
Murray, The. S Lan 4H 127
Murrell Green. Hants 1F 25
Murroes. Ang 5D 144
Murrow. Cambs 5C 76
Mursley. Buck 3G 51
Murthly. Per 5H 143
Murton. Cumb 2A 104
Murton. Dur 5G 115
Murton. Nmbd 5F 131
Murton. Swan 4E 31
Murton. York 4A 100
Musbury. Devn 3F 13
Muscoates. N Yor 1A 100
Muscott. Nptn 4D 62
Musselburgh. E Lot 2G 129
Muston. Leics 2F 75
Muston. N Yor 2E 101
Mustow Green. Worc 3C 60
Muswell Hill. G Lon 2D 39
Mutehill. Dum 5D 111
Mutford. Suff 2G 67
Muthill. Per 2A 136
Mutterton. Devn 2D 12
Muxton. Telf 4B 72
Mwmbwls. Swan 4F 31
Mybster. High 3D 168
Myddfai. Carm 2A 46
Myddle. Shrp 3G 71
Mydroilyn. Cdgn 5D 56
Myerscough. Lanc 1C 90
Mylor Bridge. Corn 5C 6
Mylor Churchtown. Corn 5C 6
Mynachlog-ddu. Pemb 1F 43
Mynydd-bach. Mon 2H 33
Mynydd Isa. Flin 4E 83
Mynyddislwyn. Cphy 2E 33
Mynydd Llandegai. Gwyn 4F 81
Mynydd Mechell. IOA 1C 80
Mynydd-y-briw. Powy 3D 70
Mynyddygarreg. Carm 5E 45
Mynytho. Gwyn 2C 68
Myrebird. Abers 4E 153
Myrelandhorn. High 3E 169
Mytchett. Surr 1G 25
Mythe, The. Glos 2D 49
Mytholmroyd. W Yor 2A 92
Myton-on-Swale. N Yor 3G 99
Mytton. Shrp 4G 71

N

Naast. High 5C 162
Na Buirgh. W Isl 8C 171
Naburn. York 5H 99
Nab Wood. W Yor 1B 92
Nackington. Kent 5F 41
Nacton. Suff 1F 55
Nafferton. E Yor 4E 101
Na Gearrannan. W Isl 3D 171
Nailbridge. Glos 4B 48
Nailsbourne. Som 4F 21
Nailsea. N Som 4H 33
Nailstone. Leics 5B 74
Nailsworth. Glos 2D 34
Nairn. High 3C 158
Nalderswood. Surr 1D 26
Nancegollan. Corn 3D 4
Nancekuke. Corn 4A 6
Nancledra. Corn 3B 4
Nangreaves. G Man 3G 91
Nanhyfer. Pemb 1E 43
Nannerch. Flin 4D 82
Nanpantan. Leics 4C 74
Nanpean. Corn 3D 6
Nanstallon. Corn 2E 7
Nant-ddu. Powy 4D 46
Nanternis. Cdgn 5C 56
Nantgaredig. Carm 3E 45
Nantgarw. Rhon 3E 33
Nant Glas. Powy 4B 58
Nantglyn. Den 4C 82
Nantgwyn. Powy 3B 58
Nantlle. Gwyn 5E 81
Nantmawr. Shrp 3E 71
Nantmel. Powy 4C 58
Nantmor. Gwyn 1F 69
Nant Peris. Gwyn 5F 81
Nantwich. Ches E 5A 84
Nant-y-bai. Carm 1A 46
Nant-y-bwch. Blae 4E 47
Nant-y-Derry. Mon 5G 47
Nant-y-dugoed. Powy 4B 70
Nant-y-felin. Cnwy 3F 81
Nantyffyllon. B'end 2B 32
Nantyglo. Blae 4E 47
Nant-y-meichiaid. Powy 4D 70
Nant-y-moel. B'end 2C 32
Nant-y-Pandy. Cnwy 3F 81
Naphill. Buck 2G 37
Nappa. Lanc 4A 98
Napton on the Hill. Warw 4B 62
Narberth. Pemb 3F 43
Narberth Bridge. Pemb 3F 43
Narborough. Leics 1C 62
Narborough. Norf 4G 77
Narkurs. Corn 3H 7
Narth, The. Mon 5A 48
Narthwaite. Cumb 5A 104
Nasareth. Gwyn 1D 68
Naseby. Nptn 3D 62
Nash. Buck 2F 51
Nash. Here 4F 59
Nash. Kent 5G 41
Nash. Newp 3G 33
Nash. Shrp 3A 60
Nash Lee. Buck 5G 51
Nassington. Nptn 1H 63
Nasty. Herts 3D 52
Natcott. Devn 4C 18
Nateby. Cumb 4A 104
Nateby. Lanc 5D 96
Nately Scures. Hants 1F 25
Natland. Cumb 1E 97
Naughton. Suff 1D 54
Naunton. Glos 3G 49
Naunton. Worc 2D 49
Naunton Beauchamp. Worc 5D 60
Navenby. Linc 5G 87
Navestock Heath. Essx 1G 39
Navestock Side. Essx 1G 39
Navidale. High 2H 165
Nawton. N Yor 1A 100
Nayland. Suff 2C 54
Nazeing. Essx 5E 53
Neacroft. Hants 3G 15
Neal's Green. W Mid 2H 61
Neap House. N Lin 3B 94
Near Sawrey. Cumb 5E 103
Neasden. G Lon 2D 38
Neasham. Darl 3A 106
Neath. Neat 2A 32
Neath Abbey. Neat 3G 31
Neatishead. Norf 3F 79
Neaton. Norf 5B 78
Nebo. Cdgn 4E 57
Nebo. Cnwy 5H 81
Nebo. Gwyn 5D 81
Nebo. IOA 1D 80
Necton. Norf 5A 78
Nedd. High 5B 166
Nedderton. Nmbd 1F 115
Nedging. Suff 1D 54
Nedging Tye. Suff 1D 54
Needham. Norf 2E 67
Needham Market. Suff 5C 66
Needham Street. Suff 4G 65
Needingworth. Cambs 3C 64
Needwood. Staf 3F 73
Neen Savage. Shrp 3A 60
Neen Sollars. Shrp 3A 60
Neenton. Shrp 2A 60
Nefyn. Gwyn 1C 68
Neilston. E Ren 4F 127
Neithrop. Oxon 1C 50
Nelly Andrews Green. Powy 5E 71
Nelson. Cphy 2E 32
Nelson. Lanc 1G 91
Nelson Village. Nmbd 2F 115
Nemphlar. S Lan 5B 128
Nempnett Thrubwell. Bath 5A 34
Nene Terrace. Linc 5B 76
Nenthall. Cumb 5A 114
Nenthead. Cumb 5A 114
Nenthorn. Bord 1A 120
Nercwys. Flin 4E 83
Neribus. Arg 4A 124
Nerston. S Lan 4H 127
Nesbit. Nmbd 1D 121
Nesfield. N Yor 5C 98
Ness. Ches W 3F 83
Nesscliffe. Shrp 4F 71
Neston. Ches W 3E 83
Neston. Wilts 5D 34
Netchwood. Shrp 1A 60
Nethanfoot. S Lan 5B 128
Nether Alderley. Ches E 3C 84
Netheravon. Wilts 2G 23
Nether Blainslie. Bord 5B 130
Netherbrae. Abers 3E 161
Netherbrough. Orkn 6C 172
Nether Broughton. Leics 3D 74
Netherburn. S Lan 5B 128
Nether Burrow. Lanc 2F 97
Netherbury. Dors 3H 13
Netherby. Cumb 2E 113
Nether Careston. Ang 3E 145
Nether Cerne. Dors 3B 14
Nether Compton. Dors 1A 14
Nethercote. Glos 3G 49
Nethercote. Warw 4C 62
Nethercott. Devn 3E 19
Nethercott. Oxon 3C 50
Nether Dallachy. Mor 2A 160
Nether Durdie. Per 1E 136
Nether End. Derbs 3G 85
Netherend. Glos 5A 48
Nether Exe. Devn 2C 12
Netherfield. E Sus 4B 28
Netherfield. Notts 1D 74
Nethergate. Norf 3C 78
Netherhampton. Wilts 4G 23
Nether Handley. Derbs 3B 86
Nether Haugh. S Yor 1B 86
Nether Heage. Derbs 5A 86
Nether Heyford. Nptn 5D 62
Netherhouses. Cumb 1B 96
Nether Howcleugh. Dum 3C 118
Nether Kellet. Lanc 3E 97
Nether Kinmundy. Abers 4H 161
Netherland Green. Staf 2F 73
Nether Langwith. Notts 3C 86
Netherlaw. Dum 5E 111
Netherley. Abers 4F 153
Nethermill. Dum 1B 112
Nethermills. Mor 3C 160
Nether Moor. Derbs 4A 86
Nether Padley. Derbs 3G 85
Netherplace. E Ren 4G 127
Nether Poppleton. York 4H 99
Netherseal. Derbs 4G 73
Nether Silton. N Yor 5B 106
Nether Stowey. Som 3E 21
Nether Street. Essx 4F 53
Netherstreet. Wilts 5E 35
Netherthird. E Ayr 3E 117
Netherthong. W Yor 4B 92
Netherton. Ang 3E 145
Netherton. Cumb 1B 102
Netherton. Devn 5B 12
Netherton. Hants 1B 24
Netherton. Here 3A 48
Netherton. Mers 1F 83
Netherton. N Lan 4A 128
Netherton. Nmbd 4D 121
Netherton. Per 3A 144
Netherton. Shrp 2B 60
Netherton. Stir 2G 127
Netherton. W Mid 2D 60
Netherton. W Yor 3C 92 (nr. Horbury)
Netherton. W Yor 3B 92 (nr. Huddersfield)
Netherton. Worc 1E 49
Nethertown. Cumb 4A 102
Nethertown. High 1F 169
Nethertown. Staf 4F 73
Nether Urquhart. Fife 3D 136
Nether Wallop. Hants 3B 24
Nether Wasdale. Cumb 4C 102
Nether Welton. Cumb 5E 113
Nether Westcote. Glos 3H 49
Nether Whitacre. Warw 1G 61
Netherwhitton. Nmbd 5F 121
Nether Worton. Oxon 2C 50
Nethy Bridge. High 1E 151
Netley. Hants 2C 16
Netley. Shrp 5G 71
Netley Marsh. Hants 1B 16
Nettlebed. Oxon 3F 37
Nettlebridge. Som 2B 22
Nettlecombe. Dors 3A 14
Nettlecombe. IOW 5D 16
Nettleden. Herts 4A 52
Nettleham. Linc 3H 87
Nettlestead. Kent 5A 40
Nettlestead Green. Kent 5A 40
Nettlestone. IOW 3E 16
Nettlesworth. Dur 5F 115
Nettleton. Linc 4E 94
Nettleton. Wilts 4D 34
Netton. Devn 4B 8
Netton. Wilts 3G 23
Neuadd. Carm 3H 45
Neuadd. Powy 5C 70
Neuk, The. Abers 4E 153
Nevendon. Essx 1B 40
Nevern. Pemb 1A 44
New Abbey. Dum 3A 112
New Aberdour. Abers 2F 161
New Addington. G Lon 4E 39
Newall. W Yor 5D 98
New Alresford. Hants 3D 24
New Alyth. Per 4B 144
Newark. Orkn 3G 172
Newark. Pet 5B 76
Newark-on-Trent. Notts 5E 87
New Arley. Warw 2G 61
Newarthill. N Lan 4A 128
New Ash Green. Kent 4H 39
New Balderton. Notts 5F 87
New Barn. Kent 4H 39
New Barnetby. N Lin 3D 94
Newbattle. Midl 3G 129
New Bewick. Nmbd 2E 121
Newbiggin. Cumb 2H 103 (nr. Appleby)
Newbiggin. Cumb 3B 96 (nr. Barrow-in-Furness)
Newbiggin. Cumb 5G 113 (nr. Cumrew)

Newbiggin—Newton Tony

Newbiggin. Cumb 2F 103 (nr. Penrith)
Newbiggin. Cumb 5B 102 (nr. Seascale)
Newbiggin. Dur 5E 115 (nr. Consett)
Newbiggin. Dur 2C 104 (nr. Holwick)
Newbiggin. Nmbd 5C 114
Newbiggin. N Yor 5C 104 (nr. Askrigg)
Newbiggin. N Yor 1F 101 (nr. Filey)
Newbiggin. N Yor 1B 98 (nr. Thoralby)
Newbiggin-by-the-Sea. Nmbd 1G 115
Newbigging. Ang 5D 145 (nr. Monikie)
Newbigging. Ang 4B 144 (nr. Newtyle)
Newbigging. Ang 5D 144 (nr. Tealing)
Newbigging. Edin 2E 129
Newbigging. S Lan 5D 128
Newbiggin-on-Lune. Cumb 4A 104
Newbold. Derbs 3A 86
Newbold. Leics 4B 74
Newbold on Avon. Warw 3B 62
Newbold on Stour. Warw 1H 49
Newbold Pacey. Warw 5G 61
Newbold Verdon. Leics 5B 74
New Bolingbroke. Linc 5C 88
Newborough. IOA 4D 80
Newborough. Pet 5B 76
Newborough. Staf 3F 73
Newbottle. Nptn 2D 50
Newbottle. Tyne 4G 115
New Boultham. Linc 3G 87
Newbourne. Suff 1F 55
New Brancepeth. Dur 5F 115
Newbridge. Cphy 2F 33
Newbridge. Cdgn 5E 57
Newbridge. Corn 3B 4
New Bridge. Dum 2G 111
Newbridge. Edin 2E 129
Newbridge. Hants 1A 16
Newbridge. IOW 4C 16
Newbridge. N Yor 1C 100
Newbridge. Pemb 1D 42
Newbridge. Wrex 1E 71
Newbridge Green. Worc 2D 48
Newbridge-on-Usk. Mon 2G 33
Newbridge on Wye. Powy 5C 58
New Brighton. Flin 4E 83
New Brighton. Hants 2F 17
New Brighton. Mers 1F 83
New Brinsley. Notts 5B 86
Newbrough. Nmbd 3B 114
New Broughton. Wrex 5F 83
New Buckenham. Norf 1C 66
Newbuildings. Devn 2A 12
Newburgh. Abers 1G 153
Newburgh. Fife 2E 137
Newburgh. Lanc 3C 90
Newburn. Tyne 3E 115
Newbury. W Ber 5C 36
Newbury. Wilts 2D 22
Newby. Cumb 2G 103
Newby. N Yor 2G 97 (nr. Ingleton)
Newby. N Yor 1E 101 (nr. Scarborough)
Newby. N Yor 3C 106 (nr. Stokesley)
Newby Bridge. Cumb 1C 96
Newby Cote. N Yor 2G 97
Newby East. Cumb 4F 113
Newby Head. Cumb 2G 103
New Byth. Abers 3F 161
Newby West. Cumb 4E 113
Newby Wiske. N Yor 1F 99
Newcastle. B'end 3B 32
Newcastle. Mon 4H 47
Newcastle. Shrp 2E 59
Newcastle Emlyn. Carm 1D 44
Newcastle International Airport. Tyne 2E 115
Newcastleton. Bord 1F 113
Newcastle-under-Lyme. Staf 1C 72
Newcastle upon Tyne. Tyne 3F 115
Newchapel. Pemb 1G 43
Newchapel. Powy 2B 58
Newchapel. Staf 5C 84
Newchapel. Surr 1E 27
New Cheriton. Hants 4D 24
Newchurch. Carm 3D 45
Newchurch. Here 5F 59
Newchurch. IOW 4D 16
Newchurch. Kent 2E 29
Newchurch. Lanc 1G 91 (nr. Nelson)
Newchurch. Lanc 2G 91 (nr. Rawtenstall)
Newchurch. Mon 2H 33
Newchurch. Powy 5E 58
Newchurch. Staf 3F 73
New Costessey. Norf 4D 78
Newcott. Devn 2F 13
New Cowper. Cumb 5C 112
Newcraighall. Edin 2G 129
New Crofton. W Yor 3D 93
New Cross. Cdgn 3F 57
New Cross. Som 1H 13
New Cumnock. E Ayr 3F 117
New Deer. Abers 4F 161
New Denham. Buck 2B 38
Newdigate. Surr 1C 26
New Duston. Nptn 4E 62
New Earswick. York 4A 100
New Edlington. S Yor 1C 86
New Elgin. Mor 2G 159
New Ellerby. E Yor 1E 95
Newell Green. Brac 4G 37
New Eltham. G Lon 3F 39
New End. Warw 4F 61
New End. Worc 5E 61
Newenden. Kent 3C 28
New England. Essx 1H 53
New England. Pet 5A 76
Newent. Glos 3C 48
New Ferry. Mers 2F 83
Newfield. Dur 4F 115 (nr. Chester-le-Street)
Newfield. Dur 1F 105 (nr. Willington)
Newfound. Hants 1D 24
New Fryston. W Yor 2E 93
New Galloway. Dum 2D 110
Newgate. Norf 1C 78
Newgate. Pemb 2C 42
Newgate Street. Herts 5D 52
New Greens. Herts 5B 52
New Grimsby. IOS 1A 4
New Hainford. Norf 4E 78
Newhall. Ches E 1A 72
Newhall. Staf 3G 73
Newham. Nmbd 2F 121
New Hartley. Nmbd 2G 115
Newhaven. Derbs 4F 85
Newhaven. E Sus 5F 27
Newhaven. Edin 2F 129
New Haw. Surr 4B 38
New Hedges. Pemb 4F 43
New Herrington. Tyne 4G 115
Newhey. G Man 3H 91
New Holkham. Norf 2A 78
New Holland. N Lin 2D 94
Newholm. N Yor 3F 107
New Houghton. Derbs 4C 86
New Houghton. Norf 3G 77
Newhouse. N Lan 3A 128
New Houses. N Yor 2H 97
New Hutton. Cumb 5G 103
New Hythe. Kent 5B 40
Newick. E Sus 3F 27
Newingreen. Kent 2F 29
Newington. Edin 2F 129
Newington. Kent 2F 29 (nr. Folkestone)
Newington. Kent 4C 40 (nr. Sittingbourne)
Newington. Notts 1D 86
Newington. Oxon 2E 36
Newington Bagpath. Glos 2D 34
New Inn. Carm 2E 45
New Inn. Mon 5H 47
New Inn. N Yor 2H 97
New Inn. Torf 5G 47
New Invention. Shrp 3E 59
New Kelso. High 4B 156
New Lanark. S Lan 5B 128
Newland. Glos 5A 48
Newland. Hull 1D 94
Newland. N Yor 2G 93
Newland. Som 3B 20
Newland. Worc 1C 48
Newlandrig. Midl 3G 129
Newlands. Cumb 1E 103
Newlands. Essx 2C 40
Newlands. High 4B 158
Newlands. Nmbd 4D 115
Newlands. Notts 4C 86
Newlands. Staf 3E 73
Newlands of Geise. High 2C 168
Newlands of Tynet. Mor 2A 160
Newlands Park. IOA 2B 80
New Lane. Lanc 3C 90
New Lane End. Warr 1A 84
New Langholm. Dum 1E 113
New Leake. Linc 5D 88
New Leeds. Abers 3G 161
New Lenton. Nott 2C 74
New Longton. Lanc 2D 90
Newlot. Orkn 6E 172
New Luce. Dum 3G 109
Newlyn. Corn 4B 4
Newmachar. Abers 2F 153
Newmains. N Lan 4B 128
New Mains of Ury. Abers 5F 153
New Malden. G Lon 4D 38
Newman's Green. Suff 1B 54
Newmarket. Suff 4F 65
Newmarket. W Isl 4G 171
New Marske. Red C 2D 106
New Marton. Shrp 2F 71
New Micklefield. W Yor 1E 93
New Mill. Abers 4E 160
New Mill. Corn 3B 4
New Mill. Herts 4H 51
Newmill. Mor 3B 160
Newmill. Bord 3G 119
New Mill. W Yor 4B 92
New Mill. Wilts 5G 35
Newmillerdam. W Yor 3D 92
New Mills. Corn 3C 6
New Mills. Derbs 2E 85
Newmills. Fife 1D 128
Newmills. High 2A 158
New Mills. Mon 5A 48
New Mills. Powy 5C 70
Newmiln. Per 5A 144
Newmilns. E Ayr 1E 117
New Milton. Hants 3H 15
New Mistley. Essx 2E 54
New Moat. Pemb 2E 43
Newmore. High 3H 157 (nr. Dingwall)
Newmore. High 1A 158 (nr. Invergordon)
Newnham. Cambs 5D 64
Newnham. Glos 4B 48
Newnham. Hants 1F 25
Newnham. Herts 2C 52
Newnham. Kent 5D 40
Newnham. Nptn 5C 62
Newnham. Warw 4F 61
Newnham Bridge. Worc 4A 60
New Ollerton. Notts 4D 86
New Oscott. W Mid 1F 61
Newpark. Fife 2G 137
New Park. N Yor 4E 99
New Pitsligo. Abers 3F 161
New Polzeath. Corn 1D 6
Newport. Corn 4D 10
Newport. Devn 3F 19
Newport. E Yor 1B 94
Newport. Essx 2F 53
Newport. Glos 2B 34
Newport. High 1H 165
Newport. IOW 4D 16
Newport. Newp 3G 33
Newport. Norf 4H 79
Newport. Pemb 1E 43
Newport. Som 4G 21
Newport. Telf 4B 72
Newport-on-Tay. Fife 1G 137
Newport Pagnell. Mil 1G 51
Newpound Common. W Sus 3B 26
New Prestwick. S Ayr 2C 116
New Quay. Cdgn 5C 56
Newquay. Corn 2C 6
Newquay Airport. Corn 2C 6
New Rackheath. Norf 4E 79
New Radnor. Powy 4E 58
New Rent. Cumb 1F 103
New Ridley. Nmbd 4D 114
New Romney. Kent 3E 29
New Rossington. S Yor 1D 86
New Row. Cdgn 3G 57
New Row. Lanc 1E 91
New Row. N Yor 3D 106
New Sauchie. Clac 4A 136
Newsbank. Ches E 4C 84
Newseat. Abers 5E 160
Newsham. Lanc 1D 90
Newsham. Nmbd 2G 115
Newsham. N Yor 3E 105 (nr. Richmond)
Newsham. N Yor 1F 99 (nr. Thirsk)
New Sharlston. W Yor 3D 93
Newsholme. E Yor 2H 93
Newsholme. Lanc 4H 97
New Shoreston. Nmbd 1F 121
New Springs. G Man 4D 90
Newstead. Notts 5C 86
Newstead. Bord 1H 119
New Stevenston. N Lan 4A 128
New Street. Here 5F 59
Newstreet Lane. Shrp 2A 72
New Swanage. Dors 4F 15
New Swannington. Leics 4B 74
Newthorpe. N Yor 1E 93
Newthorpe. Notts 1B 74
Newton. Arg 4H 133
Newton. B'end 4B 32
Newton. Cambs 1E 53 (nr. Cambridge)
Newton. Cambs 4D 76 (nr. Wisbech)
Newton. Ches W 4G 83 (nr. Chester)
Newton. Ches W 5H 83 (nr. Tattenhall)
Newton. Cumb 2B 96
Newton. Derbs 5B 86
Newton. Dors 1C 14
Newton. Dum 2D 112 (nr. Annan)
Newton. Dum 5D 118 (nr. Moffat)
Newton. G Man 1D 84
Newton. Here 2G 47 (nr. Ewyas Harold)
Newton. Here 5H 59 (nr. Leominster)
Newton. High 2B 158 (nr. Cromarty)
Newton. High 4B 158 (nr. Inverness)
Newton. High 5C 166 (nr. Kylestrome)
Newton. High 4F 169 (nr. Wick)
Newton. Lanc 2E 97 (nr. Carnforth)
Newton. Lanc 4F 97 (nr. Clitheroe)
Newton. Lanc 1C 90 (nr. Kirkham)
Newton. Linc 2H 75
Newton. Mers 2E 83
Newton. Mor 2F 159
Newton. Norf 4H 77
Newton. Nptn 2F 63
Newton. Nmbd 3D 114
Newton. Notts 1D 74
Newton. Bord 2A 120
Newton. Shrp 1B 60 (nr. Bridgnorth)
Newton. Shrp 2G 71 (nr. Wem)
Newton. Som 3E 20
Newton. S Lan 3H 127 (nr. Glasgow)
Newton. S Lan 1B 118 (nr. Lanark)
Newton. Staf 3E 73
Newton. Suff 1C 54
Newton. Swan 4F 31
Newton. Warw 3C 62
Newton. W Lot 2D 129
Newton. Wilts 4H 23
Newton Abbot. Devn 5B 12
Newtonairds. Dum 1F 111
Newton Arlosh. Cumb 4D 112
Newton Aycliffe. Dur 2F 105
Newton Bewley. Hart 2B 106
Newton Blossomville. Mil 5G 63
Newton Bromswold. Bed 4G 63
Newton Burgoland. Leics 5A 74
Newton by Toft. Linc 2H 87
Newton Ferrers. Devn 4B 8
Newton Flotman. Norf 1E 66
Newtongrange. Midl 3G 129
Newton Green. Mon 2A 34
Newton Hall. Dur 5F 115
Newton Hall. Nmbd 3D 114
Newton Harcourt. Leics 1D 62
Newton Heath. G Man 4G 91
Newtonhill. Abers 4G 153
Newtonhill. High 4H 157
Newton Hill. W Yor 2D 92
Newton Ketton. Darl 2A 106
Newton Kyme. N Yor 5G 99
Newton-le-Willows. Mers 1H 83
Newton-le-Willows. N Yor 1E 98
Newton Longville. Buck 2G 51
Newton Mearns. E Ren 4G 127
Newtonmore. High 4B 150
Newton Morrell. N Yor 4F 105
Newton Mulgrave. N Yor 3E 107
Newton of Ardtoe. High 1A 140
Newton of Balcanquhal. Per 2D 136
Newton of Beltrees. Ren 4E 127
Newton of Falkland. Fife 3E 137
Newton of Mountblairy. Abers 3E 160
Newton of Pitcairns. Per 2C 136
Newton-on-Ouse. N Yor 4H 99
Newton-on-Rawcliffe. N Yor 5F 107
Newton on the Hill. Shrp 3G 71
Newton-on-the-Moor. Nmbd 4F 121
Newton on Trent. Linc 3F 87
Newton Poppleford. Devn 4D 12
Newton Purcell. Oxon 2E 51
Newton Regis. Warw 5G 73
Newton Reigny. Cumb 1F 103
Newton Rigg. Cumb 1F 103
Newton St Cyres. Devn 3B 12
Newton St Faith. Norf 4E 78
Newton St Loe. Bath 5C 34
Newton St Petrock. Devn 1E 11
Newton Solney. Derbs 3G 73
Newton Stacey. Hants 2C 24
Newton Stewart. Dum 3B 110
Newton Toney. Wilts 2H 23
Newton Tony. Wilts 2H 23

Newton Tracey—North Warnborough

Newton Tracey. *Devn* 4F 19
Newton under Roseberry. *Red C* 3C 106
Newton Unthank. *Leics* 5B 74
Newton upon Ayr. *S Ayr* 2C 116
Newton upon Derwent. *E Yor* 5B 100
Newton Valence. *Hants* 3F 25
Newton-with-Scales. *Lanc* 1B 90
Newtown. *Abers* 2E 160
Newtown. *Cambs* 4H 63
Newtown. *Corn* 5C 10
Newtown. *Cumb* 5B 112 (nr. Aspatria)
Newtown. *Cumb* 3G 113 (nr. Brampton)
Newtown. *Cumb* 2G 103 (nr. Penrith)
Newtown. *Derbs* 2D 85
Newtown. *Devn* 4A 20
Newtown. *Dors* 2H 13 (nr. Beaminster)
New Town. *Dors* 1E 15 (nr. Sixpenny Handley)
New Town. *E Lot* 2H 129
Newtown. *Falk* 1C 128
Newtown. *Glos* 5B 48 (nr. Lydney)
Newtown. *Glos* 2E 49 (nr. Tewkesbury)
Newtown. *Hants* 1D 16 (nr. Bishop's Waltham)
Newtown. *Hants* 1A 16 (nr. Lyndhurst)
Newtown. *Hants* 5C 36 (nr. Newbury)
Newtown. *Hants* 4B 24 (nr. Romsey)
Newtown. *Hants* 2C 16 (nr. Warsash)
Newtown. *Hants* 1E 16 (nr. Wickham)
Newtown. *Here* 2B 48 (nr. Ledbury)
Newtown. *Here* 2A 48 (nr. Little Dewchurch)
Newtown. *Here* 1B 48 (nr. Stretton Grandison)
Newtown. *High* 3F 149
Newtown. *IOM* 4C 108
Newtown. *IOW* 3C 16
Newtown. *Lanc* 3D 90
New Town. *Lutn* 3A 52
Newtown. *Nmbd* 4E 121 (nr. Rothbury)
Newtown. *Nmbd* 2E 121 (nr. Wooler)
Newtown. *Pool* 3F 15
Newtown. *Powy* 1D 58
Newtown. *Rhon* 2D 32
Newtown. *Shrp* 2G 71
Newtown. *Som* 1F 13
Newtown. *Staf* 4D 84 (nr. Biddulph)
Newtown. *Staf* 5D 73 (nr. Cannock)
Newtown. *Staf* 4E 85 (nr. Longnor)
New Town. *W Yor* 2E 93
Newtown. *Wilts* 4E 23
Newtown-in-St Martin. *Corn* 4E 5
Newtown Linford. *Leics* 4C 74
Newtown St Boswells. *Bord* 1H 119
New Tredegar. *Cphy* 5E 47
Newtyle. *Ang* 4B 144
New Village. *E Yor* 1D 94
New Village. *S Yor* 4F 93
New Walsoken. *Cambs* 5D 76
New Waltham. *NE Lin* 4F 95
New Winton. *E Lot* 2H 129
New World. *Cambs* 1C 64
New Yatt. *Oxon* 4B 50
Newyears Green. *G Lon* 2B 38
New York. *Linc* 5B 88
New York. *Tyne* 2G 115
Nextend. *Here* 5F 59
Neyland. *Pemb* 4D 42
Nib Heath. *Shrp* 4G 71
Nicholashayne. *Devn* 1E 12
Nicholaston. *Swan* 4E 31
Nidd. *N Yor* 3F 99
Niddrie. *Edin* 2F 129
Niddry. *Edin* 2D 129
Nigg. *Aber* 3G 153
Nigg. *High* 1C 158
Nigg Ferry. *High* 2B 158
Nightcott. *Som* 4B 20
Nimmer. *Som* 1G 13
Nine Ashes. *Essx* 5F 53
Ninebanks. *Nmbd* 4A 114
Nine Elms. *Swin* 3G 35
Ninemile Bar. *Dum* 2F 111
Nine Mile Burn. *Midl* 4E 129
Ninfield. *E Sus* 4B 28
Ningwood. *IOW* 4C 16
Nisbet. *Bord* 2A 120
Nisbet Hill. *Bord* 4D 130
Niton. *IOW* 5D 16
Nitshill. *E Ren* 4G 127
Niwbwrch. *IOA* 4D 80
Noak Hill. *G Lon* 1G 39
Nobold. *Shrp* 4G 71
Nobottle. *Nptn* 4D 62
Nocton. *Linc* 4H 87
Nogdam End. *Norf* 5F 79
Noke. *Oxon* 4D 50
Nolton. *Pemb* 3C 42
Nolton Haven. *Pemb* 3C 42
No Man's Heath. *Ches W* 1H 71
No Man's Heath. *Warw* 5G 73
Nomansland. *Devn* 1B 12
Nomansland. *Wilts* 1A 16
Noneley. *Shrp* 3G 71
Nonikiln. *High* 1A 158
Nonington. *Kent* 5G 41
Nook. *Cumb* 2F 113 (nr. Longtown)
Nook. *Cumb* 1E 97 (nr. Milnthorpe)
Noranside. *Ang* 2D 144
Norbreck. *Bkpl* 5C 96
Norbridge. *Here* 1C 48
Norbury. *Ches E* 1H 71
Norbury. *Derbs* 1F 73
Norbury. *Shrp* 1F 59
Norbury. *Staf* 3B 72
Norby. *N Yor* 1G 99
Norby. *Shet* 6D 173
Norcross. *Lanc* 5C 96
Nordelph. *Norf* 5E 77
Norden. *G Man* 3G 91
Nordley. *Shrp* 1A 60
Norham. *Nmbd* 5F 131
Norland Town. *W Yor* 2A 92
Norley. *Ches W* 3H 83
Norleywood. *Hants* 3B 16
Normanby. *N Lin* 3B 94
Normanby. *N Yor* 1B 100
Normanby. *Red C* 3C 106
Normanby-by-Spital. *Linc* 2H 87
Normanby le Wold. *Linc* 1A 88
Norman Cross. *Cambs* 1A 64
Normandy. *Surr* 5A 38
Norman's Bay. *E Sus* 5A 28
Norman's Green. *Devn* 2D 12
Normanton. *Derb* 2H 73
Normanton. *Leics* 1F 75
Normanton. *Linc* 1G 75
Normanton. *Notts* 5E 86
Normanton. *W Yor* 2D 93
Normanton le Heath. *Leics* 4A 74
Normanton on Soar. *Notts* 3C 74
Normanton-on-the-Wolds. *Notts* 2D 74
Normanton on Trent. *Notts* 4E 87
Normoss. *Lanc* 1B 90
Norrington Common. *Wilts* 5D 35
Norris Green. *Mers* 1F 83
Norris Hill. *Leics* 4H 73
Norristhorpe. *W Yor* 2C 92
Northacre. *Norf* 1B 66
Northall. *Buck* 3H 51
Northallerton. *N Yor* 5A 106
Northam. *Devn* 4E 19
Northam. *Sotn* 1C 16
Northampton. *Nptn* 4E 63
North Anston. *S Yor* 2C 86
North Ascot. *Brac* 4A 38
North Aston. *Oxon* 3C 50
Northaw. *Herts* 5C 52
Northay. *Som* 1F 13
North Baddesley. *Hants* 4B 24
North Balfern. *Dum* 4B 110
North Ballachulish. *High* 2E 141
North Barrow. *Som* 4B 22
North Barsham. *Norf* 2B 78
Northbeck. *Linc* 1H 75
North Benfleet. *Essx* 2B 40
North Bersted. *W Sus* 5A 26
North Berwick. *E Lot* 1B 130
North Bitchburn. *Dur* 1E 105
North Blyth. *Nmbd* 1G 115
North Boarhunt. *Hants* 1E 16
North Bockhampton. *Dors* 3G 15
Northborough. *Pet* 5A 76
Northbourne. *Kent* 5H 41
Northbourne. *Oxon* 3D 36
North Bovey. *Devn* 4H 11
North Bowood. *Dors* 3H 13
North Bradley. *Wilts* 1D 22
North Brentor. *Devn* 4E 11
North Brewham. *Som* 3C 22
Northbrook. *Oxon* 3C 50
North Brook End. *Cambs* 1C 52
North Broomhill. *Nmbd* 4G 121
North Buckland. *Devn* 2E 19
North Burlingham. *Norf* 4F 79
North Cadbury. *Som* 4B 22
North Carlton. *Linc* 3G 87
North Cave. *E Yor* 1B 94
North Cerney. *Glos* 5F 49
North Chailey. *E Sus* 3E 27
Northchapel. *W Sus* 3A 26
North Charford. *Hants* 1G 15
North Charlton. *Nmbd* 2F 121
North Cheriton. *Som* 4B 22
North Chideock. *Dors* 3H 13
Northchurch. *Herts* 5H 51
North Cliffe. *E Yor* 1B 94
North Clifton. *Notts* 3F 87
North Close. *Dur* 1F 105
North Cockerington. *Linc* 1C 88
North Coker. *Som* 1A 14
North Collafirth. *Shet* 3E 173
North Common. *E Sus* 3E 27
North Commonty. *Abers* 4F 161
North Coombe. *Devn* 1B 12
North Corbelly. *Dum* 3A 112
North Cornelly. *B'end* 3B 32
North Cotes. *Linc* 4G 95
Northcott. *Devn* 3D 10 (nr. Boyton)
Northcott. *Devn* 1D 12 (nr. Culmstock)
Northcourt. *Oxon* 2D 36
North Cove. *Suff* 2G 67
North Cowton. *N Yor* 4F 105
North Craigo. *Ang* 2F 145
North Crawley. *Mil* 1H 51
North Cray. *G Lon* 3F 39
North Creake. *Norf* 2A 78
North Curry. *Som* 4G 21
North Dalton. *E Yor* 4D 100
North Deighton. *N Yor* 4F 99
North Dronley. *Ang* 5C 144
North Duffield. *N Yor* 1G 93
Northedge. *Derbs* 4A 86
North Elkington. *Linc* 1B 88
North Elmham. *Norf* 3B 78
North Elmsall. *W Yor* 3E 93
Northend. *Buck* 2F 37
North End. *E Yor* 1F 95
North End. *Essx* 4G 53 (nr. Great Dunmow)
North End. *Essx* 2A 54 (nr. Great Yeldham)
North End. *Hants* 5C 36
North End. *Leics* 4C 74
North End. *Linc* 1B 76
North End. *Norf* 1B 66
North End. *N Som* 5H 33
North End. *Port* 2E 17
Northend. *Warw* 5A 62
North End. *W Sus* 5C 26
North End. *Wilts* 2F 35
North Erradale. *High* 5B 162
North Evington. *Leic* 5D 74
North Fambridge. *Essx* 1C 40
North Fearns. *High* 5E 155
North Featherstone. *W Yor* 2E 93
North Feorline. *N Ayr* 3D 122
North Ferriby. *E Yor* 2C 94
Northfield. *Aber* 3F 153
Northfield. *Hull* 2D 94
Northfield. *Som* 3F 21
Northfield. *W Mid* 3E 61
Northfleet. *Kent* 3H 39
North Frodingham. *E Yor* 4F 101
Northgate. *Linc* 3A 76
North Gluss. *Shet* 4E 173
North Gorley. *Hants* 1G 15
North Green. *Norf* 2E 66
North Green. *Suff* 4F 67 (nr. Framlingham)
North Green. *Suff* 3F 67 (nr. Halesworth)
North Green. *Suff* 4F 67 (nr. Saxmundham)
North Greetwell. *Linc* 3H 87
North Grimston. *N Yor* 3C 100
North Halling. *Medw* 4B 40
North Hayling. *Hants* 2F 17
North Hazelrigg. *Nmbd* 1E 121
North Heasley. *Devn* 3H 19
North Heath. *W Sus* 3B 26
North Hill. *Corn* 5C 10
North Hinksey Village. *Oxon* 5C 50
North Holmwood. *Surr* 1C 26
North Huish. *Devn* 3D 8
North Hykeham. *Linc* 4G 87
Northiam. *E Sus* 3C 28
Northill. *C Beds* 1B 52
Northington. *Hants* 3D 24
North Kelsey. *Linc* 4D 94
North Kelsey Moor. *Linc* 4D 94
North Kessock. *High* 4A 158
North Killingholme. *N Lin* 3E 95
North Kilvington. *N Yor* 1G 99
North Kilworth. *Leics* 2D 62
North Kyme. *Linc* 5A 88
North Lancing. *W Sus* 5C 26
Northlands. *Linc* 5C 88
Northleach. *Glos* 4G 49
North Lee. *Buck* 5G 51
North Lees. *N Yor* 2E 99
Northleigh. *Devn* 3G 19 (nr. Barnstaple)
Northleigh. *Devn* 3E 13 (nr. Honiton)
North Leigh. *Kent* 1F 29
North Leigh. *Oxon* 4B 50
North Leverton. *Notts* 2E 87
Northlew. *Devn* 3F 11
North Littleton. *Worc* 1F 49
North Lopham. *Norf* 2C 66
North Luffenham. *Rut* 5G 75
North Marden. *W Sus* 1G 17
North Marston. *Buck* 3F 51
North Middleton. *Midl* 4G 129
North Middleton. *Nmbd* 2E 121
North Molton. *Devn* 4H 19
North Moor. *N Yor* 1D 100
Northmoor. *Oxon* 5C 50
Northmoor Green. *Som* 3G 21
North Moreton. *Oxon* 3D 36
Northmuir. *Ang* 3C 144
North Mundham. *W Sus* 2G 17
North Murie. *Per* 1E 137
North Muskham. *Notts* 5E 87
North Ness. *Orkn* 8C 172
North Newbald. *E Yor* 1C 94
North Newington. *Oxon* 2C 50
North Newnton. *Wilts* 1G 23
North Newton. *Som* 3F 21
Northney. *Hants* 2F 17
North Nibley. *Glos* 2C 34
North Oakley. *Hants* 1D 24
North Ockendon. *G Lon* 2G 39
Northolt. *G Lon* 2C 38
Northop. *Flin* 4E 83
Northop Hall. *Flin* 4E 83
North Ormesby. *Midd* 3C 106
North Ormsby. *Linc* 1B 88
Northorpe. *Linc* 4H 75 (nr. Bourne)
Northorpe. *Linc* 2B 76 (nr. Donington)
Northorpe. *Linc* 1F 87 (nr. Gainsborough)
North Otterington. *N Yor* 1F 99
Northover. *Som* 3H 21 (nr. Glastonbury)
Northover. *Som* 4A 22 (nr. Yeovil)
North Owersby. *Linc* 1H 87
Northowram. *W Yor* 2B 92
North Perrott. *Som* 2H 13
North Petherton. *Som* 3F 21
North Petherwin. *Corn* 4C 10
North Pickenham. *Norf* 5A 78
North Piddle. *Worc* 5D 60
North Poorton. *Dors* 3A 14
North Port. *Arg* 1H 133
Northport. *Dors* 4E 15
North Queensferry. *Fife* 1E 129
North Radworthy. *Devn* 3A 20
North Rauceby. *Linc* 1H 75
Northrepps. *Norf* 2E 79
North Rigton. *N Yor* 5E 99
North Rode. *Ches E* 4C 84
North Roe. *Shet* 3E 173
North Ronaldsay Airport. *Orkn* 2G 172
North Row. *Cumb* 1D 102
North Runcton. *Norf* 4F 77
North Sannox. *N Ayr* 5B 126
North Scale. *Cumb* 2A 96
North Scarle. *Linc* 4F 87
North Seaton. *Nmbd* 1F 115
North Seaton Colliery. *Nmbd* 1F 115
North Sheen. *G Lon* 3C 38
North Shian. *Arg* 4D 140
North Shields. *Tyne* 3G 115
North Shoebury. *S'end* 2D 40
North Shore. *Bkpl* 1B 90
North Side. *Cumb* 2B 102
North Skelton. *Red C* 3D 106
North Somercotes. *Linc* 1D 88
North Stainley. *N Yor* 2E 99
North Stainmore. *Cumb* 3B 104
North Stifford. *Thur* 2H 39
North Stoke. *Bath* 5C 34
North Stoke. *Oxon* 3E 36
North Stoke. *W Sus* 4B 26
Northstowe. *Cambs* 4D 64
North Street. *Hants* 3E 25
North Street. *Kent* 5E 40
North Street. *Medw* 3C 40
North Street. *W Ber* 4E 37
North Sunderland. *Nmbd* 1G 121
North Tamerton. *Corn* 3D 10
North Tawton. *Devn* 2G 11
North Thoresby. *Linc* 1B 88
North Town. *Devn* 2F 11
North Tuddenham. *Norf* 4C 78
North Walbottle. *Tyne* 3E 115
North Walney. *Cumb* 3A 96
North Walsham. *Norf* 2E 79
North Waltham. *Hants* 2D 24
North Warnborough. *Hants* 1F 25

North Water Bridge—Onslow Green

North Water Bridge. *Ang* 2F 145
North Watten. *High* 3E 169
Northway. *Glos* 2E 49
Northway. *Swan* 4E 31
North Weald Bassett. *Essx* 5F 53
North Weston. *N Som* 4H 33
North Weston. *Oxon* 5E 51
North Wheatley. *Notts* 2E 87
North Whilborough. *Devn* 2E 9
Northwich. *Ches W* 3A 84
North Wick. *Bath* 5A 34
Northwick. *Som* 2G 21
Northwick. *S Glo* 3A 34
North Widcombe. *Bath* 1A 22
North Willingham. *Linc* 2A 88
North Wingfield. *Derbs* 4B 86
North Witham. *Linc* 3G 75
Northwold. *Norf* 1G 65
Northwood. *Derbs* 4G 85
Northwood. *G Lon* 1B 38
Northwood. *IOW* 3C 16
Northwood. *Kent* 4H 41
Northwood. *Shrp* 2G 71
Northwood. *Stoke* 1C 72
Northwood Green. *Glos* 4C 48
North Wootton. *Dors* 1B 14
North Wootton. *Norf* 3F 77
North Wootton. *Som* 2A 22
North Wraxall. *Wilts* 4D 34
North Wroughton. *Swin* 3G 35
North Yardhope. *Nmbd* 4D 120
Norton. *Devn* 3E 9
Norton. *Glos* 3D 48
Norton. *Hal* 2H 83
Norton. *Herts* 2C 52
Norton. *IOW* 4B 16
Norton. *Mon* 3H 47
Norton. *Nptn* 4D 62
Norton. *Notts* 3C 86
Norton. *Powy* 4F 59
Norton. *Shrp* 2G 59
(nr. Ludlow)
Norton. *Shrp* 5B 72
(nr. Madeley)
Norton. *Shrp* 5H 71
(nr. Shrewsbury)
Norton. *S Yor* 3F 93
(nr. Askern)
Norton. *S Yor* 2A 86
(nr. Sheffield)
Norton. *Stoc T* 2B 106
Norton. *Suff* 4B 66
Norton. *Swan* 4F 31
Norton. *W Sus* 5A 26
(nr. Arundel)
Norton. *W Sus* 3G 17
(nr. Selsey)
Norton. *Wilts* 3D 35
Norton. *Worc* 1F 49
(nr. Evesham)
Norton. *Worc* 5C 60
(nr. Worcester)
Norton Bavant. *Wilts* 2E 23
Norton Bridge. *Staf* 2C 72
Norton Canes. *Staf* 5E 73
Norton Canon. *Here* 1G 47
Norton Corner. *Norf* 3C 78
Norton Disney. *Linc* 5F 87
Norton East. *Staf* 5E 73
Norton Ferris. *Wilts* 3C 22
Norton Fitzwarren. *Som* 4F 21
Norton Green. *IOW* 4B 16
Norton Green. *Stoke* 5D 84
Norton Hawkfield. *Bath* 5A 34
Norton Heath. *Essx* 5G 53
Norton in Hales. *Shrp* 2B 72
Norton in the Moors. *Stoke* 5C 84
Norton-Juxta-Twycross. *Leics* 5H 73
Norton-le-Clay. *N Yor* 2G 99
Norton Lindsey. *Warw* 4G 61
Norton Little Green. *Suff* 4B 66
Norton Malreward. *Bath* 5B 34
Norton Mandeville. *Essx* 5F 53
Norton-on-Derwent. *N Yor* 2B 100
Norton St Philip. *Som* 1C 22
Norton Subcourse. *Norf* 1G 67
Norton sub Hamdon. *Som* 1H 13
Norton Woodseats. *S Yor* 2A 86
Norwell. *Notts* 4E 87
Norwell Woodhouse. *Notts* 4E 87
Norwich. *Norf* 5E 79
Norwich International Airport.
Norf 4E 79
Norwick. *Shet* 1H 173
Norwood. *Derbs* 2B 86
Norwood Green. *W Yor* 2B 92
Norwood Hill. *Surr* 1D 26
Norwood Park. *Som* 3A 22
Norwoodside. *Cambs* 1D 64
Noseley. *Leics* 1E 63
Noss Mayo. *Devn* 4B 8
Nosterfield. *N Yor* 1E 99
Nostie. *High* 1A 148
Notgrove. *Glos* 3G 49
Nottage. *B'end* 4B 32
Nottingham. *Nott* 1C 74
Nottington. *Dors* 4B 14
Notton. *Dors* 3B 14
Notton. *W Yor* 3D 92
Notton. *Wilts* 5E 35
Nounsley. *Essx* 4A 54
Noutard's Green. *Worc* 4B 60
Nox. *Shrp* 4G 71
Noyadd Trefawr. *Cdgn* 1C 44
Nuffield. *Oxon* 3E 37
Nunburnholme. *E Yor* 5C 100
Nuncargate. *Notts* 5B 86
Nunclose. *Cumb* 5F 113
Nuneaton. *Warw* 1A 62
Nuneham Courtenay. *Oxon* 2D 36
Nun Monkton. *N Yor* 4H 99
Nunnerie. *S Lan* 3B 118
Nunney. *Som* 2C 22
Nunnington. *N Yor* 2A 100
Nunnykirk. *Nmbd* 5E 121
Nunsthorpe. *NE Lin* 4F 95
Nunthorpe. *Red C* 3C 106
Nunthorpe. *York* 5H 99
Nunton. *Wilts* 4G 23
Nunwick. *Nmbd* 2B 114
Nunwick. *N Yor* 2F 99
Nupend. *Glos* 5C 48
Nursling. *Hants* 1B 16
Nursted. *W Sus* 4F 25
Nursteed. *Wilts* 5F 35
Nurston. *V Glam* 5D 32
Nutbourne. *W Sus* 2F 17
(nr. Chichester)
Nutbourne. *W Sus* 4B 26
(nr. Pulborough)
Nutfield. *Surr* 5E 39
Nuthall. *Notts* 1C 74
Nuthampstead. *Herts* 2E 53
Nuthurst. *Warw* 3F 61
Nuthurst. *W Sus* 3C 26
Nutley. *E Sus* 3F 27
Nuttall. *G Man* 3F 91
Nutwell. *S Yor* 4G 93
Nybster. *High* 2F 169
Nyetimber. *W Sus* 3G 17
Nyewood. *W Sus* 4G 25
Nymet Rowland. *Devn* 2H 11
Nymet Tracey. *Devn* 2H 11
Nympsfield. *Glos* 5D 48
Nynehead. *Som* 4E 21
Nyton. *W Sus* 5A 26

O

Oadby. *Leics* 5D 74
Oad Street. *Kent* 4C 40
Oakamoor. *Staf* 1E 73
Oakbank. *Arg* 5B 140
Oakbank. *W Lot* 3D 129
Oakdale. *Cphy* 2E 33
Oakdale. *Pool* 3F 15
Oake. *Som* 4E 21
Oaken. *Staf* 5C 72
Oakenclough. *Lanc* 5E 97
Oakengates. *Telf* 4B 72
Oakenholt. *Flin* 3E 83
Oakenshaw. *Dur* 1F 105
Oakenshaw. *W Yor* 2B 92
Oakerthorpe. *Derbs* 5A 86
Oakford. *Cdgn* 5D 56
Oakford. *Devn* 4C 20
Oakfordbridge. *Devn* 4C 20
Oakgrove. *Ches E* 4D 84
Oakham. *Rut* 5F 75
Oakhanger. *Ches E* 5B 84
Oakhanger. *Hants* 3F 25
Oakhill. *Som* 2B 22
Oakington. *Cambs* 4D 64
Oaklands. *Powy* 5C 58
Oakle Street. *Glos* 4C 48
Oakley. *Bed* 5H 63
Oakley. *Buck* 4E 51
Oakley. *Fife* 1D 128
Oakley. *Hants* 1D 24
Oakley. *Suff* 3D 66
Oakley Green. *Wind* 3A 38
Oakley Park. *Powy* 2B 58
Oakmere. *Ches W* 4H 83
Oakridge. *Glos* 5E 49
Oaks. *Shrp* 5G 71
Oaksey. *Wilts* 2E 35
Oaks Green. *Derbs* 2F 73
Oakshaw Ford. *Cumb* 2G 113
Oakshott. *Hants* 4F 25
Oakthorpe. *Leics* 4H 73
Oak Tree. *Darl* 3A 106
Oakwood. *Derb* 2A 74
Oakwood. *W Yor* 1D 92
Oakwoodhill. *Surr* 2C 26
Oakworth. *W Yor* 1A 92
Oape. *High* 3B 164
Oare. *Kent* 4E 40
Oare. *Som* 2B 20
Oare. *W Ber* 4D 36
Oare. *Wilts* 5G 35
Oareford. *Som* 2B 20
Oasby. *Linc* 2H 75
Oath. *Som* 4G 21
Oathlaw. *Ang* 3D 145
Oatlands. *N Yor* 4F 99
Oban. *Arg* 1F 133
Oban. *W Isl* 7D 171
Oborne. *Dors* 1B 14
Obsdale. *High* 2A 158
Obthorpe. *Linc* 4H 75
Occlestone Green. *Ches W* 4A 84
Occold. *Suff* 3D 66
Ochiltree. *E Ayr* 2E 117
Ochtermuthill. *Per* 2H 135
Ochtertyre. *Per* 1H 135
Ockbrook. *Derbs* 2B 74
Ockeridge. *Worc* 4B 60
Ockham. *Surr* 5B 38
Ockle. *High* 1G 139
Ockley. *Surr* 1C 26
Ocle Pychard. *Here* 1A 48
Octofad. *Arg* 4A 124
Octomore. *Arg* 4A 124
Octon. *E Yor* 3E 101
Odcombe. *Som* 1A 14
Odd Down. *Bath* 5C 34
Oddingley. *Worc* 5D 60
Oddington. *Oxon* 4D 50
Oddsta. *Shet* 2G 173
Odell. *Bed* 5G 63
Odiham. *Hants* 1F 25
Odsey. *Cambs* 2C 52
Odstock. *Wilts* 4G 23
Odstone. *Leics* 5A 74
Offchurch. *Warw* 4A 62
Offenham. *Worc* 1F 49
Offenham Cross. *Worc* 1F 49
Offerton. *G Man* 2D 84
Offerton. *Tyne* 4G 115
Offham. *E Sus* 4F 27
Offham. *Kent* 5A 40
Offham. *W Sus* 5B 26
Offleyhay. *Staf* 3C 72
Offley Hoo. *Herts* 3B 52
Offleymarsh. *Staf* 3B 72
Offord Cluny. *Cambs* 4B 64
Offord D'Arcy. *Cambs* 4B 64
Offton. *Suff* 1D 54
Offwell. *Devn* 3E 13
Ogbourne Maizey. *Wilts* 4G 35
Ogbourne St Andrew. *Wilts* 4G 35
Ogbourne St George. *Wilts* 4H 35
Ogden. *G Man* 3H 91
Ogle. *Nmbd* 2E 115
Ogmore. *V Glam* 4B 32
Ogmore-by-Sea. *V Glam* 4B 32
Ogmore Vale. *B'end* 2C 32
Okeford Fitzpaine. *Dors* 1D 14
Okehampton. *Devn* 3F 11
Okehampton Camp. *Devn* 3F 11
Okus. *Swin* 3G 35
Old. *Nptn* 3E 63
Old Aberdeen. *Aber* 3G 153
Old Alresford. *Hants* 3D 24
Oldany. *High* 5B 166
Old Arley. *Warw* 1G 61
Old Basford. *Nott* 1C 74
Old Basing. *Hants* 1E 25
Oldberrow. *Warw* 4F 61
Old Bewick. *Nmbd* 2E 121
Old Bexley. *G Lon* 3F 39
Old Blair. *Per* 2F 143
Old Bolingbroke. *Linc* 4C 88
Oldborough. *Devn* 2A 12
Old Brampton. *Derbs* 3H 85
Old Bridge of Tilt. *Per* 2F 143
Old Bridge of Urr. *Dum* 3E 111
Old Buckenham. *Norf* 1C 66
Old Burghclere. *Hants* 1C 24
Oldbury. *Shrp* 1B 60
Oldbury. *Warw* 1H 61
Oldbury. *W Mid* 2D 61
Oldbury-on-Severn. *S Glo* 2B 34
Oldbury on the Hill. *Glos* 3D 34
Old Byland. *N Yor* 1H 99
Old Cassop. *Dur* 1A 106
Oldcastle. *Mon* 3G 47
Oldcastle Heath. *Ches W* 1G 71
Old Catton. *Norf* 4E 79
Old Clee. *NE Lin* 4F 95
Old Cleeve. *Som* 2D 20
Old Clipstone. *Notts* 4D 86
Old Colwyn. *Cnwy* 3A 82
Oldcotes. *Notts* 2C 86
Old Coulsdon. *G Lon* 5E 39
Old Dailly. *S Ayr* 5B 116
Old Dalby. *Leics* 3D 74
Old Dam. *Derbs* 3F 85
Old Deer. *Abers* 4G 161
Old Dilton. *Wilts* 2D 22
Old Down. *S Glo* 3B 34
Oldeamere. *Cambs* 1C 64
Old Edlington. *S Yor* 1C 86
Old Eldon. *Dur* 2F 105
Old Ellerby. *E Yor* 1E 95
Old Fallings. *W Mid* 5D 72
Oldfallow. *Staf* 4D 72
Old Felixstowe. *Suff* 2G 55
Oldfield. *Shrp* 2A 60
Oldfield. *Worc* 4C 60
Old Fletton. *Pet* 1A 64
Oldford. *Som* 1C 22
Old Forge. *Here* 4A 48
Old Glossop. *Derbs* 1E 85
Old Goole. *E Yor* 2H 93
Old Gore. *Here* 3B 48
Old Graitney. *Dum* 3E 112
Old Grimsby. *IOS* 1A 4
Oldhall. *High* 3E 169
Old Hall Street. *Norf* 2F 79
Oldham. *G Man* 4H 91
Oldhamstocks. *E Lot* 2D 130
Old Heathfield. *E Sus* 3G 27
Old Hill. *W Mid* 2D 60
Old Hunstanton. *Norf* 1F 77
Old Hurst. *Cambs* 3B 64
Old Hutton. *Cumb* 1E 97
Old Kea. *Corn* 4C 6
Old Kilpatrick. *W Dun* 2F 127
Old Kinnernie. *Abers* 3E 152
Old Knebworth. *Herts* 3C 52
Oldland. *S Glo* 4B 34
Old Laxey. *IOM* 3D 108
Old Leake. *Linc* 5D 88
Old Lenton. *Nott* 2C 74
Old Llanberis. *Gwyn* 5F 81
Old Malton. *N Yor* 2B 100
Oldmeldrum. *Abers* 1F 153
Old Micklefield. *W Yor* 1E 93
Old Mill. *Corn* 5D 10
Oldmixon. *N Som* 1G 21
Old Monkland. *N Lan* 3A 128
Old Newton. *Suff* 4C 66
Old Park. *Telf* 5A 72
Old Pentland. *Midl* 3F 129
Old Philpstoun. *W Lot* 2D 128
Old Quarrington. *Dur* 1A 106
Old Radnor. *Powy* 5E 59
Old Rayne. *Abers* 1D 152
Oldridge. *Devn* 3B 12
Old Romney. *Kent* 3E 29
Old Scone. *Per* 1D 136
Oldshore Beg. *High* 3B 166
Oldshoremore. *High* 3C 166
Old Snydale. *W Yor* 2E 93
Old Sodbury. *S Glo* 3C 34
Old Somerby. *Linc* 2G 75
Old Spital. *Dur* 3C 104
Oldstead. *N Yor* 1H 99
Old Stratford. *Nptn* 1F 51
Old Swan. *Mers* 1F 83
Old Swarland. *Nmbd* 4F 121
Old Tebay. *Cumb* 4H 103
Old Town. *Cumb* 5F 113
Old Town. *E Sus* 5G 27
Oldtown. *High* 5C 164
Old Town. *IOS* 1B 4
Old Town. *Nmbd* 5C 120
Oldtown of Ord. *Abers* 3D 160
Old Trafford. *G Man* 1C 84
Old Tupton. *Derbs* 4A 86
Oldwall. *Cumb* 3F 113
Oldwalls. *Swan* 3D 31
Old Warden. *C Beds* 1B 52
Oldways End. *Som* 4B 20
Old Westhall. *Abers* 1D 152
Old Weston. *Cambs* 3H 63
Oldwhat. *Abers* 3F 161
Old Windsor. *Wind* 3A 38
Old Wives Lees. *Kent* 5E 41
Old Woking. *Surr* 5B 38
Oldwood Common. *Worc* 4H 59
Old Woodstock. *Oxon* 4C 50
Olgrinmore. *High* 3C 168
Oliver's Battery. *Hants* 4C 24
Ollaberry. *Shet* 3E 173
Ollerton. *Ches E* 3B 84
Ollerton. *Notts* 4D 86
Ollerton. *Shrp* 3A 72
Olmarch. *Cdgn* 5F 57
Olmstead Green. *Cambs* 1G 53
Olney. *Mil* 5F 63
Olrig. *High* 2D 169
Olton. *W Mid* 2F 61
Olveston. *S Glo* 3B 34
Ombersley. *Worc* 4C 60
Ompton. *Notts* 4D 86
Omunsgarth. *Shet* 7E 173
Onchan. *IOM* 4D 108
Onecote. *Staf* 5E 85
Onehouse. *Suff* 5C 66
Onen. *Mon* 4H 47
Ongar Hill. *Norf* 3E 77
Ongar Street. *Here* 4F 59
Onibury. *Shrp* 3G 59
Onich. *High* 2E 141
Onllwyn. *Neat* 4B 46
Onneley. *Shrp* 1B 72
Onslow Green. *Essx* 4G 53

Onslow Village—Park Corner

Onslow Village. *Surr* 1A 26
Onthank. *E Ayr* 1D 116
Openwoodgate. *Derbs* 1A 74
Opinan. *High* 1G 155
(nr. Gairloch)
Opinan. *High* 4C 162
(nr. Laide)
Orasaigh. *W Isl* 6F 171
Orbost. *High* 4B 154
Orby. *Linc* 4D 89
Orchard Hill. *Devn* 4E 19
Orchard Portman. *Som* 4F 21
Orcheston. *Wilts* 2F 23
Orcop. *Here* 3H 47
Orcop Hill. *Here* 3H 47
Ord. *High* 2E 147
Ordhead. *Abers* 2D 152
Ordie. *Abers* 3B 152
Ordiquish. *Mor* 3H 159
Ordley. *Nmbd* 4C 114
Ordsall. *Notts* 3E 86
Ore. *E Sus* 4C 28
Oreham Common. *W Sus* 4D 26
Oreton. *Shrp* 2A 60
Orford. *Linc* 1B 88
Orford. *Suff* 1H 55
Orford. *Warr* 1A 84
Organford. *Dors* 3E 15
Orgil. *Orkn* 7B 172
Orgreave. *Staf* 4F 73
Oridge Street. *Glos* 3C 48
Orlestone. *Kent* 2D 28
Orleton. *Here* 4G 59
Orleton. *Worc* 4A 60
Orleton Common. *Here* 4G 59
Orlingbury. *Nptn* 3F 63
Ormacleit. *W Isl* 5C 170
Ormathwaite. *Cumb* 2D 102
Ormesby. *Midd* 3C 106
Ormesby St Margaret. *Norf* 4G 79
Ormesby St Michael. *Norf* 4G 79
Ormiscaig. *High* 4C 162
Ormiston. *E Lot* 3H 129
Ormsaigbeg. *High* 2F 139
Ormsaigmore. *High* 2F 139
Ormsary. *Arg* 2F 125
Ormsgill. *Cumb* 2A 96
Ormskirk. *Lanc* 4C 90
Orphir. *Orkn* 7C 172
Orpington. *G Lon* 4F 39
Orrell. *Lanc* 4D 90
Orrell. *Mers* 1F 83
Orrisdale. *IOM* 2C 108
Orsett. *Thur* 2H 39
Orslow. *Staf* 4C 72
Orston. *Notts* 1E 75
Orthwaite. *Cumb* 1D 102
Orton. *Cumb* 4H 103
Orton. *Mor* 3H 159
Orton. *Nptn* 3F 63
Orton. *Staf* 1C 60
Orton Longueville. *Pet* 1A 64
Orton-on-the-Hill. *Leics* 5H 73
Orton Waterville. *Pet* 1A 64
Orton Wistow. *Pet* 1A 64
Orwell. *Cambs* 5C 64
Osbaldeston. *Lanc* 1E 91
Osbaldwick. *York* 4A 100
Osbaston. *Leics* 5B 74
Osbaston. *Shrp* 3F 71
Osbournby. *Linc* 2H 75
Osclay. *High* 5E 169
Oscroft. *Ches W* 4H 83
Ose. *High* 4C 154
Osgathorpe. *Leics* 4B 74
Osgodby. *Linc* 1H 87
Osgodby. *N Yor* 1E 101
(nr. Scarborough)
Osgodby. *N Yor* 1G 93
(nr. Selby)
Oskaig. *High* 5E 155
Oskamull. *Arg* 4F 139
Osleston. *Derbs* 2G 73
Osmaston. *Derb* 2A 74
Osmaston. *Derbs* 1G 73
Osmington. *Dors* 4C 14
Osmington Mills. *Dors* 4C 14
Osmondthorpe. *W Yor* 1D 92
Osmotherley. *N Yor* 5B 106
Osnaburgh. *Fife* 2G 137
Ospisdale. *High* 5E 164
Ospringe. *Kent* 4E 40
Ossett. *W Yor* 2C 92
Ossington. *Notts* 4E 87
Ostend. *Essx* 1D 40
Ostend. *Norf* 2F 79
Osterley. *G Lon* 3C 38
Oswaldkirk. *N Yor* 2A 100
Oswaldtwistle. *Lanc* 2F 91
Oswestry. *Shrp* 3E 71
Otby. *Linc* 1A 88
Otford. *Kent* 5G 39
Otham. *Kent* 5B 40
Otherton. *Staf* 4D 72
Othery. *Som* 3G 21
Otley. *Suff* 5E 66
Otley. *W Yor* 5E 98
Otterbourne. *Hants* 4C 24
Otterburn. *Nmbd* 5C 120
Otterburn. *N Yor* 4A 98
Otterburn Camp. *Nmbd* 5C 120
Otterburn Hall. *Nmbd* 5C 120
Otter Ferry. *Arg* 1H 125
Otterford. *Som* 1F 13
Otterham. *Corn* 3B 10
Otterhampton. *Som* 2F 21
Otterham Quay. *Kent* 4C 40
Ottershaw. *Surr* 4B 38
Otterspool. *Mers* 2F 83
Otterswick. *Shet* 3G 173
Otterton. *Devn* 4D 12
Otterwood. *Hants* 2C 16
Ottery St Mary. *Devn* 3E 12
Ottinge. *Kent* 1F 29
Ottringham. *E Yor* 2F 95
Oughterby. *Cumb* 4D 112
Oughtershaw. *N Yor* 1A 98
Oughterside. *Cumb* 5C 112
Oughtibridge. *S Yor* 1H 85
Oughtrington. *Warr* 2A 84
Oulston. *N Yor* 2H 99
Oulton. *Cumb* 4D 112
Oulton. *Norf* 3D 78
Oulton. *Staf* 3B 72
(nr. Gnosall Heath)
Oulton. *Staf* 2D 72
(nr. Stone)
Oulton. *Suff* 1H 67
Oulton. *W Yor* 2D 92
Oulton Broad. *Suff* 1H 67
Oulton Street. *Norf* 3D 78
Oundle. *Nptn* 2H 63
Ousby. *Cumb* 1H 103
Ousdale. *High* 1H 165
Ousden. *Suff* 5G 65
Ousefleet. *E Yor* 2B 94
Ouston. *Dur* 4F 115
Ouston. *Nmbd* 4A 114
(nr. Bearsbridge)
Ouston. *Nmbd* 2D 114
(nr. Stamfordham)
Outer Hope. *Devn* 4C 8
Outertown. *Orkn* 7B 172
Outgate. *Cumb* 5E 103
Outhgill. *Cumb* 4A 104
Outlands. *Staf* 2B 72
Outlane. *W Yor* 3A 92
Out Newton. *E Yor* 2G 95
Out Rawcliffe. *Lanc* 5D 96
Outwell. *Norf* 5E 77
Outwick. *Hants* 1G 15
Outwood. *Surr* 1E 27
Outwood. *W Yor* 2D 92
Outwood. *Worc* 3D 60
Outwoods. *Leics* 4B 74
Outwoods. *Staf* 4B 72
Ouzlewell Green. *W Yor* 2D 92
Ovenden. *W Yor* 2A 92
Over. *Cambs* 3C 64
Over. *Ches W* 4A 84
Over. *Glos* 4D 48
Over. *S Glo* 3A 34
Overbister. *Orkn* 3F 172
Over Burrows. *Derbs* 2G 73
Overbury. *Worc* 2E 49
Overcombe. *Dors* 4B 14
Over Compton. *Dors* 1A 14
Over End. *Cambs* 1H 63
Over Finlarg. *Ang* 4D 144
Overgreen. *Derbs* 3H 85
Over Green. *W Mid* 1F 61
Over Haddon. *Derbs* 4G 85
Over Hulton. *G Man* 4E 91
Over Kellet. *Lanc* 2E 97
Over Kiddington. *Oxon* 3C 50
Overleigh. *Som* 3H 21
Overley. *Staf* 4F 73
Over Monnow. *Mon* 4A 48
Over Norton. *Oxon* 3B 50
Over Peover. *Ches E* 3B 84
Overpool. *Ches W* 3F 83
Overscaig. *High* 1B 164
Overseal. *Derbs* 4G 73
Over Silton. *N Yor* 5B 106
Oversland. *Kent* 5E 41
Overstone. *Nptn* 4F 63
Over Stowey. *Som* 3E 21
Overstrand. *Norf* 1E 79
Over Stratton. *Som* 1H 13
Over Street. *Wilts* 3F 23
Overthorpe. *Nptn* 1C 50
Overton. *Aber* 2F 153
Overton. *Ches W* 3H 83
Overton. *Hants* 2D 24
Overton. *High* 5E 169
Overton. *Lanc* 4D 96
Overton. *N Yor* 4H 99
Overton. *Shrp* 2A 60
(nr. Bridgnorth)
Overton. *Shrp* 3H 59
(nr. Ludlow)
Overton. *Swan* 4D 30
Overton. *W Yor* 3C 92
Overton. *Wrex* 1F 71
Overtown. *N Lan* 4B 128
Overtown. *Swin* 4G 35
Over Wallop. *Hants* 3A 24
Over Whitacre. *Warw* 1G 61
Over Worton. *Oxon* 3C 50
Oving. *Buck* 3F 51
Oving. *W Sus* 5A 26
Ovingdean. *Brig* 5E 27
Ovingham. *Nmbd* 3D 115
Ovington. *Dur* 3E 105
Ovington. *Essx* 1A 54
Ovington. *Hants* 3D 24
Ovington. *Norf* 5B 78
Ovington. *Nmbd* 3D 114
Owen's Bank. *Staf* 3G 73
Ower. *Hants* 2C 16
(nr. Holbury)
Ower. *Hants* 1B 16
(nr. Totton)
Owermoigne. *Dors* 4C 14
Owlbury. *Shrp* 1F 59
Owler Bar. *Derbs* 3G 85
Owlerton. *S Yor* 2H 85
Owlsmoor. *Brac* 5G 37
Owlswick. *Buck* 5F 51
Owmby. *Linc* 4D 94
Owmby-by-Spital. *Linc* 2H 87
Ownham. *W Ber* 4C 36
Owrytn. *Wrex* 1F 71
Owslebury. *Hants* 4D 24
Owston. *Leics* 5E 75
Owston. *S Yor* 3F 93
Owston Ferry. *N Lin* 4B 94
Owstwick. *E Yor* 1F 95
Owthorne. *E Yor* 2G 95
Owthorpe. *Notts* 2D 74
Owton Manor. *Hart* 2B 106
Oxborough. *Norf* 5G 77
Oxbridge. *Dors* 3H 13
Oxcombe. *Linc* 3C 88
Oxen End. *Essx* 3G 53
Oxenhall. *Glos* 3C 48
Oxenholme. *Cumb* 5G 103
Oxenhope. *W Yor* 1A 92
Oxen Park. *Cumb* 1C 96
Oxenpill. *Som* 2H 21
Oxenton. *Glos* 2E 49
Oxenwood. *Wilts* 1B 24
Oxford. *Oxon* 5D 50
Oxgangs. *Edin* 3F 129
Oxhey. *Herts* 1C 38
Oxhill. *Warw* 1B 50
Oxley. *W Mid* 5C 72
Oxley Green. *Essx* 4C 54
Oxley's Green. *E Sus* 3A 28
Oxlode. *Cambs* 2D 65
Oxnam. *Bord* 3B 120
Oxshott. *Surr* 4C 38
Oxspring. *S Yor* 4C 92
Oxted. *Surr* 5E 39
Oxton. *Mers* 2E 83
Oxton. *N Yor* 5H 99
Oxton. *Notts* 5D 86
Oxton. *Bord* 4A 130
Oxwich. *Swan* 4D 31
Oxwich Green. *Swan* 4D 31
Oxwick. *Norf* 3B 78
Oykel Bridge. *High* 3A 164
Oyne. *Abers* 1D 152
Oystermouth. *Swan* 4F 31
Ozleworth. *Glos* 2C 34

P

Pabail Iarach. *W Isl* 4H 171
Pabail Uarach. *W Isl* 4H 171
Pachesham. *Surr* 5C 38
Packers Hill. *Dors* 1C 14
Packington. *Leics* 4A 74
Packmoor. *Stoke* 5C 84
Packmores. *Warw* 4G 61
Packwood. *W Mid* 3F 61
Packwood Gullett. *W Mid* 3F 61
Padanaram. *Ang* 3D 144
Padbury. *Buck* 2F 51
Paddington. *G Lon* 2D 38
Paddington. *Warr* 2A 84
Paddlesworth. *Kent* 2F 29
Paddock. *Kent* 5D 40
Paddockhole. *Dum* 1D 112
Paddock Wood. *Kent* 1A 28
Paddolgreen. *Shrp* 2H 71
Padeswood. *Flin* 4E 83
Padiham. *Lanc* 1F 91
Padside. *N Yor* 4D 98
Padson. *Devn* 3F 11
Padstow. *Corn* 1D 6
Padworth. *W Ber* 5E 36
Page Bank. *Dur* 1F 105
Pagham. *W Sus* 3G 17
Paglesham Churchend. *Essx* 1D 40
Paglesham Eastend. *Essx* 1D 40
Paibeil. *W Isl* 2C 170
(on North Uist)
Paibeil. *W Isl* 8C 171
(on Taransay)
Paignton. *Torb* 2E 9
Pailton. *Warw* 2B 62
Paine's Corner. *E Sus* 3H 27
Painleyhill. *Staf* 2E 73
Painscastle. *Powy* 1E 47
Painshawfield. *Nmbd* 3D 114
Painsthorpe. *E Yor* 4C 100
Painswick. *Glos* 5D 48
Painter's Forstal. *Kent* 5D 40
Painthorpe. *W Yor* 3D 92
Pairc Shiaboist. *W Isl* 3E 171
Paisley. *Ren* 3F 127
Pakefield. *Suff* 1H 67
Pakenham. *Suff* 4B 66
Pale. *Gwyn* 2B 70
Palehouse Common. *E Sus* 4F 27
Palestine. *Hants* 2A 24
Paley Street. *Wind* 4G 37
Palgowan. *Dum* 1A 110
Palgrave. *Suff* 3D 66
Pallington. *Dors* 3C 14
Palmarsh. *Kent* 2F 29
Palmer Moor. *Derbs* 2F 73
Palmers Cross. *W Mid* 5C 72
Palmerstown. *V Glam* 5E 33
Palnackie. *Dum* 4F 111
Palnure. *Dum* 3B 110
Palterton. *Derbs* 4B 86
Pamber End. *Hants* 1E 24
Pamber Green. *Hants* 1E 24
Pamber Heath. *Hants* 5E 36
Pamington. *Glos* 2E 49
Pamphill. *Dors* 2E 15
Pampisford. *Cambs* 1E 53
Panborough. *Som* 2H 21
Panbride. *Ang* 5E 145
Pancakehill. *Glos* 4F 49
Pancrasweek. *Devn* 2C 10
Pandy. *Gwyn* 3A 70
(nr. Bala)
Pandy. *Gwyn* 5F 69
(nr. Tywyn)
Pandy. *Mon* 3G 47
Pandy. *Powy* 5B 70
Pandy. *Wrex* 2D 70
Pandy Tudur. *Cnwy* 4A 82
Panfield. *Essx* 3H 53
Pangbourne. *W Ber* 4E 37
Pannal. *N Yor* 4F 99
Pannal Ash. *N Yor* 4E 99
Pannanich. *Abers* 4A 152
Pant. *Shrp* 3E 71
Pant. *Wrex* 1F 71
Pantasaph. *Flin* 3D 82
Pant Glas. *Gwyn* 1D 68
Pant-glas. *Shrp* 2E 71
Pantgwyn. *Carm* 3F 45
Pantgwyn. *Cdgn* 1C 44
Pant-lasau. *Swan* 3F 31
Panton. *Linc* 3A 88
Pant-pastynog. *Den* 4C 82
Pantperthog. *Gwyn* 5G 69
Pant-teg. *Carm* 3E 45
Pant-y-Caws. *Carm* 2F 43
Pant-y-dwr. *Powy* 3B 58
Pant-y-ffridd. *Powy* 5D 70
Pantyffynnon. *Carm* 4G 45
Pantygasseg. *Torf* 5F 47
Pant-y-llyn. *Carm* 4G 45
Pant-yr-awel. *B'end* 3C 32
Pant y Wacco. *Flin* 3D 82
Panxworth. *Norf* 4F 79
Papa Stour Airport. *Shet* 6C 173
Papa Westray Airport. *Orkn* 2D 172
Papcastle. *Cumb* 1C 102
Papigoe. *High* 3F 169
Papil. *Shet* 8E 173
Papple. *E Lot* 2B 130
Papplewick. *Notts* 5C 86
Papworth Everard. *Cambs* 4B 64
Papworth St Agnes. *Cambs* 4B 64
Par. *Corn* 3E 7
Paramour Street. *Kent* 4G 41
Parbold. *Lanc* 3C 90
Parbrook. *Som* 3A 22
Parbrook. *W Sus* 3B 26
Parc. *Gwyn* 2A 70
Parcllyn. *Cdgn* 5B 56
Parc-Seymour. *Newp* 2H 33
Pardown. *Hants* 2D 24
Pardshaw. *Cumb* 2B 102
Parham. *Suff* 4F 67
Park. *Abers* 4E 153
Park. *Arg* 4D 140
Park. *Dum* 5B 118
Park Bottom. *Corn* 4A 6
Parkburn. *Abers* 5E 161
Park Corner. *E Sus* 2G 27
Park Corner. *Oxon* 3E 37

Parkend—Pen-y-ffordd

Parkend. Glos 5B 48
Park End. Nmbd 2B 114
Parkeston. Essx 2F 55
Parkfield. Corn 2H 7
Parkgate. Ches W 3E 83
Parkgate. Cumb 5D 112
Parkgate. Dum 1B 112
Park Gate. Hants 2D 16
Parkgate. Surr 1D 26
Park Gate. Worc 3D 60
Parkhall. W Dun 2F 127
Parkham. Devn 4D 19
Parkham Ash. Devn 4D 18
Parkhead. Cumb 5E 113
Parkhead. Glas 3H 127
Park Hill. Mers 4C 90
Parkhouse. Mon 5H 47
Parkhurst. IOW 3C 16
Park Lane. G Man 4F 91
Park Lane. Staf 5C 72
Parkmill. Swan 4E 31
Park Mill. W Yor 3C 92
Parkneuk. Abers 1G 145
Parkside. N Lan 4B 128
Parkstone. Pool 3F 15
Park Street. Herts 5B 52
Park Street. W Sus 2C 26
Park Town. Oxon 5D 50
Park Village. Nmbd 3H 113
Parkway. Here 2C 48
Parley Cross. Dors 3F 15
Parmoor. Buck 3F 37
Parr. Mers 1H 83
Parracombe. Devn 2G 19
Parrog. Pemb 1E 43
Parsonage Green. Essx 4H 53
Parsonby. Cumb 1C 102
Parson Cross. S Yor 1A 86
Parson Drove. Cambs 5C 76
Partick. Glas 3G 127
Partington. G Man 1B 84
Partney. Linc 4D 88
Parton. Cumb 2A 102
(nr. Whitehaven)
Parton. Cumb 4D 112
(nr. Wigton)
Parton. Dum 2D 111
Partridge Green. W Sus 4C 26
Parwich. Derbs 5F 85
Passenham. Nptn 2F 51
Passfield. Hants 3G 25
Passingford Bridge. Essx 1G 39
Paston. Norf 2F 79
Pasturefields. Staf 3D 73
Patchacott. Devn 3E 11
Patcham. Brig 5E 27
Patchetts Green. Herts 1C 38
Patching. W Sus 5B 26
Patchole. Devn 2G 19
Patchway. S Glo 3B 34
Pateley Bridge. N Yor 3D 98
Pathe. Som 3G 21
Pathfinder Village. Devn 3B 12
Pathhead. Abers 2G 145
Pathhead. E Ayr 3F 117
Pathhead. Fife 4E 137
Pathhead. Midl 3G 129
Pathlow. Warw 5F 61
Path of Condie. Per 2C 136
Pathstruie. Per 2C 136
Patmore Heath. Herts 3E 53
Patna. E Ayr 3D 116
Patney. Wilts 1F 23
Patrick. IOM 3B 108
Patrick Brompton. N Yor 5F 105
Patrington. E Yor 2G 95
Patrington Haven. E Yor 2G 95
Patrixbourne. Kent 5F 41
Patterdale. Cumb 3E 103
Pattiesmuir. Fife 1D 129
Pattingham. Staf 1C 60
Pattishall. Nptn 5D 62
Pattiswick. Essx 3B 54
Patton Bridge. Cumb 5G 103
Paul. Corn 4B 4
Paulerspury. Nptn 1F 51
Paull. E Yor 2E 95
Paulton. Bath 1B 22
Pauperhaugh. Nmbd 5F 121
Pave Lane. Telf 4B 72
Pavenham. Bed 5G 63
Pawlett. Som 2G 21
Pawston. Nmbd 1C 120
Paxford. Glos 2G 49
Paxton. Bord 4F 131
Payhembury. Devn 2D 12
Paythorne. Lanc 4H 97
Payton. Som 4E 20
Peacehaven. E Sus 5F 27
Peak Dale. Derbs 3E 85
Peak Forest. Derbs 3F 85
Peak Hill. Linc 4B 76
Peakirk. Pet 5A 76
Pearsie. Ang 3C 144
Peasedown St John. Bath 1C 22
Peaseland Green. Norf 4C 78
Peasemore. W Ber 4C 36
Peasenhall. Suff 4F 67
Pease Pottage. W Sus 2D 26
Peaslake. Surr 1B 26
Peasley Cross. Mers 1H 83
Peasmarsh. E Sus 3C 28
Peasmarsh. Som 1G 13
Peasmarsh. Surr 1A 26
Peaston. E Lot 3H 129
Peastonbank. E Lot 3H 129
Peathill. Abers 2G 161
Peat Inn. Fife 3G 137
Peatling Magna. Leics 1C 62
Peatling Parva. Leics 2C 62
Peaton. Arg 1D 126
Peaton. Shrp 2H 59
Peats Corner. Suff 4D 66
Pebmarsh. Essx 2B 54
Pebworth. Worc 1G 49
Pecket Well. W Yor 2H 91
Peckforton. Ches E 5H 83
Peckham Bush. Kent 5A 40
Peckleton. Leics 5B 74
Pedair-ffordd. Powy 3D 70
Pedham. Norf 4F 79
Pedlinge. Kent 2F 29
Pedmore. W Mid 2D 60
Pedwell. Som 3H 21
Peebles. Bord 5F 129
Peel. IOM 3B 108
Peel. Bord 1G 119
Peel Common. Hants 2D 16
Peening Quarter. Kent 3C 28
Peggs Green. Leics 4B 74
Pegsdon. C Beds 2B 52
Pegswood. Nmbd 1F 115
Peinchorran. High 5E 155
Peinlich. High 3D 154
Pelaw. Tyne 3G 115
Pelcomb Bridge. Pemb 3D 42
Pelcomb Cross. Pemb 3D 42
Peldon. Essx 4C 54
Pelsall. W Mid 5E 73
Pelton. Dur 4F 115
Pelutho. Cumb 5C 112
Pelynt. Corn 3G 7
Pemberton. Carm 5F 45
Pembrey. Carm 5E 45
Pembridge. Here 5F 59
Pembroke. Pemb 4D 43
Pembroke Dock. Pemb 4D 42
Pembroke Ferry. Pemb 4D 43
Pembury. Kent 1H 27
Penallt. Mon 4A 48
Penally. Pemb 5F 43
Penalt. Here 3A 48
Penalum. Pemb 5F 43
Penare. Corn 4D 6
Penarth. V Glam 4E 33
Penbeagle. Corn 3C 4
Penberth. Corn 4B 4
Pen-bont Rhydybeddau. Cdgn 2F 57
Penbryn. Cdgn 5B 56
Pencader. Carm 2E 45
Pen-cae. Cdgn 5D 56
Pencaenewydd. Gwyn 1D 68
Pencaerau. Neat 3G 31
Pencaitland. E Lot 3H 129
Pencarnisiog. IOA 3C 80
Pencarreg. Carm 1F 45
Pencarrow. Corn 4B 10
Pencelli. Powy 3D 46
Pen-clawdd. Swan 3E 31
Pencoed. B'end 3C 32
Pencombe. Here 5H 59
Pencraig. Here 3A 48
Pencraig. Powy 3C 70
Pendeen. Corn 3A 4
Pendeford. W Mid 5D 72
Penderyn. Rhon 5C 46
Pendine. Carm 4G 43
Pendlebury. G Man 4F 91
Pendleton. G Man 1C 84
Pendleton. Lanc 1F 91
Pendock. Worc 2C 48
Pendoggett. Corn 5A 10
Pendomer. Som 1A 14
Pendoylan. V Glam 4D 32
Pendre. B'end 3C 32
Penegoes. Powy 5G 69
Penelewey. Corn 4C 6
Penffordd. Pemb 2E 43
Penffordd-Lâs. Powy 1A 58
Penfro. Pemb 4D 43
Pengam. Cphy 2E 33
Pengam. Card 4F 33
Penge. G Lon 3E 39
Pengelly. Corn 4A 10
Pengenffordd. Powy 2E 47
Pengorffwysfa. IOA 1D 80
Pengover Green. Corn 2G 7
Pengwern. Den 3C 82
Penhale. Corn 5D 5
(nr. Mullion)
Penhale. Corn 3D 6
(nr. St Austell)
Penhale Camp. Corn 3B 6
Penhallow. Corn 3B 6
Penhalvean. Corn 5B 6
Penhelig. Gwyn 1F 57
Penhill. Swin 3G 35
Penhow. Newp 2H 33
Penhurst. E Sus 4A 28
Peniarth. Gwyn 5F 69
Penicuik. Midl 3F 129
Peniel. Carm 3E 45
Penifiler. High 4D 155
Peninver. Arg 3B 122
Penisa'r Waun. Gwyn 4E 81
Penistone. S Yor 4C 92
Penketh. Warr 2H 83
Penkill. S Ayr 5B 116
Penkridge. Staf 4D 72
Penley. Wrex 2G 71
Penllech. Gwyn 2B 68
Penllergaer. Swan 3F 31
Pen-llyn. IOA 2C 80
Penmachno. Cnwy 5G 81
Penmaen. Swan 4E 31
Penmaenmawr. Cnwy 3G 81
Penmaenpool. Gwyn 4F 69
Penmaen Rhos. Cnwy 3A 82
Pen-marc. V Glam 5D 32
Penmark. V Glam 5D 32
Penmarth. Corn 5B 6
Penmon. IOA 2F 81
Penmorfa. Gwyn 1E 69
Penmyndd. IOA 3E 81
Penn. Buck 1A 38
Penn. Dors 3G 13
Penn. W Mid 1C 60
Pennal. Gwyn 5G 69
Pennan. Abers 2F 161
Pennant. Cdgn 4E 57
Pennant. Den 2C 70
Pennant. Gwyn 3B 70
Pennant. Powy 1A 58
Pennant Melangell. Powy 3C 70
Pennar. Pemb 4D 42
Pennard. Swan 4E 31
Pennerley. Shrp 1F 59
Pennington. Cumb 2B 96
Pennington. G Man 1A 84
Pennington. Hants 3B 16
Pennorth. Powy 3E 46
Penn Street. Buck 1A 38
Pennsylvania. Devn 3C 12
Pennsylvania. S Glo 4C 34
Penny Bridge. Cumb 1C 96
Pennycross. Plym 3A 8
Pennygate. Norf 3F 79
Pennyghael. Arg 1C 132
Penny Hill. Linc 3C 76
Pennylands. Lanc 4C 90
Pennymoor. Devn 1B 12
Pennyvenie. E Ayr 4D 117
Pennywell. Tyne 4G 115
Penparc. Cdgn 1C 44
Penparcau. Cdgn 2E 57
Penpedairheol. Cphy 2E 33
Penperlleni. Mon 5G 47
Penpillick. Corn 3E 7
Penpol. Corn 5C 6
Penpoll. Corn 3F 7
Penponds. Corn 3D 4
Penpont. Corn 5A 10
Penpont. Dum 5H 117
Penpont. Powy 3C 46
Penprysg. B'end 3C 32
Penquit. Devn 3C 8
Penrherber. Carm 1G 43
Penrhiw. Pemb 1C 44
Penrhiwceiber. Rhon 2D 32
Pen Rhiwfawr. Neat 4H 45
Penrhiw-llan. Cdgn 1D 44
Penrhiw-pal. Cdgn 1D 44
Penrhos. Gwyn 2C 68
Penrhos. Here 5F 59
Penrhos. IOA 2B 80
Penrhos. Mon 4H 47
Penrhos. Powy 4A 46
Penrhos Garnedd. Gwyn 3E 81
Penrhyn. IOA 1C 80
Penrhyn Bay. Cnwy 2H 81
Penrhyn-coch. Cdgn 2F 57
Penrhyndeudraeth. Gwyn 2F 69
Penrhyn Side. Cnwy 2H 81
Penrice. Swan 4D 31
Penrith. Cumb 2G 103
Penrose. Corn 1C 6
Penruddock. Cumb 2F 103
Penryn. Corn 5B 6
Pensarn. Carm 4E 45
Pen-sarn. Gwyn 3E 69
Pensax. Worc 4B 60
Pensby. Mers 2E 83
Penselwood. Som 3C 22
Pensford. Bath 5B 34
Pensham. Worc 1E 49
Penshaw. Tyne 4G 115
Penshurst. Kent 1G 27
Pensilva. Corn 2G 7
Pensnett. W Mid 2D 60
Penston. E Lot 2H 129
Penstone. Devn 2A 12
Pente-tafarn-y-fedw. Cnwy 4H 81
Pentewan. Corn 4E 6
Pentir. Gwyn 4E 81
Pentire. Corn 2B 6
Pentlepoir. Pemb 4F 43
Pentlow. Essx 1B 54
Pentney. Norf 4G 77
Penton Mewsey. Hants 2B 24
Pentraeth. IOA 3E 81
Pentre. Powy 1E 59
(nr. Church Stoke)
Pentre. Powy 2D 58
(nr. Kerry)
Pentre. Powy 2C 58
(nr. Mochdre)
Pentre. Rhon 2C 32
Pentre. Shrp 4F 71
Pentre. Wrex 2D 70
(nr. Llanfyllin)
Pentre. Wrex 1E 71
(nr. Rhosllanerchrugog)
Pentrebach. Carm 2B 46
Pentre-bach. Cdgn 1F 45
Pentrebach. Mer T 5D 46
Pentre-bach. Powy 2C 46
Pentrebach. Swan 5G 45
Pentre Berw. IOA 3D 80
Pentre-bont. Cnwy 5G 81
Pentrecagal. Carm 1D 44
Pentre-celyn. Den 5D 82
Pentre-clawdd. Shrp 2E 71
Pentreclwydau. Neat 5B 46
Pentre-cwrt. Carm 2D 45
Pentre Dolau Honddu. Powy 1C 46
Pentre-du. Cnwy 5G 81
Pentre-dwr. Swan 3F 31
Pentrefelin. Carm 3F 45
Pentrefelin. Cdgn 1G 45
Pentrefelin. Cnwy 3H 81
Pentrefelin. Gwyn 2E 69
Pentrefoelas. Cnwy 5A 82
Pentre Galar. Pemb 1F 43
Pentregat. Cdgn 5C 56
Pentre Gwenlais. Carm 4G 45
Pentre Gwynfryn. Gwyn 3E 69
Pentre Halkyn. Flin 3E 82
Pentre Hodre. Shrp 3F 59
Pentre-Llanrhaeadr. Den 4C 82
Pentre Llifior. Powy 1D 58
Pentrellwyn. IOA 2E 81
Pentre-llwyn-llwyd. Powy 5B 58
Pentre-llyn-cymmer. Cnwy 5B 82
Pentre Meyrick. V Glam 4C 32
Pentre-piod. Gwyn 2A 70
Pentre-poeth. Newp 3F 33
Pentre'r Beirdd. Powy 4D 70
Pentre'r-felin. Powy 2C 46
Pentre-ty-gwyn. Carm 2B 46
Pentre-uchaf. Gwyn 2C 68
Pentrich. Derbs 5A 86
Pentridge. Dors 1F 15
Pen-twyn. Cphy 5F 47
(nr. Oakdale)
Pentwyn. Cphy 5E 46
(nr. Rhymney)
Pentwyn. Card 3F 33
Pentyrch. Card 3E 32
Pentywyn. Carm 4G 43
Penuwch. Cdgn 4E 57
Penwithick. Corn 3E 7
Penwyllt. Powy 4B 46
Penybanc. Carm 4G 45
(nr. Ammanford)
Pen-y-banc. Carm 3G 45
(nr. Llandeilo)
Pen-y-bont. Carm 2H 43
Penybont. Powy 4D 58
(nr. Llandrindod Wells)
Pen-y-bont. Powy 3E 70
(nr. Llanfyllin)
Pen-y-Bont Ar Ogwr. B'end 3C 32
Penybontfawr. Powy 3C 70
Penybryn. Cphy 2E 33
Pen-y-bryn. Pemb 1B 44
Pen-y-bryn. Wrex 1E 71
Pen-y-cae. Powy 4B 46
Penycae. Wrex 1E 71
Pen-y-cae-mawr. Mon 2H 33
Penycaerau. Gwyn 3A 68
Pen-y-cefn. Flin 3D 82
Pen-y-clawdd. Mon 5H 47
Pen-y-coedcae. Rhon 3D 32
Penycwm. Pemb 2C 42
Pen-y-Darren. Mer T 5D 46
Pen-y-fai. B'end 3B 32
Penyffordd. Flin 4F 83
(nr. Mold)
Pen-y-ffordd. Flin 2D 82
(nr. Prestatyn)

Puttenham—Retire

Puttenham. Herts 4G 51
Puttenham. Surr 1A 26
Puttock End. Essx 1B 54
Puttock's End. Essx 4F 53
Puxey. Dors 1C 14
Puxton. N Som 5H 33
Pwll. Carm 5E 45
Pwll. Powy 5D 70
Pwllcrochan. Pemb 4D 42
Pwll-glas. Den 5D 82
Pwllgloyw. Powy 2D 46
Pwllheli. Gwyn 2C 68
Pwllmeyric. Mon 2A 34
Pwlltrap. Carm 3G 43
Pwll-y-glaw. Neat 2A 32
Pyecombe. W Sus 4D 27
Pye Corner. Herts 4E 53
Pye Corner. Newp 3G 33
Pye Green. Staf 4D 73
Pyewipe. NE Lin 3F 95
Pyle. B'end 3B 32
Pyle. IOW 5C 16
Pylle. Som 3B 22
Pymoor. Cambs 2D 65
Pymoor. Dors 3H 13
Pyrford. Surr 5B 38
Pyrford Village. Surr 5B 38
Pyrton. Oxon 2E 37
Pytchley. Nptn 3F 63
Pyworthy. Devn 2D 10

Q

Quabbs. Shrp 2E 58
Quadring. Linc 2B 76
Quadring Eaudike. Linc 2B 76
Quainton. Buck 3F 51
Quaking Houses. Dur 4E 115
Quarley. Hants 2A 24
Quarndon. Derbs 1H 73
Quarndon Common. Derbs 1H 73
Quarrendon. Buck 4G 51
Quarrier's Village. Inv 3E 127
Quarrington. Linc 1H 75
Quarrington Hill. Dur 1A 106
Quarry Bank. W Mid 2D 60
Quarry, The. Glos 2C 34
Quarrywood. Mor 2F 159
Quartalehouse. Abers 4G 161
Quarter. N Ayr 3C 126
Quarter. S Lan 4A 128
Quatford. Shrp 1B 60
Quatt. Shrp 2B 60
Quebec. Dur 5E 115
Quedgeley. Glos 4D 48
Queen Adelaide. Cambs 2E 65
Queenborough. Kent 3D 40
Queen Camel. Som 4A 22
Queen Charlton. Bath 5B 34
Queen Dart. Devn 1B 12
Queenhill. Worc 2D 48
Queen Oak. Dors 3C 22
Queensbury. W Yor 2B 92
Queensferry. Flin 4F 83
Queenstown. Bkpl 1B 90
Queen Street. Kent 1A 28
Queenzieburn. N Lan 2H 127
Quemerford. Wilts 5F 35
Quendale. Shet 10E 173
Quendon. Essx 2F 53
Queniborough. Leics 4D 74
Quenington. Glos 5G 49
Quernmore. Lanc 3E 97
Quethiock. Corn 2H 7
Quick's Green. W Ber 4D 36
Quidenham. Norf 2C 66
Quidhampton. Hants 1D 24
Quidhampton. Wilts 3G 23
Quilquox. Abers 5G 161
Quina Brook. Shrp 2H 71
Quine's Hill. IOM 4C 108
Quinton. Nptn 5E 63
Quinton. W Mid 2D 61
Quintrell Downs. Corn 2C 6
Quixhill. Staf 1F 73
Quoditch. Devn 3E 11
Quorn. Leics 4C 74
Quorndon. Leics 4C 74
Quothquan. S Lan 1B 118
Quoyloo. Orkn 5B 172
Quoyness. Orkn 7B 172

R

Rableyheath. Herts 4C 52
Raby. Cumb 4C 112
Raby. Mers 3F 83
Rachan Mill. Bord 1D 118
Rachub. Gwyn 4F 81
Rack End. Oxon 5C 50
Rackenford. Devn 1B 12
Rackham. W Sus 4B 26
Rackheath. Norf 4E 79
Racks. Dum 2B 112
Rackwick. Orkn 8A 172
(on Hoy)
Rackwick. Orkn 3D 172
(on Westray)
Radbourne. Derbs 2G 73
Radcliffe. G Man 4F 91
Radcliffe. Nmbd 4G 121
Radcliffe on Trent. Notts 2D 74
Radclive. Buck 2E 51
Radernie. Fife 2G 137
Radfall. Kent 4F 41
Radford. Bath 1B 22
Radford. Nott 1C 74
Radford. W Mid 2H 61
Radford. Worc 5E 61
Radford Semele. Warw 4H 61
Radipole. Dors 4B 14
Radlett. Herts 1C 38
Radley. Oxon 2D 36
Radnage. Buck 2F 37
Radstock. Bath 1B 22
Radstone. Nptn 1D 50
Radway. Warw 1B 50
Radway Green. Ches E 5B 84
Radwell. Bed 5H 63
Radwell. Herts 2C 52
Radwinter. Essx 2G 53
Radyr. Card 3E 33
RAF Coltishall. Norf 3E 79
Rafford. Mor 3E 159
Ragdale. Leics 4D 74
Ragdon. Shrp 1G 59
Ragged Appleshaw. Hants 2B 24
Raggra. High 4F 169
Raglan. Mon 5H 47
Ragnall. Notts 3F 87
Raigbeg. High 1C 150
Rainford. Mers 4C 90
Rainford Junction. Mers 4C 90
Rainham. G Lon 2G 39
Rainham. Medw 4C 40
Rainhill. Mers 1G 83
Rainow. Ches E 3D 84
Rainton. N Yor 2F 99
Rainworth. Notts 5C 86
Raisbeck. Cumb 4H 103
Raise. Cumb 5A 114
Rait. Per 1E 137
Raithby. Linc 2C 88
Raithby by Spilsby. Linc 4C 88
Raithwaite. N Yor 3F 107
Rake. W Sus 4G 25
Rake End. Staf 4E 73
Rakeway. Staf 1E 73
Rakewood. G Man 3H 91
Ralia. High 4B 150
Ram Alley. Wilts 5H 35
Ramasaig. High 4A 154
Rame. Corn 4A 8
(nr. Millbrook)
Rame. Corn 5B 6
(nr. Penryn)
Ram Lane. Kent 1D 28
Ramnageo. Shet 2H 173
Rampisham. Dors 2A 14
Rampside. Cumb 3B 96
Rampton. Cambs 4D 64
Rampton. Notts 3E 87
Ramsbottom. G Man 3F 91
Ramsburn. Mor 3C 160
Ramsbury. Wilts 4A 36
Ramscraigs. High 1H 165
Ramsdean. Hants 4F 25
Ramsdell. Hants 1D 24
Ramsden. Oxon 4B 50
Ramsden. Worc 1E 49
Ramsden Bellhouse. Essx 1B 40
Ramsden Heath. Essx 1B 40
Ramsey. Cambs 2B 64
Ramsey. Essx 2F 55
Ramsey. IOM 2D 108
Ramsey Forty Foot. Cambs 2C 64
Ramsey Heights. Cambs 2B 64
Ramsey Island. Essx 5C 54
Ramsey Mereside. Cambs 2B 64
Ramsey St Mary's. Cambs 2B 64
Ramsgate. Kent 4H 41
Ramsgill. N Yor 2D 98
Ramshaw. Dur 5C 114
Ramshorn. Staf 1E 73
Ramsley. Devn 3G 11
Ramsnest Common. Surr 2A 26
Ramstone. Abers 2D 152
Ranais. W Isl 5G 171
Ranby. Linc 3B 88
Ranby. Notts 2D 86
Rand. Linc 3A 88
Randwick. Glos 5D 48
Ranfurly. Ren 3E 127
Rangag. High 4D 168
Rangemore. Staf 3F 73
Rangeworthy. S Glo 3B 34
Rankinston. E Ayr 3D 116
Rank's Green. Essx 4H 53
Ranmore Common. Surr 5C 38
Rannoch Station. Per 3B 142
Ranochan. High 5G 147
Ranskill. Notts 2D 86
Ranton. Staf 3C 72
Ranton Green. Staf 3C 72
Ranworth. Norf 4F 79
Raploch. Stir 4G 135
Rapness. Orkn 3E 172
Rapps. Som 1G 13
Rascal Moor. E Yor 1B 94
Rascarrel. Dum 5E 111
Rashfield. Arg 1C 126
Rashwood. Worc 4D 60
Raskelf. N Yor 2G 99
Rassau. Blae 4E 47
Rastrick. W Yor 2B 92
Ratagan. High 2B 148
Ratby. Leics 5C 74
Ratcliffe Culey. Leics 1H 61
Ratcliffe on Soar. Notts 3B 74
Ratcliffe on the Wreake. Leics 4D 74
Rathen. Abers 2H 161
Rathillet. Fife 1F 137
Rathmell. N Yor 4H 97
Ratho. Edin 2E 129
Ratho Station. Edin 2E 129
Rathven. Mor 2B 160
Ratley. Hants 4B 24
Ratley. Warw 1B 50
Ratlinghope. Shrp 1G 59
Rattar. High 1E 169
Ratten Row. Cumb 5E 113
Ratten Row. Lanc 5D 96
Rattery. Devn 2D 8
Rattlesden. Suff 5B 66
Ratton Village. E Sus 5G 27
Rattray. Abers 3H 161
Rattray. Per 4A 144
Raughton. Cumb 5E 113
Raughton Head. Cumb 5E 113
Raunds. Nptn 3G 63
Ravenfield. S Yor 1B 86
Ravenglass. Cumb 5B 102
Ravenhills Green. Worc 5B 60
Raveningham. Norf 1F 67
Ravenscar. N Yor 4G 107
Ravensdale. IOM 2C 108
Ravensden. Bed 5H 63
Ravenseat. N Yor 4B 104
Ravenshead. Notts 5C 86
Ravensmoor. Ches E 5A 84
Ravensthorpe. Nptn 3D 62
Ravensthorpe. W Yor 2C 92
Ravenstone. Leics 4B 74
Ravenstone. Mil 5F 63
Ravenstonedale. Cumb 4A 104
Ravenstown. Cumb 2C 96
Ravenstruther. S Lan 5C 128
Ravensworth. N Yor 4E 105
Raw. N Yor 4G 107
Rawcliffe. E Yor 2G 93
Rawcliffe. York 4H 99
Rawcliffe Bridge. E Yor 2G 93
Rawdon. W Yor 1C 92
Rawgreen. Nmbd 4C 114
Rawmarsh. S Yor 1B 86
Rawnsley. Staf 4E 73
Rawreth. Essx 1B 40
Rawridge. Devn 2F 13
Rawson Green. Derbs 1A 74
Rawtenstall. Lanc 2F 91
Raydon. Suff 2D 54
Raylees. Nmbd 5D 120
Rayleigh. Essx 1C 40
Raymond's Hill. Devn 3G 13
Rayne. Essx 3H 53
Rayners Lane. G Lon 2C 38
Reach. Cambs 4E 65
Read. Lanc 1F 91
Reading. Read 4F 37
Reading Green. Suff 3D 66
Reading Street. Kent 2D 28
Readymoney. Corn 3F 7
Reagill. Cumb 3H 103
Rea Hill. Torb 3F 9
Rearquhar. High 4E 165
Rearsby. Leics 4D 74
Reasby. Linc 3H 87
Reaseheath. Ches E 5A 84
Reaster. High 2E 169
Reawick. Shet 7E 173
Reay. High 2B 168
Rechullin. High 3A 156
Reculver. Kent 4G 41
Redberth. Pemb 4E 43
Redbourn. Herts 4B 52
Redbourne. N Lin 4C 94
Redbrook. Glos 4A 48
Redbrook. Wrex 1H 71
Redburn. High 4D 158
Redburn. Nmbd 3A 114
Redcar. Red C 2D 106
Redcastle. High 4H 157
Redcliff Bay. N Som 4H 33
Red Dial. Cumb 5D 112
Redding. Falk 2C 128
Reddingmuirhead. Falk 2C 128
Reddings, The. Glos 3E 49
Reddish. G Man 1C 84
Redditch. Worc 4E 61
Rede. Suff 5H 65
Redenhall. Norf 2E 67
Redesdale Camp. Nmbd 5C 120
Redesmouth. Nmbd 1B 114
Redford. Ang 4E 145
Redford. Dur 1D 105
Redford. W Sus 4G 25
Redfordgreen. Bord 3F 119
Redgate. Corn 2G 7
Redgrave. Suff 3C 66
Redhill. Abers 3E 153
Redhill. Herts 2C 52
Redhill. N Som 5H 33
Redhill. Shrp 4B 72
Redhill. Surr 5D 39
Red Hill. Warw 5F 61
Red Hill. W Yor 2E 93
Redhouses. Arg 3B 124
Redisham. Suff 2G 67
Redland. Bris 4A 34
Redland. Orkn 5C 172
Redlingfield. Suff 3D 66
Red Lodge. Suff 3F 65
Redlynch. Som 3C 22
Redlynch. Wilts 4H 23
Redmain. Cumb 1C 102
Redmarley. Worc 4B 60
Redmarley D'Abitot. Glos 2C 48
Redmarshall. Stoc T 2A 106
Redmile. Leics 2E 75
Redmire. N Yor 5D 104
Rednal. Shrp 3F 71
Redpath. Bord 1H 119
Redpoint. High 2G 155
Red Post. Corn 2C 10
Red Rock. G Man 4D 90
Red Roses. Carm 3G 43
Red Row. Nmbd 5G 121
Redruth. Corn 4B 6
Red Street. Staf 5C 84
Redvales. G Man 4F 91
Red Wharf Bay. IOA 2E 81
Redwick. Newp 3H 33
Redwick. S Glo 3A 34
Redworth. Darl 2F 105
Reed. Herts 2D 52
Reed End. Herts 2D 52
Reedham. Linc 5B 88
Reedham. Norf 5G 79
Reedness. E Yor 2B 94
Reeds Beck. Linc 4B 88
Reemshill. Abers 4E 161
Reepham. Linc 3H 87
Reepham. Norf 3C 78
Reeth. N Yor 5D 104
Regaby. IOM 2D 108
Regil. N Som 5A 34
Regoul. High 3C 158
Reiff. High 2D 162
Reigate. Surr 5D 38
Reighton. N Yor 2F 101
Reilth. Shrp 2E 59
Reinigeadal. W Isl 7E 171
Reisque. Abers 1F 153
Reiss. High 3F 169
Rejerrah. Corn 3B 6
Releath. Corn 5A 6
Relubbus. Corn 3C 4
Relugas. Mor 4D 159
Remenham. Wok 3F 37
Remenham Hill. Wok 3F 37
Rempstone. Notts 3C 74
Rendcomb. Glos 5F 49
Rendham. Suff 4F 67
Rendlesham. Suff 5F 67
Renfrew. Ren 3G 127
Renhold. Bed 5H 63
Renishaw. Derbs 3B 86
Rennington. Nmbd 3G 121
Renton. W Dun 2E 127
Renwick. Cumb 5G 113
Repps. Norf 4G 79
Repton. Derbs 3H 73
Resaurie. High 4B 158
Rescassa. Corn 4D 6
Rescobie. Ang 3E 145
Rescorla. Corn 3E 7
(nr. Rosevean)
Rescorla. Corn 4D 6
(nr. St Ewe)
Resipole. High 2B 140
Resolfen. Neat 5B 46
Resolis. High 2A 158
Resolven. Neat 5B 46
Rest and be thankful. Arg 3B 134
Reston. Bord 3E 131
Restrop. Wilts 3F 35
Retford. Notts 2E 86
Retire. Corn 2E 6

Rettendon—Rorandle

Rettendon. *Essx* 1B 40
Retyn. *Corn* 3C 6
Revesby. *Linc* 4C 88
Rew. *Devn* 5D 8
Rewe. *Devn* 3C 12
Rew Street. *IOW* 3C 16
Rexon. *Devn* 4E 11
Reybridge. *Wilts* 5E 35
Reydon. *Suff* 3H 67
Reymerston. *Norf* 5C 78
Reynalton. *Pemb* 4E 43
Reynoldston. *Swan* 4D 31
Rezare. *Corn* 5D 10
Rhadyr. *Mon* 5G 47
Rhaeadr Gwy. *Powy* 4B 58
Rhandirmwyn. *Carm* 1A 46
Rhayader. *Powy* 4B 58
Rheindown. *High* 4H 157
Rhemore. *High* 3G 139
Rhenetra. *High* 3D 154
Rhewl. *Den* 1D 70
(nr. Llangollen)
Rhewl. *Den* 4D 82
(nr. Ruthin)
Rhewl. *Shrp* 2F 71
Rhewl-Mostyn. *Flin* 3D 82
Rhian. *High* 2C 164
Rhian Breck. *High* 3C 164
Rhicarn. *High* 1E 163
Rhiconich. *High* 3C 166
Rhicullen. *High* 1A 158
Rhidorroch. *High* 4F 163
Rhifail. *High* 4H 167
Rhigos. *Rhon* 5C 46
Rhilochan. *High* 3E 165
Rhiroy. *High* 5F 163
Rhitongue. *High* 3G 167
Rhiw. *Gwyn* 3B 68
Rhiwabon. *Wrex* 1F 71
Rhiwbina. *Card* 3E 33
Rhiwbryfdir. *Gwyn* 1F 69
Rhiwderin. *Newp* 3F 33
Rhiwlas. *Gwyn* 2B 70
(nr. Bala)
Rhiwlas. *Gwyn* 4E 81
(nr. Bangor)
Rhiwlas. *Powy* 2D 70
Rhodes. *G Man* 4G 91
Rhodesia. *Notts* 2C 86
Rhodes Minnis. *Kent* 1F 29
Rhodiad-y-Brenin. *Pemb* 2B 42
Rhondda. *Rhon* 2C 32
Rhonehouse. *Dum* 4E 111
Rhoose. *V Glam* 5D 32
Rhos. *Carm* 2D 45
Rhos. *Neat* 5H 45
Rhosaman. *Carm* 4H 45
Rhoscefnhir. *IOA* 3E 81
Rhoscolyn. *IOA* 3B 80
Rhos Common. *Powy* 4E 71
Rhoscrowther. *Pemb* 4D 42
Rhos-ddu. *Gwyn* 2B 68
Rhosdylluan. *Gwyn* 3A 70
Rhosesmor. *Flin* 4E 82
Rhos-fawr. *Gwyn* 2C 68
Rhosgadfan. *Gwyn* 5E 81
Rhosgoch. *IOA* 2D 80
Rhosgoch. *Powy* 1E 47
Rhos Haminiog. *Cdgn* 4E 57
Rhos-hill. *Pemb* 1B 44
Rhoshirwaun. *Gwyn* 3A 68
Rhoslan. *Gwyn* 1D 69
Rhoslefain. *Gwyn* 5E 69
Rhosllanerchrugog. *Wrex* 1E 71
Rhos Lligwy. *IOA* 2D 81
Rhosmaen. *Carm* 3G 45
Rhosmeirch. *IOA* 3D 80
Rhosneigr. *IOA* 3C 80
Rhos-on-Sea. *Cnwy* 2H 81
Rhossili. *Swan* 4D 30
Rhosson. *Pemb* 2B 42
Rhos, The. *Pemb* 3E 43
Rhostrenwfa. *IOA* 3D 80
Rhostryfan. *Gwyn* 5D 81
Rhostyllen. *Wrex* 1F 71
Rhoswiel. *Shrp* 2E 71
Rhosybol. *IOA* 2D 80
Rhos-y-brithdir. *Powy* 3D 70
Rhos-y-garth. *Cdgn* 3F 57
Rhos-y-gwaliau. *Gwyn* 2B 70
Rhos-y-llan. *Gwyn* 2B 68
Rhos-y-meirch. *Powy* 4E 59
Rhu. *Arg* 1D 126
Rhuallt. *Den* 3C 82
Rhubadach. *Arg* 2B 126
Rhubha Stoer. *High* 1E 163
Rhuddall Heath. *Ches W* 4H 83
Rhuddlan. *Cdgn* 1E 45
Rhuddlan. *Den* 3C 82
Rhue. *High* 4E 163
Rhulen. *Powy* 1E 47
Rhunahaorine. *Arg* 5F 125
Rhuthun. *Den* 5D 82
Rhuvoult. *High* 3C 166
Rhyd. *Gwyn* 1F 69
Rhydaman. *Carm* 4G 45
Rhydargaeau. *Carm* 3E 45
Rhydcymerau. *Carm* 2F 45
Rhydd. *Worc* 1D 48
Rhyd-Ddu. *Gwyn* 5E 81
Rhydding. *Neat* 3G 31
Rhydfudr. *Cdgn* 4E 57
Rhydlanfair. *Cnwy* 5H 81
Rhydlewis. *Cdgn* 1D 44
Rhydlios. *Gwyn* 2A 68
Rhydlydan. *Cnwy* 5A 82
Rhyd-meirionydd. *Cdgn* 2F 57
Rhydowen. *Cdgn* 1E 45
Rhyd-Rosser. *Cdgn* 4E 57
Rhydspence. *Powy* 1F 47
Rhydtalog. *Flin* 5E 83
Rhyd-uchaf. *Gwyn* 2B 70
Rhydwyn. *IOA* 2C 80
Rhyd-y-clafdy. *Gwyn* 2C 68
Rhydycroesau. *Shrp* 2E 71
Rhydyfelin. *Cdgn* 3E 57
Rhydyfelin. *Rhon* 3E 32
Rhyd-y-foel. *Cnwy* 3B 82
Rhyd-y-fro. *Neat* 5H 45
Rhydymain. *Gwyn* 3H 69
Rhyd-y-meirch. *Mon* 5G 47
Rhyd-y-meudwy. *Den* 5D 82
Rhydymwyn. *Flin* 4E 82
Rhyd-yr-onen. *Gwyn* 5F 69
Rhyd-y-sarn. *Gwyn* 1F 69
Rhyl. *Den* 2C 82
Rhymney. *Cphy* 5E 46
Rhymni. *Cphy* 5E 46
Rhynd. *Per* 1D 136
Rhynie. *Abers* 1B 152
Ribbesford. *Worc* 3B 60
Ribbleton. *Lanc* 1D 90
Ribby. *Lanc* 1C 90
Ribchester. *Lanc* 1E 91
Riber. *Derbs* 5H 85
Ribigill. *High* 3F 167
Riby. *Linc* 4E 95
Riccall. *N Yor* 1G 93
Riccarton. *E Ayr* 1D 116
Richards Castle. *Here* 4G 59
Richborough Port. *Kent* 4H 41
Richings Park. *Buck* 3B 38
Richmond. *G Lon* 3C 38
Richmond. *N Yor* 4E 105
Rickarton. *Abers* 5F 153
Rickerby. *Cumb* 4F 113
Rickerscote. *Staf* 3D 72
Rickford. *N Som* 1H 21
Rickham. *Devn* 5D 8
Rickinghall. *Suff* 3C 66
Rickleton. *Tyne* 4F 115
Rickling. *Essx* 2E 53
Rickling Green. *Essx* 3F 53
Rickmansworth. *Herts* 1B 38
Riddings. *Derbs* 5B 86
Riddlecombe. *Devn* 1G 11
Riddlesden. *W Yor* 5C 98
Ridge. *Dors* 4E 15
Ridge. *Herts* 5C 52
Ridge. *Wilts* 3E 23
Ridgebourne. *Powy* 4C 58
Ridge Lane. *Warw* 1G 61
Ridgeway. *Derbs* 5A 86
(nr. Alfreton)
Ridgeway. *Derbs* 2B 86
(nr. Sheffield)
Ridgeway. *Staf* 5C 84
Ridgeway Cross. *Here* 1C 48
Ridgeway Moor. *Derbs* 2B 86
Ridgewell. *Essx* 1H 53
Ridgewood. *E Sus* 3F 27
Ridgmont. *C Beds* 2H 51
Ridgwardine. *Shrp* 2A 72
Riding Mill. *Nmbd* 3D 114
Ridley. *Kent* 4H 39
Ridley. *Nmbd* 3A 114
Ridlington. *Norf* 2F 79
Ridlington. *Rut* 5F 75
Ridsdale. *Nmbd* 1C 114
Riemore Lodge. *Per* 4H 143
Rievaulx. *N Yor* 1H 99
Rift House. *Hart* 1B 106
Rigg. *Dum* 3D 112
Riggend. *N Lan* 2A 128
Rigmaden Park. *Cumb* 1F 97
Rigsby. *Linc* 3D 88
Rigside. *S Lan* 1A 118
Riley Green. *Lanc* 2E 90
Rileyhill. *Staf* 4F 73
Rilla Mill. *Corn* 5C 10
Rillington. *N Yor* 2C 100
Rimington. *Lanc* 5H 97
Rimpton. *Som* 4B 22
Rimsdale. *High* 4H 167
Rimswell. *E Yor* 2G 95
Ringasta. *Shet* 10E 173
Ringford. *Dum* 4D 111
Ringing Hill. *Leics* 4B 74
Ringinglow. *S Yor* 2G 85
Ringland. *Norf* 4D 78
Ringlestone. *Kent* 5C 40
Ringmer. *E Sus* 4F 27
Ringmore. *Devn* 4C 8
(nr. Kingsbridge)
Ringmore. *Devn* 5C 12
(nr. Teignmouth)
Ring o' Bells. *Lanc* 3C 90
Ring's End. *Cambs* 5C 76
Ringsfield. *Suff* 2G 67
Ringsfield Corner. *Suff* 2G 67
Ringshall. *Buck* 4H 51
Ringshall. *Suff* 5C 66
Ringshall Stocks. *Suff* 5C 66
Ringstead. *Norf* 1G 77
Ringstead. *Nptn* 3G 63
Ringwood. *Hants* 2G 15
Ringwould. *Kent* 1H 29
Rinmore. *Abers* 2B 152
Rinnigill. *Orkn* 8C 172
Rinsey. *Corn* 4C 4
Riof. *W Isl* 4D 171
Ripe. *E Sus* 4G 27
Ripley. *Derbs* 1B 74
Ripley. *Hants* 3G 15
Ripley. *N Yor* 3E 99
Ripley. *Surr* 5B 38
Riplingham. *E Yor* 1C 94
Riplington. *Hants* 4E 25
Ripon. *N Yor* 2F 99
Rippingale. *Linc* 3H 75
Ripple. *Kent* 1H 29
Ripple. *Worc* 2D 48
Ripponden. *W Yor* 3A 92
Rireavach. *High* 4E 163
Risabus. *Arg* 5B 124
Risbury. *Here* 5H 59
Risby. *E Yor* 1D 94
Risby. *N Lin* 3C 94
Risby. *Suff* 4G 65
Risca. *Cphy* 2F 33
Rise. *E Yor* 5F 101
Riseden. *E Sus* 2H 27
Riseden. *Kent* 2B 28
Rise End. *Derbs* 5G 85
Risegate. *Linc* 2B 76
Riseholme. *Linc* 3G 87
Riseley. *Bed* 4H 63
Riseley. *Wok* 5F 37
Rishangles. *Suff* 4D 66
Rishton. *Lanc* 1F 91
Rishworth. *W Yor* 3A 92
Risley. *Derbs* 2B 74
Risley. *Warr* 1A 84
Risplith. *N Yor* 3E 99
Rispond. *High* 2E 167
Rivar. *Wilts* 5B 36
Rivenhall. *Essx* 4B 54
Rivenhall End. *Essx* 4B 54
River. *Kent* 1G 29
River. *W Sus* 3A 26
River Bank. *Cambs* 4E 65
Riverhead. *Kent* 5G 39
Rivington. *Lanc* 3E 91
Roach Bridge. *Lanc* 2D 90
Roachill. *Devn* 4B 20
Roade. *Nptn* 5E 63
Road Green. *Norf* 1E 67
Roadhead. *Cumb* 2G 113
Roadmeetings. *S Lan* 5B 128
Roadside. *High* 2D 168
Roadside of Catterline. *Abers* 1H 145
Roadside of Kinneff. *Abers* 1H 145
Roadwater. *Som* 3D 20
Road Weedon. *Nptn* 5D 62
Roag. *High* 4B 154
Roa Island. *Cumb* 3B 96
Roath. *Card* 4E 33
Roberton. *Bord* 3G 119
Roberton. *S Lan* 2B 118
Robertsbridge. *E Sus* 3B 28
Robertstown. *Mor* 4G 159
Robertstown. *Rhon* 5C 46
Roberttown. *W Yor* 2B 92
Robeston Back. *Pemb* 3E 43
Robeston Wathen. *Pemb* 3E 43
Robeston West. *Pemb* 4C 42
Robin Hood. *Lanc* 3D 90
Robin Hood. *W Yor* 2D 92
Robin Hood Airport Doncaster Sheffield. *S Yor* 1D 86
Robinhood End. *Essx* 2H 53
Robin Hood's Bay. *N Yor* 4G 107
Roborough. *Devn* 1F 11
(nr. Great Torrington)
Roborough. *Devn* 2B 8
(nr. Plymouth)
Rob Roy's House. *Arg* 2A 134
Roby Mill. *Lanc* 4D 90
Rocester. *Staf* 2F 73
Roch. *Pemb* 2C 42
Rochdale. *G Man* 3G 91
Roche. *Corn* 2D 6
Rochester. *Medw* 4B 40
Rochester. *Nmbd* 5C 120
Rochford. *Essx* 1C 40
Rock. *Corn* 1D 6
Rock. *Nmbd* 2G 121
Rock. *W Sus* 4C 26
Rock. *Worc* 3B 60
Rockbeare. *Devn* 3D 12
Rockbourne. *Hants* 1G 15
Rockcliffe. *Cumb* 3E 113
Rockcliffe. *Dum* 4F 111
Rockcliffe Cross. *Cumb* 3E 113
Rock Ferry. *Mers* 2F 83
Rockfield. *High* 5G 165
Rockfield. *Mon* 4H 47
Rockford. *Hants* 2G 15
Rockgreen. *Shrp* 3H 59
Rockhampton. *S Glo* 2B 34
Rockhead. *Corn* 4A 10
Rockingham. *Nptn* 1F 63
Rockland All Saints. *Norf* 1B 66
Rockland St Mary. *Norf* 5F 79
Rockland St Peter. *Norf* 1B 66
Rockley. *Wilts* 4G 35
Rockwell End. *Buck* 3F 37
Rockwell Green. *Som* 1E 13
Rodborough. *Glos* 5D 48
Rodbourne. *Wilts* 3E 35
Rodd. *Here* 4F 59
Roddam. *Nmbd* 2E 121
Rodden. *Dors* 4B 14
Roddenloft. *E Ayr* 2D 117
Roddymoor. *Dur* 1E 105
Rode. *Som* 1D 22
Rodeheath. *Ches E* 4C 84
(nr. Congleton)
Rode Heath. *Ches E* 5C 84
(nr. Kidsgrove)
Roden. *Telf* 4H 71
Rodhuish. *Som* 3D 20
Rodington. *Telf* 4H 71
Rodington Heath. *Telf* 4H 71
Rodley. *Glos* 4C 48
Rodmarton. *Glos* 2E 35
Rodmell. *E Sus* 5F 27
Rodmersham. *Kent* 4D 40
Rodmersham Green. *Kent* 4D 40
Rodney Stoke. *Som* 2H 21
Rodsley. *Derbs* 1G 73
Rodway. *Som* 2F 21
Rodway. *Telf* 4A 72
Rodwell. *Dors* 5B 14
Roecliffe. *N Yor* 3F 99
Roe Green. *Herts* 2D 52
Roehampton. *G Lon* 3D 38
Roffey. *W Sus* 2C 26
Rogart. *High* 3E 165
Rogate. *W Sus* 4G 25
Roger Ground. *Cumb* 5E 103
Rogerstone. *Newp* 3F 33
Roghadal. *W Isl* 9C 171
Rogiet. *Mon* 3H 33
Rogue's Alley. *Cambs* 5C 76
Roke. *Oxon* 2E 37
Rokemarsh. *Oxon* 2E 36
Roker. *Tyne* 4H 115
Rollesby. *Norf* 4G 79
Rolleston. *Leics* 5E 75
Rolleston. *Notts* 5E 87
Rolleston on Dove. *Staf* 3G 73
Rolston. *E Yor* 5G 101
Rolvenden. *Kent* 2C 28
Rolvenden Layne. *Kent* 2C 28
Romaldkirk. *Dur* 2C 104
Roman Bank. *Shrp* 1H 59
Romanby. *N Yor* 5A 106
Roman Camp. *W Lot* 2D 129
Romannobridge. *Bord* 5E 129
Romansleigh. *Devn* 4H 19
Romers Common. *Worc* 4H 59
Romesdal. *High* 3D 154
Romford. *Dors* 2F 15
Romford. *G Lon* 2G 39
Romiley. *G Man* 1D 84
Romsey. *Hants* 4B 24
Romsley. *Shrp* 2B 60
Romsley. *Worc* 3D 60
Ronague. *IOM* 4B 108
Rookby. *Cumb* 3B 104
Rookhope. *Dur* 5C 114
Rooking. *Cumb* 3F 103
Rookley. *IOW* 4D 16
Rooks Bridge. *Som* 1G 21
Rooksey Green. *Suff* 5B 66
Rook's Nest. *Som* 3D 20
Rookwood. *W Sus* 3F 17
Roos. *E Yor* 1F 95
Roosebeck. *Cumb* 3B 96
Roosecote. *Cumb* 3B 96
Rootfield. *High* 3H 157
Rootham's Green. *Bed* 5A 64
Rootpark. *S Lan* 4C 128
Ropley. *Hants* 3E 25
Ropley Dean. *Hants* 3E 25
Ropsley. *Linc* 2G 75
Rora. *Abers* 3H 161
Rorandle. *Abers* 2D 152

Skinidin—South Pickenham

Skinidin. *High* 4B **154**
Skinnet. *High* 2F **167**
Skinningrove. *Red C* 2E **107**
Skipness. *Arg* 4G **125**
Skippool. *Lanc* 5C **96**
Skiprigg. *Cumb* 5E **113**
Skipsea. *E Yor* 4F **101**
Skipsea Brough. *E Yor* 4F **101**
Skipton. *N Yor* 4B **98**
Skipton-on-Swale. *N Yor* 2F **99**
Skipwith. *N Yor* 1G **93**
Skirbeck. *Linc* 1C **76**
Skirbeck Quarter. *Linc* 1C **76**
Skirlaugh. *E Yor* 1E **95**
Skirling. *Bord* 1C **118**
Skirmett. *Buck* 2F **37**
Skirpenbeck. *E Yor* 4B **100**
Skirwith. *Cumb* 1H **103**
Skirwith. *N Yor* 2G **97**
Skirza. *High* 2F **169**
Skitby. *Cumb* 3F **113**
Skitham. *Lanc* 5D **96**
Skittle Green. *Buck* 5F **51**
Skulamus. *High* 1E **147**
Skullomie. *High* 2G **167**
Skyborry Green. *Shrp* 3E **59**
Skye Green. *Essx* 3B **54**
Skye of Curr. *High* 1D **151**
Slack. *W Yor* 2H **91**
Slackhall. *Derbs* 2E **85**
Slack Head. *Cumb* 2D **97**
Slackhead. *Mor* 2B **160**
Slackholme End. *Linc* 3E **89**
Slacks of Cairnbanno. *Abers* 4F **161**
Slack, The. *Dur* 2E **105**
Slad. *Glos* 5D **48**
Slade. *Swan* 4D **31**
Slade End. *Oxon* 2D **36**
Slade Field. *Cambs* 2C **64**
Slade Green. *G Lon* 3G **39**
Slade Heath. *Staf* 5D **72**
Slade Hooton. *S Yor* 2C **86**
Sladesbridge. *Corn* 5A **10**
Slade, The. *W Ber* 5D **36**
Slaggyford. *Nmbd* 4H **113**
Slaidburn. *Lanc* 4G **97**
Slaid Hill. *W Yor* 5F **99**
Slaithwaite. *W Yor* 3A **92**
Slaley. *Derbs* 5G **85**
Slaley. *Nmbd* 4C **114**
Slamannan. *Falk* 2B **128**
Slapton. *Buck* 3H **51**
Slapton. *Devn* 4E **9**
Slapton. *Nptn* 1E **51**
Slattock. *G Man* 4G **91**
Slaugham. *W Sus* 3D **26**
Slaughterbridge. *Corn* 4B **10**
Slaughterford. *Wilts* 4D **34**
Slawston. *Leics* 1E **63**
Sleaford. *Hants* 3G **25**
Sleaford. *Linc* 1H **75**
Sleagill. *Cumb* 3G **103**
Sleap. *Shrp* 3G **71**
Sledmere. *E Yor* 3D **100**
Sleightholme. *Dur* 3C **104**
Sleights. *N Yor* 4F **107**
Slepe. *Dors* 3E **15**
Slickly. *High* 2E **169**
Sliddery. *N Ayr* 3D **122**
Sligachan. *High* 1C **146**
Slimbridge. *Glos* 5C **48**
Slindon. *Staf* 2C **72**
Slindon. *W Sus* 5A **26**
Slinfold. *W Sus* 2C **26**
Slingsby. *N Yor* 2A **100**
Slip End. *C Beds* 4A **52**
Slipton. *Nptn* 3G **63**
Slitting Mill. *Staf* 4E **73**
Slochd. *High* 1C **150**
Slockavullin. *Arg* 4F **133**
Sloley. *Norf* 3E **79**
Sloncombe. *Devn* 4H **11**
Sloothby. *Linc* 3D **89**
Slough. *Slo* 2A **38**
Slough Green. *Som* 4F **21**
Slough Green. *W Sus* 3D **27**
Sluggan. *High* 1C **150**
Slyne. *Lanc* 3D **97**
Smailholm. *Bord* 1A **120**
Smallbridge. *G Man* 3H **91**
Smallbrook. *Devn* 3B **12**
Smallburgh. *Norf* 3F **79**
Smallburn. *E Ayr* 2F **117**
Smalldale. *Derbs* 3E **85**
Small Dole. *W Sus* 4D **26**
Smalley. *Derbs* 1B **74**
Smallfield. *Surr* 1E **27**
Small Heath. *W Mid* 2E **61**
Smallholm. *Dum* 2C **112**
Small Hythe. *Kent* 2C **28**
Smallrice. *Staf* 2D **72**
Smallridge. *Devn* 2G **13**
Smallwood Hey. *Lanc* 5C **96**
Smallworth. *Norf* 2C **66**
Smannell. *Hants* 2B **24**
Smardale. *Cumb* 4A **104**
Smarden. *Kent* 1C **28**
Smarden Bell. *Kent* 1C **28**
Smart's Hill. *Kent* 1G **27**
Smeatharpe. *Devn* 1F **13**
Smeeth. *Kent* 2E **29**
Smeeth, The. *Norf* 4E **77**
Smeeton Westerby. *Leics* 1D **62**
Smeircleit. *W Isl* 7C **170**
Smerral. *High* 5D **168**
Smestow. *Staf* 1C **60**
Smethwick. *W Mid* 2E **61**
Smirisary. *High* 1A **140**
Smisby. *Derbs* 4H **73**
Smitham Hill. *Bath* 1A **22**
Smith End Green. *Worc* 5B **60**
Smithfield. *Cumb* 3F **113**
Smith Green. *Lanc* 4D **97**
Smithies, The. *Shrp* 1A **60**
Smithincott. *Devn* 1D **12**
Smith's Green. *Essx* 3F **53**
Smithstown. *High* 1G **155**
Smithton. *High* 4B **158**
Smithwood Green. *Suff* 5B **66**
Smithy Bridge. *G Man* 3H **91**
Smithy Green. *Ches E* 3B **84**
Smithy Lane Ends. *Lanc* 3C **90**
Smockington. *Warw* 2B **62**
Smyth's Green. *Essx* 4C **54**
Snaigow House. *Per* 4H **143**
Snailbeach. *Shrp* 5F **71**
Snailwell. *Cambs* 4F **65**
Snainton. *N Yor* 1D **100**
Snaith. *E Yor* 2G **93**
Snape. *N Yor* 1E **99**
Snape. *Suff* 5F **67**
Snape Green. *Lanc* 3B **90**
Snapper. *Devn* 3F **19**
Snarestone. *Leics* 5H **73**
Snarford. *Linc* 2H **87**
Snargate. *Kent* 3D **28**
Snave. *Kent* 3E **28**
Sneachill. *Worc* 5D **60**
Snead. *Powy* 1F **59**
Snead Common. *Worc* 4B **60**
Sneaton. *N Yor* 4F **107**
Sneatonthorpe. *N Yor* 4G **107**
Snelland. *Linc* 2H **87**
Snelston. *Derbs* 1F **73**
Snetterton. *Norf* 1B **66**
Snettisham. *Norf* 2F **77**
Snibston. *Leics* 4B **74**
Sniseabhal. *W Isl* 5C **170**
Snitter. *Nmbd* 4E **121**
Snitterby. *Linc* 1G **87**
Snitterfield. *Warw* 5G **61**
Snitton. *Shrp* 3H **59**
Snodhill. *Here* 1G **47**
Snodland. *Kent* 4A **40**
Snods Edge. *Nmbd* 4D **114**
Snowshill. *Glos* 2F **49**
Snow Street. *Norf* 2C **66**
Snydale. *W Yor* 3E **93**
Soake. *Hants* 1E **17**
Soar. *Carm* 3G **45**
Soar. *Gwyn* 2F **69**
Soar. *IOA* 3C **80**
Soar. *Powy* 2C **46**
Soberton. *Hants* 1E **16**
Soberton Heath. *Hants* 1E **16**
Sockbridge. *Cumb* 2F **103**
Sockburn. *Darl* 4A **106**
Sodom. *Den* 3C **82**
Soham. *Cambs* 3E **65**
Soham Cotes. *Cambs* 3E **65**
Solas. *W Isl* 1D **170**
Soldon Cross. *Devn* 1D **10**
Soldridge. *Hants* 3E **25**
Solent Breezes. *Hants* 2D **16**
Sole Street. *Kent* 4A **40**
(nr. Meopham)
Sole Street. *Kent* 1E **29**
(nr. Waltham)
Solihull. *W Mid* 3F **61**
Sollers Dilwyn. *Here* 5G **59**
Sollers Hope. *Here* 2B **48**
Sollom. *Lanc* 3C **90**
Solva. *Pemb* 2B **42**
Somerby. *Leics* 4E **75**
Somerby. *Linc* 4D **94**
Somercotes. *Derbs* 5B **86**
Somerford. *Dors* 3G **15**
Somerford. *Staf* 5C **72**
Somerford Keynes. *Glos* 2F **35**
Somerley. *W Sus* 3G **17**
Somerleyton. *Suff* 1G **67**
Somersal Herbert. *Derbs* 2F **73**
Somersby. *Linc* 3C **88**
Somersham. *Cambs* 3C **64**
Somersham. *Suff* 1D **54**
Somerton. *Oxon* 3C **50**
Somerton. *Som* 4H **21**
Somerton. *Suff* 5H **65**
Sompting. *W Sus* 5C **26**
Sonning. *Wok* 4F **37**
Sonning Common. *Oxon* 3F **37**
Sookholme. *Notts* 4C **86**
Sopley. *Hants* 3G **15**
Sopworth. *Wilts* 3D **34**
Sorbie. *Dum* 5B **110**
Sordale. *High* 2D **168**
Sorisdale. *Arg* 2D **138**
Sorn. *E Ayr* 2E **117**
Sornhill. *E Ayr* 1E **117**
Sortat. *High* 2E **169**
Sotby. *Linc* 3B **88**
Sots Hole. *Linc* 4A **88**
Sotterley. *Suff* 2G **67**
Soudley. *Shrp* 1G **59**
(nr. Church Stretton)
Soudley. *Shrp* 3B **72**
(nr. Market Drayton)
Soughton. *Flin* 4E **83**
Soulbury. *Buck* 3G **51**
Soulby. *Cumb* 3A **104**
(nr. Appleby)
Soulby. *Cumb* 2F **103**
(nr. Penrith)
Souldern. *Oxon* 2D **50**
Souldrop. *Bed* 4G **63**
Sound. *Shet* 7F **173**
Soundwell. *Bris* 4B **34**
Sourhope. *Bord* 2C **120**
Sourin. *Orkn* 4D **172**
Sourton. *Devn* 3F **11**
Soutergate. *Cumb* 1B **96**
South Acre. *Norf* 4H **77**
Southall. *G Lon* 3C **38**
South Allington. *Devn* 5D **9**
South Alloa. *Falk* 4A **136**
Southam. *Glos* 3E **49**
Southam. *Warw* 4B **62**
South Ambersham. *W Sus* 3A **26**
Southampton. *Sotn* 1C **16**
Southampton International Airport. *Hants* 1C **16**
Southannan. *N Ayr* 4D **126**
South Anston. *S Yor* 2C **86**
South Ascot. *Wind* 4A **38**
South Baddesley. *Hants* 3B **16**
South Balfern. *Dum* 4B **110**
South Ballachulish. *High* 3E **141**
South Bank. *Red C* 2C **106**
South Barrow. *Som* 4B **22**
South Benfleet. *Essx* 2B **40**
South Bents. *Tyne* 3H **115**
South Bersted. *W Sus* 5A **26**
Southborough. *Kent* 1G **27**
Southbourne. *Bour* 3G **15**
Southbourne. *W Sus* 2F **17**
South Bowood. *Dors* 3H **13**
South Brent. *Devn* 2D **8**
South Brewham. *Som* 3C **22**
South Broomage. *Falk* 1B **128**
South Broomhill. *Nmbd* 4G **121**
Southburgh. *Norf* 5B **78**
South Burlingham. *Norf* 5F **79**
Southburn. *E Yor* 4D **101**
South Cadbury. *Som* 4B **22**
South Carlton. *Linc* 3G **87**
South Cave. *E Yor* 1C **94**
South Cerney. *Glos* 2F **35**
South Chard. *Som* 2G **13**
South Charlton. *Nmbd* 2F **121**
South Cheriton. *Som* 4B **22**
South Church. *Dur* 2F **105**
Southchurch. *S'end* 2D **40**
South Cleatlam. *Dur* 3E **105**
South Cliffe. *E Yor* 1B **94**
South Clifton. *Notts* 3F **87**
South Clunes. *High* 4H **157**
South Cockerington. *Linc* 2C **88**
South Common. *Devn* 2G **13**
South Common. *E Sus* 4E **27**
South Cornelly. *B'end* 3B **32**
Southcott. *Devn* 1E **11**
(nr. Great Torrington)
Southcott. *Devn* 3F **11**
(nr. Okehampton)
Southcott. *Wilts* 1G **23**
Southcourt. *Buck* 4G **51**
South Cove. *Suff* 2G **67**
South Creagan. *Arg* 4D **141**
South Creake. *Norf* 2A **78**
South Crosland. *W Yor* 3B **92**
South Croxton. *Leics* 4D **74**
South Dalton. *E Yor* 5D **100**
South Darenth. *Kent* 4G **39**
Southdean. *Bord* 4A **120**
Southdown. *Bath* 5C **34**
South Duffield. *N Yor* 1G **93**
Southease. *E Sus* 5F **27**
South Elkington. *Linc* 2B **88**
South Elmsall. *W Yor* 3E **93**
Southend. *Arg* 5A **122**
South End. *Cumb* 3B **96**
Southend. *Glos* 2C **34**
South End. *N Lin* 2E **94**
South End. *W Ber* 4D **36**
Southend (London) Airport. *Essx* 2C **40**
Southend-on-Sea. *S'end* 2C **40**
Southerfield. *Cumb* 5C **112**
Southerly. *Devn* 4F **11**
Southernden. *Kent* 1C **28**
Southerndown. *V Glam* 4B **32**
Southerness. *Dum* 4A **112**
South Erradale. *High* 1G **155**
Southerton. *Devn* 3D **12**
Southery. *Norf* 1F **65**
Southey Green. *Essx* 2A **54**
South Fambridge. *Essx* 1C **40**
South Fawley. *W Ber* 3B **36**
South Feorline. *N Ayr* 3D **122**
South Ferriby. *N Lin* 2C **94**
South Field. *E Yor* 2D **94**
Southfleet. *Kent* 3H **39**
South Garvan. *High* 1D **141**
Southgate. *Cdgn* 2E **57**
Southgate. *G Lon* 1E **39**
Southgate. *Norf* 3D **78**
(nr. Aylsham)
Southgate. *Norf* 2A **78**
(nr. Fakenham)
Southgate. *Swan* 4E **31**
South Godstone. *Surr* 1E **27**
South Gorley. *Hants* 1G **15**
South Green. *Essx* 1A **40**
(nr. Billericay)
South Green. *Essx* 4D **54**
(nr. Colchester)
South Green. *Kent* 4C **40**
South Hanningfield. *Essx* 1B **40**
South Harting. *W Sus* 1F **17**
South Hayling. *Hants* 3F **17**
South Hazelrigg. *Nmbd* 1E **121**
South Heath. *Buck* 5H **51**
South Heath. *Essx* 4E **54**
South Heighton. *E Sus* 5F **27**
South Hetton. *Dur* 5G **115**
South Hiendley. *W Yor* 3D **93**
South Hill. *Corn* 5D **10**
South Hill. *Som* 4H **21**
South Hinksey. *Oxon* 5D **50**
South Hole. *Devn* 4C **18**
South Holme. *N Yor* 2B **100**
South Holmwood. *Surr* 1C **26**
South Hornchurch. *G Lon* 2G **39**
South Huish. *Devn* 4C **8**
South Hykeham. *Linc* 4G **87**
South Hylton. *Tyne* 4G **115**
Southill. *C Beds* 1B **52**
Southington. *Hants* 2D **24**
South Kelsey. *Linc* 1H **87**
South Kessock. *High* 4A **158**
South Killingholme. *N Lin* 3E **95**
South Kilvington. *N Yor* 1G **99**
South Kilworth. *Leics* 2D **62**
South Kirkby. *W Yor* 3E **93**
South Kirton. *Abers* 3E **153**
South Knighton. *Devn* 5B **12**
South Kyme. *Linc* 1A **76**
South Lancing. *W Sus* 5C **26**
South Ledaig. *Arg* 5D **140**
Southleigh. *Devn* 3F **13**
South Leigh. *Oxon* 5B **50**
South Leverton. *Notts* 2E **87**
South Littleton. *Worc* 1F **49**
South Lopham. *Norf* 2C **66**
South Luffenham. *Rut* 5G **75**
South Malling. *E Sus* 4F **27**
South Marston. *Swin* 3G **35**
South Middleton. *Nmbd* 2E **121**
South Milford. *N Yor* 1E **93**
South Milton. *Devn* 4D **8**
South Mimms. *Herts* 5C **52**
Southminster. *Essx* 1D **40**
South Molton. *Devn* 4H **19**
South Moor. *Dur* 4E **115**
Southmoor. *Oxon* 2B **36**
South Moreton. *Oxon* 3D **36**
South Mundham. *W Sus* 2G **17**
South Muskham. *Notts* 5E **87**
South Newbald. *E Yor* 1C **94**
South Newington. *Oxon* 2C **50**
South Newsham. *Nmbd* 2G **115**
South Newton. *N Ayr* 4H **125**
South Newton. *Wilts* 3F **23**
South Normanton. *Derbs* 5B **86**
South Norwood. *G Lon* 4E **39**
South Nutfield. *Surr* 1E **27**
South Ockendon. *Thur* 2G **39**
Southoe. *Cambs* 4A **64**
Southolt. *Suff* 4D **66**
South Ormsby. *Linc* 3C **88**
Southorpe. *Pet* 5H **75**
South Otterington. *N Yor* 1F **99**
South Owersby. *Linc* 1H **87**
Southowram. *W Yor* 2B **92**
South Oxhey. *Herts* 1C **38**
South Perrott. *Dors* 2H **13**
South Petherton. *Som* 1H **13**
South Petherwin. *Corn* 4D **10**
South Pickenham. *Norf* 5A **78**

South Pool—Staveley

South Pool. *Devn* 4D **9**
South Poorton. *Dors* 3A **14**
South Port. *Arg* 1H **133**
Southport. *Mers* 3B **90**
South Queensferry. *Edin* 2E **129**
South Radworthy. *Devn* 3A **20**
South Rauceby. *Linc* 1H **75**
South Raynham. *Norf* 3A **78**
Southrepps. *Norf* 2E **79**
South Reston. *Linc* 2D **88**
Southrey. *Linc* 4A **88**
Southrop. *Glos* 5G **49**
Southrope. *Hants* 2E **25**
South Runcton. *Norf* 5F **77**
South Scarle. *Notts* 4F **87**
Southsea. *Port* 3E **17**
South Shields. *Tyne* 3G **115**
South Shore. *Bkpl* 1B **90**
Southside. *Orkn* 5E **172**
South Somercotes. *Linc* 1D **88**
South Stainley. *N Yor* 3F **99**
South Stainmore. *Cumb* 3B **104**
South Stifford. *Thur* 3G **39**
Southstoke. *Bath* 5C **34**
South Stoke. *Oxon* 3D **36**
South Stoke. *W Sus* 4B **26**
South Street. *E Sus* 4E **27**
South Street. *Kent* 5E **41**
(nr. Faversham)
South Street. *Kent* 4F **41**
(nr. Whitstable)
South Tawton. *Devn* 3G **11**
South Thoresby. *Linc* 3D **88**
South Tidworth. *Wilts* 2H **23**
South Town. *Devn* 4C **12**
South Town. *Hants* 3E **25**
Southtown. *Norf* 5H **79**
Southtown. *Orkn* 8D **172**
Southwaite. *Cumb* 5F **113**
South Walsham. *Norf* 4F **79**
South Warnborough. *Hants* 2F **25**
Southwater. *W Sus* 3C **26**
Southwater Street. *W Sus* 3C **26**
Southway. *Som* 2A **22**
South Weald. *Essx* 1G **39**
South Weirs. *Hants* 2A **16**
Southwell. *Dors* 5B **14**
Southwell. *Notts* 5D **86**
South Weston. *Oxon* 2F **37**
South Wheatley. *Corn* 3C **10**
South Wheatley. *Notts* 2E **87**
Southwick. *Hants* 2E **17**
Southwick. *Nptn* 1H **63**
Southwick. *Tyne* 4G **115**
Southwick. *W Sus* 5D **26**
Southwick. *Wilts* 1D **22**
South Widcombe. *Bath* 1A **22**
South Wigston. *Leics* 1C **62**
South Willingham. *Linc* 2A **88**
South Wingfield. *Derbs* 5A **86**
South Witham. *Linc* 4G **75**
Southwold. *Suff* 3H **67**
South Wonston. *Hants* 3C **24**
Southwood. *Norf* 5F **79**
Southwood. *Som* 3A **22**
South Woodham Ferrers. *Essx* 1C **40**
South Wootton. *Norf* 3F **77**
South Wraxall. *Wilts* 5D **34**
South Zeal. *Devn* 3G **11**
Sowerby. *N Yor* 1G **99**
Sowerby. *W Yor* 2A **92**
Sowerby Bridge. *W Yor* 2A **92**
Sowerby Row. *Cumb* 5E **113**
Sower Carr. *Lanc* 5C **96**
Sowley Green. *Suff* 5G **65**
Sowood. *W Yor* 3A **92**
Sowton. *Devn* 3C **12**
Soyal. *High* 4C **164**
Soyland Town. *W Yor* 2A **92**
Spacey Houses. *N Yor* 4F **99**
Spa Common. *Norf* 2E **79**
Spalding. *Linc* 3B **76**
Spaldington. *E Yor* 1A **94**
Spaldwick. *Cambs* 3A **64**
Spalford. *Notts* 4F **87**
Spanby. *Linc* 2H **75**
Sparham. *Norf* 4C **78**
Sparhamhill. *Norf* 4C **78**
Spark Bridge. *Cumb* 1C **96**
Sparket. *Cumb* 2F **103**
Sparkford. *Som* 4B **22**
Sparkwell. *Devn* 3B **8**
Sparrow Green. *Norf* 4B **78**
Sparrowpit. *Derbs* 2E **85**
Sparrow's Green. *E Sus* 2H **27**
Sparsholt. *Hants* 3C **24**
Sparsholt. *Oxon* 3B **36**
Spartylea. *Nmbd* 5B **114**
Spath. *Staf* 2E **73**
Spaunton. *N Yor* 1B **100**
Spaxton. *Som* 3F **21**
Spean Bridge. *High* 5E **149**
Spear Hill. *W Sus* 4C **26**
Speen. *Buck* 2G **37**
Speen. *W Ber* 5C **36**
Speeton. *N Yor* 2F **101**
Speke. *Mers* 2G **83**
Speldhurst. *Kent* 1G **27**
Spellbrook. *Herts* 4E **53**
Spelsbury. *Oxon* 3B **50**
Spencers Wood. *Wok* 5F **37**
Spennithorne. *N Yor* 1D **98**
Spennymoor. *Dur* 1F **105**
Spernall. *Warw* 4E **61**
Spetchley. *Worc* 5C **60**
Spetisbury. *Dors* 2E **15**
Spexhall. *Suff* 2F **67**
Speybank. *High* 3C **150**
Spey Bay. *Mor* 2A **160**
Speybridge. *High* 1E **151**
Speyview. *Mor* 4G **159**
Spilsby. *Linc* 4C **88**
Spindlestone. *Nmbd* 1F **121**
Spinkhill. *Derbs* 3B **86**
Spinney Hills. *Leic* 5D **74**
Spinningdale. *High* 5D **164**
Spital. *Mers* 2F **83**
Spitalhill. *Derbs* 1F **73**
Spital in the Street. *Linc* 1G **87**
Spithurst. *E Sus* 4F **27**
Spittal. *Dum* 4A **110**
Spittal. *E Lot* 2A **130**
Spittal. *High* 3D **168**
Spittal. *Nmbd* 4G **131**
Spittal. *Pemb* 2D **43**
Spittalfield. *Per* 4A **144**
Spittal of Glenmuick. *Abers* 5H **151**
Spittal of Glenshee. *Per* 1A **144**
Spittal-on-Rule. *Bord* 3H **119**
Spixworth. *Norf* 4E **79**
Splatt. *Corn* 4C **10**
Spofforth. *N Yor* 4F **99**
Spondon. *Derb* 2B **74**
Spon End. *W Mid* 3H **61**
Spooner Row. *Norf* 1C **66**
Sporle. *Norf* 4H **77**
Spott. *E Lot* 2C **130**
Spratton. *Nptn* 3E **62**
Spreakley. *Surr* 2G **25**
Spreyton. *Devn* 3H **11**
Spridlington. *Linc* 2H **87**
Springburn. *Glas* 3H **127**
Springfield. *Dum* 3E **113**
Springfield. *Fife* 2F **137**
Springfield. *High* 2A **158**
Springfield. *W Mid* 2E **61**
Springhill. *Staf* 5D **73**
Springholm. *Dum* 2F **111**
Springside. *N Ayr* 1C **116**
Springthorpe. *Linc* 2F **87**
Spring Vale. *IOW* 3E **16**
Spring Valley. *IOM* 4C **108**
Springwell. *Tyne* 4F **115**
Sproatley. *E Yor* 1E **95**
Sproston Green. *Ches W* 4B **84**
Sprotbrough. *S Yor* 4F **93**
Sproughton. *Suff* 1E **55**
Sprouston. *Bord* 1B **120**
Sprowston. *Norf* 4E **79**
Sproxton. *Leics* 3F **75**
Sproxton. *N Yor* 1A **100**
Sprunston. *Cumb* 5E **113**
Spurstow. *Ches E* 5H **83**
Squires Gate. *Bkpl* 1B **90**
Sraid Ruadh. *Arg* 4A **138**
Srannda. *W Isl* 9C **171**
Sron an t-Sithein. *High* 2C **140**
Sronphadruig Lodge. *Per* 1E **142**
Sruth Mor. *W Isl* 2E **170**
Stableford. *Shrp* 1B **60**
Stackhouse. *N Yor* 3H **97**
Stackpole. *Pemb* 5D **43**
Stackpole Elidor. *Pemb* 5D **43**
Stacksford. *Norf* 1C **66**
Stacksteads. *Lanc* 2G **91**
Staddiscombe. *Plym* 3B **8**
Staddlethorpe. *E Yor* 2B **94**
Staddon. *Devn* 2D **10**
Staden. *Derbs* 3E **85**
Stadhampton. *Oxon* 2E **36**
Stadhlaigearraidh. *W Isl* 5C **170**
Stafainn. *High* 2D **155**
Staffield. *Cumb* 5G **113**
Staffin. *High* 2D **155**
Stafford. *Staf* 3D **72**
Stafford Park. *Telf* 5B **72**
Stagden Cross. *Essx* 4G **53**
Stagsden. *Bed* 1H **51**
Stag's Head. *Devn* 4G **19**
Stainburn. *Cumb* 2B **102**
Stainburn. *N Yor* 5E **99**
Stainby. *Linc* 3G **75**
Staincliffe. *W Yor* 2C **92**
Staincross. *S Yor* 3D **92**
Staindrop. *Dur* 2E **105**
Staines. *Surr* 3B **38**
Stainfield. *Linc* 3H **75**
(nr. Bourne)
Stainfield. *Linc* 3A **88**
(nr. Lincoln)
Stainforth. *N Yor* 3H **97**
Stainforth. *S Yor* 3G **93**
Staining. *Lanc* 1B **90**
Stainland. *W Yor* 3A **92**
Stainsacre. *N Yor* 4G **107**
Stainton. *Cumb* 4E **113**
(nr. Carlisle)
Stainton. *Cumb* 1E **97**
(nr. Kendal)
Stainton. *Cumb* 2F **103**
(nr. Penrith)
Stainton. *Dur* 3D **104**
Stainton. *Midd* 3B **106**
Stainton. *N Yor* 5E **105**
Stainton. *S Yor* 1C **86**
Stainton by Langworth. *Linc* 3H **87**
Staintondale. *N Yor* 5G **107**
Stainton le Vale. *Linc* 1A **88**
Stainton with Adgarley. *Cumb* 2B **96**
Stair. *Cumb* 2D **102**
Stair. *E Ayr* 2D **116**
Stairhaven. *Dum* 4H **109**
Staithes. *N Yor* 3E **107**
Stakeford. *Nmbd* 1F **115**
Stake Pool. *Lanc* 5D **96**
Stakes. *Hants* 2E **17**
Stalbridge. *Dors* 1C **14**
Stalbridge Weston. *Dors* 1C **14**
Stalham. *Norf* 3F **79**
Stalham Green. *Norf* 3F **79**
Stalisfield Green. *Kent* 5D **40**
Stallen. *Dors* 1B **14**
Stallingborough. *NE Lin* 3F **95**
Stalling Busk. *N Yor* 1B **98**
Stallington. *Staf* 2D **72**
Stalmine. *Lanc* 5C **96**
Stalybridge. *G Man* 1D **84**
Stambourne. *Essx* 2H **53**
Stamford. *Linc* 5H **75**
Stamford. *Nmbd* 3G **121**
Stamford Bridge. *Ches W* 4G **83**
Stamford Bridge. *E Yor* 4B **100**
Stamfordham. *Nmbd* 2D **115**
Stamperland. *E Ren* 4G **127**
Stanah. *Lanc* 5C **96**
Stanborough. *Herts* 4C **52**
Stanbridge. *C Beds* 3H **51**
Stanbridge. *Dors* 2F **15**
Stanbury. *W Yor* 1A **92**
Stand. *N Lan* 3A **128**
Standburn. *Falk* 2C **128**
Standeford. *Staf* 5D **72**
Standen. *Kent* 1C **28**
Standen Street. *Kent* 2C **28**
Standerwick. *Som* 1D **22**
Standford. *Hants* 3G **25**
Standford Bridge. *Telf* 3B **72**
Standingstone. *Cumb* 5D **112**
Standish. *Glos* 5D **48**
Standish. *G Man* 3D **90**
Standish Lower Ground.
G Man 4D **90**
Standlake. *Oxon* 5B **50**
Standon. *Hants* 4C **24**
Standon. *Herts* 3D **53**
Standon. *Staf* 2C **72**
Standon Green End. *Herts* 4D **52**
Stane. *N Lan* 4B **128**
Stanecastle. *N Ayr* 1C **116**
Stanfield. *Norf* 3B **78**
Stanford. *C Beds* 1B **52**
Stanford. *Kent* 2F **29**
Stanford Bishop. *Here* 5A **60**
Stanford Bridge. *Worc* 4B **60**
Stanford Dingley. *W Ber* 4D **36**
Stanford in the Vale. *Oxon* 2B **36**
Stanford-le-Hope. *Thur* 2A **40**
Stanford on Avon. *Nptn* 3C **62**
Stanford on Soar. *Notts* 3C **74**
Stanford on Teme. *Worc* 4B **60**
Stanford Rivers. *Essx* 5F **53**
Stanfree. *Derbs* 3B **86**
Stanghow. *Red C* 3D **107**
Stanground. *Pet* 1B **64**
Stanhoe. *Norf* 2H **77**
Stanhope. *Dur* 1C **104**
Stanhope. *Bord* 1D **118**
Stanion. *Nptn* 2G **63**
Stanley. *Derbs* 1B **74**
Stanley. *Dur* 4E **115**
Stanley. *Per* 5A **144**
Stanley. *Shrp* 2B **60**
Stanley. *Staf* 5D **84**
Stanley. *W Yor* 2D **92**
Stanley Common. *Derbs* 1B **74**
Stanley Crook. *Dur* 1E **105**
Stanley Hill. *Here* 1B **48**
Stanlow. *Ches W* 3G **83**
Stanmer. *Brig* 5E **27**
Stanmore. *G Lon* 1C **38**
Stanmore. *Hants* 4C **24**
Stanmore. *W Ber* 4C **36**
Stannersburn. *Nmbd* 1A **114**
Stanningfield. *Suff* 5A **66**
Stannington. *Nmbd* 2F **115**
Stannington. *S Yor* 2H **85**
Stansbatch. *Here* 4F **59**
Stansfield. *Suff* 5G **65**
Stanshope. *Staf* 5F **85**
Stanstead. *Suff* 1B **54**
Stanstead Abbotts. *Herts* 4D **53**
Stansted. *Kent* 4H **39**
Stansted (London) Airport.
Essx 3F **53**
Stansted Mountfitchet. *Essx* 3F **53**
Stanthorne. *Ches W* 4A **84**
Stanton. *Derbs* 4G **73**
Stanton. *Glos* 2F **49**
Stanton. *Nmbd* 5F **121**
Stanton. *Staf* 1F **73**
Stanton. *Suff* 3B **66**
Stanton by Bridge. *Derbs* 3A **74**
Stanton by Dale. *Derbs* 2B **74**
Stanton Chare. *Suff* 3B **66**
Stanton Drew. *Bath* 5A **34**
Stanton Fitzwarren. *Swin* 2G **35**
Stanton Harcourt. *Oxon* 5C **50**
Stanton Hill. *Notts* 4B **86**
Stanton in Peak. *Derbs* 4G **85**
Stanton Lacy. *Shrp* 3G **59**
Stanton Long. *Shrp* 1H **59**
Stanton-on-the-Wolds. *Notts* 2D **74**
Stanton Prior. *Bath* 5B **34**
Stanton St Bernard. *Wilts* 5F **35**
Stanton St John. *Oxon* 5D **50**
Stanton St Quintin. *Wilts* 4E **35**
Stanton Street. *Suff* 4B **66**
Stanton under Bardon. *Leics* 4B **74**
Stanton upon Hine Heath.
Shrp 3H **71**
Stanton Wick. *Bath* 5B **34**
Stanwardine in the Fields.
Shrp 3G **71**
Stanwardine in the Wood.
Shrp 3G **71**
Stanway. *Essx* 3C **54**
Stanway. *Glos* 2F **49**
Stanwell. *Surr* 3B **38**
Stanwell Moor. *Surr* 3B **38**
Stanwick. *Nptn* 3G **63**
Staoinebrig. *W Isl* 5C **170**
Stape. *N Yor* 5E **107**
Stapehill. *Dors* 2F **15**
Stapeley. *Ches E* 1A **72**
Stapenhill. *Staf* 3G **73**
Staple. *Kent* 5G **41**
Staple Cross. *Devn* 4D **20**
Staplecross. *E Sus* 3B **28**
Staplefield. *W Sus* 3D **27**
Staple Fitzpaine. *Som* 1F **13**
Stapleford. *Cambs* 5D **64**
Stapleford. *Herts* 4D **52**
Stapleford. *Leics* 4F **75**
Stapleford. *Linc* 5F **87**
Stapleford. *Notts* 2B **74**
Stapleford. *Wilts* 3F **23**
Stapleford Abbotts. *Essx* 1G **39**
Stapleford Tawney. *Essx* 1G **39**
Staplegrove. *Som* 4F **21**
Staplehay. *Som* 4F **21**
Staple Hill. *S Glo* 4B **34**
Staplehurst. *Kent* 1B **28**
Staplers. *IOW* 4D **16**
Stapleton. *Bris* 4B **34**
Stapleton. *Cumb* 2G **113**
Stapleton. *Here* 4F **59**
Stapleton. *Leics* 1B **62**
Stapleton. *N Yor* 3F **105**
Stapleton. *Shrp* 5G **71**
Stapleton. *Som* 4H **21**
Stapley. *Som* 1E **13**
Staploe. *Bed* 4A **64**
Staplow. *Here* 1B **48**
Star. *Fife* 3F **137**
Star. *Pemb* 1G **43**
Starbeck. *N Yor* 4F **99**
Starbotton. *N Yor* 2B **98**
Starcross. *Devn* 4C **12**
Stareton. *Warw* 3H **61**
Starkholmes. *Derbs* 5H **85**
Starling. *G Man* 3F **91**
Starling's Green. *Essx* 2E **53**
Starston. *Norf* 2E **67**
Start. *Devn* 4E **9**
Startforth. *Dur* 3D **104**
Start Hill. *Essx* 3F **53**
Startley. *Wilts* 3E **35**
Stathe. *Som* 4G **21**
Stathern. *Leics* 2E **75**
Station Town. *Dur* 1B **106**
Staughton Green. *Cambs* 4A **64**
Staughton Highway. *Cambs* 4A **64**
Staunton. *Glos* 3C **48**
(nr. Cheltenham)
Staunton. *Glos* 4A **48**
(nr. Monmouth)
Staunton in the Vale. *Notts* 1F **75**
Staunton on Arrow. *Here* 4F **59**
Staunton on Wye. *Here* 1G **47**
Staveley. *Cumb* 5F **103**

Staveley—Strathcoil

Staveley. Derbs 3B 86
Staveley. N Yor 3F 99
Staveley-in-Cartmel. Cumb 1C 96
Staverton. Devn 2D 9
Staverton. Glos 3D 49
Staverton. Nptn 4C 62
Staverton. Wilts 5D 34
Stawell. Som 3G 21
Stawley. Som 4D 20
Staxigoe. High 3F 169
Staxton. N Yor 2E 101
Staylittle. Powy 1A 58
Staynall. Lanc 5C 96
Staythorpe. Notts 5E 87
Stean. N Yor 2C 98
Stearsby. N Yor 2A 100
Steart. Som 2F 21
Stebbing. Essx 3G 53
Stebbing Green. Essx 3G 53
Stedham. W Sus 4G 25
Steel. Nmbd 4C 114
Steel Cross. E Sus 2G 27
Steelend. Fife 4C 136
Steele Road. Bord 5H 119
Steel Heath. Shrp 2H 71
Steen's Bridge. Here 5H 59
Steep. Hants 4F 25
Steep Lane. W Yor 2A 92
Steeple. Dors 4E 15
Steeple. Essx 5C 54
Steeple Ashton. Wilts 1E 23
Steeple Aston. Oxon 3C 50
Steeple Barton. Oxon 3C 50
Steeple Bumpstead. Essx 1G 53
Steeple Claydon. Buck 3E 51
Steeple Gidding. Cambs 2A 64
Steeple Langford. Wilts 3F 23
Steeple Morden. Cambs 1C 52
Steeton. W Yor 5C 98
Stein. High 3B 154
Steinmanhill. Abers 4E 161
Stelling Minnis. Kent 1F 29
Stembridge. Som 4H 21
Stemster. High 2D 169 (nr. Halkirk)
Stemster. High 2C 168 (nr. Westfield)
Stenalees. Corn 3E 6
Stenhill. Devn 1D 12
Stenhouse. Edin 2F 129
Stenhousemuir. Falk 1B 128
Stenigot. Linc 2B 88
Stenscholl. High 2D 155
Stenso. Orkn 5C 172
Stenson. Derbs 3H 73
Stenson Fields. Derbs 2H 73
Stenton. E Lot 2C 130
Stenwith. Linc 2F 75
Steòrnabhagh. W Isl 4G 171
Stepaside. Pemb 4F 43
Stepford. Dum 1F 111
Stepney. G Lon 2E 39
Steppingley. C Beds 2A 52
Stepps. N Lan 3H 127
Sterndale Moor. Derbs 4F 85
Sternfield. Suff 4F 67
Stert. Wilts 1F 23
Stetchworth. Cambs 5F 65
Stevenage. Herts 3C 52
Stevenston. N Ayr 5D 126
Stevenstone. Devn 1F 11
Steventon. Hants 2D 24
Steventon. Oxon 2C 36
Steventon End. Cambs 1G 53
Stevington. Bed 5G 63
Stewartby. Bed 1A 52
Stewarton. Arg 4A 122
Stewarton. E Ayr 5F 127
Stewkley. Buck 3G 51
Stewkley Dean. Buck 3G 51
Stewley. Som 1G 13
Stewton. Linc 2C 88
Steyning. W Sus 4C 26
Steynton. Pemb 4D 42
Stibb. Corn 1C 10
Stibbard. Norf 3B 78
Stibb Cross. Devn 1E 11
Stibb Green. Wilts 5H 35
Stibbington. Cambs 1H 63
Stichill. Bord 1B 120
Sticker. Corn 3D 6
Stickford. Linc 4C 88
Sticklepath. Devn 3G 11
Sticklinch. Som 3A 22
Stickling Green. Essx 2E 53
Stickney. Linc 5C 88
Stiffkey. Norf 1B 78
Stifford's Bridge. Here 1C 48
Stileway. Som 2H 21
Stillingfleet. N Yor 5H 99
Stillington. N Yor 3H 99
Stillington. Stoc T 2A 106
Stilton. Cambs 2A 64
Stinchcombe. Glos 2C 34
Stinsford. Dors 3C 14
Stiperstones. Shrp 5F 71
Stirchley. Telf 5B 72
Stirchley. W Mid 2E 61
Stirling. Abers 4H 161
Stirling. Stir 4G 135
Stirton. N Yor 4B 98
Stisted. Essx 3A 54
Stitchcombe. Wilts 5H 35
Stithians. Corn 5B 6
Stittenham. High 1A 158
Stivichall. W Mid 3H 61
Stixwould. Linc 4A 88
Stoak. Ches W 3G 83
Stobo. Bord 1D 118
Stobo Castle. Bord 1D 118
Stoborough. Dors 4E 15
Stoborough Green. Dors 4E 15
Stobs Castle. Bord 4H 119
Stobswood. Nmbd 5G 121
Stock. Essx 1A 40
Stockbridge. Hants 3B 24
Stockbridge. W Yor 5C 98
Stockbury. Kent 4C 40
Stockcross. W Ber 5C 36
Stockdalewath. Cumb 5E 113
Stocker's Head. Kent 5D 40
Stockerston. Leics 1F 63
Stock Green. Worc 5D 61
Stocking. Here 2B 48
Stockingford. Warw 1H 61
Stocking Green. Essx 2F 53
Stocking Pelham. Herts 3E 53
Stockland. Devn 2F 13
Stockland Bristol. Som 2F 21
Stockleigh English. Devn 2B 12
Stockleigh Pomeroy. Devn 2B 12
Stockley. Wilts 5F 35
Stocklinch. Som 1G 13
Stockport. G Man 2D 84
Stocksbridge. S Yor 1G 85
Stocksfield. Nmbd 3D 114
Stocks, The. Kent 3D 28
Stockstreet. Essx 3B 54
Stockton. Here 4H 59
Stockton. Norf 1F 67
Stockton. Shrp 1B 60 (nr. Bridgnorth)
Stockton. Shrp 5E 71 (nr. Chirbury)
Stockton. Telf 4B 72
Stockton. Warw 4B 62
Stockton. Wilts 3E 23
Stockton Brook. Staf 5D 84
Stockton Cross. Here 4H 59
Stockton Heath. Warr 2A 84
Stockton-on-Tees. Stoc T 3B 106
Stockton on Teme. Worc 4B 60
Stockton-on-the-Forest. York 4A 100
Stockwell Heath. Staf 3E 73
Stockwood. Bris 5B 34
Stock Wood. Worc 5E 61
Stodmarsh. Kent 4G 41
Stody. Norf 2C 78
Stoer. High 1E 163
Stoford. Som 1A 14
Stoford. Wilts 3F 23
Stogumber. Som 3D 20
Stogursey. Som 2F 21
Stoke. Devn 4C 18
Stoke. Hants 1C 24 (nr. Andover)
Stoke. Hants 2F 17 (nr. South Hayling)
Stoke. Medw 3C 40
Stoke. W Mid 3A 62
Stoke Abbott. Dors 2H 13
Stoke Albany. Nptn 2F 63
Stoke Ash. Suff 3D 66
Stoke Bardolph. Notts 1D 74
Stoke Bliss. Worc 4A 60
Stoke Bruerne. Nptn 1F 51
Stoke by Clare. Suff 1H 53
Stoke-by-Nayland. Suff 2C 54
Stoke Canon. Devn 3C 12
Stoke Charity. Hants 3C 24
Stoke Climsland. Corn 5D 10
Stoke Cross. Here 5A 60
Stoke D'Abernon. Surr 5C 38
Stoke Doyle. Nptn 2H 63
Stoke Dry. Rut 1F 63
Stoke Edith. Here 1B 48
Stoke Farthing. Wilts 4F 23
Stoke Ferry. Norf 1G 65
Stoke Fleming. Devn 4E 9
Stokeford. Dors 4D 14
Stoke Gabriel. Devn 3E 9
Stoke Gifford. S Glo 4B 34
Stoke Golding. Leics 1A 62
Stoke Goldington. Mil 1G 51
Stokeham. Notts 3E 87
Stoke Hammond. Buck 3G 51
Stoke Heath. Shrp 3A 72
Stoke Holy Cross. Norf 5E 79
Stokeinteignhead. Devn 5C 12
Stoke Lacy. Here 1B 48
Stoke Lyne. Oxon 3D 50
Stoke Mandeville. Buck 4G 51
Stokenchurch. Buck 2F 37
Stoke Newington. G Lon 2E 39
Stokenham. Devn 4E 9
Stoke on Tern. Shrp 3A 72
Stoke-on-Trent. Stoke 1C 72
Stoke Orchard. Glos 3E 49
Stoke Pero. Som 2B 20
Stoke Poges. Buck 2A 38
Stoke Prior. Here 5H 59
Stoke Prior. Worc 4D 60
Stoke Rivers. Devn 3G 19
Stoke Rochford. Linc 3G 75
Stoke Row. Oxon 3E 37
Stoke St Gregory. Som 4G 21
Stoke St Mary. Som 4F 21
Stoke St Michael. Som 2B 22
Stoke St Milborough. Shrp 2H 59
Stokesay. Shrp 2G 59
Stokesby. Norf 4G 79
Stokesley. N Yor 4C 106
Stoke sub Hamdon. Som 1H 13
Stoke Talmage. Oxon 2E 37
Stoke Trister. Som 4C 22
Stoke-upon-Trent. Stoke 1C 72
Stoke Wake. Dors 2C 14
Stolford. Som 2F 21
Stondon Massey. Essx 5F 53
Stone. Buck 4F 51
Stone. Glos 2B 34
Stone. Kent 3G 39
Stone. Som 3A 22
Stone. Staf 2D 72
Stone. Worc 3C 60
Stonea. Cambs 1D 64
Stoneacton. Shrp 1H 59
Stone Allerton. Som 1H 21
Ston Easton. Som 1B 22
Stonebridge. N Som 1G 21
Stonebridge. Som 2C 22
Stonebridge. Surr 1C 26
Stone Bridge Corner. Pet 5B 76
Stonebroom. Derbs 5B 86
Stonebyres. S Lan 5B 128
Stone Chair. W Yor 2B 92
Stone Cross. E Sus 5H 27
Stone Cross. Kent 2G 27
Stone-edge-Batch. N Som 4H 33
Stoneferry. Hull 1D 94
Stonefield. Arg 5D 140
Stonefield. S Lan 4H 127
Stonegate. E Sus 3A 28
Stonegate. N Yor 4E 107
Stonegrave. N Yor 2A 100
Stonehall. Worc 1D 49
Stonehaugh. Nmbd 2A 114
Stonehaven. Abers 5F 153
Stone Heath. Staf 2D 72
Stone Hill. Kent 2E 29
Stone House. Cumb 1G 97
Stonehouse. Glos 5D 48
Stonehouse. Nmbd 4H 113
Stonehouse. S Lan 5A 128
Stone in Oxney. Kent 3D 28
Stoneleigh. Warw 3H 61
Stoneley Green. Ches E 5A 84
Stonely. Cambs 4A 64
Stonepits. Worc 5E 61
Stoner Hill. Hants 4F 25
Stonesby. Leics 3F 75
Stonesfield. Oxon 4B 50
Stones Green. Essx 3E 55
Stone Street. Kent 5G 39
Stone Street. Suff 2C 54 (nr. Boxford)
Stone Street. Suff 2F 67 (nr. Halesworth)
Stonethwaite. Cumb 3D 102
Stoneyburn. W Lot 3C 128
Stoney Cross. Hants 1A 16
Stoneyford. Devn 2D 12
Stoneygate. Leic 5D 74
Stoneyhills. Essx 1D 40
Stoneykirk. Dum 4F 109
Stoney Middleton. Derbs 3G 85
Stoney Stanton. Leics 1B 62
Stoney Stoke. Som 3C 22
Stoney Stratton. Som 3B 22
Stoney Stretton. Shrp 5F 71
Stoneywood. Aber 2F 153
Stonham Aspal. Suff 5D 66
Stonnall. Staf 5E 73
Stonor. Oxon 3F 37
Stonton Wyville. Leics 1E 63
Stonybreck. Shet 1B 172
Stony Cross. Devn 4F 19
Stony Cross. Here 1C 48 (nr. Great Malvern)
Stony Cross. Here 4H 59 (nr. Leominster)
Stony Houghton. Derbs 4B 86
Stony Stratford. Mil 1F 51
Stoodleigh. Devn 3G 19 (nr. Barnstaple)
Stoodleigh. Devn 1C 12 (nr. Tiverton)
Stopham. W Sus 4B 26
Stopsley. Lutn 3B 52
Stoptide. Corn 1D 6
Storeton. Mers 2F 83
Stormontfield. Per 1D 136
Stornoway. W Isl 4G 171
Stornoway Airport. W Isl 4G 171
Storridge. Here 1C 48
Storrington. W Sus 4B 26
Storrs. Cumb 5E 103
Storth. Cumb 1D 97
Storwood. E Yor 5B 100
Stotfield. Mor 1G 159
Stotfold. C Beds 2C 52
Stottesdon. Shrp 2A 60
Stoughton. Leics 5D 74
Stoughton. Surr 5A 38
Stoughton. W Sus 1G 17
Stoul. High 4F 147
Stoulton. Worc 1E 49
Stourbridge. W Mid 2C 60
Stourpaine. Dors 2D 14
Stourport-on-Severn. Worc 3C 60
Stour Provost. Dors 4C 22
Stour Row. Dors 4D 22
Stourton. Staf 2C 60
Stourton. Warw 2A 50
Stourton. W Yor 1D 92
Stourton. Wilts 3C 22
Stourton Caundle. Dors 1C 14
Stoven. Suff 2G 67
Stow. Linc 2H 75 (nr. Billingborough)
Stow. Linc 2F 87 (nr. Gainsborough)
Stow. Bord 5A 130
Stow Bardolph. Norf 5F 77
Stow Bedon. Norf 1B 66
Stowbridge. Norf 5F 77
Stow cum Quy. Cambs 4E 65
Stowe. Glos 5A 48
Stowe. Shrp 3F 59
Stowe. Staf 4F 73
Stowe-by-Chartley. Staf 3E 73
Stowell. Som 4B 22
Stowey. Bath 1A 22
Stowford. Devn 2G 19 (nr. Combe Martin)
Stowford. Devn 4D 12 (nr. Exmouth)
Stowford. Devn 4E 11 (nr. Tavistock)
Stowlangtoft. Suff 4B 66
Stow Longa. Cambs 3A 64
Stow Maries. Essx 1C 40
Stowmarket. Suff 5C 66
Stow-on-the-Wold. Glos 3G 49
Stowting. Kent 1F 29
Stowupland. Suff 5C 66
Straad. Arg 3B 126
Strachan. Abers 4D 152
Stradbroke. Suff 3E 67
Stradbrook. Wilts 1E 23
Stradishall. Suff 5G 65
Stradsett. Norf 5F 77
Stragglethorpe. Linc 5G 87
Stragglethorpe. Notts 2D 74
Straid. S Ayr 5A 116
Straight Soley. Wilts 4B 36
Straiton. Edin 3F 129
Straiton. S Ayr 4C 116
Straloch. Per 2H 143
Stramshall. Staf 2E 73
Strang. IOM 4C 108
Strangford. Here 3A 48
Stranraer. Dum 3F 109
Strata Florida. Cdgn 4G 57
Stratfield Mortimer. W Ber 5E 37
Stratfield Saye. Hants 5E 37
Stratfield Turgis. Hants 1E 25
Stratford. Glos 2D 49
Stratford. G Lon 2E 39
Stratford St Andrew. Suff 4F 67
Stratford St Mary. Suff 2D 54
Stratford sub Castle. Wilts 3G 23
Stratford Tony. Wilts 4F 23
Stratford-upon-Avon. Warw 5G 61
Strath. High 1G 155 (nr. Gairloch)
Strath. High 3E 169 (nr. Wick)
Strathan. High 4B 148 (nr. Fort William)
Strathan. High 1E 163 (nr. Lochinver)
Strathan. High 2F 167 (nr. Tongue)
Strathan Skerray. High 2G 167
Strathaven. S Lan 5A 128
Strathblane. Stir 2G 127
Strathcanaird. High 3F 163
Strathcarron. High 4B 156
Strathcoil. Arg 5A 140

Sydenham Damerel—Thorngrove

Sydenham Damerel. *Devn* 5E 11
Syderstone. *Norf* 2H 77
Sydling St Nicholas. *Dors* 3B 14
Sydmonton. *Hants* 1C 24
Sydney. *Ches E* 5B 84
Syerston. *Notts* 1E 75
Syke. *G Man* 3G 91
Sykehouse. *S Yor* 3G 93
Sykes. *Lanc* 4F 97
Syleham. *Suff* 3E 66
Sylen. *Carm* 5F 45
Sylfaen. *Powy* 5D 70
Symbister. *Shet* 5G 173
Symington. *S Ayr* 1C 116
Symington. *S Lan* 1B 118
Symondsbury. *Dors* 3H 13
Symonds Yat. *Here* 4A 48
Synod Inn. *Cdgn* 5D 56
Syre. *High* 4G 167
Syreford. *Glos* 3F 49
Syresham. *Nptn* 1E 51
Syston. *Leics* 4D 74
Syston. *Linc* 1G 75
Sytchampton. *Worc* 4C 60
Sywell. *Nptn* 4F 63

T

Tabost. *W Isl* 6F 171
(nr. Cearsiadar)
Tabost. *W Isl* 1H 171
(nr. Suainebost)
Tachbrook Mallory. *Warw* 4H 61
Tackley. *Oxon* 3C 50
Tacleit. *W Isl* 4D 171
Tacolneston. *Norf* 1D 66
Tadcaster. *N Yor* 5G 99
Taddington. *Derbs* 3F 85
Taddington. *Glos* 2F 49
Taddiport. *Devn* 1E 11
Tadley. *Hants* 5E 36
Tadlow. *Cambs* 1C 52
Tadmarton. *Oxon* 2B 50
Tadwick. *Bath* 4C 34
Tadworth. *Surr* 5D 38
Tafarnaubach. *Blae* 4E 46
Tafarn-y-bwlch. *Pemb* 1E 43
Tafarn-y-Gelyn. *Den* 4D 82
Taff's Well. *Rhon* 3E 33
Tafolwern. *Powy* 5A 70
Taibach. *Neat* 3A 32
Tai-bach. *Powy* 3D 70
Taigh a Ghearraidh. *W Isl* 1C 170
Tain. *High* 5E 165
(nr. Invergordon)
Tain. *High* 2E 169
(nr. Thurso)
Tai-Nant. *Wrex* 1E 71
Tai'n Lon. *Gwyn* 5D 80
Tairbeart. *W Isl* 7D 171
Tairgwaith. *Neat* 4H 45
Takeley. *Essx* 3F 53
Takeley Street. *Essx* 3F 53
Talachddu. *Powy* 2D 46
Talacre. *Flin* 2D 82
Talardd. *Gwyn* 3A 70
Talaton. *Devn* 3D 12
Talbenny. *Pemb* 3C 42
Talbot Green. *Rhon* 3D 32
Taleford. *Devn* 3D 12
Talerddig. *Powy* 5B 70
Talgarreg. *Cdgn* 5D 56
Talgarth. *Powy* 2E 47
Talisker. *High* 5C 154
Talke. *Staf* 5C 84
Talkin. *Cumb* 4G 113
Talladale. *High* 1B 156
Talla Linnfoots. *Bord* 2D 118
Tallaminnock. *S Ayr* 5D 116
Tallarn Green. *Wrex* 1G 71
Tallentire. *Cumb* 1C 102
Talley. *Carm* 2G 45
Tallington. *Linc* 5H 75
Talmine. *High* 2F 167
Talog. *Carm* 2H 43
Talsarn. *Carm* 3A 46
Talsarn. *Cdgn* 5E 57
Talsarnau. *Gwyn* 2F 69
Talskiddy. *Corn* 2D 6
Talwrn. *IOA* 3D 81
Talwrn. *Wrex* 1E 71
Tal-y-bont. *Cdgn* 2F 57
Tal-y-Bont. *Cnwy* 4G 81
Tal-y-bont. *Gwyn* 3F 81
(nr. Bangor)
Tal-y-bont. *Gwyn* 3E 69
(nr. Barmouth)
Talybont-on-Usk. *Powy* 3E 46
Tal-y-cafn. *Cnwy* 3G 81
Tal-y-coed. *Mon* 4H 47
Tal-y-llyn. *Gwyn* 5G 69
Talyllyn. *Powy* 3E 46
Talysarn. *Gwyn* 5D 81
Tal-y-waenydd. *Gwyn* 1F 69
Talywain. *Torf* 5F 47
Talywern. *Powy* 5H 69
Tamerton Foliot. *Plym* 2A 8
Tamworth. *Staf* 5G 73
Tamworth Green. *Linc* 1C 76
Tandlehill. *Ren* 3F 127
Tandridge. *Surr* 5E 39
Tanerdy. *Carm* 3E 45
Tanfield. *Dur* 4E 115
Tanfield Lea. *Dur* 4E 115
Tangasdale. *W Isl* 8B 170
Tang Hall. *York* 4A 100
Tangiers. *Pemb* 3D 42
Tangley. *Hants* 1B 24
Tangmere. *W Sus* 5A 26
Tangwick. *Shet* 4D 173
Tankerness. *Orkn* 7E 172
Tankersley. *S Yor* 1H 85
Tankerton. *Kent* 4F 41
Tan-lan. *Cnwy* 4G 81
Tan-lan. *Gwyn* 1F 69
Tannach. *High* 4F 169
Tannadice. *Ang* 3D 145
Tanner's Green. *Worc* 3E 61
Tannington. *Suff* 4E 67
Tannochside. *N Lan* 3A 128
Tan Office Green. *Suff* 5G 65
Tansley. *Derbs* 5H 85
Tansley Knoll. *Derbs* 4H 85
Tansor. *Nptn* 1H 63
Tantobie. *Dur* 4E 115
Tanton. *N Yor* 3C 106
Tanvats. *Linc* 4A 88
Tanworth-in-Arden. *Warw* 3F 61
Tan-y-bwlch. *Gwyn* 1F 69
Tan-y-fron. *Cnwy* 4B 82
Tanyfron. *Wrex* 5E 83
Tan-y-goes. *Cdgn* 1C 44
Tanygrisiau. *Gwyn* 1F 69
Tan-y-pistyll. *Powy* 3C 70
Tan-yr-allt. *Den* 2C 82
Taobh a Chaolais. *W Isl* 7C 170
Taobh a Deas Loch Aineort.
W Isl 6C 170
Taobh a Ghlinne. *W Isl* 6F 171
Taobh a Tuath Loch Aineort.
W Isl 6C 170
Taobh Tuath. *W Isl* 1E 170
Taplow. *Buck* 2A 38
Tapton. *Derbs* 3A 86
Tarbert. *Arg* 1E 125
(on Jura)
Tarbert. *Arg* 3G 125
(on Kintyre)
Tarbert. *W Isl* 7D 171
Tarbet. *Arg* 3C 134
Tarbet. *High* 4F 147
(nr. Mallaig)
Tarbet. *High* 4B 166
(nr. Scourie)
Tarbock Green. *Mers* 2G 83
Tarbolton. *S Ayr* 2D 116
Tarbrax. *S Lan* 4D 128
Tardebigge. *Worc* 4E 61
Tarfside. *Ang* 1D 145
Tarland. *Abers* 3B 152
Tarleton. *Lanc* 2C 90
Tarlogie. *High* 5E 165
Tarlscough. *Lanc* 3C 90
Tarlton. *Glos* 2E 35
Tarnbrook. *Lanc* 4E 97
Tarnock. *Som* 1G 21
Tarns. *Cumb* 5C 112
Tarporley. *Ches W* 4H 83
Tarpots. *Essx* 2B 40
Tarr. *Som* 3E 20
Tarrant Crawford. *Dors* 2E 15
Tarrant Gunville. *Dors* 1E 15
Tarrant Hinton. *Dors* 1E 15
Tarrant Keyneston. *Dors* 2E 15
Tarrant Launceston. *Dors* 2E 15
Tarrant Monkton. *Dors* 2E 15
Tarrant Rawston. *Dors* 2E 15
Tarrant Rushton. *Dors* 2E 15
Tarrel. *High* 5F 165
Tarring Neville. *E Sus* 5F 27
Tarrington. *Here* 1B 48
Tarsappie. *Per* 1D 136
Tarscabhaig. *High* 3D 147
Tarskavaig. *High* 3D 147
Tarves. *Abers* 5F 161
Tarvie. *High* 3G 157
Tarvin. *Ches W* 4G 83
Tasburgh. *Norf* 1E 66
Tasley. *Shrp* 1A 60
Taston. *Oxon* 3B 50
Tatenhill. *Staf* 3G 73
Tathall End. *Mil* 1G 51
Tatham. *Lanc* 3F 97
Tathwell. *Linc* 2C 88
Tatling End. *Buck* 2B 38
Tatsfield. *Surr* 5F 39
Tattenhall. *Ches W* 5G 83
Tatterford. *Norf* 3A 78
Tattersett. *Norf* 2H 77
Tattershall. *Linc* 5B 88
Tattershall Bridge. *Linc* 5A 88
Tattershall Thorpe. *Linc* 5B 88
Tattingstone. *Suff* 2E 55
Tattingstone White Horse. *Suff* 2E 55
Tattle Bank. *Warw* 4F 61
Tatworth. *Som* 2G 13
Taunton. *Som* 4F 21
Taverham. *Norf* 4D 78
Taverners Green. *Essx* 4F 53
Tavernspite. *Pemb* 3F 43
Tavistock. *Devn* 5E 11
Tavool House. *Arg* 1B 132
Taw Green. *Devn* 3G 11
Tawstock. *Devn* 4F 19
Taxal. *Derbs* 2E 85
Tayinloan. *Arg* 5E 125
Taynish. *Arg* 1F 125
Taynton. *Glos* 3C 48
Taynton. *Oxon* 4H 49
Taynuilt. *Arg* 5E 141
Tayport. *Fife* 1G 137
Tay Road Bridge. *Fife* 1G 137
Tayvallich. *Arg* 1F 125
Tealby. *Linc* 1A 88
Tealing. *Ang* 5D 144
Teams. *Tyne* 3F 115
Teangue. *High* 3E 147
Tebay. *Cumb* 4H 103
Tebworth. *C Beds* 3H 51
Tedburn St Mary. *Devn* 3B 12
Teddington. *Glos* 2E 49
Teddington. *G Lon* 3C 38
Tedsmore. *Shrp* 3F 71
Tedstone Delamere. *Here* 5A 60
Tedstone Wafer. *Here* 5A 60
Teesport. *Red C* 2C 106
Teesside. *Stoc T* 2C 106
Teeton. *Nptn* 3D 62
Teffont Evias. *Wilts* 3E 23
Teffont Magna. *Wilts* 3E 23
Tegryn. *Pemb* 1G 43
Teigh. *Rut* 4F 75
Teigncombe. *Devn* 4G 11
Teigngrace. *Devn* 5B 12
Teignmouth. *Devn* 5C 12
Telford. *Telf* 4A 72
Telham. *E Sus* 4B 28
Tellisford. *Som* 1D 22
Telscombe. *E Sus* 5F 27
Telscombe Cliffs. *E Sus* 5E 27
Tempar. *Per* 3D 142
Templand. *Dum* 1B 112
Temple. *Corn* 5B 10
Temple. *Glas* 3G 127
Temple. *Midl* 4G 129
Temple Balsall. *W Mid* 3G 61
Temple Bar. *Carm* 4F 45
Temple Bar. *Cdgn* 5E 57
Temple Cloud. *Bath* 1B 22
Templecombe. *Som* 4C 22
Temple Ewell. *Kent* 1G 29
Temple Grafton. *Warw* 5F 61
Temple Guiting. *Glos* 3F 49
Templehall. *Fife* 4E 137
Temple Hirst. *N Yor* 2G 93
Temple Normanton. *Derbs* 4B 86
Temple Sowerby. *Cumb* 2H 103
Templeton. *Devn* 1B 12
Templeton. *Pemb* 3F 43
Templeton. *W Ber* 5B 36
Templetown. *Dur* 5E 115
Tempsford. *C Beds* 5A 64
Tenandry. *Per* 2G 143
Tenbury Wells. *Worc* 4H 59
Tenby. *Pemb* 4F 43
Tendring. *Essx* 3E 55
Tendring Green. *Essx* 3E 55
Tenga. *Arg* 4G 139
Ten Mile Bank. *Norf* 1F 65
Tenterden. *Kent* 2C 28
Terfyn. *Cnwy* 3B 82
Terhill. *Som* 3E 21
Terling. *Essx* 4A 54
Ternhill. *Shrp* 2A 72
Terregles. *Dum* 2G 111
Terrick. *Buck* 5G 51
Terrington. *N Yor* 2A 100
Terrington St Clement. *Norf* 3E 77
Terrington St John. *Norf* 4E 77
Terry's Green. *Warw* 3F 61
Teston. *Kent* 5B 40
Testwood. *Hants* 1B 16
Tetbury. *Glos* 2D 35
Tetbury Upton. *Glos* 2D 35
Tetchill. *Shrp* 2F 71
Tetcott. *Devn* 3D 10
Tetford. *Linc* 3C 88
Tetney. *Linc* 4G 95
Tetney Lock. *Linc* 4G 95
Tetsworth. *Oxon* 5E 51
Tettenhall. *W Mid* 1C 60
Teversal. *Notts* 4B 86
Teversham. *Cambs* 5D 65
Teviothead. *Bord* 4G 119
Tewel. *Abers* 5F 153
Tewin. *Herts* 4C 52
Tewkesbury. *Glos* 2D 49
Teynham. *Kent* 4D 40
Teynham Street. *Kent* 4D 40
Thackthwaite. *Cumb* 2F 103
Thakeham. *W Sus* 4C 26
Thame. *Oxon* 5F 51
Thames Ditton. *Surr* 4C 38
Thames Haven. *Thur* 2B 40
Thamesmead. *G Lon* 2F 39
Thamesport. *Medw* 3C 40
Thanington Without. *Kent* 5F 41
Thankerton. *S Lan* 1B 118
Tharston. *Norf* 1D 66
Thatcham. *W Ber* 5D 36
Thatto Heath. *Mers* 1H 83
Thaxted. *Essx* 2G 53
Theakston. *N Yor* 1F 99
Thealby. *N Lin* 3B 94
Theale. *Som* 2H 21
Theale. *W Ber* 4E 37
Thearne. *E Yor* 1D 94
Theberton. *Suff* 4G 67
Theddingworth. *Leics* 2D 62
Theddlethorpe All Saints. *Linc* 2D 88
Theddlethorpe St Helen. *Linc* 2D 89
Thelbridge Barton. *Devn* 1A 12
Thelnetham. *Suff* 3C 66
Thelveton. *Norf* 2D 66
Thelwall. *Warr* 2A 84
Themelthorpe. *Norf* 3C 78
Thenford. *Nptn* 1D 50
Therfield. *Herts* 2D 52
Thetford. *Linc* 4A 76
Thetford. *Norf* 2A 66
Thethwaite. *Cumb* 5E 113
Theydon Bois. *Essx* 1F 39
Thick Hollins. *W Yor* 3B 92
Thickwood. *Wilts* 4D 34
Thimbleby. *Linc* 3B 88
Thimbleby. *N Yor* 5B 106
Thingwall. *Mers* 2E 83
Thirlby. *N Yor* 1G 99
Thirlestane. *Bord* 5B 130
Thirn. *N Yor* 1E 98
Thirsk. *N Yor* 1G 99
Thirtleby. *E Yor* 1E 95
Thistleton. *Lanc* 1C 90
Thistleton. *Rut* 4G 75
Thistley Green. *Suff* 3F 65
Thixendale. *N Yor* 3C 100
Thockrington. *Nmbd* 2C 114
Tholomas Drove. *Cambs* 5D 76
Tholthorpe. *N Yor* 3G 99
Thomas Chapel. *Pemb* 4F 43
Thomas Close. *Cumb* 5F 113
Thomastown. *Abers* 4E 160
Thomastown. *Rhon* 3D 32
Thompson. *Norf* 1B 66
Thomshill. *Mor* 3G 159
Thong. *Kent* 3A 40
Thongsbridge. *W Yor* 4B 92
Thoralby. *N Yor* 1C 98
Thoresby. *Notts* 3D 86
Thoresway. *Linc* 1A 88
Thorganby. *Linc* 1B 88
Thorganby. *N Yor* 5A 100
Thorgill. *N Yor* 5E 107
Thorington. *Suff* 3G 67
Thorington Street. *Suff* 2D 54
Thorlby. *N Yor* 4B 98
Thorley. *Herts* 4E 53
Thorley Street. *Herts* 4E 53
Thorley Street. *IOW* 4B 16
Thormanby. *N Yor* 2G 99
Thorn. *Powy* 4E 59
Thornaby-on-Tees. *Stoc T* 3B 106
Thornage. *Norf* 2C 78
Thornborough. *Buck* 2F 51
Thornborough. *N Yor* 2E 99
Thornbury. *Devn* 2E 11
Thornbury. *Here* 5A 60
Thornbury. *S Glo* 3B 34
Thornby. *Cumb* 4D 112
Thornby. *Nptn* 3D 62
Thorncliffe. *Staf* 5E 85
Thorncombe. *Dors* 2G 13
Thorncombe Street. *Surr* 1A 26
Thorncote Green. *C Beds* 1B 52
Thorndon. *Suff* 4D 66
Thorndon Cross. *Devn* 3F 11
Thorne. *S Yor* 3G 93
Thornehillhead. *Devn* 1E 11
Thorner. *W Yor* 5F 99
Thorne St Margaret. *Som* 4D 20
Thorney. *Notts* 3F 87
Thorney. *Pet* 5B 76
Thorney. *Som* 4H 21
Thorney Hill. *Hants* 3G 15
Thorney Toll. *Cambs* 5C 76
Thornfalcon. *Som* 4F 21
Thornford. *Dors* 1B 14
Thorngrafton. *Nmbd* 3A 114
Thorngrove. *Som* 3G 21

Thorngumbald—Tomdoun

Thorngumbald. E Yor 2F 95
Thornham. Norf 1G 77
Thornham Magna. Suff 3D 66
Thornham Parva. Suff 3D 66
Thornhaugh. Pet 5H 75
Thornhill. Cphy 3E 33
Thornhill. Cumb 4B 102
Thornhill. Derbs 2G 85
Thornhill. Dum 5A 118
Thornhill. Sotn 1C 16
Thornhill. Stir 4F 135
Thornhill. W Yor 3C 92
Thornhill Lees. W Yor 3C 92
Thornhills. W Yor 2B 92
Thornholme. E Yor 3F 101
Thornicombe. Dors 2D 14
Thornington. Nmbd 1C 120
Thornley. Dur 1A 106 (nr. Durham)
Thornley. Dur 1E 105 (nr. Tow Law)
Thornley Gate. Nmbd 4B 114
Thornliebank. E Ren 4G 127
Thornroan. Abers 5F 161
Thorns. Suff 5G 65
Thornsett. Derbs 2E 85
Thornthwaite. Cumb 2D 102
Thornthwaite. N Yor 4D 98
Thornton. Ang 4C 144
Thornton. Buck 2F 51
Thornton. E Yor 5B 100
Thornton. Fife 4E 137
Thornton. Lanc 5C 96
Thornton. Leics 5B 74
Thornton. Linc 4B 88
Thornton. Mers 4B 90
Thornton. Midd 3B 106
Thornton. Nmbd 5F 131
Thornton. Pemb 4D 42
Thornton. W Yor 1A 92
Thornton Curtis. N Lin 3D 94
Thorntonhall. S Lan 4G 127
Thornton Heath. G Lon 4E 39
Thornton Hough. Mers 2F 83
Thornton in Craven. N Yor 5B 98
Thornton in Lonsdale. N Yor 2F 97
Thornton-le-Beans. N Yor 5A 106
Thornton-le-Clay. N Yor 3A 100
Thornton-le-Dale. N Yor 1C 100
Thornton le Moor. Linc 1H 87
Thornton-le-Moor. N Yor 1F 99
Thornton-le-Moors. Ches W 3G 83
Thornton-le-Street. N Yor 1G 99
Thorntonloch. E Lot 2D 130
Thornton Rust. N Yor 1B 98
Thornton Steward. N Yor 1D 98
Thornton Watlass. N Yor 1E 99
Thornwood Common. Essx 5E 53
Thornythwaite. Cumb 2E 103
Thoroton. Notts 1E 75
Thorp Arch. W Yor 5G 99
Thorpe. Derbs 5F 85
Thorpe. E Yor 5D 101
Thorpe. Linc 2D 89
Thorpe. Norf 1G 67
Thorpe. N Yor 3C 98
Thorpe. Notts 1E 75
Thorpe. Surr 4B 38
Thorpe Abbotts. Norf 3D 66
Thorpe Acre. Leics 3C 74
Thorpe Arnold. Leics 3E 75
Thorpe Audlin. W Yor 3E 93
Thorpe Bassett. N Yor 2C 100
Thorpe Bay. S'end 2D 40
Thorpe by Water. Rut 1F 63
Thorpe Common. S Yor 1A 86
Thorpe Common. Suff 2F 55
Thorpe Constantine. Staf 5G 73
Thorpe End. Norf 4E 79
Thorpe Fendike. Linc 4D 88
Thorpe Green. Essx 3E 55
Thorpe Green. Suff 5B 66
Thorpe Hall. N Yor 2H 99
Thorpe Hamlet. Norf 5E 79
Thorpe Hesley. S Yor 1A 86
Thorpe in Balne. S Yor 3F 93
Thorpe in the Fallows. Linc 2G 87
Thorpe Langton. Leics 1E 63
Thorpe Larches. Dur 2A 106
Thorpe Latimer. Linc 1A 76
Thorpe-le-Soken. Essx 3E 55
Thorpe le Street. E Yor 5C 100
Thorpe Malsor. Nptn 3F 63
Thorpe Mandeville. Nptn 1D 50
Thorpe Market. Norf 2E 79
Thorpe Marriott. Norf 4D 78
Thorpe Morieux. Suff 5B 66
Thorpeness. Suff 4G 67
Thorpe on the Hill. Linc 4G 87
Thorpe on the Hill. W Yor 2D 92
Thorpe St Andrew. Norf 5E 79
Thorpe St Peter. Linc 4D 89
Thorpe Salvin. S Yor 2C 86
Thorpe Satchville. Leics 4E 75
Thorpe Thewles. Stoc T 2B 106
Thorpe Tilney. Linc 5A 88
Thorpe Underwood. N Yor 4G 99
Thorpe Waterville. Nptn 2H 63
Thorpe Willoughby. N Yor 1F 93
Thorpland. Norf 5F 77
Thorrington. Essx 3D 54
Thorverton. Devn 2C 12
Thrandeston. Suff 3D 66
Thrapston. Nptn 3G 63
Thrashbush. N Lan 3A 128
Threapland. Cumb 1C 102
Threapland. N Yor 3B 98
Threapwood. Ches W 1G 71
Threapwood. Staf 1E 73
Three Ashes. Here 3A 48
Three Bridges. Linc 2D 88
Three Bridges. W Sus 2D 27
Three Burrows. Corn 4B 6
Three Chimneys. Kent 2C 28
Three Cocks. Powy 2E 47
Three Crosses. Swan 3E 31
Three Cups Corner. E Sus 3H 27
Threehammer Common. Norf 3F 79
Three Holes. Norf 5E 77
Threekingham. Linc 2H 75
Three Leg Cross. E Sus 2A 28
Three Legged Cross. Dors 2F 15
Three Mile Cross. Wok 5F 37
Threemilestone. Corn 4B 6
Three Oaks. E Sus 4C 28
Threlkeld. Cumb 2E 102
Threshfield. N Yor 3B 98
Thrigby. Norf 4G 79
Thringarth. Dur 2C 104
Thringstone. Leics 4B 74
Thrintoft. N Yor 5A 106
Thriplow. Cambs 1E 53
Throckenholt. Linc 5C 76
Throcking. Herts 2D 52
Throckley. Tyne 3E 115
Throckmorton. Worc 1E 49
Throop. Bour 3G 15
Throphill. Nmbd 1E 115
Thropton. Nmbd 4E 121
Throsk. Stir 4A 136
Througham. Glos 5E 49
Throughgate. Dum 1F 111
Throwleigh. Devn 3G 11
Throwley. Kent 5D 40
Throwley Forstal. Kent 5D 40
Throxenby. N Yor 1E 101
Thrumpton. Notts 2C 74
Thrumster. High 4F 169
Thrunton. Nmbd 3E 121
Thrupp. Glos 5D 48
Thrupp. Oxon 4C 50
Thrushelton. Devn 4E 11
Thrushgill. Lanc 3F 97
Thrussington. Leics 4D 74
Thruxton. Hants 2A 24
Thruxton. Here 2H 47
Thrybergh. S Yor 1B 86
Thulston. Derbs 2B 74
Thundergay. N Ayr 5G 125
Thundersley. Essx 2B 40
Thundridge. Herts 4D 52
Thurcaston. Leics 4C 74
Thurcroft. S Yor 2B 86
Thurdon. Corn 1C 10
Thurgarton. Norf 2D 78
Thurgarton. Notts 1D 74
Thurgoland. S Yor 4C 92
Thurlaston. Leics 1C 62
Thurlaston. Warw 3B 62
Thurlbear. Som 4F 21
Thurlby. Linc 3D 89 (nr. Alford)
Thurlby. Linc 4A 76 (nr. Baston)
Thurlby. Linc 4G 87 (nr. Lincoln)
Thurleigh. Bed 5H 63
Thurlestone. Devn 4C 8
Thurloxton. Som 3F 21
Thurlstone. S Yor 4C 92
Thurlton. Norf 1G 67
Thurmaston. Leics 5D 74
Thurnby. Leics 5D 74
Thurne. Norf 4G 79
Thurnham. Kent 5C 40
Thurning. Norf 3C 78
Thurning. Nptn 2H 63
Thurnscoe. S Yor 4E 93
Thursby. Cumb 4E 113
Thursford. Norf 2B 78
Thursford Green. Norf 2B 78
Thursley. Surr 2A 26
Thurso. High 2D 168
Thurso East. High 2D 168
Thurstaston. Mers 2E 83
Thurston. Suff 4B 66
Thurston End. Suff 5G 65
Thurstonfield. Cumb 4E 112
Thurstonland. W Yor 3B 92
Thurton. Norf 5F 79
Thurvaston. Derbs 2F 73 (nr. Ashbourne)
Thurvaston. Derbs 2G 73 (nr. Derby)
Thuxton. Norf 5C 78
Thwaite. Dur 3D 104
Thwaite. N Yor 5B 104
Thwaite. Suff 4D 66
Thwaite Head. Cumb 5E 103
Thwaites. W Yor 5C 98
Thwaite St Mary. Norf 1F 67
Thwing. E Yor 2E 101
Tibbermore. Per 1C 136
Tibberton. Glos 3C 48
Tibberton. Telf 3A 72
Tibberton. Worc 5D 60
Tibenham. Norf 2D 66
Tibshelf. Derbs 4B 86
Tibthorpe. E Yor 4D 100
Ticehurst. E Sus 2A 28
Tichborne. Hants 3D 24
Tickencote. Rut 5G 75
Tickenham. N Som 4H 33
Tickhill. S Yor 1C 86
Ticklerton. Shrp 1G 59
Ticknall. Derbs 3H 73
Tickton. E Yor 5E 101
Tidbury Green. W Mid 3F 61
Tidcombe. Wilts 1A 24
Tiddington. Oxon 5E 51
Tiddington. Warw 5G 61
Tiddleywink. Wilts 4D 34
Tidebrook. E Sus 3H 27
Tideford. Corn 3H 7
Tideford Cross. Corn 2H 7
Tidenham. Glos 2A 34
Tideswell. Derbs 3F 85
Tidmarsh. W Ber 4E 37
Tidmington. Warw 2A 50
Tidpit. Hants 1F 15
Tidworth. Wilts 2H 23
Tidworth Camp. Wilts 2H 23
Tiers Cross. Pemb 3D 42
Tiffield. Nptn 5D 62
Tifty. Abers 4E 161
Tigerton. Ang 2E 145
Tighnabruaich. Arg 2A 126
Tigley. Devn 2D 8
Tilbrook. Cambs 4H 63
Tilbury. Thur 3H 39
Tilbury Green. Essx 1H 53
Tilbury Juxta Clare. Essx 1A 54
Tile Cross. W Mid 2F 61
Tile Hill. W Mid 3G 61
Tilehurst. Read 4E 37
Tilford. Surr 2G 25
Tilgate Forest Row. W Sus 2D 26
Tillathrowie. Abers 5B 160
Tillers Green. Glos 2B 48
Tillery. Abers 1G 153
Tilley. Shrp 3H 71
Tillicoultry. Clac 4B 136
Tillingham. Essx 5C 54
Tillington. Here 1H 47
Tillington. W Sus 3A 26
Tillington Common. Here 1H 47
Tillybirloch. Abers 3D 152
Tillyfourie. Abers 2D 152
Tilmanstone. Kent 5H 41
Tilney All Saints. Norf 4E 77
Tilney Fen End. Norf 4E 77
Tilney High End. Norf 4E 77
Tilney St Lawrence. Norf 4E 77
Tilshead. Wilts 2F 23
Tilstock. Shrp 2H 71
Tilston. Ches W 5G 83
Tilstone Fearnall. Ches W 4H 83
Tilsworth. C Beds 3H 51
Tilton on the Hill. Leics 5E 75
Tiltups End. Glos 2D 34
Timberland. Linc 5A 88
Timbersbrook. Ches E 4C 84
Timberscombe. Som 2C 20
Timble. N Yor 4D 98
Timperley. G Man 2B 84
Timsbury. Bath 1B 22
Timsbury. Hants 4B 24
Timsgearraidh. W Isl 4C 171
Timworth Green. Suff 4A 66
Tincleton. Dors 3C 14
Tindale. Cumb 4H 113
Tindale Crescent. Dur 2F 105
Tingewick. Buck 2E 51
Tingley. W Yor 2C 92
Tingrith. C Beds 2A 52
Tingwall. Orkn 5D 172
Tinhay. Devn 4D 11
Tinshill. W Yor 1C 92
Tinsley. S Yor 1B 86
Tinsley Green. W Sus 2D 27
Tintagel. Corn 4A 10
Tintern Parva. Mon 5A 48
Tintinhull. Som 1A 14
Tintwistle. Derbs 1E 85
Tinwald. Dum 1B 112
Tinwell. Rut 5H 75
Tippacott. Devn 2A 20
Tipperty. Abers 1G 153
Tipps End. Cambs 1E 65
Tiptoe. Hants 3A 16
Tipton. W Mid 1D 60
Tipton St John. Devn 3D 12
Tiptree. Essx 4B 54
Tiptree Heath. Essx 4B 54
Tirabad. Powy 1B 46
Tircoed. Swan 5G 45
Tiree Airport. Arg 4B 138
Tirinie. Per 2F 143
Tirley. Glos 3D 48
Tirnewydd. Flin 3D 82
Tiroran. Arg 1B 132
Tirphil. Cphy 5E 47
Tirril. Cumb 2G 103
Tirryside. High 2C 164
Tir-y-dail. Carm 4G 45
Tisbury. Wilts 4E 23
Tisman's Common. W Sus 2B 26
Tissington. Derbs 5F 85
Titchberry. Devn 4C 18
Titchfield. Hants 2D 16
Titchmarsh. Nptn 3H 63
Titchwell. Norf 1G 77
Tithby. Notts 2D 74
Titley. Here 5F 59
Titlington. Nmbd 3F 121
Titsey. Surr 5F 39
Titson. Corn 2C 10
Tittensor. Staf 2C 72
Tittleshall. Norf 3A 78
Titton. Worc 4C 60
Tiverton. Ches W 4H 83
Tiverton. Devn 1C 12
Tivetshall St Margaret. Norf 2D 66
Tivetshall St Mary. Norf 2D 66
Tivington. Som 2C 20
Tixall. Staf 3D 73
Tixover. Rut 5G 75
Toab. Orkn 7E 172
Toab. Shet 10E 173
Toadmoor. Derbs 5H 85
Tobermory. Arg 3G 139
Toberonochy. Arg 3E 133
Tobha-Beag. W Isl 1E 170 (on North Uist)
Tobha Beag. W Isl 5C 170 (on South Uist)
Tobha Mor. W Isl 5C 170
Tobson. W Isl 4D 171
Tocabhaig. High 2E 147
Tocher. Abers 5D 160
Tockenham. Wilts 4F 35
Tockenham Wick. Wilts 3F 35
Tockholes. Bkbn 2E 91
Tockington. S Glo 3B 34
Tockwith. N Yor 4G 99
Todber. Dors 4D 22
Todding. Here 3G 59
Toddington. C Beds 3A 52
Toddington. Glos 2F 49
Todenham. Glos 2H 49
Todhills. Cumb 3E 113
Todmorden. W Yor 2H 91
Todwick. S Yor 2B 86
Toft. Cambs 5C 64
Toft. Linc 4H 75
Toft Hill. Dur 2E 105
Toft Monks. Norf 1G 67
Toft next Newton. Linc 2H 87
Toftrees. Norf 3A 78
Tofts. High 2F 169
Toftwood. Norf 4B 78
Togston. Nmbd 4G 121
Tokavaig. High 2E 147
Tokers Green. Oxon 4F 37
Tolastadh a Chaolais. W Isl 4D 171
Tolladine. Worc 5C 60
Tolland. Som 3E 20
Tollard Farnham. Dors 1E 15
Tollard Royal. Wilts 1E 15
Toll Bar. S Yor 4F 93
Toller Fratrum. Dors 3A 14
Toller Porcorum. Dors 3A 14
Tollerton. N Yor 3H 99
Tollerton. Notts 2D 74
Toller Whelme. Dors 2A 14
Tollesbury. Essx 4C 54
Tolleshunt D'Arcy. Essx 4C 54
Tolleshunt Knights. Essx 4C 54
Tolleshunt Major. Essx 4C 54
Tollie. High 3H 157
Tollie Farm. High 1A 156
Tolm. W Isl 4G 171
Tolpuddle. Dors 3C 14
Tolstadh bho Thuath. W Isl 3H 171
Tolworth. G Lon 4C 38
Tomachlaggan. Mor 1F 151
Tomaknock. Per 1A 136
Tomatin. High 1C 150
Tombuidhe. Arg 3H 133
Tomdoun. High 3D 148

Tomich—Triangle

Tomich. *High* 1F **149** (nr. Cannich)
Tomich. *High* 1B **158** (nr. Invergordon)
Tomich. *High* 3D **164** (nr. Lairg)
Tomintoul. *Mor* 2F **151**
Tomnavoulin. *Mor* 1G **151**
Tomsleibhe. *Arg* 5A **140**
Ton. *Mon* 2G **33**
Tonbridge. *Kent* 1G **27**
Tondu. *B'end* 3B **32**
Tonedale. *Som* 4E **21**
Tonfanau. *Gwyn* 5E **69**
Tong. *Shrp* 5B **72**
Tonge. *Leics* 3B **74**
Tong Forge. *Shrp* 5B **72**
Tongham. *Surr* 2G **25**
Tongland. *Dum* 4D **111**
Tong Norton. *Shrp* 5B **72**
Tongue. *High* 3F **167**
Tongue End. *Linc* 4A **76**
Tongwynlais. *Card* 3E **33**
Tonmawr. *Neat* 2B **32**
Tonna. *Neat* 2A **32**
Tonnau. *Neat* 2A **32**
Ton-Pentre. *Rhon* 2C **32**
Ton-Teg. *Rhon* 3D **32**
Tonwell. *Herts* 4D **52**
Tonypandy. *Rhon* 2C **32**
Tonyrefail. *Rhon* 3D **32**
Toot Baldon. *Oxon* 5D **50**
Toot Hill. *Essx* 5F **53**
Toot Hill. *Hants* 1B **16**
Topcliffe. *N Yor* 2G **99**
Topcliffe. *W Yor* 2C **92**
Topcroft. *Norf* 1E **67**
Topcroft Street. *Norf* 1E **67**
Toppesfield. *Essx* 2H **53**
Toppings. *G Man* 3F **91**
Toprow. *Norf* 1D **66**
Topsham. *Devn* 4C **12**
Torbay. *Torb* 2F **9**
Torbeg. *N Ayr* 3C **122**
Torbothie. *N Lan* 3B **128**
Torbryan. *Devn* 2E **9**
Torcross. *Devn* 4E **9**
Tore. *High* 3A **158**
Torgyle. *High* 2F **149**
Torinturk. *Arg* 3G **125**
Torksey. *Linc* 3F **87**
Torlum. *W Isl* 3C **170**
Torlundy. *High* 1F **141**
Tormarton. *S Glo* 4C **34**
Tormitchell. *S Ayr* 5B **116**
Tormore. *High* 3E **147**
Tormore. *N Ayr* 2C **122**
Tornagrain. *High* 4B **158**
Tornaveen. *Abers* 3D **152**
Torness. *High* 1H **149**
Toronto. *Dur* 1E **105**
Torpenhow. *Cumb* 1D **102**
Torphichen. *W Lot* 2C **128**
Torphins. *Abers* 3D **152**
Torpoint. *Corn* 3A **8**
Torquay. *Torb* 2F **9**
Torr. *Devn* 3B **8**
Torra. *Arg* 4B **124**
Torran. *High* 4E **155**
Torrance. *E Dun* 2H **127**
Torrans. *Arg* 1B **132**
Torranyard. *E Ayr* 5E **127**
Torre. *Som* 3D **20**
Torre. *Torb* 2E **9**
Torridon. *High* 3B **156**
Torrin. *High* 1D **147**
Torrisdale. *Arg* 2B **122**
Torrisdale. *High* 2G **167**
Torrish. *High* 2G **165**
Torrisholme. *Lanc* 3D **96**
Torroble. *High* 3C **164**
Torroy. *High* 4C **164**
Tor Royal. *Devn* 5G **11**
Torry. *Aber* 3G **153**
Torryburn. *Fife* 1D **128**
Torthorwald. *Dum* 2B **112**
Tortington. *W Sus* 5B **26**
Tortworth. *S Glo* 2C **34**
Torvaig. *High* 4D **155**
Torver. *Cumb* 5D **102**
Torwood. *Falk* 1B **128**
Torworth. *Notts* 2D **86**
Toscaig. *High* 5G **155**
Toseland. *Cambs* 4B **64**
Tosside. *Lanc* 4G **97**
Tostock. *Suff* 4B **66**
Totaig. *High* 3B **154**
Totardor. *High* 5C **154**
Tote. *High* 4D **154**
Totegan. *High* 2A **168**
Tothill. *Linc* 2D **88**
Totland. *IOW* 4B **16**
Totley. *S Yor* 3H **85**
Totnell. *Dors* 2B **14**
Totnes. *Devn* 2E **9**
Toton. *Derbs* 2B **74**
Totronald. *Arg* 3C **138**
Totscore. *High* 2C **154**
Tottenham. *G Lon* 1E **39**
Tottenhill. *Norf* 4F **77**
Tottenhill Row. *Norf* 4F **77**
Totteridge. *G Lon* 1D **38**
Totternhoe. *C Beds* 3H **51**
Tottington. *G Man* 3F **91**
Totton. *Hants* 1B **16**
Touchen-end. *Wind* 4G **37**
Toulvaddie. *High* 5F **165**
Towans, The. *Corn* 3C **4**
Toward. *Arg* 3C **126**
Towcester. *Nptn* 1E **51**
Towednack. *Corn* 3B **4**
Tower End. *Norf* 4F **77**
Tower Hill. *Mers* 4C **90**
Tower Hill. *W Sus* 3C **26**
Towersey. *Oxon* 5F **51**
Towie. *Abers* 2B **152**
Towiemore. *Mor* 4A **160**
Tow Law. *Dur* 1E **105**
Town End. *Cambs* 1D **64**
Town End. *Cumb* 4F **103** (nr. Ambleside)
Town End. *Cumb* 2H **103** (nr. Kirkby Thore)
Town End. *Cumb* 1D **96** (nr. Lindale)
Town End. *Cumb* 1C **96** (nr. Newby Bridge)
Town End. *Mers* 2G **83**
Townend. *W Dun* 2F **127**
Townfield. *Dur* 5C **114**
Towngate. *Cumb* 5G **113**
Towngate. *Linc* 4A **76**
Town Green. *Lanc* 4B **90**
Town Head. *Cumb* 4E **103** (nr. Grasmere)
Town Head. *Cumb* 3H **103** (nr. Great Asby)
Townhead. *Cumb* 1G **103** (nr. Lazonby)
Townhead. *Cumb* 1B **102** (nr. Maryport)
Townhead. *Cumb* 1H **103** (nr. Ousby)
Townhead. *Dum* 5D **111**
Townhead of Greenlaw. *Dum* 3E **111**
Townhill. *Fife* 1E **129**
Townhill. *Swan* 3F **31**
Town Kelloe. *Dur* 1A **106**
Town Littleworth. *E Sus* 4F **27**
Town Row. *E Sus* 2G **27**
Towns End. *Hants* 1D **24**
Townsend. *Herts* 5B **52**
Townshend. *Corn* 3C **4**
Town Street. *Suff* 2G **65**
Town, The. *IOS* 1A **4**
Town Yetholm. *Bord* 2C **120**
Towthorpe. *E Yor* 3C **100**
Towthorpe. *York* 4A **100**
Towton. *N Yor* 1E **93**
Towyn. *Cnwy* 3B **82**
Toxteth. *Mers* 2F **83**
Toynton All Saints. *Linc* 4C **88**
Toynton Fen Side. *Linc* 4C **88**
Toynton St Peter. *Linc* 4D **88**
Toy's Hill. *Kent* 5F **39**
Trabboch. *E Ayr* 2D **116**
Traboe. *Corn* 4E **5**
Tradespark. *High* 3C **158**
Trafford Park. *G Man* 1B **84**
Trallong. *Powy* 3C **46**
Tranent. *E Lot* 2H **129**
Tranmere. *Mers* 2F **83**
Trantlebeg. *High* 3A **168**
Trantlemore. *High* 3A **168**
Tranwell. *Nmbd* 1E **115**
Trapp. *Carm* 4G **45**
Traquair. *Bord* 1F **119**
Trash Green. *W Ber* 5E **37**
Trawden. *Lanc* 1H **91**
Trawscoed. *Powy* 2D **46**
Trawsfynydd. *Gwyn* 2G **69**
Trawsgoed. *Cdgn* 3F **57**
Treaddow. *Here* 3A **48**
Trealaw. *Rhon* 2D **32**
Treales. *Lanc* 1C **90**
Trearddur. *IOA* 3B **80**
Treaslane. *High* 3C **154**
Treator. *Corn* 1D **6**
Trebanog. *Rhon* 2D **32**
Trebanos. *Neat* 5H **45**
Trebarber. *Corn* 2C **6**
Trebartha. *Corn* 5C **10**
Trebarwith. *Corn* 4A **10**
Trebetherick. *Corn* 1D **6**
Treborough. *Som* 3D **20**
Trebudannon. *Corn* 2C **6**
Trebullett. *Corn* 5D **10**
Treburley. *Corn* 5D **10**
Treburrick. *Corn* 1C **6**
Trebyan. *Corn* 2E **7**
Trecastle. *Powy* 3B **46**
Trecenydd. *Cphy* 3E **33**
Trecott. *Devn* 2G **11**
Trecwn. *Pemb* 1D **42**
Trecynon. *Rhon* 5C **46**
Tredaule. *Corn* 4C **10**
Tredavoe. *Corn* 4B **4**
Tredegar. *Blae* 5E **47**
Trederwen. *Powy* 4E **71**
Tredington. *Glos* 3E **49**
Tredington. *Warw* 1A **50**
Tredinnick. *Corn* 2F **7** (nr. Bodmin)
Tredinnick. *Corn* 3G **7** (nr. Looe)
Tredinnick. *Corn* 1D **6** (nr. Padstow)
Tredogan. *V Glam* 5D **32**
Tredomen. *Powy* 2E **46**
Tredunnock. *Mon* 2G **33**
Tredustan. *Powy* 2E **47**
Treen. *Corn* 4A **4** (nr. Land's End)
Treen. *Corn* 3B **4** (nr. St Ives)
Treeton. *S Yor* 2B **86**
Trefaldwyn. *Powy* 1E **58**
Trefasser. *Pemb* 1C **42**
Trefdraeth. *IOA* 3D **80**
Trefdraeth. *Pemb* 1E **43**
Trefecca. *Powy* 2E **47**
Trefechan. *Mer T* 5D **46**
Trefeglwys. *Powy* 1B **58**
Trefeitha. *Powy* 2E **46**
Trefenter. *Cdgn* 4F **57**
Treffgarne. *Pemb* 2D **42**
Treffynnon. *Flin* 3D **82**
Treffynnon. *Pemb* 2C **42**
Trefil. *Blae* 4E **46**
Trefilan. *Cdgn* 5E **57**
Trefin. *Pemb* 1C **42**
Treflach. *Shrp* 3E **71**
Trefnant. *Den* 3C **82**
Trefonen. *Shrp* 3E **71**
Trefor. *Gwyn* 1C **68**
Trefor. *IOA* 2C **80**
Treforest. *Rhon* 3D **32**
Trefrew. *Corn* 4B **10**
Trefriw. *Cnwy* 4G **81**
Tref-y-Clawdd. *Powy* 3E **59**
Trefynwy. *Mon* 4A **48**
Tregada. *Corn* 4D **10**
Tregadillett. *Corn* 4D **10**
Tregare. *Mon* 4H **47**
Tregarne. *Corn* 4E **5**
Tregaron. *Cdgn* 5F **57**
Tregarth. *Gwyn* 4F **81**
Tregear. *Corn* 3C **6**
Tregeare. *Corn* 4C **10**
Tregeiriog. *Wrex* 2D **70**
Tregele. *IOA* 1C **80**
Tregeseal. *Corn* 3A **4**
Tregiskey. *Corn* 4E **6**
Tregole. *Corn* 3B **10**
Tregolwyn. *V Glam* 4C **32**
Tregonetha. *Corn* 2D **6**
Tregonhawke. *Corn* 3A **8**
Tregony. *Corn* 4D **6**
Tregoodwell. *Corn* 4B **10**
Tregorrick. *Corn* 3E **6**
Tregoss. *Corn* 2D **6**
Tregowris. *Corn* 4E **5**
Tregoyd. *Powy* 2E **47**
Tregrehan Mills. *Corn* 3E **7**
Tre-groes. *Cdgn* 1E **45**
Tregullon. *Corn* 2E **7**
Tregurrian. *Corn* 2C **6**
Tregynon. *Powy* 1C **58**
Trehafod. *Rhon* 2D **32**
Trehan. *Corn* 3A **8**
Treharris. *Mer T* 2E **32**
Treherbert. *Rhon* 2C **32**
Trehunist. *Corn* 2H **7**
Trekenner. *Corn* 5D **10**
Trekenning. *Corn* 2D **6**
Treknow. *Corn* 4A **10**
Trelales. *B'end* 3B **32**
Trelan. *Corn* 5E **5**
Trelash. *Corn* 3B **10**
Trelassick. *Corn* 3C **6**
Trelawnyd. *Flin* 3C **82**
Trelech. *Carm* 1G **43**
Treleddyd-fawr. *Pemb* 2B **42**
Trelewis. *Mer T* 2E **32**
Treligga. *Corn* 4A **10**
Trelights. *Corn* 1D **6**
Trelill. *Corn* 5A **10**
Trelissick. *Corn* 5C **6**
Trelleck. *Mon* 5A **48**
Trelleck Grange. *Mon* 5H **47**
Trelogan. *Flin* 2D **82**
Trelystan. *Powy* 5E **71**
Tremadog. *Gwyn* 1E **69**
Tremail. *Corn* 4B **10**
Tremain. *Cdgn* 1C **44**
Tremaine. *Corn* 4C **10**
Tremar. *Corn* 2G **7**
Trematon. *Corn* 3H **7**
Tremeirchion. *Den* 3C **82**
Tremore. *Corn* 2E **6**
Tremorfa. *Card* 4F **33**
Trenance. *Corn* 5D **4** (nr. Helston)
Trenance. *Corn* 2C **6** (nr. Newquay)
Trenance. *Corn* 1D **6** (nr. Padstow)
Trenarren. *Corn* 4E **7**
Trench. *Telf* 4A **72**
Trencreek. *Corn* 2C **6**
Trendeal. *Corn* 3C **6**
Trenear. *Corn* 5A **6**
Treneglos. *Corn* 4C **10**
Trenewan. *Corn* 3F **7**
Trengune. *Corn* 3B **10**
Trent. *Dors* 1A **14**
Trentham. *Stoke* 1C **72**
Trentishoe. *Devn* 2G **19**
Trentlock. *Derbs* 2B **74**
Treoes. *V Glam* 4C **32**
Treorchy. *Rhon* 2C **32**
Treorci. *Rhon* 2C **32**
Tre'r-ddol. *Cdgn* 1F **57**
Tre'r llai. *Powy* 5E **71**
Trerulefoot. *Corn* 3H **7**
Tresaith. *Cdgn* 5B **56**
Trescott. *Staf* 1C **60**
Trescowe. *Corn* 3C **4**
Tresham. *Glos* 2C **34**
Tresigin. *V Glam* 4C **32**
Tresillian. *Corn* 4C **6**
Tresimwn. *V Glam* 4D **32**
Tresinney. *Corn* 4B **10**
Treskillard. *Corn* 5A **6**
Treskinnick Cross. *Corn* 3C **10**
Tresmeer. *Corn* 4C **10**
Tresparrett. *Corn* 3B **10**
Tresparrett Posts. *Corn* 3B **10**
Tressady. *High* 3D **164**
Tressait. *Per* 2F **143**
Tresta. *Shet* 6E **173**
Treswell. *Notts* 3E **87**
Treswithian. *Corn* 3D **4**
Tre Taliesin. *Cdgn* 1F **57**
Trethomas. *Cphy* 3E **33**
Trethosa. *Corn* 3D **6**
Trethurgy. *Corn* 3E **7**
Tretio. *Pemb* 2B **42**
Tretire. *Here* 3A **48**
Tretower. *Powy* 3E **47**
Treuddyn. *Flin* 5E **83**
Trevadlock. *Corn* 5C **10**
Trevalga. *Corn* 3A **10**
Trevalyn. *Wrex* 5F **83**
Trevance. *Corn* 1D **6**
Trevanger. *Corn* 1D **6**
Trevanson. *Corn* 1D **6**
Trevarrack. *Corn* 3B **4**
Trevarren. *Corn* 2D **6**
Trevarrian. *Corn* 2C **6**
Trevarrick. *Corn* 4D **6**
Tre-vaughan. *Carm* 3E **45** (nr. Carmarthen)
Trevaughan. *Carm* 3F **43** (nr. Whitland)
Treveighan. *Corn* 5A **10**
Trevellas. *Corn* 3B **6**
Trevelmond. *Corn* 2G **7**
Treverva. *Corn* 5B **6**
Trevescan. *Corn* 4A **4**
Trevethin. *Torf* 5F **47**
Trevia. *Corn* 4A **10**
Trevigro. *Corn* 2H **7**
Trevilley. *Corn* 4A **4**
Treviscoe. *Corn* 3D **6**
Trevivian. *Corn* 4B **10**
Trevone. *Corn* 1C **6**
Trevor. *Wrex* 1E **71**
Trevor Uchaf. *Den* 1E **71**
Trew. *Corn* 4D **4**
Trewalder. *Corn* 4A **10**
Trewarlett. *Corn* 4D **10**
Trewarmett. *Corn* 4A **10**
Trewassa. *Corn* 4B **10**
Treween. *Corn* 4C **10**
Trewellard. *Corn* 3A **4**
Trewen. *Corn* 4C **10**
Trewennack. *Corn* 4D **5**
Trewern. *Powy* 4E **71**
Trewetha. *Corn* 5A **10**
Trewidland. *Corn* 2G **7**
Trewint. *Corn* 3B **10**
Trewithian. *Corn* 5C **6**
Trewoofe. *Corn* 4B **4**
Trewoon. *Corn* 3D **6**
Treworthal. *Corn* 5C **6**
Trewyddel. *Pemb* 1B **44**
Treyarnon. *Corn* 1C **6**
Treyford. *W Sus* 1G **17**
Triangle. *Staf* 5E **73**

West Murkle—Whitgift

West Murkle. High 2D 168
West Ness. N Yor 2A 100
Westnewton. Cumb 5C 112
West Newton. E Yor 1E 95
West Newton. Norf 3F 77
Westnewton. Nmbd 1D 120
West Newton. Som 4F 21
West Norwood. G Lon 3E 39
Westoe. Tyne 3G 115
West Ogwell. Devn 2E 9
Weston. Bath 5C 34
Weston. Ches E 5B 84
(nr. Crewe)
Weston. Ches E 3D 84
(nr. Macclesfield)
Weston. Devn 2E 13
(nr. Honiton)
Weston. Devn 4E 13
(nr. Sidmouth)
Weston. Dors 5B 14
(nr. Weymouth)
Weston. Dors 2A 14
(nr. Yeovil)
Weston. Hal 2H 83
Weston. Hants 4F 25
Weston. Here 5F 59
Weston. Herts 2C 52
Weston. Linc 3B 76
Weston. Nptn 1D 50
Weston. Notts 4E 87
Weston. Shrp 1H 59
(nr. Bridgnorth)
Weston. Shrp 3F 59
(nr. Knighton)
Weston. Shrp 3H 71
(nr. Wem)
Weston. S Lan 5D 128
Weston. Staf 3D 73
Weston. Suff 2G 67
Weston. W Ber 4B 36
Weston Bampfylde. Som 4B 22
Weston Beggard. Here 1A 48
Westonbirt. Glos 3D 34
Weston by Welland. Nptn 1E 63
Weston Colville. Cambs 5F 65
Westoncommon. Shrp 3G 71
Weston Coyney. Stoke 1D 72
Weston Ditch. Suff 3F 65
Weston Favell. Nptn 4E 63
Weston Green. Cambs 5F 65
Weston Green. Norf 4D 78
Weston Heath. Shrp 4B 72
Weston Hills. Linc 4B 76
Weston in Arden. Warw 2A 62
Westoning. C Beds 2A 52
Weston-in-Gordano. N Som 4H 33
Weston Jones. Staf 3B 72
Weston Longville. Norf 4D 78
Weston Lullingfields. Shrp 3G 71
Weston-on-Avon. Warw 5F 61
Weston-on-the-Green. Oxon 4D 50
Weston-on-Trent. Derbs 3B 74
Weston Patrick. Hants 2E 25
Weston Rhyn. Shrp 2E 71
Weston Subedge. Glos 1G 49
Weston-super-Mare. N Som 5G 33
Weston Town. Som 2C 22
Weston Turville. Buck 4G 51
Weston under Lizard. Staf 4C 72
Weston under Penyard. Here 3B 48
Weston under Wetherley. Warw 4A 62
Weston Underwood. Derbs 1G 73
Weston Underwood. Mil 5F 63
Westonzoyland. Som 3G 21
West Orchard. Dors 1D 14
West Overton. Wilts 5G 35
Westow. N Yor 3B 100
Westown. Per 1E 137
West Panson. Devn 3D 10
West Park. Hart 1B 106
West Parley. Dors 3F 15
West Peckham. Kent 5H 39
West Pelton. Dur 4F 115
West Pennard. Som 3A 22
West Pentire. Corn 2B 6
West Perry. Cambs 4A 64
West Pitcorthie. Fife 3H 137
West Plean. Stir 1B 128
West Poringland. Norf 5E 79
West Porlock. Som 2B 20
Westport. Som 1G 13
West Putford. Devn 1D 10
West Quantoxhead. Som 2E 20
Westra. V Glam 4E 33
West Rainton. Dur 5G 115
West Rasen. Linc 2H 87
West Ravendale. NE Lin 1B 88
Westray Airport. Orkn 2D 172
West Raynham. Norf 3A 78
Westrigg. W Lot 3C 128
West Rounton. N Yor 4B 106
West Row. Suff 3F 65
West Rudham. Norf 3H 77
West Runton. Norf 1D 78
Westruther. Bord 4C 130
Westry. Cambs 1C 64
West Saltoun. E Lot 3A 130
West Sandford. Devn 2B 12
West Sandwick. Shet 3F 173
West Scrafton. N Yor 1C 98
Westside. Orkn 5C 172
West Sleekburn. Nmbd 1F 115
West Somerton. Norf 4G 79
West Stafford. Dors 4C 14
West Stockwith. Notts 1E 87
West Stoke. W Sus 2G 17
West Stonesdale. N Yor 4B 104
West Stoughton. Som 2H 21
West Stour. Dors 4C 22
West Stourmouth. Kent 4G 41
West Stow. Suff 3H 65
West Stowell. Wilts 5G 35
West Strathan. High 2F 167
West Stratton. Hants 2D 24
West Street. Kent 5D 40
West Tanfield. N Yor 2E 99
West Taphouse. Corn 2F 7
West Tarbert. Arg 3G 125
West Thirston. Nmbd 4F 121
West Thorney. W Sus 2F 17
West Thurrock. Thur 3G 39
West Tilbury. Thur 3A 40
West Tisted. Hants 4E 25
West Tofts. Norf 1H 65
West Torrington. Linc 2A 88
West Town. Bath 5A 34
West Town. Hants 3F 17
West Town. N Som 5H 33
West Tytherley. Hants 4A 24
West Tytherton. Wilts 4E 35
West View. Hart 1C 106
Westville. Notts 1C 74
West Walton. Norf 4D 76
Westward. Cumb 5D 112
Westward Ho!. Devn 4E 19
Westwell. Kent 1D 28
Westwell. Oxon 5H 49
Westwell Leacon. Kent 1D 28
West Wellow. Hants 1A 16
West Wemyss. Fife 4F 137
Westwick. Cambs 4D 64
Westwick. Dur 3D 104
Westwick. Norf 3E 79
West Wick. N Som 5G 33
West Wickham. Cambs 1G 53
West Wickham. G Lon 4E 39
West Williamston. Pemb 4E 43
West Willoughby. Linc 1G 75
West Winch. Norf 4F 77
West Winterslow. Wilts 3H 23
West Wittering. W Sus 3F 17
West Witton. N Yor 1C 98
Westwood. Devn 3D 12
Westwood. Kent 4H 41
Westwood. Pet 1A 64
Westwood. S Lan 4H 127
Westwood. Wilts 1D 22
West Woodburn. Nmbd 1B 114
West Woodhay. W Ber 5B 36
West Woodlands. Som 2C 22
West Woodside. Cumb 5E 112
Westwoodside. N Lin 4H 93
West Worldham. Hants 3F 25
West Worlington. Devn 1A 12
West Worthing. W Sus 5C 26
West Wratting. Cambs 5F 65
West Wycombe. Buck 2G 37
West Wylam. Nmbd 3E 115
West Yatton. Wilts 4D 34
West Yell. Shet 3F 173
West Youlstone. Corn 1C 10
Wetheral. Cumb 4F 113
Wetherby. W Yor 5G 99
Wetherden. Suff 4C 66
Wetheringsett. Suff 4D 66
Wethersfield. Essx 2H 53
Wethersta. Shet 5E 173
Wetherup Street. Suff 4D 66
Wetley Rocks. Staf 1D 72
Wettenhall. Ches E 4A 84
Wetton. Staf 5F 85
Wetwang. E Yor 4D 100
Wetwood. Staf 2B 72
Wexcombe. Wilts 1A 24
Wexham Street. Buck 2A 38
Weybourne. Norf 1D 78
Weybourne. Surr 2G 25
Weybread. Suff 2E 67
Weybridge. Surr 4B 38
Weycroft. Devn 3G 13
Weydale. High 2D 168
Weyhill. Hants 2B 24
Weymouth. Dors 5B 14
Weythel. Powy 5E 59
Whaddon. Buck 2G 51
Whaddon. Cambs 1D 52
Whaddon. Glos 4D 48
Whaddon. Wilts 4G 23
Whale. Cumb 2G 103
Whaley. Derbs 3C 86
Whaley Bridge. Derbs 2E 85
Whaley Thorns. Derbs 3C 86
Whalley. Lanc 1F 91
Whalton. Nmbd 1E 115
Wham. N Yor 3G 97
Whaplode. Linc 3C 76
Whaplode Drove. Linc 4C 76
Whaplode St Catherine. Linc 3C 76
Wharfe. N Yor 3G 97
Wharles. Lanc 1C 90
Wharley End. C Beds 1H 51
Wharncliffe Side. S Yor 1G 85
Wharram-le-Street. N Yor 3C 100
Wharton. Ches W 4A 84
Wharton. Here 5H 59
Whashton. N Yor 4E 105
Whasset. Cumb 1E 97
Whatcote. Warw 1A 50
Whateley. Warw 1G 61
Whatfield. Suff 1D 54
Whatley. Som 2G 13
(nr. Chard)
Whatley. Som 2C 22
(nr. Frome)
Whatlington. E Sus 4B 28
Whatmore. Shrp 3A 60
Whatstandwell. Derbs 5H 85
Whatton. Notts 2E 75
Whauphill. Dum 5B 110
Whaw. N Yor 4C 104
Wheatacre. Norf 1G 67
Wheatcroft. Derbs 5A 86
Wheathampstead. Herts 4B 52
Wheathill. Shrp 2A 60
Wheatley. Devn 3B 12
Wheatley. Hants 2F 25
Wheatley. Oxon 5D 50
Wheatley. S Yor 4F 93
Wheatley. W Yor 2A 92
Wheatley Hill. Dur 1A 106
Wheatley Lane. Lanc 1G 91
Wheatley Park. S Yor 4F 93
Wheaton Aston. Staf 4C 72
Wheatstone Park. Staf 5C 72
Wheddon Cross. Som 3C 20
Wheelerstreet. Surr 1A 26
Wheelock. Ches E 5B 84
Wheelock Heath. Ches E 5B 84
Wheelton. Lanc 2E 90
Wheldrake. York 5A 100
Whelford. Glos 2G 35
Whelpley Hill. Buck 5H 51
Whelpo. Cumb 1E 102
Whelston. Flin 3E 82
Whenby. N Yor 3A 100
Whepstead. Suff 5H 65
Wherstead. Suff 1E 55
Wherwell. Hants 2B 24
Wheston. Derbs 3F 85
Whetsted. Kent 1A 28
Whetstone. G Lon 1D 38
Whetstone. Leics 1C 62
Whicham. Cumb 1A 96
Whichford. Warw 2B 50
Whickham. Tyne 3F 115
Whiddon. Devn 2E 11
Whiddon Down. Devn 3G 11
Whigstreet. Ang 4D 145
Whilton. Nptn 4D 62
Whimble. Devn 2D 10
Whimple. Devn 3D 12
Whimpwell Green. Norf 3F 79
Whinburgh. Norf 5C 78
Whin Lane End. Lanc 5C 96
Whinnyfold. Abers 5H 161
Whinny Hill. Stoc T 3A 106
Whippingham. IOW 3D 16
Whipsnade. C Beds 4A 52
Whipton. Devn 3C 12
Whirlow. S Yor 2H 85
Whisby. Linc 4G 87
Whissendine. Rut 4F 75
Whissonsett. Norf 3B 78
Whisterfield. Ches E 3C 84
Whistley Green. Wok 4F 37
Whiston. Mers 1G 83
Whiston. Nptn 4F 63
Whiston. S Yor 1B 86
Whiston. Staf 1E 73
(nr. Cheadle)
Whiston. Staf 4C 72
(nr. Penkridge)
Whiston Cross. Shrp 5B 72
Whiston Eaves. Staf 1E 73
Whitacre Heath. Warw 1G 61
Whitbeck. Cumb 1A 96
Whitbourne. Here 5B 60
Whitburn. Tyne 3H 115
Whitburn. W Lot 3C 128
Whitburn Colliery. Tyne 3H 115
Whitby. Ches W 3F 83
Whitby. N Yor 3F 107
Whitbyheath. Ches W 3F 83
Whitchester. Bord 4D 130
Whitchurch. Bath 5B 34
Whitchurch. Buck 3G 51
Whitchurch. Card 4E 33
Whitchurch. Devn 5E 11
Whitchurch. Hants 2C 24
Whitchurch. Here 4A 48
Whitchurch. Pemb 2C 42
Whitchurch. Shrp 1H 71
Whitchurch Canonicorum. Dors 3G 13
Whitchurch Hill. Oxon 4E 37
Whitchurch-on-Thames. Oxon 4E 37
Whitcombe. Dors 4C 14
Whitcot. Shrp 1F 59
Whitcott Keysett. Shrp 2E 59
Whiteash Green. Essx 2A 54
Whitebog. High 2B 158
Whitebridge. High 2G 149
Whitebrook. Mon 5A 48
Whitecairns. Abers 2G 153
White Chapel. Lanc 5E 97
Whitechurch. Pemb 1F 43
White Colne. Essx 3B 54
White Coppice. Lanc 3E 90
White Corries. High 3G 141
Whitecraig. E Lot 2G 129
Whitecroft. Glos 5B 48
White Cross. Corn 4D 5
(nr. Mullion)
Whitecross. Corn 1D 6
(nr. Wadebridge)
Whitecross. Falk 2C 128
White End. Worc 2C 48
Whiteface. High 5E 164
Whitefarland. N Ayr 5G 125
Whitefaulds. S Ayr 4B 116
Whitefield. Dors 3E 15
Whitefield. G Man 4G 91
Whitefield. Som 4D 20
Whiteford. Abers 1E 152
Whitegate. Ches W 4A 84
Whitehall. Devn 1E 13
Whitehall. Hants 1F 25
Whitehall. Orkn 5F 172
Whitehall. W Sus 3C 26
Whitehaven. Cumb 3A 102
Whitehaven. Shrp 3E 71
Whitehill. Hants 3F 25
Whitehill. N Ayr 4D 126
Whitehills. Abers 2D 160
Whitehills. Ang 3D 144
White Horse Common. Norf 3F 79
Whitehough. Derbs 2E 85
Whitehouse. Abers 2D 152
Whitehouse. Arg 3G 125
Whiteinch. Glas 3G 127
Whitekirk. E Lot 1B 130
White Kirkley. Dur 1D 104
White Lackington. Dors 3C 14
Whitelackington. Som 1G 13
White Ladies Aston. Worc 5D 60
White Lee. W Yor 2C 92
Whiteley. Hants 1D 16
Whiteley Bank. IOW 4D 16
Whiteley Village. Surr 4B 38
Whitemans Green. W Sus 3E 27
White Mill. Carm 3E 45
Whitemire. Mor 3D 159
Whitemoor. Corn 3D 6
Whitenap. Hants 4B 24
Whiteness. Shet 7F 173
White Notley. Essx 4A 54
Whiteoak Green. Oxon 4B 50
Whiteparish. Wilts 4H 23
White Pit. Linc 3C 88
Whiterashes. Abers 1F 153
White Rocks. Here 3H 47
White Roding. Essx 4F 53
Whiterow. High 4F 169
Whiterow. Mor 3E 159
Whiteshill. Glos 5D 48
Whiteside. Nmbd 3A 114
Whiteside. W Lot 3C 128
Whitesmith. E Sus 4G 27
Whitestaunton. Som 1F 13
Whitestone. Abers 4D 152
Whitestone. Devn 3B 12
White Stone. Here 1A 48
Whitestones. Abers 3F 161
Whitestreet Green. Suff 2C 54
Whitewall Corner. N Yor 2B 100
White Waltham. Wind 4G 37
Whiteway. Glos 4E 49
Whitewell. Lanc 5F 97
Whitewell Bottom. Lanc 2G 91
Whiteworks. Devn 5G 11
Whitewreath. Mor 3G 159
Whitfield. D'dee 5D 144
Whitfield. Kent 1H 29
Whitfield. Nptn 2E 50
Whitfield. Nmbd 4A 114
Whitfield. S Glo 2B 34
Whitford. Devn 3F 13
Whitford. Flin 3D 82
Whitgift. E Yor 2B 94